Charles Seale-Hayne Library
University of Plymouth
(01752) 588 588
LibraryandITenquiries@plymouth.ac.uk

THE PSYCHOLOGY
OF EVALUATION

Affective Processes in Cognition and Emotion

THE PSYCHOLOGY OF EVALUATION

Affective Processes in Cognition and Emotion

Edited by

Jochen Musch
Karl Christoph Klauer
University of Bonn

LEA LAWRENCE ERLBAUM ASSOCIATES, PUBLISHERS
2003 Mahwah, New Jersey   London

Lawrence Erlbaum Associates, Inc., Publishers
10 Industrial Avenue
Mahwah, New Jersey 07430

Cover design by Kathryn Houghtaling Lacey

Library of Congress Cataloging-in-Publication Data

The psychology of evaluation: affective processes in cognition and emotion,
edited by Jochen Musch and Karl Christoph Klauer.
Includes bibliographical references and indexes.
ISBN 0-8058-4047-8 (c) ✓

Copyright information for this volume can be obtained by contacting the Library of Congress.

Books published by Lawrence Erlbaum Associates are printed on acid-free paper,
and their bindings are chosen for strength and durability.

Printed in the United States of America
10 9 8 7 6 5 4 3 2 1

Contents

List of Contributors

Frank Baeyens, Department of Psychology, University of Leuven, Belgium

Rainer Banse, Department of Psychology, Humboldt University, Berlin, Germany

John Bargh, Department of Psychology, New York University, USA

Gerald Clore, Department of Psychology, University of Virginia, USA

Stanley Colcombe, Department of Psychology, University of Illinois, USA

Emily Crawford, Department of Psychology, University of Illinois, USA

Nathalie Dalle, Department of Psychology, University of Clermont-Ferrand, France

Jan De Houwer, Department of Psychology, University of Southampton, United Kingdom

Paul Eelen, Department of Psychology, University of Leuven, Belgium

Tedra Fazendeiro, Department of Psychology, University of Denver, USA

Melissa Ferguson, Department of Psychology, New York University, USA

Klaus Fiedler, Department of Psychology, University of Heidelberg, Germany

Jens Förster, Department of Psychology, University of Würzburg, Germany

Jack Glaser, Goldman School of Public Policy, University of California, Berkeley, USA

Dirk Hermans, Department of Psychology, University of Leuven, Belgium

Karl Christoph Klauer, Department of Psychology, University of Bonn, Germany

Jochen Musch, Department of Psychology, University of Bonn, Germany

Roland Neumann, Department of Psychology, University of Würzburg, Germany

Paul Niedenthal, CNRS and the University of Clermont-Ferrand, France

Rolf Reber, Department of Psychology, University of Bern, Switzerland

Michael Robinson, Department of Psychology, North Dakota State University, USA

Anette Rohmann, Department of Psychology, University of Münster, Germany

Klaus Rothermund, Department of Psychology, University of Trier, Germany

Norbert Schwarz, Institute for Social Research, University of Michigan, USA

Fritz Strack, Department of Psychology, University of Würzburg, Germany

Patrick Vargas, Department of Psychology, University of Illinois, USA

Dirk Wentura, Department of Psychology, University of Münster, Germany

Piotr Winkielman, Department of Psychology, University of Denver, USA

Chapter 1

The Psychology of Evaluation: An Introduction

Jochen Musch
Karl Christoph Klauer
Rheinische Friedrich-Wilhelms-Universität Bonn

Evaluative and affective information processing in individuals has long been a fundamental issue in social and cognitive psychology. The concepts *affect, valence,* and *attitude* are all fundamentally linked to the most basic psychological dimensions of good versus bad, positive versus negative, approach versus avoidance. The processing of stimulus valence, that is, the act of determining the location of a stimulus on the affective dimension, is at the heart of most current theories in cognition and emotion. Accordingly, there has been a dramatic increase in interest in evaluative processes in the late 20th century. Research on the nature of evaluative processes is now one of the most rapidly growing endeavours of psychology and provides a unifying focus for researchers working in a variety of disciplines such as social, cognitive, and personality psychology.

Of particular interest has been the question whether evaluations are elicited automatically, without intent, effort, and conscious awareness, and how these evaluations influence subsequent information processing. Much of this research has been conducted in the framework of the affective priming paradigm and has sought to identify conditions under which evaluations are processed automatically. Another major concern has been the consequences of the activated evaluations on the perceiver's judgments and behaviors. In addition, theoretical progress has revealed a number of surprising parallels and connections between affective priming and other paradigms such as evaluative conditioning, Stroop-analogous tasks, the Simon task, and the mere exposure paradigm, to name just a few. Finally, these insights have been used to develop unobtrusive measures of implicit attitudes such as the Implicit Association Test (IAT) and other tasks based on the affective priming paradigm. Out of this work, a common theoretical foundation for evaluative information processing is beginning to emerge. The present book seeks to provide an informative, scholarly, yet readable overview of what we know today about the nature of evaluation and affective processes in cognition and emotion. It summarizes all recent advances in the field, based on invited contributions from an eminent group of investigators.

However, this is not simply an edited book in the usual sense. Rather, it is the result of an ongoing discussion between a number of researchers united by a joint and continued interest in the psychology of evaluation. Accordingly, the idea for this book evolved in a number of interconnected forums and is the result of extensive and fruitful theoretical exchanges that took place on various occasions. In particular, from 1994 to 2000, several research projects within the research program "Information processing in its social context", which was initiated by Klaus Fiedler and Fritz Strack and implemented by the German Research Foundation DFG, dealt with affective and emotional processes. In June 1997, many of the contributors to the present volume met in Konstanz at a symposium on affective priming hosted by the social psychology division of the German Psychological Society. In 1998, a special issue of the German *Zeitschrift für Experimentelle Psychologie* was devoted to affective priming. In December 1998, Jan De Houwer and Dirk Hermans organized a workshop on affective processing in Leuven, as a part of the Scientific Research Network "Acquisition and representation of evaluative judgments and emotions". In June 1999, a symposium on affective priming took place in Kassel at the occasion of the biannual meeting of the German social psychologists. Finally, in March 2001, a special issue of *Cognition and Emotion* dealt with the psychology of evaluation, and in May 2001, another workshop supported by the Fund for Scientific Research (Flanders, Belgium) was being held in Le Lignely.

The book is organised into four main sections. The first section deals with the mechanisms, boundary conditions, and theories of automatic evaluation processes. In a comprehensive review of findings obtained in the affective priming paradigm, Klauer and Musch examine the evidence for different mechanisms that have been proposed to underlie automatic evaluation effects. Their review is structured around the impacts of the major procedural variables: Prime variables, target variables, variables related to the prime-target pairs, list-context variables, and task-related variables. Major explanations of affective priming effects and their respective empirical support are explored. The chapter concludes with a model of the evaluative system that comprises a process of automatic evaluation activation and two mechanisms, assumed to operate in parallel, that mediate the effects of activated evaluations on subsequent evaluative and noneval-uative processing.

In chapter 3, Wentura and Rothermund discuss consequences of the au-tomatic processing of valence that go beyond temporarily increasing the ac-cessibility of associated concepts. Because of its global relevance, they argue, the automatic processing of valence is strongly tied to response proc-esses and is therefore likely to interrupt ongoing behavior by modifying the probability of responses and redirecting behavior. Wentura and Rother-mund make a strong case for this power of positive and negative stimuli to *meddle* with ongoing processes of behavior formation, and present a theo-retical framework in which this *meddling-in* of valent stimuli is seen as the common ground to several automatic evaluation phenomena, including af-fective priming, Simon, and Stroop effects.

In chapter 4, dealing with boundary conditions of automatic evaluation processes, Glaser suggests that the automatic evaluative response is more complex than a simple binary orientation. Specifically, he argues that auto-matic evaluative responses can be automatically overridden when the prim-ing stimulus is obtrusive and when accuracy motivation is high. Such find-ings have implications for the important debate on the conditionality of automatic evaluation. Glaser suggests that positions holding that automatic evaluation will occur only for those stimuli toward which a reasonably strong attitude is held, and positions holding that automatic evaluation is unconditional and will occur with equal facility for strong and weak attitude objects, may represent a false dichotomy. According to Glaser, all stimuli can elicit an automatic evaluative response, but the strength of the attitude will moderate the magnitude of the response.

In a thought-provoking chapter that concludes the more theoretically oriented first section of the book (chapter 5), Fiedler points to hidden vicis-situdes of the priming paradigm in evaluative judgment research in a re-view that integrates findings from different priming paradigms ranging from simple perception and word-recognition experiments to more com-plex measures of decision making, manifest action, and goal orientation. Fiedler outlines an enriched framework for studying priming effects on evaluative judgments. Within this framework, he argues for the separation of the evaluative judgment domain from the original paradigm of priming in associative memory and highlights the distinction between afferent and efferent process components.

The second section of the book investigates how evaluations are ac-quired and how evaluative judgments are arrived at. Hermans, Baeyens, and Eelen (chapter 6) highlight parallels between evaluative learning and affective priming research and demonstrate the relevance of the study of evaluative conditioning for a better understanding of the processes that are involved in the cycle that encompasses the acquisition, the representation, and the activation of evaluative information in memory. In particular, they show that associative acquisition procedures are capable of inducing evaluative changes that can be assessed by indirect measures of stimulus valence such as the IAT and the affective priming procedure.

Ferguson and Bargh (chapter 7) argue against the assumption that an evaluation consists of a single, affective representation associated in memory with the object. Studies showing that participants are able to automatically evaluate novel, unfamiliar objects for which there are no previously stored, corresponding representations, are consistent with the claim that an evaluation represents a combination of numerous evaluations of various features of the object. In addition, these studies suggest that automatic evaluations can be spontaneously and immediately constructed on the spot, rather than being dependent on previous experience with, and conscious appraisal of, the objects.

Winkielman, Schwarz, Fazendeiro, and Reber (chapter 8) propose that one particular source of relevant information for the assessment of valence is the fluency with which information about the target can be processed. They propose that high fluency is associated with more favorable evaluations and present empirical evidence consistent with their proposal. Subsequently, they explore possible reasons for the link between fluency and affective reactions and discuss boundary conditions of the fluency-affect link.

The third section of the book considers indirect measures of individual differences in the evaluation of social objects. In his structural analysis of different indirect measures, De Houwer (chapter 9) focuses on four reaction time tasks that provide potential ways to measure attitudes indirectly: affective priming tasks, the emotional Stroop task, the Implicit Association Test, and the affective Simon task. De Houwer presents a taxonomy of these indirect measures of attitudes that reveals the essential similarities and differences between them, as well as their relation to existing compatibility tasks. He concludes by discussing the implications of this structural analysis for the measurement of attitudes.

In chapter 10, Banse presents the results of his research on unobtrusive measures of relationship quality. In an overview of experimental methods that have been used in relationship research, it is shown how attachment theories can be tested using indirect measures based on implicit associations and automatic evaluations that are not distorted by self-presentation concerns. However, problems and limitations of the priming approach to the investigation of the mental representation of relationships are also considered.

Robinson, Vargas, and Crawford (chapter 11) explore individual differences in evaluative processing. These differences in, for example, the speed to recognize rewards or threats have the potential to influence emotional behavior and experience. The authors therefore recommend to supplement self-report measures of personality traits by evaluative processing paradigms in order to develop a more complete understanding of how and why people differ in their emotional reactions. An agenda is set for future evaluative processing research in which individual differences play a central role.

The relationship between evaluations on one hand and mood, emotion and behavior on the other hand is explored in the fourth section of the book. Niedenthal, Rohmann, and Dalle (chapter 12) review the research on the automatic activation of evaluative responses and emotional states and discuss the theoretical distinction between evaluations and emotional responses. They report experimental evidence suggesting that the experience of emotional feelings and the activation of emotion concepts do not have the same consequences for subsequent information processing. They argue that a powerful theory of conceptual representation and processing is required in order to understand the conditions under which the processing of emotional words and concepts will result in the reexperience of some affect.

Clore and Colcombe (chapter 13) discuss the mood-like effects that sometimes occur when evaluative concepts are unconsciously primed. They propose that moods and primed evaluative concepts have parallel effects, because affective feelings and affective meaning obey the same rules. Both, affective feelings engendered by mood states, as well as unconsciously primed affective meaning can exert broad influence, because the implied evaluation is not tied to a particular source. Moreover, they argue that the information from affective mood and the information from affective priming share an important phenomenological quality that make them both especially compelling: in the absence of a salient, external source, they are experienced as internally generated.

In the concluding chapter, Neumann, Förster, and Strack (chapter 14) discuss how emotions and attitudes serve adaptive functions in preparing individuals to act in accordance with their needs and the requirements of their environment. In their view, evaluative processes underlying emotions and attitudes are directly linked to motor representations of either approach or avoidance responses. Approach or avoidance behavior is facilitated whenever compatible evaluative contents are processed. This link between evaluation and behavioral dispositions seems to be bidirectional in nature, however, in the sense that the execution of approach or avoidance behavior facilitates compatible evaluative processes. From this perspective, approach and avoidance behavior is not only a consequence, but also a cause of evaluative processes.

I: Mechanisms, Boundary Conditions, and Theories of Automatic Evaluation

Chapter 2

Affective Priming:
Findings and Theories

Karl Christoph Klauer
Jochen Musch
Rheinische Friedrich-Wilhelms-Universität Bonn

Environmental events directly and automatically activate three interactive but distinct psychological systems, responsible, respectively, for perceptual, evaluative, and motivational analysis according to a model proposed by Bargh (1997). These systems' automatic reactions to environmental events influence perceptual interpretations of other people's behavior, they color the evaluations of perceived objects and persons, and they inhibit or energize behavioral responses. Automaticity of a social phenomenon is a powerful finding because it implies that a person is not in conscious control of the behavior or perception in question, cannot escape the automatic processing once it is elicited by appropriate trigger stimuli, and ultimately cannot be held fully responsible for the ensuing biases in perceptions, judgments, and behavior (Bargh, 1999; Greenwald & Banaji, 1995).

Bargh (1997) distinguished preconscious from postconscious and goal-dependent forms of automaticity. Preconscious effects require only the presence of the triggering environmental event. They do not depend on a prepared or receptively tuned cognitive state. In contrast, postconscious and goal-dependent effects require special mental states in addition to the mere presence of triggering objects or events. For example, goal-dependent automaticity is conditioned on the individual intending to perform the mental function, but given this intention, the processing occurs immediately and autonomously in the presence of the triggering stimulus (e.g., Pendry & Macrae, 1996).

The evaluative system comprises a process of automatic activation of evaluations that is triggered by the mere presence of an object in one's field of perception. A major tenet is therefore that the process of evaluation activation is preconscious. A second postulate is that the evaluative system is functionally dissociable from the perceptual and the motivational system. The evidence for both assumptions stems in large part from the affective priming paradigm.

Affective priming refers to the phenomenon that processing of an evaluatively polarized target word (e.g., love) is facilitated, that is, proceeds faster and more accurately, when it is preceded by an evaluatively consistent prime word (e.g., sunshine) rather than an evaluatively inconsistent prime word (e.g., death). Since the seminal demonstrations by Fazio, Sanbonmatsu, Powell, and Kardes (1986), more than 80 studies have been conducted in that paradigm extending it in many ways and probing deeply into the dynamics and mechanisms of evaluative processing. An overview of the studies reviewed in this chapter is given in the appendix. Affective priming effects contrast evaluatively consistent and inconsistent prime-target pairs: They are defined by the interaction of prime and target valence. Both evaluatively consistent and inconsistent prime-target pairs comprise positive and negative words and thus, affective priming can be expected to provide a relatively pure measure of evaluative processing uncontaminated by nonevaluative differences between the sets of positive and negative stimuli in, for example, familiarity, informational diagnosticity, concreteness, and others. In recent years, the paradigm has also received attention as providing an unobtrusive measure for assessing evaluations (Banse, chap. 10, this volume; De Houwer, chap. 9, this volume; Fazio, Jackson, Dunton, & Williams, 1995; Hermans, Baeyens, & Eelen, chap. 6, this volume; Hermans, Vansteenwegen, Crombez, Baeyens, & Eelen, in press; Otten & Wentura, 1999).

The present chapter is organized as follows. We begin with a review of findings obtained in the affective priming paradigm. The review is structured around the impacts of the major procedural variables: Prime variables, target variables, variables related to the prime-target pairs, list-context variables, and task-related variables. The next section introduces the major explanations of affective priming effects and explores their respective empirical support vis à vis the just-reviewed findings. The chapter concludes with a model of the evaluative system that comprises a process of automatic evaluation activation and two mechanisms, assumed to operate in parallel, that mediate the effects of activated evaluations on subsequent evaluative and nonevaluative processing.

AFFECTIVE PRIMING: FINDINGS

In Fazio's (1989) attitude theory, attitudes are seen as object-evaluation associations stored in memory. The strength of the association determines the likelihood that the evaluation will be activated on encountering the attitude object. The associative strength is termed *attitude accessibility*, and it is measured by the speed with which attitude objects can be evaluated.

In Fazio et al.'s (1986) seminal demonstrations of affective priming, there were two experimental phases. In the first phase, attitude accessibilities of a number of attitude objects were assessed, and attitude objects high and low in accessibility were selected for each participant to serve as primes in the second phase of the experiment. In the second phase, evaluatively consistent and inconsistent prime-target pairs as well as pairs with neutral primes were presented. The participants' task was to classify the target word as good or bad as fast as possible; a task that we will refer to as the evaluative decision task. Targets were 10 clearly positive and 10 clearly negative adjectives. Primes were nouns that referred to attitude objects. There was also a baseline condition, in which primes were presumably neutral letter strings such as BBB.

In Experiment 1, prime-target onset asynchrony (SOA) was 300 ms. A priming effect emerged for primes high in attitude accessibility as assessed and selected in the first phase, but not for primes low in attitude accessibility. This effect was replicated in Experiment 2. A new condition realized a long SOA of 1000 ms and revealed an absence of affective priming effects both for low-accessibility as well as for high-accessibility primes. In Experiment 3, attitude accessibility was manipulated experimentally in the first phase in which participants evaluated some attitude objects repeatedly, thereby momentarily increasing these objects' attitude accessibility. Affective priming occurred at the short SOA (300 ms), but not at the long SOA, and it was stronger for the primes with heightened attitude accessibility.

Generality of Affective Priming

Subsequent research confirmed and extended many of the original findings. For example, whereas Fazio et al. (1986) asked participants to memorize the prime word and to recite it aloud after they had evaluated the target, many subsequent studies showed that the affective priming effect is not dependent on this requirement. In fact, in the majority of studies reviewed below participants were simply asked to ignore the prime word. In Hermans, Van den Broeck, and Eelen's (1998) Experiment 4 as well as in Bargh, Chaiken, Govender, and Pratto's (1992) Experiment 3, one group of participants was required to memorize and recite the prime word, whereas no such requirement was given for the participants of a second group. In both experiments, affective priming effects were not affected by the memory instruction. In a related experiment, Hermans, Crombez, and Eelen (2000) found that affective priming effects were not moderated by the requirement to hold a number of digits in memory for the duration of each priming trial.

Similarly, the effect can be obtained when there is no first phase of accessibility assessment or manipulation and when primes are instead selected from evaluation norms as having strong affective connotations. In fact, affective priming effects have now been obtained with a variety of positively and negatively evaluated stimuli as primes: With color slides of objects, persons, and animals (which were also used as targets; Hermans, De Houwer, & Eelen, 1994, Exp. 1); with photographs of self, significant others, and disliked persons (Banse, 2000); with black-and-white line drawings (Giner-Sorolla, Garcia, & Bargh, 1999); with non-words that were presented as Turkish translations of positive or negative words before the priming trials (De Houwer, Hermans, & Eelen, 1998); with positive and negative odors (Hermans, Baeyens, & Eelen, 1998). Finally, the effect does not appear to depend on the number of letters of prime and target words. Musch, Elze, and Klauer (1998) compared priming by short and long primes crossed with either short or long targets and found no moderating effect of prime and target length on the affective priming effect.

In a related paradigm that is also often called an affective-priming paradigm, Murphy and Zajonc (1993) presented smiling and scowling faces for either 4 ms or 1000 ms followed immediately by Chinese ideographs. Liking and evaluative ratings of Chinese ideographs were found to be assimilated to the affect displayed by the prime face under the brief, but not the long presentation duration. Similarities and differences between affective priming sensu Fazio et al. (1986) and related priming paradigms are discussed by Fiedler (chap. 5, this volume).

A recent innovation in procedure is the response window technique proposed by Greenwald, Draine, and Abrams (1996). The response window technique pushes participants toward responding within a narrow time frame after the presentation of the target. As Greenwald et al. (1996) pointed out, it has the major benefit of controlling for speed-accuracy tradeoff problems by forcing all response latencies to be relatively similar, thereby avoiding the dilution of the priming effect amongst both response latency and accuracy. The dependent variable with this procedure is the percentage of correct responses, and the technique typically leads to a large increase in the size of accuracy priming. It has been used extensively by Abrams and Greenwald (2000), Klauer and Musch (in press), Klinger, Burton, and Pitts (2000), Musch (2000), and Musch and Klauer (2001) to secure affective priming effects under a wide range of conditions.

Prime Strength

An early debate concerned the question of whether affective priming is found only for strongly accessible primes (Glaser, chap. 4, this volume). Fazio et al. (1986) consistently found stronger effects for strongly accessible than for weakly accessible primes given a short SOA of 300 ms. These effects were replicated by Bargh et al. (1992; Exp. 1). Interestingly, strong affective priming effects also emerged for primes selected for consistency in evaluations across participants rather than for strong accessibility (Bargh et al., 1992; Exps. 1 & 2). Moreover, when the first phase of accessibility assessment was separated from the priming trials by two days, the moderation by accessibility was eliminated (Exp. 2), as further supported by a study by Chaiken and Bargh (1993). Thus, it appears to make a difference whether prime accessibility is assessed two days in advance of, or immediately before, the priming trials. A parsimonious explanation might be that the evaluation latencies used to assess accessibility are themselves only moderately stable over a period of 2 days. If so, a regression effect would work to attenuate the accessibility manipulation and any effects associated with it over that period.

De Houwer et al. (1998) had participants learn translations of ostensibly Turkish words that were unknown to the participants. The translations were strongly positive or negative words. In three experiments with the evaluative decision task and an SOA of 300 ms, the Turkish words engendered affective priming effects when used as primes after the learning phase. When their evaluation latencies, the measure of attitude accessibility, were assessed in a separate study (Exp. 5), the Turkish words' evaluations were found to be less accessible than those associated with strongly and even with only moderately positive and negative words. It was concluded that affective priming can also be obtained even when attitude accessibility is low.

Just as attitude objects can differ in the strength of the object-evaluation association, people may differ in the chronic accessibility of evaluations. Building on this idea, Hermans, De Houwer, and Eelen (2001; Exp. 3) used the Need to Evaluate Scale (NES) by Jarvis and Petty (1996) to form two groups that differed in their disposition to engage in evaluative responding. Under an SOA of 300 ms, affective priming emerged in evaluative decisions of the group with high NES scores, but not in the group with low NES scores.

Although the strength of the object-evaluation association is logically independent of the extremity of the evaluation itself, accessibility and evaluation extremity tend to be correlated and therefore, studies that have manipulated the extremity of prime evaluations are also relevant to this debate. Giner-Sorolla et al. (1999) used line drawings that were either strongly or weakly polarized in normative evaluations and found a tendency for affective priming to be stronger for strong rather than weak primes in their Experiment 1. A number of studies have used the pronunciation task, in which participants are asked to name the target as quickly as possible, and manipulated prime accessibility and/or extremity to obtain weak, moderate, and strong primes. Bargh, Charken, Raymond, and Hymes (1996) consistently found equivalent affective priming effects for weak and strong primes in naming latencies as did Giner-Sorolla et al. (1999) in their Experiment 2. Glaser and Banaji (1999), on the other hand, obtained *reversed* affective priming effects with extreme primes (i.e. faster responses for inconsistent rather than consistent prime-target pairs), and normal or no affective priming effects for trials based on moderately evaluated primes. Using Bargh et al.' s (1996) procedures and stimuli, Glaser (chap. 4, this volume) in contrast finds a weak normal effect for both weak and strong primes. Finally, in an attempt to replicate the Bargh, et al. (1996) findings, Klauer and Musch (2000; Exp. 3) did not obtain affective priming effects in the pronunciation task irrespective of prime strength.

To summarize, there is some evidence that affective priming in the evaluative decision task is moderated by attitude accessibility and related indicators of prime strength. However, affective priming can also be obtained with primes low in accessibility and strength. Based on their findings with the pronunciation task, Bargh et al. (1996) have argued that the impact of accessibility and extremity is modulated by the presence of a goal to evaluate. Such a goal is clearly present in the evaluative decision task, where accessibility effects are typically found, and presumably absent in the pronunciation task, where accessibility effects are often not found. The pattern of findings obtained with the pronunciation task is however complex and will be discussed further in subsequent sections.

Prime Presentation Parameters: Masked Priming

In this section, studies of two kinds are considered. The first kind is given by studies that seek to establish the existence of affective priming effects when primes are rendered invisble by suitable masks. The second class of studies aim at demonstrating functional dissociations between visible and masked priming effects by showing that they are differentially affected by experimental manipulations.

Does Subliminal Affective Priming Occur?   Studies demonstrating affective priming when primes are rendered invisible by suitable masks provide strong support for a role of automatic processes. Greenwald, Klinger, and Liu (1989) report three experiments in which primes were masked dichoptically by presentation of a random letter-fragment pattern to the dominant eye, either rapidly following the prime (Exp. 1) or presented simultaneously with the prime (Exps. 2 and 3). The effectiveness of the masking procedure was demonstrated by participants' inability to discriminate the left versus right position of a test series of words viewed under the same masking conditions as the prime stimuli. In each experiment, there were additional trials in which the prime words were presented without masks and thus were clearly visible. In all three experiments, significant masked priming effects were obtained with the chosen SOA of 500 ms, whereas affective priming by visible primes was not obtained in Experiment 2.

Studies of unconscious cognition typically compare direct and indirect measures of stimulus effects. Indirect effects are uninstructed influences of the task stimuli on behavior. Direct effects measure instructed influences of the relevant stimuli. In the Greenwald et al. (1989) studies, for example, indirect effects were the priming effects, and direct effects of prime words were measured by the position discrimination task. Under the assumption that the sensitivity of the direct measure for conscious stimulus effects is at least as great as that of the indirect measure (Reingold & Merikle, 1988), an indirect-without-direct effect pattern provides evidence for unconscious stimulus processing.

Greenwald, Klinger, and Schuh (1995) proposed a regression method to secure the desired indirect-without-direct effect pattern. In that technique, an indirect measure is regressed on an appropriate direct measure. It is tested whether the intercept of this regression function is significantly larger than zero, implying indirect effects in the absence of a direct effect. The new method has instigated considerable debate (Dosher, 1998; Greenwald & Draine, 1998; Klauer, Greenwald, & Draine, 1998; Klauer & Greenwald, 2000; Merikle & Reingold, 1998; Miller, 2000), and refinements of the method were proposed by Klauer, Draine, and Greenwald (1998). Using the new method, Greenwald et al. (1995) compared visible and masked priming over an impressive series of experiments. With SOAs between 250 ms and 300 ms, there was no priming by visible primes and only weak evidence for some amount of priming in the masked condition that was present to the extent to which there was also evidence for direct effects (i.e., zero intercept, but positive slope of the regression function relating indirect and direct measure). These results thus provide little evidence for subliminal affective priming.

Recent research has tended to use so-called sandwich masks rather than dichoptical masking. In sandwich masking, the prime word is preceded by a meaningless letter string (forward mask), and is followed by another meaningless letter string (backward mask). Combining sandwich masking with the response window technique, Draine and Greenwald (1998; cf. Greenwald et al., 1996) studied affective priming for masked primes. Direct effects were assessed by participants' ability to discriminate between prime words and letter strings of alternating Xs and Gs viewed under the same masking conditions as were used in the priming trials (Exps. 1 to 3). In Experiment 4, another direct measure was also realized, namely to make evaluative decisions on the masked prime words. With SOAs between 34 ms and 67 ms and masked primes presented for 17 ms, 33 ms, or 50 ms, intercepts significantly larger than zero were reliably obtained for the larger presentation durations of 33 ms and 50 ms in four experiments. An analysis of the aggregated data revealed the desired indirect-without-direct pattern also for the 17 ms prime duration (cf. also Klauer et al., 1998).

Thus, affective priming effects can be obtained with primes rendered invisible by suitable masks. Extending this work, Abrams and Greenwald (2000) investigated which aspects of prime words were crucial for these masked effects and found that letter strings composed of subword fragments of earlier-viewed targets functioned as effective evaluative primes. For example, after repeated evaluation of the targets *angle* and *warm*, the nonword *anrm* acted as an evaluatively positive prime (Exp. 1), and there were indications that when fragments were combined to yield words with evaluations that were the opposite of the parent words, the evaluation of the parent words prevailed in priming effects (Exp. 2). Thus, *smile* worked as an evaluatively negative prime after repeated classification of the targets *smut* and *bile*. In addition, priming was obtained only when primes did contain parts of earlier targets (Exp. 3), a finding that is further discussed in the section on open questions.

Functional Dissociations Between Masked and Visible Affective Priming. A number of studies have compared visible and masked priming and found that both kinds of priming effects were affected differently by experimental manipulations. Musch (2000) used the response window technique and sandwich masking to compare the so-called consistency proportion effect for masked and visible primes. The consistency proportion effect refers to the observation that affective priming effects tend to increase as the proportion of evaluatively consistent prime-target pairs increases relative to the proportion of inconsistent pairs (Klauer, Roßnagel, & Musch, 1997). With an SOA of 71 ms, Musch (2000; Exp. 5) obtained the consistency proportion effect for visible primes, thereby replicating findings of his previous experiments in this series. However, when primes were masked, the effect did not show although a substantial priming effect was found, and this difference in the consistency proportion effects for masked and visible primes was significant.

Greenwald et al. (1996) contrasted visible and masked priming as a function of SOA using the response window technique and sandwich masks. They found a rapid decline in masked priming for SOAs exceeding 100 ms, whereas priming by visible primes was undiminished over SOAs varying from 100 ms to 400 ms. A dissociation between visible and masked priming was also demonstrated with respect to a so-called sequential effect in the studies summarized by Greenwald et al. (1996). When the trial preceding the current trial had presented an evaluatively inconsistent rather than consistent prime-target pair, affective priming was diminished in the current trial. This effect occurred with visible primes and an SOA of 150 ms, but was absent when primes were masked by sandwich masks and SOA was 67 ms in experiments that employed the response window procedure.

Another interesting dissociation has recently been reported by Banse (2000; Exp. 2). Comparing priming engendered by pictures and names of a liked person (Charlie Chaplin), a disliked person (Saddam Hussein), and a neutral stranger, normal priming was found when primes were visible whereas *reversed* effects emerged when primes were masked (SOA 42 ms; evaluative decision task). Similarly, Hermans (1996), obtained indications of reversed effects in masked priming in two of three studies under conditions that led to normal priming effects when primes were visible (Hermans et al., 1994, Exp. 1).

To summarize, indirect without direct effects of prime words can be reliably produced when short SOAs and the response window technique are used. In addition, local sequential effects and consistency proportion effects occur for visible, but not for masked primes.

Target Presentation Parameters

Only a few studies have looked at effects of target variables. Musch and Klauer (2001) presented primes and targets simultaneously at different locations on the screen. For half of the participants, the location of the upcoming target was signalled by an advance cue appearing 600 ms and 150 ms before target onset in Experiments 1 and 2, respectively; for the other half, the advance cue was uninformative with respect to target location. In both experiments, affective priming was observed only in the latter group (i.e. under locational uncertainty), but not when participants could prepare for the target's location.

While prime and target were always shown in different locations in these experiments, Hermans et al. (2001; Exp. 3) compared centered versus uncentered presentation of prime and target. In centered trials, primes and targets were presented at the same central location on the screen with an SOA of 300 ms. In uncentered trials, primes and targets were written on different adjacent lines, one above the other. Affective priming was obtained for the centered, but not for the uncentered trials. It appears from these studies that affective priming effects are weakened when a perceptual and/or attentional separation of primes and targets is supported by the manner of presentation.

In an experiment by De Houwer, Hermans, and Spruyt (2001), half of the participants were presented targets in a degraded fashion (e.g., %U%G%L%Y%) and the other half saw undegraded targets (e.g., UGLY). Using the pronunciation task and an SOA of 250 ms, affective priming ef-

fects were found in the degraded condition, but not in the standard undegraded condition.

SOA: The Time Course of Affective Priming

Stimulus-onset asynchrony is an important moderator of affective priming
effects as already indicated by the original Fazio et al. (1986) studies.
Klauer, Roßnagel, and Musch (1997; Exp. 1) varied SOA in six steps (-100
ms, 0 ms, 100 ms, 200 ms, 600 ms, and 1200 ms) in a between-participants
design. SOA had a significant effect, and individually significant priming effects were found at SOAs 0 ms and 100 ms, but not at the other SOAs. These
findings were corroborated in a study by Hermans et al. (2001; Exp. 1) using a within-participants design and five levels of SOA (-150 ms, 0 ms, 150
ms, 300 ms, 450 ms). Individually significant priming effects emerged at the
short SOAs of 0 ms and 150 ms and were absent at the other SOA levels.
Using the pronunciation task and SOAs of 150 ms, 300 ms, and 1000 ms in a
second experiment, an individually significant priming effect was obtained
at the SOA 150 ms, but not at the longer SOAs. Taken together with the
above-reviewed findings by Greenwald et al. (1996; section on masked
priming), these different findings indicate that affective priming effects are
obtained most robustly for short SOAs well below 300 ms. Thus, the activation of prime evaluations appears to be quite short-lived.

List Context Effects

Is affective priming a local phenomenon that depends only on the characteristics of the current trial, or is it modulated by the wider context in which
the prime-target pair is placed? As already explained, sequential effects of
the trial preceding the current one were in fact found with visible primes in
the experiments by Greenwald et al. (1996). Wentura (1999) also demonstrated that responses to the target of a given trial are influenced by characteristics of the preceding trial in the evaluative decision task. Specifically,
when the prime in the preceding trial matched the current target in valence, responses were inhibited in two experiments with SOA 300 ms; a pattern of results that is known as negative priming (e.g., Fox, 1995).

Klauer et al. (1997) manipulated the proportion of evaluatively consistent prime-target pairs presented in the evaluative decision task. In a between-participants design, three proportions were realized in their Experiment 2: 25%, 50%, and 75%. A second between-participants factor was SOA
(0 ms, 200 ms, and 1000 ms). As already explained, a consistency proportion (CP) effect is given if affective priming increases as a function of consistency proportion. A CP effect was found in the latency data for the 0 ms

SOA and in the error data for the 200 ms SOA, but not at the long SOA of 1000 ms. Musch and Klauer (1997) replicated the CP effect at SOA 0 ms.

In a series of experiments employing the response window procedure and the evaluative decision task with SOA 71 ms, Musch (2000) further explored the CP effect. In a first experiment, the CP effect was again replicated. The second experiment addressed the question whether local sequential contingencies were responsible for the effect. It has been argued that participants can shift the weight given to the prime information on a trial-by-trial basis. Specifically, they might rely more strongly on the prime information when it has just been seen to provide valid information regarding the target valence in the last trial, that is, when that trial presented an evaluatively consistent prime-target pair, as is indeed suggested by the sequential effect observed by Greenwald et al. (1996; cf. Greenwald & Rosenberg, 1978). In lists with a high CP, trials are frequently preceded by trials with evaluatively consistent prime-target pairs, simply because such pairs are generally more frequent when CP is high. Therefore, the CP effect could reflect a trial-by-trial adjustment of the weight given to the prime information. In Experiment 2, CP was manipulated in three steps (25%, 50%, and 75%) between participants. A subset of trials was, however, balanced with respect to evaluative consistency versus inconsistency of the preceding prime-target pair in each CP condition. Nevertheless, the CP effect emerged in full strength even when only the balanced subset of trials was considered. The notion that the CP effect reflects context-dependencies that extend over a wider range than just the preceding trial was further supported by Experiment 3, in which a final block of trials realized a 50% CP regardless of the CP that was given in the previous five blocks (either 25%, 50%, and 75%). The CP effect was found to be as strong in this last block as in the ones preceding it. Because the actual CP was 50% in this block, a local explanation of the effect is ruled out. In a fourth experiment, only inconsistent prime-target pairs and pairs with neutral letter string primes were employed to explore the extent to which the CP effect might eliminate affective priming. Although the CP was 0% in this study, a residual affective priming effect was nevertheless found. In a final experiment (Exp. 5), masked and visible primes were compared in a between-participants design that also varied CP. The usual CP effect emerged for visible primes, but was absent in the masked priming groups, and this difference was reliable. To summarize, the CP effect moderates affective priming, but cannot override it. In addition, it appears to rely on learning processes that extend over a wider range of trials and require prime visibility to occur.

It can be concluded that visible affective priming in the evaluative decision task is modulated both by the local trial-by-trial context in which a given trial is placed and by the global list context in which the trials are embedded.

Task

Another kind of context-dependency is given by task-dependence. The pattern of findings differs pronouncedly between tasks. It is helpful to categorize tasks in three groups: Tasks requiring the identification of certain target attributes, tasks that require affirmative and negative responses, and the pronunciation task.

Identifying Target Attributes.   Most of the studies have relied on the original evaluative decision task in which the prime valence has a direct relationship to the required response. When targets had to be classified with respect to nonevaluative features, however, affective priming usually did not occur. For example, Hermans, Van den Broeck, and Eelen (1998; Exp. 3) contrasted evaluative decisions with a color-naming task. Targets appeared in one of four colors, and in the color naming trials, participants were to name the color in which the target was written. Affective priming effects were found for the evaluative decision task, but not in the color naming task, and this difference between the two kinds of trials was significant. Previous experiments in this series had used only the color-naming task and did not obtain affective priming as was the case in two experiments conducted by Rothermund and Wentura (1998) with the color-naming task.

In a related study, De Houwer, Hermans, Rothermund, and Wentura (2000; Exp. 2) contrasted two groups. In the first group, participants categorized targets as persons versus animals (semantic classification); in the second group, participants were required to make evaluative decisions on these same targets. An affective priming effect was found for the evaluative decision task, but not for the semantic-classification task. This difference between tasks in the pattern of priming effects was significant. Similarly, Klinger et al. (2000; Exp. 2) had members of different groups either classify targets as denoting living versus nonliving things (animacy decisions) or make evaluative decisions on targets. Affective priming effects were found in evaluative decisions, but not in the animacy decisions. Conversely, the animacy category of the prime elicited congruency effects in the animacy decision task, but not in the evaluative decision task. That is, deciding whether a target denoted a living versus nonliving thing was facilitated when prime and target were congruent (both living versus both nonliving) rather than incongruent (one living, the other nonliving) in this respect; this kind of congruency had no effect on evaluative decisions, however.

Double dissociations of this kind constitute strong evidence for the task-dependence of affective priming. In four experiments by Klauer and Musch (in press), primes and targets could vary orthogonally with respect to their valence and with respect to their values on a second dimension. The second dimension was spanned, respectively, by two presentation locations of prime and target stimuli (an upper vs. a lower line; Exp. 1), by two colors in which prime and target were presented (blue vs. brown; Exp. 2), by letter case (small vs. capital letters; Exp. 3), and by grammatical category (adjective vs. noun; Exp. 4). In each experiment, one group was asked to make evaluative decisions on targets, whereas members of the second group were required to decide which of the two values of the second dimension was realized by a given target. In each experiment, affective priming effects were found in evaluative decisions, but not for the group making decisions on nonevaluative target features. Conversely, equivalent nonevaluative congruency effects engendered by the prime value on the second dimension were found in the group making decisions with respect to that dimension, but not in the group making evaluative decisions across all four experiments.

Tasks Requiring Affirmative and Negative Responses. Thus, affective priming effects were reliably found only when the task itself was focused on evaluations. An exception to this rule may, however, be given by tasks that require affirmative and negative responses as in yes/no decisions. For example, in the lexical decision task, targets can be words or meaningless letter strings. Participants are asked to decide whether or not the target is a word and to respond "yes, word" in the first case and "no, not a word" in the second case. In trials in which primes and targets are words, evaluative consistency of prime and target can be manipulated to test for affective priming effects. Klinger et al. (2000, Exp. 2) used masked primes and found no evidence for affective priming in the lexical decision task. With visible primes, however, Wentura (1998, 2000) reported effects of affective priming in that task. In addition, priming was moderated by the assignment of "yes" and "no" responses to words and nonwords, respectively. In the usual "word=yes" condition, Wentura (1998, 2000) obtained affective priming effects in three experiments. These effects were however reversed in tendency (Wentura, 1998) and significantly (Wentura, 2000; Exp. 2) when participants were required to respond "no" if the target was a word and "yes" if it was a nonword. A similar reversal of affective priming effects from trials requiring yes-responses to those requiring no-responses was reported by Klauer and Stern (1992) in an early study based on grammatical classifications of prime-target pairs.

In Experiments 5 to 8 by Klauer and Musch (in press), primes and targets varied with respect to evaluations and orthogonally with respect to the same nonevaluative second dimensions used in Experiment 1 to 4, respectively, as just detailed previously. Participants were required to compare primes and targets with respect to valence (first group) or with respect to their values on the second dimension realized in each experiment (second group) and to respond "yes, same" in the case of a match and "no, different" in the case of a mismatch. Pervasive affective priming effects (i.e. facilitatory effects of a match of prime and target valence), were found in the group making nonevaluative comparisons for trials requiring "yes, same" responses. The affective priming effects were eliminated or reversed in tendency for the "no, different" response. Equivalent congruency effects of matches versus mismatches on the second, nonevaluative dimension were not found in the group making evaluative comparisons. In a ninth study, participants made decisions on the grammatical category of the target and were required to respond "yes" for one category (e.g., in the case of a noun) and "no" for the other category of targets (e.g., in the case of an adjective). Again, affective priming was found for trials requiring "yes" responses, and the effect was reversed in tendency for trials requiring "no" responses. This is a remarkable finding as there were no effects of the irrelevant evaluations in a previous study in this series (Exp. 4) that used exactly the same task with the only difference that the responses were directly labelled *adjective* and *noun*, respectively. Taken together, there is some evidence that the affective match (mismatch) of prime and target can bias nonevaluative "yes" ("no") responses.

The Naming Task.   Finally, a number of studies have employed the pronunciation task to study affective priming. Hermans et al. (1994; Exp. 2) found an affective priming effect using that task and an SOA of 300 ms. As already mentioned, Hermans et al. (2001; Exp. 2) manipulated SOA in three levels (150 ms, 300 ms, 1000 ms) in a study that found no overall affective priming effect and no main effect of SOA. An individually significant effect emerged at the short SOA, however. Bargh et al. (1996; Exps. 1 to 3) and Giner-Sorolla et al. (1999; Exp. 2) consistently observed affective priming effects in the pronunciation task for weak and strong primes using SOAs between 250 ms and 300 ms. Klauer and Musch (2001) ran five statistically powerful experiments with the pronunciation task that varied prime-set size (10 primes vs. infinite set size) and target-set size (2, 10, infinite; SOA 200 ms; Exp. 1a and 1b), SOA (0 ms, 50 ms, 100 ms; Exp. 2), prime strength (weak vs. strong; SOA 300 ms; Exp. 3) and language of primes and targets (English vs. German; SOA 300 ms; Exp. 4) and did not observe affective priming in any of these experiments although traditional semantic priming (Neely, 1991) was obtained. De Houwer, Hermans, and Spruyt (2001) found affective priming when targets were presented in a degraded manner, but not under the standard undegraded presentation mode with SOAs of 250 ms. Similarly, De Houwer et al. (1998; Exp. 2) did not obtain an affective priming effects for stimuli that were associated with positively and negatively valenced words in the experimental context although these stimuli engendered priming effects in evaluative decisions (Exps. 1, 3, and 4). Finally, in a series of five experiments with SOA 150 ms and the pronunciation task, Glaser and Banaji (1999) found reversed affective priming effects by strong primes (Exps. 1 to 5), and normal (Exps. 2 and 3) or no (Exps. 4 and 5) affective priming effects for moderately strong primes. Using stimuli and procedures more similar to the Bargh et al. (1996) experiments, Glaser (chap. 4, this volume) in contrast finds a weak normal priming effect for both weak and strong primes. There are also many unpublished studies that failed to obtain an affective priming effect in the pronunciation task (e.g., Hermans, 1996). We are not aware of published studies that have compared the pronunciation task to other tasks within one experiment.

This review of the effects of task settings supports the following conclusions:

- When targets have to be classified into a small number of categories, there are priming effects engendered by task-relevant prime categories, but prime categories that are not task-relevant do not give rise to priming effects. There are no differences between evaluative and non-evaluative classifications in this respect.
- When the task requires affirmative or negative responses, affective priming effects occur for trials requiring affirmative responses, and they tend to be eliminated or reversed for trials requiring negative responses.
- The pattern of findings obtained with the naming task is mixed and complex, and there appear to be as yet unidentified factors determining whether normal priming effects, reversed effects, or no effects are obtained.

AFFECTIVE PRIMING: EXPLANATIONS

Several mechanisms have been considered as underlying affective priming effects (cf. De Houwer, chap. 9, this volume; Fiedler, chap. 5, this volume; Wentura & Rothermund, chap. 3, this volume). The most prominent are (1) a mechanism based on an analogy with the semantic priming paradigm (Neely, 1991) and the notion of spreading activation, (2) a mechanism based on an analogy with the Stroop paradigm (MacLeod, 1991) and the notions of selective attention and response competition (Klauer, 1998; Klauer, Roßnagel, & Musch, 1997; Musch, 2000; Rothermund & Wentura, 1998), and (3) an affective-matching hypothesis proposed by Klauer (1991; Klauer, 1998; Klauer & Stern, 1992). In the account by spreading activation, primes exert an influence by preactivating related target nodes in a lexical or semantic network. In the Stroop mechanism, irrelevant evaluations exert an effect by virtue of the observed response having an evaluative component. In the affective-matching mechanism, irrelevant evaluations exert an effect by virtue of biasing yes/no-responses.

The Account by Spreading Activation

An early explanation of affective priming drew an analogy between affective priming and semantic priming (Neely, 1991) using the concept of spreading activation. Roughly, perceiving the prime is assumed to activate its representing node in a lexical or semantic network (Bower, 1991; Fazio et al., 1986), and the activation then spreads to nodes of evaluatively consistent targets, but not of inconsistent targets, thereby facilitating processing of the target whenever prime and target are evaluatively consistent. Spreading activation can thereby account for affective priming effects.

Yet, there are many findings that are difficult to reconcile with the notion of spreading activation. According to the account by spreading activation, pervasive and context-independent facilitation of target processing should be a consequence of evaluative consistency of prime and target at least when lexical processing of the target is required. This expectation is not borne out by the findings of strong task-dependence (e.g., De Houwer et al., 2000; Klauer & Musch, in press; Klinger et al., 2000; Rothermund & Wentura, 1998) reviewed earlier. Nor does it agree well with the finding that in tasks with affirmative and negative responses, the effects of evaluative consistency are less pronounced and in tendency *reversed* when negative responses are required (Klauer & Musch, in press; Klauer & Stern, 1992; Wentura, 1998, 2000).

Similarly, list-context effects are also difficult to explain from the perspective of a spread of activation. Thus, the sequential effects observed by Wentura (1999) and Greenwald et al. (1996) as well as the CP effects found by Klauer et al. (1997; Musch, 2000; Musch & Klauer, 1997) at short SOAs cannot be accounted for by this mechanism. For these and other, more theoretical reasons (e.g., Bargh, 1997; Klauer & Musch, 2001), the account by spreading activation has been abandoned by most researchers in the field.

Hermans et al. (1998) proposed an affective-motivational account of affective priming according to which evaluative inconsistency, but not evaluative consistency, of two incoming stimuli delays any kind of cognitive processing, irrespective of the participants' current goals. This mechanism also leads one to expect affective priming effects on target processing regardless of the nature of the task that participants are required to perform on the target word, and it encounters the same difficulties as the account by spreading activation.

Spreading activation is, however, still relevant as a methodological caveat. Spreading activation is often argued to underlie the reliable and largely task-independent priming effects observed for strongly associated primes and targets (e.g., bread and butter; Neely, 1991). Many researchers have therefore taken explicit measures to control for associative relatedness in prime-target pairs used in affective priming studies. In our own research, we prepare large and diverse pools of positive and negative words, from which each participant's list is randomly sampled. This is to ensure that evaluative consistent and inconsistent word pairs do not differ systematically and substantially within and across participants in associative relatedness. Another possibility is to look at each list of prime-target pairs and to screen out associatively related pairs before presentation (e.g., Rothermund & Wentura, 1998). In some circumstances, a third possibility is to analyze the data by items rather than by participants. If an affective priming effect goes back to a few targets that by accident are paired with highly associated primes for all participants, then the effect should not generalize over targets although it might generalize over participants. That is, instead of computing an affective priming effect for each participant by averaging over items, the analysis by items computes the effect for each target by averaging over participants (Clark, 1973; for examples in the context of affective priming, see Wentura, 2000). The target-wise priming effects are then subjected to an analysis of variance with targets taking the role of participants to see whether the effects generalize over items or are concentrated on a few unusual, or unusually paired, targets.

The Stroop Mechanism

In the classical Stroop task, words are presented in different colors. Naming the color is delayed when the word itself denotes a color that differs from the one that the word is written in (MacLeod, 1991). There are many variants of the task, some of which are structurally similar to the evaluative decision task in affective priming research. The so-called flanker task in particular works with two sets of stimuli (e.g., the letters H and K versus S and C), which are assigned different responses (e.g., pressing the left key for H and K, and pressing the right key for S and C). Irrelevant letters from the wrong response set interfere with the response to the target (Eriksen & Eriksen, 1974) when they flank the target letter. Flanker effects are also found with words from different categories (Shaffer & LaBerge, 1979) and the task to categorize the target word (e.g., as a piece of furniture vs. a metal). When primes are identified with flankers, affective priming in the evaluative decision task can thus be seen as an instance of flanker effects (cf. De Houwer, chap. 9, this volume; Klauer et al., 1997; Rothermund & Wentura, 1998; Wentura & Rothermund, chap. 3, this volume).

Adapting a prominent model of Stroop effects (Logan & Zbrodoff, 1979) to the present case, Musch (2000) assumed that both prime and target evaluations are activated and integrated in a random-walk process on a decision dimension related to the responses. Two response thresholds are located on the decision dimension, and a response is made as soon as the accumulated evidence falls outside the interval spanned by the two thresholds. At each point in time, the available evidence is given by a weighted sum of the accrued prime information and the accrued target information. The weights themselves are sums of automatic and strategic components. An automatic component of the prime weight is positive and reflects the automatic influence of irrelevant prime evaluations as found in masked priming. The prime weight also has a strategic component that reflects strategies of attention allocation, requiring some amount of strategic, conscious processing, as occurs in contexts where the prime information is generally valid and helpful (Cheesman & Merikle, 1986). The integration of prime and target evaluations proceeds in a random-walk process in which the impacts of prime and target are accrued in proportion to their weights.

The Stroop mechanism thereby explains visible and masked affective priming in evaluative decisions, and its time course agrees well with analogous findings from other Stroop-like tasks (MacLeod, 1991). In addition, consistency proportion effects and sequential effects of the Greenwald et al. (1996) variety can be explained through learning-induced, strategic shifts in prime weights that require visibility of the irrelevant prime stimulus (Cheesman & Merikle, 1986; cf. Musch, 2000). Similarly, separating prime and target location, and allowing participants to prepare for the target location supports a strategy of attention allocation in which to-be-ignored prime information is given a small weight because it can be more effectively ignored when perceivers can prepare for the location of the target (Musch & Klauer, 2001). On the other hand, presenting prime and target at the same rather than different locations is likely to hinder the strategic screening out of prime information, thereby explaining larger priming in the former condition (Hermans et al., 2001). Furthermore, negative priming effects as demonstrated by Wentura (1999) for affective priming are generally found in Stroop-like tasks and thus fall under the scope of effects that can be explained by the set of mechanisms that underlie findings in Stroop tasks. Effects of prime strength follow naturally from Musch's (2000) model in which prime and target evaluations are integrated in the form of a weighted sum. Effects of prime accessibility follow from the temporal dynamics of this random-walk model, in which evaluations that are available quickly are likely to exert a greater influence.

Finally, the mechanism is easily reconciled with the absence of affective priming in tasks that require nonevaluative classification of target stimuli (cf. section on task-dependence), because only response-relevant prime information is integrated. But for the same reason, it cannot explain affective priming in nonevaluative tasks that require affirmative or negative responses such as the lexical decision task. Nor can it account for affective priming in the pronunciation task for which task the pattern of findings is, however, complex and mixed. To summarize, the Stroop mechanism integrates the results obtained with the evaluative decision task, but fares less well in accounting for affective priming in nonevaluative tasks.

The Affective-Matching Mechanism

A mechanism that predicts a broader range of effects of irrelevant evaluations is the affective-matching mechanism. It was originally proposed to account for tendencies toward evaluative consistency in social judgments (e.g., Abelson & Rosenberg, 1958; Cooper, 1981; cf. Klauer, 1991; Klauer & Stern, 1992; Nisbett & Wilson, 1977) and is adapted from so-called post-lexical mechanisms as discussed in the context of semantic priming (e.g., de Groot, 1984; Neely, Keefe, & Ross, 1989).

The affective-matching model makes three assumptions:

1. It is assumed that the evaluations of both prime and target are activated automatically and are spontaneously compared for evaluative consistency regardless of the perceiver's current goals or tasks.

2. Evaluative consistency of two words (e.g., sunshine, friendly) gives rise to a feeling of plausibility, evaluative inconsistency (e.g., sunshine, sick) engenders a feeling of implausibility.

3. A spontaneous feeling of plausibility facilitates making *affirmative* responses, whereas a spontaneous feeling of implausibility inhibits such responses. Conversely, a spontaneous feeling of implausibility facilitates making *negative* responses, whereas a spontaneous feeling of plausibility inhibits such responses. That is, a feeling of plausibility biases affirmative responses and a feeling of implausibility biases negative responses.

An effect of evaluative consistency is predicted by this mechanism whenever affirmative or negative responses are required with respect to both evaluatively consistent as well as inconsistent word pairs. Consider, for example, the case of lexical decisions. In the lexical decision task, participants decide whether target letter strings constitute words or not. When prime and target are evaluatively consistent words, the "yes, word" response is facilitated, via a feeling of plausibility, according to the affective-matching model. The "yes" response is inhibited, via a feeling of implausibility, when prime and target are evaluatively inconsistent words. As a result, an affective priming effect is predicted for word targets although the evaluations of prime and target are irrelevant in the lexical decision task.

Wentura (1998, 2000) has used the lexical decision task to perform tests of this model. As just explained, affective priming effects for word targets are expected and were in fact obtained. The crucial test of the model consisted of a condition in which the assignment of "yes" responses and "no" responses to words and nonwords, respectively, was reversed. Because of Assumption 3, the affective-matching model predicts a reversal of priming effects as a consequence of this manipulation. For the original "word=yes" condition, the affective priming effect emerged, whereas the data pattern was in fact reversed for the "word=no" condition. That is, "no" responses to word targets preceded by evaluatively inconsistent rather than consistent primes were now made faster. The model predicts this reversal because evaluative inconsistency is expected to facilitate negative responses via a feeling of implausibility, whereas evaluative consistency should inhibit negative responses. Analogous reversals of the effects of irrelevant evaluations were reported by Klauer and Stern (1992) and using a different task by Klauer and Musch (in press).

Applying the mechanism to the evaluative decision task is somewhat complicated. The response *good* or *positive* for positive words can be classified as affirmative, the response *bad* or *negative* for negative words is negative. A priming effect is therefore expected for positive targets, and a *reversed* priming effect is expected for negative targets. The priming effect is expected to be reversed for negative targets, because the required response *negative* is negative, and negative responses are facilitated by evaluative inconsistency and inhibited by evaluative consistency under the affective-matching model. Overall, the net priming effect, averaged over positive and negative targets, should be zero. In addition, it is not easy to test the prediction of reversed priming effects for positive versus negative targets in the evaluative decision task. Any difference between priming for positive targets and priming for negative targets is perfectly confounded with the main effect of prime valence as is not difficult to see. It is therefore impossible to disentangle possible effects of prime valence from differences caused by affective matching. Even the absence of a difference between priming for positive targets and priming for negative targets cannot be interpreted unambiguously because of this confounding.

To summarize, the affective-matching model predicts affective priming in tasks requiring responses that can be classified as affirmative or negative, the paradigmatic case being binary "yes/no" decisions, and it explains the reversal of affective priming from trials requiring "yes" responses to those requiring "no" responses. The affective-matching mechanism is thereby less task-dependent than the Stroop mechanism in the sense that it does not presuppose an intention to evaluate the stimuli themselves as good or bad. It cannot, however, account for the pattern of findings obtained with the evaluative decision task.

A MODEL OF THE EVALUATIVE SYSTEM

A large portion of the research is integrated by a model of the evaluative system that has at its core a process of preconscious evaluation activation. The evaluations, once activated, exert their influence on subsequent processes through mediating mechanisms. We assume that there are at least two such mechanisms that were termed the *Stroop mechanism* and the *affective-matching mechanism*. Both are assumed to operate simultaneously and in parallel. By their properties they determine the scope and generality of observable priming effects.

As already discussed, the Stroop mechanism explains most of the findings obtained with the evaluative decision task, but because of its strong task-dependence it fails to account for affective priming in tasks without a strong evaluative component. Neumann (1984) reviewed findings on goal dependence obtained in classical Stroop paradigms and concluded that "to a large degree, a distractor causes interference not because of its intrinsic properties but because it is related to the intended action" (p. 269). At this point, the affective-matching model comes into play to explain affective priming in wider contexts. As detailed above, the affective-matching mechanism is not expected to contribute to affective priming in the evaluative decision task itself. However, it complements the Stroop mechanism to account for affective priming in tasks that require nonevaluative affirmative and negative responses, the paradigmatic case being binary yes/no decisions. Considerable evidence for its operation has by now accrued in the form of the telltale pattern of a reversal of priming effects from trials requiring an affirmative response to those requiring a negative response.

This model, comprising a preconscious process of evaluation activation and two mediating mechanisms, offers differentiated answers to two issues of considerable debate: (a) The extent to which the effects of irrelevant evaluations are goal-dependent, and (b) whether the processing of evaluative information must be assumed to differ from cognitive processing.

Goal Dependence of Affective Priming

Turning first to the issue of goal dependence, Holender (1992) has pointed out that a necessary condition for Stroop-like congruity effects such as flanker effects is an overlap between the ensemble of task-relevant attributes of the target stimuli or the required responses on the one hand and the attributes of the irrelevant primes on the other hand. The overlap endows irrelevant primes with the power to prime a response from the set of responses, either the same response as that required by the target or a different one, thereby facilitating or inhibiting, respectively, the task-appropriate response. The Stroop mechanism (i.e., the mechanisms that underlie Stroop-like congruity effects) can thereby explain affective priming in *evaluative* responses, but is goal-dependent and fails to account for affective priming in nonevaluative tasks such as the lexical decision task. When the evaluations of targets are not relevant for the task at hand and when there is no implicit or explicit evaluative component in the required responses, irrelevant evaluations are not expected to exert an influence under this mechanism.

The Stroop mechanism readily explains affective priming in the evaluative decision task, but it also accounts for effects of irrelevant evaluations in a number of situations that at first hand appear to demonstrate goal independence. For example, in Experiment 2 by Chen and Bargh (1999), participants were required to move a lever as soon as an evaluatively polarized word was presented in what was presented as a reaction time test. In half of the trials, participants were to move the lever toward them and in the other half, they moved the lever away from themselves. It was found that the lever was pulled faster for positive than negative words, and that it was pushed faster for negative than positive words. Following Chen and Bargh's (1999) interpretation that pushing is part of an appetitive system linked to positive evaluations and pulling is part of an aversive system linked to negative evaluations (e.g., Lang, 1995; Neumann, Förster & Strack, chap. 14, this volume), the Stroop mechanism naturally applies to explain these effects as Stroop-like congruity effects. Similarly, effects of irrelevant evaluations in De Houwer and Eelen's (1998) affective Simon paradigm (De Houwer, chap. 9, this volume) fall under the range of this mechanism. In that paradigm, participants identify nonevaluative attributes of words such as their grammatical category, but respond with evaluative labels. For example, nouns might be mapped onto the response *good* and adjectives might be mapped onto the response *bad*. Again, the irrelevant evaluations of the stimuli interfere with the responses: Responding *good* is easier for positive than negative words, irrespective of grammatical category, and vice versa for the response *bad* (De Houwer & Eelen, 1998).

Another set of effects that have been argued to demonstrate goal independence can be explained by the affective-matching model. According to that model, irrelevant evaluations exert an influence by virtue of biasing yes/no-responses. As explained earlier, affective priming in the lexical decision task can be accounted for by the affective-matching model, and Wentura (1998, 2000) provided direct evidence for the role of affective matching in the lexical decision task. Likewise, Klauer and Stern (1992) and Klauer and Musch (in press) demonstrated affective priming effects in situations in which there was no goal to evaluate, but affirmative and negative responses were required for both evaluatively congruent and incongruent stimulus combinations.

More importantly, the present framework integrates *failures* to obtain affective priming in other nonevaluative tasks. When there is no evaluative component in the required response and when affirmative or negative responses are not required, neither the Stroop mechanism nor the affective-matching model predict effects of irrelevant evaluations. Many findings have demonstrated an absence of affective priming effects in such tasks, often in the form of strong double dissociations as a function of task, as reviewed in the above section on the role of the participants' task. Thus, the present framework can account for the mixed pattern of findings on goal dependence in a principled manner.

Dissociation of Evaluative and Cognitive Processing

Like for the issue of goal dependence, the present view of the evaluative system offers a differentiated answer to the question of whether evaluative processes can be dissociated from cognitive processes. The answer is no for the Stroop mechanism and yes for the affective-matching model.

The Stroop mechanism accepts evaluative information just like any other kind of information. All that is required is some amount of overlap between task-relevant features of targets and/or responses on the one hand and features of irrelevant distractors on the other hand. Whether task-relevant overlap is given by an evaluative component shared by primes and targets, or by nonevaluative features of primes and targets makes no difference whatsoever for the pattern of results (cf. section on Task). It appears then that the Stroop mechanism is a general-purpose mechanism that is part of a general system of attention allocation and response selection and that can be recruited by the evaluative system as well as by any other system under the conditions just outlined.

A different story is related by the findings for the affective-matching model. For example, Klauer and Musch (in press) required participants to make yes/no decisions on prime-target pairs that varied with respect to valence or gender as well as a second orthogonal dimension across five experiments. Evidence for a spontaneous comparison of stimulus pairs was found only with respect to evaluating the affective match of prime and target, but not with respect to any other dimension. This finding contrasts with the just-mentioned findings for the Stroop mechanism in which these other dimensions were just as influential as irrelevant evaluations were. In the present instance, yes/no-decisions based on nonevaluative features of the word pairs were biased by the irrelevant affective match of prime and target, but there was never any evidence for an analogous effect of prime-target matches on other dimensions such as gender. It can be concluded that affective matching is an integral component of only the evaluative system and that a dissociation with the cognitive processes comprising Bargh's (1997) perceptual system has been identified.

OPEN QUESTIONS

We conclude this chapter by briefly discussing two open issues. The first concerns the locus at which Stroop-like congruity effects operate in evaluative decisions, the second the pattern of findings obtained with the pronunciation task.

Locus of Affective Priming Effects

An open question is whether affective priming in the evaluative decision task reflects synergy and conflict of *response tendencies* triggered by primes and targets, or whether synergy and conflict at a more central level of *categorizing stimuli* as good or bad are also involved. Klinger et al. (2000) strongly argued for a peripheral locus of the effect (i.e., for response synergy and conflict), although their data are really silent with respect to this issue. Musch (2000; Exp. 8) attempted to assess peripheral and central components of affective priming effects separately. He presented first names and evaluatively polarized adjectives as primes and targets. Participants were required to make gender decisions if the target was a first name, and evaluative decisions on adjectives. Each response key was assigned one gender and one evaluation; for example, female first names and positive adjectives were mapped onto the right response key and male first names and negative adjectives on the left response key. Some of the trials thereby presented primes (e.g., a first name) and targets (e.g., an adjective) that had diminished potential of interfering with each other at a central level of categorization, but could still trigger the same or different responses. Other trials shared this potential for peripheral synergy and conflict, but also had the potential for eliciting central synergy and conflict in categorization (both prime and target first names, or both adjectives). Contrasting the different kinds of trials, it was found that a major component of priming effects was due to peripheral response congruency, but there was also a significant and substantial component going back to central facilitation engendered by prime and target sharing the same evaluation or gender.

A related point was recently made by Abrams, Klinger, and Greenwald (in press). As discussed previously, Abrams and Greenwald (2000) obtained stronger affective priming effects in a study on masked affective priming when primes were composed of subword parts of previously evaluated targets than when the primes, nor any parts of them, had not been seen before. Abrams et al. (in press) built on this work and aim at testing whether the effect of previous evaluations goes back to an automatic activation of a practiced stimulus-response mapping (peripheral locus) or to a facilitation of the unconscious classification of the prime (central locus). Abrams et al. (in press) had participants practice classifying visible targets as *pleasant* or *unpleasant*, before these targets were used as subliminal primes in a second phase of the experiment. Of importance, the association of response keys with valences was reversed from practice to test phase. Nevertheless, the subliminal primes engendered normal priming effects indicating that the practice effect has a central rather than peripheral locus. In Fazio et al's (1986) words, the practice effect might thus be seen as an instance of an accessibility effect.

The Puzzle of the Naming Task

A second open question is given by the pattern of findings in the pronunciation task (Glaser, chap. 4, this volume; Wentura & Rothermund, chap. 3, this volume). As reviewed earlier, some authors consistently found affective priming in that task irrespective of prime strength and accessibility. Others did not observe any priming effect whether strong or weak primes were used. Still others found reversed priming engendered by extreme primes. What could be the cause of this contradictory set of findings? One point of departure could be the recent finding by De Houwer et al. (2001) according to which affective priming effects were obtained in the naming task when targets were presented in a degraded manner, but not under the standard presentation condition. This result suggests that priming in the naming task is augmented if the phase of target identification is made more difficult. This points to a possible post-lexical origin of the effect in which prime and candidate targets are considered as a pair and in which their relationship *biases the decision* on target identification. For example, the affective-matching model postulates that evaluatively consistent prime-target pairs elicit a spontaneous feeling of plausibility, whereas inconsistent pairs engender a feeling of implausibility. If so, the decision that an internally represented candidate target is indeed the correct target to be named might be facilitated under evaluative consistency and inhibited by evaluative inconsistency. This mechanism is likely to exert an impact in naming to the extent to which identification constitutes a real decision problem, rather than an automatic and unconditional response, explaining the stronger effects obtained under degraded conditions and the frequent absence of the effect under standard presentation conditions (Klauer & Musch, 2001). Another classical way to manipulate the difficulty of the naming task is to contrast word-naming (highly over-learned and automatic) with picture-naming (less well-practiced and automatic; e.g., MacLeod, 1991), and it is interesting to note that Spruyt, Hermans, De Houwer, and Eelen (2001) have recently demonstrated replicable normal affective priming effects in picture naming.

However, this account still leaves open the puzzling findings of reversed priming for extreme primes that were documented by Glaser and Banaji (1999). One possibility is that list context and/or instructions in these experiments made it salient that targets differ pronouncedly from primes and thereby made participants focus on detecting differences between primes and target. As argued previously, the decision about whether the target has been correctly identified might again be supported by a routine similarity check of primes and targets. In this situation, participants would however proceed to naming the target as soon as the similarity hypothesis had to be rejected for a given prime-target pair. For "no, different" judgments, however, the affective-matching model predicts facilitation by evaluative mismatches rather than matches and thereby a reversal of priming effects.

Clearly, these considerations are speculative at this point, and other principled accounts for the pattern of findings in the naming task are proposed by Glaser (chap. 4, this volume) and Rothermund and Wentura (chap. 3, this volume). Future research in this very active field is likely to bring as much light to the puzzle of the naming task as has already been brought to the evaluative decision task. It seems likely that the present model of the evaluative system will have to be enriched by additional mechanisms as a consequence of this research.

REFERENCES

Abelson, R. P., & Rosenberg, M. J. (1958). Symbolic psycho-logic: A model of attitudinal cognition. *Behavioral Science, 3,* 1–13.

Abrams, R. L., & Greenwald, A. G. (2000). Parts outweigh the whole (word) in unconscious analysis of meaning. *Psychological Science, 11,* 118–124.

Abrams, R. L., Klinger, M. R., & Greenwald, A. G. (in press). Subliminal words activate semantic categories (not automatic motor responses). *Psychonomic Bulletin and Review.*

Banse, R. (2000). *Affective priming with liked and disliked persons: Prime visibility determines congruency and incongruency effects.* Manuscript submitted for publication, Humbold Universität, Berlin, Germany.

Bargh, J. A. (1997). The automaticity of everyday life. In R. S. Wyer (Ed.), *Advances in social cognition* (Vol. 10, pp. 1–49). Mahwah, NJ: Lawrence Erlbaum Associates.

Bargh, J. A. (1999). The cognitive monster: The case against the controllability of automatic stereotype effects. In S. Chaiken & Y. Trope (Eds.), *Dual process theories in social psychology* (pp. 361–382). New York: Guilford Press.

Bargh, J. A., Chaiken, S., Govender, R., & Pratto, F. (1992). The generality of the automatic attitude activation effect. *Journal of Personality and Social Psychology, 62,* 893–912.

Bargh, J. A., Chaiken, S., Raymond, P., & Hymes, C. (1996). The automatic evaluation effect: Unconditional automatic attitude activation with a pronunciation task. *Journal of Experimental Social Psychology, 32,* 104–128.

Bower, G. H. (1991). Mood congruity of social judgments. In J. Forgas (Ed.), *Emotion and social judgments* (pp. 31–53). Oxford: Pergamon.

Chaiken, S., & Bargh, J. A. (1993). Occurrence versus moderation of the automatic attitude activation effect: Reply to Fazio. *Journal of Personality and Social Psychology, 64,* 759–765.

Cheesman, J., & Merikle, P. M. (1986). Distinguishing conscious from unconscious perceptual processes. *Canadian Journal of Psychology, 40,* 343–367.

Chen, M., & Bargh, J. A. (1999). Consequences of automatic evaluation: Immediate behavioral predispositions to approach or avoid the stimulus. *Personality and Social Psychology Bulletin, 25,* 215–224.

Clark, H. H. (1973). The language-as-fixed-effect fallacy: A critique of language statistics in psychological research. *Journal of Verbal Learning and Verbal Behavior, 12,* 335–359.

Cooper, W. H. (1981). Ubiquitous halo. *Psychological Bulletin, 90,* 218–244.

de Groot, A. M. B. (1984). Primed lexical decision: Combined effects of the proportion of related prime-target pairs and the stimulus-onset asynchrony of prime and target. *Quarterly Journal of Experimental Psychology, 36A,* 253–280.

De Houwer, J., & Eelen, P. (1998). An affective variant of the Simon paradigm. *Cognition & Emotion, 12,* 45–61.

De Houwer, J., Hermans, D., & Eelen, P. (1998). Affectivity and identity priming with episodically associated stimuli. *Cognition & Emotion, 12,* 145–169.

De Houwer, J., Hermans, D., Rothermund, K., & Wentura, D. (2000). *Affective priming of semantic categorization responses.* Manuscript submitted for publication.

De Houwer, J., Hermans, D., & Spruyt, A. (2001). Affective priming of pronunciation responses: Effects of target degradation. *Journal of Experimental Social Psychology, 37,* 85–91.

Dosher, B. A. (1998). The response-window regression method—some problematic assumptions: Comment on Draine and Greenwald (1998). *Journal of Experimental Psychology: General, 127,* 311–317.

Draine, S. C., & Greenwald, A. G. (1998). Replicable unconscious semantic priming. *Journal of Experimental Psychology: General, 127,* 286–303.

Eriksen, B. A., & Eriksen, C. W. (1974). Effects of noise letters upon the identification of a target letter in a nonsearch task. *Perception and Psychophysics, 16,* 143–149.

Fazio, R. H. (1989). On the power and functionality of attitudes: The role of attitude accessibility. In A. R. Pratkanis, S. J. Breckler, & A. G. Greenwald (Eds.), *Attitude structure and function* (pp. 153–179). Hillsdale, NJ: Lawrence Erlbaum Associates.

Fazio, R. H., Jackson, J. R., Dunton, B. C., & Williams, C. J. (1995). Variability in automatic activation as an unobtrusive measure of racial attitudes: A bona fide pipeline? *Journal of Personality and Social Psychology, 69,* 1013–1027.

Fazio, R. H., Sanbonmatsu, D. M., Powell, M. C., & Kardes, F. R. (1986). On the automatic activation of attitudes. *Journal of Personality and Social Psychology, 50,* 229–238.

Fox, E. (1995). Negative priming from ignored distractors in visual selection: A review. *Psychonomic Bulletin and Review, 2,* 145–173.

Giner-Sorolla, R., Garcia, M. T., & Bargh, J. A. (1999). The automatic evaluation of pictures. *Social Cognition, 17,* 76–96.

Glaser, J., & Banaji, M. R. (1999). When fair is foul and foul is fair: Reverse priming in automatic evaluation. *Journal of Personality and Social Psychology, 77,* 669–687.

Greenwald, A. G., & Banaji, M. R. (1995). Implicit social cognition: Attitudes, self-esteem, and stereotypes. *Psychological Review, 102,* 4–27.

Greenwald, A. G., & Draine, S. C. (1998). Distinguishing unconscious from conscious cognition: Reasonable assumptions and replicable findings: Reply to Merikle and Reingold (1998) and Dosher (1998). *Journal of Experimental Psychology: General, 127,* 320–324.

Greenwald, A. G., Draine, S. C., & Abrams, R. L. (1996). Three cognitive markers of unconscious semantic activation. *Science, 273,* 1699–1702.

Greenwald, A. G., Klinger, M. R., & Liu, T. J. (1989). Unconscious processing of dichoptically masked words. *Memory & Cognition, 17,* 35–47.

Greenwald, A. G., Klinger, M. R., & Schuh, E. (1995). Activation by marginally perceptible ("subliminal") stimuli: Dissociation of unconscious from conscious cognition. *Journal of Experimental Psychology: General, 124,* 22–42.

Greenwald, A. G., & Rosenberg, K. E. (1978). Sequential effects of distracting stimuli in a selective attention reaction time task. In J. Requin (Ed.), *Attention and performance* (Vol. VII, pp. 487–504). Hillsdale, NJ: Lawrence Erlbaum Associates.

Hermans, D. (1996). *Automatische stimulusevaluatie. Een experimentele analyse van de voorwaarden voor evaluatieve stimulusdiscriminatie aan de hand van het affectieve-priming paradigma. [Automatic stimulus evaluation. An experimental analysis of the preconditions for evaluative stimulus discrimination using an affective priming paradigm].* Unpublished doctoral dissertation, University of Leuven, Belgium.

Hermans, D., Baeyens, F., & Eelen, P. (1998). Odours as affective-processing context for word evaluation: A case of cross-modal affective priming. *Cognition & Emotion, 12,* 601–613.

Hermans, D., Crombez, G., & Eelen, P. (2000). Automatic attitude activation and efficiency: The fourth horseman of automaticity. *Psychologica Belgica, 40,* 3–22.

Hermans, D., De Houwer, J., & Eelen, P. (1994). The affective priming effect: Automatic activation of evaluative information in memory. *Cognition and Emotion, 8,* 515–533.

Hermans, D., De Houwer, J., & Eelen, P. (1996). Evaluative decision latencies mediated by induced affective states. *Behavior Research and Therapy, 34,* 483–488.

Hermans, D., De Houwer, J., & Eelen, P. (2001). A time course analysis of the affective priming effect. *Cognition & Emotion, 15,* 143–165.

Hermans, D., Van den Broeck, A., & Eelen, P. (1998). Affective priming using a color-naming task: A test of an affective-motivational account of affective priming effects. *Zeitschrift für Experimentelle Psychologie, 45,* 136–148.

Hermans, D., Vansteenwegen, D., Crombez, G., Baeyens, F., & Eelen, P. (in press). Expectancy-learning and evaluative learning in human classical conditioning: Affective priming as an indirect and unobtrusive measure of conditioned stimulus valence. *Behavior Research and Therapy.*

Holender, D. (1992). Expectancy effects, congruity effects, and the interpretation of response latency measurement. In J. Alegria, D. Holender, J. Junça de Morais, & M. Radeau (Eds.), *Analytic approaches to human cognition* (pp. 351–375). North Holland: Elsevier.

Jarvis, W. B. G., & Petty, R. E. (1996). The need to evaluate. *Journal of Personality and Social Psychology, 70,* 172–194.

Klauer, K. C. (1991). *Einstellungen: Der Einfluß der affektiven Komponente auf das kognitive Urteilen [Attitudes: The influence of the affective component on cognitive judgments].* Göttingen, Germany: Hogrefe.

Klauer, K. C. (1998). Affective priming. *European Review of Social Psychology, 8,* 67–103.

Klauer, K. C., & Greenwald, A. G. (2000). Measurement error in subliminal perception experiments: Simulation analyses of two regression methods—comment on Miller (2000). *Journal of Experimental Psychology: Human Perception and Performance, 26,* 1–3.

Klauer, K. C., Greenwald, A. G., & Draine, S. C. (1998). Correcting for measurement error in detecting unconscious cognition: Comment on Draine and Greenwald (1998). *Journal of Experimental Psychology: General, 127,* 318–319.

Klauer, K. C., & Musch, J. (in press). Goal-dependent and goal-independent effects of irrelevant evaluations. *Personality and Social Psychology Bulletin.*

Klauer, K. C. & Musch, J. (2001). Does sunshine prime loyal? Affective priming in the naming task. *Quarterly Journal of Experimental Psychology, 54A,* 727–751.

Klauer, K. C., Roßnagel, C., & Musch, J. (1997). List-context effects in evaluative priming. *Journal of Experimental Psychology: Learning, Memory, and Cognition, 23,* 246–255.

Klauer, K. C., & Stern, E. (1992). How attitudes guide memory-based judgments: A two-process model. *Journal of Experimental Social Psychology, 28,* 186–206.

Klinger, M. R., Burton, P. C., & Pitts, G. S. (2000). Mechanisms of unconscious priming: I. Response competition not spreading activation. *Journal of Experimental Psychology: Learning, Memory, and Cognition, 26,* 441–455.

Lang, P. J. (1995). The emotion probe: Studies of motivation and attention. *American Psychologist, 50,* 372–385.

Logan, G. D., & Zbrodoff, N. J. (1979). When it helps to be misled: Facilitative effects of increasing the frequency of conflicting stimuli in a Stroop-like task. *Memory & Cognition, 7,* 166–174.

MacLeod, C. M. (1991). Half a century of research on the Stroop effect: An integrative review. *Psychological Bulletin, 109,* 163–203.

Merikle, P. M., & Reingold, E. M. (1998). On demonstrating unconscious perception: Comment on Draine and Greenwald (1998). *Journal of Experimental Psychology: General, 127,* 304–310.

Miller, J. (2000). Measurement error in subliminal perception experiments: Simulation analyses of two regression methods. *Journal of Experimental Psychology: Human Perception and Performance, 26,* 1461–1477.

Murphy, S. T., & Zajonc, R. B. (1993). Affect, cognition, and awareness: Affective priming with optimal and suboptimal stimulus exposures. *Journal of Personality and Social Psychology, 64,* 723–739.

Musch, J. (2000). *Affektives Priming: Kongruenzeffekte bei der evaluativen Bewertung [Affective priming: Congruency effects in evaluative decisions].* Unpublished doctoral dissertation, Universität Heidelberg, Germany.

Musch, J., Elze, A., & Klauer, K. C. (1998). Gibt es Wortlängeneffekte in der evaluativen Entscheidungsaufgabe? [Are there word-length effects in the evaluative decision task?] *Zeitschrift für Experimentelle Psychologie, 45,* 109–119.

Musch, J., & Klauer, K. C. (1997). Der Anteilseffekt beim affektiven Priming: Replikation und Bewertung einer theoretischen Erklärung [The consistency proportion effect in affective priming: Replication and evaluation of a theoretical explanation]. *Zeitschrift für Experimentelle Psychologie, 44,* 266–292.

Musch, J., & Klauer, K. C. (2001). Locational uncertainty moderates affective congruency effects in the evaluative decision task. *Cognition & Emotion, 15,* 167–188.

Neely, J. H. (1991). Semantic priming effects in visual word recognition: A selective review of current findings and theories. In D. Besner & G. W. Humphreys (Eds.), *Basic processes in reading: Visual word recognition* (pp. 264–336). Hillsdale, NJ: Lawrence Erlbaum Associates.

Neely, J. H., Keefe, D. E., & Ross, K. L. (1989). Semantic priming in the lexical decision task: Roles of prospective prime-generated expectancies and retrospective semantic matching. *Journal of Experimental Psychology: Learning, Memory, and Cognition, 15,* 1003–1019.

Neumann, O. (1984). Automatic processing: A review of recent findings and a plea for an old theory. In W. Prinz & A. F. Sanders (Eds.), *Cognition and motor processes* (pp. 255–293). Berlin, Germany: Springer.

Nisbett, R. E., & Wilson, T. D. (1977). The halo effect: Evidence for unconscious alteration of judgments. *Journal of Personality and Social Psychology, 35,* 250–256.

Otten, S., & Wentura, D. (1999). About the impact of automaticity in the Minimal Group Paradigm: Evidence from affective priming tasks. *European Journal of Social Psychology, 29,* 1049–1071.

Pendry, L. F., & Macrae, C. N. (1996). What the disinterested perceiver overlooks: Goal-directed social categorization. *Personality and Social Psychology Bulletin, 22,* 249–256.

Reingold, E. M., & Merikle, P. M. (1988). Using direct and indirect measures to study perception without awareness. *Perception and Psychophysics, 44,* 563–575.

Rothermund, K., & Wentura, D. (1998). Ein fairer Test für die Aktivationsausbreitungshypothese: Untersuchung affektiver Kongruenzeffekte in der Stroop-Aufgabe [An unbiased test of a spreading activation account of affective priming: Analysis of affective congruency effects in the Stroop task]. *Zeitschrift für Experimentelle Psychologie, 45,* 120–135.

Shaffer, W. O., & LaBerge, D. (1979). Automatic semantic processing of unattended words. *Journal of Verbal Learning and Verbal Behavior, 18,* 413–426.

Spruyt, A., Hermans, D., De Houwer, J., & Eelen, P. (2001). *Explaining the affective priming effect: Affective priming in a picture-naming task.* Manuscript submitted for publication, University of Leuven, Belgium.

Wentura, D. (1998). Affektives Priming in der Wortentscheidungsaufgabe: Evidenz für postlexikalische Urteilstendenzen [Affective priming in the lexical decision task: Evidence for postlexical judgmental tendencies]. *Sprache und Kognition, 17,* 125–137.

Wentura, D. (1999). Activation and inhibition of affective information: Evidence for negative priming in the evaluation task. *Cognition and Emotion, 13,* 65–91.

Wentura, D. (2000). Dissociative affective and associative priming effects in the lexical decision task: Responding with "yes" vs. "no" to word targets reveal evaluative judgment tendencies. *Journal of Experimental Psychology: Learning, Memory, and Cognition, 26,* 456–469.

Study	N	Primes	Targets	No. of pairs	SOA (ms)	Procedure	Factors	Task	Effects
Abrams & Greenwald (2000); Exp. 1	12	24 hybrids composed of parts of targets	24 parent words (norms)	6*48	66	Response window; sandwich mask		Evaluative decisions	Affective priming.
Abrams & Greenwald (2000); Exp. 2	34	20 tumor-type hybrids (see effects)	40 parent words (norms)	6*48	66	Response window; sandwich mask		Evaluative decisions	Affective priming by tumor-type primes in the direction implied by parents (tulip and amor).
Abrams & Greenwald (2000); Exp. 3	27	16 words	16 new words vs. 16 primes (b.p.)	6*48	66	Response window; sandwich mask	Prime type (b.p.)	Evaluative decisions	Affective priming when primes were previous targets, but not for new primes.
Abrams, Klinger, & Greenwald (in press); Exp. 1	62	50 words	50 different words	5*50	67	Response window; sandwich mask; practice in evaluating primes; then priming with reversed response key assignment		Evaluative decisions	Affective priming.
Abrams, Klinger, & Greenwald (in press); Exp. 2	50	50 words	50 different words	5*50	50	Response window; sandwich mask; practice in evaluating primes; then priming with reversed response key assignment		Evaluative decisions	Affective priming.
Banse (2000); Exp. 1	37	Self, partner, Hussein, stranger: faces and names	40 nouns, 40 adjectives (norms)	320	42		Prime visibility (masked vs. visible); prime modality (face vs. name)	Evaluative decisions	Normal affective priming for visible primes; for masked primes: partner and Hussein engender more positive priming than self and stranger.

(Continued)

37

APPENDIX (Continued)

Study	N	Primes	Targets	No. of pairs	SOA (ms)	Procedure	Factors	Task	Effects
Banse (2000); Exp. 2	40	Chaplin, Hussein, stranger: faces and names	40 nouns, 40 adjectives (norms)	320	42		Prime visibility (masked vs. visible); prime modality (face vs. name)	Evaluative decisions	Relatively normal affective priming for visible primes; for masked primes: more positive priming for Hussein than for Chaplin, although both positive.
Bargh, Chaiken, Govender, & Pratto (1992); Exp. 1	23	24 nouns; 4 letter strings (bbb)	28 adjectives	196	300	Accessibility assessment, then priming	Prime type (fast, slow, consistent, neutral)	Evaluative decisions	Affective priming for fast and consistent, but not for slow primes.
Bargh, Chaiken, Govender, & Pratto (1992); Exp. 2	24	24 nouns; 4 letter strings (bbb)	28 adjectives	196	300	Accessibility assessment; two-days delay, then priming	Prime type (fast, slow, consistent, neutral)	Evaluative decisions	Affective priming for fast and consistent primes, marginal for slow primes.
Bargh, Chaiken, Govender, & Pratto (1992); Exp. 3	59	16 nouns; 4 letter strings (bbb)	28 adjectives	140?	300	Accessibility assessment, then priming	Prime type (fast, slow, neutral); memory vs. no memory instruction for primes (b.p.)	Evaluative decisions	Affective priming for fast and slow, stronger for fast. No effect of memory instruction.
Bargh, Chaiken, Raymond, & Hymes (1996); Exp. 1	43	16 nouns; 4 letter strings (bbb)	20 adjectives	100	300	Accessibility assessment, then priming	Prime type (fast, slow, neutral)	Pronunciation	Affective priming for fast and slow primes. No effect of accessibility.
Bargh, Chaiken, Raymond, & Hymes (1996); Exp. 2	25	16 nouns; 4 letter strings (bbb)	20 adjectives	100	300	No accessibility assessment	Prime type (strong, weak as based on norms, neutral)	Pronunciation	Affective priming for weak and strong primes. No effect of strength.
Bargh, Chaiken, Raymond, & Hymes (1996); Exp. 3	30	16 nouns; 4 letter strings (bbb)	20 moderately polarized nouns	100	300	No accessibility assessment	Prime type (strong, weak as based on norms, neutral)	Pronunciation	Affective priming for weak and strong primes. No effect of strength.

Study	N	Primes	Targets	Trials	Procedure	SOA	Variable	Task	Results
Chaiken & Bargh (1993)	45	24 nouns; 4 letter strings (bbb)	28 adjectives	196	Accessibility assessment, then priming	300	Prime type (fast, slow, consistent, neutral); immediate vs. two-days delay of accessibility assessment (b.p.)	Evaluative decisions	Affective priming for fast and consistent, but not for slow primes under no-delay condition. Smaller effect of accessibility with delayed accessibility assessment.
De Houwer, Hermans, & Eelen (1998); Exp. 1	30	10 nonwords	10 words (norms)	120	Nonwords associated with target words through learning, then priming	300	Prime-target relation: previously associated, affectively consistent, inconsistent	Evaluative decisions	Affective priming and additional identity priming by associated nonwords.
De Houwer, Hermans, & Eelen (1998); Exp. 2	24	10 nonwords	10 words (norms)	120	Nonwords associated with target words through learning then priming	300	Prime-target relation: previously associated, affectively consistent, inconsistent	Pronunciation	No affective priming, but identity priming by associated nonwords.
De Houwer, Hermans, & Eelen (1998); Exp. 3	33	8 nonwords	8 words (norms)	2*72	Nonwords associated with target words through learning, then priming	300 and 1000	Prime-target relation and SOA	Evaluative decisions	Affective priming with short SOA, but not at the long SOA. No identity priming by associated nonwords.
De Houwer, Hermans, & Eelen (1998); Exp. 4	26	8 nonwords	32 adjectives (norms)	2*32	Nonwords associated with words through learning, then priming with new targets	300	Prime-target relation	Evaluative decisions	Affective priming.
De Houwer, Hermans, Rothermund, & Wentura (2000); Exp. 1	94	20 nouns (norms)	20 animal names, 20 person names	2*40		250		Categorize as person vs. animal	No affective priming.

(Continued)

APPENDIX (Continued)

Study	N	Primes	Targets	No. of pairs	SOA (ms)	Procedure	Factors	Task	Effects
De Houwer, Hermans, Rothermund, & Wentura (2000); Exp. 2	48	64 verbs (norms)	32 animal names, 32 person names	2*64	250		Evaluative decisions vs. categorizing as person vs. animal	See factors	No affective priming for semantic categorization; affective priming for evaluative decisions.
De Houwer, Hermans, & Spruyt (2001)	56	20 nouns (norms)	20 adjectives (norms)	2*40	250		Targets degraded or not (b.p.)	Pronunciation	Affective priming for degraded, but not for undegraded targets.
Draine & Greenwald (1998); Experiments 2–4	66	50 words (norms)		6*50	34, 50, 67	Adaptive response window; sandwich mask	SOA	Evaluative decisions	Affective priming at all SOAs.
Fazio, Sanbonmatsu, Powell, & Kardes (1986); Exp. 1	22	16 nouns; 4 letter strings (bbb)	20 adjectives	5*20	300	Accessibility assessment, then priming	Prime type (fast, slow, neutral)	Evaluative decisions	Affective priming for fast, but not for slow primes.
Fazio, Sanbonmatsu, Powell, & Kardes (1986); Exp. 2	23	16 nouns; 4 letter strings (bbb)	20 adjectives	5*20	300 vs. 1000	Accessibility manipulation, then priming	Prime type (fast, slow, neutral); SOA	Evaluative decisions	Affective priming for fast, but not for slow primes at short SOA. No priming at long SOA.
Fazio, Sanbonmatsu, Powell, & Kardes (1986); Exp. 3	18	16 nouns; 4 letter strings (bbb)	20 adjectives	5*20	300 vs. 1000	Accessibility manipulation, then priming	Prime type (strong, weak, neutral); SOA	Evaluative decisions	Affective priming for strong and weak primes at short SOA. Greater effect for strong than for weak primes. No priming at long SOA.
Giner-Sorolla, Garcia, & Bargh (1999); Exp. 1	41	20 pictures of simple objects (norms)	20 adjectives	96	250		Moderate vs. strong primes	Evaluative decisions	Affective priming for strong and weak pictures; tendentially stronger for strong pictures.

Giner-Sorolla, Garcia, & Bargh (1999); Exp. 2	38	16 pictures of simple objects (norms)	4*16	250	Moderate vs. strong primes	Pronunciation	Affective priming for strong and weak pictures.
Glaser (this volume)	120	16 nouns (norms); 20 adjectives	80	300	Prime type (strong vs weak); accuracy instruction (high vs. low; b.p.)	Pronunciation	Affective priming for weak and strong primes. Little evidence for moderation by accuracy instruction.
Glaser & Banaji (1999); Exp. 1	43?	160 black, white, generic, food words.	?	150	Prime and target category	Pronunciation	Affective priming for food primes; reverse effects for extreme primes.
Glaser & Banaji (1999); Exp. 2	19	160 black, white, moderate, extreme words (norms).	5*128	150	Prime and target category	Pronunciation	Affective priming for moderate primes; reverse effects for extreme primes.
Glaser & Banaji (1999); Exp. 3	17	160 black, white, moderate, extreme words (norms).	5*128	300	Prime and target category	Pronunciation	Affective priming for moderate primes; reverse effects for extreme primes.
Glaser & Banaji (1999); Exp. 4	31	80 moderate and extreme words (norms).	2*80	300	Prime and target category	Pronunciation	No priming for moderate primes, reverse effects for extreme primes.
Glaser & Banaji (1999); Exp. 5	15	80 moderate and extreme words (norms).	2*80	300	Prime and target category	Pronunciation	No priming for moderate primes, reverse effects for extreme primes.
Glaser & Banaji (1999); Exp. 6	36	80 moderate and extreme words (norms).	2*80	300	Prime and target category; fixation point vs not (b.p.)	Pronunciation	No priming for moderate primes, reverse effects for extreme primes.

(Continued)

APPENDIX *(Continued)*

Study	N	Primes	Targets	No. of pairs	SOA (ms)	Procedure	Factors	Task	Effects
Greenwald, Draine, & Abrams (1996); several experiments	?	Words (norms) or first names		?	67–400	Response window	Prime masked vs. not (b.p.); SOA; gender decisions vs. evaluative decisions (b.p.)	See factors	Masked priming weaker than visible priming; masked priming absent at SOAs above 100 ms; visible priming undiminished up to 400 ms; sequential effect for visible, but not for masked primes.
Greenwald, Klinger, & Liu (1989); Exp. 1	20	12 extreme, 6 neutral words (norms)	72 words (norms)	2*72	500		Prime masked vs. not	Evaluative decisions	Priming for both visible and masked primes.
Greenwald, Klinger, & Liu (1989); Exp. 2	12	12 extreme words (norms), blank as neutral.	72 words (norms)	6*36	500		Prime masked vs. not	Evaluative decisions	Priming for masked, but not visible primes.
Greenwald, Klinger, & Liu (1989); Exp. 3	12	12 extreme words (norms), blank as neutral.	72 words (norms)	6*36	500		Prime masked (40-ms), masked (80-ms) vs. not; high vs. low-frequency primes	Evaluative decisions	Priming for masked (80-ms) and visible, but not for masked (40-ms).
Greenwald, Klinger, & Schuh (1995); Exps. 4, 13, 15–17	180	Extreme words (norms)	Less extreme words (norms)	100–224	250 or 300			Evaluative decisions	No priming effect with dichoptically masked primes.
Greenwald, Klinger, & Schuh (1995); Exps. 18–20	166	Extreme words (norms)	Less extreme words (norms)	4*25	300			Evaluative decisions	Weak priming effect in error data, none in latency data with dichoptically masked primes.
Greenwald, Klinger, & Schuh (1995); Exps. 5, 8, 9	185	Extreme words (norms)	Less extreme words (norms)	100–224	250			Evaluative decisions	No priming effect with visible primes.

Study	N	Primes	Targets	Design	SOA	Procedure	Manipulated variables	Task	Results
Hermans (1996); Exp. 4	28	12 extreme, 6 neutral color pictures.	18 color pictures	2*63	70	Selection of targets and primes out of 100; sandwich-masked primes	Block (1 vs. 2); state anxiety (high vs. low; b.p.); trait anxiety (high vs. low; b.p.)	Evaluative decisions	No affective priming.
Hermans (1996); Exp. 5	33	12 extreme, 6 neutral color pictures.	18 nouns	2*54	70	Selection of targets and primes out of, respectively, 100 pictures and 75 nouns; sandwich-masked primes	Block (1 vs. 2); trait anxiety (high vs. low; b.p.)	Evaluative decisions	Reversed affective priming effect in second block of trials; no priming effect in first block.
Hermans (1996); Exp. 6	14	12 extreme, 6 neutral color pictures.	18 nouns	2*54	70	Selection of targets and primes out of, respectively, 100 pictures and 75 nouns; dichoptically masked primes	Block (1 vs. 2); trait anxiety (high vs. low; b.p.)	Evaluative decisions	Reversed affective priming effect in second block of trials; no priming effect in first block.
Hermans, Baeyens, & Eelen (1998)	40	10 odours	20 nouns	2*20	10200	Prime selection; target selection out of 50	Gender (b.p.)	Evaluative decisions	Affective priming for female participants, but not for males.
Hermans, Crombez, & Eelen (2000)	24	20 extreme, 10 neutral nouns (norms)	30 adjectives (norms)	6*30	150		Digit load (no, low, high; blocked)	Evaluative decisions	Affective priming, not moderated by load.
Hermans, De Houwer, & Eelen (1994); Exp. 1	24	12 extreme, 6 neutral color pictures.	18 color pictures	2*54	300, 1000	Selection of targets and primes out of 100; then priming	SOA	Evaluative decisions	Priming at SOA 300 ms, but not at SOA 1000 ms.
Hermans, De Houwer, & Eelen (1994); Exp. 2	24	20 nouns (norms), 10 letter strings (bbb)	30 adjectives (norms)	4*30	300			Pronunciation	Affective priming
Hermans, De Houwer, & Eelen (1996)	40	Mood states	16 extreme color pictures; 8 neutral ones.	4*24	n.a.	Selection of targets, then priming		Evaluative decisions	No interaction of induced mood state and target valence; however, mood change and target valence interacted in the expected manner.

(Continued)

APPENDIX (Continued)

Study	N	Primes	Targets	No. of pairs	SOA (ms)	Procedure	Factors	Task	Effects
Hermans, DeHouwer, & Eelen (2001); Exp. 1	49	20 nouns, 10 neutral nouns	30 adjectives (norms)	2*150	Five levels	Prime selection based on ratings	SOA (−150, 0, 150, 300, 450 ms)	Evaluative decisions	Affective priming at 0 and 150 ms, but not at −150, 300, and 450 ms.
Hermans, De Houwer, & Eelen (2001); Exp. 2	49	20 nouns (norms)	20 adjectives (norms)	2*60	Five levels	Prime selection based on ratings	SOA (150, 300, 1000 ms)	Pronunciation	Affective priming at 150 ms, but not at 300 or 1000 ms.
Hermans, De Houwer, & Eelen (2001); Exp. 3	22	20 nouns (norms)	20 adjectives (norms)	2*40	300		Centered vs. uncentered presentation of primes and targets; NES-scores (b.p.)	Evaluative decisions	Affective priming for centered, but not for uncentered. Affective priming for high NES-group, but not for low NES-group.
Hermans, Van den Broeck, & Eelen (1998); Exp. 1	36	20 nouns, 10 neutral nouns	30 adjectives (norms)	4*30	150	Selection of primes, then priming.		Color naming	No affective priming.
Hermans, Van den Broeck, & Eelen (1998); Exp. 2	36	20 nouns, 10 neutral nouns (norms)	30 adjectives (norms)	6*30	150		Onset of target color after 0, 150, or 300 ms	Color naming	No affective priming.
Hermans, Van den Broeck, & Eelen (1998); Exp. 3	36	20 nouns, 10 neutral nouns (norms)	20 nouns (norms)	6*30	150		Onset of target color after 100, 150, or 200 ms	Color naming	No affective priming.
Hermans, Van den Broeck, & Eelen (1998); Exp. 4	37	20 fixed prime-target pairs		8*20	150	Onset of target color after 150 ms	Prime recall vs. not (b.p.); task	Color naming vs. evaluative decisions	Affective priming for evaluative decisions, but not for color naming.
Klauer & Musch (in press); Exp. 1a	180	344 adjectives (norms); neutral letter strings (bbbb)		2*60	200		Prime-set size (ten, infinite; b.p.); target-set size (2, ten, infinite; b.p.)	Pronunciation	No affective priming.
Klauer & Musch (in press); Exp. 1b	180	160 nouns (noms); neutral letter strings (Bbbb)	344 adjectives (norms)	2*60	200		Prime-set size (ten, infinite; b.p.); target-set size (2, ten, infinite; b.p.)	Pronunciation	No affective priming.

				SOA (b.p.)				
Klauer & Musch (in press); Exp. 2	90	344 adjectives (norms); neutral letter strings (bbbb)	2*60	0, 50, 100			Pronunciation	No affective priming.
Klauer & Musch (in press); Exp. 3	180	16 nouns; 4 letter strings (bbb); 20 adjectives	100	300		Prime type (strong, weak, as based on norms, neutral)	Pronunciation	No affective priming.
Klauer & Musch (in press); Exp. 4	50	50 nouns (norms); 50 adjectives (norms)	4*100	300	2*100 trials each with associatively related vs. unrelated word pairs.	Language (German vs. English); relatedness (affective vs. associative)	Pronunciation	No affective priming; associative priming in both the English and the German language.
Klauer & Musch (in press); Exp. 1	32	140 adjectives (norms)	6*48	71	Response window	Task (evaluative decisions vs. decisions about target location; b.p.)	See factors	Affective priming for evaluative, but not for location decisions. Reverse pattern for location priming.
Klauer & Musch (in press); Exp. 2	32	140 adjectives (norms)	6*48	71	Response window	Task (evaluative decisions vs. decisions about target color; b.p.)	See factors	Affective priming for evaluative, but not for color decisions. Reverse pattern for color priming.
Klauer & Musch (in press); Exp. 3	32	140 adjectives (norms)	6*48	71	Response window	Task (evaluative decisions vs. decisions about target letter case; b.p.)	See factors	Affective priming for evaluative, but not for case decisions. Reverse pattern for letter case priming.
Klauer & Musch (in press); Exp. 4	32	60 adjectives; 60 nouns (norms)	6*48	71	Response window	Task (evaluative decisions vs. decisions about target grammatical category; b.p.)	See factors	Affective priming for evaluative, but not for grammatical decisions. Reverse pattern for grammar priming.
Klauer & Musch (in press); Exp. 5	32	140 adjectives (norms)	6*48	71	Response window	Task (evaluative prime-target comparisons vs. location comparisons; b.p.)	See factors	Affective priming in location comparisons; no effects of location congruity on evaluative comparisons.

(Continued)

APPENDIX (Continued)

Study	N	Primes	Targets	No. of pairs	SOA (ms)	Procedure	Factors	Task	Effects
Klauer & Musch (in press); Exp. 6	32	140 adjectives (norms)		6*48	71	Response window	Task (evaluative prime-target comparisons vs. color comparisons; b.p.)	See factors	Affective priming in color comparisons; no effects of color congruity on evaluative comparisons.
Klauer & Musch (in press); Exp. 7	32	140 adjectives (norms)		6*48	71	Response window	Task (evaluative prime-target comparisons vs. case comparisons; b.p.)	See factors	Affective priming in letter case comparisons; no effects of case congruity on evaluative comparisons.
Klauer & Musch (in press); Exp. 8	32	60 adjectives; 60 nouns (norms)		6*48	71	Response window	Task (evaluative prime-target comparisons vs. grammatical comparisons; b.p.)	See factors	Affective priming in grammatical comparisons; no effects of grammatical congruity on evaluative comparisons.
Klauer & Musch (in press); Exp. 9	16	60 adjectives; 60 nouns (norms)		6*48	71	Response window	Response labeled as yes versus no	Grammatical decisions	Affective priming and effects of grammar congruity in grammatical decisions.
Klauer, Roßnagel, & Musch (1997); Exp. 1	180	390 adjectives (norms)		4*32	−100, 0, 100, 200, 600, 1200	75% evaluatively consistent prime-target pairs	SOA (b.p.)	Evaluative decisions	Affective priming at 0 and 100 ms
Klauer, Roßnagel, & Musch (1997); Exp. 2	270	390 adjectives (norms)		4*32	0, 200, 1200		SOA (b.p.) and consistency proportion (25%, 50%, and 75%; b.p.).	Evaluative decisions	Consistency proportion effect at SOA 0 ms, but not at higher SOAs. Reversed affective priming at SOA 1200 ms.

46

Study	N	Primes	Targets	Design		Procedure	Independent variables	Dependent variable	Findings
Klauer & Stern (1992); Exp. 1	45	48 adjectives (Peabody quadruples)	16 names of politicians	4*32	0	Target selection; then priming.	Response (correct vs. false) for grammatical categories (b.p.)	Grammatical classification of prime-target pairs	Affective priming for response "correct"; reversed affective priming for response "false".
Klinger, Burton, & Pitts (2000); Exp. 1	29	50 words (norms)		4*50	67	Response window; masked primes		Evaluative decisions	Affective priming effect.
Klinger, Burton, & Pitts (2000); Exp. 2	41	50 words (norms) and 50 nonwords		4*50	67	Response window; masked primes	Affective vs. word/nonword congruency	Lexical decisions	Congruency effects of word/nonword status of prime and target; no affective priming.
Klinger, Burton, & Pitts (2000); Exp. 4	90	48 nouns (evaluative and living/nonliving)		4*48	67	Response window; masked primes	Task (b.p.): Evaluative decisions vs. animacy decisions	See factors	Affective priming in evaluative decisions, but not in animacy decisions. Reverse pattern for animacy priming.
Murphy & Zajonc (1993); Exp. 1	32	20 smiling and scowling faces; random polygons	45 Chinese ideographs	45	4 vs. 1000		Optimal exposure to prime (1000 ms) vs. suboptimal exposure (4 ms)	Liking ratings	Affective priming effect under suboptimal presentation, but not with optimally visible primes.
Murphy & Zajonc (1993); Exp. 1	32	20 smiling and scowling faces; random polygons	45 Chinese ideographs	45	4 vs. 1000		Optimal exposure to prime (1000 ms) vs. suboptimal exposure (4 ms)	Evaluative ratings	Affective priming effect under suboptimal presentation, but not with optimally visible primes.
Musch (2000); Exp. 1	48	140 adjectives (norms)		6*48	71	Response window	Consistency proportion (25%, 50%, 75%; b.p.)	Evaluative decisions	Consistency proportion effect.
Musch (2000); Exp. 2	48	140 adjectives (norms)		6*48	71	Response window; trials balanced for sequential effects	Consistency proportion (25%, 50%, 75%; b.p.)	Evaluative decisions	Consistency proportion effect.

(Continued)

APPENDIX (Continued)

Study	N	Primes	Targets	No. of pairs	SOA (ms)	Procedure	Factors	Task	Effects
Musch (2000); Exp. 3	24	140 adjectives (norms)		6*48	71	Response window	Consistency proportion (25%, 50%, 75%; b.p.); last block 50%	Evaluative decisions	Consistency proportion effect even in last block.
Musch (2000); Exp. 4	16	140 adjectives (norms); letter strings as primes (bbtfghp)		6*48	71	Response window; only incongruent and neutral-prime trials		Evaluative decisions	Affective priming effect.
Musch (2000); Exp. 5	96	140 adjectives (norms); letter strings as primes (bbtfghp)		4*48	71	Response window	Consistency proportion (17%, 42%, 67%; b.p.); masked vs. visible primes	Evaluative decisions	Consistency proportion effect for visible primes, but not for masked primes; affective priming under all conditions.
Musch (2000); Exp. 8	16	140 adjectives (norms); 140 first names (first names)		10*48	71	Response window	Prime type: names vs. adjectives; Target type: names vs. adjectives	Evaluative and gender decisions depending on target	Affective and gender congruency effects over and above response congruency effect; i.e. priming at a central level.
Musch, Elze, & Klauer (1998); Exp. 1	24	126 adjectives (norms) < 9 letters, 140 > 10 letters.	< 9 letters,	4*32	100		Lenghts (short vs. long) of primes and targets	Evaluative decisions	No affective priming.
Musch, Elze, & Klauer (1998); Exp. 2	24	66 adjectives (norms) < 10 letters, 45 > 10 letters.	96 adjectives (norms) < 9 letters, 96 > 11 letters	4*32	0		Lenghts (short vs. long) of primes and targets	Evaluative decisions	Affective priming; no interactions with prime or target length.
Musch & Klauer (1997)	40	390 adjectives (norms)		2*32	0		Consistency proportion (25% vs. 75%; b.p.)	Evaluative decisions	Consistency proportion effect.
Musch & Klauer (2001); Exp. 1	32	140 adjectives (norms)		6*48	0	Response window; changing locations of stimuli	Cue about target location vs. neutral cue (b.p.)	Evaluative decisions	Affective priming under locational uncertainty, but not under certainty.

Study	N				SOA			Task	Results
Musch & Klauer (2001); Exp. 2	32	140 adjectives (norms)		6*48	0	Response window; changing locations of stimuli	Cue about target location vs. neutral cue (b.p.)	Evaluative decisions	Affective priming under locational uncertainty, but not under certainty.
Rothermund & Wentura (1998); Exp. 1	36	96 nouns (norms); 96 associated prime-target pairs; neutral bbbbb primes		2*48	300		Relatedness (affective vs. associative; b.p.), block	Color naming	Associative relation: inhibition in first block, facilitation in second. Affective relation: no effects.
Rothermund & Wentura (1998); Exp. 2	48	96 nouns (norms); 96 associated prime-target pairs; neutral bbbbb primes		2*2*48	500	Reproduce prime after target decision	Relatedness (affective vs. associative; w.p.), order (affective, then associative or vice versa), block	Color naming	Associative relation: inhibition. Affective relation: no effects.
Wentura (1998)	91	120 words (norms), including 40 neutral ones; 40 pseudo-words	80 adjectives (norms) and 80 pseudo-words	4*40	300		Response assignment (word=yes vs. word=no; b.p.)	Evaluative decisions	Affective priming, in tendency reversed for word=no condition.
Wentura (1999); Exp. 1	35	80 nouns (norms), letter strings (BBBB)	120 adjectives (norms)	120	300	Double-trial negative priming paradigm	Relation of trial n-1 prime to trial n target (same vs. different valence)	Evaluative decisions	Affective priming effect and negative trial n-1 priming.
Wentura (1999); Exp. 2	72	80 nouns (norms), letter strings (BBBB)	120 adjectives (norms)	120	0 vs. 300	Double-trial negative priming paradigm	Relation of trial n-1 prime to trial n target (same vs. different valence); SOA	Evaluative decisions	Affective priming effect and negative trial n-1 priming.
Wentura (2000); Exp. 1	55	120 nouns (norms), including 40 neutral and 40 pseudo-words	80 adjectives (norms) and 80 pseudo-words	160	300		Response assignment: Word=yes vs. word=no; b.p.	Lexical decisions	Affective priming.
Wentura (2000); Exp. 2	46	120 nouns (norms), including 40 neutral and 40 pseudo-words	96 adjectives (norms) and 96 pseudo-words	192	300		Response assignment: Word=yes vs. word=no; b.p.	Lexical decisions	Affective priming, reversed for word=no condition.

Notes. When norms are mentioned, they refer to evaluative norms. N = number of participants retained for analysis; b.p. = between-participants.

Chapter 3

The "Meddling-In" of Affective Information: A General Model of Automatic Evaluation Effects

Dirk Wentura
University of Jena, Germany

Klaus Rothermund
University of Trier, Germany

In a recent text on visual cognition, Houghton, Tipper, Weaver, and Shore (1996) illustrated the basic problem of selective attention by inviting their readers to imagine a fictitious peanut-eater, whose only aim is to eat peanuts. Equipped with a sensory apparatus to locate peanuts in his visual field and an effector to grasp one peanut at a time, the problem arises how this organism will behave in the case of two peanuts placed in front of its sensory system. What mechanisms will prevent the peanut-eater from endlessly grasping into the emptiness between the two peanuts, thereby starving to death? An adequate cognitive apparatus must be tuned to process objects in its visual field in an asymmetrical manner, that is, to respond efficiently to target objects while ignoring distractor objects (see also Neumann, 1987). But what is the target and what is the distractor? Because one peanut is just as good as the other, higher order goals (like the wish to eat peanuts) do not sufficiently determine which of the objects is to be considered as the target of the next action, thereby defining other objects as distractors.

In this regard, the peanut-eater simile reminds one of the old allegory of Buridan's ass who starved to death in the midst of two bundles of hay because of its inability to come to a decision about which bundle it should eat. In contrast to the donkey, we as humans are equipped with the ability to decide; it seems as if we are not only able to pursue top-down higher-order goals that determine target objects (like bundles of hay) but are also outfitted with a bottom-up sensitivity for differences in valence between potential targets.

Moreover, what is the distractor with regard to the current goal might be a potential target for some other even more important goal. For example, besides the wish to eat peanuts until the end of his days, the peanut-eater might have the goal to escape his strongest enemy, the peanut-eater eater. Thus, pursuing only one goal at a time would leave us with the risk of overlooking signals of chance and signals of danger in the environment, which are related to other personal goals. Therefore it seems our cognitive system must have the necessary equipment to automatically process the valence of objects in the environment to prevent such an oversight.

In this regard, it is interesting to note that in a variety of experimental paradigms evidence was found for the automaticity of evaluation. For example, if the color of positive and negative words has to be named, interference effects (i.e., longer color naming times) were found for valent stimuli, thus indicating an automatic processing of valence ("affective Stroop task"; e.g., Pratto & John, 1991; Wentura, Rothermund, & Bak, 2000; White, 1996; see also Rothermund, Wentura, & Bak, 2001). If positive and negative words that are preceded by a positive or negative prime word have to be categorized with regard to their valence, affective congruency effects (i.e., quicker responses in case of prime and target being of same valence) can be reliably obtained, thus indicating an automatic processing of prime valence ("affective priming"; e.g., Fazio, Sanbonmatsu, Powell, & Kardes, 1986; Hermans, De Houwer, & Eelen, 1994; Klauer, Roßnagel, & Musch, 1997). If stimulus features of positive and negative words, which are independent of valence (e.g., noun vs. adjective), are categorized by responding with "Positive!" (e.g., for nouns) and "Negative!" (e.g., for adjectives), affective congruency effects (i.e., quicker responses if the response matches the valence of the word) were found, thus indicating an automatic processing of valence ("affective Simon task"; De Houwer & Eelen, 1998).

The consequences of an automatic processing of information, however, might be rather superficial. For example, as we know from cognitive psychology, processing of a neutral word will automatically cause a heightened accessibility of its associates, a phenomenon known as associative priming (for a review see Neely, 1991). This increases the probability of using one of the preactivated words in an appropriate context. But typically, the heightened accessibility will fade out quickly with no further consequences.

In the following, we argue that the automatic processing of valence has consequences that go beyond temporarily increasing the accessibility of associated concepts. Because of its global relevance, automatic processing of valence is strongly tied to response processes (i.e., interrupting ongoing behavior, modifying the probability of responses, redirecting behavior, or specifying certain action parameters). Thus, processes that are triggered by positive and negative stimuli are most dominantly located at a response formation stage. Speaking metaphorically, positive and negative stimuli have the power to meddle with ongoing processes of behavior formation.

This "meddling-in" of valent stimuli seems to be the common ground to all automatic evaluation phenomena, like affective Stroop effects, affective priming (in its diverse variations), and affective Simon effects. We argue that because of task demands and stimulus features, different action schemas are involved in these experimental tasks, thereby receiving different effects of an affective "meddling-in."

In the first part of the chapter, we briefly review evidence found in the different paradigms. Then, we elaborate on the "meddling-in" metaphor. Using the framework of a general model of selective attention (Houghton & Tipper, 1994), we describe this metaphor in more detail. The different results are then explained within this theoretical framework.

PARADIGMS OF AUTOMATIC EVALUATION

Affective Priming

Fazio, Sanbonmatsu, Powell, and Kardes (1986) were instrumental in stimulating research on what can be called *affective priming* (e.g., Bargh, Chaiken, Govender, & Pratto, 1992; Greenwald, Klinger, & Liu, 1989; Hermans, De Houwer, & Eelen, 1994; Kemp-Wheeler & Hill, 1992; Klauer et al., 1997; Wentura, 1997b; for reviews see Fazio, 2001; Klauer, 1998; Klauer & Musch, chap. 2, this volume). They presented valenced adjectives (e.g., *repulsive*; *appealing*) on a CRT screen and participants had to classify these target words as *positive* or *negative* as quickly as possible (*evaluation task*). Shortly before each target (300 ms), a valenced prime word was presented (e.g., *death*; *gift*). The decision latency for the target words was shorter when the prime and target were congruent in terms of valence.

Subsequently, a research guiding principle of explanation for this effect was an increased accessibility of those valent target stimuli that followed a congruent prime. This principle was borrowed from the research tradition of semantic priming (for a review see Neely, 1991). In terms of theoretical models, it might be assumed, for example, that in a semantic memory network presentation of a positive or negative prime word activates the corresponding node; activation spreads via global positivity or negativity nodes to all concept nodes with the same valence, which makes them more accessible (e.g., Bower, 1981, 1991). In terms of parallel distributed memory models, it might be assumed that a subset of nodes corresponds to the valence of a concept. Thus, in the case of a congruent prime-target pair, updating the activation pattern on target presentation will be shortened if a related prime has instantiated a somewhat similar pattern just before (Masson, 1995; see also McRae, de Sa, & Seidenberg, 1997). To fully examine this principle of explanation, several different tasks were used.

Evaluation Task. Although in principle the affective priming effect in the evaluation task can be explained by increased accessibility of congruent targets, there are some results that do not fit this explanation. Klauer and colleagues (Klauer et al., 1997; Musch & Klauer, 1997) varied the proportion of congruent to incongruent prime-target pairs thereby getting a variation in the affective priming effect at stimulus-onset asynchronies (SOA) of 0 ms and 200 ms. A high proportion (i.e., 75%) yielded a marked priming effect whereas the effect decreased to a nonsignificant level for the low proportion condition (i.e., 25%). From semantic priming research, it is known that the proportion of related to unrelated prime-target pairs affects semantic priming effects only at SOAs of 500 ms and above (see Neely, 1991). Thus, Klauer and colleagues (Klauer et al., 1997; Musch & Klauer, 1997) argued that a data pattern that is comparable to what they found is known from Stroop-like tasks (Logan & Zbrodoff, 1979). We return to this issue later.

Pronunciation Task. In accordance with the principle of increased accessibility, some evidence for affective priming effects in the *pronunciation task* was found as well (Bargh, Chaiken, Raymond; & Hymes, 1996; Giner-Sorolla, Garcia, & Bargh, 1999; Hermans et al., 1994; Spruyt, Hermans, De Houwer, & Eelen, 2001). This is especially noteworthy because in semantic priming research this task is reputed to be a means for assessing "pure" automatic activation processes instead of so-called *postlexical* processes (see Neely, 1991). However, in some recent studies, affective priming effects only emerged under restricted conditions (Hermans, De Houwer, & Eelen, 2001, De Houwer, Hermans, & Spruyt, 2001, De Houwer & Randell, 2001), showing the effect to be more conditional than initially thought. Moreover, there are some studies that fail to show the affective-priming effect in the pronunciation task (De Houwer & Hermans, 1999; De Houwer, Hermans, & Eelen, 1998; Hermans, 1996; Klauer & Musch, 2001). For example, in an extensive series of experiments, Klauer and Musch found no evidence for affective priming effects in the pronunciation task. Glaser and Banaji (1999) found even reversed effects (see also Glaser, chap. 4, this volume).

Lexical Decision Task. Hill and Kemp-Wheeler (1989; Kemp-Wheeler & Hill, 1992) were the first to provide some evidence for affective priming in the *lexical decision task*. Unfortunately, these authors compared only negative to neutral primes with respect to their effect on negative targets. Thus, an effect due to the prime-target relationship cannot be disentangled from a main effect of primes. Using adjective–adjective pairs, Klauer, Roßnagel, and Musch (1995) obtained no effects. Wentura (1998, 2000) found a congruence effect with noun primes and adjective targets. Interestingly, he could show that the effect depended on response modalities. If participants were trained to respond with "Yes" to words and "No" to nonwords, a congruence effect was found. If, however, participants were trained to respond with "Yes" to nonwords and "No" to words, an incongruence effect was found. Of course, this variation was not done for exploratory reasons. The research was guided by a theory of Klauer and Stern (1992) that made assumptions about automatic judgmental tendencies. Again, we return to this issue later.

Color-Naming Task. Warren (1972, 1974) used the color-naming task for the analysis of associative and semantic priming effects. In this type of task, a prime word is presented in a white color, followed by a target word presented in a nonwhite color that has to be named. If the target word is preactivated by an associatively or semantically related prime word, this typically leads to an increase in the color naming latencies because the content of the target word is irrelevant for the color naming task (Warren, 1972, 1974; see also Burt, 1994; Oden & Spira, 1983). An important feature of the color-naming task is that priming effects cannot be explained by response facilitation or interference because neither the prime nor the prime–target relation is in any way related to the color-naming response. Therefore, Rothermund and Wentura (1998) used the color-naming task to test for affective congruency effects that are not located at the response stage. In their experiments, priming effects of associatively related/unrelated prime–target pairs were compared to the effects of affectively congruent/incongruent prime–target pairs. Although significant associative priming effects were found in two experiments[1], color naming latencies were virtually identical for affectively congruent and incongruent prime–target pairs. In another series of experiments, Hermans, Van den Broeck, and Eelen (1998) also found no reliable effects of affective congruency with the color-naming task. The results of these experiments question an interpretation of affective congruency effects in terms of spreading activation.

Semantic Categorization Task. A direct implication of the spreading activation account of affective priming effects is that facilitation effects should not only be observed in the evaluation task. If presentation of a valent prime word leads to an automatic preactivation of other concepts of the same valence, facilitation effects of affectively congruent primes should also

---

[1]In the first experiment, participants developed a strategy to inhibit the prime words during the experiment, so whereas significant increases in color naming latencies for associatively related prime-target pairs were observed in the first half of trials, a significant decrease for associatively related word pairs emerged in the second half of the trials (similar inhibitory effects were reported by Pratto, 1994). To control for these strategic effects, participants had to memorize the primes during the color-naming task in a second experiment (see Warren, 1972, 1974). In this experiment, color-naming latencies were significantly increased for associatively related prime-target pairs throughout the experiment.

be observed in other tasks that require a semantic processing of the target words (e.g., determine whether the target word is a noun or an adjective, determine whether the target word refers to something animate or inanimate). This implication is important because in nonevaluative semantic categorization tasks, response compatibility/incompatibility of prime and target words can be counterbalanced within the affectively congruent and incongruent prime-target pairs. A mediation of affective priming effects by response compatibility/incompatibility of prime and target can thus effectively be ruled out. In a recent series of experiments, De Houwer, Hermans, Rothermund, and Wentura (in press) compared affective congruency effects in the evaluation task with affective congruency effects in semantic categorization tasks (e.g., deciding whether the target word refers to a person or an object). Although significant priming effects emerged in the evaluation task, no significant affective congruency effects were observed in the semantic categorization tasks despite the fact that apart from the task, the conditions were identical (De Houwer et al., in press).

A different technique to estimate the contribution of central (spreading activation) and peripheral (response compatibility) loci of affective priming with the help of nonevaluative semantic classifications was used by Musch (2000, Exp. 8; see also Klauer & Musch, chap. 2, this volume). In this experiment, first names had to be classified as male or female together with valent words that had to be classified as positive or negative. Classification responses of both tasks were mapped onto two keys according to a 4 to 2 reduction paradigm (i.e., each response key was assigned one gender and one evaluation; see also Shaffer & LaBerge, 1979). Effects of response compatibility/incompatibility can be estimated by using male and female first names as primes for positive and negative target words. Subtracting these cross-category priming effects from the priming effects that were obtained when valent prime words were used yields an adjusted measure of affective priming effects that is free from peripheral effects of response compatibility. Musch (2000) found a significant effect of response compatibility across categories, but—at odds with the results of De Houwer et al. (2000)—priming effects were significantly stronger when valent primes were used instead of first names.

Affective Stroop Paradigm

A paradigm that is closely related to the affective priming task is the affective Stroop task (Pratto, 1994; Pratto & John, 1991; Wentura et al., 2000; White, 1995). Valent stimuli are presented in different colors, which have to be named. Pratto and John found increased color-naming latencies for negative trait words compared to positive ones. They discussed this effect in terms of an automatic vigilance to negative social information.

Meanwhile, other studies questioned whether this attention-grabbing effect is restricted to the negative valence category (e.g., Roskos-Ewoldsen & Fazio, 1992; Wentura et al., 2000). Wentura et al. (2000), for example, provided evidence that negative trait terms associated with avoidance as well as positive trait terms associated with approach produced Stroop-interference. In detail, we referred to a distinction introduced by Peeters (1983; 1992; Peeters & Czapinski, 1990). Peeters argued that the evaluation of a given trait depends on the perspective of the evaluators—whether they evaluate the trait from the perspective of someone who has to interact with the trait-holder or from the perspective of the trait-holder him or herself. There are two basic questions tied to these perspectives: (a) "Is it good or bad for me that person X possesses the characteristic Y?" and (b) "Is it good or bad for person X him or herself to possess the characteristic Y?" Given these two perspectives, we can differentiate between traits like *brutal, deceitful, reckless* (negative other-relevant), *kind, comradely, just* (positive other-relevant) on the one hand and *desperate, lonely, dull* (negative possessor-relevant), *intelligent, optimistic, versatile* (positive possessor-relevant) on the other hand. With regard to question a only traits like *brutal* (*comradely*) are strongly tied to the answer "It is bad (good) for me to interact with someone who is brutal (comradely)!" On the contrary, there is no definitive answer to question a for *lonely* and *intelligent*, for example: Lonely individuals might have developed quirky traits leading to less positive interactions. However, they might be especially thankful for social contact, such that it is rather positive to interact with them. The intelligence of others will be seen as positive as long as they are considered as friends. However, an intelligent enemy is especially threatening. As should be evident, the reverse holds for question b. Now, *loneliness* and *intelligence* are strongly tied to the answer "It is bad (good) for me to be lonely (intelligent)!" whereas *brutal* and *comradely* will be met with an "it depends" answer. Brutality is negatively sanctioned in most circumstances, although it might help sometimes to achieve a certain objective. To be comradely is positively sanctioned in most circumstances, although the comradely person might be more easily taken advantage of.

We argued that it is more vital for an organism to scan the environment with regard to question a compared to question b (Wentura et al., 2000). Therefore, other-relevant trait terms (e.g., *brutal, comradely*) should attract attention to a greater extent than possessor-relevant trait terms (e.g., *lonely, intelligent*). Confirming this hypothesis, in a 2 (valence: positive vs. negative) × 2 (relevance: other vs. possessor) design we found increased color-naming latencies for negative and positive other-relevant trait terms compared to possessor-relevant ones. Moreover, this effect seems to be rather robust with regard to context manipulations. Interspersing color-naming trials with a rating task for the same words (presented in white color), which was either "To what extent do others suffer or profit by interacting with a person who possesses this characteristic?" (other-relevant perspective) or "To what extent does the person him or herself suffer or profit by possessing this characteristic?" (possessor-relevant perspective) does not moderate the automatic vigilance to other-relevant stimuli.

Affective Simon Paradigm

De Houwer and Eelen (1998) recently introduced an affective variant of the Simon paradigm as another technique for the study of automatic processes of evaluation. In this kind of task, a valent response (e.g., say "Positive", say "Negative") is given on the basis of an arbitrarily selected stimulus attribute (e.g., grammatical category or color). Stimulus valence is always irrelevant for the task. In spite of this, response latencies are faster when stimulus valence and response valence match compared to when they are incongruent (De Houwer & Eelen, 1998). Affective Simon effects have been demonstrated across a wide range of different relevant task features and response types (De Houwer, Crombez, Baeyens, & Hermans, 2001; De Houwer & Eelen, 1998; De Houwer, Hermans, & Eelen, 1998; see also De Houwer, chap. 9, this volume).

This compatibility effect of stimulus valence and valent characteristics of the response is additional evidence that stimulus valence is processed automatically even when it is completely irrelevant for the task. But most important for purposes of the present article, affective Simon effects demonstrate that the valence of stimuli is strongly linked to response tendencies like evaluation or approach/avoidance. The latter point is nicely illustrated by an experiment by De Houwer and colleagues (2001) in which a manikin had to be moved toward or away from a valent word depending on its grammatical category (noun vs. adjective). Response latencies were delayed when the manikin had to be moved away from positive words or toward negative words. This unintended interaction of stimulus valence and response valence can most readily be explained by assuming an automatic mapping of valent information onto evaluative response tendencies.

In the following, we want to integrate this diverse set of phenomena and effects into a larger framework. The leading metaphor is the capability of affective stimuli to "meddle" with ongoing processes, because it lies at the heart of affective and emotional processing to fulfill the function of signaling chances and risks for an organism (e.g., Frijda, 1988; Lang, 1995; Simon, 1967). One may assume that the valence of stimuli indicates the general relevance of stimuli for the individual. Information processing is not geared simply toward the acquisition of knowledge, but enables the organism to act in an environment full of opportunities and risks. Thus, the "meddling-in" of affective stimuli will cause interference with ongoing processes if these are unrelated to the stimulus; "meddling-in" will mean an integration with other information if the affective component is relevant in this context.

If the hypothesis is correct that presentation of an affective stimulus meddles with ongoing processes and the formation of actual behavior, the experimental task at hand has to be taken into consideration. Different mechanisms could be operative, for example, in the evaluation and lexical decision task of the affective priming paradigm, respectively. These mechanisms must be described in detail.

To do this, we will move beyond the "meddling-in" metaphor (MIM) to examine the functional organization of cognitive processes involved in affective priming. Therefore, we investigate whether a general model of selective attention as proposed by Houghton and Tipper (1994) is suited to capture the "meddling-in" assumption. First, we will explain the model as proposed by Houghton and Tipper. Second, we will supplement it with mechanisms for processing affective information.

THE HOUGHTON AND TIPPER (1994) MODEL OF SELECTIVE ATTENTION

Houghton and Tipper (1994, 1996, 1999; Houghton et al., 1996) developed their model of selective attention in response to the basic question of "how [does] an organism selectively respond to an object when other objects evoke competing responses?" (Houghton et al., 1996, p. 119). To give an answer, Houghton and Tipper (1994) developed a neural network model that is heavily based on the interplay of activation and inhibition of mental representations. They postulated four highly interrelated subsystems (see Fig. 3.1): (a) The *object field*, containing the property units representing external world objects, which is connected to (b) the *response system*, containing basic response schemata (like grasping, naming, categorization etc.) with their variable slots; (c) a *target field*, representing the properties of an internally generated attentional target, that is, the specification of the properties of to-be-selected objects with regard to a current goal (e.g., color of a stimulus in a Stroop task); (d) a *match/mismatch detector*, integrating inputs from both the object field and the target field and linked through backward channels with the object field to enhance relevant and inhibit irrelevant object representations. Additionally, a supervisory system specifies the features of the current task (i.e., which kind of targets have to be selected and which kind of response schemas are adequate).

In an input situation where relevant stimuli (targets) as well as irrelevant stimuli (distractors) are presented, both will activate corresponding property units in the object field. For example, in each trial of a categorisation experiment two words are presented simultaneously on the computer screen. Participants are instructed to categorise the red one (the target) as either denoting a person or an object by keypresses and to ignore the green

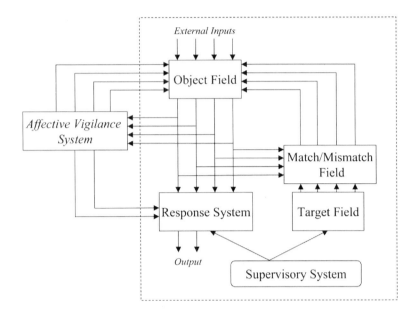

FIG. 3.1.   A schematic view of Houghton and Tipper's model of selective attention (1994, 1996; depicted within the broken line), supplemented with an "Affective Vigilance System" (see text for further explantion).

one (the distractor). Initially, both stimuli will activate their corresponding mental representation (i.e., a set of interrelated property units) in the object field. In a parallel cascade-like process (see, e.g., McClelland & Rumelhart, 1981), activated property units compete for activation of response schemas, filling their variable slots. With regard to the example, the response schema will be "Press the _____ key!", which has one variable slot (i.e., whether the left or right key has to be pressed). If target and distractor belong to different semantic categories, both possible responses would be activated. To channel this process and to prevent chaotic or paralysed behavior, the object field is coupled through parallel forward and backward links to the match/mismatch system. Besides the forward activation from the property units of the object field, this system gets activation from internally driven inputs (i.e., from the representation of current goals and plans in the target field.) To simulate our simple categorisation task, the target field consists of only two units—one corresponding to the feature *red,* which is a constant source of activation and one corresponding to the feature *green,* which is constantly inactive. Then, in the match/mismatch-field, a "match unit" receives input from the target field unit corresponding to the feature *red* and from the property unit, which represents the color red of the target stimulus. Activation of the "match unit" will initiate a process of backward activation of property units representing the relevant stimulus. In addition, a "mismatch unit" in the match/mismatch field is activated by the property unit, which represents the color green of the distractor stimulus (i.e., mismatch units are only activated if corresponding property units of the object field are active but corresponding units of the target field are inactive). Activation of the "mismatch unit" will initiate a process of backward inhibition of property units representing the irrelevant stimulus. Interference (i.e., the initial activation of both the relevant and irrelevant information), will vanish, and only the relevant information will have access to the response system.

> For the sake of completeness, we briefly sketch how these backward processes are implemented. At a more finely-grained level of modeling, each property unit (representing the presence of some feature in the input) is linked to gain-control units ("on-" and "off-cells"). Thus, if a property unit is activated by external input, it equally activates both its corresponding on- and off-cell. Through feedback loops the on-cell increases the activation of the property unit whereas the off-cell decreases it, with a default net effect of zero. However, the match/mismatch system is linked to both the on-cell and off-cell and can create imbalance in this micro-system by activating either the one or the other. Because on-cells and off-cells, respectively, of those property units that in sum represent the whole object are excitatorily linked, an imbalance with regard to one property unit spreads to all other units, thus activating or inhibiting the whole distributed representation of a stimulus.

AUTOMATIC EVALUATION
AS A MEDDLING-IN PROCESS

An affective vigilance subsystem can be added to the model of Houghton and Tipper (1994), connected with forward and backward links to the object field and with forward links to the response system (see Fig. 3.1). Affective connotation of stimuli corresponds to excitatory links from the property units representing the stimulus to units either representing the positive or the negative connotation within the affective subsystem. Backward links will strengthen activation of the property units of the object, thereby reflecting the unspecific relevance of the stimulus. Note that this does not necessarily imply that the representations of all objects being affectively congruent to the one presented are activated (see, e.g., the interplay of bottom-up and top-down processes in the model of Grossberg, 1987; Grossberg & Stone, 1986).

In addition, the affective subsystem has access to the response system. As Houghton and Tipper (1994) pointed out, there is a "competitive variable binding" of property units to slots in action schemas (see earlier discussion). Moreover, it can be assumed that there is a competition between the schemas themselves. The affective subsystem might be linked to various action schemas, from rather unspecific approach (e.g., grasping, touching) or avoidance (e.g., pushing, withdrawal) schemas to more specific, linguistic forms (e.g., judgments, evaluations). How can the different results of automatic evaluation paradigms be reconciled with this model?

MIM and the Evaluation Task: Stroop-Like Interference Processes

The primes in the evaluation task can be classified as positive or negative just as easily as the targets. Thus, the affective congruency effect can be explained by interference processes. In other words, in the evaluation task, presentation of a prime might trigger a response process due to its affective value. Therefore, when prime and target are affectively congruent, facilitation of the correct response may occur. An even more likely event is interference in cases of incongruency (e.g., Bargh et al., 1996; Klauer et al., 1997; Wentura, 1997b).

Therefore, the evaluation task has much more in common with the Stroop interference paradigm (MacLeod, 1991; Stroop, 1935;) than with the semantic priming paradigm. The classical Stroop task requires the naming of the color of a stimulus. In cases where this stimulus is a color word, which is incongruent to the to-be-named color, reaction times are decreased. Since the original work of Stroop (1935), many studies have been published that show the phenomenon to be generalizable (for a review see MacLeod, 1991). By designating the to-be-named dimension of the stimulus configuration as the target and the to-be-ignored dimension as the distractor, the type, modality, local, and temporal discriminability of target and distractor can be varied (e.g., Glaser & Glaser, 1989). For example, typical Stroop interference effects emerge in cases where targets as well as distractors are color words, separated by a SOA (Glaser & Glaser, 1982, 1989). Moreover, La Heij, van der Heijden, and Schreuder (1985) demonstrated interference effects with other types of distractors (e.g., *day* as distractor for *night*; *uncle* for *aunt*). Thus, in the evaluation task the prime is better termed a distractor stimulus that competes with the target for specifying the relevant action (i.e., pressing the positive or negative key).

In terms of the model, the relevant action schema for the evaluation task has two variable slots: The word that is to be evaluated (the object slot) and the evaluation itself as either positive or negative (the evaluation slot). The affective subsystem will deliver the evaluation information whereas the cascade process from the object field to the response system will result in filling the object slot. Due to one or more features (temporal sequence, noun vs. adjective, upper case vs. lower case letters), one stimulus is task-relevant (the target), the other task-irrelevant (the prime/distractor). In the case of a neutral prime, the match/mismatch-system will swiftly create the necessary imbalance because the units representing the prime will receive only inhibitory signals. The affective subsystem has no conflicting input and therefore will provide the response system with the adequate activation very quickly. Now take the case of affective congruency. Concerning the object slot, the match/mismatch-system will solve the conflict as usual, maybe somewhat delayed due to the additional activation of the irrelevant stimulus from the affective subsystem. In the affective subsystem only the positive or the negative component will be activated. Therefore the variable binding for the evaluation slot of the action schema will be provided easily. In the context of a response time experiment with its instruction for a fast response, it is not necessary to wait for solving the conflict in the object field (but see below). In contrast to this, in cases of *incongruency* there is a conflict in the object field as well as in the affective subsystem. The slots of the action schema cannot be filled until the backward process from the match/mismatch-system has created an imbalance of activation for the relevant and irrelevant properties, including the components of the affective subsystem. This slows down the response in the actual trial. While this makes the question of why the usual affective congruency effect emerges understandable, the Stroop analogy and its description in terms of the model provides us with some further predictions.

Relatedness-Proportion Effects. As was briefly described above, Klauer and colleagues (Klauer et al., 1997; Musch & Klauer, 1997) tested one of these special predictions (see Musch & Klauer, 2001, for a second one). They found the affective priming effect to be dependent on the proportion of congruent prime-target pairs in the trial list. The congruence effect was larger in magnitude if the proportion was, for example, 75% compared to, for example, 25%. A comparable pattern is known from Stroop-like tasks (see Logan & Zbrodoff, 1979). The authors (see also Klauer, 1998) favor an explanation given by Logan and Zbrodoff (1979). Thereafter, attention is divided between the prime and target. The cue validity of the prime is used by assigning the prime information a positive weight (in cases of a high proportion of congruent pairs) or a negative weight (in cases of a high proportion of incongruent pairs). To account for this result in terms of the Houghton and Tipper model, it has to be assumed that, given high cue validity, the prime can no longer be considered a distractor (i.e., a stimulus that is by definition a nonattended one). Now, the compound of prime and target is accounted for by top-down processes. Below, we give an alternative account that is more closely tied to the model favoured here.

Negative Affective Priming.   Wentura (1999a) predicted from the Stroop analogy a negative affective priming effect. The influence of congruence or incongruence in a first trial on the response in a subsequent trial was studied. If there is interference in incongruent trials, this should result in a negative priming effect like those that are known from Stroop-like paradigms (for reviews, see Fox, 1995; May, Kane, & Hasher, 1995; Neill, Valdes, & Terry, 1995). According to this assumption, an affective incongruence of prime and target in a first trial would result in a slowing of the response on the next trial if that target was affectively congruent to the prime of the former trial. This result was found in the experiments of Wentura (1999a).

In general, Houghton and Tipper (1994) accounted for negative priming effects in the following way. As was explained previously, the backward process of spreading activation and inhibition from the match/mismatch system decreases interference in the actual trial. That is, the initial activation of the distractor's units due to external stimulation vanishes. However, while the distractor is present, inhibition from the match/mismatch system and external activation will establish a state of equilibrium. Thus, following offset of the external input, activation of the distractor's property units will diminish to below resting levels. If the current distractor is the target of the next trial, this initial inihibition will produce a somewhat delayed dissolving of the interference. In the evaluation task, those units in the affective vigilance system that represent the valence of the distractor are involved in this backward inhibition process. Thus, presenting a target in the next trial that corresponds in valence to the distractor of the foregoing trial will result in longer latencies because the activation of the relevant property units has to be shifted from a level below baseline.

MIM and the Lexical Decision Task:
Judgmental Tendency Mechanisms

As should be clear from the preceding considerations, interference mechanisms cannot be applied to the lexical decision task. At least for noun–adjective pairings, however, an alternative account can be made for affective priming effects in the lexical decision task. Klauer and Stern (1992; Klauer, 1991; see also Klauer & Musch, 1998, Klauer & Musch, chap. 2, this volume) proposed a model of affective-cognitive links in judgmental processes. According to their model, when judging statements of the form (noun) is (adjective) (e.g., Einstein is fond of animals), a process with three components—two automatic and one controlled—will take place. First, the affective components of both the noun and the adjective are activated. Second, the affective components are compared with respect to affective consistency. Both processes are supposed to be automatic. The result of the second process is an a priori hypothesis about the correct answer and therefore a judgmental tendency to affirm (in cases of affective congruency) or to reject (in cases of incongruency) the relation in question will be established. Third, in a controlled process, relevant information will be recalled to form an adequate answer on the basis of the a priori hypothesis and the available information. Note that in the context of judgmental processes, the meddling-in character of affective stimuli does not cause an interference or an interruption of ongoing processes; instead the automatic evaluation of stimuli will be used to solve the judgmental task.

An experimental procedure to test the hypothesis of an automatic comparison of affective components was constructed as follows (see Klauer & Stern, 1992): Participants were required to classify pairs of stimuli (either the name of a politician paired with a trait word, two names or two traits; pairs were presented simultaneously) according to some formal characteristic ("Does this pair consist of a person and a trait?") requiring a yes/no response (actually, Klauer & Stern, 1992, used the labels *correct* and *false*). Politicians as well as traits were evaluated as positive or negative so that affective congruency could be varied. In accordance with the model, response latencies for person/trait pairs were facilitated in cases of affective congruency and inhibited in cases of incongruency. But, by reversing the question so that person/trait pairs required a no-response ("Does this pair consist of either two persons or two traits?"), the pattern of latencies was reversed (Klauer & Stern, 1992). This second order interaction was critical in supporting the theory.

In the lexical decision task, the affective components are not relevant to the task. The action schema has only one slot: Because a word—compared to a nonword—will produce more "resonance" in the object field (i.e., will activate more property units), the decision will largely be based on this flow of activation to the response system. (In more introspectively couched terms: The decision will largely be based on "familiarity".) This reconstruction does not explain why affectively congruent and incongruent prime-target pairs should make a difference on response times because it is a conflict in the object field that has to be resolved. The match (in cases of congruency) or mismatch (in cases of incongruency) in the affective subsystem does not matter. However, given the background of Klauer and Stern (1992), we can predict the following scenario. An alternative action schema is largely supported by a series of features: Pairs of words (feature one) consisting of a noun and an adjective (feature two) that are affectively connotated (feature three) were presented in close succession (feature four), thereby triggering a judgmental action schema. Response generation in this schema is susceptible to signals of the affective subsystem in the way outlined above: Affective congruency is transferred into a tendency to respond with "yes", affective incongruency to respond with "no". Given the assumption that the lexical decision task is implicitly coded as requiring "yes" (word) and "no" (nonword) responses (see, e.g., West & Stanovich, 1982), it can be assumed that the two action schemas—the judgmental action schema and the word decision schema—will both be activated and compete for triggering the motor response. Thus, the affective congruency effect in the lexical decision task may be a mere by-product of the judgmental tendencies caused by the compound of prime and target.

Wentura (1998, 2000) tested this assumption by manipulating the assignment of the response categories "yes" and "no" to either words or nonwords. That is, instructions emphasized the respective "yes" category ("You have to respond with YES to words [or to nonwords], otherwise with NO"). To counteract the tendency to view words as the natural "yes" category, nonwords were given a Gestalt-like character by naming them "SIWOBs" (a German acronym for "senseless wordlike strings") in the word=no condition and by giving some examples. The ease of detecting SIWOBs was emphasized. In accordance with the assumption, he found an affective congruency effect in the lexical decision task under standard instructions (i.e., responding with "yes" to words) but a reversal of this effect by instructing the participants to respond with "no" to words (and "yes" to nonwords). Using the same manipulation with associatively related, but affectively neutral materials resulted in the usual semantic priming effect that was not moderated by the "yes/no" variation.

Recently, Klauer and Musch (in press) provided further evidence for the judgment model by presenting prime–target pairs and asking their participants to judge whether prime and target (that were either affectively congruent or incongruent) were the same or different with respect to some task-relevant dimension (i.e., locality, color, letter case, or grammatical category). The judgment model predicts an affective congruency effect for same judgments because the tendency to affirm supports the response that is needed, whereas an affective incongruency effect is predicted for different judgments because now the tendency to negate supports the response that is needed. The pattern of results was largely supportive for the judgment model: For same judgments, significant affective congruency effects emerged, whereas for different judgments, a mixture of null effects and weak incongruency effects were found. This asymmetry in effect size is probably due to some basic differences in giving same and different responses (see Klauer & Musch, in press, for a discussion).

MIM and the Pronunciation Task

As mentioned in the introduction, some evidence for affective priming effects in the pronunciation task was found as well (Bargh et al., 1996; De Houwer et al., 2001; Hermans et al., 1994). In semantic priming research the pronunciation task is reputed to be a means for assessing "pure" automatic activation processes instead of "postlexical" processes (see Neely, 1991). Therefore spreading activation seemed to be the most parsimonious explanation for affective priming effects in this task, and we cannot entirely rule out this possibility. However, there are some studies that fail to show the affective-priming effect in the pronunciation task (De Houwer & Hermans, 1999; De Houwer et al., 1998; Hermans, 1996; Klauer & Musch, in press). Glaser and Banaji (1999) even found reversed effects. That is, a proponent of a spreading activation account is faced by results that are hard to accommodate. Additionally, even in semantic priming research there is some evidence of priming effects that can only be attributed to the production stage of the pronunciation task (Balota, Boland, & Shields, 1989), thereby casting some doubts on the reputation described earlier. Thus, some speculations might be allowed with regard to the pronunciation effects in light of the present results and theories.

Although there are obvious discrepancies, the pronunciation task resembles both the evaluation task and the lexical decision task in some respects, and thus any results obtained using this task will remain somewhat ambiguous. However, assume for a moment, that in the pronunciation task there is essentially the same rivalry between prime and target as in the evaluation task. It might be assumed that there are some basic differences in the way positive and negative words (taken as a whole) are typically pronounced (see Gardner, 1985, for indications), that is, in terms of the model—some variable slots of the corresponding action schema are connected to the affective subsystem. In cases of affective incongruency this will result in an interference. On the other hand, looking at the pronunciation task from the perspective of the jugmental tendency version of the meddling-in metaphor, one might speculate whether speaking aloud the attribute in question in a judgmental context is something like an affirmative answer. Then, we will get the same blending of action schemas as was described previously.

Although both assumptions explain affective congruency effects, the Glaser and Banaji (1999) results showing a reversed affective priming effect remain a puzzle. Additionally, recently De Houwer and colleagues (2001) found affective congruency effects in the pronunciation task moderated by the type of presentation. Whereas there was no effect for a normal presentation of targets, an affective congruency effect emerged for a degraded target presentation (e.g., presenting "ugly" as %U%G%L%Y%). This result is not easily accommodated by interference in the response system (see also more recent thus far unpublished results of De Houwer & Randell, 2001, and Spruyt et al., 2001). Therefore, we provide a different account further.

MIM and the Affective Stroop Task: Approach and Avoidance Tendencies

In the affective Stroop task the heightened interference for (certain types of) affective stimuli might be explained by the working of the affective subsystem. In contrast to neutral words, the affective words will receive not only inhibitory signals from the match/mismatch-system but also an activation from the affective vigilance mechanism. Therefore, establishing the required imbalance between relevant (i.e, color) and irrelevant (i.e., content) features of the stimulus will take longer. Moreover, action schemas other than the (color-)naming schema might be activated by the affective subsystem and will produce interference in the response system as well. In fact, there is some evidence in the literature for subtle approach and avoidance tendencies that are automatically evoked by the mere presence of valenced stimuli (Brendl, 1997; Chen & Bargh, 1999; Solarz, 1960).

This last point is especially suited to explain the finding of Wentura et al. (2000), which shows that it is not the valence by itself that causes interference in the affective Stroop-task, but certain subtypes of valence. As mentioned, the effect was restricted to those stimuli that are tied directly to approach or avoidance in social contexts. In terms of the model, the content of these words fits more easily to approach or avoidance schemas triggered by the affective subsystem, thereby causing more interference in the response system.

To test this assumption more directly, we used a different experimental task (Wentura et al., 2000; Experiment 3). In a go–nogo lexical decision task participants were presented with the words used in the affective Stroop-task as well as with nonwords. Participants were asked to respond only in the case of word stimulus. Half of the participants had to press a key that was stuck to the screen just below the position of the stimulus. Thus, their reaction is similar to an approach behavior like, for example, touching a pet. The other half of the participants were instructed to press the key permanently and to withdraw it in case of a word stimulus. Thus, their reaction is similar to an avoidance behavior like, for example, withdrawing the finger from a hot-plate. We found a triple interaction of valence, relevance, and type of behavior: Whereas type of behavior did not moderate responses to possessor-relevant words, there was an interaction of valence and response within the subset of other-relevant words: Avoidance behavior (i.e., the "withdraw" reaction in our experiment) relatively favors the processing of negative other-relevant words whereas approach behavior (i.e., the "touch" reaction) favors the processing of positive other-relevant words.

To test for further applicability of the results from the word-stimuli tests discussed earlier, we carried out an additional experiment (thus far unpublished) using affective Stroop tasks; stylized faces were used (see Rothermund, Wentura, & Bak, 1996, for a report).

In this experiment (N = 42), the manipulation of other-relevant negativity versus possessor-relevant negativity was pictured by an angry versus sad face, the manipulation of other-relevant positivity versus possessor-relevant positivity was realized by a friendly versus satisfied face (see Fig. 3.2, top row). To

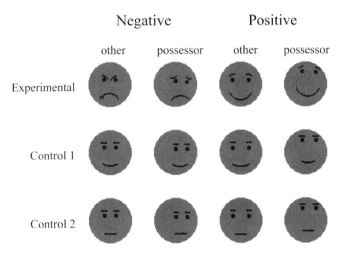

FIG. 3.2.   Face stimuli used in an affective Stroop experiment.

control for effects of the different visual features of the faces (beyond their emotional Gestalt), two types of neutral control faces were used (see Fig. 3.2, middle and bottom row). Eyes, eye brows, and mouth were presented in either a red or blue color on a light grey face. Participants had to categorize each face with regard to its color either by naming the color or by keypresses.[2] Interference scores for each experimental face were calculated by subtracting mean response times for the two control faces from the response times of the experimental face.

What we found was a significant interaction of valence and relevance (see Fig. 3.3). Significant interference was found only for the other-relevant negative face (i.e., the angry face; $M = 14$ ms, $SD = 36$, $t[41] = 2.53$, $p < .05$). Thus, the result for the word stimuli (i.e., higher color naming latencies for both negative *and* positive other-relevant words) was only partially replicated. However, a simple hypothesis might reconcile the diverging results. With reference to older theories about motivational processes (e.g., Miller, 1951), it might be assumed that the relative magnitude of behavioral tendencies of approach and avoidance depend on the distance between the stimulus and the perceiver. Thus, within a short distance avoidance tendencies are relatively stronger than approach tendencies, whereas the reverse holds for longer distances. If there is some truth to this hypothesis, it can

---

[2]Results were roughly comparable for the two response conditions. However, the keypress results were somewhat more pronounced. This was expected for visual stimuli compared to words given a rationale of Glaser and Glaser (1989; see Rothermund et al., 1996, for further explanation).

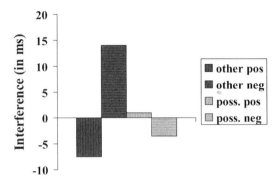

FIG. 3.3.   Mean interference scores (in ms) for face stimuli in an affective
Stroop experiment.

be hypothesized that given the experimental parameters (i.e, the faces in
their dimensions, the visual angle etc.) the avoidance tendency in the face
experiment reported previously was relatively stronger than the approach
tendency.

> In a recent pilot experiment (N = 21), we manipulated distance in the easiest
> way: In this new experiment, the computer screen was placed in a nearer posi-
> tion to half of the participants (compared to the experiment reported previ-
> ously), and farther away for the other half of the sample. In the far condition,
> we found a main effect of valence with higher interference for positive faces.
> Moreover, for positive faces, mean interference deviates significantly from
> zero, $M = 10$ ms ($SD = 15$ ms), $t(9) = 2.21$, $p = .05$. Taking into account that the
> two positive faces were not easily distinguishable with regard to their rele-
> vance (see Fig. 3.2 and Rothermund et al., 1996, for ratings), we are faced
> with a result that is quite compatible with the view that at longer distances—
> everything else being equal—approach tendencies outweigh avoidance ten-
> dencies. However, at odds with our assumption, there were no significant in-
> terference scores in the near condition.[3]

Of course, it is premature to take these results too seriously. However, it
would certainly be beneficial to make more rigorous tests with this simple

---

[3]This was possibly due to the fact that decreasing the distance too much will alter the perceptual situation from focusing on the Gestalt to focusing on some features of the face. There
is indeed evidence for this assumption. Neither in the former experiment (Rothermund et al.,
1996) nor in the *far* condition of the recent experiment, a main effect of relevance for the absolute response times was observed. In the *near* condtion, however, this was the only significant
effect, with shorter latencies for the other-relevant conditions. With regard to Fig. 3.2, it can be
easily seen that such an effect means nothing more than faster response times for those faces
with symmetrically arranged components.

manipulation. That applies as well to visual search experiments with stylized faces that were conducted to examine a "pop-out" of other-relevant negative faces (see Fox, Lester, Russo, Bowles, Pichler, & Dutton, 2000; White, 1995).

MIM and the Affective Simon Task

The expanded version of the Hougthon and Tipper model can also be used to explain congruency effects in affective Simon tasks (De Houwer & Eelen, 1998). As explained earlier, in this kind of task, participants have to make a valent response on the basis of an arbitrarily selected stimulus attribute and must ignore the valence of the stimulus valence. In spite of this, response latencies are typically delayed when stimulus valence and response valence are incongruent (De Houwer et al., 2001).

According to the model, congruency effects in the affective Simon task can be explained by interference in the response system. Interference can arise because the responses required in this kind of task overlap with the response sets of automatic evaluative action schemas. Stimulus valence will activate the affective subsystem that in turn will activate corresponding evaluative tendencies in the response system. In the case of a congruent trial (e.g., say "Positive"/"Negative" to a positive/negative stimulus, respectively), this might speed up the response because the correct response will receive additional support from the affective subsystem. In the case of an incongruent trial (e.g., say "Negative" to a positive stimulus or vice versa), on the other hand, different evaluative responses will become activated by the task-relevant stimulus feature and valence. This interference is particularly strong because variable binding in the automatic evaluation schema is easy and natural whereas values of the task-relevant feature are assigned to evaluative responses arbitrarily and the assignment rules first have to be retrieved from working memory (e.g., Mayr & Kliegl, 2000). An automatic evaluation of the stimulus might thus reach the variable slots of the evaluative response system before the relevant feature has been translated into the respective response codes.

To resolve this conflict, stimulus valence has to be inhibited by negative feedback from the match/mismatch detector. Although valence is a task-irrelevant feature, it will be difficult to establish an inhibition because the affective subsystem is constantly activated by the property units representing the stimulus. In the case of an incongruent trial, responding will thus be delayed until inhibitory effects of the match/mismatch system with respect to stimulus valence have overcome the positive feedback of the affective subsystem.

BEYOND OUTPUT INTERFERENCE: PREDICTING AFFECTIVE INCONGRUENCY EFFECTS IN THE EVALUATION AND PRONUNCIATION TASKS

Up to this point, the explanations for the different phenomena were focused on the affective subsystem's ability to trigger response schemas. However, some thoughts are directly derivable from the model that rely heavily on the backward links from the affective subsystem to the object field. First, we return to the evaluation task and spell out some arguments that lead to the prediction of affective incongruency effects under specified circumstances. We report on some new experiments with regard to these predictions.

In the second part of the section, we return to the pronunciation task with its rather bizarre pattern of results. Here, we give some speculations that follow from the considerations about the evaluation task in the first part of the section.

Object Field Interference and the Evaluation Task

As argued previously, the relevant action schema for the evaluation task has two variable slots: The word that is to be evaluated (the *object slot*) and the evaluation itself as positive or negative (the *evaluation slot*). Of course, as soon as the evaluation slot is filled, a response can be given. In the case of target-congruent priming, the affective vigilance subsystem delivers an unequivocal activation of one of the response alternatives, whereas this is only the case for target-incongruent priming when the basic interference between prime and target in the object field has been resolved.

However, there is a certain ambiguity in this explanation. Releasing a response can be dependent on two different response criteria. First, participants might respond as soon as the evaluation slot is filled. Second, participants might not respond until both slots—the object slot as well the evaluation slot—are filled. The difference between the two response criteria might be framed in terms of different strategies that participants might adopt. In principle, they can adopt one of two strategies (Milliken, Joordens, Merikle, & Seiffert, 1998). First, they can respond on the basis of accumulated evidence in favor of one of the two response alternatives, whatever the source of this evidence might be. That is, as soon as the evaluation slot is filled they will emit a response. Second, they can select "a response *that is accessible for the right reason* [italics added]; namely, because it corresponds to the current target" (Milliken et al., 1998, p. 225). Thus, they will wait for evidence that unequivocally fills the object slot.

More interesting, whereas the first strategy will clearly predict an affective congruency effect because the release of a response is based only on filling the evaluation slot, which is finished earlier in the case of congruent prime/distractor-target pairs compared to an incongruent pairing, the second strategy is associated with more complex predictions. In the case of an incongruent prime/distractor-target pair, there is rivalry in the object field as well as in the affective subsystem. In the case of a congruent prime/distractor-target pair, there is rivalry only in the object field. At first sight, it seems obvious to predict that the more rivalry, the longer the process of conflict resolution will last. However, it should be noticed that the affective subsystem activates the property units of the object field via backward links. Possibly, the interference in the object field is prolonged in the case of affective congruency because the property units of both distractor and target are constantly activated by the backward links of the affective vigilance system without having inhibitory processes within this subsystem. Or—to say it the other way round—presenting affectively incongruent stimulus pairs triggers interference within the affective subsystem. This interference is resolved in parallel to solving the interference in the object field. Thus, backward activation of the distractor's property units is limited.

Thus, under circumstances that have to be specified, affective congruency effects in the evaluation task should be diminished or even reversed. Given this backdrop, it is interesting to note that in one subdomain of affective priming research with the evaluation task (i.e., by examining whether affective congruency effects will emerge under conditions of a masked presentation of primes), mixed results were reported. In early attempts to find reliable subliminal effects, Greenwald, Klinger, and Schuh (1995) reported very small effects. However, by using a somewhat different technique, Draine and Greenwald (1998, Greenwald, Draine, & Abrams, 1996) found large and replicable masked affective priming (see also Otten & Wentura, 1999, Exp. 2). In contrast, Hermans (1996) was the first to find reversed affective priming under conditions of subliminal priming. In an unpublished experiment (see Wentura, 1997a, for a brief report), the reliability of this last result was corroborated.

In this experiment (N = 12), by using a prime duration of 28 ms, a mask (a row of @) for about 50 ms and a SOA of 100 ms, a reversed affective congruency effect (i.e., the difference between the congruent prime-target pairings and the incongruent prime-target pairings) of M = –23 ms (SD = 37 ms), t(11) = 2.14, p = .055, emerged. That is, if one is willing to ignore the slight deviation from the conventional criterion of statistical significance, there was in fact evidence for increased response times after the priming with a stimulus of the same valence compared to a priming with a stimulus of a different valence, thereby replicating Hermans (1996).

How can the different results be reconciled? In a further unpublished experiment, Wentura (1999b) provided evidence for moderating conditions. The main argument was that the different strategies can be induced by different instructions with regard to the speed-accuracy trade-off. Strategy 1 ("Base your response on accumulated evidence for one of the response alternatives, whatever the source of this evidence might be!") should be induced by putting strong emphasis on speed. Strategy 2 ("Base your response only on evidence coming from the correct source!") should be induced by putting strong emphasis on accuracy. In this experiment (N = 57), half of the participants were assigned to the emphasis-on-speed (EOS) instructions, the other half to the emphasis-on-accuracy (EOA) instructions. Parameters of presentation were roughly comparable to those of the experiment reported above (see Wentura, 1999b, for details).

With regard to affective priming, there was a significant interaction of instruction and affective priming (see Fig. 3.4), $F(1,55) = 5.08$, $p < .05$. As expected, in the emphasis-on-speed sample, the affective priming effect was 13 ms ($SD = 27$ ms), which was significantly different from zero, $t(27) = 2.60$, $p < .05$. In the emphasis-on-accuracy sample, however, the affective priming

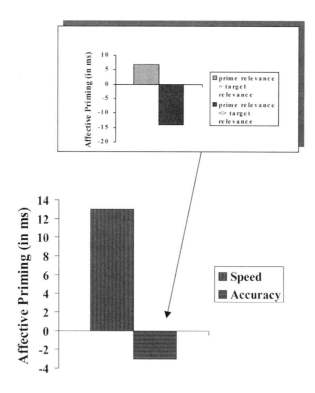

FIG. 3.4.   Mean affective priming (in ms) as a function of speed vs. accuracy instructions and match vs. nonmatch in prime-target relevance (insert figure; see text for further explanations).

effect reduced to −3 ms (SD = 29 ms), which was not significantly different from zero, $t(28)$ = 0.63, *n.s.*

Moreover, Wentura (1999b) used an additional variable in this experiment. With reference to our studies with the Stroop-color naming latencies (Wentura et al., 2000), the *type* of negativity and positivity (in the sense of Peeters, 1983) of the adjectives (i.e., whether they are other-relevant or possessor-relevant), was manipulated (see earlier discussion). If the affective vigilance system is sensitive to the difference between the two types of relevance (which is indicated by our Stroop experiments), it can be argued that, given strategy 2, the congruent pairs that consist of two stimuli of different relevance (e.g., depressive/brutal) are especially problematic: The affective subsystem delivers slightly ambiguous information (i.e., it fills the evaluation slot with the response "other *or* possessor negative!)" This ambiguity signals that there are two sources of evidence. As is the case for incongruent pairs, a response can only be given after the interference process in the object field is finished. However, the process of differentiation between the two stimuli in the object field is prolonged compared to the incongruent condition because there is less rivalry within the affective subsystem such that both the property units of distractor and target will continuously be activated through the backward links from the affective subsystem.

In fact, in the emphasis-on-accuracy sample, the affective congruency effect was −14 ms (SD = 36 ms) if the relevance type of prime and target was different, which was significantly below zero (see Fig. 3.4), $t(28)$ = −2.07, $p <$ .05. In cases where prime and target relevance were the same, the affective congruency effect was 7 ms (SD = 46 ms), which was not significantly different from zero, $t(28)$ = .82, *ns.* In the emphasis-on-speed sample, the positive affective congruency effect (see previous discussion) was not moderated by prime-target relevance.

It should be added that, surprisingly, the different instructions (speed vs. accuracy) in the experiment did not lead to gross differences with regard to the overall speed and error rate. This might be seen as a failure to prove manipulation efficiency. However, given this result it cannot be claimed that the actual performance with regard to speed and accuracy is the causal factor for different results in affective priming. It rather seems to be case that the adoption of the different criteria for success led to the different strategies that were hypothesized.

Thus, given these considerations about different strategies, it is possible to accommodate the different results that were found with masked affective priming. In this regard, it is interesting that Draine and Greenwald (1998; see also Musch, 2000; Otten & Wentura, 1999, Exp. 2) proposed a so-called *response window* technique to get robust subliminal priming effects. With this technique, participants are trained to respond to the target stimulus within a time span that is too fast to respond to with high accuracy. That is, the response should be given within, for example, 333 to 450 ms after presentation onset of the target stimulus. The error rate dramatically rises and its variation with regard to the prime-target relationship is a reliable and powerful indicator of affective priming. The argument given by Draine and Greenwald (1998) for this boost in power is that with the response window technique, treatment variance is focused on one instead of two dependent variables (i.e., all participants contribute to a priming effect in the error rate instead of some contributing to a response time effect and some to an error effect). Given the background suggested here, the story is the following: Forcing participants to give their response within the response window is equivalent to encouraging the adoption of Strategy 1: Base your response on any evidence whatever the reason for this evidence might be. The evidence accumulated up to the start of the response window, however, is evidence largely based on the prime. What is diminished by using this technique is the proportion of participants who choose Strategy 2 on their own (i.e., the strategy to discriminate between successive inputs in order to use only the correct evidence).

The "two-strategies" approach can also be used to provide an alternative account for the relatedness proportion effect shown by Klauer et al. (1997). It can be argued that the relatedness proportion is a predictor of the strategy chosen by a participant. Given a relatedness proportion of more than 50%, Strategy 1 will be very efficient because the prime valence is a good predictor of the target valence. Thus, it is a good strategy to wait only for filling of the evaluation slot. But given a relatedness proportion of less than 50%, it would be better to discriminate between prime and target display (i.e., to base a response only on correct evidence). Please note that choosing this strategy will not necessarily predict an incongruence effect. Whether positive, negative, or null results will be observed is a question of the ease with which prime and target can be differentiated within the object field. The experiment of Wentura (1999b) provides one possibility of manipulating this feature (see also Wentura, 2002).

Object Field Interference and the Pronunciation Task

As mentioned above, Glaser and Banaji (1999) gave replicable evidence for reversed affective priming in the pronunciation task. For strongly valenced primes, naming is delayed in cases of congruent priming. The framework proposed here offers a speculation with regard to this intriguing phenomenon. For filling the response schema for the pronunciation task, it is absolutely necessary to have a clear asymmetry in the object field with the property units of the target activated and the property units of the prime/distractor inhibited. In this regard, the pronunciation task resembles the evaluation task, given Strategy 2 ("Base your response only on evidence coming from the correct source!"; see earlier discusion). That is, in case of an incongruent prime/distractor-target pair, there is a rivalry both within the object field and the affective subsystem. With regard to the latter, property units that represent "positivity" are inhibitorily linked to units that represent "negativity." As was argued earlier for the evaluation task, this two-fold rivalry might lead to an intense but quick settlement process.

Fig. 3.5a visualizes this process in a snapshot. Both the distractor "brutal" and the target "lovely" had initially activated corresponding property units in the object field. (The external activation is depicted by the hatched nodes). For solving the task (i.e, to pronounce the target), the units corresponding to the distractor must be fully inhibited whereas the units corresponding to the target must be fully activated. There are two sources of inhibition for the distractor units: The first source of inhibition stems from the match/mismatch-system (M/M) that works on the basis of instructional features distinguishing targets from distractors (e.g., locality, color). This asymmetry is visualized by the status of the right-most property units of distractor and target (using black for full activation of a unit and white for full inhibition). Whereas the unit corresponding to the distractor feature is

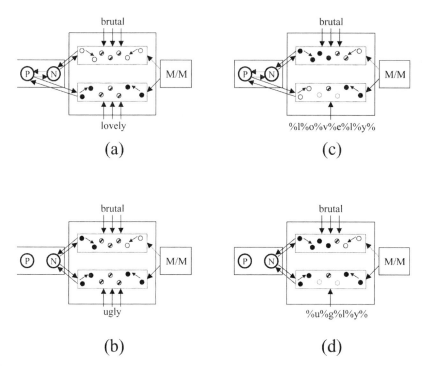

FIG. 3.5.   Explaining positive and reversed priming effects by processes in the object field (see text for further explanations).

inhibited by the match/mismatch-system, the unit corresponding to the target feature is activated. Inhibition as well as activation spread through excitatory links between corresponding units. Then, establishing a full-blown asymmetry (i.e., full activation of the target pattern and full inhibition of the distractor pattern) is supported by the inhibitory links within the affective subsystem.

Now, consider the case of a congruent prime/distractor-target pair (see Fig. 3.5b). Here, establishing an asymmetry in the object field will be delayed because of two reasons. First, there is only one source of inhibition—the match/mismatch-system. Second, because there is no rivalry within the affective subsystem, the property units of both the distractor and the target are continuously activated by the backward links from the affective subsystem. Additionally, assuming that the feature of being "strongly valenced" is equivalent to strong forward and backward links between the property units in the object field and the property units representing valence in the affective subsystem, we are faced by a strongly activated prime/distractor especially in the case of a congruent prime/distractor-target pair.

But what about the results of De Houwer and colleagues (2001) who found affective congruency effects for degraded target presentations (see previous discussion)? First of all, it should be noticed that mean absolute response times in the experiments of Glaser and Banaji (1999) were about 550 ms whereas mean response times in the essential condition of the experiment of De Houwer and colleagues (2001) were above 1000 ms. That is, the filling of the object slot cost about twice the time compared to Glaser and Banaji. Is there any argument that a distractor condition that is of help in a fast settlement process will be a hurdle in a slow settlement process and vice versa? We will try to give one.

The external activation of the target's property units in the object field is severely limited because of the degradation. Thus, the forward activation of the affective subsystem by the target's property units is low. Now consider the case of presenting an incongruent prime/distractor (see Fig. 3.5c). This stimulus fully activates the units in the affective subsystem representing its valence. For a while these units undermine effectively the delicate forward activation of the target's valence. The settlement process that ultimately ends with a full-blown activation of the target's property units (because of the top-down specification of task requirements) is delayed compared to congruent priming because in the latter case forward activation of the target's valence in the affective subsystem (and then backward support) will not be obstructed (see Fig. 3.5d).

To summarize these considerations with regard to the diverging results of Glaser and Banaji (1999) on the one hand and De Houwer and colleagues (2001) on the other hand, we can discriminate between two cases: (a) If both the distractor and target initially create a balanced activation of their corresponding property units in the object field, both valences are initially activated by the property units. In return, they provide supporting activation for the corresponding property units through backward links. However, because the match/mismatch field creates an imbalance in favor of the target's units that is propagated into the affective subsystem, the activation of the incongruent distractor's units will be quickly inhibited. In contrast, in the case of a congruent distractor, this process will last somewhat longer because the distractor's units will continuously be activated from the valence units that are not in conflict with the target's valence. Thus, an affective incongruency effect is predicted; (b) If there is an imbalanced initial activation in the object field, the incongruent distractor causes an imbalance in the affective subsystem as well, thereby suppressing a slow-rising activation of the units representing the target's valence for a while. Thus, while the backward activation from the match/mismatch field is effective in activating the target's representation and inhibiting the distractor's representation, the representation of the incongruent distractor gets support from the affective subsystem, which is not the case for the target's property units. Thus, an affective congruency effect is predicted.

Old Wine in New Bottles? Object Field Interference and the Principle of Increased Accessibility

The question might arise whether by focusing on processes at the level of object representations some kind of principle of increased accessibility of targets, caused by congruent priming, is reintroduced. Yes and no. In our model the role of (some sort of) such a process is very limited. Most of the congruency effects, especially the robust ones found with the evaluation task, are explained by response competition. If processes located in the object field are made responsible for any effects, we would expect them dominantly to be of the reversed type because the rivalry between the distractor and target representation is prolonged in cases of a feature overlap (e.g., congruent valence; see also Houghton & Tipper, 1994, for this argument). There are two cases that remain. The first one is given if perceiving the "gestalt" of the target is hampered. Then, inhibiting the valence component of the target by an incongruent distractor delays target activation and naming. This case is exemplified by the experiment of De Houwer and colleagues (2001) with their degraded target presentation (see previous discussion). The second case is given if a distractor strongly activates its corresponding valence but does not strongly activate a naming response. In this case, there will be no (strong) interference between distractor and target in the object field with regard to the naming response but strong rivalry in the affective subsystem. Then, in the case of an incongruent prime-target pair, activation of the valence component of the target is hampered and a full-blown activation of the target's representation—a precondition for naming—is prolonged. This case might be exemplified by the results of Giner Sorolla et al. (1999) and Spruyt et al. (2001), who found congruency effects with picture primes. At an abstract level we might describe priming by a nonneutral picture as a strong activation of the corresponding valence accompanied by a weak activation of the response-related part: A nonneutral picture will clearly activate its corresponding valence; however, it will not strongly activate those property units that are most closely tied to giving the adequate naming response (at least compared to word stimuli).

Of course, in both cases facilitation by a congruent distractor within the affective subsystem can be assumed as well. Therefore, in some sense, the old principle of increased target accessibility has reentered the scene. However, in at least two aspects we have left behind the spreading activation account depicted in a semantic network. First, in the model favorized here much emphasis is put on inhibitory processes. In fact, it is an open (empirical) question whether increased accessibility of congruent targets or decreased accessibility of incongruent targets is the dominant process under those (rare) circumstances leading to congruency effects in the pronunciation task. Second, even more important, using a model of selective attention to explain automatic evaluative processes makes clear that the rivalry between a distractor and a target (and not priming) might be the dominant process in affective priming tasks. If the process of response generation is focused on the valence category only (which is the case in the evaluation task, given Strategy 1), congruency effects will be expected from this rivalry (see earlier discussion). If, however, response generation is focused on the identity of the target (which is the case in the pronunciation task and, partly, in the evaluation task, given Strategy 2), incongruency effects will be (dominantly) expected, because the rivalry in the object field is more easily solved in the case of incongruent stimulus pairs.

CONCLUSIONS

We have tried to integrate a set of findings that have been published in recent years under the topic of automatic evaluation. By using and adapting a general model on selective attention (Houghton & Tipper, 1994, 1996), we have pointed out two characteristics of an affective subsystem that are suited to explain most of the phenomena. First, the affective subsystem has a privileged access to response schemata of avoidance and approach, as well as evaluation and judgment. In most experimental tasks, this feature causes interference effects if incongruent prime/distractors are presented just before or in parallel with a target stimulus.

Second, the affective subsystem is not only automatically activated by presenting a positive or negative stimulus. Additionally, the activation of the units that represent this stimulus is increased by backward links from the affective subsystem, thereby accounting for the unspecific relevance of valent stimuli. This feature makes it understandable why under specific conditions (i.e., accuracy instructions in the evaluation task and presenting strong primes in the pronunciation task), reversed affective priming effects emerge.

However, thus far we have not implemented the expanded model in a computer simulation (as Houghton & Tipper, 1994, did for the original model). Yet this would clearly offer more specific predictions for, the conditions of normal and reversed affective priming effects in the pronunciation task, for example.

Another theme that has to be discussed in the future is the status of the affective subsystem. It might be argued that it is enough to assume some property units that represent valence (like any other category) within the object field. However, Houghton and Tipper (1994) related their model to neuropsychological evidence. In this regard, it might be worthwhile to have a look on neuropsychological theories on affect and emotion as well (e.g., LeDoux, 1995, 1998). Evidence from this field might support the assumption of an affective subsystem in attentional regulation.

ACKNOWLEDGMENTS

We are grateful to Dirk Hemans and an annonymous reviewer for their comments and suggestions on an earlier version of this manuscript.

Correspondence concerning this article should be addressed to Dirk Wentura, Universitat Jena, Institut fur Psychologie, Am Steiger 3, Haus1, D-07743 Jena, Germany, e-mail: d.wentura@uni-jena.de

REFERENCES

Balota, D. A., Boland, J. E., & Shields, L. W. (1989). Priming in pronunciation: Beyond pattern recognition and onset latency. *Journal of Memory and Language, 28*, 14–36.

Bargh, J. A., Chaiken, S., Govender, R., & Pratto, F. (1992). The generality of the automatic attitude activation effect. *Journal of Personality and Social Psychology, 62*, 893–912.

Bargh, J. A., Chaiken, S., Raymond, P., & Hymes, C. (1996). The automatic evaluation effect: Unconditional automatic attitude activation with a pronunciation task. *Journal of Experimental Social Psychology, 32*, 104–128.

Bargh, J. A., Chen, M., & Burrows, L. (1996). Automaticity of social behavior: Direct effects of trait construct and stereotype activation on action. *Journal of Personality and Social Psychology, 71*, 230–244.

Bower, G. H. (1981). Mood and memory. *American Psychologist, 36*, 129–148.

Bower, G. H. (1991). Mood congruity of social judgments. In J. P. Forgas (Ed.), *Emotion and social judgments* (pp. 31–53). Oxford: Pergamon Press.

Brendl, C. M. (1997, June). *Geschwindigkeit von Armstreckung und Armbeugung: Annäherungs-Vermeidungsmotivation und Einstellungen implizit messen?* [Speed of arm extension vs. arm flexion: Implicitly assessing approach/avoidance motivation and attitudes?]. Paper presented at the 6th meeting of the Division of Social Psychology, Konstanz, Germany.

Burt, J. S. (1994). Identity primes produce facilitation in a colour naming task. *Quarterly Journal of Experimental Psychology, 47A,* 957–1000.

Chen, M., & Bargh, J. A. (1999). Consequences of automatic evaluation: Immediate behavioral predispositions to approach or avoid the stimulus. *Personality and Social Psychology Bulletin, 25,* 215–224.

De Houwer, J., Crombez, G., Baeyens, F., & Hermans, D. (2001). On the generality of the affective Simon effect. *Cognition and Emotion, 15,* 189–206.

De Houwer, J., & Eelen, P. (1998). An affective variant of the Simon paradigm. *Cognition and Emotion, 8,* 45–61.

De Houwer, J., & Hermans, D. (1999, June). *Nine attempts of find affective priming of pronunciation responses: Effects of SOA, degradation, and language.* Paper presented at the 7th meeting of the Division of Social Psychology, Kassel, Germany.

De Houwer, J., Hermans, D., & Eelen, P. (1998). Affective and identity priming with episodically associated stimuli. *Cognition and Emotion, 12,* 145–169.

De Houwer, J., Hermans, D., Rothermund, K., & Wentura, D. (in press). Affective priming of semantic categorization responses. *Cognition and Emotion.*

De Houwer, J., Hermans, D., & Spruyt, A. (2001). Affective priming of pronunciation responses: Effects of target degradation. *Journal of Experimental Social Psychology, 37,* 85–91.

De Houwer, J., & Randell, T. (2001). *Attention to primes modulates affective priming of pronunciation responses.* Unpublished manuscript.

Draine, S. C., & Greenwald, A. G. (1998). Replicable unconscious semantic priming. *Journal of Experimental Psychology: General, 127,* 286–303.

Fazio, R. H. (2001). On the automatic activation of associated evaluations: An overview. *Cognition and Emotion, 15,* 115–141.

Fazio, R. H., Sanbonmatsu, D. M., Powell, M. C., & Kardes, F. R. (1986). On the automatic activation of attitudes. *Journal of Personality and Social Psychology, 50,* 229–238.

Fox, E. (1995). Negative priming from ignored distractors in visual selection: A review. *Psychonomic Bulletin & Review, 2,* 145–173.

Fox, E., Lester, V., Russo, R., Bowles, R. J., Pichler, A., & Dutton, K. (2000). Facial expressions of emotion: Are angry faces detected more efficiently? *Cognition and Emotion, 14,* 61–92.

Frijda, N. H. (1988). The laws of emotion. *American Psychologist, 43,* 349–358.

Gardner, R. M. (1985). The Reverse Affect Test: A new interference task. *Perceptual and Motor Skills, 60,* 384–386.

Giner-Sorolla, R., Garcia, M., & Bargh, J. A. (1999). The automatic evaluation of pictures. *Social Cognition, 17,* 76–96.

Glaser, J., & Banaji, M. R. (1999). When fair is foul and foul is fair: Reverse priming in automatic evaluation. *Journal of Personality and Social Psychology, 77,* 669–687.

Glaser, M. O., & Glaser, W. R. (1982). Time course analysis of the Stroop phenomenon. *Journal of Experimental Psychology: Human Perception and Performance, 8,* 875–894.

Glaser, W. R., & Glaser, M. O. (1989). Context effects in Stroop-like word and picture processing. *Journal of Experimental Psychology: General, 118,* 13–42.

Greenwald, A. G., Draine, S. C., & Abrams, R. L. (1996). Three cognitive markers of unconscious semantic activation. *Science, 273,* 1699–1702.

Greenwald, A. G., Klinger, M. R., & Liu, T. J. (1989). Unconscious processing of dichoptically masked words. *Memory & Cognition, 17,* 35–47.

Greenwald, A. G., Klinger, M. R., & Schuh, E. S. (1995). Activation by marginally perceptible ("subliminal") stimuli: Dissociation of unconscious from conscious cognition. *Journal of Experimental Psychology: General, 124,* 22–42.

Grossberg, S. (1987). Competitive learning: From interactive activation to adaptive resonance. *Cognitive Science, 11*, 23–63.

Grossberg, S., & Stone, G. (1986). Neural dynamics of word recognition and recall: Attentional priming, learning, and resonance. *Psychological Review, 93*, 46–74.

Hermans, D. (1996). *Automatische stimulusevaluatie. Een experimentele analyse van de voorwaarden voor evaluatieve stimulusdiscriminatie aan de hand van het affectieve-primingparadigma.* [Automatic stimulus evaluation. An experimental analysis of the preconditions for evaluative stimulus discrimination using an affective priming paradigm]. Unpublished doctoral dissertation, University of Leuven, Belgium.

Hermans, D., De Houwer, J., & Eelen, P. (1994). The affective priming effect: Automatic activation of evaluative information in memory. *Cognition and Emotion, 8*, 515–533.

Hermans, D., De Houwer, J., & Eelen, P. (2001). A time course analysis of the affective priming effect. *Cognition and Emotion, 15*, 143–165.

Hermans, D., Van den Broeck, A., & Eelen, P. (1998). Affective priming using a colour-naming task: A test of an affective-motivational account of affective priming effects. *Zeitschrift für Experimentelle Psychologie, 45*, 136–148.

Hill, A. B., & Kemp-Wheeler, S. M. (1989). The influence of context on lexical decision times for emotionally aversive words. *Current Psychology Research and Reviews, 8*, 219–227.

Houghton, G., & Tipper, S. P. (1994). A model of inhibitory mechanisms in selective attention. In D. Dagenbach & T. H. Carr (Eds.), *Inhibitory processes in attention, memory, and language* (pp. 53–112). San Diego, CA: Academic Press.

Houghton, G., & Tipper, S. P. (1996). Inhibitory mechanisms of neural and cognitive control: Applications to selective attention and sequential action. *Brain and Cognition, 30*, 20–43.

Houghton, G., & Tipper, S. P. (1999). A model of selective attention as a mechanism of cognitive control. In J. Grainger & A. M. Jacobs (Eds.), *Localist connectionist approaches to human cognition* (pp. 39–74). Mahwah, NJ: Lawrence Erlbaum Associates.

Houghton, G., Tipper, S. P., Weaver, B., & Shore, D. I. (1996). Inhibition and interference in selective attention: Some tests of a neural network model. *Visual Cognition, 3*, 119–164.

Kemp-Wheeler, S. M., & Hill, A. B. (1992). Semantic and emotional priming below objective detection threshold. *Cognition and Emotion, 6*, 113–128.

Klauer, K. C. (1991). *Einstellungen. Der Einfluß der affektiven Komponente auf das kognitive Urteilen* [Attitudes: The influence of the affective component on cognitive judgments]. Göttingen, Germany: Hogrefe.

Klauer, K. C. (1998). Affective Priming. *European Review of Social Psychology, 8*, 67–103.

Klauer, K. C., & Musch, J. (in press). Goal-dependent and goal-independent effects of irrelevant evaluations. *Personality and Social Psychology Bulletin.*

Klauer, K. C., & Musch, J. (2001). Does sunshine prime loyal? Affective priming in the naming task. *Quarterly Journal of Experimental Psychology, 54A*, 727–751.

Klauer, K. C., Roßnagel, C., & Musch, J. (1995). *Affective priming effects: Evidence for assimilation and contrast.* Unpublished manuscript.

Klauer, K. C., Roßnagel, C., & Musch, J. (1997). List context effects in evaluative priming. *Journal of Experimental Psychology: Learning, Memory, and Cognition, 23*, 246–255.

Klauer, K. C., & Stern, E. (1992). How attitudes guide memory-based judgments: A two-process model. *Journal of Experimental Social Psychology, 28*, 186–206.

La Heij, W., van der Heijden, A. H., & Schreuder, R. (1985). Semantic priming and Stroop-like interference in word-naming tasks. *Journal of Experimental Psychology: Human Perception and Performance, 11*, 62–80.

Lang, P. J. (1995). The emotion probe. Studies of motivation and attention. *American Psychologist, 50*, 372–385.

LeDoux, J. (1995). Emotion: clues from the brain. *Annual Review of Psychology, 46*, 209–235.

LeDoux, J. (1998). *The emotional brain.* New York: Simon and Schuster.

Logan, G. D., & Zbrodoff, N. J. (1979). When it helps to be misled: Facilitative effects of increasing the frequency of conflicting stimuli in a Stroop-like task. *Memory and Cognition, 7,* 166–174.

MacLeod, C. M. (1991). Half a century of research on the Stroop effect: An integrative review. *Psychological Bulletin, 109,* 163–203.

Masson, M. E. J. (1995). A distributed memory model of semantic priming. *Journal of Experimental Psychology: Learning, Memory, and Cognition, 21,* 3–23.

May, C. P., Kane, M. J., & Hasher, L. (1995). Determinants of negative priming. *Psychological Bulletin, 118,* 35–54.

Mayr, U., & Kliegl, R. (2000). Task-set switching and long-term memory retrieval. *Journal of Experimental Psychology: Learning, Memory, and Cognition, 26,* 1124–1140.

McClelland, J. L., & Rumelhart, D. E. (1981). An interactive activation model of context effects in letter perception: Part 1. An account of basic findings. *Psychological Review, 88,* 375–407.

McRae, K., de Sa, V. R., & Seidenberg, M. S. (1997). On the nature and scope of featural representations of word meaning. *Journal of Experimental Psychology: General, 126,* 99–130.

Miller, N. E. (1951). Learnable drives and rewards. In S. S. Stevens (Ed.), *Handbook of experimental psychology* (pp. 435–472). New York: Wiley.

Milliken, B., Joordens, S., Merikle, P., & Seiffert, A. (1998). Selective attention: A re-evaluation of the implications of negative priming. *Psychological Review, 105,* 203–229.

Musch, J. (2000). *Affektives Priming: Kongruenzeffekte bei der evaluativen Bewertung* [Affective priming: Congruency effects in evaluative judgments]. Unpublished doctoral dissertation, University of Bonn, Germany.

Musch, J., & Klauer, K. C. (1997). Der Anteilseffekt beim affektiven Priming: Replikation und Bewertung einer theoretischen Erklärung [The consistency proportion effect in affective priming: Replication and evaluation of a theoretical account]. *Zeitschrift für Experimentelle Psychologie, 44,* 266–292.

Musch, J., & Klauer, K. C. (2001). Locational uncertainty moderates affective congruency effects in the evaluative decision task. *Cognition and Emotion, 15,* 167–188.

Neely, J. H. (1991). Semantic priming effects in visual word recognition: A selective review of current findings and theories. In D. Besner & G. W. Humphreys (Eds.), *Basic processes in reading. Visual word recognition* (pp. 264–336). Hillsdale, NJ: Lawrence Erlbaum Associates.

Neill, W. T., Valdes, L. A., & Terry, K. M. (1995). Selective attention and the inhibitory control of cognition. In F. N. Dempster & C. J. Brainerd (Eds.), *Interference and inhibition in cognition* (pp. 207–261). San Diego, CA: Academic Press.

Neumann, O. (1987). Beyond capacity: A functional view of attention. In H. Heuer & A. F. Sanders (Eds.), *Perspectives on perception and action* (pp. 361–394). Hillsdale, NJ: Lawrence Erlbaum Associates.

Oden, G. C., & Spira, J. L. (1983). Influence of context on the activation and selection of ambiguous word senses. *Quarterly Journal of Experimental Psychology, 35A,* 51–64.

Otten, S., & Wentura, D. (1999). About the impact of automaticity in the Minimal Group Paradigm: Evidence from affective priming tasks. *European Journal of Social Psychology, 29,* 1049–1071.

Peeters, G. (1983). Relational and informational patterns in social cognition. In W. Doise & S. Moscovici (Eds.), *Current Issues in European Social Psychology* (Vol. 1, pp. 201–237). Cambridge, UK: Cambridge University Press.

Peeters, G. (1992). Evaluative meanings of adjectives in vitro and in context: Some theoretical implications and practical consequences of positive-negative asymmetry and behavioral-adaptive concepts of evaluation. *Psychologica Belgica, 32,* 211–231.

Peeters, G., & Czapinski, J. (1990). Positive–negative asymmetry in evaluations: The distinction between affective and informational negativity effects. *European Review of Social Psychology, 1,* 33–60.

Pratto, F. (1994). Consciousness and automatic evaluation. In P. M. Niedenthal & S. Kitayama (Eds.), *The heart's eye* (pp. 115–143). New York: Academic Press.

Pratto, F., & John, O. P. (1991). Automatic vigilance: The attention-grabbing power of negative social information. *Journal of Personality and Social Psychology, 61,* 380–391.

Roskos-Ewoldsen, D. R., & Fazio, R. H. (1992). On the orienting value of attitudes: Attitude accessibility as a determinant of an object's attraction of visual attention. *Journal of Personality and Social Psychology, 63,* 198–211.

Rothermund, K., & Wentura, D. (1998). Ein fairer Test für die Aktivationsausbreitungshypothese: Affektives Priming in der Stroop-Aufgabe [An unbiased test of a spreading activation account of affective priming: Analysis of affective congruency effects in the Stroop task]. *Zeitschrift für Experimentelle Psychologie, 45,* 120–135.

Rothermund, K., Wentura, D., & Bak, P. (1996). *Automatische Vigilanz: Aufmerksamkeitsbindung durch verhaltensrelevante soziale Informationen* [Automatic Vigilance: The attention-grabbing power of behavior-related social information] (Trierer Psychologische Berichte, 23, Heft 1). Trier: Universität Trier, Fachbereich I - Psychologie.

Rothermund, K., Wentura, D., & Bak, P. (2001). Automatic attention to stimuli signalling chances and dangers: Moderating effects of positive and negative goal and action contexts. *Cognition and Emotion, 15,* 231–248.

Shaffer, W. O., & LaBerge, D. (1979). Automatic semantic processing of unattended words. *Journal of Verbal Learning and Verbal Behavior, 18,* 413–426.

Simon, H. A. (1967). Motivational and emotional controls of cognition. *Psychological Review, 74,* 29–39.

Solarz, A. K. (1960). Latency of instrumental responses as a function of compatibility with the meaning of eliciting verbal signs. *Journal of Experimental Psychology, 59,* 239–245.

Spruyt, A., Hermans, D., De Houwer, J., & Eelen, P. (2001). *Explaining the affective priming effect: Affective priming in a picture naming task.* Unpublished manuscript.

Stroop, J. R. (1935). Studies of interference in serial verbal reactions. *Journal of Experimental Psychology, 18,* 643–662.

Warren, R. E. (1972). Stimulus encoding and memory. *Journal of Experimental Psychology, 94,* 90–100.

Warren, R. E. (1974). Association, directionality, and stimulus encoding. *Journal of Experimental Psychology, 102,* 151–158.

Wentura, D. (1997a). *Subliminales affektives Priming: Evidenz für Inkongruenzeffekte* [Subliminal affective priming: Evidence for incongruence effects]. Unpublished manuscript.

Wentura, D. (1997b). Zur mentalen Repräsentation affektiv-evaluativer Komponenten: die Netzwerkmetapher und das Paradigma des "affektiven Primings" [The mental representation of affective-evaluative components: the network metaphor and the "affective priming" paradigm]. In H. Mandl (Ed.), *Bericht über den 40. Kongreß der Deutschen Gesellschaft für Psychologie in München 1996* (pp. 446–453). Göttingen, Germany: Hogrefe.

Wentura, D. (1998). Affektives Priming in der Wortentscheidungsaufgabe: Evidenz für postlexikalische Urteilstendenzen [Affective priming in the lexical decision task: Evidence for post-lexical judgmental tendencies]. *Sprache und Kognition, 17,* 125–137.

Wentura, D. (1999a). Activation and inhibition of affective information: Evidence for negative priming in the evaluation task. *Cognition and Emotion, 13,* 65–91.

Wentura, D. (1999b). *Masked priming in the evaluation task: A switch from positive to negative priming due to speed-accuracy instructions.* Unpublished manuscript.

Wentura, D. (2000). Dissociative affective and associative priming effects in the lexical decision task: Yes vs. no responses to word targets reveal evaluative judgment tendencies. *Journal of Experimental Psychology: Learning, Memory, and Cognition, 26,* 456–469.

Wentura, D. (2002). Ignoring "brutal" will make "numid" more pleasant but "uyuvu" more unpleasant: The role of a priori pleasantness of unfamiliar stimuli in affective priming tasks. *Cognition and Emotion, 16,* 269–298.

Wentura, D., Rothermund, K., & Bak, P. (2000). Automatic vigilance: The attention-grabbing power of approach- and avoidance-related social information. *Journal of Personality and Social Psychology, 78,* 1024–1037.

West, R. F., & Stanovich, K. E. (1982). Source of inhibition in experiments on the effect of sentence context on word recognition. *Journal of Experimental Psychology: Learning, Memory, and Cognition, 8,* 385–399.

White, M. (1995). Preattentive analysis of facial expressions of emotion. *Cognition and Emotion, 9,* 439–460.

White, M. (1996). Automatic affective appraisal of words. *Cognition and Emotion, 10,* 199–211.

Chapter 4

Reverse Priming: Implications for the (Un)conditionality of Automatic Evaluation

Jack Glaser
University of California, Berkeley

The first demonstration of automatic attitude activation (a.k.a., automatic evaluation) (Fazio, Sanbonmatsu, Powell, & Kardes, 1986) marked a turning point in the study of social cognition. From that point forward it was evident that our most fundamental social psychological construct, the attitude, something typically measured with direct questions, could be elicited indirectly, and triggered and displayed unintentionally and uncontrollably. Since then there has been considerable research on the topic (see Fazio, 2001; Klauer, 1998; Klauer & Musch, chap. 2, this volume, for reviews) and as a result we know a lot about the nature of automatic evaluation and how it gives rise to affective priming. Furthermore, the automatic attitude activation paradigm has lent itself nicely to the study of implicit attitudes and indirect attitude measurement (see De Houwer, chap. 9, this volume) even at the level of individual differences (e.g., Fazio, Jackson, Dunton, & Williams, 1995).

One prominent unresolved question regarding automatic evaluation has to do with its conditionality (i.e., under what conditions it will and will not occur), and one important aspect of this question has to do with the degree to which attitude strength affects automatic evaluation. Does it occur with weak as well as strong attitudes, and if so, does it occur with different likelihood for attitudes of different strengths? This question has been the source of controversy in the field (Bargh, Chaiken, Govender, & Pratto, 1992; Bargh, Chaiken, Raymond, & Hymes, 1996; Chaiken & Bargh, 1993; Fazio, 1993a, 1993b; Fazio et al., 1986), with disparate published findings leaving it unresolved. Recent demonstrations of *reverse priming* (Glaser & Banaji, 1999), however, promise to illuminate a feature of automatic evaluation, specifically *automatic correction*, which may be applied to reconcile the discordant positions. This chapter reviews the relevant literature, focusing on the issue of attitude strength and conditionality of automatic activation, and describes recent affective priming findings, applying their significance to the question at hand.

AUTOMATIC EVALUATION AND ATTITUDE STRENGTH

Fazio and colleagues (1986; Fazio, Chen, McDonel, & Sherman, 1982) defined an attitude as an "object-evaluation association" and specified that the strength of such associations could vary along a continuum from a "nonattitude" to a well-learned, highly accessible attitude. They contended that whether or not an attitude would be activated in memory would depend on where it lay on that continuum, that is, the strength of the object-evaluation association (Fazio et al., 1986, p. 230). This they tested by adopting a sequential semantic priming paradigm in which pairs of words were presented, one word right after the other, in rapid succession, the second word (an adjective) being categorized, with the press of a designated button, as positive or negative in meaning. This paradigm for measuring automatic evaluation is what has come to be known as *affective priming* because the affect (evaluation) associated with the first word (the prime) serves to "prime" the affective categorization response to the second word (the target). Indeed, Fazio et al. (1986) found that people tended to evaluate target adjectives faster when they had been preceded by affectively congruent primes. From this they inferred that the attitude toward the prime must have been activated.

Fazio et al. (1986) employed a 300 millisecond stimulus onset asynchrony (SOA; the time from the onset of the appearance of the prime to the onset of the appearance of the target), the prime being presented for 200 ms, followed by a 100 millisecond blank screen, and then the target appearing in the same location as the prime had been. Citing past cognitive research on automaticity (Neely, 1977; Posner & Snyder, 1975), Fazio et al. adopted this short SOA to increase the likelihood that the effect of the prime on the response latency to evaluate the target was due to automatic processes.

There were two conditions under which Fazio et al., as they had predicted, did not obtain affective priming effects: (a) when the SOA was 1,000 ms, allowing sufficient time for deliberate response processes to overwhelm the automatic process; and (b) when the primes represented objects toward which attitudes were "weak" (i.e., possessing a tenuous object-evaluation association). Attitude strength was operationalized by the speed with which participants had evaluated the primes in a pretesting task prior to the priming task. Those words participants took a relatively long time to evaluate, reflecting poorer attitude accessibility, were categorized as representing weak attitude objects, whereas those that were evaluated quickly (high accessibility) were categorized as representing strong attitude objects. In the subsequent priming task, each participant was assigned weak and strong primes based on their own response latencies during pretesting. Because significant priming effects were obtained only for strong primes, Fazio et al. concluded, "the likelihood of such automatic activation of an attitude appears to depend upon the strength of the association between the attitude object and the evaluation" (p. 236), and further that a "weak association," which they differentiated from a "nonattitude" is nevertheless, "unlikely to be capable of automatic activation" (p. 236).

Greenwald and his colleagues (Greenwald, Klinger, & Liu, 1989) soon after obtained affective priming effects when the primes were presented subliminally (i.e., below the participant's threshold of conscious perception), making a very strong case for the automaticity of evaluation. They have since found the subliminal effect, with the correct procedures, to be highly replicable (Greenwald, Draine, & Abrams, 1996; see also Glaser, 1999), but have recently expressed concerns about the spontaneity of such automatic evaluations of subliminal stimuli (Abrams & Greenwald, 2000).

Fazio's initial findings have resulted in a veritable cottage industry of research on affective priming, much of which is discussed elsewhere in this volume. Explanations of how and why affective priming occurs vary, from spreading activation accounts to expectancy and response competition effects (see Fazio, 2001; Klauer, 1998; Klauer & Musch, chap. 2, this volume; Wentura & Rothermund, chap. 3, this volume). The present investigation, however, is not so much concerned with affective priming as it is with automatic evaluation. Specifically, the theories explaining why responses to target words preceded by evaluatively congruent or incongruent primes are speeded or delayed, important as they are for understanding fundamental aspects of human cognition, are not of central interest here, as long as they all agree that in order for affective priming to occur, the evaluative valence of the prime has to be activated automatically. This chapter is primarily dedicated to exploring the possibility that nonconscious accuracy motivation can explain counterintuitive, "reverse priming" effects, and, of even greater interest, the implications of reverse priming for the conditionality, or lack thereof, of automatic evaluation.

Unconditional Automaticity. Arguing that automatic attitude activation is a "pervasive and relatively unconditional phenomenon," Bargh et al. (1992, p. 893) replicated the automatic evaluation effect, but, in accordance with their theoretical perspective, found that it occurred for weak as well as strong attitude object primes, particularly for those attitudes toward which participants responded consistently (i.e., tended to evaluate the same way across time). The effects were larger, however, for strong primes and consistent (but evaluatively midrange) primes than they were for weak primes.

Bargh et al. (1992) also demonstrated that the automatic attitude activation effect did not rely on a prime memorization and repetition instruction that Fazio et al. (1986) had included to ensure that participants would attend to the primes. This finding, in conjunction with the others, made a stronger case for the unconditionality of automatic attitude activation, suggesting that it is a truly automatic process that occurs in the mere presence of the eliciting stimulus. Finally, Bargh et al. (1992) submitted their data to multiple regression analyses and determined, among other things, that normative ambivalence (i.e., the degree to which participants in general were inconsistent in their evaluations of the primes; the flip side of consistency) moderated the automatic attitude activation effect—high ambivalence (low consistency) predicted smaller automatic evaluation effects. They also found that normative attitude accessibility or strength (as indexed by latency to evaluate an object) was more predictive of affective priming than was idiosyncratic (i.e., an individual's own, unique) accessibility.

Fazio (1993b) took issue with Bargh et al.'s (1992) findings and their interpretations of them. First and foremost, he revisited Bargh et al.'s dataset and regression analyses, correcting some important data analytic assumptions (e.g., transforming reaction time data to normalize distributions) and found the data supported his expectation that idiosyncratic measures accounted for most of the variance in affective priming. More important, for the present purposes, Fazio recognized that automatic attitude activation did appear to obtain for weak primes, although not as robustly as with strong primes, and revised his position accordingly, to avoid implying a false-dichotomy. Fazio maintained, however, that attitude strength should moderate automatic evaluation, with stronger (i.e., more accessible) attitudes being more readily activated.

Chaiken and Bargh (1993) rejoined[1] that not only can automatic attitude activation occur with weak attitudes, but that it should occur no less so than with strong attitudes. To support this contention they cited the results of one of their experiments (Bargh et al., 1992, Experiment 2) in which they had added a 2-day delay between the attitude strength/accessibility assessment phase and the affective priming procedure, finding that under these conditions there was no moderating effect of strength. Their explana-

---

[1]They agreed with Fazio's critique with regard to the effect of reaction time data transformation on the regression results for idiosyncratic versus normative ratings as predictors.

tion was that the recent rehearsal of the attitudes (in prescreening) somehow moderated the likelihood of their subsequent activation as a function of strength. The recent rehearsal enhanced attitude activation for strong attitudes but not for weak attitudes. As to why and how this might occur, they could only speculate. Nevertheless, with a sufficient delay, they argued, attitude strength would not moderate the priming effect. In a new experiment, Chaiken and Bargh (1993) replicated the effect of delay, this time manipulating it within a single experiment. They found, as predicted, that without a delay between attitude assessment and priming task, attitude strength moderated the attitude activation—the effect obtained with strong and midrange, but not with weak primes. When there was a delay, however, attitude strength did not moderate the affective priming effect—it was as large with weak primes as it was with strong primes. They concluded from this that attitude strength may, under some conditions, moderate attitude activation, but that under conditions of mere presence (i.e., without recent rehearsal), which is an important criterion for automaticity, it does not appear to.

In yet another salvo in this debate, Fazio (1993a) asserted that the theoretical rationale was lacking for why (a) attitude accessibility would not moderate activation, and (b) recent attitude expression (i.e., in the no-delay condition) would affect the subsequent activation of strong and weak attitudes differentially. He also cited new data of his own that, in contradiction to Chaiken and Bargh's (1993) findings, showed that attitude strength did moderate attitude activation in an affective priming paradigm, even after a 3-month delay following attitude strength assessment.

Minimal Conditions: The Pronunciation Task. The discussion did not end there. Building on the idea that automatic evaluation ought to occur in the mere presence of the attitude object, and that removing evaluation-relevant features (e.g., attitude expression, an inherently evaluative task) from the experimental procedure would enhance the automaticity of evaluation and diminish the moderating role of attitude strength, Bargh et al. (1996) conducted an elegant series of experiments in which they successively removed evaluative cues from the experimental procedures. In the first experiment, they replaced the good/bad judgment of the priming task with a word pronunciation response (see also Hermans, DeHouwer, & Eelen, 1994). All other aspects of the procedure were identical to those used in previous experiments, but now participants simply read the target words out loud as they appeared. Despite the absence of an evaluative demand, this procedure revealed clear affective priming effects. Importantly, the effects did not vary as a function of prime strength. In the second experiment, Bargh et al. (1996) further removed evaluative components from the participants' experience by eliminating the idiosyncratic prepriming word evaluation task, instead relying on previously obtained, normative data to select the primes. The pronunciation task was again employed, and participants were that much less likely to notice evaluative cues. Nevertheless, in this as in the first experiment, robust priming effects were obtained, and again they were not moderated by prime strength. Finally, in their third experiment, Bargh et al. (1996) replaced the strongly valenced target adjectives with more moderately valenced words, further removing evaluative cues and demands from the procedure. Once again, clear priming effects were obtained and they were not at all moderated by prime strength. Bargh et al. (1996) drew a strong conclusion about conditionality, stating that, "automatic evaluation is the general case, moderation is the special case" (p. 125). Questions about the comparability of effects with an evaluative judgment task versus those with a pronunciation task notwithstanding, this conclusion stood in contrast to Fazio's position and findings, and to date the debate over the conditionality of automatic attitude activation, and specifically the role of attitude strength, has remained unresolved.

REVERSE PRIMING, AUTOMATIC CORRECTION, AND A POSSIBLE SYNTHESIS

It should be noted that, although Hermans et al. (1994) and Bargh et al. (1996) clearly succeeded in demonstrating automatic evaluation with a pronunciation task, more recent reports have featured repeated failures to obtain such effects (see Klauer & Musch, chap. 2, this volume, for a review). For example, De Houwer, Hermans, and Spruyt (2001) observed them only when target words were degraded (i.e., obscured with other stimuli) but not when target words were presented in normal fashion. Klauer and Musch (2001) carried out a series of experiments, with a variety of procedures, taking pains to achieve ample statistical power, and failed to obtain any affective priming effects with the pronunciation task. Clearly, affective priming with a pronunciation task is not a perfectly reliable or easily obtained result.

Failing to anticipate the capriciousness of the effect, and inspired by the effectiveness of the Bargh et al. (1996) affective priming with a pronunciation task procedure, Mahzarin Banaji and I (Glaser & Banaji, 1999) set out to adopt and adapt the paradigm to measure implicit race prejudice unobtrusively.[2] Using normative ratings, we expanded the stimulus categories to include words and names that were stereotypically associated with African American and European American subcultures (e.g., basketball, homeboy,

---

[2]As it turns out, Fazio and colleagues (Fazio et al., 1995) had already initiated a similar project.

Cosby and golf, hippies, Letterman). In addition to these, we used a list of extremely positive and negative, but race-neutral words (e.g., accident, tumor, kindness, puppy) that we termed *generic* stimuli, and another set of race-neutral words that were all related to food (e.g., beets, meatloaf, fudge, soup). By pairing these categories of words in all possible types of combinations we could test for automatic evaluation (race-neutral primes with race-neutral targets), race categorization (race primes with race targets), and race prejudice (race-neutral primes with race targets, or vice versa). These multiple possible tests within one paradigm promised to bolster the internal validity of our findings. For example, if generic or food primes and targets produced automatic evaluation effects, and race primes and targets produced race categorization effects (e.g., faster responding to Black-Black and White-White pairings) that would support the interpretation of an interaction of the valence of race-neutral (generic or food) primes with the race associated with targets (e.g., faster responding to negative-Black and positive-White than to negative-White and positive-Black prime-target pairings) as reflecting race prejudice (i.e., an association between evaluations and groups; an evaluative bias or preference).

Indeed, we found support for all three types of association, and we found it with both types of race-neutral stimuli (generic and food). However, when the generic words served as primes (but not when they were targets), we obtained perplexing, counterintuitive results. The effects were in the opposite direction of what we had predicted and of what we had obtained with the food words. Specifically, when the generic words served as primes, participants were faster to respond to evaluatively *in*congruent targets than to congruent targets. Similarly, while with the food primes participants were faster to pronounce Black-associated and White-associated targets when preceded by negative and positive primes, respectively, the opposite was true for generic primes. We dubbed such effects *reverse priming*. Importantly, these effects were very large and highly significant. When we inspected the data more closely it was evident that virtually all subjects showed this pattern, and that the pattern of results was very consistent across trials, with participants showing reverse priming with generic primes, and normal priming with food primes in the early, middle, and late phases of the task. Consequently, we were not inclined to dismiss this finding as random.

We set about trying to determine what caused these counterintuitive results. What was it about the food and generic words that led to such dramatically different patterns? One thing that was evident immediately was that the food and the generic words differed in evaluative extremity. Because food words can never be extremely negative (anything that is extremely aversive is probably not edible, or at least not considered a food), and because we had sought to have negative and positive words balanced on evaluative extremity, our food words tended to be only mildly valenced

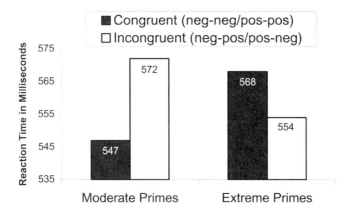

FIG. 4.1. Automatic evaluation by prime extremity in Glaser & Banaji (1999), Experiment 3 (with racial stimuli present, but not in the trials represented by these data). Neg = negative; pos = positive. From "When Fair is Foul and Foul is Fair: Reverse Priming in Automatic Evaluation," by J. Glaser and M. R. Banaji, 1999, *Journal of Personality and Social Psychology*, 77, pp. 669–687. Copyright © 1999 by American Psychological Association. Reprinted with permission.

(–1.0 for negative and +1.03 for positive food words on an 11-point evaluation scale from –5 to +5). In contrast, the generic words were fairly extreme in valence (–3.7 and +3.85 on the same scale). Subsequent, post hoc analyses revealed that the most extremely valenced of the generic primes showed an even more exaggerated reverse priming effect, while the least extreme of them (still considerably more extreme than the food primes) showed a flat line—no priming effect at all.

The post hoc analyses were suggestive, but a priori replication was required to isolate prime extremity as the determinant of reverse priming. Accordingly, we replicated this experiment selecting race-neutral stimuli that varied only in evaluative extremity. The results (see Fig. 4.1) matched those of the first experiment almost precisely, with mild primes leading to normal effects and extreme primes yielding reversed effects (Glaser & Banaji, 1999, Experiment 2).[3]

Considering that the presence of the racial stimuli might be causing the participants to react in an unusual manner (even on trials where there were no racial stimuli, as when prime and target were race-neutral, as presented in Fig. 4.1), we replicated the experiment without any racial stimuli in any

[3]Although the first two experiments in Glaser & Banaji (1999) used an SOA of 150 ms in order to better ensure automaticity, we replicated Experiment 2 with a 300 ms SOA in order to comply with the procedures used by Bargh et al. (1996) and most affective priming tests. We obtained results that were virtually identical to those of Experiments 1 and 2 and have used a 300 ms SOA in all subsequent experiments.

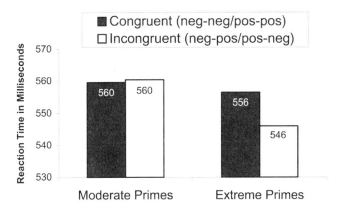

FIG. 4.2. Automatic evaluation by prime extremity in Glaser & Banaji (1999), Experiment 4 (with no racial stimuli present). Neg = negative; pos = positive. From "When Fair is Foul and Foul is Fair: Reverse Priming in Automatic Evaluation," by J. Glaser and M. R. Banaji, 1999, *Journal of Personality and Social Psychology*, 77, pp. 669–687. Copyright © 1999 by by American Psychological Association. Reprinted with permission.

of the trials. This had the effect of making our procedure very similar to that of Bargh et al. (1996). As Fig. 4.2 illustrates, whereas with racial stimuli present (see Fig. 4.1) we had obtained normal priming with mild primes and reverse priming with extreme primes, in the absence of racial stimuli we no longer obtained any priming effect with the mild primes, but with the extreme primes the reverse priming effect was still evident and robust, although somewhat less so than before. We replicated this finding in two additional experiments with subtle procedural variances (the intertrial interval and the presence/absence of a preprime focusing stimulus) also designed to better approximate the Bargh et al. (1996) procedure. We can only speculate at this stage, but it seems plausible that the presence of the racial stimuli served to enhance the salience of the evaluative aspect of the stimuli, thereby enabling even mild primes to activate an associated attitude. Importantly, however, reverse priming (i.e., priming in the opposite direction of that predicted given the valence of the prime) persisted when the primes were evaluatively extreme, across the full series of six[4] experiments, with various samples, stimulus sets, and procedures.

Obtrusiveness, Correction, and Contrast. This is not the first time that prime extremity has led to counterintuitive results. In fact, in the literature relating

---

[4]A seventh experiment, included as a footnote in Glaser & Banaji (1999), wherein we replicated Experiment 3 with a sample at a different American university, yielded the same pattern of results.

to priming and construct activation (Higgins, 1996; Higgins, Rholes, & Jones, 1977) so central to social cognition, several groups have found that obtrusive, blatant, or salient (either in presentation or memory) primes lead to contrast effects in judgments (e.g., Lombardi, Higgins, & Bargh, 1987; Newman & Uleman, 1990; Strack, Schwarz, Bless, Kübler, & Wänke, 1993). Although the comparison between contrast effects in judgments and reverse priming effects in a reaction time paradigm should be made cautiously, the parallels are striking, and the possibility of a related explanatory mechanism warrants consideration. Most relevant to prime extremity and the reverse priming findings, Herr, Sherman, & Fazio (1983) found that when guessing the size of an animal, people tended to make assimilative judgments when primed with an animal of moderate (either large or small) size, but they tended to make contrasted judgments when primed with an extremely large or small animal. For example, if primed with a lion or a cow (moderately large), estimations of the size of the target animal would be somewhat larger than if not primed at all. If primed with a cat or raccoon, estimates would be on the small side. But if primed with elephant or whale, estimates tend to be on the small side, and flea and minnow primes would lead to relatively large estimates.

Many explanations of contrast effects invoke the role of comparison standards, wherein extreme standards set by primes will lead percepts to be judged contrarily by comparison (e.g., Sherif & Hovland, 1961). Several theorists have argued that contrast effects can result from corrective processes engaged when the prime (an unintended percept) threatens to bias the response to the intended target of judgment. Martin (1986; Martin, Seta, & Crelia, 1990) theorized that contrast effects result from overgeneralized attempts to counteract the biasing influence of priming stimuli. Similarly, Strack (1992; Strack & Hannover, 1996) contended that awareness of the influence of primes leads to corrective measures that can engender contrast effects. Perhaps most directly relevant to the reverse priming effect, Stapel, Martin, and Schwarz (1998) have demonstrated that corrections that lead to contrast effects are made when biasing information is blatant, but not when it is subtle. It seems most likely that such corrective processes would be driven by a motivation to respond accurately. Consistent with this, studies that have manipulated accuracy motivation have found it to attenuate assimilation effects (Ford & Kruglanski, 1995; Stapel, Koomen, & Zeelenberg, 1998; Thompson, Roman, Moskowitz, Chaiken, & Bargh, 1994). In the realm of automatic evaluation, because the effect reflects automatic processes, such correction would have to occur outside of conscious intention. Thus, the reverse priming effects may represent unconscious accuracy motivation. Although evidence for nonconscious motivation (e.g., Bargh & Gollwitzer, 1994; Chartrand & Bargh, 1996) is still sparse, it is consistent with compelling arguments that the totality of mental life (e.g., affect, cognition, and motivation) can operate outside of conscious awareness and control (Bargh, 1997; Kihlstrom, 1987). The experiment described next tests this proposition with regard to nonconscious accuracy motivation and reverse priming. First, however, I consider another important issue with regard to discrepancies among past findings.

Synthesis: Reconciling Effects. Although the reverse priming effect obtained with extreme primes replicated consistently (Glaser & Banaji, 1999), it stands in contrast to the results obtained by Bargh et al. (1996), which were also very consistent across experiments. This is especially troubling when we consider the similarity between the two approaches. In both cases, latency to pronounce the target word was the dependent variable, a 300 ms SOA was employed, and evaluatively strong and weak primes were used. With regard to this latter feature, in the case of Glaser and Banaji, although the words were selected on the basis of the extremity of ratings and not the speed of evaluative response (as in Bargh's and Fazio's experiments), our "extreme" and "moderate" words are very comparable to their "strong" and "weak" words. Words that are evaluatively extreme tend to be evaluated more quickly because their valence is more readily recognized. Furthermore, in Bargh et al. (1996) experiments 2 and 3, extremity was one of several explicit criteria (including response latency and consistency) used to select the stimuli. This leaves us wondering why the results are so discrepant, with Bargh et al. (1996) finding normal priming effects for both weak and strong primes, and Glaser and Banaji (1999) finding, in the absence of racial stimuli, no effect for moderate primes and reversed effects for extreme primes.

There are a few potentially important differences between these experiments. First, we had more trials per participant (160 vs. 80) and more stimuli per category (80 total; 20 extreme-positive, 20 extreme-negative, 20 moderate-positive, 20 moderate-negative vs. Bargh et al.'s 16 primes, four per category, and 10 positive and 10 negative target adjectives), meaning that participants saw each stimulus fewer times and with less frequency. Furthermore, the words we used as primes served as targets as well, although a word would never serve as the prime and target in the same trial, nor in any proximal trials.

Another feature of the Glaser and Banaji procedure may differentiate it importantly from other affective priming experiments. Specifically, we instructed our participants that trials on which they made errors (e.g., misstated the target word) would be repeated later in the experiment, so it was in their interest to respond accurately. To my knowledge, this instruction has not been used in other experiments. We had included it in order to increase the likelihood that participants would carry out the procedure conscientiously, but, in retrospect, it could be that this instruction enhanced accuracy motivation enough to engender the corrective processes that we theorize underlie reverse priming. Given the possibility that the reverse priming effect reflects accuracy-motivated correction, such an instruction may have been instrumental.

The Role of Accuracy Motivation: A New Experiment. Having identified the remaining discrepancies described earlier, I set out to reconcile the findings of Glaser and Banaji (1999) with those of Bargh et al. (1996) and to test the effect of accuracy motivation by replicating the Bargh et al. (1996) procedure, manipulating the presence of the instruction that trials with errors would be repeated. This experiment might serve not only to determine a critical difference explaining the discrepancy between Bargh et al. (1996) and Glaser and Banaji (1999), but may also explain their difference with Fazio et al. (1986; Fazio, 1993a). Specifically, given the similarities between the procedures of Bargh et al. (1996) and Glaser and Banaji, it is possible that reverse priming could occur in both procedures, to a greater or lesser extent, depending on some procedural variances. If, in the absence of a strong accuracy demand, Bargh et al. had nevertheless had some reverse priming (i.e., correction) occurring with their strong primes (as with our "extreme" primes) this may have served to dilute their priming effects, making them seem equivalent to those with the weak primes. This potential artifact could lead to an erroneous conclusion that, counterintuitively, attitude strength does not moderate attitude activation.

I adopted Bargh et al.'s (1996) procedures as closely as possible, using the exact prime and target words they used in their Experiment 2 (wherein, unlike Experiment 1, primes were chosen normatively, and unlike Experiment 3, the targets were not subtly valenced), having 80 trials (20 per condition) per participant, and a 300 ms SOA. Importantly, the presence of the accuracy-enhancing instructions was varied between subjects.

Participants. One hundred and forty (140) UC Berkeley undergraduates from the psychology department subject pool participated for course credit. Data from 20 of these were excluded because they did not meet Bargh et al.'s (1996) language criterion of having begun speaking English by 5 years of age. This left 120 participants in the dataset. Sixty-one (61) of these were assigned to the "high accuracy motivation" condition, and 59 were in the "low accuracy motivation" condition.

Stimuli. As indicated previously, we used the same primes and targets as Bargh et al. (1996) had used in their Experiment 2.

Procedure. Participants were seated at a computer and given a brief, oral, general overview of the experiment. They were then asked to read the written instructions on screen, and were left alone in the lab room. The instructions in the two accuracy motivation conditions were identical, asking participants to read aloud only the second word in each pair, quickly and clearly. However, for those in the high accuracy condition, one additional sentence was added, stating: "Trials on which you make errors will be repeated at some point later in the experiment, so it is in your interest to respond accurately."[5] Participants were given a set of 10 practice trails, followed by a break during which they could open the door and ask the experimenter questions (none did). After the break, when they hit a space bar to continue the experiment, the first six trials were buffers, included to absorb any adaptation variance. These were followed by 80 experimental trials. There were 10 trials per condition for the 2 (prime strength: weak, strong) by 2 (prime valence: good, bad) by 2 (target valence: good, bad) within-subjects design. For the purposes of examining the central question of automatic evaluation and the effect of prime extremity, this can be simplified to a simple 2 (prime strength: weak, strong) by 2 (prime-target congruence: congruent, incongruent) design, wherein there were 20 trials per condition. The SOA was 300 ms, comprised of a 200 ms prime presentation period and a 100 ms interstimulus interval (ISI). The intertrial interval (ITI; the time between the disappearance of a target and the appearance of the prime for the next trial), was 3 seconds.

RESULTS AND DISCUSSION

As with Bargh et al. (1996), response times that were less than 300 ms or greater than 1000 ms were excluded from analyses because they most likely represent meaningless data wherein the participant was either making an extraneous noise, such as coughing, yielding an improbably fast response (< 300 ms) or said the target word too quietly and had to repeat it, yielding an improbably slow response (> 1000 ms). Furthermore, removing such response times serves to normalize the distribution in accordance with the assumptions of the analysis of variance (ANOVA) to be conducted. Similarly, the data were logarithmically transformed, to further remove the positive skew that typically plagues latency data. As with Bargh et al. (1996), the analyses were conducted on this log-transformed data, but reaction times presented in the results are based on the pretransformed data, in the millisecond metric, in order to facilitate interpretation and comparison with other studies.

The data were submitted to a mixed-factor ANOVA to determine the effect of prime-target evaluative congruence as well as prime strength (both

---

[5]In neither condition was this actually true—an element of deception that would doubtless be appreciated by the participants, given the alternative (i.e., a longer procedure).

within-subjects variables) and accuracy motivation (a between-subjects variable). Overall, combining both accuracy motivation conditions and weak and strong primes, an affective priming effect was obtained ($F_{(1,119)} = 9.4$, $p <$ .005). This effect, in millisecond terms, was small—just a 3.5 ms difference between the average response latency for congruent and incongruent prime target pairs. The effect size calculated in terms of Pearson's r is .27. The reason such a small effect (in terms of milliseconds) is significant is in part because of the relatively large participant sample size, but also because of the large sample of trials per condition (40 per participant, because I have collapsed across the prime strength variable), leading to reasonably stable mean response times.

Separating out the effects for weak and strong primes (see Fig. 4.3) we find that the separate 3 ms effect for weak primes is also significant ($F_{(1,119)} =$ 4.24, $p < .05$) as is the 4 ms effect for strong primes ($F_{(1,119)} = 5.71$, $p < .02$). Not surprisingly, given a mere 1 ms difference between the effects for these two conditions, prime strength (i.e., extremity) did not moderate the congruence effect ($F < 1$). These results indicate primarily, as did those of Bargh et al. (1996) and Glaser and Banaji (1999) experiments wherein there were race primes, that automatic evaluation can occur under relatively minimal conditions (e.g., a nonevaluative task, and with moderately valenced primes), although these results are not as robust as past ones have been. From these findings, in further accord with Bargh et al. (1996), because the priming effect was only slightly, and nonsignificantly, larger with strong than with weak primes, we would not want to conclude that attitude strength moderates affective priming.

Of greater interest, however, is the issue of accuracy motivation and its effect on automatic evaluation and affective priming. When we look at the priming effects for the "high" and "low" accuracy motivation participants

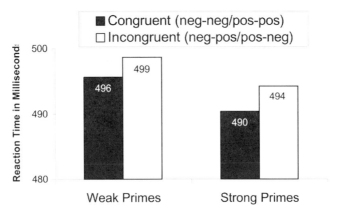

FIG. 4.3. Automatic evaluation by prime strength. Neg = negative; pos = positive.

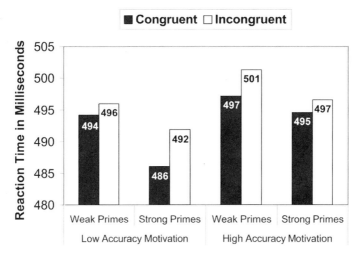

FIG. 4.4. Automatic evaluation by prime strength and accuracy motivation.

separately, we see distinct patterns emerge (see Fig. 4.4). Specifically, for those who were not instructed that they would have to repeat trials on which they had made errors (the "low accuracy motivation" condition), weak primes did not appear to affect response times to targets as a function of evaluative match ($F < 1$), but there was a significant priming effect with strong primes ($F_{(1,58)} = 8.1$, $p < .01$, $r = .35$). Those in the high accuracy motivation condition, however, exhibit affective priming with weak primes ($F_{(1,60)} = 4.29$, $p < .05$, $r = .26$). But while the accuracy instruction may be enhancing the effect with weak primes, it is doing the opposite when the primes are strong, essentially washing out the effect ($F < 1$).

Higher order interaction ANOVAs indicated that, while overall the affective priming effect is clearly not moderated by motivation condition ($F < 1$) (not surprisingly, given the symmetrical reversal of patterns, which cancel each other out), the 3-way accuracy motivation by prime extremity by valence match interaction is suggestive ($F_{(1,118)} = 1.74$, $p < .2$). This reflects that, as indicated by the simple comparisons reported earlier, accuracy motivation moderates the relative priming effect of weak and strong primes. Specifically, under relatively low accuracy motivation, weak primes do not serve to activate attitudes, but strong primes do, while under relatively high accuracy motivation, the opposite is true. The accuracy instruction appears to affect affective priming, and specifically to undermine priming with extreme primes while, if anything, enhancing it with moderate primes. Despite the relatively clear simple comparisons, the results with regard to the moderating role of instructions need to be taken with a grain of salt because the predicted higher order interaction was not statistically significant. It should be noted, however, that between-subjects comparisons are relatively low in power, particularly when testing for differences in small, within-subjects effects. And it should be further noted that the accuracy motivation manipulation—the presence or absence of a single sentence indicating that trials with errors will have to be repeated—was subtle, at most, failing to achieve even a marginally significant difference in overall response latencies between conditions. This subtlety is largely an indirect consequence of my intention to systematically identify procedural differences between previous experiments, but future attempts could investigate the effects of more powerful manipulations.

The pattern of results is consistent with an accuracy-motivated correction explanation. The enhanced accuracy motivation, engendered by a reasonably subtle manipulation may cause participants to attempt to correct for the biasing influence of the primes. As seen in the Glaser & Banaji (1999) experiments, this occurs only when the prime is evaluatively extreme, and therefore obtrusively valenced.

To understand how and why people might overcorrect for the evaluative judgment of a prime they are ignoring in the process of merely reading a target word aloud, one must consider how affective priming with the pronunciation task can occur in the first place. As Banaji and I (1999) argued, except in the most orthographically shallow (i.e., phonetic) languages, in which English is clearly not included, the pronunciation of a word typically involves the recognition of its meaning. Doubtless, whether something is good or bad is a crucial aspect of meaning, one particularly prone to spontaneous determination (Fazio et al., 1986; Zajonc, 1980), even "vigilance" (Pratto & John, 1991). If someone is attempting to process the meaning of a stimulus, therefore, its value will likely play a large role in that determination. Our model holds that if, in the act of trying to process one word, someone is presented with an extraneous word that is extreme in its evaluative valence, he or she may recognize the potential of that ostensibly irrelevant stimulus to interfere with the recognition, with regard to valence, and consequently meaning in general, of the intended target of response. An attempt to correct for that extraneous stimulus may lead, as do many corrections in psychological findings, to an overcompensation. Thus, extreme primes can activate evaluations opposite to their own meaning and consequently result in reverse priming effects. At this stage, we have no conclusive evidence for this explanation, but the present results are consistent with it, and we have gone to pains elsewhere (Glaser & Banaji, 1999) to consider alternative explanations, none of which fit the extant data.

Having said that, Wentura and Rothermund (chap. 3, this volume) provide a plausible alternative explanation for affective priming with the pronunciation task, suggesting that pronouncing the target word is an act of "affirmation" of sorts and that, consequently responses will be made faster to positive stimuli, especially if preceded by positive primes. This explanation is also consistent with the idea of a nonconscious correction for the valence of the prime leading to reverse priming. In either model, Wentura and Rothermund's or mine, the automatic evaluation of the prime is driving the congruency effects, and in either case an automatic correction for the evaluation of the prime can explain reverse priming.

With regard to the importance of automaticity, we know that in order for affective priming to occur, the prime must be automatically evaluated, although there is no intentional (i.e., conscious) goal to attend to the prime, let alone evaluate it. Any correction for a consciously uncontrollable process would logically be automatic as well, especially given the unobtrusive nature of the pronunciation task and the response latency dependent variable. Thus, it appears that in addition to perception, categorization, and evaluation, correction can occur without conscious intention. The present finding, that accuracy instructions serve to negate affective priming, suggests that the reverse priming effects obtained by Glaser and Banaji (1999) reflect an unconscious accuracy motivation.

Conditionality of Automatic Evaluation. With regard to implications for the effect of attitude strength on automatic evaluation, the present findings suggest a middle ground between the position that only strong attitudes will be activated automatically and the contention that attitudes of all strengths will be activated equally. These results indicate that lack of priming effects with strong attitudes can be achieved through an accuracy goal manipulation, and, perhaps, the corrections it engenders. In the Glaser and Banaji (1999) experiments, the same subtle instruction may have given rise to sufficient correction to completely overwhelm the priming effect, leading to reverse priming. Just as in the present experiment the accuracy instruction served only to negate the priming effect (with strong primes), it could be that with more middling accuracy motivation, affective priming with strong primes would be only somewhat diminished. This could lead to the perfectly reasonable, but nevertheless spurious conclusion that activation of strong attitudes is weaker than it really is, perhaps as weak as with weak attitudes. This may be the case with the Bargh et al. (1996) data.

The existence of priming effects with weak primes when accuracy motivation is high, and more strongly, in the case of Glaser and Banaji (1999), when racial stimuli are present, also suggests that, as Bargh et al. (1992; 1996; Chaiken & Bargh, 1993) argued, attitudes of all strengths, even the very weak, are capable of being activated automatically, they just may not be as consistent or detectable. In contrast to the perplexing disparity between studies showing no moderating effect of attitude strength on automatic attitude activation (e.g., Bargh et al., 1996), and those showing a clear moderating effect (e.g., Fazio et al., 1986), We now face a more intuitively appealing state of affairs: Attitudes, being object-evaluation associations, can, like other mental associations, be activated automatically, regardless of strength, provided they are not totally ambivalent. However, to the extent that strong attitudes are more accessible, and that is how they have been operationalized (Bargh et al., 1992; e.g., Fazio et al., 1986), they will have a higher probability of being activated.

Further Reconciliation Needed. It should be noted that the present results do not provide a perfect reconciliation of the Bargh et al. (1996) and Glaser and Banaji (1999) findings. The former study found only normal (assimilative) priming effects, whereas the latter found only reverse effects with strong primes. The present study, using the exact stimuli and procedures Bargh et al. (1996) had used, found, for strong primes, a normal effect with low accuracy motivation and no effect with high accuracy motivation. We might have expected to see reverse priming in the high accuracy condition and therefore must consider that the null result might reflect that the accuracy instruction simply dampened the priming. However, this seems unlikely because in the Glaser and Banaji (1999) experiments the same instruction yielded clear priming effects (normal for moderate primes and reversed for extreme primes). Furthermore, the accuracy instruction appears to have had something of an enhancing effect on priming with the weak primes. The more likely explanation is that, as with Glaser and Banaji (1999), some correction was occurring, but in this case it was sufficient only to negate the effect, not to reverse it.

There are some remaining differences between the Bargh et al. (1996) methods, which were adopted for the present experiment, and those of Glaser and Banaji (1999), and these differences could serve to explain the lack of reverse priming in the present experiment. For one, in Glaser and Banaji (1999) we used the same words as primes and targets (although never in the same trial), while Bargh et al. (1996), and the present experiment, did not. However, post hoc analyses of the Glaser and Banaji (1999) data revealed that the reverse priming effect occurred at all stages of the experiments, including the beginning, before any word had served as both prime and target, so this difference is most likely not critical. Another difference involves the total number of stimuli. The Bargh et al. (1996) and present methods involved many fewer primes and targets than did Glaser and Banaji (1999), and these stimuli were, therefore, repeated with greater frequency. This could have allowed participants to habituate to the primes, thus eroding any reverse priming.

Such procedural variances cannot be ruled out entirely. However, it seems most likely that, given the impact of instructions within the present experiment, differences in instructions account for the discrepancy between experiments. According to Bargh et al. (1996), participants were instructed to pronounce the second word in each trial as quickly as possible, but also that "accuracy as well as speed was emphasized" (p. 110). The exact instructions used by Bargh et al. are not available, but it seems possible that their instructions, with regard to accuracy, fell somewhere in between the two conditions in the present experiment, where accuracy was not emphasized at all, and where it was emphasized and even, ostensibly, rewarded. This could explain why, for Bargh et al. (1996), priming with strong primes might have been diminished, but not negated or reversed. Furthermore, their moderate emphasis on accuracy may have been enough to give rise to priming effects with weak primes. However, at this stage this is only conjecture and more direct testing will be needed to fully reconcile the disparate findings. What is striking is that such a subtle instructional manipulation could yield such dramatically different priming effects. This suggests that presumably trivial variances in instructions and other motivation-relevant procedures (e.g., the presence or absence of the experimenter in the testing room) might moderate, even qualitatively, priming effects, and potentially mask automatic processes.

CONCLUSION: THE IMPORTANCE OF EVALUATION *AND* STRENGTH

The present findings with regard to the moderating role of accuracy motivation, in conjunction with reverse priming effects previously observed by Glaser and Banaji (1999), offer a hope of reconciliation of the disparate positions of Fazio and Bargh and their colleagues with regard to the conditionality of automatic evaluation. While Fazio had originally argued that attitude strength will moderate automatic attitude activation to the extent that only reasonably well-rehearsed attitudes will activate automatically, Bargh has contended that any object for which there is an attitude will elicit an automatic evaluation and that this will occur equally for strong and weak attitudes. Both have provided compelling data to support their theses. But the findings reported here suggest a compromise; that indeed all attitudes can be activated automatically, but the likelihood and extent of that activation will be determined by the strength of the object-evaluation association.

ACKNOWLEDGMENTS

Production of this chapter was supported by a National Research Service Award Postdoctoral Fellowship from the National Institute of Mental Health (NIMH), grant number MH12195, as well as institutional support from the Institute of Personality and Social Research at the University of California, Berkeley. I thank Eric D. Knowles, Brian Nosek, and Dirk

Wentura for their incisive comments on an earlier draft, and Miranda Chiu and Teresa Docker for their help with research. Correspondence should be sent to Jack Glaser, Goldman School of Public Policy, University of California, Berkeley, CA 94720-7320, U. S. A., or electronic mail to *glaserj@socrates. berkeley.edu.*

REFERENCES

Abrams, R. L., & Greenwald, A. G. (2000). Parts outweigh the whole (word) in unconscious analysis of meaning. *Psychological Science, 11,* 118–124.

Bargh, J. A. (1997). The automaticity of everyday life. In Wyer, R. (Ed.), *Advances in Social Cognition, Vol. X.* Mahwah, NJ: Lawrence Erlbaum Associates.

Bargh, J. A., Chaiken, S., Govender, R., & Pratto, F. (1992). The generality of the automatic attitude activation effect. *Journal of Personality and Social Psychology, 62,* 893–912.

Bargh, J. A., Chaiken, S., Raymond, P., & Hymes, C. (1996). The automatic evaluation effect: Unconditional automatic attitude activation with a pronunciation task. *Journal of Experimental Social Psychology, 32,* 104–128.

Bargh, J. A., & Gollwitzer, P. M. (1994). Environmental control of goal-directed action: Automatic and strategic contingencies between situations and behavior. In W. D. Spaulding (Ed.), *Nebraska Symposium on Motivation: Vol. 41, Integrative views of motivation, cognition, and emotion* (pp. 71–124). Lincoln, NE: University of Nebraska Press.

Chaiken, S., & Bargh, J. A. (1993). Occurrence versus moderation of the automatic attitude activation effect: Reply to Fazio. *Journal of Personality and Social Psychology, 64,* 759–764.

Chartrand, T. L., & Bargh, J. A. (1996). Automatic activation of impression formation and memorization goals: Nonconscious goal priming reproduces effects of explicit task instructions. *Journal of Personality and Social Psychology, 71,* 464–478.

De Houwer, J., Hermans, D., & Spruyt, A. (2001). Affective priming of pronunciation responses: Effects of target degradation. *Journal of Experimental Social Psychology, 37,* 85–91.

Fazio, R. H. (1993a). Addendum: Reply to Chaiken and Bargh. *Journal of Personality and Social Psychology, 64,* 764–765.

Fazio, R. H. (1993b). Variability in the likelihood of automatic attitude activation: Data reanalysis and commentary on Bargh, Chaiken, Govender, and Pratto. *Journal of Personality and Social Psychology, 64,* 753–758.

Fazio, R. H. (2001). On the automatic activation of associated evaluations: An overview. *Cognition & Emotion, 15,* 115–142.

Fazio, R. H., Chen, J., McDonel, E. C., & Sherman, S. J. (1982). Attitude accessibility, attitude-behavior consistency, and the strength of the object-evaluation association. *Journal of Experimental Social Psychology, 18,* 339–357.

Fazio, R. H., Jackson, J. R., Dunton, B. C., & Williams, C. J. (1995). Variability in automatic activation as an unobtrusive measure of racial attitudes: A bona fide pipeline? *Journal of Personality and Social Psychology, 69,* 1013–1027.

Fazio, R. H., Sanbonmatsu, D. M., Powell, M. C., & Kardes.F. R. (1986). On the automatic activation of attitudes. *Journal of Personality and Social Psychology, 50,* 229–238.

Ford, T. E., & Kruglanski, A. W. (1995). Effects of epistemic motivations on the use of accessible constructs in social judgment. *Personality and Social Psychology Bulletin, 21,* 950–962.

Glaser, J. (1999). *The relation between stereotyping and prejudice: Measures of newly formed automatic associations.* Unpublished Doctoral Dissertation, Yale University.

Glaser, J., & Banaji, M. R. (1999). When fair is foul and foul is fair: Reverse priming in automatic evaluation. *Journal of Personality and Social Psychology, 77,* 669–687.

Greenwald, A. G., Draine, S. C., & Abrams, R. L. (1996). Three cognitive markers of unconscious semantic activation. *Science, 273,* 1699–1702.

Greenwald, A. G., Klinger, M. R., & Liu, T. J. (1989). Unconscious processing of dichoptically masked words. *Memory and Cognition, 17,* 35–47.

Hermans, D., de Houwer, J., & Eelen, P. (1994). The affective priming effect: Automatic activation of evaluative information in memory. *Cognition and Emotion, 8,* 515–533.

Herr, P. M., Sherman, S. J., & Fazio, R. H. (1983). On the consequences of priming: Assimilation and contrast effects. *Journal of Experimental Social Psychology, 19,* 323–340.

Higgins, E. T. (1996). Knowledge activation: Accesibility, applicability, and salience. In E. T. Higgins & A. W. Kruglanski (Eds.), *Social psychology: Handbook of basic principles* (pp. 133–168). New York: Guilford Press.

Higgins, E. T., Rholes, W. S., & Jones, C. R. (1977). Category accessibility and impression formation. *Journal of Experimental Social Psychology, 13,* 141–154.

Kihlstrom, J. F. (1987). The cognitive unconscious. *Science, 237,* 1445–1452.

Klauer, K. C. (1998). Affective priming. In W. Stroebe & M. Hewstone (Eds.), *European Review of Social Psychology.* New York: John Wiley & Sons.

Klauer, K. C., & Musch, J. (2001). Does sunshine prime loyal? Affective priming in the naming task. *Quarterly Journal of Experimental Psychology: Human Experimental Psychology, 54,* 727–751.

Lombardi, W. J., Higgins, E. T., & Bargh, J. A. (1987). The role of consciousness in priming effects on categorization: Assimilation versus contrast as a function of awareness of the priming task. *Personality and Social Psychology Bulletin, 13,* 411–429.

Martin, L. L. (1986). Set/reset: Use and disuse of concepts in impression formation. *Journal of Personality and Social Psychology, 51,* 493–504.

Martin, L. L., Seta, J. J., & Crelia, R. A. (1990). Assimilation and contrast as a function of people's willingness and ability to expend effort on forming an impression. *Journal of Personality and Social Psychology, 59,* 27–37.

Neely, J. H. (1977). Semantic priming and retrieval from lexical memory: Roles of inhibitionless spreading activation and limited-capacity attention. *Journal of Experimental Psychology: General, 106,* 225–254.

Newman, L. S., & Uleman, J. S. (1990). Assimilation and contrast effects in spontaneous trait inference. *Personality and Social Psychology Bulletin, 16,* 224–240.

Posner, M. I., & Snyder, C. R. R. (1975). Facilitation and inhibition in the processing of signals. In P. M. A. Rabbit & S. Dornic (Eds.), *Attention and performance V.* New York: Academic Press.

Pratto, F., & John, O. P. (1991). Automatic vigilance: The attention-grabbing power of negative social information. *Journal of Personality & Social Psychology, 61,* 380–391.

Sherif, M., & Hovland, C. I. (1961). *Social judgment: Assimilation and contrast effects in communication and attitude change.* New Haven, CT: Yale University Press.

Stapel, D. A., Koomen, W., & Zeelenberg, M. (1998). The impact of accuracy motivation on interpretation, comparison, and correction processes: Accuracy X knowledge accessibility effects. *Journal of Personality and Social Psychology, 74,* 878–893.

Stapel, D. A., Martin, L. L., & Schwarz, N. (1998). The smell of bias: What instigates correction processes in social judgments? *Personality and Social Psychology Bulletin, 24,* 797–806.

Strack, F. (1992). The different routes to social judgment: Experiential versus informational strategies. In L. L. Martin and A. Tesser (Eds.), *The construction of social judgments* (pp. 249–275). Hillsdale, NJ: Lawrence Erlbaum Associates.

Strack, F., & Hannover, B. (1996). Awareness of influence as a precondition for implementing correctional goals. In P. M. Gollwitzer & J. A. Bargh (Eds.), *The psychology of action: Linking cognition and motivation to behavior* (pp. 579–596). New York: Guilford Press.

Strack, F., Schwarz, N., Bless, H., Kübler, A., & Wänke, M. (1993). Awareness of the influence as a determinant of assimilation versus contrast. *European Journal of Social Psychology, 23,* 53–62.

Thompson, E. P., Roman, R. J., Moskowitz, G. B., Chaiken, S., & Bargh, J. A. (1994). Accuracy motivation attenuates covert priming: The systematic *re*processing of social information. *Journal of Personality and Social Psychology, 66,* 474–489.

Zajonc, R. B. (1980). Feeling and thinking: Preferences need no inferences. *American Psychologist, 35*(2), 151–175.

Chapter 5

The Hidden Vicissitudes
of the Priming Paradigm
in Evaluative Judgment Research

Klaus Fiedler
University of Heidelberg, FRG

How the stories of the genesis and maturation of theoretical ideas resemble each other. When we consider the course of theory development from a metatheoretical perspective, we soon encounter a persistent bias in theoretical thinking that has intrigued Karl Popper (1935) and that was neatly illustrated by Paul Wason (1960) many decades ago. When asked to find out the rule underlying a series of numbers such as the series 2, 4, 8, ?, people would typically engage in positive tests of sensible but too restrictive "theories". For instance, they might assume the rule is 2^N (with N denoting increasing natural numbers) and test whether choosing 16 for the next number fulfills the rule. The feedback would be positive and so they are already quite confident that the theory is correct. Another positive test, 32, would also be met with a positive feedback, and confidence would rise close to certainty. In this positively reinforcing research process, hardly anybody finds out that the underlying generic rule is much less restricted and leaves room for a much broader variety of numerals. Thus, the "true theory" may be any positive accelerated function of N, or any series that increases monotonically, or even any series of numbers, or any alphanumeric symbols.

Note that once such a more general rule is recognized to underlie the phenomenon, the nature of the phenomenon itself changes. The sequence 2, 4, 8, . . . is no longer perceived with the same eyes. Note also that now the restrictive rule does not simply become invalid. In fact, 2^N is also consistent with the true rule and describes the available data more completely, and in an esthetically nicer way. Nevertheless, the habit of positive testing of re-

109

strictive theories and the failure to take a broader perspective will retard the discovery of underlying principles.

In this chapter, I try to point out an analogy between Wason's famous paradigm and the recent history of research and theorizing about priming effects on evaluative judgments. Priming—that is, the impact of activated knowledge structures on subsequent reactions—has become a popular research topic, and a major experimental tool, in contemporary cognitive and social psychology. Priming effects serve to investigate the nature of associative memory (Johnston & Dark, 1986), language comprehension and reading (McKoon & Ratcliff, 1992), misunderstandings (Shafto & MacKay, 2000), to diagnose attitudes (Fazio, Jackson, Dunton, & Williams, 1995) and prejudice (Dovidio, Evans, & Tyler, 1986; Lepore & Brown, 1997), to uncover implicit cognitive processes (Ratcliff & McKoon, 1996), or to study emotional processes (Fiedler, Nickel, Muehlfriedel, & Unkelbach, 2001). Aside from using priming experiments as a research tool, the direct influence of priming on decision-making, social judgment, and manifest behavior has become an interesting research goal in its own right. Priming effects have immediate content validity for all kinds of hedonic, evaluative processes of the approach-avoidance type. It is possible to induce pro- or anti-votes, optimistic or pessimistic appraisals, positive versus negative evaluations using priming treatments that are often weak and subtle and outside the person's awareness (Gilovich, 1981; Johnson & Tversky, 1983; Srull & Wyer, 1980). The very possibility of unconscious priming effects, and their quasi-automatic nature, affords important ingredients to the popularity and the attractiveness of this phenomenon. In this chapter, I am concerned with semantic priming as a direct means of influencing evaluations, or judgments and behavioral decisions with a clear evaluative component.

In the next section, I first argue that in psychological approaches to higher-order cognitive processes references to priming run the risk of being caught in the same positive-testing trap as Wason's (1960) participants. Although the notion of a priming effect, as imported from cognitive research on language comprehension, appears to be consistent with and applicable to many phenomena in social judgment and behavior, and despite this notion's simplistic appeal, it may fail to capture the full nature of context effects on evaluative judgments. For several reasons, evaluative judgments are less restrictive, allowing for more possibilities than suggested by the original demonstrations of priming word recognition and lexical-decision paradigms. Due to the habit of positive testing, researchers have mainly studied whether the basic priming rule works in the area of evaluative judgment, thereby missing broader evidence on other rules that are also valid and that supplement and moderate priming processes in evaluative judgment. These might be termed negative priming, antipriming, inhibition, or contrast effects, as will be explained shortly. To complete the analogy, realizing a broader rule to underlie priming in evaluative judgment also helps us to recognize that this variant of "priming" is no longer the same as in the original paradigms.

PRIMING IN ITS ORIGINAL CONTEXT
AND IN EVALUATIVE JUDGMENT TASKS

To give a preview, an enriched framework for studying priming effects on evaluative judgments will be outlined, within which the following points become apparent: (a) The evaluative judgment domain should be clearly separated from the original paradigm of priming in associative memory; (b) Two process components, or stages, should be usefully distinguished, the afferent and the efferent component; (c) Both process stages turn out to be less restrictive than originally expected, albeit for different reasons; (d) within such a refined framework, a number of new research topics and theoretical insights about priming might be inspired.

Let us first consider the original demonstrations of priming effects in lexical decision experiments. In an often-cited study, Meyer and Schvaneveldt (1971) measured the time required to decide if a briefly presented letter string is a word or not. They found a facilitation of such lexical decisions when words were preceded by semantically related primes. For example, when the target stimulus is the word *building*, the time required to decide that it is a word is reduced when the semantically related prime word *house* is presented prior to the target stimulus. This facilitation effect apparently reflects activation of semantic knowledge structures that are shared by the prime and the target.

This very simple and straightforward process is depicted in Fig. 5.1. Being exposed to the prime word (house), a rather specific part of semantic memory is activated. Of course, we cannot determine the associative consequences of the prime in all detail. But whatever is activated will be somehow related to the semantic features associated with a house. Associations can refer to different aspects of a house, its parts, functions, costs, concrete imagery, or architecture, and also to phonetic aspects (e.g., a rhyme with mouse). However, on average, at group data level, or across many similar trials, one can be sure that semantic priming of the category *house* is part of the associative pattern, thereby preparing memory for a subsequent task involving the target *building*.

Note also that there is nothing like an opposite or antonym of house, or similar reasons for misguided associations (e.g., homonyms, nonliteral meanings, etc.) that could complicate the activation product. Lexical decision is a monadic, qualitative task. To recognize a word is a task that has only one argument, the presented word itself, and does not involve any syn-

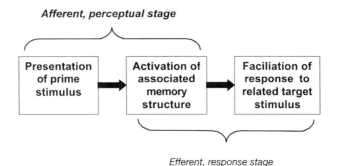

FIG. 5.1.   Graphical illustration of a priming effect, decomposed into an afferent, perceptual stage and an efferent, response stage.

tactical or interpretational problems. For both process stages in Fig. 5.1
there is only one reasonable candidate. In the "afferent" process stage,
there is only one semantic structure to be activated by the prime (viz., the
concept of a *house*). In the efferent stage, there is only one bit of a binary decision (viz., to respond "Yes, it is a word"). The restrictive experimental task
does not leave more degrees of freedom, or uncertainty.

A similar situation holds in other unproblematic priming paradigms. In
reading or word identification tasks, there is but one reasonable response
(i.e., to name the target word). Or, when the interpretation of a homonym
with two meanings (e.g., light) depends on previous priming (e.g., of the
concept *weight* vs. *illumination*), the disambiguation task leaves only one degree of freedom, as in a forced choice task. In the evaluative domain, too,
experimental control over the priming process is quite high in specific paradigms, such as affective priming (Hermans, DeHouwer, & Eelen, 1994;
Klauer, Rossnagel, & Musch, 1997; Musch, 2000). When many prime-target
pairs are presented sequentially, reactions to the target are regularly faster
when the preceding prime has been of the same valence. Pooling over numerous prime-target pairs, the chief systematic influence is due to valence,
which can be isolated as the only sensible determinant.

In contrast, the situation is quite different in the typical priming-and-
evaluative judgments experiment in social cognition. In this paradigm, the
experimental task involves a judgment target presented after a single complex priming treatment, and the cognitive process is much less restrictive
than in the classic paradigms. For illustration, let us consider the "classic"
priming experiment of Higgins, Rholes, and Jones (1977). Prior to the
judgment task, participants were first asked to encode and memorize particular words as part of an alleged verbal-learning experiment. The meaning of the words selected for this verbal task constituted the priming manipulation. In one condition, the words to be memorized had positive
connotations (adventurous, self-confident, independent, persistent); in an-

other condition, the words were of negative valence (reckless, conceited, aloof, stubborn). Afterward, a social judgment task was presented, based on a written sketch of the target person's habits, interests, and behaviors. This sketch was typically ambiguous, leaving room for positive as well as negative interpretation. The major finding was that evaluative judgments of the same constant target person became more benevolent when the preceding verbal priming treatment had entailed positive rather than negative word meanings.

In several respects, the task situation is much less clear-cut than in the original lexical-decision task context. On one hand, the afferent activation stage (cf. Fig. 5.1) is complicated by the fact that the complex priming treatment covers multiple words from which many different aspects could be extracted. Activating the semantic meaning of particular words may require the simultaneous inhibition of other meaning aspects. The primed words may be connected to a story line, an analogy to a living person, or superordinate person schema, and this self-generated knowledge structure may exert uncontrolled complex priming influences that go beyond the manipulated word meanings or even act in an opposite direction. In any case, the question of what is activated (or inhibited at the same time) has become complex.

On the other hand, the efferent reaction stage is complicated as well. Assuming that positive concepts have been activated, this might of course influence the manner in which the personality sketch about the target person is disambiguated. A behavior like *criticizing others* might be seen as quite likeable when the meaning of *self-confident* has been primed, but more unlikable when the meaning of *conceited* has been primed. However, a number of different outcomes are possible. In the positive priming condition, the overall evaluative tone of the stimulus sketch may appear relatively negative when compared to the positive tone of the preceding verbal learning task, thus leading to more negative judgments. Similarly, the primed positive words may invoke thoughts about a highly likeable well-known person that lets the target person in the sketch appear relatively neutral or even negative.

In any case, it should be obvious that the structure of meaningful judgment tasks leaves more latitude for different outcomes of both process stages. This is not merely due to the increased complexity of information. Another distinctive feature that sets evaluative judgment tasks apart from the classic priming tasks is richer inferential processes and voluntary control. During the activation stage, judges are not only exposed to an isolated experimenter-provided prime stimulus, but they are encouraged to actively do something, often with a rather rich prime input: to memorize and reproduce words (Higgins et al., 1977), unscramble sentences (Wenzlaff & Bates, 2000), describe a skinhead (Macrae, Bodenhausen, Milne, & Jetten, 1994), suppress thoughts (Wegner, 1994) and so on. These rich priming tasks invite active inferences, intrusions of world knowledge, eliciting various second-order priming processes. Thus, the effective priming treatment is not confined to a circumscribed, reflex-like activation of a singular concept, but open to active inference and elaboration. Later, too, the efferent stage is open to a much larger repertoire of reactions, part of which can be controlled voluntarily. Unlike the responses on a word recognition or lexical decision task, which are largely determined by automatic associations to the prime stimuli and hardly open to strategic and voluntary processes, evaluative judgments studies are open to a wider repertoire of responses. Evaluations must be represented on reference scales with anchors and comparison standards. Output norms (of politeness or fairness) may regulate judgments. Judges may decide to correct for any affective influences they feel might bias their judgments. Rather than derogating target persons, judges' coping with the situation might involve controlled voluntary behaviors involving humor, irony, and other culturally approved techniques. In general, quantitative evaluative judgments are much more remote from primed cues than just reading a related word, or making a lexical decision.

How to Refine the Theoretical Framework?

In view of so many complicating factors that loosen the associative chain from an initial prime to a resulting judgment, it almost comes as a surprise that systematic priming effects on evaluative social judgments are still obtained. Part of the evidence comes from experiments that were deliberately modeled after the original priming paradigm, leaving little room for uncontrolled inferences and voluntary action. Indeed, the lexical-decision task itself was employed in recent stereotype research to demonstrate, say, that processing of negative (as opposed to positive) words is facilitated when the word *Black* was primed a few seconds before (Wittenbrink, Judd, & Park, 1997). In some studies, subliminal priming of group labels (e.g., Black, Female) ruled out conscious correction and inference processes (Blair & Banaji, 1996; Dovidio et al. 1986; Fazio et al., 1995; Wittenbrink et al., 1997).

However, notably, priming effects on direct judgment tasks or even on overt motor behavior have been shown in much less constrained situations as well. The impact of processing words or sentences of positive or negative meaning on subsequent person judgments was replicated in numerous experiments (Bargh, 1994). Mood priming was shown to influence evaluative judgments (Forgas, 1991). Keeping in memory words related to social cooperation was sufficient to enhance cooperation in dilemma games (Hertel & Fiedler, 1994; Neuberg, 1988). Goal-priming succeeded in eliciting behaviors related to those goals (Bargh, 1992). Subtle priming of historical analogies (to either World War II or the Vietnam War) was sufficient to influence decisions about whether the United States should help an allied State in a hostile conflict or not (Gilovich, 1981). And subtle, subliminal priming of concepts (e.g., hostile) was shown to induce manifest actions (e.g., aggressions toward the experimenter), as demonstrated in several recent studies (Bargh, Chen, & Burrows, 1996; Dijksterhuis, Spears, Postmes, Stapel, Koomen, van Knippenberg, & Scheepers, 1998).

Although the growing body of empirical evidence is impressive, the danger remains that the homogeneity of this evidence may be, to an unknown degree, the result of positive testing. Just as Wason's participants, most researchers look for, and succeed in publishing, positive evidence for typical priming. They rarely search actively for something else, or for alternative rules. To be sure, several opposite outcomes have been published and interpreted creatively. For instance, the occasional finding of contrast effects—negative judgments after positive priming and vice versa—was explained in terms of correction processes when awareness of the primes was high (Lombardi, Higgins, & Bargh, 1987; Wilson & Brekke, 1994). Or, when an exemplar (Einstein) rather than a generic category (Professor) was used for priming, the participants' appraisal of their own intelligence went down, rather than up (Dijksterhuis et al., 1998), the ad-hoc interpretation being that exemplars are more prone to comparison and to evoking contrast effects. However, it appears as if these reversals were originally unexpected, and the offered explanations—although intriguing—were post hoc. Although some of these reversals are replicable, there was no cogent theoretical framework from which those reversals could be derived in the first place. Moreover, until today, it would appear that theorists in the priming-social-judgment paradigm have not been very concerned about conceptual frameworks that might broaden the scope of priming research.

In the remainder of this chapter, I argue that once a broader theoretical perspective is taken, a number of important insights become immediately apparent: (a) as a matter of rule, all priming can involve both facilitation and inhibition; (b) priming can simultaneously facilitate or inhibit access to more than one category, or knowledge structure; (c) priming not only has a perceptual component (being passively exposed to a stimulus) but also an operative component (actively doing something with the prime); different psychological laws apply to these two components; (d) priming effects neither conform to the rules of propositional logic nor the rules of pragmatics; as explained in the next paragraph, they are not truth-conserving and they are pragmatically blind; and (e) most important, informed explanations of priming effects on specific evaluative-judgment tasks require more than the reflex-like associative link from one prime to one response.

With reference to Fig. 5.1, I try to demonstrate that in the context of higher cognitive processes of evaluation and decision making the priming process is less restrictive than usually assumed. There are two different aspects to this statement. First, priming of a category (i.e., the afferent process) is not dependent on strong and valid information. To prime the category *aggressive*, it matters little whether aggressiveness is observed in reality or imagined in a dream, considered true or false, whether the information source is credible or not, whether priming comes as an assertion or as a question. This should clarify the phrase that priming processes are pragmatically blind, and not truth-conserving. In analogy to an implication of the form *if x, then y*, priming means to follow an invitation to assume the if-clause proposition, *x*, regardless of whether there is strong evidence for *x*. Even when primes are obviously false, come from unauthorized persons, or when primes are subliminally weak and short, they may nevertheless start the process. Second, the efferent judgmental inferences elicited by the primed category or knowledge structure are nonrestrictive in a different sense. They are not confined to a single judgment target; to gain full understanding it is important to look at several influences at the same time. Thus, once the if-part is granted, the then-phrase is not restricted to a single inference, but can involve multiple, sometimes conflicting, inferences at the same time.

I report findings from our own research as well as selected examples from the pertinent literature. Although the broadened perspective will lead to a more refined, less simplistic view of priming effects, I hope the outcome will result in clarification and a better understanding of priming in the context of higher cognitive processes. The purpose is first to outline a framework within which usual and unusual priming results can be integrated. Next I deal with evidence that opens a broader view of the afferent process stage. Later on, I present evidence that serves to refine the efferent stage.

EMPIRICAL EVIDENCE

Facilitation AND Inhibition

An old topic of attention research says that increased attention to one stimulus goes along with decreased attention to another (cf. Greenwald, 1972). By analogy, attaching one interpretation to a prime stimulus may block alternative interpretations. Although not directly related to evaluative judgment, this was illustrated by Ratcliff and McKoon (1996), who argued that, as a matter of principle, both benefits and costs of priming must be kept in mind, that is, facilitation of one interpretation but, at the same time, inhibition of others. One of their experiments involved picture naming. Pictures of mundane objects were presented and remained on the computer screen until the participants named the object. Naming latencies were recorded by voice key. The priming treatment, employing the same picture-naming task, had been administered a whole week earlier. The crucial independent variable was whether a target object to be named in the second session matched a prime object already named in the first session or the prime object was a perceptually similar but semantically different competitor. For instance, when the target was a light bulb, the prime could have been also a light bulb or a graphically very similar drawing of a balloon. Both conditions, priming of the target itself versus a similar picture, as well as a no-priming control condition, were varied within participants across a longer series of 30 stimulus objects. Analyses of naming latencies confirmed both facilitation *and* inhibition effects. The mean response time in the second session for the control condition was 809 ms. In comparison, when the identical target had been named previously, there was a marked facilitation effect (720 ms). In contrast, prior exposure to a perceptually similar competitor resulted in an inhibition effect of approximately the same size (879 ms).

Ratcliff and McKoon (1996) reported equivalent findings for various other implicit memory tasks, such as forced-choice picture identification, word-stem completion, fragment completion, visual, and auditory word-identification tasks. Priming served to facilitate one interpretive response and to inhibit others. Having attached one interpretation to a prime, access to other, competing interpretations is hindered.

Simple and straightforward as this demonstration appears, it was hardly ever caught on and applied to priming effects on social judgment. One notable exception comes from Macrae, Bodenhausen, and Milne (1995). These authors had their participants watch a videotape of a Chinese woman reading a book; that is, the target person could be categorized both as a Woman or as a Chinese. Depending on whether in a preceding parafoveal priming task the category name *Woman* or *Chinese* had been primed (presented for 75 ms), watching the same constant target person facilitated access to the primed category and inhibited access to the unprimed category on a subsequent lexical decision task. When the Woman category was primed, lexical decision times were shorter for words related to the female stereotype (514 ms) than for words related to Chinese (794 ms). After priming the Chinese category, latencies were shorter for Chinese (529 ms) than for woman-related words (763 ms). In a control condition, latencies for words related to Woman and Chinese were approximately equal and intermediate (631 ms and 649 ms, respectively). These findings corroborate the notion that priming involves benefits and costs at the same time, and that an incomplete picture of priming will arise from positive testing (i.e., considering only the facilitative effect on the focal category).

An intriguing aspect of Ratcliff and McKoon's research was that the inhibition of unprimed stimulus interpretations may not be confined to opposite or semantically distant meanings. It is commonly granted that the activation of one concept (e.g., *masculine*; *liking*) may be incompatible with the simultaneous activation of an opposite or antonymous concept (*feminine*; *disliking*). However, the above findings suggest, vividly, that alternative interpretations of very similar competitors can be blocked as well.

Facilitative and Inhibitive Priming Effects on Social Judgments

In the context of evaluative judgments, this means that priming of one semantic category (e.g., *polite*) to interpret an observed stimulus behavior might block the activation of other, even evaluatively consistent interpretations (e.g., *friendly*). Having already occupied the stimulus behavior with one meaningful label (*polite*), subsequent impression ratings concerning the alternative, but strongly related, meaning (*friendly*) might be reduced. Such a seemingly paradoxical side effect would appear to be quite unexpected in social cognition.

Picture Superiority Effect in Trait Attribution. Pertinent evidence comes from a recent investigation on spontaneous trait inferences from pictorially presented behaviors. Immediate, spontaneous inferences from an observed behavior to a correspondent trait disposition within the actor have been a very prominent topic of research on attribution in general and the fundamental attribution bias (toward internal causes) in particular. Unlike previous work (Winter & Uleman, 1984) with verbally presented behavior descriptions and indirect measures of trait inference (delayed cued recall; savings in relearning), we (Fiedler & Schenck, 2001) developed a paradigm that uses pictorially presented behaviors as primes and direct measures of trait inference immediately afterward. Each trial involved the presentation of a black and white silhouette-like photograph displaying a positive or negative social behavior (see Fig. 5.2). The encoding task during picture presentation was manipulated between participants. In an initial experiment, participants either had to provide a verbal interpretation of the picture contents or to make a purely graphical judgment, namely, to judge the proportion of black area in the picture. We also ran one condition with the graphical judgment plus a distracter task supposed to increase cognitive load (i.e., memorizing a letter string during picture presentation). A few seconds afterward, participants had to identify a positive or negative trait word (written in large letters) that was gradually appearing behind a rectangular mask (see Fig. 5.2). At first the word was fully covered, but as pieces of the mask disappeared in a mosaic-like fashion over a period of several seconds, the trait could be identified eventually. If a corresponding trait had been inferred spontaneously from the preceding picture, then the time re-

FIG. 5.2.   An example of a stimulus picture used by Fiedler and Schenck (2001). The bottom part shows three stages of a corresponding trait word appearing gradually behind a mask on the subsequent trait identification task.

quired to identify the trait word should decrease, relative to a no-match condition in which the preceding picture did not match the subsequent trait.

The rather challenging set of findings can be summarized as follows. When the traits to be identified matched the preceding pictures contents, a facilitation effect was obtained in all three encoding conditions, for both positive and negative valence. In comparison to the no-match condition (mean latency = 4450 ms), the identification latency decreased to 3976 ms on average in the verbal-interpretation condition. However, surprisingly, facilitation was strongest in the purely graphical encoding task (3817 ms) in which the black proportion had to be judged. Even when an additional distracter was added to graphical coding, facilitation was still in the same magnitude (4032 ms) as in the explicit verbal interpretation condition.

One possible explanation of the relative inferiority of verbal recoding is in terms of the inhibition effect illustrated earlier. Any verbal interpretation attached to the stimulus picture during presentation might have blocked access to alternative trait categories on the subsequent trait identification task. After all, given the multitude of verbal recodings that might be used to describe the same pictures (cf. Fig. 5.2), it is unlikely that the verbally coded trait exactly matched the trait to be identified later. An intriguing implication of this analysis is that a kind of *picture superiority effect*, as it is long known for episodic memory (Seifert, 1997; Weldon & Roediger, 1987), may also hold for trait attributions.[1] Pictures, as long as they are not occupied by particular verbal labels, induce perceptual priming while avoiding the blocking side effect of verbal labeling. This may be one of the reasons underlying the widely accepted claim that pictures provide privileged access to categorical codes. What holds for semantic categories in general should hold for trait categories as well.

In further experiments, we tried to replicate this phenomenon and to validate this interpretation. Of particular interest was the role of evaluative consistency. When traits are more accessible after exposure to a picture showing a matching behavior than after seeing a nonmatching behavior, one question is whether match versus mismatch is confounded with valence. In the aforementioned experiment, nonmatching pictures were simply chosen at random so that part of the picture-trait pairs were of opposite valence. Thus, evaluative inconsistency alone might have been responsible for the effect. In another experiment, however, nonmatching behaviors were always of the same valence as the subsequent trait words. Moreover, the proportion of matching picture-trait pairs in the whole series was reduced to one sixth, and trials involving traits were allegedly filler trials among a majority of geometric-symbol trials that concealed the purpose of the study and minimized the chance of planned, strategic inferences. Nevertheless, merely perceiving pictures and deciding whether the black or the white area is larger facilitated access to subsequent matched traits.

Concreteness Effect on Social Judgment.   The two tasks of verbal interpretation and purely graphical encoding decisions differ in several respects (modality, mental load, demand characteristics, and so on), making direct comparison of such an unequal pair rather complex and difficult to understand. Therefore, in another experiment, the qualitative encoding task was

---

[1] Weldon & Roediger's (1987) finding that the picture superiority effect may disappear for implicit word fragment completion tasks may reflect the use of specific pictures that serve to prime very specific objects, unlike the pictures used in the present study.

held constant, requiring verbal encoding in all conditions. We only manipulated the degree to which either perceptual encoding of picture contents or semantic interpretation was called for. Each picture was followed by a verification task; that is, participants had to decide on the presence versus absence of a specific attribute in the picture. The linguistic level of the attribute to be verified was manipulated. According to the linguistic category model (Fiedler & Semin, 1988; Semin & Fiedler, 1988), descriptive action verbs are linguistic devices that refer to the objective characteristics and refrain from any interpretation and evaluation (e.g., shake hands, hit, comb). To verify shaking hands means to decide on what actually is in the picture, with little need to draw inferences beyond the perceptual level. Such a decision can be made regardless of whether shaking hands is benevolent or malevolent, and what purpose or goal it serves. In contrast, other linguistic categories involve interpretation and evaluation. Interpretive action verbs (welcome, attack, care for) entail attributions of action goals and intentions. Adjectives (friendly, hostile, helpful) entail attributions of traits and dispositions.

If our reasoning is correct, then the identification of a subsequent trait word should be facilitated most when the preceding picture verification task is concrete and confined to the perceptual analysis of the picture. If, however, the verification task entails attaching semantic interpretations to the pictures, the subsequent identification of other traits might suffer from relative inhibition. Accordingly, we manipulated the language level of the initial verification task—descriptive action verbs, interpretive action verbs, or trait adjectives—between participants. When traits were to be verified, they were always different from, but strongly related to, the traits to be identified later.

Indeed, what could be demonstrated for the crude comparison of verbal recoding and purely graphical decisions held for concrete versus interpretive attributes as well. Verification of a purely descriptive, concrete aspect of the manifest picture content caused more facilitation than verifying an interpretive attribute, as evident from Fig. 5.3. The average time required to identify the same set of 24 traits preceded by the same 24 matching pictures was around 4700 ms after verifying descriptive action verbs, about 4850 ms after verifying interpretive action verbs, and also 4850 ms after verifying a highly related trait.[2]

Such a pattern is opposite to the common intuition that priming of one trait should facilitate inferences of a semantic associate. How can thinking about *shake hands* (i.e., a descriptive action verb) cause more facilitation on a subsequent task to identify the trait *friendly* than thinking about the

---

[2]In this experiment, latencies were generally somewhat higher than in the former experiment, due to a constant delay factor in the computer program.

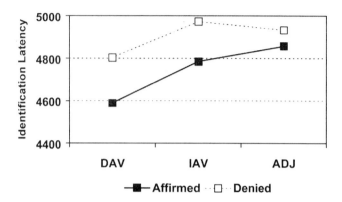

FIG. 5.3.   Mean identification latencies for traits implicitly inferred from pictures after affirming or denying a related behavior in a preceding picture verification task (DAV = Descriptive Action Verb; IAV = Interpretive Action Verb; ADJ = Adjective).

strongly related trait *polite*? However, these findings are consistent with the earlier analysis of benefits and costs, facilitative and inhibitive priming effects. Having occupied a stimulus picture with one interpretation reduces access to alternative interpretations, causing a kind of lateral inhibition.[3] Note that such a result is not really incompatible with previous results showing that priming of trait adjectives can bias subsequent perceptions of persons and groups (cf. Higgins et al., 1977). When the dependent measure is an open one, asking for multiple judgments, free descriptions, or free associations, the inhibition effect of prior trait priming is hardly manifested. Inhibition should only occur when a convergent, restrictive dependent measure is used, such as identifying one specific trait word, if this word is different from, or overshadowed by the prime word.

The present findings are also consistent with and perhaps intrinsically related to other recent evidence on the so-called concreteness effect (Marschak & Surian, 1992). Based on McClelland, McNaughton, and Reilly's (1995) distinction of a fast-learning system (triggered by pictures) and a slow-learning system (triggered by tedious associative processes), Sweeney (2000) found that concrete descriptions of behavior not only led to stronger inferences but were also recalled better than abstract trait descriptions. For instance, using descriptive action verbs as in "Michael Brown *cried* while watching a documentary of famine in Africa" were obviously processed to a deeper level than corresponding trait descriptions like "Michael Brown is *empathetic*". Thus, just as pictures open deeper categorical processing than

---

[3]The term *lateral inhibition* is used here in its broadest sense, independent of its specific implications in the perceptual literature.

words, concrete terms show a similar advantage over abstract terms (cf. Fiedler & Schenck, 2001).

Theoretically, the advantage of pictorial priming may be understood in terms of the inhibitory side effects of priming. A purely graphical encoding task (e.g., judging the proportion of black area) forces the participant to adhere to the picture contents and distracts her from categorical interpretation. Because no specific semantic category is primed (ideally), other categories cannot be blocked. Consequently, identifying another trait related to the picture cannot be inhibited. Although the well-known picture-superiority effect (Weldon & Roediger, 1987) in episodic memory has been explained in terms of pictures providing privileged access to categorical memory codes, such privileged access may in part reflect freedom of inhibitory side effects of verbal priming.

Priming Social Categories Versus Instances.   The following finding gives a new twist to the *concrete versus abstract* distinction, which may not precisely capture the crucial determinant of whether priming causes facilitation or inhibition. In several experiments conducted by Stapel and his colleagues (Dijksterhuis et al., 1998; Stapel, Koomen, & van der Pligt, 1996), priming of a social category led to an assimilation effect (i.e., judgments moving in the direction of the prime) whereas priming of a specific exemplar from the category produced contrast. This finding not only held for evaluative judgments but also influenced the participants' overt behavior. For example, priming of the category *professor* led participants to judge their own intellectual ability higher (assimilation). But priming of the specific exemplar *Albert Einstein* led them to judge their own intelligence lower (contrast) than in a control condition. At first glance, this appears to contradict the earlier finding that concrete language leads to stronger correspondent inferences than abstract language.

Here we meet a point where ordinary language may be too vague to convey precise theoretical arguments. The graphical illustration in Fig. 5.4 may help to reconcile both sets of seemingly contradictory findings. Reading the notation from left to right, the (afferent part of the) process starts with exposure to the (verbal or pictorial) prime, which solicits some knowledge structure in memory. The activated structure varies in specificity versus inclusiveness. That is, the activated structure may either afford a specific, restrictive interpretation, confining the prime stimulus to a distinct knowledge unit that gives rise to one trait inference, but not others (upper panel). Or the activated structure may be less restrictive and activate a more diffuse structure causing inferences to several traits at the same time (lower panel). Whether the outcome is an assimilation or contrast effect (or, alternatively, facilitation or inhibition), depends on the relationship between the activated structure and the target-judgment task. If the (information re-

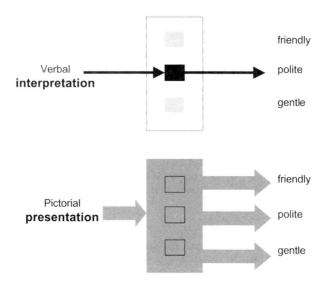

FIG. 5.4.   Two cases of priming differing in restrictiveness versus inclusiveness. A verbal encoding task is assumed to activate a restrictive knowledge structure bound to a specific inference, whereas a pictorial encoding task activates a more inclusive structure that allows for multiple inferences.

quired to judge the) target is included in the activated structure, facilitation (assimilation) can be expected. If, however, the target lies outside the activated structure (Schwarz & Bless, 1992), in a different or even in a neighboring structure, the information required for the task may be blocked and the outcome may be an inhibition effect (contrast).[4]

Within such a framework, both phenomena can be reconciled. Judging the intelligence of one instance (Klaus Fiedler) after priming a different instance (Albert Einstein) from the same category (professors) should produce contrast because different instances from the same category are typically represented by their distinctive features. Therefore, the specific structure activated by *Albert Einstein* is unlikely to include references to *Klaus Fiedler*. In contrast, using a super-ordinate category such as *professor* for priming enhances the likelihood that semantic features of a professor are carried over to the target (see Tversky & Hutchinson, 1986), resulting in higher judgments of intellectual ability (assimilation).

---

[4]Note that such an inhibition mechanism is conceptually different from the usual reference scale, or comparison anchor account of contrast effects, which refers to the efferent part of the process.

The seemingly opposite superiority of concrete over abstract encoding tasks may reflect the same principle. Being exposed to a picture showing two persons who shake hands, and being asked only to verify whether the picture shows *shake-hands* should activate a knowledge structure that is both informative and flexible. On a subsequent trait identification task, access to a number of other traits (polite, friendly, warm, etc.) should be facilitated. However, when the encoding task requires the judge to decide whether the picture shows the trait *polite*, then a much more constrained memory structure may be activated and a restrictive category label may occupy the representation of the stimulus. Subsequent exposure to another trait (*friendly*) may thus be inhibited.

A number of well-known findings from the social-judgment literature can be covered by this principle. It was long known that a boomerang (contrast) effect might be obtained if the prime stimulus is too distant from the target, thus reducing the likelihood that the target falls within the domain of the activated category (Herr, Sherman, & Fazio, 1983). Also, the remarkable finding that priming effects on social judgment may disappear or even reverse (into a contrast effect) when judges remember the priming treatment (Lombardi et al., 1987) makes perfect sense within this framework. Being aware of, or remembering, the priming treatment reminds the judge that the prime stimulus belonged to a distinct task context (e.g., a prior verbal learning task), making the activated structure less likely to carry over to subsequent social judgment tasks that are different from the priming episode.

By this analysis, one can also integrate the *applicability* condition (Higgins et al., 1977), that is, the failure of primes that are not applicable to the judgment target. In such a case, the primed knowledge structure cannot assimilate the target and it therefore can neither facilitate nor inhibit access to target-relevant information. Consistent with this conjecture, we (Fiedler & Schenck, 2001) did not find an inhibition effect of a nonmatching picture prime on the identification of a completely independent trait (e.g., the trait *polite* after seeing a picture of one person punishing the other). On such a strange trial, the applicability condition is not met.

One implication that suggests itself is that priming of a broader category should more likely affect subsequent judgments of specific attributes than vice versa. This hardly surprising but rarely ever studied implication (for an exception, see Stapel & Koomen, 1998) was applied to evaluative person judgments by Fiedler, Semin, and Bolten (1989). A target person was first described in a brief written vignette. Participants in different experimental conditions were then engaged in two successive judgment tasks. Each task consisted of ratings of the extent to which 12 behaviors or traits were descriptive of the target person. Both judgment tasks involved either only positive attributes or only negative attributes. Moreover, we manipulated the breadth or linguistic abstractness of the first and the second judgment. Judgments at the most specific level involved 12 positive or negative interpretive action verbs (IAV: does the target help, encourage; hurt, insult etc. others?), the middle level used 12 state verbs (SV: like, admire; hate, abhor), and the most abstract level involved 12 positive or negative trait adjectives (ADJ: friendly, tolerant; aggressive, arrogant). All upward and downward transitions (of the same valence) were established for the two successive judgment tasks (i.e., adjectives → state verbs; adjectives → action verbs; state verbs → action verbs; action verbs → adjectives; action verbs → state verbs; state verbs → adjectives).

The central hypothesis was that prior general judgments would to greater extent bias subsequent specific judgments of the same valence than vice versa. In other words, priming of general categories should influence specific target judgments more than priming of specific categories should affect judgments of general attributes. These predictions are nicely borne out in the empirical data. The three curves in Fig. 5.5 all refer to the extremity of secondary judgments at one level as a function of increasing abstractness of the primary judgments. Thus, judgments of IAV attributes remained at the lowest level when given first but were enhanced when preceded by more abstract SVs and ADJs of the same valence. SV ratings were lowest when preceded by specific IAV ratings, moderate when not preceded by other ratings, and became most extreme when preceded by most abstract ADJs. Finally, judgments of ADJs were less extreme when preceded by judgments of less abstract IAVs or SVs of the same valence than when unpreceded. This top-down transfer effect was more pronounced for the negative than positive valence condition, presumably due to the higher diagnosticity of negative information in the social-behavior domain (Reeder & Brewer, 1979).

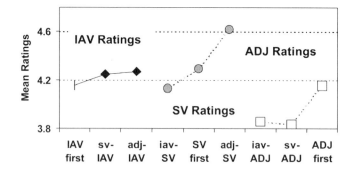

FIG. 5.5. Top-down asymmetry in priming influences on evaluative judgments. The three curves refer to judgments at different linguistic levels (IAV, SV, ADJ). At each level, target judgment extremity increases with the abstractness of the preceding prime.

Relation Between Prime Stimulus and Activated Structure

Having emphasized repeatedly that priming can have benefits and costs, we can now turn to an equally important question: How precisely does the prime determine the knowledge being activated? Most previous research seems to assume a one-to-one relation between prime and activated category. Exposure to the word *Black* activates the stereotype of *Black* people, exposure to *Woman* a *female* stereotype. In this section, it is seen that priming can have unwanted effects. The activated structure can be opposite to what was presented, because the afferent priming component is insensitive to logical and pragmatic constraints.

Priming Denied Interpretations. This point can be illustrated with reference to *primed denials* as well as *denied primes.* Imagine what would happen when the primary judgment task would involve a list of questions about denied negative traits: Is the target person *not* aggressive, *not* rude, *not* intolerant, *not* selfish etc.? Logically, the negation of negative traits amounts to posing positive assumptions. However, would such a treatment result in more positive judgments? Intuition alone suggests the opposite. After all, the substantive semantic meanings that are being primed are the negative trait terms. The pallid syntactical devices used for negation would appear to be rather unlikely to reverse the effect. To put it more generally, there is by now rather strong evidence that the associative process underlying priming is not a truth-conserving, logically sensitive process. The previous example refers to the case of priming of denials; a related case that is even more compelling refers to denied primes, for which I can offer some empirical evidence.

For instance, in the picture-priming experiments by Fiedler and Schenck (2001), it was found that even when the initial reaction on the verification task was negative (i.e., participants denied seeing an aggression in a picture), the subsequent identification of a related trait was facilitated. More direct evidence for counter-dictional effects of denied primes comes from a series of experiments using a questioning paradigm (Fiedler, Armbruster, Nickel, Walther, & Asbeck, 1996; Fiedler, Walther, Armbruster, Fay, Kuntz, & Naumann, 1996). In one study (Fiedler, Armbruster, et al., 1996; Experiment 1), participants saw a videotaped TV group discussion on a topic related to healthy food. They were instructed to focus on a male target person who played the active role of the discussion leader, or talk master. Immediately after seeing the film (about 7 min), participants were asked to verify whether the target person had shown 12 positive behaviors (e.g., encourage, support, help others) or 12 negative behaviors (e.g., insult, provoke, interrupt others), depending on the experimental condition. This initial verification task constituted the priming treatment. Several minutes later, judges were asked to convey their evaluative impression of the target person on two sets of 12 positive and 12 negative trait adjectives that were matched in meaning to the behaviors verified previously (e.g., *aggressive* after verifying *to attack*; *helpful* after verifying *to support* etc.). Although the authentic information given about the target person in the video film was held constant, judging positive behaviors led to more benevolent trait judgments than considering negative attributes (see Fig. 5.6, left chart).

More important, however, this held even when responses to the initial verification task had been negative. Aggregating impression judgments for particular traits only across those judges who had denied seeing the corresponding behavior in the film resulted in the same priming influence (Fig. 5.6, right part). Thus, even when judges had initially denied that the target *delighted others* or that the target had *listened to others*, they would subsequently judge the target higher on related traits such as *gentle* or *attentive*. Merely considering positive behaviors was sufficient to create positive impressions, regardless of the truth-value ascribed to the primed attributes. Conceptually similar findings, which could be termed antipriming, have been obtained in several other experiments using recall and recognition measures by Fiedler, Walther et al. (1996). This failure to take the truth value of primed information into account is also reminiscent of the so-called innuendo effect (Wegner, Wenzlaff, Kerker & Beattie, 1981), the perseverance effect (Ross, Lepper, & Hubbard, 1975) and the work of Gilbert, Krull, and Malone (1990) on default truth inferences.

Priming as an Operant Instruction.   This demonstration that denying or rejecting a prime as false does not prevent the prime from exerting its influence clarifies the phrase "priming effects are not truth-conserving." Logical

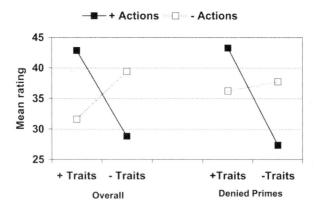

FIG. 5.6.   Mean ratings of positive and negative traits after merely considering the possibility of having observed positive versus negative actions in the target. The left panel refers to all data; the right panel only refers to judgments of traits after judges have denied corresponding actions.

rules are not obeyed and logical transformations are not conveyed in the afferent process; negating the prime does not negate the priming effect. Furthermore, the afferent process is pragmatically blind for the epistemological status of the priming information. As we have seen, it matters little whether the primed category (e.g., the notion of attacking or offending against others) comes from a valid source (e.g., a credible informant who knows the target well and who affirms the prime deliberately) or whether the prime is nothing but a possibility that is considered and even rejected as false. This low threshold of validity is parallel to the low, subliminal presentation threshold that is sufficient for priming effects.

However, this liberality only holds for the afferent side of priming, the cooperation with the if-phrase. Regarding the then-phrase, or efferent side, priming effects can have a rather strict inferential and operative grammar. In fact, there is quite compelling evidence for operative, procedural constraints imposed on priming effects. The cognitive process is not confined to the activation of a category but often includes an operant instruction that "tells" the individual *what to do with the primed category.*

For example, the operant component may rely on the priming of schematic structures that impose specific constraints on subsequent inferences. Pertinent evidence comes again from the videotaped talk-show study just reported (Fiedler, Armbruster et al., 1996). Note that in the aforementioned experimental conditions, the primed behaviors were represented by positive and negative action verbs (*encourage, support; attack, insult*). According to the principle of implicit verb causality (Brown & Fish, 1983; Fiedler & Semin, 1988), action verbs elicit a causal schema that supports internal attributions to factors within the sentence subject, or behavioral agent. In line with this prediction, priming of positive action verbs facilitated the attribution of positive traits to the target person, who was in the agent role.

In further experimental conditions, priming involved positive or negative state verbs (*like, admire; hate, abhor*) that are known to invoke schemas supporting external attributions. Thus, if Person A hates or abhors Person B, this raises stronger inferences about the object B than the subject A. Accordingly, when participants who had viewed the TV discussion were asked to verify, say, negative state verbs (Did the target hate, abhor others?), this led to external attributions. After considering negative target states, negative target behaviors were excused as due to provocations by other persons, resulting in relatively more positive target impressions after judging negative states. This rather sophisticated effect of priming verb-specific causal schemas was replicable, and it could be extinguished when the focus of external attribution (the alleged provocateur) was removed from the stimulus film.

That priming can impose quite distinct restrictions on what should be done with the primed memory contents is apparent in the notion of *procedural priming* (Smith & Lerner, 1986). It is not only possible to prime a concept, but also a procedure to be applied on that concept. Perhaps the first demonstrations of this fact can be found in Luchins' (1942) famous experiments with numerical calculation problems. When several successive calculation problems could be solved by the same solution path, the carry-over of that path inhibited performance on a new problem requiring a different solution path.

The so-called *negative-priming paradigm* provides further, telling evidence for the operant component of priming processes. In this paradigm (Tipper, 1985; Tipper & Cranston, 1985), priming is operationalized as an active cognitive process that involves both the positive choice of one stimulus interpretation and the suppression of another, competing interpretation. For example, a priming task may involve two superimposed letters printed in different colors, the instruction being to read the red letter and to ignore the green letter. When the suppressed green letter is then presented in red on the next trial, the recognition latency increases, reflecting a learned inhibition effect, or negative-priming side effect. More interesting, the learned suppression effect occurs only when the problem involves a forced choice, that is, when the probe is presented together with another letter from which it has to be selected. If the probe is presented alone, without a choice, no effect is observed, suggesting that the negative priming effect entails a specific choice operation.

The negative-priming paradigm promises to offer refined investigations of the ironical consequences of thought suppression—one of the most popular topics of contemporary social cognition research. Many recent experiments have demonstrated that instructions to suppress unwanted thoughts may have an opposite effect. Trying not to think of a white bear (Wegner, 1994), to avoid sexist language, or to suppress stereotypes or depressive thoughts (Wenzlaff & Bates, 2000) can result in enhanced accessibility of the suppressed cognitive contents. According to a wide-spread theory advanced by Wegner (1994), this ironic effect reflects the fact that the monitoring loop that is necessary to avoid specific thoughts has the side effect of keeping these very thoughts permanently in mind, if only at a low, preconscious level. From the present point of view, this provides further strong evidence for the contention that the afferent priming component is insensitive to logical and pragmatic constraints. The instruction "Do NOT think of negative topics" serves to maintain the accessibility of negative topics. Negation is in vain, as in the studies reported before. After all, the cognitive function of the afferent activation process is to prompt information in memory that is linked to the prime. Such a process component must be as sensitive as possible; it must be not truth-conserving or dependent on logical flexions and transformations, or strong evidence.

However, the negative-priming effect suggests an interesting way in which the operant component of priming might be exploited to accomplish more effective thought suppression. As suggested by Tipper and Cranston (1985), offering participants positive topics to concentrate on, rather than merely instructing them to suppress negative topics, may be more successful, especially when the task involves a forced choice, thereby training the participants in the mental operation of choosing a positive and suppressing a negative topic.

Exactly this task situation was recently adopted by Wenzlaff and Bates (2000) to achieve an efficient means of avoiding negative contents without a rebound effect (i.e., a subsequent release of negative content after the active attempt is over). They presented their participants with scrambled sets of six words (e.g., equal am others I inferior to) that could be unscrambled as a negative, depressive five-word sentence (I am inferior to others) or as a positive sentence (I am equal to others). In different experimental conditions, participants were instructed NOT to produce negative sentences (suppression), to produce positive sentences (concentration) while suppressing negative ones, or to unscramble the word sets spontaneously (control condition). Given this stimulus material—that offers a forced choice between a positive and a negative interpretation—choosing the positive option was not only the most preferred spontaneous strategy (in the control group), but could still be enhanced by the positive instruction to concentrate on positive meanings. Moreover, the forced-choice concentration on positive and avoidance of negative contents did not result in a rebound-like release of negative contents on a second unscrambling task series. Future research within Tipper's paradigm may figure out the conditions under which a positive focus on a repeated forced-choice task may cause an operant, procedural priming effect that serves to suppress negative thoughts persistently.

Once more, the negative-priming phenomenon substantiates the double assumption that the afferent, activation component of the priming effect does not obey logical constraints (what should be suppressed is nevertheless activated), but that the efferent component leaves room for deliberate instruction. To provide a theoretically sound analysis of priming effects, one has to explain why one particular outcome was obtained rather than the other. Unfortunately, empirical reports of priming phenomena rarely meet this requirement, especially when the outcome is congruent with the prime, thus appearing plausible and not requiring any further comments. It is here that theorists fall prey to Wason's positive testing strategy. For the reasons outlined here, however, alternative, less plausible, or even paradoxical outcomes of the efferent process might have been possible as well, due to the complex, simultaneous influence of priming on more than one target.

One radical implication of this insight is that one should not consider assimilation and contrast as alternative outcomes of a unitary priming influence on social judgment, but one should acknowledge—as a matter of principle—that both assimilation and contrast are present at the same time (Petzold, 1992; Wänke, Bless, & Igou, 2001). As long as a one-to-one association is assumed from a prime to a single activated category, the typical implication is that *either* assimilation *or* contrast will be obtained. For instance, when judging the intelligence of target person X, priming Albert Einstein may *either* cause assimilation (enhance X's perceived intelligence) when linked to the target category, or *contrast* (reduce X's relative intelligence) when linked to the comparison standard of the intelligence judgment scale (cf. Schwarz & Bless, 1992).

However, all we know about the parallel processing capacities of associative processes suggests that the prime will presumably activate several categories simultaneously. Thus, Albert Einstein will be associated with both the target person category *as well as* the comparison standard category.[5] In the absence of strong evidence to the contrary, one has to assume, as a default, that the prime may in principle influence both categories, albeit to different degrees. Thus, there is always assimilation (using the prime to construe the target category) and contrast (using the prime to construe the comparison standard), at the same time. Both processes are not mutually exclusive but reflect qualitatively independent aspects of every judgment process; each judgment involves a target and a reference scale with a comparison standard. Whether the net judgment outcome resembles an assimilation effect or a contrast effect depends on the relative strength of the two associative effects and should not be taken as evidence for a monadic priming effect that impacts only the target or only the comparison standard. Needless to repeat that the common practice of treating assimilation and contrast as exclusive outcomes is again reminiscent of Wason.

TOWARD A MORE COMPREHENSIVE APPROACH TO PRIMING AND EVALUATIVE JUDGMENT

The only sensible alternative to positive testing of the Wason type is not to start from given positive examples when reasoning about a (theoretical) rule, but trying to consider the full problem space of all reasonable rules from a broader perspective. What might such a broader approach to priming look like? And which reasonable assumptions could restrict the priming process in a theoretically fruitful way? The evidence reviewed in this chap-

---

[5]To be sure, accepting the claim that assimilation and contrast can occur at the same time, as a matter of principle, does not strictly rule out the possibility of a competitive interaction between assimilation and contrast, which could also be included in a comprehensive model.

ter, on the hidden vicissitudes in priming research, suggests the following outline.

First, the paradigmatic domain of evaluative person judgments should be clearly defined and well distinguished from priming effects in other domains, such as lexical decisions, word recognition, or even affective priming.

Second, within the evaluative judgment domain, it should be useful to distinguish two stages, referred to as the afferent and efferent component, that are governed by distinct psychological rules.

Third, the theoretical arguments and empirical evidence advanced in the present chapter highlight that both process stages might be less restrictive than expected, albeit in different ways. On one hand, the afferent stage is governed by very basic associative rules that are unrestrained by logical and pragmatic rules. To activate a cognitive schema of aggressive behavior, it matters little whether aggression in the target is affirmed or denied, stated or asked, whether the judge believes in the truth of a proposition stating that the target is aggressive, whether aggression has been observed or merely imagined (Koehler, 1991), validated or vaguely suggested, whether the prime is presented super- or subliminally. Even a denied prime still activates the structure being denied. Nevertheless, not all primes are equally effective; their ability to activate knowledge structures that trigger subsequent judgments depends on such factors as concrete versus abstract primes, pictorial versus verbal priming, and individual exemplars versus generic categories. One intriguing finding in this regard was the picture-superiority effect, suggesting that pictures cause less interference than verbal primes, resulting in stronger activation effects.

On the other hand, the efferent stage from the activated knowledge structure to the resulting judgment is also less restrictive than often suggested, although in a different sense. This part of the process is not at all insensitive to logical and pragmatic constraints. What operation is applied on the activated knowledge and what kind of inference is drawn can be influenced quite specifically. Judgmental inferences are sensitive to schematic rules, to the abstractness of categories, and to procedural constraints, as evident in procedural priming and the negative-priming effect. The influence of the activated structure can be canalized into the confines of the specific judgment task (rating, format-free communication, choice, etc.). Most important, one must take for granted, as a matter of rule, that the same activated knowledge structure will have more than one implication at a time. In particular, one should expect primed categories to interact with both the target category and the comparison standard, thus producing assimilation and contrast at the same time. If the outcome of an experiment happens to resemble a simpler priming model, mimicking a one-to-one relation between prime and response, only assimilation, or a direct influence of a prime on overt action, theorists should be alerted that Wason is around and nevertheless look out for a more differentiated effect pattern.[6]

Finally, such a refined framework, with its distinct assumptions about the afferent and the efferent priming component, might instigate a number of new research topics that may eventually further our understanding of priming in evaluative judgments. Some of these novel implications have been already tackled in the recent experiments reported in this chapter, such as the impact of mere considering (Fiedler, 2000) and denied priming, priming of verb causality, and the intriguing advantage of pictorial information. Other implications suggest themselves for future research, such as the elaboration of negative-priming effects, refinement of thought suppression, and experiments designed to disentangle the simultaneous operation of assimilation and contrast effects. Based on such an enriched framework, it ought to be realized that referring to the primed word *aggressive* is as inadequate as an explanation of an overt aggressive act as the rule 2^N is to explain the series 2, 4, 8 in Wason's seminal reasoning studies.

ACKNOWLEDGMENTS

The research underlying the present chapter was supported by various grants from the German research foundation (Deutsche Forschungsgemeinschaft). Correspondence concerning this chapter should be addressed to Klaus Fiedler, Department of Psychology, University of Heidelberg, Hauptstrasse 47–51, 69117 Heidelberg, FRG. Email: klaus.fiedler@psychologie.uni-heidelberg.de. Valuable comments on a draft of this chapter came from Claude Messner, Paula Niedenthal, and Piotr Winkielman. Thanks are also due to Matthias Bluemke for proofreading.

REFERENCES

Bargh, J. A. (1992). The ecology of automaticity: Toward establishing the conditions needed to produce automatic processing effects. *American Journal of Psychology, 105*, 181–199.
Bargh, J. A. (1994). The Four Horsemen of automaticity. In R. S. Wyer & T. K. Srull (Eds.), *Handbook of social cognition* (pp. 1–40). Hillsdale, NJ: Lawrence Erlbaum Associates.
Bargh, J. A., Chen, M., & Burrows, L. (1996). Automaticity of social behavior: Direct effects of trait construct and stereotype activation on action. *Journal of Personality and Social Psychology, 71*, 230–244.
Blair, I. V., & Banaji, M. R. (1996). Automatic and controlled processes in stereotype priming. *Journal of Personality and Social Psychology, 70*, 1142–1163.

---

[6]It should be apparent that automatic versus controlled processes can be hardly separated in this complex interaction of associative, volitional, and meta-cognitive processes.

Brown, R., & Fish, D. (1983). The psychological causality implicit in language. *Cognition, 14*, 233–274.

Dijksterhuis, A., Spears, R., Postmes, T., Stapel, D. A., Koomen, W., van Knippenberg, A., & Scheepers, D. (1998). Seeing one thing and doing another: Contrast effects in automatic behavior. *Journal of Personality and Social Psychology, 75*, 862–871.

Dovidio, J. F., Evans, N., & Tyler, R. B. (1986). Racial stereotypes: the contents of their cognitive representations. *Journal of Experimental Social Psychology, 22*, 22–37.

Fazio, R. H., Jackson, J. R., Dunton, B. C., & Williams, C. J. (1995). Variability in automatic activation as an unobtrusive measure of racial attitudes: A bona fide pipeline? *Journal of Personality and Social Psychology, 69*, 1013–1027.

Fiedler, K. (2000). On mere considering: The subjective experience of truth. In H. Bless & J. P. Forgas (Eds.), *The message within: The role of subjective experience in social cognition and behavior* (pp. 13–36). Philadelphia, PA: Taylor & Francis.

Fiedler, K., Armbruster, T., Nickel, S., Walther, E., & Asbeck, J. (1996). Constructive biases in social judgment: Experiments on the self-verification of question contents. *Journal of Personality and Social Psychology, 71*, 861–873.

Fiedler, K., Nickel, S., Muehlfriedel, T., & Unkelbach, C. (2001). Is mood congruency a genuine memory effect or a matter of response bias? *Journal of Experimental Social Psychology, 37*, 201–214.

Fiedler, K., & Schenck, W. (2001). Spontaneous inferences from pictorially presented behaviors. *Personality and Social Psychology Bulletin, 27*, 1533–1546.

Fiedler, K., & Semin, G. R. (1988). On the causal information conveyed by different interpersonal verbs. *Social Cognition, 6*, 21–39.

Fiedler, K., Semin, G. R., & Bolten, S. (1989). Language use and reification of social information: Top-down and bottom-up processing in person cognition. *European Journal of Social Psychology, 19*, 271–295.

Fiedler, K., Walther, E., Armbruster, T., Fay, D., Kuntz, H., & Naumann, U. (1996). Do you really know what you have seen? Intrusion errors and presupposition effect in constructive memory. *Journal of Experimental Social Psychology, 32*, 484–511.

Forgas, J. P. (1991). *Emotion and social judgment.* Cambridge, UK: Cambridge University Press.

Gilbert, D. T., Krull, D. S., & Malone, P. S. (1990). Unbelieving the unbelievable: Some problems in the rejection of false information. *Journal of Personality and Social Psychology, 59*, 601–613.

Gilovich, T. (1981). Seeing the past in the present: The effect of associations to familiar events on judgments and decisions. *Journal of Personality and Social Psychology, 40*, 797–808.

Greenwald, A. G. (1972). Evidence for both perceptual filtering and response suppression for rejected messages in selective attention. *Journal of Experimental Psychology, 94*, 58–67.

Hermans, D., DeHouwer, J., & Eelen, P. (1994). The affective priming effect: Automatic activation of evaluative information in memory. *Cognition & Emotion, 8*, 515–533.

Herr, P. M., Sherman, S. J., & Fazio, R. H. (1983). On the consequences of priming: Assimilation and contrast effects. *Journal of Experimental Social Psychology, 19*, 323–340.

Hertel, G., & Fiedler, K. (1994). Affective and cognitive influences in a social dilemma game. *European Journal of Social Psychology, 24*, 131–145.

Higgins, E. T., Rholes, W. S., & Jones, C. R. (1977). Category accessibility and impression formation. *Journal of Experimental Social Psychology, 13*, 141–154.

Johnson, E. J., & Tversky, A. (1983). Affect, generalization, and the perception of risk. *Journal of Personality and Social Psychology, 45*, 20–31.

Johnston, W. A., & Dark, V. J. (1986). Selective attention. *Annual Review of Psychology, 37*, 43–75.

Klauer, K. C., Rossnagel, C., & Musch, J. (1997). List-context effects in evaluative priming. *Journal of Experimental Psychology: Learning, Memory & Cognition, 23*, 246–255.

Koehler, D. J. (1991). Explanation, imagination, and confidence in judgment. *Psychological Bulletin, 110*, 499–519.

Lepore, L., & Brown, R. (1997). Category and stereotype activation: Is prejudice inevitable? *Journal of Personality and Social Psychology, 72*, 275–287.

Lombardi, W. J., Higgins, E. T., & Bargh, J. A. (1987). The role of consciousness in priming effects on categorization: Assimilation versus contrast as a function of awareness of the priming task. *Personality and Social Psychology Bulletin, 13*, 411–429.

Luchins, A. S. (1942). Mechanization in problem solving. *Psychological Monographs, Volume 54.*

Macrae, C. N., Bodenhausen, G. V., & Milne, A. B. (1995). The dissection of selection in person perception: Inhibitory processes in social stereotyping. *Journal of Personality and Social Psychology, 69*, 397–407.

Macrae, C. N., Bodenhausen, G. V., Milne, A. B., & Jetten, J. (1994). Out of mind but back inside: Stereotypes on the rebound. *Journal of Personality and Social Psychology, 67*, 808–817.

Marschak, M., & Surian, L. (1992). Concreteness effects in free recall: The roles of imaginal and relational processing. *Memory and Cognition, 20*, 612–620.

McClelland, J. L., Naughton, B. L., & O'Reilly, R. C. (1995). Why there are complementary learning systems in the hippocampus and neocortex: Insights from the successes and failures of connectionist models of learning and memory. *Psychological Review, 102*, 419–437.

McKoon, G., & Ratcliff, R. (1992). Inference during reading. *Psychological Review, 99*, 440–466.

Meyer, D. E., & Schvaneveldt, R. W. (1971). Facilitation in recognising pairs of words: Evidence of a dependence between retrieval operations. *Journal of Experimental Psychology, 90*, 227–234.

Musch, J. (2000). *Affektives Priming: Kongruenzeffekte bei der evaluativen Bewertung.* (Affective priming: Congruency effects in evaluation). Dissertation, University of Heidelberg.

Neuberg, S. L. (1988). Behavioral implications of information presented outside of conscious awareness: The effect of subliminal presentation of trait information on behavior in the Prisoner's Dilemma Game. *Social Cognition, 6*, 207–230.

Petzold, P. (1992). Context effects in judgments of attributes: An information integration approach. In H. G. Geissler, S. W. Link & J. T. Townsend (Eds.), *Cognition, information processing and psychophysics: Basic issues* (pp. 175–205). Hillsdale, NJ: Lawrence Erlbaum Associates.

Popper, K. R. (1935). *Logik der Forschung.* Tübingen: J. C. B. Mohr.

Ratcliff, R., & McKoon, G. (1996). Bias effects in implicit memory tasks. *Journal of Experimental Psychology: General, 125*, 403–421.

Reeder, G., & Brewer, M. (1979). A schematic model of dispositional attribution in interpersonal perception. *Psychological Review, 86*, 61–79.

Ross, L., Lepper, M. R., & Hubbard, M. (1975). Perseverance in self-perception and social perception: Biased attribution processes in the debriefing paradigm. *Journal of Personality and Social Psychology, 32*, 880–892.

Schwarz, N., & Bless, H. (1992). Constructing reality and its alternatives: An inclusion-exclusion model of assimilation and contrast effects in social judgment. In L. L. Martin & A. Tesser (Eds.), *The construction of social judgment* (pp. 217–245). Hillsdale, NJ: Lawrence Erlbaum Associates.

Seifert, L. S. (1997). Activating representations in semantic memory: Different benefits for pictures and words. *Journal of Experimental Psychology: Learning, Memory and Cognition, 23*, 1106–1121.

Semin, G. R., & Fiedler, K. (1988). The cognitive functions of linguistic categories in describing persons: Social cognition and language. *Journal of Personality and Social Psychology, 54*, 558–568.

Shafto, M., & MacKay, D. G. (2000). The Moses, Mega-Moses, and Armstrong illusions: Integrating language comprehension and semantic memory. *Psychological Science, 11*, 372–378.

Smith, E. R., & Lerner, M. (1986). The development of automatism of social judgments. *Journal of Personality and Social Psychology, 50*, 246–259.

Srull, T. K., & Wyer, R. S. (1980). The role of category accessibility in the interpretation of information about persons: Some determinants and implications. *Journal of Personality and Social Psychology, 37*, 1660–1672.

Stapel, D. A., Koomen, W., & van der Pligt, J. (1996). The referents of trait inferences: The impact of trait concepts versus actor-trait links on subsequent judgments. *Journal of Personality and Social Psychology, 70*, 437–450.

Sweeney, L. T. (2000). *Abstraction, representation, and social cognition.* Unpublished dissertation, Free University of Amsterdam.

Tipper, S. P. (1985). The negative priming effect: Inhibitory priming by ignored objects. *Quarterly Journal of Experimental Psychology, 37A*, 571–590.

Tipper, S. P., & Cranston, M. (1985). Selective attention and priming: Inhibitory and facilitatory effects of ignored primes. *Quarterly Journal of Experimental Psychology, 37A*, 591–611.

Tversky, A., & Hutchinson, J. W. (1986) Nearest neighbor analysis of psychological spaces. *Psychological Review, 93*, 3–22.

Wänke, M., Bless, H., & Igou, E. (2001). Next to a star: Paling, shining, or both? Turning interexamplar contrast into interexemplar assimilation. *Personality and Social Psychology Bulletin, 27*, 14–29.

Wason, P. C. (1960). On the failure to eliminate hypotheses in a conceptual task. *Quarterly Journal of Experimental Psychology, 12*, 129–140.

Wegner, D. M. (1994). Ironic processes of mental control. *Psychological Review, 101*, 34–52.

Wegner, D. M., Wenzlaff, R., Kerker, R. M., & Beattie, A. E. (1981). Incrimination through innuendo: Can media questions become public answers? *Journal of Personality and Social Psychology, 40*, 822–832.

Weldon, M. S., & Roediger, H. L. (1987). Altering retrieval demands reverses the picture-superiority effect. *Memory and Cognition, 15*, 269–280.

Wenzlaff, R. M., & Bates, D. E. (2000). The relative efficacy of concentration and suppression strategies of mental control. *Personality and Social Psychology Bulletin, 26*, 1200–1212.

Wilson, T. D., & Brekke, N. (1994). Mental contamination and mental correction: Unwanted influences on judgments and evaluations. *Psychological Bulletin, 116*, 117–142.

Winter, L., & Uleman, J. S. (1984). When are social judgments made? Evidence for the spontaneousness of trait inferences. *Journal of Personality and Social Psychology, 47*, 237–252.

Wittenbrink, B, Judd, C. M., & Park, B. (1997). Evidence for racial prejudice at the implicit level and its relationship with questionnaire measures. *Journal of Personality and Social Psychology, 72*, 262–274.

II: Evaluative Judgments and the Acquisition of Evaluations

On the Acquisition and Activation of Evaluative Information in Memory: The Study of Evaluative Learning and Affective Priming Combined

Dirk Hermans
Frank Baeyens
Paul Eelen*
University of Leuven, Belgium

THE AUTOMATIC EVALUATION HYPOTHESIS

Theoretical contributions from domains as diverse as learning psychology (Martin & Levey, 1978), social psychology (Zajonc, 1980), neurophysiology (Le Doux, 1989), and cognitively inspired emotion research (e.g., Öhman, 1987; Scherer, 1993) have put forward the idea that the human cognitive system is endowed with a mechanism that automatically evaluates all incoming stimulus information as "good/positive/pleasant" or "bad/negative/unpleasant." This evaluative process is assumed to occur very early in the track of information processing operations, to be rather crude and undifferentiated, and to occur independently of the conscious awareness of the instigating stimulus, an evaluative processing goal, and the presence of ample cognitive resources (Hermans, 1996). Also, the output of this affective decision mechanism is believed to color our perception and (evaluative) responses toward the activating stimuli or events (e.g., Fazio, Roskos-Ewoldsen, & Powell, 1994). The assumption of such a basic automatic evaluative

*Dirk Hermans and Frank Baeyens are postdoctoral researchers for the Fund for Scientific Research (Flanders, Belgium), Department of Psychology, University of Leuven, Belgium; Paul Eelen, Department of Psychology, University of Leuven, Belgium.

Correspondence concerning this manuscript should be addressed to Dirk Hermans, Department of Psychology, University of Leuven, Tiensestraat 102, B-3000 Leuven, Belgium. Electronic mail may be sent to Dirk.Hermans@psy.kuleuven.ac.be mechanism or process is certainly not new. Authors like Arnold (1960), Lazarus (1966) and even Wundt advocated its existence.

Given the significance of this automatic stimulus evaluation hypothesis within several domains of psychology, its seemingly functional importance, and the fact that is quite an "old" hypothesis, it is rather surprising that the experimental analysis of automatic stimulus evaluation only commenced about 15 years ago (Hermans & Eelen, 1997). Without doubt it has been the original publication by Russell Fazio and coworkers on automatic attitude activation that has fueled this research (Fazio, Sanbonmatsu, Powell, & Kardes, 1986). They reported a series of studies in which a variant of the standard sequential priming procedure was used. In this variant the affective relation between primes and targets was manipulated. On each trial, a noun was presented for 200 ms on a computer monitor. This prime stimulus could be either positive, negative, or a string of three identical letters (e.g., BBB), and was followed by the target after a 100 ms blank-screen interval. Participants were instructed to indicate whether the target-adjective had a positive or negative connotation by pressing one of two keys as quickly as possible. It was found that responses to the target words were facilitated if both prime and target had the same valence, but were inhibited if they were of opposite valence, as compared to the control trials for which the prime was a three-letter string. These results were observed in three succeeding experiments and provided support for the authors' assumption that attitudes can be activated on the mere presentation of the attitude object (c.q., the prime).

Fazio's contribution to the study of automatic stimulus evaluation is not restricted to the development of this elegant research paradigm, but also pertains to the way he conceptualized attitudes and their automatic activation (e.g., Fazio, 1986, 1990). According to Fazio, attitudes should be viewed as "an association in memory between a given object and one's evaluation of that object" (Fazio, 1990a, p. 81). When perceiving an attitude object, the memory representation of this stimulus or event will be activated, which in turn automatically leads to the activation of the evaluation associated with it. This evaluation can be considered as a kind of general positive or negative evaluative tag directly linked to the memory representation of the relevant stimulus/event (for similar accounts, see Bower, 1991; De Houwer & Hermans, 1994; Fiske & Pavelchak, 1986). According to Fazio, automatic attitude activation is dependent on the strength of the association between the memory representation of the attitude object and this evaluative tag. He argued that only in cases of relatively highly accessible attitudes (i.e., in case of strong object-evaluation associations), the mere observation of an attitude object would lead to its automatic evaluation.

It was only after 6 years that new studies were published that further elaborated on this first clear empirical evidence for the automatic stimulus evaluation hypothesis. In 1992, John Bargh and colleagues (Bargh, Chaiken, Govender, & Pratto, 1992) reported a series of studies that examined Fazio's claim that automatic activation effects are confined to stimuli for which there exists a relatively highly accessible attitude. Without going into the details of the subsequent debate (see Bargh, Chaiken, Raymond, & Hymes, 1996; Fazio, 1993a, 1993b, 1995; Chaiken & Bargh, 1993), we simply want to highlight that—although relevant for other domains in psychology—the priming experiments reported by Fazio and Bargh and the related discussion on the generality of this priming effect remained largely unknown to researchers outside the domain of attitude research. In a similar vein, later research with this priming paradigm has been mainly carried out by a strong group of experimental social psychologists interested in attitude research and social cognition (e.g., Greenwald, Klinger, & Schuh, 1995; Klauer, Rossnagel, & Musch, 1997; Otten & Wentura, 1999; Rothermund & Wentura, 1998; Wentura, 1999, 2000).

Given our own interest in the study of the processes that are involved in the generation of emotions (e.g., Hermans & De Houwer, 1993), we were highly interested in the automatic attitude research because it supported the idea of automatic stimulus evaluation that is part of several major models on emotion generation (e.g., Scherer, 1993; Öhman, 1987). And, because it was our conviction that results from the priming procedure that was developed by Fazio could be of great interest for emotion researchers, we have sent our first data from this paradigm to journals like *Cognition and Emotion* and *Behaviour Research and Therapy* (Hermans, De Houwer, & Eelen, 1994, 1996). It was also within this attempt to introduce this literature to emotion researchers that we chose to use the term *affective priming paradigm* rather than *attitude activation paradigm* (Hermans et al., 1994).

But, given that the automatic evaluation idea is an "old" and quite general hypothesis that is prevalent in several domains of psychology, and given that its strongest empirical support stems from affective priming research, we believe that this research deserves an even more widespread translation. Conversely, other areas of research may provide an interesting input to the study of attitudes and their automatic activation. For instance, it is interesting to note that research on the *activation* of attitudes from memory has developed quite separately from the study of how these attitudes are *acquired.* With respect to this latter issue, recent research on evaluative conditioning is highly relevant, as it provides an insight of how evaluative information gets stored in memory. Although these evaluative conditioning studies are rooted in learning psychology, it is our conviction that attitude as well as emotion research might benefit from a better understanding of these studies. And more specifically, we believe that a fruitful cross-fertilization would result from the combination of research on evaluative learning and automatic stimulus evaluation. These points will be elucidated in the remainder of this chapter.

There are essentially two pathways to the acquisition of evaluation that have received attention from within learning psychology. The first pathway pertains to a nonassociative way of evaluative acquisition due to repeated exposure to a stimulus or event. This phenomenon is also more generally known as the *mere exposure effect*, and will be discussed only briefly. For a more extensive review of this literature, we refer to Winkielman, Schwarz, Fazendeiro, & Reber (chap. 8, this volume). The second route will be discussed in more detail in the first part of the chapter (On the acquisition of evaluative information) and mainly pertains to the studies on evaluative learning that have been conducted at our laboratory in Leuven. This vast amount of experimental work has provided fundamental knowledge about the processes by which originally neutral stimuli acquire a positive or negative meaning. In the second part of the chapter (On the activation of evaluative information) we discuss the representation of evaluation in memory and will provide a short overview of the paradigms that have been employed in the study of automatic stimulus evaluation (for a more detailed discussion we refer to Klauer & Musch, chap. 2, this volume, and De Houwer, chap. 9, this volume). In a final round (Acquisition and activation of evaluative information combined) we discuss a series of very recent studies in which the automatic activation of recently acquired stimulus valence was investigated. We end with a discussion on how the combined study of acquisition and activation of evaluative information might proceed.

ON THE ACQUISITION OF EVALUATIVE INFORMATION

Evaluative Conditioning as an Associative Route to Valence Acquisition

Learning theories essentially describe two routes of valence acquisition. The first route can be characterized as a nonassociative route, and is typically illustrated by studies that show that repeated unreinforced exposure to a stimulus has been found to lead to an increase in liking for that stimulus (e.g., Bornstein & D'Agostino, 1994; Mandler, Nakamura, & van Zandt, 1987; Zajonc, 1968, 1980). This finding is referred to as the mere exposure effect and has repeatedly been demonstrated in supraliminal as well as subliminal versions of the mere exposure paradigm (e.g., Bornstein, 1989; Bornstein & D'Agostino, 1994). Mere exposure can be viewed as a nonassociative way of valence acquisition. In contrast to the associative type of valence acquisition, which is essentially based on the learning of an association between two stimuli/events, mere exposure is based on the (repeated) presentation of a single stimulus. Although different procedures of valence acquisition do not necessarily involve different underlying processes, it can be assumed that processes of mere exposure are quite different from the processes that are involved in associative valence acquisition. For a more detailed discussion on the processes that are responsible for mere exposure effects we refer to Klinger and Greenwald (1994), Seamon, Williams, Crowley, and Kim (1995), and Winkielman et al. (chap. 8, this volume).

The remainder of this chapter is focused on the second route to the acquisition of valence. This route is associative in nature, and is essentially based on the contiguous or contingent pairing of originally neutral stimuli with events that already have some positive or negative valence. For instance, children may learn to like orange flavor because of the mere repeated spatio-temporal co-occurrence of orange flavor with the agreeable sweetness of sugar, abundantly being present in the average orange soft drink. It needs no argument that this path to stimulus valence may be approached from the Pavlovian associative learning perspective. As such, the concept of *evaluative conditioning* (or *evaluative learning*) was introduced precisely to refer to the observation that the mere spatio-temporal co-occurrence of a neutral stimulus X (Conditioned Stimulus, CS) with a valenced stimulus Y (Unconditioned Stimulus, US), may result in the originally neutral stimulus X itself acquiring an evaluative meaning that is congruent with the valence of Y.

Without doubt, this form of learning can be considered as a major source of acquired stimulus valence. Moreover, the firm and empirically rich research tradition on evaluative conditioning that has its foundation at our laboratory in Leuven (for an overview, see Baeyens, Vansteenwegen, Hermans, & Eelen, 2001) not only gained a lot of interest within learning psychology over the last decade, but also forms the basis of one of the few empirically grounded psychological theories that explain and give a detailed account of the origins of stimulus valence.

In the first series of experiments on evaluative conditioning, Baeyens and colleagues made use of a modified version of an experimental procedure that was originally developed by Levey and Martin (1975). In a prototypical experiment (see for example Baeyens, Eelen, & Van den Bergh, 1990a), a cover story was used in which research participants were led to believe that they participated in a psychophysiological study investigating the relationship between the subjective evaluation of and electrodermal responding to visual stimuli. In order to increase the plausibility of the cover story, participants got a detailed explanation of the measurement of skin conductance responses, electrodes were actually attached to participants' hand, and all further instructions were centered on the so-called psychophysiological measurement. Color pictures of human faces were used as stimulus materials. In the first phase, participants were invited to evaluate each of these pictures based on their first, spontaneous, and overall impression. Next, the experimenter selected the 12 most neutral (N), the 3 most liked (L) and the 3 most disliked (D) pictures, and constructed 9 stimulus pairs out of this stimulus set: 3 N-L pairs, 3 N-D pairs, and finally 3 N-N control pairs. The real hypothesis was that the repeated pair-wise presentation of a neutral picture of a face with a picture of a face that already had a strong negative or positive value, would be a sufficient condition to change the originally neutral picture into a stimulus with negative or positive valence. Hence, during the second phase of the experiment, color slides of the 9 CS–US pairs were projected 10 times in a random order (CS and US presentation duration = 1 sec.; inter-stimulus-interval (ISI) = 3 sec.), while the participant was watching attentively and "skin conductance changes were registered throughout the stimulus presentation series". In the third and final phase, the participant was asked to rate the pictures again. As a justification of this second evaluative rating, it was explained that "for a correct interpretation of the electrodermal responses, the current subjective evaluation of each of the pictures had to be known, whereby it did not matter whether the evaluation of the faces had remained the same or had changed in comparison to the first rating: The only thing that mattered was to indicate how they felt about the pictures right now."

Results that stem from such evaluative conditioning procedure typically show that after a neutral picture of a human face has repeatedly been paired with a liked (or disliked) picture of another face, research participants demonstrate an acquired liking (or disliking) for the originally neutral face. This basic phenomenon has now been documented in forward, backward, and simultaneous conditioning preparations, using CSs and USs of visual, auditory, and gustatory-olfactory sensory modalities (for an overview, see Baeyens et al., 2001; De Houwer, Thomas, & Baeyens, 2001; Hermans & Baeyens, in press).

Characteristics of Evaluative Conditioning

Although the procedural similarities with human Pavlovian autonomic conditioning preparations are obvious, evidence is accumulating indicating that the processes and the representational structure underlying evaluative conditioning are different from those involved in the prototypical tone-shock conditioning paradigm, measuring autonomic responses (heart rate or skin conductance) as indices of learning (e.g., Dawson & Shell, 1987). As argued elsewhere (Baeyens, Eelen, & Crombez, 1995b), this last type of learning may be properly conceived of as an instance of signal-learning referring to the process by which a CS acquires the capacity to generate the expectation of a US-going-to-occur-here-and-now. In the spirit of the information processing approach, this type of classical conditioning can be conceptualized as a phenomenon the quintessence of which is the acquisition of (propositional) knowledge about predictive relations between stimuli in the environment (Davey, 1987; Dawson & Shell, 1985, 1987; Öhman, 1986). According to this view, the most important function of Pavlovian conditioning is the detection of reliable predictors or signals (CSs) for the occurrence of biologically significant environmental stimuli (USs)—hence the label *signal learning* or *expectancy-learning*. This type of learning (at least in humans) depends on the participants' awareness of the crucial CS–US relation; it is sensitive to extinction manipulations, and it is determined by the objective statistical nature of the CS–US contingency (Dawson & Shell, 1987).

The results of research concerning these three functional properties in evaluative conditioning justify distinguishing evaluative learning from expectancy-learning (Baeyens et al., 1995b). The first issue bears on the role of explicit knowledge about the CS–US relation, (i.e., *contingency-awareness*). In contrast to expectancy learning, which has repeatedly been shown to require awareness of the CS–US contingency, evidence is accumulating from several paradigms that contingency awareness is *not* a necessary condition for evaluative conditioning (e.g., Baeyens, Eelen, & Van den Bergh, 1990a; De Houwer, Baeyens, & Eelen, 1994). For instance, evaluative flavor–flavor learning has been demonstrated to be possible in the complete absence of the conscious identification of the CS–US flavor contingencies (Baeyens, Eelen, Van den Bergh, & Crombez, 1990b; Baeyens, Crombez, De Houwer, & Eelen, 1996).

The two other relevant properties of evaluative conditioning pertain to the interrelated phenomena of *extinction* and *contingency-sensitivity*. Indeed, in contrast with expectancy-learning, evaluative learning seems not to be influenced by unreinforced CS presentations, either during (contingency–sensitivity) or after acquisition (extinction).

First, with respect to the procedure of *extinction*, Baeyens, Crombez, Van den Bergh, and Eelen (1988) found that 5 or even 10 unreinforced presentations of the CS did not have any influence on the evaluative value that was acquired as the result of 10 previous CS–US pairings. The conditioned valence was completely unaffected by the nonreinforced CS presentations. Also, 2 months after the acquisition/extinction phase, the evaluative conditioning effect was still observed, both for a subgroup tested in the original acquisition/extinction context and for a subgroup tested in a new test room. Baeyens and colleagues replicated these results in a study in which, after 10 CS–US acquisition trials, on a within-subject base some CSs were given 10 unreinforced extinction presentations, some CSs were no longer presented, and some CSs were involved in a 10-trial counterconditioning contingency (Baeyens, Eden, Van den Bergh, & Crombez, 1989). The same amount of evaluative differentiation was observed for CSs that had been involved in the extinction treatment as for CSs that had no longer been presented in the second phase of the experiment; quite differently, the counterconditioning procedure clearly was effective in altering the acquired CS valence. This finding seems not restricted to the picture–picture pairing paradigm. In a recent series of evaluative flavor–flavor association experiments, in which a flavor CS (e.g., Apricot) is presented during acquisition in compound with a very disliked flavor US (Tween20 = Polysorbate 20), we repeatedly observed that the acquired dislike for the CS-flavor is still present in an unattenuated form after an extended number of nonreinforced test presentations (e.g., Baeyens, Crombez, Hendrickx, & Eelen, 1995a; see also Baeyens et al., 1996; and for further critical discussion, see De Houwer, Baeyens, Vansteenwegen, & Eelen, 2000).

Second, with respect to the role of *contingency* (which refers to the statistical correlation between the CS and US, and which is the best criterion to distinguish between stimuli (CSs) that may or may not function as predictors of US occurrence), Baeyens, Hermans, and Eelen (1993) demonstrated that different levels of CS–US contingency did not result in significantly different levels of conditioning. Even more conclusive with respect to the idea that effects of evaluative conditioning are not dependent on statistical contingencies stem from the flavor-flavor conditioning paradigm. For instance, Baeyens et al. (1996) showed that an acquisition schedule containing an equal number of reinforced and nonreinforced flavor trials results in an equally strong acquired flavor dislike as an acquisition schedule containing the same number of reinforced but no unreinforced learning trials.

These findings with respect to contingency-awareness, extinction, and manipulations of the statistical contingency between the CS and UCS have been the basis on which evaluative conditioning has been defined as a prototypical example of *referential learning* (Baeyens et al., 1995b; Baeyens, Vansteenwegen, Hermans, & Eelen, 2001). This type of learning is assumed to result from the (conscious or unconscious) registration of co-occurrences between neutral and valenced events. At the subjective level, it may give rise to "intrinsic" changes in CS valence. At the level of the underlying representational structure, it is based on an association between CS and US representations, such that the activation of the CS activates the US representation (makes the S "think of the US"), without additionally creating the expectation that the US is really going-to-occur-in-the-immediate-future. The synchronous activation of CS and US representations results in an increase of associative strength, whereas the activation of the representation of the CS alone (or of the US alone) is causally ineffective.

Interim Conclusion Concerning the Acquisition of Stimulus Valence

Research suggests that there are associative as well as nonassociative routes to the acquisition of stimulus valence. The mere exposure effect is an example of a nonassociative account: The mere presentation of a stimulus leads to a change in evaluation. The second route that has been described here—

evaluative conditioning—is a case example of an associative account of valence acquisition. This research domain encompasses a rich empirical literature and offers a theoretical model for the understanding of valence acquisition in terms of learned associations between memory representations of previously neutral and positively or negatively valenced stimuli or events.

ON THE ACTIVATION OF EVALUATIVE INFORMATION

Before discussing the reaction time paradigms that have been used to study the automatic activation of (recently acquired) evaluations, we first discuss the representational structures that underlie this automatic activation. Although related, this question is different from the question of how automatic evaluation influences subsequent behavior in these reaction time procedures (see Moss, Ostrin, Tyler, & Marslen-Wilson, 1995). For further discussion on the mechanisms of affective priming and related tasks, we refer to De Houwer (chap. XX, this volume), Klauer and Musch (chap. XX, this volume), and Wentura and Rothermund (chap. XX, this volume). The issue of the representational structures underlying the automatic activation of evaluative information essentially pertains to the way evaluative information is represented in memory (Hermans, Van den Broeck, & Eelen, 1998).

The Representation of Evaluative Information

Given that evaluative conditioning research indicates that evaluative meaning can be acquired by way of associative processes, the question arises of where and how this acquired evaluative information is stored in memory. The answer to this question is codetermined by the broader perspective that one holds on human memory. For instance, the representation of stimulus valence has recently been framed within a connectionist framework (Spruyt, Hermans, De Houwer, & Eelen, 2002). Most often, however, the representation of evaluation (c.q., affect, attitudes) has been discussed in terms of associative network models of human memory (e.g., Bower, 1981, 1991; Fiske & Pavelchak, 1986).

Based on their research concerning the differences in the affective processes of words and pictures, De Houwer and Hermans (1994) have argued that evaluative information is stored in semantic memory. This research was inspired by a theory of Glaser and Glaser (1989), who proposed a distinction between a semantic and a lexical memory system. The semantic system controls, via an executive system, the perception of pictures and the action on physical objects. Likewise, the lexicon is thought to be responsible for the perception and production of spoken and written language. As a consequence of this architecture, De Houwer and Hermans (1994) argued that unless semantic responses have to be provided about words, the processing of words can proceed without any interference of evaluative information (or other types of semantic information). In contrast, because pictures have privileged access to the semantic system, their processing is much more easily influenced by all kinds of semantic information, including evaluative information. These assumptions have been sustained by research employing affective variants of the Stroop paradigm (De Houwer & Hermans, 1994) and the priming paradigm (De Houwer, Hermans, & Spruyt, 2001; Spruyt, Hermans, De Houwer, & Eelen, 2002).

Given that evaluative information is stored in a semantic system and not in the lexicon, and given that we proceed from an associative view on human memory, how then should the representation of evaluative information be conceptualised? We start this discussion with the attitude accessibility model (Fazio, 1986) that was described before. According to Fazio, attitudes should be viewed as an association in memory between the representation of a stimulus or event and its summary evaluation (in terms of the positive–negative dimension) (Fazio, 1995). The strength of this association is different for different attitude objects and can change over time due to new experiences with the attitude object. Automatic attitude activation hence refers to the situation in which the presentation of the attitude object results in the activation of its memory representation and immediately leads to the automatic activation of the related attitude/evaluation.[1]

The model proposed by Fazio, however, does not tell how these summary evaluations are acquired and structured. The reformulation of Bower's original theory on mood and memory (Bower, 1981) is interesting from this perspective. The way in which stimulus valence is represented within this model (Bower, 1991) shows striking similarity with the view proposed by Fazio. Yet, one of the differences is that not one, but two evaluative labels are associated to memory representations, which correspond to positive and negative valence respectively. This double evaluative representation allows concepts to have an ambiguous evaluative meaning, and corresponds with the view of Cacioppo and Berntson (1994) that a single bipolar evaluative dimension (positive–negative) is not sufficient to comprehensively portray the evaluative meaning of stimuli. These authors prefer to define stimuli by situating them in a two-dimensional evaluative space, in

---

[1]Although Fazio's model is framed in terms of *attitudes* and *attitude objects*, it basically pertains to the activation of positive or negative *evaluations*. Besides *attitude* and *evaluation*, a term that has sometimes been used in a way that makes it interchangeable with the two previous concepts is *affect*. For instance, referring to his own research, Fazio stated that: "Thus, the research essentially addresses how *affect* might be activated from memory." (Fazio et al., 1986, p. 236, italics added). It is our belief that although these concepts are highly compatible, the use of different terms within different types of literature has hindered translation between these domains.

which each stimulus can be positioned according to the amount of positive and negative affect associated with it. Hence, *more positive* does not necessarily imply *less negative.*

According to Bower (1991), positive and/or negative experiences with a specific stimulus or event will lead to a stronger positive and/or negative valence of that stimulus or event. This valence is not necessarily mediated by the representations of those specific experiences, as there also may exist a direct link between the memory representation of the stimulus/event and the positive and negative evaluative labels. An important implication of this model is that even if the specific individual experiences are forgotten, a strong evaluative meaning can remain attached to the memory representation. Due to the repeated strengthening, the direct association with the global positive or negative label can become stronger than the associations with the individual events that were the basis for this positive/negative evaluation. A related (but not identical) point has been made by learning theorists who have argued that a US should be conceived of as a multiproperty event involving several levels of representation, each of which can entertain separate associative links with a CS. Wagner and Brandon (1989), for example, proposed a distinction between *emotional-affective* and *sensory-descriptive* properties and corresponding levels of a US representation. The emotional representation is argued to be more general than the sensory representation of a US, in that it may be shared by several, perceptually different discrete USs. For example, quinine and salt solutions have clearly distinctive perceptual characteristics and as such involve different sensory-descriptive representations, but probably share the same emotional-affective representation, in that both are bad-tasting, disliked USs. Of direct concern to our present discussion is that these dual US-representation models thus allow for the possibility that a CS is *only* associated with the emotional-affective representation, or *also* with the sensory-descriptive representation of a US, paralleling Bowers distinction between direct associations between a CS and positive/negative evaluative labels, versus associations between the CS and specific US experiences or events.

The direct link between the memory representation and the evaluative label(s) is analogous to the object-evaluation association described by Fazio (1986; Fazio et al., 1986). An important advantage of the model by Bower is, however, that it also gives an account of the way this association is built up. Positive or negative encounters with a stimulus/event lead to associations in memory between the representation of the stimulus/event and the representation of these positive or negative experiences. So far, the model parallels what we have said about evaluative conditioning: Co-occurrence of a neutral (CS) and a positive or negative stimulus (US) leads to the formation of CS-US associations, and presentation of the CS will activate the representation of the US and hence its evaluative meaning. When one has had different kinds of experiences (USs) associated with a specific stimulus (CS), the model of Bower additionally states that the evaluative meaning of that stimulus can be directly accessible without the involvement of the different, specific CS–US associations. At the moment being there is, however, not much research that supports this latter assumption. Given that in most studies on evaluative conditioning CSs were coupled with only one (positive or negative) US, this literature also has little to say about the possibility that such direct object-evaluation associations develop after time. In this respect, it would be interesting if future studies on evaluative conditioning would also employ CSs that are associated with multiple USs.

Given that most research on the automatic activation of evaluative information as yet did not deal with the "acquisition" part, this research has mainly employed stimulus materials for which quite strong, stable, and relatively highly accessible attitudes exist. Traditional affective priming studies, for example, have used stimuli that were either normatively or ideographically selected because of their clear positive or negative valence. In our own research, we have employed words like *love, disease,* and *humor* (Hermans, Crombez, & Eelen, 2000c), odors like citrus, cinnamon, or peppermint (Hermans, Baeyens, & Eelen, 1998), and pictures of persons and objects like a shotgun, a flower, or an atom bomb explosion (Hermans, De Houwer, & Eelen, 1994, 1996). There is no doubt that for these kinds of stimuli there exists an elaborate series of experiences that have accumulated over different kinds of situations and sources (direct experience, observation, information), which have shaped the positive or negative evaluative meaning that is associated to them. Or, in terms of Bowers model, for these stimuli there will most probably exist an object-evaluation association that is much stronger than the associations between the stimulus and the various separate experiences.

The central question of this chapter is now whether stimuli for which a positive or negative evaluative meaning was only recently acquired, also elicit their valence in an automatic fashion. For these stimuli there is no extensive learning history and their valence might be merely based on a few occasional contiguous presentations with a positive (or negative) stimulus. In the final part of this chapter we review the evidence for the automatic evaluation of recently acquired stimulus valence. But before doing so, we first briefly discuss the paradigms that have been used to study automatic stimulus evaluation.

The Activation of Evaluative Information: The Research Paradigms

Several paradigms have been employed to study the activation of evaluative information from memory. All are reaction time tasks in which participants have to respond to specific stimuli or stimulus features, and in which the facilitating or inhibiting influence of the valence of an irrelevant stimulus or stimulus feature is investigated. As such, these tasks can be considered as indirect measures of stimulus valence. The four most widely used paradigms are the affective priming task, the implicit association test, the emotional Stroop task (e.g., Pratto & John, 1991), and the affective Simon task (e.g., De Houwer & Eelen, 1998; De Houwer, Hermans, & Eelen, 1998b). As our focus, in the remainder of this chapter, will be more on the affective priming task and the implicit association test, we refer to De Houwer (chap. XX, this volume) for a more detailed discussion on the affective Simon task and the emotional Stroop task.

The *Implicit Association Test* (IAT; Greenwald, McGhee, & Schwartz, 1998), measures the degree to which a participant associates two conceptual categories, without requiring a direct, conscious evaluation of the association. The presumption of the task is that, generally speaking, when a task requires the same response (e.g., pressing a particular key) to be used for two associated stimuli, response times should be faster than when the identical response is used for two unrelated stimuli. In a first experiment by Greenwald et al. (1998), participants viewed a series of flower names (e.g., azalea, crocus, iris), insect names (e.g., bedbug, centipede, fly), positive words (e.g., laughter, paradise, vacation), and negative words (e.g., grief, poison, stink). Participants were asked to press one of two keys depending on the category of the word (flower, insect, positive, negative). Because instances of the category "flower" generally have a more positive valence than instances of the "insect" category, one would expect a stronger association in memory between insects and negative valence, and between flowers and positive valence. Hence, Greenwald et al. (1998) predicted better reaction time performance when responses to flowers and positive words were assigned to the same key (and insects and negative words to the other key), than when flowers and negative words are mapped to the same key (and insects and positive words to the other key). Confirming expectation, consistently superior performance was indeed observed when associatively compatible (compared with associatively noncompatible) categories were mapped onto the same response.

Since the original publication by Greenwald et al. (1998), the IAT has been successfully employed in a number of research domains, including the study of prejudice (e.g., Rudman et al., 1999), self-esteem (e.g., Greenwald & Farnham, 2000), attitude–behaviour consistency (Swanson, Rudman, & Greenwald, 2001), and vulnerability to recurrence in depression (Gemar, Segal, Sagrati, & Kennedy, 2001). More research is needed to reveal the exact nature of the processes that are responsible for IAT effects (see also De Houwer, chap. XX, this volume).

The *affective priming task* is probably the most influential of the procedures that have been employed to study automatic stimulus evaluation.

Since Fazio et al. (1986) introduced this procedure (see introduction), literally dozens of affective priming studies have been conducted and reported. A rather complete overview of these studies has been provided by Klauer and Musch (chap. XX, this volume). Hence, we confine ourselves to a short overview on the generality of the affective priming effect.

Affective priming has been demonstrated for stimuli as diverse as ideographically as well as normatively selected *words* (e.g., Bargh et al., 1992; Hermans et al., 2000c; Klauer, Rossnagel, & Musch, 1997), *simple line drawings* (Giner-Sorolla, Garcia, & Bargh, 1999), *complex real life colour pictures* (Fazio, Jackson, Dunton, & Williams, 1995; Hermans et al., 1994), *regular versus atonal combinations of tones* (Reber, Haerter, & Sollberger, 1999), and *odors* (Hermans, Baeyens, & Eelen, 1998). Moreover, affective priming effects have been demonstrated using different types of tasks, such as *evaluative categorization* (e.g., Bargh et al., 1992; Fazio et al., 1986; Hermans et al., 1994; Klauer, Rossnagel, & Musch, 1997), *lexical decisions* (Wentura, 2000), and *naming* (Bargh et al., 1996; De Houwer, Hermans, & Spruyt, 2001; Hermans et al., 1994; Hermans, De Houwer, & Eelen, 2001; Giner-Sorolla et al., 1999; Glaser & Banaji, 1999; Spruyt et al., 2000; but see Klauer & Musch, 2000).

Also, there is ample research that indicates that the processes on which the affective priming effect are based are automatic in the sense that they are fast and short-lived (Hermans et al., 2001; Klauer et al., 1997), do not depend on an explicit evaluative goal (*intention characteristic of automaticity*; e.g., Bargh et al., 1996; Hermans et al., 1994), or on the presence of ample processing resources (*efficiency characteristic*; Hermans, Crombez, & Eelen, 2000c), and can even be observed for subliminally presented primes (*awareness characteristic*; e.g., Draine & Greenwald, 1998; Greenwald, Klinger, & Liu, 1989; Greenwald, Klinger, & Schuh, 1995; Hermans, 1996).

Indirect but reliable support for the automatic character of affective priming effects stems from studies in which the stimulus onset asynchrony (SOA; i.e., the interval between the onset of the prime and the onset of the target) was manipulated (e.g., Fazio et al., 1986; Hermans et al., 1994, 2001; Klauer et al., 1997). In a standard affective priming study, the prime is presented for only 200 milliseconds and is followed by the target after an interval of 50 or 100 milliseconds, resulting in an SOA of 250 or 300 milliseconds. When in the aforementioned studies the SOA was prolonged to 1000 ms, the priming effects disappeared. This absence of priming effects at the longer SOAs provides indirect, but rather strong evidence for the idea that priming effects at the short SOAs (SOA 0, 150, 300; see Hermans et al., 2001) are not the product of specific, conscious response strategies, because one would predict stronger or at least similar results if participants are provided with more time to process the prime-target relation (i.e., at the longer SOAs). This is because such controlled strategies are generally assumed to be time-consuming (Hermans et al., 2001). Hence, when short SOAs are employed, the affective priming procedure is an ideal research instrument to investigate automatic stimulus evaluation.

ACQUISITION AND ACTIVATION OF EVALUATIVE INFORMATION COMBINED

After this brief overview on the IAT and the affective priming procedure, we now discuss some very recent research in which both procedures were used to study the automatic evaluation of stimulus valence that was recently acquired by means of associative acquisition procedures.[2]

Affective Priming of Evaluatively Conditioned Stimuli

In a series of experiments by De Houwer, Hermans, and Eelen (1998a), the affective priming procedure was used as an index of stimulus valence that was acquired by means of a prior associative learning phase. These experiments started with a learning phase during which participants had to learn nonword–word pairs. Participants were told that they would see Turkish words (i.e., the nonwords) together with their Dutch translations. The cover story was that we wanted to investigate how fast they could learn the meaning of the Turkish words. For each individual subject, the computer program randomly assigned each nonword (e.g., bayram) with either an ex-

---

[2]With respect to research in which IAT or priming paradigms were used to assess evaluative stimulus meaning that was acquired by means of a nonassociative procedure, we are only aware of recent work by Mitchell, Anderson, and McDonough (2000). These authors employed the IAT to investigate whether a procedure of mere exposure effectively leads to changes in the affective character of the previously exposed stimuli. In a first study, Mitchell et al. were able to demonstrate that nonwords that had been previously presented nine times each, were more easily classified when the response that had to be emitted (pressing left or right for "novel" or "familiar") for these stimuli was the same as the response (pressing left or right for "nice" or "nasty") that was assigned for the classification of positive personality trait words (as compared to negative words). An opposite pattern was present for the stimuli to which participants were not pre-exposed. These IAT results could hence be seen as evidence for the fact that unreinforced exposure to stimuli increases the preference for those stimuli. In two subsequent studies, Mitchell ruled out some possible alternative explanations and further improved the paradigm. In a final experiment, Mitchell asked participants to categorise pictures of mountains or food as "mountain" or "food", and to categorise positive and negative personality trait words as "nice" and "nasty" respectively. This was done after the participants were familiarised to the pictures of the mountains or the pictures of the food stimuli. Although this procedure precluded specific alternative interpretations with respect to response effects, IAT data again indicated that pre-exposed stimuli were preferred to novel stimuli. These data led Mitchell to conclude that effects of mere exposure should not solely be attributed to a nonaffective and nonspecific activation account (Mandler, Nakamura, & Van Zandt, 1987).

isting positive (e.g., honest) or an existing negative word (e.g., death). Each of these 10 pairs was presented four times. After a recall task during which we tested whether the participant had actually learned the translation of the "Turkish" words, a priming phase was run using the nonwords and words of the learning phase. Nonwords always served as primes, existing words as targets. Prime and target were presented sequentially and could be related in three ways: The target could be (a) the word that was associated to the nonword-prime during the learning phase (e.g., bayram-death; identity congruent), (b) a different word but with the same affective connotation (e.g., bayram - lonely; affectively congruent), (c) a word with a different affective connotation (e.g., bayram-happy; incongruent). Results showed a significant effect of identity priming. But more important, there was also a significant affective priming effect (De Houwer et al., 1998a, Experiments 1 & 3). If participants had previously learned that "bayram" denoted something negative, this Turkish word facilitated evaluative responses to negative targets relative to positive targets, while the opposite was true when the participant had learned that "bayram" was the translation of a more positive word (e.g., soft). In a further experiment it was demonstrated that this affective priming effect for recently acquired stimulus valence was sensitive to a manipulation of the SOA (De Houwer et al., 1998a, Experiment 3). In this study a reliable priming effect was observed at SOA 300, but not at SOA 1000. This further substantiates the automatic character of the observed priming effects. Hence, it can be concluded from these studies that stimulus valence that is recently acquired by means of an instructed learning task can be automatically activated. Given that the accessibility of this acquired valence was only weak (Experiment 4), these data cast doubt on Fazio's (Fazio, 1986, Fazio et al., 1986) claim that the automatic processing of stimulus valence requires the presence of a strong stimulus-valence association in memory.

In the experiments reported by De Houwer et al. (1998a) an acquisition procedure was employed that somewhat differs from the procedures that are typically used in evaluative conditioning research, in that participants were "instructed" to learn a relation between the CS and the US. In traditional evaluative conditioning research, participants are merely exposed to the contingent presentation of the CS and the US. An important question is then whether such "instructed" learning phase is a necessary precondition to obtain affective priming effects.

Results from a study by reported by Hermans and Baeyens (in press) shed some light on this issue. In this study, it was investigated whether it is possible to (1) effectively use positive and negative odors as USs in a an evaluative conditioning procedure with neutral pictures of objects as CSs, and (2) whether the newly acquired valence of the picture-CSs in turn exert an automatic affective influence, as measured by an affective priming procedure. A group of students from different faculties participated in this study. Because gender differences in odor perception have been abundantly reported (see also, Hermans, Baeyens, & Eelen, 1998), half of the participants were female. The CSs used in this study were four different color pictures of a bottle of washing-up liquid. Each picture displayed a different bottle. These pictures were placed in separate plastic, transparent freezer bags, together with a piece of cotton wool. For one of these pictures (CSpositive) a pleasant odor was dropped on the cotton wool, whereas for a second picture (CSnegative) a negative odor was dropped on the piece of cotton wool. For the last two pictures (CSneutral) that served as controls, there was no odor. As part of the cover story an electrode was attached to the participants' right hand, and they were told "the experiment was designed to determine whether there is a relationship between preferences for complex sensory stimuli and physiological (skin conductance) responses to those stimuli, and whether these skin conductance responses depend on preferences for these visual and olfactory stimuli." The order in which the four CS–US pairs were presented, was randomized for each participant. On each trial, the participant was asked to look at the picture, to open the bag and to sniff it, to close the bag again, and finally to take a second look at the picture. For each CS–US pair, there were eight acquisition trials. At the end of the acquisition phase, participants were asked to rate each of the four CSs for valence and attractiveness.

Results showed that there was a strong effect of evaluative conditioning. The CSpositive was generally rated as more attractive and pleasant than the CSnegative. We can thus conclude from these data that the mere pairing of relatively neutral pictorial CSs with a positive or negative US-odor can result in an evaluative shift for these visual CSs. It can however not be excluded that these effects were (partly) due to demand effects. Most participants were probably aware of the specific CS–US contingencies and it is possible that effects of social desirability or other demand effects may have influenced their ratings. Therefore, in the second phase of the experiment, the four CSs were entered as primes in an affective priming procedure. During this priming phase, participants were asked to evaluate a series of positive and negative target words that were preceded by one of the four CSs. Results from this affective priming procedure (SOA 300) showed a significant effect of affective congruence for the male subgroup. For the female participants an effect of affective congruence was, however, absent. We have no valid explanation for this gender difference in the affective priming data, but the data from the male subgroup are a clear indication that the mere contingent pairing of a neutral visual CS with a positive or negative odor-US can result in genuine evaluative shifts for these nonodor CSs. Moreover, this newly acquired valence can be automatically activated, as was indexed by the results of the affective priming procedure. Recently, this effect could be replicated using pictures of food items instead of bottles of washing-up liquid. In this experiment the significant priming effect was not mediated by gender (Hermans, Baeyens, & Lamote, 2000d).

Similar results have been reported by Glautier & De Houwer (2000). An interesting feature of their research is that multiple USs were used in association with the CSs. The CSs in these studies were blue, green, or yellow colored circles of approximately 8 cm diameter, whereas the USs were positive and negative pictures that were normatively selected from the IAPS picture set (Lang, Bradley, & Cuthbert, 1997). During the acquisition phase, the CSpositive and the CSnegative were presented nine times each (12 times in Experiment 2), and were always immediately followed by a positive or a negative picture respectively. These pictures were randomly selected from a larger pool of 14 positive and 12 negative pictures. In contrast with the previous studies, in the experiments by Glautier and De Houwer (2000) each CS could be followed by different USs of the same valence over several trials. Although this procedure will most certainly not lead to strong associations between the CS and specific USs, the authors nevertheless reported significant affective priming effects.

Other interesting results have been reported by Díaz, Baeyens, Ruiz, & Sánchez (2000). In this study, participants were shown three Japanese characters on the computer screen. Either a positive, a neutral or a negative word followed each character on 10 out of the 14 acquisition trials that were scheduled for each CS–US pair. The same word-US was used for each of the three characters during acquisition. As in the study by Hermans et al. (2000d) and in contrast with the studies by De Houwer et al. (1998a), no explicit instructions were given to learn the contingencies between the specific CSs and USs. Before and after acquisition, participants were asked to provide evaluative ratings for the CSs. As predicted, the Japanese character that was presented contingent with a negative word was rated more negatively than the Japanese character that was associated with a positive word.

More interesting, in the next phase of the experiment, Diaz et al. (2000) tested the hypothesis that evaluative conditioning is resistant to extinction. In this phase, half of the participants (extinction group) were presented with a total of 48 extinction trials, which included 24 unreinforced presentations of the CSpositive and 24 unreinforced presentations of the CSnegative. The control group received 24 unreinforced presentations of two neutral filler characters. After extinction, evaluative ratings of the CSpositive and CSnegative were again assessed. Results showed that the affective discrimination between the CSpositive and CSnegative that was present after conditioning remained unaltered after extinction. There were no differences between the extinction and the control group with respect to these data. Moreover, when the Japanese character CSs were subsequently used as primes in an affective priming procedure (SOA 300, evaluation task, positive and negative target words), a significant priming effect emerged that did not interact with the group variable (extinction/control). These data not only provide further evidence for the fact that recently acquired stimulus valence can be automatically evaluated, but also provide an empirical validation of the idea that evaluative learning is resistant to extinction.

Evaluative Learning and the IAT

In a recent study by Olson and Fazio (2001), evaluatively conditioned stimulus valence was assessed by means of the IAT. Participants were first presented a series of 430 trials. Only 40 of these trials consisted of the crucial CS–US presentations, including 20 trials during which a Pokémon cartoon character was paired with one of a number of positively valenced words and pictures, and 20 trials of another Pokémon character paired with one of a number of negatively valenced words and pictures. The remaining 390 trials consisted of other Pokémon, blank screens, and neutrally valenced words and images presented individually and in pairs. In the second phase of the experiment, the participants rated a series of stimuli (including the two CSs) for the evaluative dimension, and completed an IAT designed to assess evaluative changes for the two CSs. The order of the IAT and the evaluative ratings was counterbalanced over participants. Results showed that there was a significant evaluative conditioning effect in both the IAT and the explicit ratings, which was not influenced by the order of the tasks.

This study is also interesting because of its presentation parameters. Instead of presenting the CS and US sequentially and segmented from other stimuli by a relatively lengthy intertrial interval, each CS–US pair was presented simultaneously and embedded within a stream of similar perceptual events. In a study that preceded the IAT study, it could be demonstrated that this acquisition procedure precluded awareness of the contingency between the specific CSs and the type (positive/negative) of US they were associated with. The authors hence conclude that the results of their study provide additional evidence for the fact that contingency awareness is not a necessary precondition for evaluative learning.

Affective Priming of Aversively Conditioned Stimuli

The USs that have been employed in the previously described studies can not be considered as "unconditional" stimuli in a strict sense, as they do not unconditionally lead to a specific response. This should not be viewed as a limitation of these studies. In fact, there are only very few stimuli that elicit "unconditional" responses. Pain stimuli such as heat and high local pressure are examples of negatively valenced USs, but also bitter tastes in most children. On the other hand, specific food stimuli can be regarded as unconditionally positive stimuli in case of hunger. Yet, most stimuli that we regard as highly pleasant/positive or highly unpleasant/negative have received their positive or negative valence by way of the processes that have been described before, and should therefore not be considered as "unconditional stimuli" in a strict sense.

There is however a long-standing tradition in learning psychology in which such strict unconditional stimuli have been employed, the most prototypical of which is without any doubt the fear-conditioning research in animal as well as human populations (for an overview, see Mackintosh, 1983). In its most basic form, a fear-acquisition preparation entails the contingent presentation of an external CS (tone, light) immediately followed by the presentation of an aversive electrocutaneous stimulus (US). As a result of this procedure the organism essentially learns that the CS is a valid predictor for the US (signal learning). Based on this knowledge, the organism is capable of anticipating this event, and to (behaviorally) prepare for it. This newly acquired knowledge can be reflected in behavioral (e.g., avoidance behavior) as well as in psychophysiological (e.g., increased heart rate, increased skin conductance response) or verbal indices of fear.

In a recent series of studies, Hermans and colleagues (Hermans, Crombez, Vansteenwegen, Baeyens, & Eelen, 2002; Hermans, Spruyt, & Eelen, in pressa; Hermans, Vansteenwegen, Crombez, Baeyens, & Eelen, 2002; Vansteenwegen, Crombez, Baeyens, & Eelen, 1998) demonstrated that such a differential aversive conditioning procedure not only leads to signal learning, but also induces changes in the evaluation of the CS+. In these studies, individually selected neutral pictures of human faces were used as conditioned stimuli (CS). During the acquisition phase the CS+ was contingently followed by an aversive electrocutaneous stimulus, while this was never the case for the CS–. This procedure altered the meaning of the CS+ in two different ways. First, the CS+ became a valid predictor for the US. This was evident from the fact that on verbal ratings of US-expectancy, participants indicated that they strongly expected to receive an electrocutaneous stimulus after the CS+, but not after the CS–. Second, besides this acquired "signal value", the CS+ by itself became a more negative stimulus. The CS–, on the other hand, usually became slightly more positive, which can be attributed to the fact that it had acquired the status of a safety signal (i.e. the CS– signalled the absence of the electrocutaneous stimulus). These affective changes were not only evident from the fact that participants now rated the CS+ (CS–) more negatively (positively) on the evaluative ratings scales, but also from the data of an affective priming procedure that was performed at the end of the experiment.

In a first study by Hermans, Spruyt, and Eelen (in press), an individually selected neutral picture (CS+) was contingently followed by an electrocutaneous stimulus during 8 acquisition trials, whereas a second picture (CS–) that was also presented 8 times, was never followed by this US. Postacquisition ratings not only revealed that, due to this learning phase, the CS+ had become a valid predictor for the US (signal learning), but also that the CS+ induced higher levels of fear and arousal. Moreover, the CS+ was now rated more negative than before acquisition. Correspondingly, the CS- became more positive. This evaluative learning did not only emerge in the evaluative rating scales, but was also evident from the affective priming procedure that was conducted at the end of the experiment. During this phase, the CS+ and CS-, together with four other pictures that were rated as neutral at the beginning of the experiment, were used as primes in a picture-word variant of the affective priming paradigm. Participants were simply asked to evaluate the target words as quickly as possible as either "positive" or "negative." The stimulus onset asynchrony was manipulated over two levels: SOA 300 and SOA 1000. This SOA-manipulation interacted significantly with the affective priming effect. As predicted, there was a significant priming effect at the short but not at the long SOA. At SOA 300, response latencies toward negative targets were shorter if the target was preceded by the CS+ as compared to the CS-, whereas the opposite was true for positive targets.

The fact that affective shifts for the CS+ and CS– could be confirmed by the data of the affective priming procedure is an interesting observation for several reasons. First of all, these data provide additional support for the thesis that evaluative learning can be observed within a human differential aversive conditioning preparation. Second, these priming data—and in particular the differential effect at the two SOA levels—cannot easily be discounted as an effect of demand characteristics. Such an alternative explanation can, however, not be excluded with respect to the data of the evaluative ratings, because only two CSs were used and all participants were aware of the contingency between the CS+ and the US. Given that such a transparent acquisition procedure might easily lead to demand effects in verbal ratings, the affective priming effects are hence even more important from this perspective.

In a second study by Hermans et al. (2002b), the aversive conditioning procedure was directly compared with a conditioning procedure in which nonaversive positive and negative USs were used. This latter procedure consisted of the simultaneous auditory presentation of a neutral picture of a human face with a series of five positive (honest, sensitive, friendly, broadminded, spontaneous) or five negative adjectives (intolerant, imperious, hypocritical, unreliable, egoistic), and is more similar to the procedures that have been typically used to study evaluative conditioning (see also Baeyens, Eelen, Van den Bergh, & Crombez, 1992). Hence, during the acquisition phase of this experiment four CSs were employed: one CS (CS+) was always followed by an electrocutaneous stimulus while a second CS (CS–) was never followed by this US (aversive conditioning procedure), and a third ($CS_{positive}$) and fourth ($CS_{negative}$) stimulus were presented together with positive or negative adjectives respectively (nonaversive conditioning procedure). As was expected, the aversive conditioning procedure induced stronger changes in arousal and fear ratings. Both procedures however led to similar and reliable changes in the evaluation of the CSs. These evaluative shifts were again evident from the subjective rating scales as well as the affective priming procedure, and did not differ in strength for both acquisition procedures.

Together with the data of Hermans et al. (in pressa), the results of this experiment suggest that the mere contingent presentation (8 trials) of a previously neutral stimulus with a positive or negative stimulus is sufficient to alter the evaluative meaning of this stimulus to the extent that the subsequent (unreinforced) presentation of this stimulus automatically activates its valence from memory.

In a final series of experiments, Hermans et al. (2002a) investigated the impact of an extinction procedure on expectancy-learning as well as evaluative learning. Based on previous research, it has been suggested that although expectancy-learning is highly sensitive to extinction, this procedure has no impact on evaluative learning. Although the data of several studies indeed suggest that evaluative learning is resistant to extinction (for an overview, see De Houwer, Thomas, & Baeyens, 2001), the differential impact of extinction on both types of learning has never been observed within one single paradigm. Therefore, in the studies reported by Hermans et al. (2002a) the acquisition phase was followed by an extinction phase during which the CS+ and CS– were both presented eight times without being followed by the US. Confirming our prediction, these unreinforced presentations had a massive impact on the expectancy ratings ($F = 260$; Experiment 1) and even reduced expectancy ratings to the pre-acquisition baseline (Experiment 2). The acquired valence, however, was unaffected by this extinction procedure. In both experiments the acquired difference in valence ratings between the CS+ and the CS– remained unchanged ($F < 1$) from postacquisition to postextinction ratings. The persistence of these acquired evaluative changes could be confirmed by the affective priming procedure, which was conducted after extinction, and which again produced reliable priming effects for the CS+ and CS–.

These results have recently been replicated in a study by Francken, Vansteenwegen, Hermans, Van Calster, Declercq, and Eelen (2002). An interesting feature of this study was that the number of extinction trials was now increased to three times the number of acquisition trials (8 versus 24). Although this extinction procedure returned indicators of expectancy-learning (US-expectancy ratings and skin conductance measures) to baseline level, the evaluative shifts remained highly significant after extinction.

This could again be confirmed by the results of the affective priming procedure.

On the basis of these data we can conclude (a) that the mere contingent presentation of a neutral stimulus together with an aversive stimulus induces evaluative changes in these previously neutral stimuli, (b) that these evaluative changes are comparable to evaluative shifts that are obtained by means of more traditional evaluative conditioning procedures in which nonaversive USs are employed, (c) that these newly acquired valences can be automatically activated from memory, (d) that evaluative learning and expectancy learning can co-occur, and (e) that extinction has a differential impact on both forms of learning: It reduces expectancy learning, while leaving the acquired valence unchanged.

DISCUSSION

Within several domains of psychology the idea of automatic stimulus evaluation has been put forward. Although this hypothesis has been quite consequential, empirical evidence for this type of evaluative processing has long been lacking. With the development of research procedures like the affective priming and the affective Simon paradigm, support for the idea that humans automatically evaluate stimuli in an automatic fashion has been accumulating.

This research on the "activation" of evaluative information has, however, largely proceeded independently from research that focussed on the "acquisition" of this evaluative information in memory. Without doubt, recent contributions from learning psychology are highly relevant in this context. From a learning perspective one can distinguish nonassociative accounts of evaluative acquisition (e.g., mere exposure) from associative accounts. A good example of the latter is the study of evaluative conditioning. At the moment, a large body of empirical work indeed demonstrates that the mere spatio-temporal co-occurrence of a neutral stimulus (CS) with a valenced stimulus (US) may result in the originally neutral stimulus acquiring an evaluative meaning that is congruent with the valence of the US. In addition, research on the characteristics of evaluative conditioning has demonstrated that it concerns a form of associative learning that is qualitatively different from other types of learning. In contrast with expectancy-learning, evaluative learning has been shown not to be dependent on awareness of the CS–US contingencies, not to be sensitive to manipulations of the statistical contingency between the CS and the US, and—perhaps most important—not to be sensitive to procedures of extinction. The process that underlies these evaluative changes can be conceptualised as the formation of an association between the memory representations of the CS and the US. Presentations of the CS in the absence of the US (extinction) do not diminish the strength of this association and, hence, leave the acquired valence unchanged. Only counterconditioning—which implies the subsequent presentation of the CS with a US of opposite valence—seems to be sufficient to alter the acquired evaluative meaning of the CS (e.g., Baeyens et al., 1989).

It is our conviction that the study of evaluative conditioning can be highly relevant for a better understanding of the processes that are involved in the cycle that encompasses the acquisition, the representation and the activation of evaluative information in memory. In this context, we have discussed a series of studies in which automatic activation was demonstrated for recently acquired stimulus valence. In summary, these findings show that associative acquisition procedures are capable of inducing evaluative changes that can be assessed by indirect measures of stimulus valence such as the IAT and the affective priming procedure. Significant effects of SOA manipulations indicate that these evaluative activation effects are automatic.

These findings are interesting because of several reasons. First, these data add to the generality of the automatic evaluation effect. Second, they challenge the idea that automatic stimulus evaluation can only be observed for stimuli for which there exists a strong object-evaluation association in memory (Fazio, 1986, 1995). Given that in most studies reported here, the acquired valence was based on only a few contingent presentations of the CS and the US, it is quite reasonable to assume that these newly acquired associations are not really strong and highly accessible. The studies by Glautier and De Houwer (2000) are particularly interesting from this perspective as their acquisition procedure involved the association of the CS with multiple similarly valenced USs, while employing only a very limited number of trials for each individual US.

Future research on the activation of recently acquired valence may follow different routes simultaneously. It would for instance be interesting to investigate possible differences between acquisition procedures that employ one single US for each CS and procedures that employ multiple similarly valenced USs. Are there differences in the ease with which the acquired valence can subsequently be activated from memory? Are there differences in resistance to extinction? Second, it would be interesting to investigate whether priming effects for acquired stimulus valence are also replicable when there is a longer delay between the acquisition phase and the activation phase. In all studies reported here, there was most often an interval of only a few minutes between both experimental phases. It might be that this newly acquired information needs to be consolidated over time and that activation effects would only get stronger. Or conversely, it might be that the accessibility of the evaluative information is partly dependent on the recency of the acquisition phase, and that accessibility and activation would fade out over time. Still other research could aim at employing more "implicit" acquisition procedures (see for instance the study by Olson & Fazio, in press). In most of the studies reported here only a few CSs and USs were used and most participants were aware of the contingency between those stimuli. But, as contingency awareness is not a necessary precondition for evaluative learning, one could employ procedures that lead to less or no contingency awareness. Affective priming for stimulus valence that is acquired in this way would provide an elegant example of an entirely implicit cycle of acquisition, representation and activation of evaluative information. Finally, one could employ other versions of the affective priming procedure than the evaluative categorisation variant that has been used so far. It would, for instance, be interesting to employ the pronunciation task if one would apply the acquisition/activation paradigm to further explore the way in which stimulus valence is represented.

REFERENCES

Arnold, M. B. (1960). *Emotion and personality, Vol. 1, Psychological aspects.* New York: Columbia University Press.

Baeyens, F., Crombez, G., De Houwer, J., & Eelen, P. (1996). No evidence for modulation of evaluative flavor-flavor associations in humans. *Learning and Motivation, 27,* 200–241.

Baeyens, F., Crombez, G., Hendrickx, H., & Eelen, P. (1995a). Parameters of human evaluative flavor-flavor conditioning. *Learning and Motivation, 26,* 141–160.

Baeyens, F., Crombez, G., Van den Bergh, O., & Eelen, P. (1988). Once in contact always in contact: Evaluative conditioning is resistant to extinction. *Advances in Behaviour Research and Therapy, 10,* 179–199.

Baeyens, F., Eelen, P., & Crombez, G. (1995b). Pavlovian associations are forever: On classical conditioning and extinction. *Journal of Psychophysiology, 9,* 127–141.

Baeyens, F., Eelen, P., & Van den Bergh, O. (1990a). Contingency awareness in evaluative conditioning: A case for unaware affective-evaluative learning. *Cognition and Emotion, 4,* 3–18.

Baeyens, F., Eelen, P., Van den Bergh, O., & Crombez, G. (1989). Acquired affective-evaluative value: Conservative but not unchangeable. *Behaviour Research and Therapy, 27,* 279–287.

Baeyens, F., Eelen, P., Van den Bergh, O., & Crombez, G. (1990b). Flavor-flavor and color-flavor conditioning in humans. *Learning and Motivation, 21,* 434–455.

Baeyens, F., Eelen, P., Van den Bergh, O., & Crombez, G. (1992). The content of learning in human evaluative conditioning: Acquired valence is sensitive to US-revaluation. *Learning and Motivation, 23,* 200–224.

Baeyens, F., Hermans, D., & Eelen, P. (1993). The role of CS–US contingency in human evaluative conditioning. *Behaviour Research and Therapy, 31,* 731–737.

Baeyens, F., Vansteenwegen, D., Hermans, D., & Eelen, P. (2001). Chilled white wine, when all of a sudden the doorbell rings: Mere reference and evaluation versus expectancy and preparation in human Pavlovian learning. In F. Columbus (Ed.), *Advances in Psychology Research* (Vol. 4, pp. 241–277), Huntington, NY: Nova Science Publishers, Inc.

Bargh, J. A., Chaiken, S., Govender, R., & Pratto, F. (1992). The generality of the attitude activation effect. *Journal of Personality and Social Psychology, 62,* 893–912.

Bargh, J. A., Chaiken, S., Raymond, P., & Hymes, C. (1996). The automatic evaluation effect: Unconditional automatic attitude activation with a pronunciation task. *Journal of Experimental Social Psychology, 32,* 104–128.

Bornstein, R. F. (1989). Exposure and affect: Overview and meta-analysis of research, 1968–1987. *Psychological Bulletin, 106,* 265–289.

Bornstein, R. F. (1992). Subliminal mere exposure effects. In R. F. Bornstein & T. S. Pittman (Eds.), *Perception without awareness: Cognitive, Clinical, and Social Perspectives* (pp. 191–210). New York: The Guilford Press.

Bornstein, R. F., & D'Agostino, P. R. (1994). The attribution and discounting of perceptual fluency: Preliminary tests of a perceptual fluency/attributional model of the mere exposure effect. *Social Cognition, 12,* 103–128.

Bower, G. H. (1981). Mood and memory. *American Psychologist, 36,* 129–148.

Bower, G. H. (1991). Mood congruity of social judgements. In J. P. Forgas (Ed.), *Emotion and social judgments* (pp. 31–54). Oxford: Pergamon Press.

Cacioppo, J. T., & Berntson, G. G. (1994). Relationship between attitudes and evaluative space: A critical review, with emphasis on the separability of positive and negative substrates. *Psychological Bulletin, 115,* 401–423.

Chaiken, S., & Bargh, J. A. (1993). Occurrence versus modification of the automatic activation effect: Reply to Fazio. *Journal of Personality and Social Psychology, 64,* 759–765.

Davey, G. C. L. (1987). An integration of human and animal models of Pavlovian conditioning: Associations, cognitions and attributions. In G. Davey (Ed.), *Cognitive processes and Pavlovian conditioning in humans* (pp. 83–113). New York: John Wiley & Sons.

Dawson, M. E., & Shell, A. M. (1985). Information processing and human autonomic classical conditioning. In P. K. Ackles, J. R. Jennings, & M. G. H. Coles (Eds.), *Advances in Psychophysiology* (Vol. 1, pp. 89–165). Greenwich, CT: JAI Press.

Dawson, M. E., & Shell, A. M. (1987). Human autonomic and skeletal classical conditioning: The role of conscious factors. In G. Davey (Ed.), *Cognitive processes and Pavlovian conditioning in humans* (pp. 27–57). New York: John Wiley & Sons.

De Houwer, J., Baeyens, F., & Eelen, P. (1994). Verbal evaluative conditioning with undetected US presentations. *Behaviour Research and Therapy, 32,* 629–633.

De Houwer, J., Baeyens, F., Vansteenwegen, D., Eelen, P. (2000). Evaluative conditioning in the picture–picture paradigm with random assignment of conditioned stimuli to unconditioned stimuli. *Journal of Experimental Psychology: Animal Behaviour Processes, 26,* 237–242.

De Houwer, J., & Eelen, P. (1998). An affective variant of the Simon paradigm. *Cognition and Emotion, 8,* 45–61.

De Houwer, J., & Hermans, D. (1994). Differences in the affective processing of words and pictures. *Cognition and Emotion, 8,* 1–20.

De Houwer, J., Hermans, D., & Eelen, P. (1998a). Affective and identity priming with episodically associated stimuli. *Cognition and Emotion, 12,* 145–169.

De Houwer, J., Hermans, D., & Eelen, P. (1998b). Affective Simon effects using facial expressions as affective stimuli. *Zeitschrift für Experimentelle Psychologie, 45,* 88–98.

De Houwer, J., Hermans, D., & Spruyt, A. (2001). Affective priming of pronunciation responses: Effects of target degradation. *Journal of Experimental Social Psychology, 37,* 85–91.

De Houwer, J., Thomas, S., & Baeyens, F. (2001). Associative learning of likes and dislikes: A review of 25 years of research on human evaluative conditioning. *Psychological Bulletin, 127,* 853–869.

Díaz, E., Baeyens, F., Ruiz, G., & Sánchez, N. (2000, September). *Resistencia a la extinción del condicionamiento evaluativo en diseños entre-grupos [Resistance to extinction of evaluative conditioning with a between-group design].* Abstract of paper presented at the XIIth Congress of the Spanish Society of Comparative Psychology, First International Reunion, Granada.

Draine, S. C., & Greenwald, A. G. (1998). Replicable unconscious semantic priming. *Journal of Experimental Psychology: General, 127,* 286–303.

Fazio, R. H. (1986). How do attitudes guide behavior? In R. M. Sorrentino & E. T. Higgins (Eds.), *The handbook of motivation and cognition: Foundations of social behavior* (pp. 204–243). New York: Guilford Press.

Fazio, R. H. (1990). Multiple processes by which attitudes guide behavior: The MODE model as an integrative framework. In M. P. Zanna (Ed.), *Advances in experimental social psychology* (Vol. 23, pp. 75–109). New York: Academic Press.

Fazio, R. H. (1993a). Variability in the likelihood of automatic attitude activation: Data reanalysis and commentary on Bargh, Chaiken, Govender, and Pratto (1992). *Journal of Personality and Social Psychology, 64,* 753–758.

Fazio, R. H. (1993b). Addendum: Reply to Chaiken and Bargh by Russell H. Fazio. *Journal of Personality and Social Psychology, 64,* 764–765.

Fazio, R. H. (1995). Attitudes as object-evaluation associations: Determinants, consequences, and correlates of attitude accessibility. In R. E. Petty & J. A. Krosnick (Eds.), *Attitude strength: Antecedents and consequences.* Hillsdale, NJ: Lawrence Erlbaum Associates.

Fazio, R. H., Jackson, J. R., Dunton, B. C. & Williams, C. J. (1995). Variability in automatic activation as an unobtrusive measure of racial attitudes: A bona fide pipeline? *Journal of Personality and Social Psychology, 69,* 1013–1027.

Fazio, R. H., Roskos-Ewoldsen, D. R., & Powell, M. C. (1994). Attitudes, perception, and attention. In P. M. Niedenthal & S. Kitayama (Eds.), *The heart's eye: Emotional influences in perception and attention* (pp. 197–216). San Diego: Academic Press.

Fazio, R. H., Sanbonmatsu, D. M., Powell, M. C., & Kardes, F. R. (1986). On the automatic activation of attitudes. *Journal of Personality and Social Psychology, 50,* 229–238.

Fiske, S. T., & Pavelchak, M. A. (1986). Category-based versus piecemeal-based affective responses: Developments in schema-triggered affect. In R. M. Sorrentino & E. T. Higgins (Eds.), *Handbook of Motivation and Cognition* (pp. 167–203). New York: Wiley.

Francken, G. Vansteenwegen, D., Hermans, D., Van Calster, B., Declercq, A., & Eelen, P. (2002). Pavlovian associations remain intact through extinction. (submitted for publication).

Gemar, M. C., Segal, Z. V., Sagrati, S., & Kennedy, S. J. (2001) Contributions of effortful and automatic measures of cognition to a risk marker for depressive relapse/recurrence: The Implicit Association Task in depression. *Journal of Abnormal Psychology, 110,* 282–289.

Giner-Sorolla, R., Garcia, M. T., & Bargh, J. A. (1999). The automatic evaluation of pictures. *Social Cognition, 17,* 76–96.

Glaser, J., & Banaji, M. R. (1999). When fair is foul and foul is fair: Reverse priming in automatic evaluation. *Journal of Personality and Social Psychology, 77,* 669–687.

Glaser, W. R., & Glaser, M. O. (1989). Context effects in Stroop-like word and picture processing. *Journal of Experimental Psychology: General, 118,* 13–42.

Glautier, S., & De Houwer, J. (2000). *Classical conditioning of facial electromyographic and affective responses using emotionally significant visual images as unconditioned stimuli.* Manuscript submitted for publication.

Greenwald, A. G., & Farnham, S. D. (2000). Using the Implicit Association Test to measure self-esteem and self–concept. *Journal of Personality and Social Psychology, 79,* 1022–1038.

Greenwald, A. G., Klinger, M. R., & Liu, T. J. (1989). Unconscious processing of dichoptically masked words. *Memory and Cognition, 17,* 35–47.

Greenwald, A. G., Klinger, M. R., & Schuh, E. S. (1995). Activation by marginally perceptible ("subliminal") stimuli: Dissociation of unconscious from conscious cognition. *Journal of Experimental Psychology: General, 124,* 22–42.

Greenwald, A. G., McGhee, D. E., & Schwartz, J. L. K. (1998). Measuring individual differences in implicit cognition: The Implicit Association Test. *Journal of Personality and Social Psychology, 74,* 1464–1480.

Hermans, D. (1996). *Automatische stimulusevaluatie. Een experimentele analyse van de voorwaarden voor evaluatieve stimulusdiscriminatie aan de hand van het affectieve-primingparadigma.* [Automatic stimulus evaluation. An experimental analysis of the preconditions for evaluative stimulus discrimination using an affective priming paradigm]. Unpublished doctoral dissertation, University of Leuven, Belgium.

Hermans, D., & Baeyens, F. (in press). The acquisition and activation of odour hedonics in everyday situations: Conditioning and priming studies. In C. Rouby, B. Schaal, D. Dubois, R. Gervais, & A. Holley (Eds.), *Olfaction, taste, & cognition.* Cambridge, UK: Cambridge University Press.

Hermans, D., Baeyens, F., & Eelen, P. (1998). Odours as affective processing context for word evaluation: A case of cross-modal affective priming. *Cognition and Emotion, 12,* 601–613.

Hermans, D., Baeyens, F., & Lamote, S. (2000d). *Evaluative conditioning of brand CS with odor USs: A demonstration using the affective priming technique.* (Manuscript in preparation).

Hermans, D., Crombez, G., & Eelen, P. (2000c). Automatic attitude activation and efficiency: The fourth horseman of automaticity. *Psychologica Belgica, 40,* 3–22.

Hermans, D., Crombez, G., Vansteenwegen, D., Baeyens, F., & Eelen, P. (2000a). Expectancy-learning and evaluative learning in human classical conditioning: Differential effects of extinction. In S. P. Shohov (Ed.). *Advances in Psychology Research* (Vol. 12, pp. 21–45). Huntington. NY: Nova Science Publishers, Inc.

Hermans, D., Vansteenwegen, D., Crombez, G., Baeyens, F., & Eelen, P. (2000b). Expectancy-learning and evaluative learning in human classical conditioning: Affective priming as an indirect and unobtrusive measure of conditioned stimulus valence. *Behaviour Research and Therapy, 40,* 217–234

Hermans, D., & De Houwer, J. (1993). Angstproblematiek en diagnostiek: Ontwikkelingen binnen de experimentele cognitieve psychologie. [Anxiety disorder and its assessment: recent developments in experimental cognitive psychology]. *Psychotherapeutisch Paspoort, 2,* 5–23.

Hermans, D., De Houwer, J., & Eelen, P. (1994). The affective priming effect: Automatic activation of evaluative information in memory. *Cognition and Emotion, 8,* 515–533.

Hermans, D., De Houwer, J., & Eelen, P. (1996). Evaluative decision latencies mediated by induced affective states. *Behaviour Research and Therapy, 34,* 483–488.

Hermans, D., De Houwer, J., & Eelen, P. (2001). A time course analysis of the affective priming effect. *Cognition and Emotion, 15,* 143–165.

Hermans, D., & Eelen, P. (1997). Automatische stimulusevaluatie: Experimentele evidentie voor een oude hypothese. [Automatic stimulus evaluation: experimental evidence for an old hypothesis]. *Nederlands Tijdschrift voor de Psychologie en haar Grensgebieden, 52,* 57–66.

Hermans, D., Spruyt, A., & Eelen, P. (in pressa). *Automatic affective priming of recently acquired stimulus valence: Priming at SOA 300 but not at SOA 1000.*

Hermans, D., Van den Broeck, A., & Eelen, P. (1998). Affective priming using a colour-naming task: A test of an affective-motivational account of affective priming effects. *Zeitschrift für Experimentelle Psychologie, 45,* 136–148.

Klauer, K. C., & Musch, J. (in press). Does sunshine prime loyal? Affective priming in the naming task. *Quarterly Journal of Experimental Psychology.*

Klauer, K. C., Rossnagel, C., & Musch, J. (1997). List-context effects in evaluative priming. *Journal of Experimental Psychology: Learning, Memory, and Cognition, 23,* 246–255.

Klinger, M. R., & Greenwald, A. G. (1994). Preferences need no inferences?: The cognitive basis of unconscious mere exposure effects. In P. M. Niedenthal & S. Kitayama (Eds.), *The heart's eye: Emotional influences in perception and attention* (pp. 67–85). San Diego: Academic Press.

Lang, P. J., Bradley, M. M., & Cuthbert, B. N. (1997.) *International Affective Picture System (IAPS): Technical Manual and Affective Ratings.* NIMH Center for the Study of Emotion and Attention, Gainesville, Florida.

LeDoux, J. E. (1989). Cognitive-emotional interactions in the brain. *Cognition and Emotion, 3,* 267–289.

Levey, A. B., & Martin, I. (1975). Classical conditioning of human "evaluative" responses. *Behaviour Research and Therapy, 13*, 221–226.

Mackintosh, N. J. (1983). *Conditioning and associative learning*. New York: Oxford University Press.

Mandler, G., Nakamura, Y., & Van Zandt, B. J. S. (1987). Nonspecific effects of exposure to stimuli that cannot be recognized. *Journal of Experimental Psychology: Learning, Memory, and Cognition, 13*, 646–648.

Martin, I., & Levey, A. B. (1978). Evaluative Conditioning. *Advances in Behaviour Research and Therapy, 1*, 57–102.

Mitchell, C. J., Anderson N. E., & McDonough, J. (2000). *Mere exposure increases preferences for non-words and pictures as measured in the implicit association test: Implications for the non-specific activation hypothesis*. Manuscript submitted for publication.

Moss, H. E., Ostrin, R. K., Tyler, L. K., Marslen-Wilson, W. D. (1995). Accessing different types of lexical semantic information: Evidence from priming. *Journal of Experimental Psychology: Learning, Memory and Cognition, 21*, 863–883.

Öhman, A. (1986). Face the beast and fear the face: Animal and social fears as prototypes for evolutionary analyses of emotion. (Presidential Address, 1985). *Psychophysiology, 23*, 123–145.

Öhman, A. (1987). The psychophysiology of emotion: an evolutionary-cognitive perspective. *Advances in Psychophysiology, 2*, 79–127.

Olson, M. A., & Fazio, R. H. (2001). Implicit attitude formation through classical conditioning. *Psychological Science, 12*, 413–417.

Otten, S., & Wentura, D. (1999). About the impact of automaticity in the Minimal Group Paradigm: Evidence from affective priming tasks. *European Journal of Social Psychology, 29*, 1049–1071.

Pratto, F., & John, O. P. (1991). Automatic vigilance: The attention grabbing power of negative social information. *Journal of Personality and Social Psychology, 61*, 380–391.

Reber, R., Haerter, A., & Sollberger, B. (1999, June). *Unbewusstes affektives Priming: Zwei neue experimentelle paradigmen*. Paper presented at the 7. Tagung der Fachgruppe Sozialpsychologie, Universität Kassel, Kassel, Germany.

Rothermund, K., & Wentura, D. (1998). Ein fairer Test für die Aktivationsausbreitungshypothese: affektives Priming in der Stroop-Aufgabe [An unbiased test of a spreading activation account of affective priming: Analysis of affective congruency effects in the Stroop task]. *Zeitschrift für Experimentelle Psychologie, 45*, 120–135.

Rudman, L. A., Greenwald, A. G., Mellott, D. S., & Schwartz, J. L. K. (1999). Measuring the automatic components of prejudice: Flexibility and generality of the Implicit Association Test. *Social Cognition, 17*, 437–465.

Scherer, K. R. (1993). Neuroscience projections to current debates in emotion psychology. *Cognition and Emotion, 7*, 1–42.

Seamon, J. G., Williams, P. C., Crowley, M. J., & Kim, I. J. (1995). The mere exposure effect is based on implicit memory: Effects of stimulus type, encoding conditions, and number of exposures on recognition and affect judgments. *Journal of Experimental Psychology: Learning, Memory, and Cognition, 21*, 711–721.

Spruyt, A., Hermans, D., De Houwer, J., & Eelen, P. (2002). *Explaining the affective priming effect: Affective priming in a picture naming task*. (submitted for publication).

Swanson, J. E., Rudman, L. A., & Greenwald, A. G. (2001). Using the Implicit Association Test to investigate attitude-behaviour consistency for stigmatised behaviour. *Cognition and Emotion, 15*, 207–230.

Vansteenwegen, D., Crombez, G., Baeyens, F., & Eelen, P. (1998). Extinction in fear conditioning: Effects on startle modulation and evaluative self-reports. *Psychophysiology, 35*, 729–736.

Wagner, A. R., & Brandon, S. E. (1989). Evolution of a structured connectionist model of Pavlovian conditioning (AESOP). In S. B. Klein & R. R. Mowrer (Eds.), *Contemporary learning theories: Pavlovian conditioning and the status of traditional learning theory.* Hillsdale, NJ: Lawrence Erlbaum Associates.

Wentura, D. (1999). Activation and inhibition of affective information: Evidence for negative priming in the evaluation task. *Cognition and Emotion, 13,* 65–91.

Wentura, D. (2000). Dissociative affective and associative priming effects in the lexical decision task: Yes vs. no responses to word targets reveal evaluative judgment tendencies. *Journal of Experimental Psychology: Learning, Memory, and Cognition, 26,* 456–469.

Zajonc, R. B. (1968). Attitudinal effects of mere exposure. *Journal of Personality and Social Psychology (Monograph Supplement), 9,* 1–28.

Zajonc, R. B. (1980). Feeling and thinking. Preferences need no inferences. *American Psychologist, 35,* 151–175.

Chapter 7

The Constructive Nature of Automatic Evaluation

Melissa J. Ferguson
John A. Bargh
New York University

Previous research concerning automatic evaluation has largely focused on when an evaluation is activated versus when it is not, as well as the possible mechanisms by which automatic evaluation leads to evaluative priming (Bargh, Chaiken, Govender, & Pratto, 1992; Bargh, Chaiken, Raymond, & Hymes, 1996; Fazio, 2000; Fazio, Jackson, Dunton, & Williams, 1995; Fazio, Sanbonmatsu, Powell, & Kardes, 1986; Fiske & Pavelchak, 1986; Giner-Sorolla, Garcia, & Bargh, 1999; Greenwald, Draine, & Abrams, 1996; Greenwald, Klinger, & Liu, 1989; Wittenbrink, Judd, & Park, 1997). This chapter, instead, describes two sets of recent studies that concern the underlying process of the activation of the evaluation itself, rather than the ways in which such an evaluation can then influence subsequent stimuli.

We first review the phenomenon of automatic evaluation and the paradigm in which it is frequently measured—evaluative priming—and then summarize current theorizing about the mechanisms underlying evaluative priming. Next, we describe the assumption in the evaluative priming literature that an evaluation consists of a single, affective representation associated in memory with the object. We then argue against this model, and describe an alternative that is in accord with many current perspectives on memory, in both cognitive and social psychology (e.g., Anderson & Rosenfeld, 1988; Bechtel & Abrahamsen, 1991; Carlston & Smith, 1996; Fiedler, 1996; E. R. Smith, 1996, 1997; Smith & DeCoster, 1999). This alternative hypothesis holds that an observed automatic evaluation of an object represents an integration of multiple sources of affective information, possibly associated both to the object and to other objects or representations. We discuss various reasons why this alternative claim is more consistent with frameworks concerning how the utility of attitude objects varies from situation to situation (e.g., Lewin, 1926; Rosenberg, 1956).

In order to consider evidence consistent with this alternative hypothesis, we first turn to studies that demonstrate that participants are able to automatically evaluate objects for which there are no previously stored, corresponding representations (i.e., novel, unfamiliar objects). This set of findings is consistent with the claim that an evaluation, of either a novel or familiar object, represents a combination of numerous evaluations of various features of the object, rather than a solitary tag associated with the object representation (see Fiske & Pavelchak, 1986). In addition, these findings suggest that automatic evaluations can be spontaneously and immediately constructed on the spot, rather than being dependent on previous experience with, and conscious appraisal of, the objects.

We then consider the second set of studies, which examined the context-sensitivity of automatic evaluations. If an automatic evaluation is a function of multiple representations, it should be sensitive to situational constraints that delimit the kind of information that is contributive during the construction process (e.g., see Anderson, 1974; Tesser, 1978). Comparatively, if an evaluation reflects a solitary, preexisting representation that is associated with the attitude object, it might be less sensitive to the kind of attitude object-relevant information that is available during the perception of the object. The findings show that the same attitude object can evoke different automatic evaluations depending on the nature of previously activated, semantically related knowledge. This research therefore suggests that automatic evaluation is constructive and thus subject to a number of situational factors that have previously been ascribed only to explicitly measured evaluations (i.e., attitudes).

AUTOMATIC EVALUATION AND EVALUATIVE PRIMING

According to much experimental social psychological research, people seem to automatically (i.e., immediately and unintentionally; see Bargh, 1989) evaluate objects in their environment within a fraction of a second after perceiving them (e.g., Bargh et al., 1992; Bargh et al., 1996; Fazio, 2000; Fazio et al., 1995; Fazio et al., 1986; Giner-Sorolla et al., 1999; Greenwald et al., 1996; Greenwald et al., 1989; Wittenbrink et al., 1997). Most of this work employs a sequential priming paradigm (Neely, 1976, 1977) wherein participants are presented with otherwise semantically unrelated prime-target pairings that either share or do not share the same valence. The critical dependent measure is the speed with which participants respond to the targets as a function of the valence of the preceding attitude objects. Results have shown, across a wide spectrum of methodologies, an evaluative priming effect; that is, people are faster to respond to target stimuli when they are preceded by similarly (versus dissimilarly) valenced prime stimuli.

The automaticity of the activation is based on the fact that the typical stimulus onset asynchrony (SOA) in this research is too brief a delay to allow strategic responding to occur (see Fazio et al., 1986; cf. Klauer, Rossnagel, & Musch, 1997). Specifically, research demonstrates that the phenomenon only occurs when the SOA is less than 300 milliseconds (e.g., De Houwer, Hermans, & Eelen, 1998; Fazio, et al., 1986; Hermans, De Houwer, & Eelen, 1994) and work in semantic priming suggests that participants are unable to strategically respond to stimuli when the SOA is less than 500 ms (Neely, 1977).

Furthermore, Fazio et al. (1986) found that the evaluative priming effect occurred when the SOA was 300 milliseconds but not when the SOA was 1000 milliseconds. Because the effect did not occur when strategic processing was possible (i.e., when the SOA was 1000 ms), they concluded that the effect is not due to strategic processing. In addition, the automaticity of the evaluation is also suggested by evidence showing that the effect obtains even when the primes are subliminally presented (Greenwald et al., 1996; Greenwald et al., 1989; Wittenbrink et al., 1997).

Much research has addressed various parameters of the evaluative priming effect. Researchers have concluded that the effect can be replicated using a variety of response tasks, such as lexical decision (e.g., Hill & Kemp-Wheeler, 1989; Wittenbrink et al., 1997; cf. Wentura, 2000), evaluation (e.g., Bargh et al., 1992; Fazio et al., 1986), pronunciation (e.g., Bargh et al., 1996), and arm movements (Chen & Bargh, 1999). Furthermore, the effect also replicates using different prime materials, including visually presented nouns (e.g., Bargh et al., 1992; Fazio et al., 1986) and pictures (e.g., Fazio et al., 1995; Giner-Sorolla et al., 1999), auditory stimuli (e.g., De Houwer et al., 1998), and even olfactory stimuli such as pleasant and unpleasant odors (Hermans, Baeyens, & Eelen, 1998). Although research continues to explore the occurrence of the effect, resolution of the possible process mechanisms underlying the effect has proven more elusive. There seem to be two predominant mechanisms that can account for at least some of the extant data.

PROCESS MODELS OF THE EVALUATIVE PRIMING EFFECT

Spreading Activation Models

One proposed mechanism of the evaluative priming effect entails the automatic spreading of activation from the representation of the attitude object to its corresponding attitude and then to either representations that are synonymous with positive or negative (e.g., wonderful, awful; Fazio, 2000; Fazio et al., 1986) or possibly to all similarly valenced representations (e.g.,

Bargh et al., 1996; Ferguson & Bargh, 2001a). According to this proposal, similarly valenced representations are more accessible as a result of the spreading activation from the prime, and thus are more readily used to encode subsequent information (e.g., Anderson, 1983; Anderson & Bower, 1973; Collins & Loftus, 1975), such as similarly valenced target stimuli.

Although some researchers working on automatic evaluation have interpreted their data in line with a spreading activation mechanism (e.g., Bargh et al., 1996), the claim that the activation of an attitude increases the accessibility of all similarly valenced representations in memory appears unlikely given tenets of spreading activation models. In particular, theorists of spreading activation models argued that the magnitude of a priming effect will depend on the degree to which the relevant feature (the prime stimulus) is common to many versus few concepts in memory (i.e., the fan effect; e.g., N. H. Anderson, 1974; Collins & Loftus, 1975; E. E. Smith, Adams, & Schorr, 1978). If the prime stimulus contains features shared by numerous concepts (e.g., *red*), the amount of activation theoretically disperses over many pathways, making the increased activation level, and therefore facilitation, for any one representation rather minimal. In comparison, a feature that is relatively unique would activate a relatively smaller number of concepts, and those related concepts would be facilitated due to the previous perception of the prime stimulus. Assuming that there is a limited amount of activation available and that nearly all concepts contain either the feature *good*, or the feature *bad*, a priming effect due to valence theoretically should be weak.

Due to such difficulties, Fazio (2000) has argued that perhaps the spreading activation that results from the activation of an attitude only extends to those concepts that are synonymous with the feature of good or bad, such as obviously evaluative adjectives such as *pleasant* or *repulsive*. The activation might not, however, automatically spread to concepts that are not as synonymous with positive and negative, such as *wise* or *lonely*. This possibility is speculative at the moment and the precise nature of a hypothetical associative network of evaluative concepts, including the relative strength of the links between them, is not yet clear.

Although the evaluative priming effect cannot be easily explained by spreading activation through an associative network, the claim that the presentation of a prime stimulus renders similarly valenced concepts more accessible could instead be explained by a connectionist model of memory (see Ferguson & Bargh, 2001a; Wentura, 2000). Such models assume that a given representation consists of a pattern of activation distributed across a subset of processing units. These processing units are updated with new patterns of activation on perception of a new stimulus. If a group of the processing units is responsible for the valence of a stimulus, then the perception of a stimulus that has the same valence as the previous stimulus would require less of an update, and therefore less time to respond (Wentura, 2000). Researchers have begun to consider connectionist explanations of evaluative priming (E. R. Smith, 1997, 2000).

Response Competition Models

Other researchers have endorsed response competition models that do not make any assumptions regarding the spreading of activation from the attitude of the object to similarly valenced representations (see Hermans et al., 1994; Klauer, 1998; Klauer et al., 1997; Klinger, Burton, & Pitts, 2000; Wentura, 1999, 2000). According to this perspective, the activation of the attitude associated with the attitude object suggests a response that either facilitates or inhibits the response to the following target word. Participants are thus faster to respond to target words when the preceding prime words activate the same (versus different) responses.

Wentura (1999) has also recently argued that when the response to the prime and the response to the target are in competition, the response to the prime is inhibited. Findings showed that the presentation of a negative attitude object before a positive target word, for instance, resulted in a longer reaction time to identify the next, subsequently presented, negative target word. This research demonstrates that both facilitation and inhibition processes can occur during evaluative priming according to the compatibility of responses to the prime and target stimuli.

As another example of a response competition explanation, Klauer and colleagues (Klauer, 1998; Klauer et al., 1997; Wentura, 2000) explain evaluative priming effects in a lexical decision task according to a judgmental tendency. These authors assert that when the prime word is a noun and the target word is an adjective, people automatically try to integrate the two stimuli into a sentence (Is object X adjective Y?). People purportedly go through three stages: They first automatically evaluate both the prime and the target, and then they automatically assess the similarity of these evaluations. This comparison process provides a priori evidence for the question of whether the strategic answer to the target word will be affirmative or negative. When the two words are similarly valenced, an affirmative response, such as in a lexical decision task (i.e., "yes, target is a word"), is facilitated, compared to when the two stimuli are dissimilarly valenced. In the third stage, people then use the a priori evidence, as well as controlled searches for evidence, in order to respond to the target stimulus.

Wentura (2000) recently tested the tenet that a match in valence should facilitate an affirmative response by asking participants to say "yes" when the target was a nonword and "no" when the target was a word (i.e., reversing the typical response in lexical decision). When the correct response to the word targets was "no," those trials in which the prime and target mismatched in valence were facilitated compared to trials in which the prime and target matched in valence (i.e., the typical effect was reversed). This recent research seems to support the judgmental tendency proposal by Klauer and colleagues (Klauer, 1998; Klauer et al., 1997), at least for those paradigms that use the lexical decision task, and employ nouns as prime stimuli and adjectives as target stimuli.

Wentura also concluded that the findings did not support a spreading activation account of evaluative priming. He reasoned that the typical evaluative priming effect should have emerged even when the response to the target stimuli was varied. However, the unusual nature of the task, involving a reversal of the natural response, means that it heavily involved strategic processing. Previous research has demonstrated that strategic processing in a lexical decision task can obscure effects of accessibility (e.g., Balota & Lorch, 1986). Moreover, several researchers have concluded that immediate affective responses are obscured to the degree that conscious, strategic processes are involved (Bargh et al., 1996; Bornstein, 1989; Chaiken & Bargh, 1993). Finally, studies that have used the lexical decision task but not adjectives as target stimuli (Bargh et al., 1996, Exp. 3) have still found evidence for evaluative priming, which would not be predicted by the judgmental tendency model.

Overall, the extant literature concerning the evaluative priming effect is inconclusive with regard to these two general types of process mechanisms. For example, the studies that have used an evaluation task can be explained by either a spreading activation account or a response competition account. Because the response in an evaluation task (i.e., positive or negative) is confounded with the attitude that is activated (i.e., positive or negative), it remains unclear whether the facilitation to the target stimuli when the prime and target match in valence is due to faster *perception* of the target stimuli or to faster *responding* to the target stimuli. Fazio (2000) has suggested that perhaps the spreading activation and the response competition account are both responsible in some way (i.e., both necessary conditions), possibly under different circumstances, for the evaluative priming effect.

Although much research has therefore examined possible proposals for mechanisms underlying the evaluative priming effect, there has heretofore been very little discussion in the evaluative priming literature of the precise ways in which the evaluation itself is activated, rather than how that activation then influences subsequent responses. We now consider the ways in which an evaluation itself might be activated.

THE AUTOMATIC ACTIVATION OF AN EVALUATION

Single Affective Tag

It has been generally assumed in the evaluative priming literature that an implicitly observed (i.e., measured) evaluation reflects the activation of a solitary, previously stored, evaluative representation associated with the attitude object (e.g., Bargh et al., 1992; Bargh et al., 1996; Fazio et al., 1986; Fiske & Pavelchak, 1986). For example, Fazio et al. (1986) stated that "Just as a knowledge structure concerning some object may consist of bits of information organized in a network of associations to the object, so too may affect be linked to the object. Furthermore, just as activation can spread from one node in the network to another, the present data indicate a spontaneous spreading of activation from the object to the affective association" (p. 236).

This perspective is compatible with localist, symbolic models of memory that postulate associative networks of memory wherein isolated nodes represent individual constructs, exemplars, or features of an object, such as the evaluative summary of an object (e.g., Anderson, 1983; Anderson & Bower, 1973; Collins & Loftus, 1975). These nodes are interconnected via associative links according to the degree of (semantic) relation between the nodes, and activation spreads along these links automatically on perception of an object (e.g., Meyer & Schvaneveldt, 1971; Neely, 1976, 1977; Posner & Snyder, 1975; Shiffrin & Schneider, 1977).

This conceptualization of the evaluation representation has remained generally unquestioned in the evaluative priming literature, with few exceptions (e.g., E. R. Smith, 2000). Although some researchers in this area have discussed the interconnections between the representation of the evaluation and other concepts in memory (Fazio, 2000), there has been little critical discussion of whether the observed evaluation of an attitude object reflects an associated evaluative tag stored in memory or is a function of numerous evaluative *tags* (cf. Bargh et al., 1992). That is, whereas there has been much discussion concerning the various processes that follow the activation of an attitude associated with an object, there has been very little examination of the activation of the attitude itself.

Problems With Single Affective Tag

According to the *single-tag* perspective, the stimulus is categorized into the category to which it is most similar and then acquires the valence that is associated with the category (Fiske & Pavelchak, 1986). This possibility seems to be assumed in the previously discussed process models of automatic evaluation along with the supposition that a category is associated with a solitary representation that denotes the valence of the members of that category.

However, it seems unlikely that a category has a single associated valence that serves to reflect the evaluation of all of its members. For one thing, categories often consist of subtypes that could each be associated with different attitudes (e.g., see Kunda, 1999). For example, within the category of *dogs*, there may be subcategories such as *attack dogs* and *puppies* with possibly opposite associated attitudes. Even within subcategories however, exemplars may differ from one another with regard to their associated attitudes. Some memories of puppies might be quite positive while others may be quite negative, for instance. Recent theories of categorization (e.g., see Kunda, 1999 for a review) suggest that both prototypes and exemplars exist within categories and there does not seem to be an a priori reason why exemplars should not each have associated attitudes. Thus, the claim that a category, or subcategory, is associated with a summary, affective tag that can be applied to each category member seems unlikely.

Furthermore, even if a subcategory was associated with its own summary evaluative tag, the utility of any object will vary depending on the person's goals, needs, and the situation, respective of the subcategory. Therefore, a subcategory, such as *attack dogs*, should theoretically reflect different utilities of the attitude object across time and situations (see Brendl & Higgins, 1996; Lewin, 1926; Rosenberg, 1956) and have different evaluations according to the utility. For example, when one is trying to protect oneself from a mugger, *attack dog* fulfills the need for protection and thus should be evaluated positively. When one is taking a stroll through a neighborhood without being mauled by the neighbor's Doberman, *attack dog* is likely quite negative because it impedes the goal of safety and comfort.

Assuming the claim that an evaluation is associated with the respective attitude object, *attack dog* must be repeatedly represented according to its specific utility; in other words, each instantiation of the object according to different utilities would have its own associated evaluation. This assumption of such repeated representation seems uneconomic but is nevertheless necessary for the claim that any observed evaluation represents the activation of an affective tag associated to the respective attitude object.

Finally, the "single-tag" perspective cannot represent attitudinal ambivalence, wherein both a positive and negative evaluation are associated in memory with the representation of the attitude object (Bargh et al., 1992). Attitude objects that are ambiguous or ambivalent likely evoke different evaluative information, even within the same measurement context (e.g., see Eagly & Chaiken, 1993), and therefore could not be explained by a model that presumes a single, summary evaluative tag.

Integration of Affective Information

In light of these considerations, a second possibility of how a stimulus is evaluated is that an evaluative system computes a valence based on various representations, possibly including multiple categories that relate to the attitude object in various ways (E. R. Smith, 1997). In this way, the valence that is measured (and that influences subsequent processing such as reaction time to targets) does not represent the activation of a solitary evaluative tag as a function of only the attitude object but is instead a composite of multiple, affective tags. That is, the observable response reflects the result of a function that incorporates various stored valences with regard to many different objects, plans, and behaviors in memory. An evaluation can be thought of, from this perspective, as an index of the goodness or badness of that object with regard to the person's current goals, beliefs, and needs within the situation (Katz, 1960; Katz & Stotland, 1959; Lewin, 1926; Rosenberg, Smith, et al., 1956). Such an integrative process could be considered constructive.

For example, a person who is strolling down the street might have patterns of activation regarding the goal of safety and tranquility in place (e.g., Bruner, 1957). On the perception of growling from the Doberman Pincher in the next yard, the automatic evaluation of the dog is computed based on situationally specific features of the dog that are selected according to the goals of safety and tranquility (e.g., can bite me, can hurt me, is going to chase me). The automatic evaluation of the dog in this case will probably be quite negative.

In contrast, when one is walking down the street and is confronted by a mugger, the automatic evaluation of the growling dog in the neighbor's yard would again be based on situationally specific features of the dog according to the goal of getting help, and defending oneself against the mugger (e.g., will scare the mugger, may bite the mugger, may distract the mugger). The automatic evaluation of the dog in this case might be extremely positive.

This computation, on the basis of numerous representations of current goals as well as object-relevant features and functions, is what constitutes the person's immediate evaluation of the attack dog. The observed evaluation would prepare the person to react to the attitude object in a manner that is appropriate to the situation-specific meaningfulness of the object (e.g., Barsalou, 1992; Fiske, 1992; Glenberg, 1997; Lakoff; 1987). Instead of every possible instantiation of *attack dog* and its associated evaluation being represented according to instrumentality, the evaluation of attack dog is computed across context-relevant sources of information, such as current goals and needs.

Memory Models for the Integration of Affective Information

Although there has not been extensive consideration of this issue in the evaluative priming literature, much current research in cognitive and social psychology suggest an underlying architecture in cognition that requires such an integration of affective information from numerous sources, rather than a single affective association to the object. Parallel-distributed processing perspectives inherently support contextually dependent perceptions, such as attitudes, due to the fact that many representations contribute to any one psychological state (e.g., Anderson & Rosenfeld, 1988; Bechtel & Abrahamsen, 1991; Masson, 1995; McClelland, Rumelhart, & PDP Research Group, 1986; E. R. Smith, 1996, 1997). According to these types of models, then, an automatic evaluation would (sometimes or always) reflect a pattern of activation across numerous objects, or features of objects.

As another example, Fiedler (1996) argued that judgment tasks depend on an aggregation of information across multiple cues in the environment, resulting in a probabilistic computation. Although Fiedler (1996) addressed how such a framework explains explicit judgmental biases, such as out-group homogeneity and group polarization, it could naturally extend to automatic evaluative processes. Such a model would assume that an evaluation represents a combination of affective information regarding multiple features and exemplar information in the environment.

EVIDENCE FOR AN INTEGRATIVE MECHANISM

Beyond a consideration of the theoretical advantages of an integrative mechanism, there are two lines of research that are compatible with the claim that an observed behavior (i.e., an evaluation) represents a function of multiple sources of information, rather than a solitary affective piece of information regarding the attitude object. We first review research that bears on the necessity of a stored evaluation for the attitude object in order for automatic evaluation of the object to occur. Next, we review other research that addresses the fluctuation in evaluation of an object based solely on the context in which the object is perceived. Both sets of studies suggest a more constructive orientation in process accounts of the activation of an evaluation, as would be suggested by recent models of memory.

Stored Object-Evaluations Unnecessary

Because the "single affective tag" claim presupposes that an object is associated with a summary evaluative association, people should be theoretically unable to automatically evaluate objects for which there are no preexisting, corresponding affective tags. It would therefore be informative to know whether people are able to automatically evaluate such objects in order to assess the strength of the single-tag claim.

Furthermore, although various theorists have asserted that evaluation is sometimes computed across attributes or representations, the consensus seems to be that such integrative work cannot occur automatically and requires conscious deliberation (e.g., Fiske & Pavelchak, 1986; Wilson & Hodges, 1992; Wilson et al., 2000). For example, Wilson et al. (2000) considered the literature on attitude stability and concluded that some attitudes are stored evaluations and thus can be automatically activated, whereas other attitudes are constructed on the spot according to new information, and these attitudes require at least some degree of effort. Therefore, according to these authors, people are able to automatically evaluate objects with which they have had experience, and this is accomplished through stored evaluations that can be automatically activated without awareness or effort. When people encounter new objects, such automatic evaluation is not possible, presumably because of the effort required to construct an attitude for a new stimulus. According to this perspective, then, such integration should not be possible without strategic cognitive work.

In order to test these claims, the first set of studies explored whether people can automatically evaluate novel objects. At first glance, it might seem as if this possibility has already been established by previous empirical work. For example, Zajonc and colleagues (e.g., Monahan, Murphy, & Zajonc, 2000; Murphy & Zajonc, 1993; Zajonc, 2000) have demonstrated that people seem to evaluate novel stimuli and that the (explicit) liking for the stimuli increases as a function of the amount of exposure to the stimuli. According to this work, liking of stimuli increases as the exposure of the stimuli increases. Although this work attests to how the experience of frequently (vs. infrequently) perceiving stimuli influences people's positivity, which is then attributed to the stimuli (Monahan et al., 2000; Zajonc, 2000), it does not address the extent to which participants automatically evaluated the stimuli. In other words, although this work suggests that there is positive affect associated with the experience of stimulus frequency, it does not examine whether participants are able to immediately and unintentionally appraise the novel stimuli as positive or negative.

According to previous research and theory therefore, there is actually no empirical work that suggests that people can automatically evaluate novel stimuli. In a series of four experiments, Duckworth, Bargh, Garcia, and Chaiken (in press) found evidence that participants were able to nonconsciously and automatically evaluate both novel auditory stimuli and novel visual stimuli. In the first two studies, participants were asked to pronounce a series of adjectives that appeared one at a time in the center of a computer screen. Each adjective was preceded by a positive or negative word or nonsense word. The words were nouns that have been used in previous automatic evaluation studies (e.g., *cancer, music;* see Bargh et al., 1992). The nonsense words were composed of two-syllable utterances and were completely unfamiliar to the participants. The valence of the novel words was determined by a pilot study in which participants explicitly evaluated the novel stimuli (as was the case across all four experiments).

The findings demonstrate that, irrespective of the novelty of the prime stimuli, participants were faster at pronouncing the target adjectives when the preceding prime stimuli were of the same (vs. opposite) valence. These first two studies demonstrated that people seem able to automatically evaluate novel sounds as good or bad without any representation of the meaning of those novel sounds in memory.

In their third study, Duckworth et al. (in press) used visual, pictorial stimuli as prime stimuli. Both familiar pictures of attitude objects and novel attitude objects were included. The novel pictures consisted of abstract art images with which participants were unfamiliar, akin to the random polygons or Chinese ideographs used by Monahan et al. (2000). That is, the novel stimuli could not evoke any corresponding representational meaning in memory for participants. Still, participants were able to pronounce the target adjectives more quickly when they were preceded by prime stimuli of the same (vs. opposite) valence, regardless of the novelty of the pictures. Thus, the third study replicated the findings of the first two studies and demonstrated that participants are able to immediately and automatically appraise novel images as positive or negative.

Duckworth et al. (in press) also conducted a fourth study in order to generalize the findings to a situation in which the response task differed from pronunciation. In their fourth study, participants were asked to make either approach motions by pulling a lever toward them or avoidance motions by pushing a lever away from them (see Chen & Bargh, 1999; Wentura, Rothermund, & Bak, 2000). Duckworth et al. predicted that positive evaluations would facilitate approach motions compared to negative evaluations and that negative evaluations would facilitate avoidance motions relative to positive evaluations. Participants were presented with novel, abstract art images, one at a time, and were told either to push or pull the lever as quickly as possible in reaction to the image. The results demonstrate that participants were able to make approach motions (i.e., pulling the level) more quickly when they were in response to positive art images compared to negative art images. Similarly, participants were able to make avoidance motions (i.e., pushing the lever) more quickly when they were in response to negative art images relative to positive art images. This fourth study again suggests that people are able to automatically evaluate novel stimuli and that this evaluation influences the speed with which participants can behave toward the prime stimuli.

As these four studies suggest, participants were able to automatically evaluate words and pictures with which they were completely unfamiliar. This set of studies suggests two tentative corollaries concerning the automatic evaluation phenomenon. One corollary is that people are able to evaluate stimuli for which there is no corresponding representation stored in memory. This finding suggests that an automatic evaluation does not require a preexisting, stored affective tag associated with the object.

Beyond the implication of this research for the nature of the underlying representations, these studies also suggest the corollary that constructive processes in evaluation do not require effortful processing. Contrary to recent theorizing about the necessity of deliberative processing when encountering a novel array, scene or object (Wilson & Hodges, 1992; Wilson et al., 2000), this recent research suggests that people can immediately and effortlessly respond to novelty with positivity or negativity.

Temporary Patterns of Activation

Another way to investigate the process underlying the activation of evaluations is to examine the degree to which an evaluation is sensitive to the context in which it is measured. Explicit attitudes are thought to be constructive largely due to their context-sensitivity. For example, there has been much research demonstrating that explicit attitudes fluctuate according to contextual factors such as mood, previously activated attitude-relevant information, and experimental expectations, for instance (e.g., see Anderson, 1974; Bem, 1972; Chaiken & Yates, 1985; Fazio, 1987; Feldman & Lynch, 1988; Forgas, 1992; Millar & Tesser, 1986; Olson, 1990; Schwarz & Clore, 1983; Schwarz & Bless, 1992; Schuman & Presser, 1981; Strack, 1992; Tesser, 1978; Tourangeau & Rasinski, 1988; Wilson, Dunn, Kraft, & Lisle, 1989; Wilson & Hodges, 1992). For example, researchers have illustrated how people's attitudes about the health of their marriage can depend on whether it is sunny outside (Schwarz & Clore, 1983) and that a person's self-reported religiosity depends on the nature of the preceding question (Salancik & Conway, 1975). Because the contextual dependence of explicit attitudes has led to the view that they are constructed on the spot (see Anderson, 1974; Tesser, 1978), it seems fruitful to explore the extent to which automatically activated evaluations are also contextually dependent, and therefore perhaps the result of a constructive process.

This next set of studies explored the dependence of automatically activated evaluations on the nature of recently activated, evaluation-relevant information. The widely accepted notion that many attitude objects are associated with a complex array of memories, some of which may differ in valence, suggests that even automatically activated evaluations might be contingent on the particular selection of activated memories (e.g., Abelson, 1976, 1981; Bower, 1981; Eagly & Chaiken, 1993; Fishbein & Ajzen, 1975; Fiske & Pavelchak, 1986; Schank & Abelson, 1977). In this way, one would expect automatically activated evaluations to vary across time and contexts, depending on the ways in which the attitude object is perceived and what has recently been activated with regard to the attitude object. That is, just as the context in which one explicitly answers a question about religiosity influences the reported attitude, the context in which one perceives the word *religion* should likewise influence the implicit response to the stimulus.

Two studies addressed the extent to which automatically activated evaluations are context-dependent (Ferguson & Bargh, 2001b). These studies examined attitude objects that have traditionally been classified as provoking unambivalent, corresponding evaluations (e.g., *dentist, chocolate*; e.g., see Bargh et al., 1992). In these studies, the first word in a trial (i.e., the prime word) was an attitude object (e.g., *sunshine, poison*) and the second word was an adjective that participants rated as good or bad. In both studies, information that was semantically related to each attitude object was manipulated. Each target trial (i.e., those trials that contained the attitude objects whose implicit attitudes were measured) was yoked with a preceding trial in which the attitude object was semantically related to the attitude object in the target trial.

In one of the two between-subject conditions, participants received semantically related information in preceding trials that matched in valence with the traditional evaluation of the target attitude object. For example, these participants might first see a trial with the attitude object *Drill* followed by an adjective, and then in the following trial see the attitude object *Dentist* followed by an adjective. Participants in the other condition received semantically related information that mismatched in valence with the traditional evaluation of the target attitude object. These participants would first see *Doctor* followed by an adjective, and then, in the next trial, see *Dentist* followed by an adjective. Participant's automatically activated evaluations toward the target attitude objects, such as *Dentist,* were measured by comparing response times to the adjectives in the target trials. The critical analysis was whether the valence of an attitude changed depending on the valence of the previously presented, semantically related information in the preceding trial.

According to both studies, in the condition in which attitude objects in the preceding trials matched in valence with the following target attitude objects, automatic evaluations toward attitude objects seemed consistent with traditional conceptions. The word *Dentist* seemed to evoke a negative evaluation, for instance. However, in the condition in which the previously presented attitude objects mismatched in valence with the following target attitude objects, evaluations were reliably and strongly reversed compared to the other condition. The word *Dentist* now apparently evoked a positive evaluation.

Together, these studies demonstrated that automatically activated evaluations can be completely reversed by manipulating the nature of recently activated, semantically related (to the attitude object) information. Therefore, automatically activated attitudes seem to be sensitive to contextual factors and hence might be considered as *constructed.* From this perspective, it seems unlikely that an observed automatic evaluation is based on a single affective tag associated with the object. Instead, the evaluation might consist of the integration of multiple affective tags associated with various attitude-relevant memories.

REPERCUSSIONS OF SINGLE-TAG VERSUS
INTEGRATIVE MECHANISM

Both sets of studies suggest that the process underlying the automatic activation of an evaluation is constructive, in that it does not consist of the activation of a single affective tag associated with the attitude object. The process is instead flexible and can respond to novelty based on some integration of affective information across familiar features of the novel object. Additionally, such a process is sensitive to situational constraints on patterns of activation, and in this way is similar to the constructive nature of explicit evaluation. We now discuss the implications of such a process, both for the stability of automatic evaluations and for models of evaluative processing.

Contextual Dependence and Stability

The degree of contextual dependence of an evaluation will determine the stability of that evaluation across measurement contexts. Just as there is sometimes low reliability of explicit attitudes across time due to its underlying constructive nature (e.g., Eagly & Chaiken, 1993), an automatic evaluation will be similarly bound by contextual factors. And, an evaluation that depends on different measurement contexts would influence subsequent judgments, feelings, and behaviors according to the context.

The single-tag perspective might also argue that evaluations are context-dependent. For example, if the evaluation that is observed is a reflection of the evaluation of the category into which the object is classified, then fluctuations in measurement across time and situations could result from different ways in which the object can be categorized. However, this means that the evaluation should be stable across time and situations as long as the object is categorized in a similar fashion across time. If, on the other hand, the evaluation reflects a composite function of numerous active representations, then one might assume considerable fluctuation across time, even when the categorization of the object is the same, as long as factors such as mood, goals, task demands, or previously activated information co-vary with measurement contexts. Thus, if the activation process is constructive, with multiple factors affecting the observed evaluation, then the evaluation should be more sensitive to previous and current processing demands.

Data that address the stability of automatically activated evaluations seem timely considering recent research on attitudes (e.g., Wilson et al., 2000). For example, Wilson et al. (2000) argued that automatically activated attitudes should be quite stable across time and situations, and should be impervious to change. An analysis of exactly how evaluations are activated might address this discussion.

Possible Inferences About Data Meaningfulness

The inferences that researchers can draw about the contents of memory directly depend on what they believe an observed evaluation reflects. If it reflects an evaluative tag associated with the category, or even with the exemplar to which the object is most similar, then researchers can infer that the representation of the object in memory includes a valence of the type that was observed. If, however, the evaluation that is observed reflects a composite of numerous representations (and therefore possibly numerous evaluations), then researchers have no basis on which to posit what is included in the representation of that object in memory in terms of valence. These two possibilities suggest different degrees of freedom for interpreting the meaning of data concerning the automatic attitudes toward objects. For example, explicit attitudes are known to be context-sensitive and thus any given explicit report of an attitude does not represent the total sum of attitudinal-relevant information associated with the object in memory.

CONCLUSIONS

The current chapter provided a cursory review of the literature on automatic evaluation and in particular discussed the importance of exploring the precise ways in which an evaluation itself is represented and automatically activated. Previous research largely seems to assume that an automatic evaluation reflects the valence of the category into which it is classified. This suggests that an automatic evaluation is based on a stable, preexisting representation of valence. In contrast, we considered the possibility that an automatic evaluation reflects instead a composite of multiple representations and is thus flexible and sensitive to current goals and patterns of object-relevant activation.

Two important predictions that would derive from the latter possibility are (1) that people would be able to automatically evaluate stimuli for which they have no corresponding representations in memory and (2) that evaluations should be sensitive to the currently activated set of information in the situation in which they are measured. We reviewed two sets of studies that each suggest preliminary support for these two predictions, and thus for the possibility that an automatic evaluation reflects multiple sources of affective information.

The first set of studies, which demonstrated that people are able to automatically evaluate novel objects, also challenges the theoretical premise that the constructive process required to evaluate a novel object depends on conscious deliberation (e.g., see Fiske & Pavelchak, 1986; Wilson et al, 2000). This set of studies suggests that, on the contrary, a constructive process can occur automatically and thus without intention or effort.

The second set of studies also seems to challenge the claim that a constructive process requires conscious deliberation and effort, by demonstrating that automatic evaluation is context-dependent. In contrast to recent research that has asserted that such automatically activated attitudes are stable and largely invariant (e.g., Fazio, 1995; Wilson et al., 2000), this set of studies demonstrated that such attitudes are a function of recently activated, object-relevant information. This pattern of results also suggests that the perspective of context-dependency and constructivism that characterizes explicit attitudes might be also reasonably extended to automatically activated attitudes as well.

REFERENCES

Abelson, R. P. (1976). Script processing in attitude formation and decision making. In J. S. Carroll & J. W. Payne (Eds.), *Cognition and social behavior* (pp. 33–45). Hillsdale, NJ: Lawrence Erlbaum Associates.

Abelson, R. P. (1981). Psychological status of the script concept. *American Psychologist, 36,* 715–729.

Anderson, J. R. (1983). *The architecture of cognition.* Cambridge, MA: Harvard University Press.

Anderson, J. R., & Bower, G. H. (1973). *Human associative memory.* Washington, DC: Winston and Sons.

Anderson, J. A., & Rosenfeld, E. (1988). *Neurocomputing: Foundations of research.* Cambridge, MA: MIT Press.

Anderson, N. H. (1974). Cognitive algebra: Integration theory applied to social attribution. In L. Berkowitz (Ed.), Advances in experimental social psychology (Vol. 7, pp. 1–101). New York: Academic Press.

Balota, D. A., & Lorch, R. F. (1986). Depth of automatic spreading activation: Mediated priming effects in pronunciation but not in lexical decision. *Journal of Experimental Psychology: Learning, Memory, and Cognition, 12,* 336–345.

Bargh, J. A. (1989). Conditional automaticity: Varieties of automatic influence in social perception and cognition. In J. S. Uleman & J. A. Bargh (Eds.), *Unintended thought* (pp. 3–51). New York: Guilford.

Bargh, J. A., Chaiken, S., Govender, R., & Pratto, F. (1992). The generality of the automatic attitude activation effect. *Journal of Personality and Social Psychology, 62,* 893–912.

Bargh, J. A., Chaiken, S., Raymond, P., & Hymes, C. (1996). The automatic evaluation effect: Unconditional automatic attitude activation with a pronunciation task. *Journal of Experimental Social Psychology, 32,* 104–128.

Barsalou, L. W. (1992). *Cognitive psychology: An overview for cognitive scientists.* Hillsdale, NJ: Lawrence Erlbaum Associates.

Bechtel, W., & Abrahamsen, A. (1991). *Connectionism and the mind: An introduction to parallel processing in networks.* Oxford, England UK: Basil Blackwell, Inc.

Bem, D. J. (1972). Self-perception theory. In L. Berkowitz (Ed.), Advances in experimental social psychology (Vol. 6, pp. 1–62). New York: Academic Press.

Bornstein, R. F. (1989). Exposure and affect: Overview and meta-analysis of research, 1968–1987. *Psychological Bulletin, 106,* 265–289.

Bower, G. H. (1981). Mood and memory. *American Psychologist, 36,* 129–148.

Brendl, C. M., & Higgins, E. T. (1996). Principles of judging valence: What makes events positive or negative? *Advances in Experimental Social Psychology, 28,* 95–160.

Bruner, J. S. (1957). On perceptual readiness. *Psychological Review, 64,* 123–152.

Carlston, D. E., & Smith, E. R. (1996). Principles of mental representation. In E. T. Higgins, & A. W. Kruglanski (Eds.), *Social psychology: Handbook of basic principles* (pp. 184–210). New York, NY: Guilford Press.

Chaiken, S., & Bargh, J. A. (1993). Occurrence versus moderation of the automatic attitude activation effect: Reply to Fazio. *Journal of Personality and Social Psychology, 64,* 759–765.

Chaiken, S., & Yates, S. M. (1985). Attitude schematicity and thought-induced attitude polarization. *Journal of Personality and Social Psychology, 49,* 1470–1481.

Chen, M., & Bargh, J. A. (1999). Consequences of automatic evaluation: Immediate behavioral predispositions to approach or avoid the stimulus. *Personality and Social Psychology Bulletin, 25,* 215–224.

Collins, A. M., & Loftus, E. F. (1975). A spreading activation theory of semantic processing. *Psychological Review, 82,* 407–428.

DeHouwer, J., Hermans, D., & Eelens, P. (1998). Affective and identity priming with episodically associated stimuli. *Cognition and Emotion, 12,* 145–169.

Duckworth, K., Bargh, J. A., Garcia, M., & Chaiken, S. (in press). The automatic evaluation of novel stimuli. *Psychological Science.*

Eagly, A. H., & Chaiken, S. (1993). *The psychology of attitudes.* Fort Worth, TX: Harcourt Brace Jovanovich College.

Fazio, R. H. (1987). Self-perception theory: A current perspective. In M. P. Zanna, J. M. Olson, & C. P. Herman (Eds.), *Social influence: The Ontario Symposium* (Vol. 5, pp. 129–150). Hillsdale, NJ: Lawrence Erlbaum Associates.

Fazio, R. H. (1995). Attitudes as object-evaluation associations: Determinants, consequences and correlates of attitude accessibility. In R. E. Petty & J. A. Krosnick (Eds.), *Attitude strength: Antecedents and consequences* (pp. 247–282). Mahwah, NJ: Lawrence Erlbaum Associates.

Fazio, R. H. (2000). On the automatic activation of associated evaluations: An overview. *Cognition and Emotion, 14,* 1–27.

Fazio, R. H., Jackson, J. R., Dunton, B. C., & Williams, C. J. (1995). Variability in automatic activation as an unobtrusive measure of racial attitudes. A bona fide pipeline? *Journal of Personality and Social Psychology, 69,* 1013–1027.

Fazio, R. H., Sanbonmatsu, D. M., Powell, M. C., & Kardes, F. R. (1986). On the automatic activation of attitudes. *Journal of Personality and Social Psychology, 50,* 229–238.

Feldman, J. M., & Lynch, J. G. Jr. (1988). Self-generated validity and other effects of measurement on belief, attitude, intention, and behavior. *Journal of Applied Psychology, 73,* 421–435.

Ferguson, M. J., & Bargh, J. A. (2001a). *Beyond response time: Consequences of automatic evaluative processes for the interpretation of subsequent stimuli.* Unpublished manuscript, New York University.

Ferguson, M. J., & Bargh, J. A. (2001b). *Markers of meaningfulness: A motivational perspective on automatic attitudes.* Unpublished manuscript, New York University.

Fiedler, K. (1996). Explaining and simulating judgment biases as an aggregation phenomenon in probabilistic, multiple-cue environments. *Psychological Review, 103,* 193–214.

Fishbein, M., & Ajzen, I. (1975). *Belief, attitude, intention, and behavior: An introduction to theory and research. Reading, MA: Addison-Wesley.*

Fiske, S. T. (1992). Thinking is for doing: Portraits of social cognition from Daguerreotype to laserphoto. *Journal of Personality and Social Psychology, 63,* 877–889.

Fiske, S. T., & Pavelchak, M. A. (1986). Category-based versus piecemeal-based affective responses: Development in schema-triggered affect. In R. M. Sorrentino & E. T. Higgins (Eds.), *Handbook of motivation and cognition: Foundations of social behavior* (pp. 167–203). New York: Guilford.

Forgas, J. P. (1992). Affect in social judgments and decisions: A multiprocess model. In M. P. Zanna (Ed.), *Advances in experimental social psychology* (Vol. 25, pp. 227–275). San Diego, CA: Academic Press.

Giner-Sorolla, R., Garcia, M. T., & Bargh, J. A. (1999). The automatic evaluation of pictures. *Social Cognition, 17,* 76–96.

Glenberg, A. M. (1997). What memory is for. *Behavioral and Brain Sciences, 20,* 1–55.

Greenwald, A. G. (1990). What cognitive representations underlie social attitudes? *Bulletin of the Psychonomic Society, 28,* 254–260.

Greenwald, A. G., Draine, S. C., & Abrams, R. L. (1996). Three cognitive markers of unconscious semantic activation. *Science, 273,* 1699–1702.

Greenwald, A. G., Klinger, M. R., & Liu, T. J. (1989). Unconscious processing of dichoptically masked words. *Memory and Cognition, 17,* 35–47.

Hermans, D., Baeyens, F., & Eelen, P. (1998). Odours as affective processing context for word evaluation: A case of cross-modal affective priming. *Cognition and Emotion, 12,* 601–613.

Hermans, D., DeHouwer, J., & Eelen, P. (1994). The affective priming effect: Automatic activation of evaluative information in memory. *Cognition and Emotion, 8,* 515–533.

Hill, A. B., & Kemp-Wheeler, S. M. (1989). The influence of context on lexical decision times for emotionally aversive words. *Current psychology research and reviews, 8,* 219–227.

Katz, D. (1960). The functional approach to the study of attitudes. *Public Opinion Quarterly, 24,* 163–204.

Katz, D., & Stotland, E. (1959). A preliminary statement to a theory of attitude structure and change. In S. Koch (Ed.), *Psychology: A study of a science* (Vol. 3, pp. 423–475). New York: McGraw-Hill.

Klauer, K. C. (1998). Affective priming. *European Review of Social Psychology, 8,* 63–107.

Klauer, K. C., Rossnagel, C., & Musch, J. (1997). List-context effects in evaluative priming. *Journal of Experimental Psychology: Learning, Memory, and Cognition, 23,* 246–255.

Klinger, M. R., Burton, P. C., & Pitts, G. S. (2000). Mechanisms of unconscious priming: I. Response competition, not spreading activation. *Journal of Experimental Psychology, 26,* 441–455.

Kunda, Z. (1999). *Social cognition: Making sense of people.* Cambridge, MA: Mit Press.

Lakoff, G. (1987). *Women, fire, and dangerous things: What categories reveal about the mind.* Chicago, IL: University of Chicago Press.

Lewin, K. (1926). Vorsatz, Wille, und Bedürfnis [Intention, will, and need]. *Psychologische Forschung, 7,* 330–385.

Masson, M. E. J. (1995). A distributed memory model of semantic priming. *Journal of Experimental Psychology: Learning, Memory, and Cognition, 21,* 3–23.

McClelland, J. L., Rumelhart, D. E., & PDP Research Group (Eds.). (1986). *Parallel distributed processing: Vol. 2. Explorations in the microstructure of cognition.* Cambridge, MA: MIT Press.

Meyer, D. E., & Schvaneveldt, R. W. (1971). Facilitation in recognizing pairs of words: Evidence of a dependence between retrieval operations. *Journal of Experimental Psychology, 90,* 227–234.

Millar, M. G., & Tesser, A. (1986). Thought-induced attitude change: The effects of schema structure and commitment. *Journal of Personality and Social Psychology, 51,* 259–275.

Monahan, J. L., Murphy, S. T., & Zajonc, R. B. (2000). Subliminal mere exposure: Specific, general, and diffuse effects. *Psychological Science, 11,* 462–466.

Murphy, S. T., & Zajonc, R. B. (1993). Affect, cognition, and awareness: Affective priming with optimal and suboptimal stimulus exposures. *Journal of Personality and Social Psychology, 64,* 723–739.

Neely, J. H. (1976). Semantic priming and retrieval from lexical memory: Evidence for faciliatory and inhibitory processes. *Memory and Cognition, 4,* 648–654.

Neely, J. H. (1977). Semantic priming and retrieval from lexical memory: Roles of inhibitionless spreading activation and limited-capacity attention. *Journal of Experimental Psychology: General, 106,* 225–254.

Olson, J. M. (1990). Self-inference processes in emotion. In J. M. Olson & M. P. Zanna (Eds.), *Self-inference processes: The Ontario Symposium* (Vol. 6, pp. 17–42). Hillsdale, NJ: Lawrence Erlbaum Associates.

Posner, M. I., & Snyder, C. R. R. (1975). Attention and cognitive control. In R. L. Solso (Ed.), *Information processing and cognition: The Loyola symposium* (pp. 55–85). Hillsdale, NJ: Lawrence Erlbaum Associates.

Rosenberg, M. J. (1956). Cognitive structure and attitudinal affect. *Journal of Abnormal and Social Psychology, 53,* 367–372.

Salancik, G. R., & Conway, M. (1975). Attitude inferences from salient and relevant cognitive content about behavior. *Journal of Personality and Social Psychology, 32,* 829–840.

Schank, R. C., & Abelson, R. P. (1977). *Scripts, plans, goals, and understanding: An inquiry into human knowledge structures.* Hillsdale, NJ: Lawrence Erlbaum Associates.

Schuman, H., & Presser, S. (1981). *Questions and answers in attitude surveys.* New York: Academic Press.

Schwarz, N., & Bless, H. (1992). Scandals and the public's trust in politicians: Assimilation and contrast effects. *Personality and Social Psychology Bulletin, 18,* 574–579.

Schwarz, N., & Clore, G. L. (1983). Mood, misattribution, and judgment of well-being: Informative and directive functions of affective states. *Journal of Personality and Social Psychology, 45,* 513–523.

Shiffrin, R. M., & Schneider, W. (1977). Controlled and automatic human information processing: II. Perceptual learning, automatic attending, and a general theory. *Psychological Review, 84,* 127–190.

Smith, E. E., Adams, N., & Schorr, D. (1978). Fact retrieval and the paradox of interference. *Cognitive Psychology, 10,* 438–464.

Smith, E. R. (1996). What do connectionism and social psychology offer each other? *Journal of Personality and Social Psychology, 70,* 893–912.

Smith, E. R. (1997). Preconscious automaticity in a modular connectionist system. In R. S. Wyer Jr. (Ed.), *Advances in social cognition* (Vol. 10, pp. 187–202). Mahwah, NJ: Lawrence Erlbaum Associates.

Smith E. R. (2000, February). *Connectionist representation of evaluation.* Paper presented at the meeting of the Society for Personality and Social Psychology, Nashville, TN.

Smith, E. R., & DeCoster, J. (1999). Associative and rule-based processing: A connectionist interpretation of dual-process models. In S. Chaiken & Y. Trope (Eds.), *Dual-process theories in social psychology* (pp. 323–336). New York, NY: Guilford Press.

Smith, M. B., Bruner, J. S., & White, R. W. (1956). *Opinions and personality.* New York: Wiley.

Strack, F. (1992). The different routes to social judgments: Experiential versus informational strategies. In L. L. Martin & A. Tesser (Eds.), *The construction of social judgments* (pp. 249–276). Hillsdale, NJ: Lawrence Erlbaum Associates.

Tesser, A. (1978). Self-generated attitude change. In L. Berkowitz (Ed.), *Advances in experimental social psychology* (Vol. 11, pp. 289–338). New York: Academic Press.

Tourangeau, R., & Rasinski, K. A. (1988). Cognitive processes underlying context effects in attitude measurement. *Psychological Bulletin, 103,* 299–314.

Wentura, D. (1999). Activation and inhibition of affective information: Evidence for negative priming in the evaluation task. *Cognition and Emotion, 13,* 65–91.

Wentura, D. (2000). Dissociative affective and associative priming effects in the lexical decision task: Yes versus no responses to word targets reveal evaluative judgment tendencies. *Journal of Experimental Psychology: Learning, Memory, and Cognition, 26,* 456–469.

Wentura, D., Rothermund, K., & Bak, P. (2000). Automatic vigilance: The attention grabbing power of approach- and avoidance-related social information. *Journal of Personality and Social Psychology, 78,* 1024–1037.

Wilson, T. D., Dunn, D. S., Kraft, D., & Lisle, D. J. (1989). Introspection, attitude change, and attitude-behavior consistency: The disruptive effects of explaining why we feel the way we do. In L. Berkowitz (Ed.), *Advances in experimental social psychology* (Vol. 22, pp. 287–343). Orlando, FL: Academic Press.

Wilson, T. D., & Hodges, S. D. (1992). Attitudes as temporary constructions. In A. Tesser & L. Martin (Eds.), *The construction of social judgment* (pp. 37–65). Hillsdale, NJ: Lawrence Erlbaum Associates.

Wilson, T. D., Lindsey, S., Schooler, T. Y. (2000). A model of dual attitudes. *Psychological Review, 107,* 101–126.

Wittenbrink, B., Judd, C. M., & Park, B. (1997). Evidence for racial prejudice at the implicit level and its relationship with questionnaire measures. *Journal of Personality and Social Psychology, 72,* 262–274.

Zajonc, R. B. (2000). Feeling and thinking: Closing the debate over the independence of affect. In J. P. Forgas (Ed.), *Feeling and thinking: The role of affect in social cognition. Studies in emotion and social interaction, second series* (pp. 31–58). New York, NY: Cambridge University.

Chapter 8

The Hedonic Marking of Processing Fluency: Implications for Evaluative Judgment

Piotr Winkielman
University of Denver

Norbert Schwarz
University of Michigan

Tedra A. Fazendeiro
University of Denver

Rolf Reber
University of Berne

Each organism faces a variety of evaluative tasks. We need to distinguish what is hospitable and what is hostile, what to approach and what to avoid, what is valuable and what is worthless, what to pursue and what to abandon. We make these judgments often, we make them throughout life, we make them about trivial issues, and about issues of substantial consequences. Psychological research echoes these observations and increasingly adds to the image of the social perceiver as the evaluating human—*homo evaluaticus.* Given the importance and variety of situations that call for an assessment of valence, it is not surprising that people's evaluative toolbox includes mechanisms that draw on different sources of information, ranging from attributes of the target of judgment to the person's own feelings and phenomenal experiences. In this chapter, we propose that one source of relevant information is the fluency with which information about the target can be

*We thank John Cacioppo, Jerry Clore, Paula Niedenthal, Andrzej Nowak, Randy O'Reilly, Bruce Whittlesea, and the University of Denver Cognitive Research Group for discussion and comments. Preparation of this chapter was supported by a fellowship from the Center for Advanced Study in the Behavioral Sciences to Norbert Schwarz.

Correspondence should be addressed to: Piotr Winkielman, Department of Psychology, University of Denver, 2155 S. Race St., Denver, CO 80208, U.S.A.; e-mail: pwinkiel@du.edu; phone: (303) 871-3638; fax: (303) 871-4747.

processed. We further propose that high fluency is associated with positive affect and results in more favorable evaluations.

We first consider the range of evaluative mechanisms and locate our proposal in that context. Next, we elaborate on the concept of fluency and discuss possible reasons for the link between fluency and affective reactions. Subsequently, we present empirical evidence consistent with our proposal. Finally, we discuss boundary conditions of the fluency-affect link.

DECLARATIVE AND EXPERIENTIAL BASES OF JUDGMENT

To form evaluative judgments, people can draw on a range of different processes. These processes vary in complexity and automaticity and use different sources of information as their primary input. In a nutshell, we can distinguish between evaluative judgments that are primarily based on declarative information, such as features of the target, and evaluative judgments that are primarily based on experiential information, such as the person's feelings or phenomenal experiences. Moreover, declarative as well as experiential information may be integral as well as incidental to the target of judgment, as will become apparent further on in this chapter.

Traditionally, models of evaluative judgment have focused on declarative information about the target. According to these models, we attend to features of the target, assess their evaluative implications and integrate them to arrive at an overall judgment. This process has been prototypically described in the theory of information integration (Anderson, 1981). Which features of the target we attend to, or recall from memory, may be a function of the target itself (i.e., integral to the target) or may depend on influences that are incidental to the target. Thus, preceding events (e.g., Schwarz & Bless, 1992) or our mood at the time of judgment (e.g., Bower, 1981) can render some aspects of the target more accessible than others. Moreover, incidental influences can determine how ambiguous features are interpreted, as illustrated by the rich literature on knowledge accessibility effects (for a review see Higgins, 1996). Finally, inferences about the features of the target may be qualified by experiential information, like the ease or difficulty with which some content can be recalled. For example, we may conclude that the target does not have many positive features when we find it difficult to bring relevant examples to mind (for a review see Schwarz, 1998).

Alternatively, evaluative judgments may be primarily based on experiential information, at the expense of declarative information about the target (for a review see Schwarz & Clore, 1996). It is useful to distinguish between experiential information that is feature-based and nonfeature-based. Feature-based affective responses reflect the analysis of the evaluative implications of the stimulus attributes (e.g., Ortony, Clore, & Collins, 1988). Such an analysis may range from sophisticated appraisals resulting in complex emotions (e.g., Frijda, 1988; Smith & Ellsworth, 1985) to the detection of rudimentary attributes resulting in a fairly undifferentiated response (Bargh, Chaiken, Raymond, & Hymes, 1996; LeDoux, 1996). Furthermore, the stimulus that elicits the affective response may be the target itself, in which case the response constitutes *integral affect* in Bodenhausen's (1993) terminology. Alternatively, the affective response may be "incidental" to the target and may have been elicited by a previously viewed movie, a compliment, or the valence of a priming word (see Schwarz & Clore, 1996).

On the other hand, some affective responses are not based on stimulus features. This possibility is best documented for the role of various biological variables that underlie affective states. For example, transient feelings can be influenced by changes in neurotransmitter levels (e.g., Berridge, 1999), electrical brain activity (e.g., Davidson, 1993), brain temperature (e.g., Zajonc, Murphy, & Inglehart, 1989), body posture (e.g., Stepper & Strack, 1993) or facial expressions (e.g., Strack, Martin, & Stepper, 1988). However, nonfeature-based influences on affective reactions are not limited to biological factors. The possibility explored in our chapter is that affective responses may also result from the dynamics of information processing itself. Specifically, we propose that individuals monitor the *fluency* with which they can extract information from the presented stimulus. We further propose that the fluency signal is hedonically marked and that high fluency elicits a positive affective reaction. In fact, this affective reaction can be captured with psychophysiological measures, as reviewed later. This reaction, in turn, contributes to a more positive evaluation when a given stimulus can be processed with high rather than low fluency.

It is worth noting that fluency-based affective reactions are *not* a function of stimulus attributes in the same way that regular feature-based affective reactions are. Although some attributes of a stimulus, like figure-ground contrast or semantic predictability may themselves facilitate fluent processing, the same positive influence is observed when fluency of processing is enhanced through variables that do not affect the features of the stimulus, but only the dynamics of its processing. For example, exposure frequency, exposure duration, or perceptual priming have been found to influence recognition speed as well as evaluations. This work, discussed in more detail further in this chapter, highlights that it is useful to distinguish fluency-based affective reactions from feature-based affective reactions. This distinction is also important because it contributes to an understanding of some otherwise paradoxical phenomena. For example, this distinction suggests that an organism can have affective reactions to stimuli that are neutral, simply because processing of *any* stimulus can generate a fluency signal, which itself leads to an affective response. Furthermore, this distinction suggests that organisms can have affective reactions to stimuli before fully extracting their attributes because the fluency signal may be generated and trigger an affective response at a very early stage of information processing, as discussed later.

Note, however, that the assumption that fluency-based affective reactions do not *derive* from stimulus features does not entail that the affective reaction is not *perceived* as a response to the meaning of the stimulus. As Higgins (1998) suggested, the influence of incidental experiential or declarative information reflects the operation of a tacit *aboutness* principle: We assume that any feelings we experience, or any information that comes to mind, while we think about a target bears on the target—or why else would we feel like this, or think these thoughts, at this point? Accordingly, the respective influence is typically eliminated when we become aware of its incidental nature (e.g., when we realize that some information may only come to mind due to a preceding priming episode; e.g., Strack, Schwarz, Bless, Kübler, & Wänke, 1993) or are aware that our mood may be due to a source unrelated to the target (e.g., Schwarz & Clore, 1983). At present, the only known exception to this rule are affective responses that are too subtle to be consciously experienced, which precludes their discounting (Winkielman, Zajonc, & Schwarz, 1997). It is therefore not surprising that at least some fluency-based affective reactions are also subject to misattribution effects, as we shall see later on in this chapter.

A Preview

In the remainder of this chapter we review our research into the role of processing fluency in evaluative judgment. We show that conditions that facilitate fluent processing result in more positive evaluations of the stimulus, as reflected in judgments as well as physiological responses. We provide a comprehensive review of this robust finding, which has been obtained across a range of different experimental procedures. What is less clear, however, is why processing fluency would have this effect? We propose that the fluency signal is hedonically marked and present empirical evidence in support of this conjecture. We also highlight that the impact of fluency on evaluative judgments reflects the operation of the "aboutness" principle in which participants, by default, rely on their affective responses in forming evaluative judgments, but discount them when they are aware of their incidental nature. The chapter concludes with a discussion of boundary conditions that shape the role of fluency in evaluative judgment.

MONITORING INTERNAL PROCESSING DYNAMICS

The Concept of Fluency

Stimulus processing is characterized by a variety of internal mental events that are nonspecific to the stimulus content. For example, mental representations carrying the same content may differ in the degree of activation

(Mandler, 1980), and processing of the same content may differ in speed (Jacoby, 1983) or effort (Schwarz, 1998). Although there are substantial differences between these various parameters, it is useful to encompass them under a general term of *fluency* (for reviews see Clore, 1992; Jacoby, Kelley, & Dywan, 1989; Schwarz, 1998). It is generally assumed that the *fluency* of processing can be read by the perceiver via some internal metacognitive feedback mechanism (Mazzoni & Nelson, 1998; Metcalfe & Shimamura, 1994). Such a feedback mechanism can make the fluency signal available to other processing modules, including the affect system (Fernandez-Duque, Baird, & Posner, 2000). The signal can be available to the other processing modules either directly, presumably via an automatic process, or indirectly, in the form of a conscious experience of processing ease. It is also interesting that the availability of the fluency signal may not require the simultaneous availability of the stimulus content, and may occasionally precede it, as we discuss below (Curran, 2000; Koriat, 2000; Seamon, Brody, & Kauff, 1983).[1]

A few additional distinctions are useful. First, fluency may or may not be reflected in conscious experience. We use the term *objective* fluency to refer to a mental process characterized by high speed, low resource demands, high accuracy, or other indicators of efficient processing, without necessarily assuming that these processes are reflected on a subjective level. Conversely, we use the term *subjective* fluency, to refer to a conscious experience of processing ease, low effort, high speed, and so on. One consequence of this distinction is that objective and subjective fluency may become dissociated under some conditions. For example, a well-practiced, automatic mental process may have a high objective fluency, but it may not elicit an experience of processing ease. Furthermore, it is possible that objective and subjective fluency may even go in opposite directions, as in cases where alcohol slows down the actual processing, yet creates a strong experience of subjective fluency. Finally, objective fluency may function differently in judgments than subjective fluency. Whereas objective fluency may enter judgments via automatic processes, subjective fluency may enter judgments via theory-driven interpretations of its source, meaning, and diagnosticity. Accordingly, the judgmental impact of subjective fluency may depend on (mis)attributions and theory-driven processes (Skurnik, Schwarz, & Winkielman, 2000).

Second, fluency can reflect processes and manipulations occurring at different levels. *Perceptual* fluency reflects the ease of low-level, data-driven operations that deal primarily with surface features of the stimulus, or its perceptual form. As a consequence, perceptual fluency is influenced by

---

[1]This possibility accounts for metacognitive states in which a person has a strong cognitive "experience", but is not aware of the specific content responsible for that experience.

variables like simple repetition, form priming, contrast, duration, and so on. These manipulations have been shown to influence responses primarily by changing the speed and accuracy of perceptual identification (Jacoby, 1983; Roediger, 1990; Tulving & Schachter, 1990). On the other hand, *conceptual* fluency reflects the ease of high-level operations concerned primarily with categorization and processing of a stimulus' relation to semantic knowledge structures. Accordingly, conceptual fluency is influenced by variables like semantic priming, semantic predictability, context congruity, rhyme, and so on (e.g., Kelley & Jacoby; 1998; McGlone & Tofighbakhsh, 2000; Poldrack & Logan, 1998; Roediger, 1990; Whittlesea, 1993). Of course, perceptual and conceptual processes usually operate in concert, and support each other, especially when the information about the stimulus is "poor" (brief, degraded, ambiguous, etc.). However, this distinction is validated by evidence of a perceptual representation system, the operation of which is most sensitive to manipulations of form processing, and a conceptual representation system, the operation of which is most sensitive to manipulations of semantic processing (Schacter, 1992; Squire, 1992). These systems can be dissociated on the level of manipulations and judgmental consequences as well as on the level of underlying neural structures (Desimone, Miller, Chelazzi, & Lueschow, 1995). For example, neuroimaging and single-cell recording studies suggest that perceptual priming and simple repetition decrease neural responses in brain areas responsible for processing stimulus form, such as the sensory cortex (Desimone et al., 1995). On the other hand, conceptual priming decreases activation in brain areas responsible for processing stimulus meaning, such as the prefrontal cortex (Demb, Desmond, Wagner, Vaidya, Glover & Gabrieli, 1995).[2]

For the time being, however, we will subsume both perceptual and conceptual fluency under the summary term *fluency*. Such a generalization is justified by the fact that perceptual and conceptual manipulations have similar effects on judgments. For example, evaluative judgments as well as judgments of previous occurrence can be influenced by both perceptual priming as well as conceptual priming, as we shall see below. More important, perceptual and conceptual manipulations can influence judgments in the respective "other" domain. For example, simple perceptual manipulations, like repetition or figure-ground contrast, have been shown to influence conceptual judgments of fame or truth (e.g., Jacoby, Kelley, Brown, & Jasechko, 1989; Reber & Schwarz, 1999), much as conceptual manipulations like semantic priming have been shown to influence per-

---

[2]The decrease in neural activity in response to repeated stimuli has several interpretations. Some researchers view it as attenuation of a signal to higher brain systems for allocation of resources to novel stimuli (Desimone et al., 1995). It is also possible that the decrease reflects "sharpening" of the neural response, with "new" stimuli nonspecifically activating more neurons and "old" stimuli selectively activating fewer neurons (Norman, O'Reilly, & Huber, 2000).

ceptual judgments of duration and visual clarity (e.g., Masson & Caldwell, 1998). In summary, the available research suggests that conceptual and perceptual manipulations of processing ease tend to result in a similar signal of "fluency."

The Fluency-Affect Link

As noted earlier, the same stimulus is evaluated more positively when it can be processed with high rather than low fluency. We propose that this is the case because the fluency signal itself is hedonically marked. In general, high fluency is indicative of positive states of the environment or the cognitive system, whereas low fluency is indicative of negative states of the environment or the cognitive system. Consistent with these conjectures, the empirical evidence suggests that high fluency selectively increases positive, but not negative evaluations of the stimulus. Furthermore, high fluency elicits positive affect, as reflected in psychophysiological measures. Empirical evidence also suggests that people "by default" assume that their fluency-based affective reactions reflect their disposition toward the stimulus. Consistent with this thesis, the positive effects of high fluency on evaluative judgment are eliminated under conditions that invite the misattribution of affect to an irrelevant source. Before we review the available evidence, however, it is useful to ask *why* fluency may be hedonically marked. Several alternatives, which are not mutually exclusive, deserve consideration.

Fluency as a Cue to Familiarity. High fluency may be positive because it is a cue that a stimulus has been encountered before, or is in some way familiar.[3] Such a fluency-familiarity link is supported by empirical findings and computer simulations that identified several differences in the processing dynamics of familiar and novel stimuli. First, familiar stimuli are processed faster than novel stimuli (e.g., Haber & Hershenson, 1965; Jacoby & Dallas, 1981). Second, familiar stimuli elicit less attentional orienting than novel stimuli (Desimone et al., 1995). Third, familiar stimuli result in a faster, sharper, and more coherent network response than novel stimuli (Lewenstein & Nowak, 1989; Norman, O'Reilly, & Huber, 2000). Fourth, familiar stimuli do not generate a global "mismatch" signal (Carpenter & Grossberg, 1995; Metcalfe, 1993). It is also important that all four differences may emerge at early stages of stimulus processing and precede the recognition of specific features. Accordingly, an organism that monitors processing fluency may be able to detect novelty/familiarity even before it can fully de-

---

[3]The link between fluency, familiarity, and affect does not assume that the process is mediated by a conscious experience of familiarity, but simply that fluency provides a reliable cue to stimulus "oldness."

code the content of the stimulus (see Lewenstein & Nowak, 1989; Norman et al., 2000; Smith, 2000; Winkielman, Schwarz, & Nowak, in press; for discussions of these mechanisms).

Why, however, would familiarity be associated with positive valence? This connection may be grounded in a biological predisposition for caution in encounters with novel, and thus potentially harmful objects (Zajonc, 1998). Such instinctual "fear of the unknown" has been observed in a variety of species with a range of different stimuli (for a review see Hill, 1978). Moreover, a strong connection between signals of familiarity and positive affect has also been demonstrated by research testing the reverse order of this link—from positive affect to familiarity. For example, subliminal positive primes tend to increase judgments of familiarity for novel stimuli (Phaf, Rotteveel, & Spijksma, 1999), whereas the induction of positive moods increases judgments of truth, presumably via the "positive = familiar = true" connection (Garcia-Marques & Mackie, 2000).

Fluency as a Cue to Prototypicality and Symmetry.   A related fluency-valence link is suggested by the observation that prototypical and symmetrical stimuli are associated with faster and less complex processing (Checkosky & Whitlock, 1973; Posner & Keele, 1968; Palmer, 1991). Again, monitoring processing fluency may allow an organism to estimate the likely prototypicality or symmetry of the stimulus at very early processing stages.

Why, however, would prototypicality or symmetry be associated with positive valence? One possible answer is based on the notion that animals (including insects) have a built-in preference for prototypicality (averageness) and symmetry due to the association of these variables with high mate quality (e.g., Thornhill & Gangestad, 1993). In humans, such preferences have been observed in several domains. For example, average and symmetrical faces are reliably preferred over alternatives (e.g., Langlois & Roggman, 1990; Rhodes & Tremewan, 1996), as are symmetrical shapes (Berlyne, 1974). Similarly, studies have observed a preference for prototypical birds, cars, watches, and colors over less prototypical ones (e.g., Halberstadt & Rhodes, 2000; Martindale & Moore, 1988). Moreover, the notion of prototypicality entails familiarity: For a given perceiver, a stimulus is prototypical for its class due to its global similarity to previously encountered stimuli. Hence, familiarity may contribute to prototypicality effects in evaluation, rendering the two difficult to separate.

Fluency as a Cue to Cognitive Progress.   Finally, fluency may trigger affective responses because it provides feedback about the ongoing cognitive operations. Specifically, highly fluent (fast, easy, coherent) processing tends to be indicative of progress toward successful recognition and interpretation of the target (Carver & Scheier, 1990; Simon, 1967; Vallacher &

Nowak, 1999). If such progress is experienced as rewarding, it may motivate bringing the cognitive activity to completion. Ramashandran and Hirnstein (1999) draw on this notion in their analysis of Capgrass Syndrome (i.e., a lack of the ability to integrate successive encounters with the same persons into a stable person representation). They suggest that this deficit may be due to limbic system damage that prevents Capgrass patients from experiencing "a warm fuzzy emotional response" to a familiar face. Ramashandran and Hirnstein (1999) proposed that "in the absence of limbic activation—the 'glow' of recognition—there is no incentive for the brain to link successive views of a face, so that the patient treats a single person as several people" (p. 31). It is worth noting that the fluency-as-progress notion suggests that preference for familiarity, symmetry, prototypicality, and many other variables is a by-product of their influence on speed, effort, and coherence of processing.

Summary: Fluency as a Hedonically Marked Signal

The just discussed notions converge on the assumption that the fluency signal is hedonically marked because it says something about a positive or negative state of affairs, either in the world or within the cognitive system. In general, high fluency indicates a positive state of affairs, whereas low fluency indicates a negative state of affairs. Consistent with this *hedonic marking* thesis, our research shows that fluency triggers genuine affective responses that can be detected with psychophysiological measures. Moreover, the impact of fluency on stimulus evaluation is eliminated when people attribute this affective response to an irrelevant source, suggesting that the affective response is a crucial mediator of the fluency-evaluation link. In the next section, we review this work. We first address the influence of perceptual fluency and subsequently turn to parallel influences of conceptual fluency. Throughout, we contrast the hedonic marking thesis with competing theoretical accounts.

PERCEPTUAL FLUENCY ENHANCES LIKING

Historically, the interest in the fluency-evaluation link was stimulated by research into the mere-exposure effect (Zajonc, 1968; i.e., the observation that repeated exposure to an initially neutral stimulus enhances liking of the stimulus; for review see Bornstein, 1989). Several authors proposed that the mere-exposure effect might be based on changes in perceptual fluency (Bornstein & D'Agostino, 1994; Klinger & Greenwald, 1994; Seamon et al., 1983). This proposal is consistent with the observation that repeated exposure speeds up stimulus recognition and enhances judgments of stimulus clarity and presentation duration (e.g., Haber & Hershenson, 1965; Jacoby & Dallas, 1981; Witherspoon & Allan, 1985; Whittlesea, Jacoby, & Girard, 1990). If so, any variable that increases perceptual fluency should result in more positive evaluations of the stimulus, even with a single exposure. Our initial studies were designed to test this conjecture.

Perceptual Fluency Facilitates Recognition and Increases Evaluative Judgments

In one of these studies (Reber, Winkielman, & Schwarz, 1998, Study 1), we presented participants with pictures of everyday objects, such as desk, bird, or plane (Snodgrass & Vanderwart, 1980). The quality of the pictures was slightly degraded and their processing fluency was manipulated through a visual priming procedure. Depending on conditions, the target was preceded by a subliminally presented, highly degraded contour of either the target picture or a different picture. We expected that a matching contour would facilitate processing (high fluency), consistent with research showing that subliminal visual primes enhance target's naming accuracy (Bar & Biederman, 1998).

Some participants were asked to indicate how much they liked the target pictures. Other participants were asked to press a key as soon as they could recognize the object in the picture, thus providing us with a measure of recognition speed, an indicator of fluency. The data were consistent with our predictions: Pictures primed by matched contours were recognized faster, indicating higher fluency, and were liked more than pictures preceded by mismatched contours. Post-experimental interviews revealed that participants were unaware of the fluency manipulation, thus eliminating the possibility of strategic responding to pictures preceded by various primes.

Additional studies replicated and extended these findings in several ways. First, we wanted to show that fluency enhances liking even when it is manipulated by means other than visual priming. This is important because the priming procedure requires a previous exposure to a similar stimulus, and thus is subject to interpretational debates on the mechanism by which repetition enhances preferences (Zajonc, 1998). Second, we wanted to show that liking can be increased by manipulations of fluency that do not rely on inhibitory influences. This is important because the matched/mismatched contour procedure may influence liking by either increasing or decreasing the fluency of processing. Third, we wanted to show that fluency could enhance liking without changes in the visual appearance of the stimulus. Again, this is important because the matched/mismatched contour procedure may potentially influence the quality of the visual input. Based on these considerations, we conducted several studies using other manipulations of perceptual fluency.

In one study (Reber et al., 1998, Study 3), we manipulated perceptual fluency through unobtrusive changes in presentation duration, taking advantage of the observation that longer presentation durations facilitate the extraction of information (Mackworth, 1963). As expected, participants evaluated the same stimulus more positively when it was presented for a longer duration. In another study (Reber et al., 1998, Study 2), we manipulated perceptual fluency through different degrees of figure-ground contrast, a variable that has been shown to influence identification speed (Checkosky & Whitlock, 1973). Again, participants liked the same stimulus more when it was presented with higher figure-ground contrast, and hence could be processed more fluently.

In combination, the just discussed studies based on visual priming, presentation duration, and figure-ground contrast consistently show that increases in perceptual fluency result in more positive evaluations of the perceived stimuli. Subsequent studies, to be reviewed further in this chapter, confirmed and extended this conclusion.

Perceptual Fluency Selectively Enhances Positive Responses: A Comparison with "Two-Step" Models

Our experiments on perceptual fluency also allowed us to further characterize the nature of the evaluative reactions elicited by processing facilitation, a question that bears on the mechanisms underlying the observed effects. As already noted, our hedonic marking thesis predicts that high fluency is associated with positive valence and hence selectively increases positive responses. This prediction is contrary to the predictions of so called *two-step models*, which hold that fluency is affectively neutral and can lead to increases in positive as well as negative responses, depending on the judgment task.

According to the nonspecific activation model proposed by Mandler and colleagues, the effects of fluency manipulations (e.g., repetition, priming) "are assumed to be content free and merely produce the greater accessibility of the activated representation" (Mandler, Nakamura, & Van Zandt, 1987, p. 646). This increased activation, in turn, leads the person to make more extreme judgments of the target, with the specific outcome depending on the judgment task. Summarizing their position regarding the mere-exposure effect, Mandler and colleagues wrote: "The hypothesis is that the prior exposure generates and activates the stimulus representations, and that such activation may then be related to any judgment about the stimuli that is stimulus relevant" (p. 647). This hypothesis predicts, for example, that increased fluency results in judgments of increased brightness when the question pertains to brightness, but of increased darkness when the question pertains to darkness. Empirically, this is the case (Mandler et al., 1987).

A related two-step model, proposed by Jacoby and colleagues, offers similar predictions. This model suggests that processing facilitation leads to an affectively neutral, "arousal-like" experience of fluency (Jacoby, Kelley, & Dywan, 1989). Based on contextual cues, this neutral fluency experience is then disambiguated and results in a more specific feeling. For example, in the context of a memory task, high fluency is presumably experienced as a feeling of familiarity, whereas in a context of a problem-solving task, the same fluency is presumably experienced as a feeling of confidence. This logic is analogous to Schachter and Singer's (1962) two-factor theory of emotion, which holds that in the presence of proper contextual cues, nonspecific arousal can lead to opposite emotions (see Jacoby et al., 1989; p. 395).

The two-step models presented by Mandler et al. (1987) and Jacoby et al. (1989) were primarily developed to account for implicit memory phenomena and discussed affective judgments rather parenthetically. Embracing the above logic, however, psychologists advanced closely related explicit models of the mere-exposure effect. For example, Bornstein and D'Agostino (1992, p. 106) suggested that the mere-exposure effect results from participants' attempts to arrive at "the most parsimonious and reasonable explanation" of "the experience of perceptual fluency, given situational constraints and the available contextual cues." In the process, the fluency experience may be attributed "to liking or, for that matter, to any variety of stimulus properties that the subject is asked to rate" (p. 107). Similarly, Klinger and Greenwald (1994) suggested that "in the context of performing liking judgments, misattributions to liking and disliking are likely because the goal of the subject is to form a preference" (p. 77). Two-step models of this type, which explicitly acknowledge their indebtedness to Schachter and Singer (1962), converge on the prediction that high fluency can result in judgments of increased liking as well as increased disliking, depending on the specific nature of the judgment task.

Yet, as Reisenzein (1983) noted in a comprehensive review, Schachter and Singer's (1962) prediction that nonspecific arousal can equally result in positive as well as negative emotions has received little empirical support. The same appears to hold true for the above extensions of the two-factor theory, which have received considerable support in the nonevaluative domain and little support in the domain of preferences. Specifically, the impact of fluency on nonevaluative judgments depends, indeed, on the focus introduced by the judgment task, as illustrated by the brightness/darkness findings of Mandler et al. (1987) and the truth/fame/recognition findings of Jacoby and colleagues (Kelley & Jacoby, 1998). Yet, attempts to demonstrate a similar focus-dependency in the evaluative domain have consistently failed. For example, in Mandler et al.'s (1987) studies, as well as a follow-up by Seamon, McKenna, and Binder (1998), increased fluency led to higher judgments of liking, but not to higher judgments of disliking. This pattern contradicts two-step accounts, but is consistent with the assumption that fluency itself is positively marked. Our own studies reiterate this observation.

In one study (Reber et al., 1998, Study 2), we asked some participants to judge the "prettiness" of the targets, but asked other participants to judge the "ugliness" of the targets. In another study (Reber et al., 1998, Study 3), we asked some participants to make "liking" judgments, but asked others to make "disliking" judgments. In both studies, increased perceptual fluency resulted in higher judgments of "prettiness" and "liking" and lower judgments of "ugliness" and "disliking," as reflected in significant interactions of fluency and judgment focus. In combination, these findings indicate that increased fluency does not facilitate more extreme judgments in general, but selectively increases positive evaluations.

Note, however, that these studies are subject to the objection that judgments of disliking or ugliness may be less "natural" than judgments of liking and prettiness. Thus, Mandler et al. (1987) suggested that, in their studies, repeated exposure did not enhance disliking because "disliking is a complex judgment, often based on the absence of a liking response. Linguistically, liking is the unmarked and disliking the marked end of the imputed continuum" (p. 647). That is, participants may always evaluate stimuli in terms of likeability/prettiness and only subsequently reverse their response to report it along a disliking/ugliness scale, which would thwart the attempt to manipulate judgment focus. Although possible in principle, this explanation cannot account for results of a study by Winkielman and Cacioppo (2001, Study 1). In this study, participants were presented with targets that varied in fluency, manipulated via a visual priming manipulation. Some participants were told to selectively monitor and report only their positive affective reactions, while other participants were told to selectively monitor and report only their negative affective reactions. We framed the question this way because it is hard to argue that it is more "natural" for participants to monitor or report positive responses than negative responses, especially because participants have been able to provide such valence-specific reports in other research (see Cacioppo & Berntson, 1994; Cacioppo, Gardner, & Berntson, 1997 for reviews). As expected, we found a selective effect of the fluency manipulation on affective responses. Specifically, participants who focused on positive affect indicated more positive responses to the stimuli under high rather than low fluency conditions. In contrast to the predictions of two-step models, however, participants who focused on negative affect did *not* indicate more negative responses under high rather than low fluency conditions.

In summary, studies that tested the predictions of two-step models in the evaluative domain, using initially neutral stimuli, failed to support the hypothesis that increased fluency may equally result in more positive as well as more negative evaluations, depending on the focus of the judgment task. Instead, the available findings are consistent with the assumption that fluency is positively marked and selectively enhances positive evaluations of the processed stimuli. The next set of studies further supports this conclusion.

Perceptual Fluency Elicits Genuine Affective Responses

Another theoretically important question concerns the nature of the evaluative responses elicited by processing facilitation. According to our hedonic marking thesis, changes in fluency lead to genuine affective responses. If so, increases in fluency should manifest themselves in psychophysiological indicators of affective activation. Demonstrating this is important for several reasons. The evidence of genuine affective responses would indicate that fluency makes "hot" contact with the affective system (Winkielman, Berntson, & Cacioppo, 2001). As such, this observation would argue against the core assumption of two-step models that fluency is associated with evaluation by virtue of "cold", context-dependent inferential processes. Furthermore, psychophysiological measures can provide evidence for the positive hedonic marking of high fluency without relying on self-reports, thus avoiding complexities inherent in interpretation of response scales discussed earlier (Mandler et al., 1987; Schwarz, 1999).

To provide such evidence, Winkielman and Cacioppo (2001) measured affective responses to fluency with facial electromyography (EMG). This technique is based on observations that affective responses are reflected in the electrical activity of facial muscles (Cacioppo, Petty, Losch, & Kim, 1986; Lang, Greenwald, Bradley, & Hamm, 1993). Specifically, positive affective responses increase activity over the region of the zygomaticus major ("smiling muscle"). On the other hand, negative affective responses increase activity over the region of the corrugator supercilli ("frowning muscle"). More important, facial EMG responses can be elicited by stimuli that vary subtly in valence and do not produce overtly visible facial expressions (Cacioppo, Bush, & Tassinary, 1992; Dimberg, Thunberg, & Elmehed 2000). In the Winkielman and Cacioppo (2001) studies, participants were again asked to watch pictures of everyday objects. The fluency with which these pictures could be processed was manipulated through visual priming in Study 1 and through variations in presentation duration in Study 2. While participants watched the pictures, the EMG activity was recorded from several muscle sites, including the zygomaticus major and corrugator supercilli. Participants were also asked to rate each picture using scales designed to tap selectively into positive and negative affect, as described previously. To avoid a contamination with spontaneous EMG responses, however, participants gave these ratings several seconds after the presentation of the picture. The results of both studies were very consistent. High fluency was associated with stronger activity over the zygomaticus region (indicative of positive affect), but was not associated with the activity of the corrugator region (indicative of negative affect). Furthermore, these differences in activity occurred in the first 3 seconds after the presentation of the stimulus, several seconds before subjects made their overt judgments, indicating a spontaneous affective response to processing fluency.

In combination, the findings of the Winkielman and Cacioppo (2001) studies suggest that manipulations of processing fluency have genuine affective consequences, thus supporting our theoretical assumption that fluency is hedonically marked and triggers the affect system. Furthermore, these findings suggest that the affect generated by processing facilitation is positive, thus providing another argument against the assumption of the two-step models that fluency is equally likely to elicit positive as well as negative responses.

Perceptual Fluency and the Mere-Exposure Effect

Research into the fluency-evaluation link was initially stimulated by debates about the mere-exposure effect (Zajonc, 1968, 1998). More than 30 years of research have shown that repetition reliably enhances liking for an initially neutral stimulus (for review see Bornstein, 1989). As noted earlier, several authors have proposed that the mere-exposure effect may be based on changes in perceptual fluency (Bornstein & D'Agostino, 1994; Jacoby et al., 1989; Seamon et al., 1983). Although our findings are incompatible with the two-factor models that have been stimulated by this assumption, they highlight that any variable that increases fluency of processing will result in more positive evaluations of the stimulus. From this perspective, repetition is just one of the many variables that increase fluency of processing and priming, duration, figure-ground contrast, and probably many other variables, are functionally equivalent.

Further supporting the parallels between effects of stimulus repetition and other manipulations of processing fluency, Monahan, Murphy, and Zajonc (2000) observed that repeated exposure elicits positive affect. In their study, participants were exposed to 25 ideographs under subliminal conditions, and were later asked to report their tonic mood. For some participants, each of the 25 ideographs was different, while for other participants, 5 different ideographs were repeated 5 times each. The results showed that participants subliminally exposed to repeated ideographs reported being in a better mood than participants exposed to 25 different ideographs. Moreover, Harmon-Jones and Allen (2001) observed that repeatedly presented stimuli elicited stronger EMG activity over the zygomaticus region, indicative of positive affect, without changing the activity over the corrugator region. These findings are consistent with the EMG results obtained by Winkielman and Cacioppo (2001), based on different manipulations of processing fluency. In combination, the Monahan et al. (2000), Harmon-Jones and Allen (2001), and Winkielman and Cacioppo (2001) studies demonstrate that stimulus repetition, as well as other manipulations of processing fluency, can elicit a positive affective response.

Although we suggest that the mere-exposure effect is driven by the impact of stimulus repetition on processing fluency, we agree with Zajonc (1998) that the mere-exposure effect cannot be fully explained by the two-step models discussed earlier (Bornstein & D'Agostino, 1994; Jacoby et al., 1989; Klinger & Greenwald, 1994; Mandler, 1980). Instead, we propose that the positive hedonic marking of the fluency signal is the crucial ingredient, consistent with the accumulating evidence that high fluency elicits positive affect. Furthermore, we suggest that the role of perceptual fluency in the mere-exposure effect is consistent with the notion of "preferences without inferences" (Zajonc, 1980, 2000). After all, affective responses may result from changes in the dynamics of perceptual processing that are generated very early and do not derive from analysis of stimulus features.

CONCEPTUAL FLUENCY ENHANCES LIKING

So far, we have focused on the consequences of *perceptual fluency*. Accordingly, the studies reviewed here relied on manipulations like visual priming, presentation duration, figure-ground contrast, or stimulus repetition, which are designed to influence low-level stages of processing, concerned with identifying the stimulus' physical identity. As the following studies indicate, parallel effects can also be observed for increases in *conceptual fluency*. These studies relied on manipulations designed to influence high-level stages of processing, concerned with identifying the meaning of the stimulus. In addition to extending the fluency-evaluation link from perceptual to conceptual fluency, these studies address theoretical issues related to the relative contributions of perceptual and conceptual fluency, the automaticity of the mediating processes, and the nature of subjective fluency experiences.

Conceptual Fluency Increases Evaluative Judgments

To our knowledge, the first experiment that directly examined the influence of conceptual fluency on evaluative judgments was conducted by Whittlesea (1993, Experiment 5). In his study, the fluency with which target words could be processed was manipulated by embedding them in a predictive or nonpredictive semantic context ("stormy seas tossed the *boat*" vs. "stormy seas tossed the *lamp*"). Words embedded in the predictive context (e.g., boat) were pronounced faster than words embedded in a nonpredictive context (e.g., lamp), indicating higher fluency. More important, when participants were asked how much they like the target words, the semantically predicted words (boat) were rated as more pleasant than the nonpredicted words (lamp). Unfortunately, Whittlesea's study is ambiguous in several respects. First, it is unclear if the preferences for target words were influenced by a facilitation of fluency in the predictive context, an impediment in fluency in the nonpredictive context, or both. Second, it is unclear to what extent participants' preferences actually reflected the fluency with which they processed the target words, rather than their reactions to the (in)congruity of the whole sentence. That is, participants may have found the sentences like "stormy seas tossed the lamp" to be ill-formed or highly unusual, and may have generalized this reaction to the word "lamp." Hence, Whittlesea's (1993) pioneering exploration of conceptual fluency is consistent with the perceptual fluency results reviewed above, but suffers from some ambiguities.

To avoid these ambiguities, we used a cross-modal semantic paradigm to test the evaluative consequences of conceptual fluency. This paradigm has previously been used to examine the contribution of conceptual fluency to recognition memory (Fazendeiro & Luo, 2000; Roediger, Srinivas, & Weldon, 1989; Weldon, 1993). Specifically, participants are first exposed to "study" stimuli (primes) that are presented in one representational form (e.g., words) and subsequently respond to "test" stimuli (targets) that are presented in a different form (e.g., pictures). The relation between test and study stimuli may be of different kinds. The stimuli can be unrelated (word "dog", picture "shovel") or they can be semantically related, based either on their associative link or membership in a common category (word "key," picture "lock"). Research using this paradigm showed that participants are more likely to erroneously recognize a test item as previously presented when the item is semantically related to study items than when it is not (Fazendeiro & Luo, 2000). It is worth emphasizing that this effect reflects the influence of primes on conceptual fluency for targets, and does not depend on changes in perceptual fluency (Roediger et al., 1989).

We used two versions of the cross-modal semantic paradigm to examine evaluative consequences of conceptual fluency (Fazendeiro & Winkielman, 2000; Winkielman & Fazendeiro, 2000). In some studies, a prime word immediately preceded each picture target (cross-modal semantic priming) whereas in other studies, a list of prime words was presented first and was followed after a small delay with a list of picture targets (cross-modal semantic memory).

Cross-Modal Semantic Priming. Participants were shown a series of pictures of common objects and animals. Each picture was preceded by a letter string consisting either of a word or a nonword. Participants were kept from focusing on the word–picture relation by performing two different tasks. First, the participants indicated, as fast as possible, if the letter string was an actual English word. Second, the participants reported their liking for the picture. The letter strings served as the manipulation of conceptual fluency. Specifically, some pictures were preceded by matched words (e.g., word "dog" - picture "dog"), introducing the highest level of fluency. Other pictures were preceded by associatively related words (e.g., word "key" - picture "lock"), introducing a medium level of fluency. Yet other pictures were preceded by an unrelated word (e.g., word "snow" - picture "desk"), introducing the lowest level of fluency. The results showed a robust effect of conceptual fluency on participants' evaluation of the target pictures. As expected, pictures preceded by matching words were liked significantly more than pictures preceded by related words, which, in turn, were liked significantly more than pictures preceded by unrelated words.

Cross-Modal Semantic Memory. We replicated and extended the above findings using a paradigm where participants first studied a list with 32 pictures and words, each presented for 250 ms. After a short delay, participants were presented with another list of items and indicated their liking for them. The items on this test list were of three different types. Some test items were previously presented on the study list in the same modality (e.g., picture "bird" - picture "bird"). Other items were semantically related to items from the study list and appeared in a different modality (e.g., word "snow" - picture "shovel"). Finally, yet other test items had no semantic relation to the study items (e.g., word "snow" - picture "desk").

We conducted several studies using this paradigm. Across these studies, we observed that participants liked pictures that were associatively related to words from the study list significantly more than pictures that had no semantic relationship to words from the study list. Moreover, participants tended to like the new, but "related" pictures as much as the previously presented "old" pictures. This finding suggests that conceptual fluency elicited by a cross-modal semantic associate may increase liking as much as perceptual fluency from previous exposure to the same stimulus in the same modality.[4] This finding is consistent with other research that observed an equal, and occasionally greater, influence of conceptual as compared to perceptual fluency (Poldrack & Logan, 1998; Whittlesea, 1993).

---

[4]In this, as in all other studies using the memory paradigm, fluency increased liking only in the "word at study - picture at test" direction. No systematic effects were observed in the "picture at study - word at test" direction. This finding suggests a picture superiority effect—very good memory for information presented in the picture form (Israel & Schachter, 1997). Specifically, because participants remember the study pictures very well, they are less likely to (mis)attribute the fluency to the related words at test (Jacoby & Whitehouse, 1989).

The Role of Automatic Processes

Our studies in the cross-modal semantic memory paradigm have also allowed us to address theoretical issues regarding the mechanisms underlying the observed influence of fluency. As discussed earlier, we assume that fluency elicits a positive affective reaction that is perceived as being about the target (Higgins, 1998). This process does not require conscious inferences about the meaning of fluency or conscious attributions of positive affect to the target. Instead, conscious inferences are only involved when the informational value of the experience is discounted, an issue to which we return further in this chapter (see Schwarz, 1990, for a discussion). Accordingly, the previously observed effects of fluency on liking judgments should be obtained even when participants' cognitive resources are limited. In fact, we may expect that fluency effects increase under resource limitations, because these limitations interfere with the integration of additional information about the stimulus. This prediction parallels the observation that mood effects increase under time pressure (Siemer & Reisenzein, 1998), consistent with the predictions of the mood-as-information model (Schwarz, 1990).

To test this prediction, we asked some participants to hold an 8-digit number in mind while evaluating the test stimuli. As expected, the impact of fluency increased under resource limitations. Specifically, participants preferred "related" pictures more strongly to "unrelated" pictures when they were under cognitive load than when they were not. This finding suggests that reliance on the hedonically marked fluency signal is automatic and does not require extensive inferences (Bargh, 1996).

The Role of Attribution

The earlier observation that reliance on the affective reactions elicited by fluency is a "default" strategy that requires few cognitive resources does not imply, however, that the observed influence is unconditional. If participants are aware that their response to the stimulus may be influenced by external variables, they may discount their response as irrelevant to the judgment at hand, as has been observed for other sources of experiential information (for a review see Schwarz & Clore, 1996). Note, however, that the informational value of the fluency signal may be undermined in two different ways. On the one hand, people may become aware that a variable like exposure duration influences the ease with which the stimulus can be processed. Such awareness may undermine the informational value of the fluency signal, along with the informational value of the affective experience that is part and parcel of the fluency signal (as suggested by the EMG studies; Winkielman & Cacioppo, 2001). On the other hand, people may attribute their affective response to an external variable, thus undermining only the informational value of the elicited affect. We addressed both of these possibilities in two studies based on the cross-modal semantic memory paradigm.

In one study, we manipulated participants' attributions by varying the presentation time for study words. For some participants, the study words were presented for 250 ms (short condition); for other participants, the words were presented for 2000 ms (long condition). We expected that participants in the long condition would be more likely to identify the true source of the enhanced fluency and would accordingly discount their fluency-based reaction to test pictures. The logic of this manipulation is based on research that shows that awareness of the priming episode undermines the otherwise observed effects (e.g., Jacoby & Whitehouse, 1989; Lombardi, Higgins, & Bargh, 1987; Strack et al., 1993). The results confirmed our predictions. Participants in the short exposure condition liked the "related" pictures more than "unrelated" pictures. Yet, no difference in liking was obtained in the long exposure condition, presumably reflecting the discounting of fluency-based reactions.

In a second study, we introduced two different misattribution manipulations designed to undermine either the informational value of the affective response or the informational value of the fluency experience. Specifically, we told participants, before they made their liking judgments, that their reactions to the stimuli might be influenced by background music played to them. The music was an ambiguous new-age piece recorded at half-speed (see Schwarz, Bless, Strack, Klump, & Rittenauer-Schatka, 1991, for details on this manipulation). Some participants were told that the music might bias how easily stimuli come to mind (i.e. their fluency experience), whereas other participants were told the music might influence how they feel about the various stimuli (i.e. their affective experience). The results were highly informative. Specifically, attributing subjective fluency to music did not eliminate the effect of processing facilitation on liking. That is, participants who were informed that the music might influence how easily things come to mind still judged pictures as more likeable when they were preceded by related rather than unrelated words, replicating our previous findings. In contrast, attributing the affective response to the music *did* eliminate the effect of processing facilitation on liking. That is, participants who were informed that the music might influence their feelings toward various stimuli no longer judged new pictures as more likeable when they were preceded by related rather than by unrelated words. We interpret this pattern of results as suggesting that processing facilitation may immediately lead to an affective reaction. It is this affective reaction, and not the fluency experience itself, that is attributed to the target picture, resulting in enhanced liking. This interpretation is consistent with the findings reviewed previously, which indicate that facilitation of perceptual processing elicits a positive affective experience, as revealed in judgment asymmetries (Reber et al., 1998; Seamon, Luo, & Gallo, 1998), electromyographic findings (Harmon-Jones & Allen, 2001; Winkielman & Cacioppo, 2001), and mood reports (Monahan et al., 2000).

CONCLUSIONS AND BOUNDARY CONDITIONS

This chapter presented theoretical and empirical arguments for a causal influence of processing fluency on evaluations. The reviewed studies demonstrate that perceptual and conceptual manipulations of processing fluency reliably influence evaluative judgments. The findings further indicate that processing fluency elicits positive affect, which can be captured with psychophysiological measures. Finally, the misattribution studies suggest that this positive affect is the crucial link between fluency and positive evaluations: When the informational value of the affective reaction is undermined, fluency effects on preference judgments are no longer obtained. Several variables are likely to moderate the impact of fluency on preference judgments and we conclude this chapter with a discussion of these variables and the identification of likely boundary conditions.

First, human findings and computer simulations suggest that the fluency signal is generated at very early stages of information processing (Curran, 2000; Lewenstein & Nowak, 1989; Norman et al., 2000; Smith, 2000). Accordingly, the fluency-based affective response might be the *first* evaluatively relevant information available. We would therefore expect fluency effects on preference judgments to be strongest under conditions that limit the extraction of additional information, which may compete with the fluency signal in the computation of a judgment. Such conditions include time pressure, limited cognitive capacity and a lack of motivation to process the stimulus in sufficient detail. So far, only the cognitive capacity prediction has been tested and has received clear support, as reviewed above.

Second, the fluency signal may be the most informative input when little other information can be extracted from the stimulus (e.g., because the stimulus is an unknown Chinese ideograph; e.g., Zajonc, 1968) or a neutral geometrical shape with little inherent meaning (e.g., Reber et al., 1998). When the stimuli are more meaningful, the impact of the fluency signal may be attenuated, provided that the conditions allow for the extraction of stimulus meaning. Consistent with these assumptions, exposure frequency, exposure duration and figure-ground contrast have been found to have the strongest influence on preference judgments when the stimuli are novel, neutral, and presented for relatively short durations (e.g., Bornstein & D'Agostino, 1992; Reber & Schwarz, 2001).

Third, by the same token, highly familiar or simple stimuli may initially elicit a positive reaction because they can be processed with high fluency but may seem uninteresting and boring once their features are extracted and attended to (Bornstein, Kale, & Cornell, 1990). The observation that fluency increases liking is therefore not at odds with the observation that people may sometimes prefer novel, complex, and surprising stimuli over simple and familiar ones (Cox & Cox, 1988). We propose, however, that the latter preference emerges at a later stage of processing and is different from, and independent of, the immediate positive affect elicited by fluency at an earlier stage.

Fourth, when fluency derives from incidental variables, like exposure duration, exposure frequency or priming manipulations, awareness of these variables is likely to undermine the perceived informational value of fluency and its accompanying affective response. This is consistent with the misattribution studies reviewed previously, as well as with the observation that mere-exposure effects decrease with increasing awareness of the manipulation (Bornstein & D'Agostino, 1992). Moreover, these findings parallel similar observations with regard to other sources of experiential information (for a review see Schwarz & Clore, 1996).

Fifth, to avoid overgeneralization, it is worth emphasizing that many evaluative judgments (e.g., judgments of morality) require a consideration of stimulus meaning. The degree to which initial fluency-based affective reactions influence such judgments is an open question, which deserves attention in future research.

Sixth, when forming *nonevaluative* judgments, individuals are likely to ignore the hedonic component of their fluency experience, but still draw on its other aspects. In that case, they need to interpret the implications of their fluency experience for the judgment at hand, as suggested by the two-step models (Jacoby et al., 1989; Mandler et al., 1987). Under these conditions, the impact of fluency depends on the focus of the judgment task and high fluency may, for example, enhance judgments of different conceptual qualities, such as fame or truth, or different perceptual qualities, such as loudness or clarity. However, such focus-of-judgment effects are not observed for evaluations, as discussed earlier.

Seventh, it is possible that the impact of experienced fluency is moderated by the person's processing expectations. Whittlesea and Williams (1998) observed, for example, that participants who initially expected a stimulus to be uninterpretable were more likely to attribute processing fluency to prior exposure than participants who did not expect interpretation difficulties. Hence, the former were more likely than the latter to conclude that they had seen the stimulus before. The role of processing expectations in the fluency-affect link has so far received no attention.

Finally, it is possible that high fluency may lead to more *negative* evaluations under some specific conditions. Although such a reversal of the usually obtained positive influence has not yet been observed, it is conceivable under two conditions. First, in an environment where, say, familiarity or prototypicality are associated with danger, fluency may become a reliable cue to negativity. A test of this possibility awaits the identification of a suitable environment. Second, and less speculative, such reversals are likely when people are lead to consciously believe that the subjective experience of processing fluency is an indicator of negative value. In this case, their initially automatic positive reaction to high fluency may be overridden by deliberate, theory-driven inference processes that result in a negative judgment. The fact that individuals' "naive" theories about the meaning of subjective experiences can determine which inferences they draw from a feeling is well documented (e.g., Skurnik, Moskowitz, & Johnson, 2000; Winkielman & Schwarz, 2001; see Skurnik, Schwarz, & Winkielman, 2000, for a discussion), but has not yet been tested for the influence of fluency on evaluative judgments.

As this discussion of moderators and boundary conditions indicates, we generally expect fluency-based affective reactions to exert their strongest influence under the conditions that are also known to give rise to pronounced mood effects in evaluative judgment: When little other information is available; when the person's processing capacity or motivation is low, thus limiting more deliberate information search and integration; and when the informational value of the affect has not been called into question (for discussions see Schwarz, 1990; Schwarz & Clore, 1996). However, these parallels should not distract from the unique character of fluency-based affect. Most important, fluency-based affect is not based on the analysis of the stimulus meaning (in contrast to specific emotions), nor does it necessarily reflect incidental influences that are completely unrelated to the stimulus (such as the weather or an earlier compliment), as is typical for moods. Instead, it results from the dynamics of information processing itself. In this sense, processing fluency allows preferences that do not depend on the affective content of the stimulus proper.

REFERENCES

Anderson, N. H. (1981). *Foundations of information integration theory.* New York: Academic Press.

Bar, M., & Biederman, I. (1998). Subliminal visual priming. *Psychological Science, 9,* 464–469.

Bargh, J. A. (1996). Automaticity in social psychology. In E. T. Higgins & A. W. Kruglanski (Ed.), *Social Psychology: Handbook of Basic Principles* (pp. 169–183). New York: Guilford Press.

Bargh, J. A., Chaiken S., Raymond, P., & Hymes, C. (1996). The automatic evaluation effect: Unconditional automatic attitude activation with a pronunciation task. *Journal of Experimental Social Psychology, 32,* 104–128.

Berlyne, D. E. (1974). *Studies in the new experimental aesthetics: Steps toward an objective psychology of aesthetic appreciation.* Washington, DC: Hemisphere Co.

Berridge, K. C. (1999). Pleasure, pain, desire, and dread: Hidden core processes of emotion. In D. Kahneman, E. Diener, & N. Schwarz (Eds.), *Well-being: The foundations of hedonic psychology* (pp. 525–557). New York, NY: Russell Sage Foundation.

Bodenhausen, G. V. (1993). Emotions, arousal, and stereotypic judgments: A heuristic model of affect and stereotyping. In D. M. Mackie & D. L. Hamilton (Eds.), *Affect, cognition, and stereotyping* (pp. 13–37). San Diego, CA: Academic Press.

Bornstein, R. F. (1989). Exposure and affect: Overview and meta-analysis of research, 1968-1987. *Psychological Bulletin, 106,* 265–289.

Bornstein, R. F., & D'Agostino, P. R. (1992). Stimulus recognition and the mere exposure effect. *Journal of Personality and Social Psychology, 63,* 545–552.

Bornstein, R. F., & D'Agostino, P. R. (1994). The attribution and discounting of perceptual fluency: Preliminary tests of a perceptual fluency/attributional model of the mere exposure effect. *Social Cognition, 12,* 103–128.

Bornstein, R. F., Kale, A. R., & Cornell, K. R. (1990). Boredom as a limiting condition on the mere exposure effect. *Journal of Personality and Social Psychology, 58,* 791–800.

Bower, G. H. (1981). Mood and memory. *American Psychologist, 36,* 129–148.

Cacioppo, J. T., & Berntson, G. G. (1994). Relationship between attitudes and evaluative space: A critical review, with emphasis on the separability of positive and negative substrates. *Psychological Bulletin, 115,* 401–423.

Cacioppo, J. T., Bush, L. K., & Tassinary, L. G. (1992). Microexpressive facial actions as a function of affective stimuli: Replication and extension. *Personality and Social Psychology Bulletin, 18,* 515–526.

Cacioppo, J. T., Gardner, W., & Berntson, G. G. (1997). Beyond bipolar conceptualizations and measures: The case of attitudes and evaluative space. *Personality and Social Psychology Review, 1,* 3–25.

Cacioppo, J. T., Petty, R. E., Losch, M. E., & Kim, H. S. (1986). Electromyographic activity over facial muscle regions can differentiate the valence and intensity of affective reactions. *Journal of Personality and Social Psychology, 50,* 260–268.

Carpenter, G. A., & Grossberg, S. (1995). Adaptive resonance theory (ART). In M. Arbib (Ed.), *The handbook of brain theory and neural networks* (pp. 79–82). Cambridge, MA: MIT press.

Carver, C. S., & Scheier, M. F. (1990). Origins and functions of positive and negative affect: A control-process view. *Psychological Review, 97,* 19–35.

Checkosky, S. F., & Whitlock, D. (1973). The effects of pattern goodness on recognition time in a memory search task. *Journal of Experimental Psychology, 100,* 341–348.

Clore, G. L. (1992). Cognitive phenomenology: Feelings and the construction of judgment. In L. L. Martin & A. Tesser (Eds.), *The construction of social judgments* (pp. 133–164). Hillsdale, NJ: Lawrence Erlbaum Associates.

Cox, D. S., & Cox, A. D. (1988). What does familiarity breed? Complexity as a moderator of repetition effects in advertisement evaluation. *Journal of Consumer Research, 15,* 111–116.

Curran, T. (2000). Brain potentials of recollection and familiarity. *Memory and Cognition, 28,* 923–938.

Davidson, R. J. (1993). Cerebral asymmetry and emotion: Conceptual and methodological conundrums. *Cognition & Emotion, 7,* 115–138.

Demb, J. B., Desmond, J. E., Wagner, A. D., Vaidya, C. J., Glover, G. H., & Gabrieli, J. D. E. (1995). Semantic encoding and retrieval in left inferior prefrontal cortex: A functional MRI study of task difficulty and process specificity. *Journal of Neuroscience, 15,* 5870–5878.

Desimone, R., Miller, E. K., Chelazzi, L., & Lueschow, A. (1995). Multiple memory systems in the visual cortex. In M. S. Gazzaniga (Ed.), *The cognitive neurosciences* (pp. 475–490). Cambridge, MA: MIT Press.

Dimberg, U., Thunberg, M., & Elmehed, K. (2000). Unconscious facial reactions to emotional facial expressions. *Psychological Science, 11,* 86–89.

Fazendeiro, T. A., & Luo, C. R. (2000). *False memory for paired-associates: Evidence for the implicit activation-fluency misattribution hypothesis.* Manuscript submitted for publication.

Fazendeiro, T. A., & Winkielman, P. (2000). *Effects of conceptual fluency on affective judgments.* Manuscript in preparation.

Fernandez-Duque, D., Baird, J. A., & Posner, M. I. (2000). Executive attention and metacognitive regulation. *Consciousness and Cognition, 9,* 288–307.

Frijda, N. H. (1988). The laws of emotions. *American Psychologist, 43,* 349–358.

Garcia-Marques, T., & Mackie, D. M. (2000). The positive feeling of familiarity: Mood as an information processing regulation mechanism. In H. Bless & J. Forgas (Eds.), *The message within: The role of subjective experience in social cognition and behavior* (pp. 240–261). Philadelphia: Psychology Press.

Haber, R. N., & Hershenson, M. (1965). The effects of repeated brief exposures on growth of a percept. *Journal of Experimental Psychology, 69,* 40–46.

Halberstadt, J., & Rhodes, G. (2000). The attractiveness of nonface averages: Implications for an evolutionary explanation of the attractiveness of average faces. *Psychological Science, 4,* 285–289.

Harmon-Jones, E., & Allen, J. J. B. (2001). The role of affect in the mere exposure effect: Evidence from psychophysiological and individual differences approaches. *Personality and Social Psychology Bulletin, 27,* 889–898.

Higgins, E. T. (1996). Knowledge activation: Accessibility, applicability, and salience. In E. T. Higgins & A. Kruglanski (Eds.), *Social psychology: Handbook of basic principles* (pp. 133–168). New York: Guilford Press.

Higgins, E. T. (1998). The aboutness principle: A pervasive influence on human inference. *Social Cognition, 16,* 173–198.

Hill, W. F. (1978). Effects of mere exposure on preferences in nonhuman animals. *Psychological Bulletin, 85,* 117–1198.

Israel, L., & Schacter, D. L. (1997). Pictorial encoding reduces false recognition of semantic associates. *Psychonomic Bulletin & Review, 4,* 577–581.

Jacoby, L. L. (1983). Perceptual enhancement: Persistent effects of an experience. *Journal of Experimental Psychology: Learning, Memory, and Cognition, 9,* 21–38.

Jacoby, L. L., & Dallas, M. (1981). On the relationship between autobiographical memory and perceptual learning. *Journal of Experimental Psychology: General, 110,* 306–340.

Jacoby, L. L., Kelley, C. M., Brown, J., & Jasechko, J. (1989). Becoming famous overnight: Limits on the ability to avoid unconscious influences of the past. *Journal of Personality and Social Psychology, 56,* 326–338.

Jacoby, L. L., Kelley, C. M., & Dywan, J. (1989). Memory attributions. In H. L. Roediger & F. I. M. Craik (Eds.), *Varieties of memory and consciousness: Essays in honour of Endel Tulving* (pp. 391–422). Hillsdale, NJ: Lawrence Erlbaum Associates.

Jacoby, L. L., & Whitehouse, K. (1989). An illusion of memory: False recognition influenced by unconscious perception. *Journal of Experimental Psychology: General, 118,* 126–135.

Kelley, C. M., & Jacoby, L. L. (1998). Subjective reports and process dissociation: Fluency, knowing, and feeling. *Acta Psychologica, 98,* 127–140.

Klinger, M. R., & Greenwald, A. G. (1994). Preferences need no inferences? The cognitive basis of unconscious mere exposure effects. In P. M. Niedenthal & S. Kitayama (Eds.), *The heart's eye* (pp. 67–85). San Diego: Academic Press.

Koriat, A. (2000). The feeling of knowing: Some metatheoretical implications for consciousness and control. *Consciousness and Cognition, 9,* 149–171.

Lang, P. J., Greenwald M. K., Bradley M. M., & Hamm A. O. (1993). Looking at pictures: Evaluative, facial, visceral, and behavioral responses. *Psychophysiology, 30,* 261–273.

Langlois, J. H., & Roggman, L. A. (1990). Attractive faces are only average. *Psychological Science, 1,* 115–121.

LeDoux, J. E. (1996). *The Emotional Brain.* New York: Touchstone.

Lewenstein, M., & Nowak, A. (1989). Recognition with self-control in neural networks. *Physical Review, 40*, 4652–4664.

Lombardi, W. J., Higgins, E. T., & Bargh, J. A. (1987). The role of consciousness in priming effects on categorization: Assimilation versus contrast as a function of awareness of the priming task. *Personality and Social Psychology Bulletin, 13*, 411–429.

Mackworth, J. F. (1963). The duration of the visual image. *Canadian Journal of Psychology, 17*, 62–81.

Mandler, G. (1980). Recognizing: The judgment of previous occurrence. *Psychological Review, 87*, 252–271.

Mandler, G., Nakamura, Y., & Van Zandt, B. J. (1987). Nonspecific effects of exposure on stimuli that cannot be recognized. *Journal of Experimental Psychology: Learning, Memory, and Cognition, 13*, 646–648.

Martindale, C., & Moore, K. (1988). Priming, prototypicality, and preference. *Journal of Experimental Psychology: Human Perception and Performance, 14*, 661–670.

Masson, M. E. J., & Caldwell, J. I. (1998). Conceptually driven encoding episodes create perceptual misattributions. *Acta Psychologica, 98*, 183–210.

Mazzoni, G., & Nelson, T. O. (1998). *Metacognition and Cognitive Neuropsychology : Monitoring and Control Processes.* Mahwah, NJ: Lawrence Erlbaum Associates.

McGlone, M. S., & Tofighbakhsh, J. (2000). Birds of a feather flock conjointly (?) Rhyme as reason in aphorisms. *Psychological Science, 11*, 424–428.

Metcalfe, J. (1993). Novelty monitoring, metacognition, and control in a composite holographic associative recall model: Implications for Korsakoff Amnesia. *Psychological Review, 100*, 3–22.

Metcalfe, J., & Shimamura, A. P. (1994). *Metacognition: Knowing about knowing.* Cambridge, MA: MIT Press.

Monahan, J. L., Murphy, S. T., & Zajonc, R. B. (2000). Subliminal mere exposure: Specific, general, and diffuse effects. *Psychological Science, 6*, 462–466.

Niedenthal, P. M., & Kitayama, S. (1994). *The heart's eye. Emotional influences in perception and attention.* San Diego, CA: Academic Press.

Norman, K. A., O'Reilly, R. C., & Huber, D. E. (2000). *Modeling hippocampal and neocortical contributions to recognition memory.* Poster presented at the Cognitive Neuroscience Society Meeting, San Francisco, CA.

Ortony, A., Clore, G. L., & Collins, A. (1988). *The cognitive structure of emotions.* New York: Cambridge University Press.

Palmer, S. E. (1991). Goodness, gestalt, groups, and Garner: Local symmetry subgroups as a theory of figural goodness. In J. R. Pomerantz & G. R. Lockhead (Eds.), *Perception of Structure.* Washington, DC: APA.

Phaf, R. H., Rotteveel, M., & Spijksma, F. P. (1999). *False recognition and affective priming.* Manuscript submitted for publication.

Poldrack, R. A., & Logan, G. D. (1998). What is the mechanism for fluency in successive recognition? *Acta Psychologica, 98*, 167–181.

Posner, M. I., & Keele, S. W. (1968). On the genesis of abstract ideas. *Journal of Experimental Psychology, 77*, 353–363.

Ramachandran, V. S., & Hirstein, W. (1999). The science of art: A neurological theory of aesthetic experience. *Journal of Consciousness Studies, 6*, 15–51.

Reber, R., & Schwarz, N. (1999). Effects of perceptual fluency on judgments of truth. *Consciousness and Cognition, 8*, 338–342.

Reber, R., & Schwarz, N. (2001). The hot fringes of consciousness: Perceptual fluency and affect. *Consciousness & Emotion, 2*, 223–231.

Reber, R., Winkielman P., & Schwarz, N. (1998). Effects of perceptual fluency on affective judgments. *Psychological Science, 9*, 45–48.

Reisenzein, R. (1983). The Schachter theory of emotion: Two decades later. *Psychological Bulletin, 94,* 239–264.

Rhodes, G., & Tremewan, T. (1996). Averageness, exaggeration, and facial attractiveness. *Psychological Science, 7,* 105–110.

Roediger, H. L. (1990). Implicit memory: Retention without remembering. *American Psychologist, 45,* 1043–1056.

Roediger, H. L., Srinivas, K., & Weldon, M. S. (1989). Dissociations between implicit measures of retention. In S. Lewandowsky, J. C. Dunn, & K. Kirsner (Eds.), *Implicit Memory: Theoretical Issues* (pp. 67–84). Hillsdale, NJ: Lawrence Erlbaum Associates.

Schachter, S. E., & Singer, J. (1962). Cognitive, social, and physiological determinants of emotional state. *Psychological Review, 69,* 379–399.

Schacter, D. L. (1992). Understanding implicit memory: A cognitive neuroscience approach. *American Psychologist, 47,* 559–569.

Schwarz, N. (1990). Feeling as information: Informational and motivational functions of affective states. In E. T. Higgins & R. M. Sorrentino (Eds.), *Handbook of motivation and cognition* (pp. 527–561). New York: Guilford Press.

Schwarz, N. (1998). Accessible content and accessibility experiences: The interplay of declarative and experiential information in judgment. *Personality and Social Psychology Review, 2,* 87–99.

Schwarz, N. (1999). Self-reports: How the questions shape the answers. *American Psychologist, 54,* 93–105.

Schwarz, N., & Bless, H. (1992). Constructing reality and its alternatives: Assimilation and contrast effect in social judgments. In L. L. Martin & A. Tesser (Eds.), *The construction of social judgments* (pp. 217–245). Hillsdale, NJ: Lawrence Erlbaum Associates.

Schwarz, N., Bless, H., Strack, F., Klumpp, G., Rittenauer-Schatka, H., & Simons, A. (1991). Ease of retrieval as information: Another look at the availability heuristic. *Journal of Personality and Social Psychology, 61,* 195–202.

Schwarz, N., & Clore, G. L. (1983). Mood, misattribution, and judgments of well-being: Informative and directive functions of affective states. *Journal of Personality and Social Psychology, 45,* 513–523.

Schwarz, N., & Clore, G. L. (1996). Feelings and phenomenal experiences. In E. T. Higgins & A. W. Kruglanski (Eds.), *Social Psychology: Handbook of Basic Principles.* New York: The Guilford Press.

Seamon, J. G., Brody, N., & Kauff, D. M. (1983). Affective discrimination of stimuli that are not recognized: Effects of shadowing, masking, and cerebral laterality. *Journal of Experimental Psychology: Learning, Memory, and Cognition, 9,* 544–555.

Seamon, J. G., Luo, C. R., & Gallo, D. A. (1998). Creating false memories of words with or without recognition of list items: Evidence for nonconscious processes. *Psychological Science, 9,* 20–26.

Seamon, J. G., McKenna, P. A., & Binder, N. (1998). The mere exposure effect is differentially sensitive to different judgment tasks. *Consciousness and Cognition, 7,* 85–102.

Siemer, M., & Reisenzein, R. (1998). Effects of mood on evaluative judgment: Influence of reduced processing capacity and mood salience. *Cognition and Emotion, 12,* 783–805.

Simon, H. A. (1967). Motivational and emotional controls of cognition. *Psychological Review, 74,* 29–39.

Skurnik, I., Moskowitz, G., & Johnson, M. K. (2000). The illusions of truth and falseness: Irrational biases or metacognitive inferences? Manuscript submitted for publication.

Skurnik, I., Schwarz, N., & Winkielman, P. (2000). Drawing inferences from feelings: The role of naive beliefs. In H. Bless & J. P. Forgas (Eds.), *The message within: The role of subjective experience in social cognition and behavior* (pp. 162–175). Philadelphia: Psychology Press.

Smith, C. A., & Ellsworth, P. C. (1985). Patterns of cognitive appraisal in emotion. *Journal of Personality and Social Psychology, 48,* 813–838.

Smith, E. R. (2000). Subjective experience of familiarity: Functional basis in connectionist memory. In H. Bless & J. P. Forgas (Eds.), *The message within: The role of subjective experience in social cognition and behavior* (pp. 109–124). Philadelphia: Psychology Press.

Snodgrass, J. G., & Vanderwart, M. (1980). A standardized set of 260 pictures: Norms for name agreement, image agreement, familiarity, and visual complexity. *Journal of Experimental Psychology: Human Learning and Memory, 6,* 174–215.

Squire, L. R. (1992). Memory and the hippocampus: A synthesis from findings with rats, monkeys, and humans. *Psychological Review, 99,* 195–231.

Stepper, S., & Strack, F. (1993). Proprioceptive determinants of emotional and nonemotional feelings. *Journal of Personality and Social Psychology, 64,* 211–220.

Strack, F., Martin, L. L., & Stepper, S. (1988). Inhibiting and facilitating condition of facial expressions: A non-obtrusive test of the facial feedback hypothesis. *Journal of Personality and Social Psychology, 54,* 768–777.

Strack, F., Schwarz, N., Bless, H., Kübler, A., & Wänke, M. (1993). Awareness of the influence as a determinant of assimilation versus contrast. *European Journal of Social Psychology, 23,* 53–62.

Thornhill, R., & Gangestad, S. W. (1993). Human facial beauty: Averageness, symmetry, and parasite resistance. *Human Nature, 4,* 237–269.

Tulving, E., & Schacter, D. L. (1990). Priming and human memory. *Science, 247,* 301–306.

Vallacher, R. R., & Nowak, A. (1999). The dynamics of self-regulation. In R. S. Wyer Jr. (Ed.), *Perspectives on behavioral self-regulation* (pp. 241–259). Mahwah: Lawrence Erlbaum Associates.

Weldon, M. S. (1993). The time course of perceptual and conceptual contributions to word fragment completion priming. *Journal of Experimental Psychology: Learning, Memory, and Cognition, 19,* 1010–1026.

Whittlesea, B. W. A. (1993). Illusions of familiarity. *Journal of Experimental Psychology: Learning, Memory, and Cognition, 19,* 1235–1253.

Whittlesea, B. W. A., Jacoby L. L., & Girard, K. (1990). Illusions of immediate memory: Evidence of an attributional basis for feelings of familiarity and perceptual quality. *Journal of Memory and Language, 29,* 716–732.

Whittlesea, B. W. A., & Williams, L. D. (1998). Why do strangers feel familiar, but friends don't? A discrepancy-attribution account of feelings of familiarity. *Acta Psychologica, 98,* 141–165.

Winkielman P., Berntson, G. G., & Cacioppo, J. T. (2001). The psychophysiological perspective on the social mind. In A. Tesser & N. Schwarz (Eds.), *Blackwell handbook of social psychology: Intraindividual processes* (pp. 89–108). Oxford: Blackwell.

Winkielman, P., & Cacioppo, J. T. (2001). Mind at ease puts a smile on the face: Psychophysiological evidence that processing facilitation increases positive affect. *Journal of Personality and Social Psychology, 81,* 989–1000.

Winkielman, P., & Fazendeiro, T. A. (2000). The role of conceptual fluency in preference and memory. Manuscript in preparation.

Winkielman, P., & Schwarz, N. (2001). How pleasant was your childhood? Beliefs about memory shape inferences from experienced difficulty of recall. *Psychological Science, 12,* 176–179.

Winkielman, P., Schwarz, N., & Nowak, A. (in press). Affect and processing dynamics: Perceptual fluency enhances evaluations. In S. Moore & M. Oaksford (Eds.), *Emotional Cognition: From brain to behavior.* Amsterdam: John Benjamins.

Winkielman, P., Zajonc, R. B., & Schwarz, N. (1997). Subliminal affective priming resists attributional interventions. *Cognition and Emotion, 11,* 433–465.

Witherspoon, D., & Allan, L. G. (1985). The effects of a prior presentation on temporal judgments in a perceptual identification task. *Memory and Cognition, 13,* 103–111.

Zajonc, R. B. (1968). Attitudinal effects of mere exposure. *Journal of Personality and Social Psychology: Monograph Supplement, 9,* 1–27.

Zajonc, R. B. (1980). Feeling and thinking: Preferences need no inferences. *American Psychologist, 35,* 117–123.

Zajonc, R. B. (1998). Emotions. In D. T. Gilbert, S. T. Fiske, & G. Lindzey (Eds.), *The Handbook of Social Psychology* (pp. 591–632). Boston, MA: McGraw-Hill.

Zajonc, R. B. (2000). Feeling and thinking: Closing the debate over the independence of affect. In J. P. Forgas (Ed.), *Feeling and thinking: The role of affect in social cognition* (pp. 31–58). Cambridge, UK: Cambridge University Press.

Zajonc, R. B., Murphy, S. T., & Inglehart, M. (1989). Feeling and facial efference: Implications of the vascular theory of emotion. *Psychological Review, 96,* 395–416.

III: Individual Differences
and Indirect Measures
of Evaluations

Chapter 9

A Structural Analysis of Indirect Measures of Attitudes

Jan De Houwer
University of Southampton

One of the most important recent developments in the study of attitudes has been the growing interest in indirect measures of attitudes. Traditionally, researchers used self-report measures that allowed respondents to reflect on and express their attitudes toward objects or object features in a conscious, deliberate way. However, such direct measures of attitudes have a number of drawbacks (e.g., Dovidio & Fazio, 1992; Greenwald & Banaji, 1995). First, direct measures of attitudes are susceptible to deception and self-presentational strategies. Second, in daily life, people often do not analyse their attitudes toward objects in a conscious and deliberate manner. In such cases, behavior can be guided by a spontaneous, automatic affective appraisal of the attitude object (e.g., Zajonc, 1980). Assuming that attitudes are stored in memory as associations between the representation of the attitude object and the representation of positive or negative valence (e.g., Fazio, 1986), such an automatic affective appraisal of objects can be regarded as equivalent to automatic attitude activation. Although there is some disagreement as to whether automatic attitude activation reflects a fundamentally different type of attitude than consciously constructed stimulus evaluations (e.g., Greenwald & Banaji, 1995), most authors agree that direct measures of attitudes are not well suited to measure the spontaneous affective reactions to attitude objects that often guide behavior.

Since the 1980s, a number of reaction time tasks have been developed that provide ways to measure attitudes indirectly. Historically, the affective priming task as developed by Fazio, Sanbonmatsu, Powell, and Kardes

(1986) can be regarded as the first and most influential of these tasks (see Klauer & Musch, chap. , this volume, for a review). In most affective priming studies, two stimuli are presented consecutively and participants are asked to evaluate the second stimulus, that is, to determine whether the second stimulus refers to something good or to something bad (e.g., by saying "good" or "bad"). Results consistently show that less time is needed to evaluate the second stimulus (also called the target) when this stimulus has the same valence as the first stimulus (also called the prime) (e.g, FLOWER - HAPPY) than when both stimuli have a different valence (e.g., CANCER - HAPPY) (e.g., Bargh, Chaiken, Govender, & Pratto, 1992; Fazio et al., 1986; Hermans, De Houwer, & Eelen, 1994).

The affective priming task can and has been used to measure attitudes. If the presentation of the prime leads to faster processing of positive than negative targets, this indicates that the participant has a positive attitude toward the prime stimulus. If a prime facilitates the processing of negative compared to positive targets, one can infer that the prime is negative for the participant. For instance, Fazio, Jackson, Dunton, and Williams (1995) used the affective priming task to measure racial attitudes. They used pictures of faces of Black or White persons as prime stimuli and selected positive and negative adjectives as target stimuli. If a participant evaluated positive adjectives more quickly when the prime was a White face than when the prime was a Black face but evaluated negative adjectives more quickly after a Black face prime than after a White face prime, Fazio et al. (1995) inferred that the participant had a bias against Black persons. Fazio et al. (1995) demonstrated the affective priming measure predicted subtle racial behavior more accurately than self-report measures of racial prejudice. This finding makes sense given that, in comparison to self-report measures, the affective priming measure (a) is less likely to be influenced by factors such as social desirability and self-presentation, (b) is more sensitive to the spontaneous, automatic evaluations of stimuli that can be assumed to guide real-life behavior.

Since the introduction of the affective priming task (Fazio et al., 1986), a number of other reaction time tasks have been introduced that also provide potential ways to measure attitudes indirectly. These tasks include the emotional Stroop task (e.g., Pratto & John, 1991), the Implicit Association Test (Greenwald, McGhee, & Schwartz, 1998), and the affective Simon task (De Houwer & Eelen, 1998). At present, it is unclear how these tasks relate to each other. In this chapter, I describe a structural analysis of these reaction time tasks. I start by presenting a taxonomy of compatibility tasks that have been developed within cognitive psychology. By applying the same taxonomy to the various indirect measures of attitudes, the essential similarities and differences between these indirect measures will be revealed as well as their relation to existing compatibility tasks. Finally, I discuss what the implications are of the structural analysis for the measurement of attitudes, in particular when and why the results of different indirect measures might diverge.

A TAXONOMY OF COMPATIBILITY TASKS

Numerous studies have demonstrated that reaction time performance depends on the compatibility between the presented stimuli and the required responses and/or the relation between (features of) the stimuli that are presented. Kornblum (Kornblum, Hasbroucq, & Osman, 1990; Kornblum & Lee, 1995) pointed out that one can distinguish three types of compatibility: (a) relevant Stimulus–Response (S–R) compatibility, (b) irrelevant S–R compatibility, and (c) Stimulus–Stimulus (S–S) compatibility. Relevant S–R compatibility refers to the similarity between on the one hand a feature of the presented stimulus that determines what the correct response should be (i.e., relevant stimulus feature) and on the other hand the response that needs to be emitted. Irrelevant S–R compatibility relates to the similarity between a task-irrelevant stimulus feature and the correct response. Finally, S–S compatibility refers to the similarity between different features of the presented stimulus or stimuli. Importantly, different compatibility tasks can be classified on the basis of the type(s) of compatibility that are manipulated (see Appendix for a discussion of how the present taxonomy differs from the taxonomy of Kornblum). I now try to clarify the taxonomy by applying it to four well known compatibility tasks (see Table 9.1 for a summary).

In traditional S–R compatibility tasks, the compatibility between the relevant feature of the presented stimulus and the correct response varies over trials. On some trials, the relevant feature of the stimulus is similar to the correct response whereas on other trials it is dissimilar from the correct re-

TABLE 9.1
A Taxonomy of the Traditional S–R Compatibility,
Simon, Priming, and Stroop Tasks.

Task	Is there a manipulation of		
	S–S Compatibility?	Irrelevant S–R Compatibility?	Relevant S–R Compatibility?
Traditional S–R Compatibility	No	No	Yes
Simon	No	Yes	No
Priming	Yes	No	No
Stroop	Yes	Yes	No

sponse. Consider a task in which a white dot is presented on the left or right side of a computer screen and participants are instructed to press a left or right key on the basis of the position of the dot. In this task, the relevant stimulus feature is the position of the dot (left or right) and the responses differ with regard to their spatial position (left or right). Participants can be instructed to either press the key that has the same spatial position as the dot (i.e., press the left key for dots on the left and the right key for dots on the right) or to press the key with the opposite spatial location (i.e., press left for dots on the right and press right for dots on the left). In the first situation, the relevant feature of the stimulus (i.e., its position on a given trial) is compatible with the position of the correct response. In the latter situation, however, the relevant feature of the stimulus is incompatible with the correct response. Therefore, both situations differ with regard to the level of relevant S–R compatibility. The results of traditional S–R compatibility tasks typically show that performance is superior on trials where the relevant feature of the presented stimulus is compatible with the correct response (e.g., Fitts & Seeger, 1953; Kornblum & Lee, 1995). Traditional S–R compatibility tasks can thus be defined as tasks in which the level of relevant S–R compatibility varies over trials.

In the Simon task, the compatibility between the required response and a task-irrelevant feature of the presented stimulus varies over trials. For instance, Craft and Simon (1970) presented a red or green stimulus on either the left or right side of the screen and asked participants to press a left or right key on the basis of the color of the stimulus. As such, the color of the stimulus was the relevant feature because it determined what the correct response should be whereas the spatial position of the stimulus was task-irrelevant because it could not be used to determine the correct response. Results showed that responses were faster and more accurate when the spatial position of the correct response matched the spatial position of the stimulus than when the spatial position of the response and stimulus differed. So although the spatial position of the stimuli was irrelevant for the task, the match between this irrelevant feature and the responses had an impact on performance. According to the present taxonomy, the Simon task can be defined as a compatibility task in which the level of irrelevant S–R compatibility varies over trials.

The well known priming task, on the other hand, is a typical example of a task in which S–S compatibility varies over trials. In a typical priming study, two stimuli are presented consecutively (e.g., the prime BREAD and the target BUTTER) and participants are asked to respond to the second stimulus (e.g., decide whether it is an existing word). Importantly, on some trials the two stimuli are in some way (e.g., semantically, associatively, or perceptually) related whereas the stimuli are unrelated on other trials. Numerous studies demonstrated that performance is superior when the stimuli are related (Neely, 1991).[1]

Sometimes two or more types of compatibility are manipulated within the same task. For instance, in a typical Stroop study (e.g., Stroop, 1935), participants are asked to name the inkcolor in which a word is written. On some trials, the word is related to the inkcolor (e.g., the word GREEN written in green ink) whereas on other trials the word and the inkcolor differ (e.g., the word RED written in green ink). As such, S–S compatibility varies over trials. However, irrelevant S–R compatibility also varies over trials. When the word and the color are related, the correct response (e.g., the response "green") is also related to the irrelevant word meaning (e.g., the word GREEN). When word and color differ, the correct response and the word meaning (e.g., the word RED) also differ. As such, there is a perfect confounding of the different levels of S–S compatibility and irrelevant S–R compatibility: When there is S–S compatibility, there is also irrelevant S–R compatibility; when there is S–S incompatibility, there is also irrelevant S–R incompatibility. The Stroop task can thus be defined as a compatibility task in which both S–S and irrelevant S–R compatibility vary over trials in such a way that the two types of compatibility are confounded. Note that the level of relevant S–R compatibility is the same on all trials. Because participants are asked to name the inkcolor, the inkcolor is always related to the correct response.

The main advantage of classifying compatibility tasks according to the type(s) of compatibility that are manipulated is that it allows one to look beyond superficial procedural task elements such as the particular type of stimuli that are used or the way in which stimuli are presented. For instance, the taxonomy encompasses the fact that the Stroop task is not limited to colors and words. There are many variants of the Stroop task that involve many different types of stimuli such as spatial position, numbers, and sounds (see MacLeod, 1991, for a review). What is common to all these variants is that both the level of S–S compatibility and the level of irrelevant S–R compatibility is manipulated in such a way that both types of compatibility are confounded.

Likewise, Simon tasks do not necessarily involve spatial information (although the vast majority of Simon studies have looked only at the process-

---

[1]It is, however, more correct to regard the wordness (word or nonword) of the target as the relevant feature. From this perspective, the compatibility between two irrelevant features of the stimulus display varies over trials (i.e., the irrelevant meaning of the prime and the irrelevant meaning of the target). One could refer to this as irrelevant S–S compatibility. In order not to complicate matters too much, I will ignore the possibility of relations between two irrelevant features in the remainder of this paper.

ing of spatial information; see Lu & Proctor, 1995, for a review). One can create many other variants of the Simon task by simply changing the nature of the stimuli that are used. For example, one can create a color Simon task by manipulating the compatibility between the task-irrelevant color of a stimulus and the meaning of the response while using a relevant stimulus feature that is unrelated to color. Assume, for instance, that participants either see the letter X or the letter A presented in green or blue ink. Their task is to say the word "green" if they see the letter X and to say "blue" if they see the letter A, regardless of the color in which the letter is presented. As such, the identity of the letter is the relevant stimulus feature, the color of the letter is a task-irrelevant stimulus feature, and the meaning of the responses is related to color. On some trials, the irrelevant feature is compatible with the correct response (e.g., say "green" in response to X presented in green ink) whereas on other trials there is no such correspondence (e.g., say "green" to the letter X presented in blue ink). Whereas the level of irrelevant S–R compatibility thus varies from trial to trial, the level of relevant S–R compatibility and S–S compatibility does not vary from trial to trial: The identity of the letter is on all trials unrelated to its color or the meaning of the responses. Therefore, this task is structurally equivalent to a standard spatial Simon task.

The example of the color Simon task can also be used to illustrate the way in which the taxonomy reveals the structural differences between various tasks. Although both the color Simon task described earlier and the color Stroop task (i.e., naming the inkcolor of color words; Stroop, 1935) look at the processing of color related information, the tasks are fundamentally different at a structural level. In the Simon task, only the level of irrelevant S–R compatibility is manipulated. In the Stroop task, however, both the level of irrelevant S–R compatibility and the level of S–S compatibility vary from trial to trial.

Finally, a structural analysis of compatibility tasks according to the type(s) of compatibility that are manipulated can also help shed light on the processes that underlie the effects that are observed in these tasks. For instance, if two tasks are structurally similar one can reasonably assume that similar processes operate in both tasks. Although such an assumption always needs to be verified empirically, it can be helpful in generating hypotheses about the processes that are involved in a certain task.

APPLYING THE TAXONOMY TO INDIRECT MEASURES OF ATTITUDES

The advantages of classifying compatibility tasks according to the type(s) of compatibility that are manipulated become clear when applying the classification to the various reaction time tasks that can be used as indirect meas-

TABLE 9.2
A Taxonomy of the Affective Priming, Emotional Stroop,
Affective Simon, and IAT Tasks.

	Is there a manipulation of		
Task	S–S Compatibility?	Irrelevant S–R Compatibility?	Relevant S–R Compatibility?
Affective Priming	Yes	Yes	No
Emotional Stroop	No	No	No
Affective Simon	No	Yes	No
IAT	No	Yes*	Yes

*But only on target concept trials.

ures of attitudes. Table 9.2 provides a summary of the classification of these tasks.

The Affective "Priming" Task

It is perhaps not surprising that Fazio et al. (1986) considered their task to be an affective variant of the priming task. At a superficial level it is quite similar to a standard associative priming task: In both cases, a task-irrelevant prime and a relevant target are presented consecutively and the prime and target are related on some but not other trials. The only difference seems to be that in Fazio et al.'s task, the affective relation between the prime and target stimulus is manipulated whereas in associative priming the associative relation between both stimuli varies.

There is, however, one important additional difference. In most associative priming studies, participants are asked to read the target or to decide whether the target is a word (e.g., by saying "yes" or "no" or by pressing one of two keys). Because these responses are related to all possible primes and targets to the same extent, neither the level of irrelevant S–R compatibility, nor the level of relevant S–R compatibility varies over trials.[2] In Fazio et al.'s (1986) affective priming task, however, participants respond on the basis of the valence of the target (e.g., by saying "good" or "bad" or by pressing one

---

[2]The fact that irrelevant and relevant S–R compatibility do not vary over trials does not exclude the possibility that those priming effects are due to processes at the response selection stage. For instance, Wentura (2000) showed that when participants are encouraged to detect nonwords ("yes" this is a nonword or "no" this is not a nonword) rather than to detect words ("yes" this is a word or "no" this is not a word), responses are slower with related than unrelated prime-target pairs. This is because related prime-target pairs induce a tendency to give affirmative responses such as "yes." When participants are encouraged to detect nonwords, the correct response for a word target is negative ("no" this is not a nonword) which differs from the automatically activated response.

of two keys). Therefore, the responses are either intrinsically or extrinsically (i.e., because of the fact that the responses are assigned to positive or negative stimuli) related to valence.[3] On some trials, the prime and response have the same valence, on other trials they differ in valence. As such, irrelevant S–R compatibility varies over trials. Moreover, in the affective priming task there is a perfect confounding of S–S compatibility and irrelevant S–R compatibility: If the prime and target have the same valence, then the prime and the response also have the same valence (e.g., say "good" to the target HAPPY that is preceded by the prime FLOWER); if there is a mismatch between the valence of the prime and the valence of the target, there is also a mismatch between the valence of the prime and the valence of the correct response (e.g., say "good" to the target HAPPY that is preceded by the prime CANCER).

According to the taxonomy, the affective priming task is thus a compatibility task in which both S–S and irrelevant S–R compatibility are manipulated in such a way that both types of compatibility are confounded. This is exactly the same definition as for the Stroop task. Therefore, at a structural level, the affective priming task should be regarded as an affective variant of the Stroop task rather than as a variant of the priming task (De Houwer & Hermans, 1994; De Houwer, Hermans, Rothermund, & Wentura, in press; Klauer, Roßnagel, & Musch, 1997; Wentura, 1999). The resemblance between the associative priming and affective priming task is merely superficial. For instance, the fact that there are two stimuli (as is the case in most priming studies) rather than one stimulus (as is the case in most Stroop studies) is irrelevant: There are also variants of the Stroop task in which there are two stimuli on each trial such as two separate words (e.g., Glaser & Glaser, 1989).

The observation that Fazio et al.'s (1986) affective priming task is more similar to the Stroop than to the priming task has important implications for theories about the processes that underlie the affective priming (or more correctly, Stroop) effect. Because the task of Fazio et al. (1986) was originally considered to be a variant of the associative priming task, many researchers assumed that popular theories of associative priming such as

---

[3]One can assume that when participants are instructed to give a certain response (e.g., press a left key) to exemplars of a concept (e.g., positive stimuli), a short-term association will be created between the representation of that response and the representation of that concept. As such, the response will become to a certain extent functionally equivalent to responses that are intrinsically associated (i.e., have long-term associations) with that concept (e.g., saying the word "good"). Rather than developing gradually as the result of practice, the short-term associations are set up mainly as a direct result of task instructions (Proctor & Lu, in press; Zorzi & Umilta, 1995). Short-term associations can be created between any response representation and any possible concept. Therefore, extrinsic response meaning is not restricted to valence.

the spreading of activation model (Collins & Quillian, 1969) were also valid models of affective priming (e.g., Bower, 1991; Hermans et al., 1994). The realization that affective priming is actually more similar to the Stroop task has recently led researchers to consider response conflict accounts similar to those that had been proposed within Stroop research (e.g., De Houwer & Hermans, 1994; De Houwer et al., in press; Klauer et al., 1997; Wentura, 1999). Recent evidence indeed supports the hypothesis that affective priming effects are largely due to the fact that prime valence influences response selection rather than the identification of the target (e.g., De Houwer et al., in press; Klauer et al., 1997; Wentura, 1999).

The Emotional "Stroop" Task

In a typical emotional Stroop task (e.g., Mathews & MacLeod, 1985; Mogg, Mathews, & Weinman, 1989; Pratto & John, 1991), words with a positive, negative, or neutral valence are presented in different colors. Participants are asked to name the inkcolor as quickly as possible. The results of some studies revealed longer latencies when the irrelevant word has a negative valence compared to when it has a positive or neutral valence (e.g., Pratto & John, 1991; but see Wentura, Rothermund, & Bak, 2000). Although it has not yet been used in this way, the emotional Stroop task could potentially be used to measure attitudes. Assume that one wants to know which of two attitude objects a person likes best. One can do this by selecting a representative word for each attitude object and asking the person to name the color in which the words are written (e.g., blue or green). Short color naming latencies point to a positive or neutral attitude, long color naming latencies are indicative of a negative attitude.[4]

At a superficial level, the emotional Stroop task is indeed similar to the Stroop color-word task. In both tasks, words are presented in different colors and participants are asked to name the color of the words. However, when one looks at the types of compatibility that are involved, it becomes clear that the emotional Stroop task is fundamentally different from the Stroop task. In the emotional Stroop task, the meaning of the words is always unrelated to the color of the words and the meaning of the responses: Regardless of whether the word has a positive valence or a negative valence, the words that are used in most emotional Stroop studies do not refer to a specific color. Therefore, unlike a true Stroop task, the emotional Stroop

---

[4]There are some indications, however, that the time needed to name the inkcolor of a word depends on the personal relevance of the attitude object represented by the word rather than on the valence of the attitude object. For instance, both positive and negative stimuli can interfere with color naming provided that they are related to important goals or concerns (e.g., Mathews & Klug, 1992; Pratto, 1994; see Williams et al., 1996, for a review).

task involves neither a manipulation of S–S compatibility nor a manipulation of irrelevant S–R compatibility. In fact, none of the three types of compatibility are manipulated in the emotional Stroop task. One might thus
even conclude that the emotional Stroop task should not be regarded as a
compatibility task at all.

Again this structural analysis has implications for theories about the
processes that underlie the emotional Stroop task. Williams, Mathews, and
MacLeod (1996) argued that the model of Cohen, Dunbar, and McClelland (1990), which is one of the most widely accepted models of the Stroop
effect, is also a good model for the emotional Stroop effect. The model of
Cohen et al. (1990) attributes Stroop effects mainly to processes that occur
at the response selection stage (see also Glaser & Glaser, 1989). Likewise,
Williams et al. (1996) postulate that emotional Stroop effects also occur at
the response selection stage: Negative words are assumed to interfere more
with naming colors (e.g., saying BLUE or GREEN) than positive or neutral
words do.

But one could argue that a response conflict account is more plausible
for Stroop effects than for emotional Stroop effects. There is strong evidence to support the hypothesis that stimuli will automatically activate compatible responses (e.g., Hommel, 1995; Kornblum & Lee, 1995; Simon,
1990). This mechanism can influence reaction times in a Stroop task because irrelevant S–R compatibility varies over trials. For instance, in the case
of the color-word Stroop task, a word will automatically activate the response alternative that is most similar to its meaning. When the word and
response are compatible (e.g., say "green" to the word GREEN in green ink),
response selection will be facilitated and reaction times short; when the
word and response are incompatible (e.g., say GREEN to BLUE in green ink),
there will be a response conflict and reaction times will be long. However,
in the emotional Stroop task, neither relevant or irrelevant S–R compatibility varies over trials. There are no reasons to assume that the level of compatibility between positive words and color responses (such as saying "blue"
or "green") is higher than that between negative words and color responses. Although I do not want to exclude the possibility that emotional
Stroop effects are due to processes at the response selection stage,[5] the

---

[5]Assume, for instance, that negative words attract more attention than positive words. As a
result, less resources will be available for selecting the correct response when the word has a
negative compared to a positive meaning. Alternatively, because a negative word receives more
attention, it is possible that the name of this word will be highly activated at the response level,
thus interfering with the selection of the correct response. These response conflict explanations differ, however, from the mechanism that is assumed to underlie stimulus–response compatibility effects. Such effects are attributed to the fact that (relevant or irrelevant) stimuli automatically activate representations of responses that belong to the set of possible responses
within the task.

structural analysis does suggest that such an account is less likely to be correct than for true Stroop effects because an important mechanism for inducing response conflicts (i.e., automatic activation of valid responses) cannot operate in a typical emotional Stroop task but can operate in real Stroop tasks. It is interesting to note that until now there have been no studies that tested the widespread assumption that emotional Stroop effects occur at the response selection stage.

Finally, I would like to point out that there are no reasons why the so-called emotional Stroop task should involve words, colors, or color naming. What is structurally unique about the emotional Stroop task is that it examines the effects of the task-irrelevant valence of stimuli in a situation where S–S and S–R compatibility are not manipulated. Other aspects of the task should not be crucial. For instance, rather than asking participants to name the color of positive and negative words, one might just as well present positive and negative tactile stimuli (e.g., a pleasant tickle or a painful electric shock) and ask participants to say a nonword such as "bayram" when they hear a high pitched tone and to say another nonword such as "mecburi" when they hear a low pitched tone that is presented in close temporal contiguity with the tactile stimulus. An emotional "Stroop" effect would be evidenced by shorter reaction times on trials with positive stimuli than on trials with negative stimuli.

The Affective Simon Task

One of the advantages of the present taxonomy is that it allows one to fully appreciate the flexibility of existing compatibility tasks because it reveals the abstract core of these tasks. My own research was in many ways inspired by this insight. Some years ago, I developed an affective variant of the Simon task (De Houwer, 1997; De Houwer & Eelen, 1998). According to the taxonomy, the Simon task is a compatibility task in which irrelevant S–R compatibility varies over trials, but not S–S compatibility or relevant S–R compatibility. Whereas in virtually all previous Simon experiments, stimuli and responses were spatially compatible or incompatible (see Kornblum & Lee, 1995, and De Houwer, 1998, for an exception), I manipulated the affective relation between the stimuli and the responses.

In a first series of experiments (De Houwer & Eelen, 1998), I presented positive and negative nouns (e.g., BABY, CANCER) and adjectives (e.g., HAPPY, SAD). Half of the participants were instructed to say the word "positive" when the presented word was a noun and to say "negative" when the word was an adjective. The response assignment was reversed for the other participants. The valence of the words was irrelevant and had to be ignored. Therefore, the grammatical category of the words was the relevant stimulus feature, the valence of the words was the irrelevant stimulus feature, and the responses were the words "positive" and "negative". As in other Simon tasks, the compatibility between the irrelevant feature of the presented stimulus and the correct response varied from trial to trial whereas the match between the relevant stimulus feature and the irrelevant stimulus feature or the responses did not vary over trials. The only important new element was that irrelevant S–R compatibility was defined in terms of stimulus valence rather than in terms of spatial position. The results of several experiments consistently showed that participants needed more time to respond when the valence of the stimulus and the correct response matched (e.g., say "positive" to the word HAPPY because it is an adjective) than when the stimulus and response differed in valence (e.g., say "positive" to UGLY because it is an adjective).

This task can be used to measure attitudes in an indirect way. In one study (De Houwer, 1997, Experiment 17), I examined the validity of the affective Simon task as a measure of attitudes by using the known group approach. This approach entails that one looks at whether a measure is able to detect differences between members of different groups that can be assumed to diverge with regard to the trait or property that is being measured. I invited students that were active members of one of four political parties. Two of those parties formed a coalition that had a majority in parliament whereas the other two parties were in the opposition. During the experiment, I presented names of senior politicians that were members of one of the four possible political parties. Half of the participants were asked to say "positive" when they saw the name of a politician that belonged to the majority and "negative" when the presented politician belonged to the opposition. The instructions were reversed for the other participants. Results showed that participants needed less time to say "positive" than to say "negative" for politicians of their own party whereas this difference was significantly smaller or reversed for responses to politicians of parties to which the participant did not belong. This study suggests that the difference between the time needed to give a positive response and the time needed to give a negative response when presented with (examples of) the same attitude object can indeed provide an valid indirect index of the attitude toward that object.

The fact that the affective Simon task was defined in terms of the type of compatibility that was manipulated revealed the flexibility of this task. In more recent experiments, I exploited this flexibility and demonstrated that affective Simon effects also occurred when photographs of objects or faces are presented (De Houwer, Crombez, Baeyens, & Hermans, 2001, Experiment 3; De Houwer, Hermans, & Eelen, 1998), when participants were asked to process a nonsemantic feature of the stimuli (De Houwer et al., 2001, Experiment 2), and when nonverbal approach-avoidance responses were used (De Houwer et al., 2001, Experiment 4).

The Implicit Association Test (IAT)

Greenwald et al. (1998) recently introduced a task that can be used to measure implicit associations between concepts. The simple idea behind the IAT is that it should be easier to map two concepts onto a single response when those concepts are somehow similar or associated in memory than when the concepts are unrelated or dissimilar. For instance, Greenwald et al. (1998, Experiment 1) presented names of flowers (e.g., TULIP), names of insects (e.g., COCKROACH), positive words (e.g., FRIEND), and negative words (e.g., MURDER). Words were presented one by one in a random order and participants were instructed to press a left or right key depending on the category of the words (flower, insect, positive, or negative). Because the concept *flower* has a more positive valence than the concept *insect*, one can assume that *flower* is more strongly associated in memory with positive valence than with negative valence whereas *insect* has stronger associations with negative valence than with positive valence. Therefore, one would expect better task performance when flowers and positive words are assigned to one key and insects and negative words are assigned to the other key than when flowers and negative words are mapped onto one key and insects and positive words are assigned to the other key. The results reported by Greenwald et al. (1998, Experiment 1) clearly confirmed this hypothesis.

Assuming that attitudes are represented in memory as associations between the representation of the attitude object and the representation of positive and/or negative valence (Fazio, 1986; Greenwald & Banaji, 1995), the IAT offers an elegant indirect measure of attitudes. For instance, Greenwald et al. (1998, Experiment 3) presented prototypical names of Black persons (e.g., JAMEL) and White persons (e.g., HANK) together with positive and negative words. Greenwald et al. argued that if a participant is faster when Black names and negative words are assigned to one key and White names and positive words are assigned to the second key than when the response assignment is reversed (first key for Black names and positive words and second key for White names and negative words), one can infer that the participant has a more negative attitude toward Black persons than toward White persons.

Unlike to what was the case for the affective priming, emotional Stroop, and affective Simon task, the IAT was not explicitly derived from an existing compatibility task. Nevertheless, a structural analysis of the IAT shows that it is highly similar to traditional S–R compatibility tasks. Consider the IAT in which flower names, insect names, positive words, and negative words are presented (Greenwald et al., 1998, Experiment 1). The relevant stimulus feature is the category to which the presented stimulus belongs. On some trials, the relevant feature of the stimulus has a positive valence (flower and positive), on other trials the relevant stimulus feature has a negative valence (insect and negative). Importantly, because of the response assignments, responses also receive an extrinsic valence (see Footnote 2). When participants are asked to press a left key for positive words and flower names (i.e., compatible response assignments), the response "press the left key" will be linked with both the concept *positive* and the concept *flower* and will thus receive an unambiguously positive meaning. Therefore, when participants see a positive word or a flower word, the relevant stimulus feature and the response are compatible because they have a similar valence: The concepts *flower* and *positive* have a positive intrinsic meaning; pressing the left key has a positive extrinsic meaning because it is associated with positive concepts during the experiment.

If, however, positive words and insect names are assigned to the left key (i.e., incompatible response assignments), the extrinsic meaning of the response "press the left key" will be ambiguous: It will be linked directly with positive valence because it is associated with the concept *positive* but indirectly with negative valence because it is also linked with the concept *insect*, a concept that has a negative valence. Therefore, when the response assignments are incompatible, the relevant stimulus feature and the response are less compatible than when the response assignments are compatible. As such, the level of relevant S–R compatibility depends on the way in which categories are assigned to responses. This is exactly the same as for traditional S–R compatibility tasks (e.g., press a key corresponding to or opposite to the spatial position of a stimulus).

The most important difference between the IAT and traditional S–R compatibility tasks is that in the latter, the compatibility between the relevant stimulus feature and an intrinsic feature of the responses varies over trials whereas in the IAT, the match between the meaning of the relevant stimulus feature and an extrinsic feature of the responses is manipulated. It would be easy to transform the IAT into a traditional stimulus–response compatibility task. For instance, one could ask participants to say "good" when they see flower names and "bad" when they see insect names (compatible response assignments) or to say "good" to insect names and "bad" to flower names (incompatible response assignments). Likewise, participants can be instructed to say "flower" in response to positive words and "insect" to negative words (compatible response assignments) or "flower" to negative words and "insect" to positive words (incompatible response assignments).

A second difference between traditional S–R compatibility tasks and the IAT is that in the IAT, irrelevant S–R compatibility also varies on some of the trials. On trials where flower and insect names are presented (the so-called target concept trials, Greenwald et al., 1998), one can make a distinction between a relevant and irrelevant stimulus feature. For instance, flower names and insect names do not only differ with regard to their semantic category but also with regard to their individual valence. Because participants do not need to process the valence of the individual flower and insect names and because they are instructed to respond to these names on the basis of the semantic category to which the names belong, one can argue that stimulus valence is an irrelevant feature of the target concept stimuli. With compatible response assignments (e.g., press left for flowers and positive words and right for insects and negative words), the valence of the individual stimuli is always the same as the extrinsic valence of the responses. With incompatible response assignments (e.g., press left for flowers and negative words and right for insects and positive words), the extrinsic valence of the responses is ambiguous. Therefore, the compatibility between an irrelevant feature of the stimuli (i.e., the valence of the individual words) and the responses is different with compatible than with incompatible response assignments.

In all IAT studies that have been published until now (e.g., Dasgupta, McGhee, Greenwald, & Banaji, 2000; Greenwald et al., 1998; Rudman, Greenwald, Mellott, & Schwartz, 1999; Swanson, Rudman, & Greenwald, 2001), irrelevant S–R and relevant S–R compatibility have been confounded. This is because all exemplars of the positive target category (e.g., the category "flowers") have a positive valence whereas all the exemplars of the negative target category (e.g., the category "insects") are negative. Therefore, when the valence of the category of the presented stimulus and the extrinsic valence of the response are compatible (as is the case with compatible response assignments), the valence of the stimulus will also be compatible with the responses. When the extrinsic valence of the responses is ambiguous (as is the case with incompatible response assignments), both the level of irrelevant and relevant S–R compatibility will be reduced.

It is important to note, however, that the distinction between irrelevant S–R and relevant S–R compatibility does not hold for trials on which positive and negative words are presented (i.e., attribute concept trials, Greenwald et al., 1998). On attribute concept trials, participants do need to process the valence of the individual stimuli in order to select the correct response. It makes little sense to say that the irrelevant stimulus feature on the attribute concept trials is the valence of the individual stimuli because this is actually the relevant stimulus feature on these trials. Therefore, the IAT can be defined as a compatibility task in which relevant S–R compatibility is manipulated on attribute concept trials and in which both relevant and irrelevant S–R compatibility vary on target concept trials. As such, the IAT is a mix of a traditional S–R compatibility task and a Simon task.

This structural analysis allows one to formulate hypotheses about the processes that underlie IAT effects. Current models of Simon and stimulus–response compatibility effects postulate that these effects occur at the stage of response selection (e.g., Hommel, 1997; Kornblum & Lee, 1995; H.

Zhang, J. Zhang, & Kornblum, 1999). According to these models, the representations of responses that are compatible with the relevant or irrelevant feature of the presented stimulus will be activated automatically on presentation of the stimulus. For instance, when a stimulus is presented on the left side, this will automatically activate response representations that are associated with a left spatial position (e.g., pressing a left key). When the automatically activated response representation differs from the representation of the correct response (e.g., press a right key in response to a stimulus presented on the left side of a screen) response selection will be delayed relative to a situation in which the response representation of the correct response is automatically activated.

On the basis of the structural similarity between the IAT and stimulus–response compatibility tasks, one could speculate that IAT effects are also due to processes that occur at the response selection stage. On target concept trials, a flower word such as "tulip" could automatically activate response representations that are extrinsically associated with positive valence either because the category to which the word belongs (i.e., "flower") has a positive valence (relevant feature account) or because the word itself has a positive valence (irrelevant feature account). Assume that participants are instructed to press a left key for flowers and positive words and a right key for insects and negative words (compatible response assignments). In this case, the left response has an unambiguous positive extrinsic valence whereas the negative key has an unambiguous negative extrinsic valence. Therefore, flower names will automatically activate the representation of the left response whereas insect names will pre-activate the representation of the right response. Because the automatically activated response representation is always the representation of the correct response, task performance will be facilitated. However, when flowers and negative words are mapped onto the right response and insects and positive words are assigned to the left response (incompatible response assignments), each response representation will be associated both with positive and negative valence. Therefore, a flower word such as TULIP will either activate both response representations, which would lead to a response conflict, or it will pre-activate the representation of the correct response to a lesser extent than when the response assignments are compatible. Likewise, on attribute concept trials, positive and negative words can also automatically activate response representations on the basis of their valence. With compatible response assignments, words will activate only the representation of the correct response whereas with incompatible response assignments, both response representations will be activated or the representation of correct response will be pre-activated to a lesser extent. As such, performance should be inferior with incompatible than with compatible response assignments.

I recently conducted two experiments that were designed to test a response conflict account of IAT effects (De Houwer, 2001; De Houwer, 2001a). Both experiments followed a procedure that was modeled after the experiments reported by Greenwald et al. (1998). The main difference was that in my studies, the valence of the individual target concept stimuli varied within each target category. That is, some exemplars of a target concept had a positive valence whereas other exemplars of the same target concept had a negative valence. Because category valence and stimulus valence were manipulated independently, I could examine the extent to which performance on target concept trials was determined by relevant S–R compatibility (i.e., the match between the valence of the category and the valence of the responses) or by irrelevant S–R compatibility (i.e., the match between the valence of the individual stimuli and the valence of the responses).

In a first experiment (De Houwer, 2001a), I prevented a possible impact of relevant S–R compatibility by using target concepts that did not differ in valence. The concepts I used were "person" and "animal". For each of the two target concepts, some exemplars had a positive valence (e.g., FRIEND, SWAN) whereas other exemplars of the same concept had a negative valence (e.g., LIAR, SPIDER). The attribute concept stimuli were positive and negative adjectives that did not refer to persons or animals. Results showed that the compatibility between the valence of the individual target concept stimuli and the responses had a significant effect on reaction times. For instance, if person names were assigned to the same key as positive words, responses were faster for positive person names (e.g., FRIEND) than for negative person names (e.g., LIAR). If, however, person names and negative words were assigned to the same key, reaction times were shorter for negative person names than for positive person names. The results thus demonstrated that the level of irrelevant S–R compatibility on target concept trials had an impact on performance.

In the second experiment (De Houwer, 2001), I did use categories that clearly differed in valence. The target concept stimuli were either names of British persons or names of Foreign persons. Because all the participants were British, it was safe to assume that our participants had a more positive attitude toward the concept *British* than toward the concept *foreign* (e.g., Farnham, Greenwald, & Banaji, 1999; Nuttin, 1985). However, most British people do not like all British persons or dislike all foreign persons. This allowed me to select for each category an equal number of liked (e.g., Princess Diana, Albert Einstein) and disliked (e.g., Margaret Thatcher, Adolf Hitler) persons. The attribute concept stimuli were again positive and negative adjectives. In contrast to what was observed in the first experiment, results showed that the match between the valence of the target concept stimuli and the valence of the response had no impact whatsoever on performance. Instead, only the match between the valence of the target concept (*British* or *foreign*) and the valence of the correct response mattered. For instance, responses to both EINSTEIN and HITLER were faster when the category "foreign" was assigned to the same response as negative words compared to when it was assigned to the same response as positive words. This result suggests that when target concepts differ in valence, IAT effects result from the fact that stimuli automatically activate those responses that are compatible with the valence of the relevant feature of the stimuli. In other words, only the level of relevant S–R compatibility seems to matter.[6] I return to this issue in the final section of this chapter.

Other Tasks

The literature on indirect measures of attitudes is expanding rapidly and new reaction time tasks are constantly being introduced. In this section, I discuss how the taxonomy can be used to structurally analyse some of these new tasks.

Chen and Bargh (1999): An Affective Traditional S–R Compatibility Task. Chen and Bargh (1999, Experiment 1; also see Solarz, 1960) asked participants to respond to the valence of stimuli by pulling or pushing a lever. Reaction times were faster when participants responded to positive stimuli by pulling the lever toward them and to negative stimuli by pushing a lever away from them compared to when the response assignments were reversed (pull for negative stimuli; push for positive stimuli).

This task can be classified in the following way. Stimulus valence is the relevant stimulus feature and the responses also differ in valence (assuming that pulling a lever is an approach behavior whereas pushing a lever is an avoidance behavior). Importantly, the compatibility between the relevant stimulus feature and the responses depends on the stimulus–response assignments. When positive stimuli are assigned to the pull response and negative stimuli are assigned to the push response, the valence of the stimuli (i.e., relevant feature) and the valence of the correct response always match. When the response assignments are reversed, there is always a mismatch between the valence of the stimulus and the valence of the response. Therefore, the level of relevant S–R compatibility varies over trials. Because

---

[6]Although the valence of the individual exemplars does not appear to have a direct impact on IAT performance when the target concepts are clearly positive or negative, it is possible that the selection of exemplars does have an indirect effect. For instance, if one only presents negative exemplars of a positive category such as "British" and positive exemplars of a negative category such as "foreign," this could temporarily alter the attitude toward the concepts "British" and "foreign" in such a way that "British" becomes less positive and "foreign" becomes less negative. This would reduce differences in relevant S–R compatibility and thus the magnitude of a British–Foreign IAT effect.

there is no obvious or systematic irrelevant stimulus feature, irrelevant S–R and S–S compatibility do not vary over trials. The task used by Chen and Bargh (1999, Experiment 1; Solarz, 1960) is thus structurally equivalent to a traditional stimulus–response compatibility effect.

Note that in a second experiment, Chen and Bargh sometimes asked participants to pull the lever as soon as a stimulus was presented on the screen and sometimes asked participants to push the lever when a stimulus was presented (see Wentura et al., 2000, Experiment 3, for a similar task). As in their first experiment, half of the stimuli had a positive valence, half had a negative valence. Despite the fact that stimulus valence was no longer relevant, participants were faster to push the lever when the stimulus had a negative valence but were faster to pull the lever when it had a negative valence. This task is a variant of the affective Simon task: The relevant feature is the presence or absence of a stimulus, the irrelevant feature is stimulus valence, the responses either have a positive or negative valence, and irrelevant S–R compatibility varies over trials.

Klauer and Musch: A Relational Stroop Task. Klauer and Musch (2001, chap. , this volume) recently conducted a number of experiments in which two stimuli were presented on each trial. Both stimuli either had the same or a different valence. Participants were asked to judge whether the two stimuli were similar with regard to a nonaffective feature that was manipulated independently of stimulus valence. In one of their experiments, the stimuli were colored and participants indicated whether the two stimuli had the same or a different color. Results showed that "same" responses were faster when the two stimuli had the same valence than when the two stimuli had a different valence. This pattern of results was reversed for the "different" responses.

At first sight, it is not easy to fit this task within the present taxonomy. The main reason is that the task involves the comparison of two stimuli rather than the processing of one particular stimulus (feature). However, one could argue that in tasks where responses need to be made on the basis of a comparison of two or more stimuli, the relevant and irrelevant task feature can be defined in terms of the match between stimuli rather than in terms of (the features of) the individual stimuli. Therefore, the relevant feature in the Klauer and Musch task can be defined as the match (same or different) between the relevant nonaffective feature of the stimuli (e.g., color) and the irrelevant feature as the match between the valence of the stimuli (same or different). The responses refer to the presence of a match (e.g., say "same") or the absence of a match (e.g., say "different").

If one accepts this point of view, the task developed by Klauer and Musch (2001) is structurally similar to a Stroop task. First, S–S compatibility varies over trials. On some trials, both the valence and the color of the stimuli (mis)match (S–S congruent) whereas on other trials the stimuli match only with regard to color or with regard to valence (S–S incongruent). Second, irrelevant S–R compatibility also varies over trials: Sometimes, a match between the valence of the stimuli is present and the meaning of the correct response refers to the presence of a match (e.g., say "same") or the valence of the stimuli differs and the correct response has the meaning "different". On other trials, the meaning of the response is different from the actual match between the valence of the stimuli (e.g., the stimuli differ in valence but the correct response is "same"). As in the Stroop task, S–S and irrelevant S–R compatibility are perfectly confounded.

As an analogue of the Klauer and Musch task, one could present two words on a computer screen, only one of which needs to be read. The relevant word is either the word SAME or the word DIFFERENT. The irrelevant word is also either SAME or DIFFERENT. On half of the trials, the relevant and irrelevant word are identical, on the other trials, they differ. The responses also have the meaning "same" or "different". As in the Klauer and Musch (chap , this volume) task, both S–S and irrelevant S–R compatibility vary over trials in a perfectly confounded manner. The only difference is that rather than presenting stimuli that symbolically represent the concepts *same* and *different* (i.e., the words SAME and DIFFERENT), in the Klauer and Musch task, stimuli are presented that provide a concrete instantiation of the concepts *same* or *different* (e.g., two stimuli that match or mismatch with regard to the relevant color and with regard to the irrelevant valence).

IMPLICATIONS FOR MEASURING ATTITUDES INDIRECTLY

I have argued that the taxonomy can help one understand the structural properties of various reaction times measures of attitudes. The analysis can also help reveal the processes that underlie these measures. But does this knowledge have any practical implications for how psychologists should use these measures? One of the reasons why psychologists are interested in the reaction time tasks that I described in this chapter is that each of these tasks offers a way to measure spontaneous affective reactions. If each of these tasks measures the same thing, one would of course expect that the results of the various measures would converge. However, preliminary studies suggest that this is not always the case (Cameron, Alvarez, & Bargh, 2000; but see Cunningham, Preacher, & Banaji, 2001). More important, the structural analysis points at some of the possible reasons why the results of different measures might diverge.

One could, for instance, expect differences between the results of an affective priming measure and an IAT measure. Although the affective priming and IAT task have in common that the level of irrelevant S–R compatibility varies over trials, the IAT task also involves a manipulation of the level of relevant S–R compatibility. Moreover, the evidence described previously suggests that IAT effects are mainly due to the impact of relevant S–R compatibility (De Houwer, 2001) whereas affective priming effects appear to be due to irrelevant S–R compatibility (De Houwer et al., 2001; Klauer et al., 1997; Wentura, 1999).

This implies that the IAT and affective priming task are measuring attitudes toward different elements of the presented stimuli. On any given trial, responses in the IAT task appear to be determined by the compatibility between the valence of one particular feature of the stimulus (i.e., the relevant stimulus feature) and the valence of the response rather than by the match between the global attitude toward the stimulus and the valence of the response. A stimulus such as EINSTEIN, for instance, appears to activate negative responses when it needs to be classified as foreign, despite the fact that most people have a global positive attitude toward the person Einstein (De Houwer, 2001). In the affective priming task, however, it is not the case that a particular feature (such as nationality or semantic category) of the prime is relevant for the task. Moreover, the only feature that is relevant for the task is the global attitude toward a different stimulus (i.e., the target) rather than the attitude toward a feature of that stimulus. Therefore, an affective priming measure most likely reflects the global attitude toward a prime stimulus.

Because the IAT and the affective priming task reflect different aspects of the attitude toward objects, these measures could produce different outcomes. Assume, for instance, that one would want to measure racial attitudes. In an affective priming task, a picture of, for instance, Martin Luther King would most likely facilitate responses to positive compared to negative targets because the global attitude toward this person is positive for most people. In an IAT where Martin Luther King needs to be classified as a Black person, however, this stimulus will most likely activate negative rather than positive responses when the participant has a negative attitude toward Black people (De Houwer, 2001). Whereas an IAT appears to measure attitudes toward the concept *Black person* (but see Footnote 6), the affective priming measure is more likely to reflect the mean of the attitudes toward the different persons that are used as exemplars of the category "Black person". Both measures would therefore not necessarily converge.

Simply presenting pictures of persons that are unknown to the participants will not completely resolve this problem. It is likely that the affective priming measure will always be influenced more by attitudes toward features of the stimuli that are not related to race (e.g., gender, physical appearance, . . .). However, a possible solution would be to use the category labels as primes in a priming task rather than exemplars of those categories.

Another way to make the affective priming task more similar to the IAT task would be to direct attention toward one feature of the primes. For instance, one could ask participants to name the race associated with the prime stimulus after they have responded to the target stimulus. Although this idea still needs to be tested, it is possible that priming effects will then reflect attitudes toward race rather than the global attitude toward the prime.

One would expect a better convergence between the results of an affective priming task and an affective Simon task. In both tasks, the level of irrelevant S–R compatibility varies from trial to trial. Although the level of S–S compatibility is also manipulated in the affective priming task, research has demonstrated that affective priming effects are mainly due to the impact of irrelevant S–R compatibility (e.g., De Houwer et al., 2001; Klauer et al., 1997; Wentura, 1999). Moreover, because neither task involves relevant S–R compatibility, both affective priming and affective Simon effects should reflect global attitudes rather than attitudes toward a specific feature of the presented stimuli. Provided that an affective priming and affective Simon measure of attitudes prove to be reliable, one would thus expect that there will be a high correlation between the outcome of both measures.

ACKNOWLEDGMENTS

The ideas put forward in this chapter were first presented at a workshop on indirect measures of attitudes that was organized by Tony Greenwald and Marzu Banaji, Chicago, May 1999. Correspondence concerning this chapter should be addressed to Jan De Houwer, Department of Psychology, University of Ghent, H. Dunantlaan2, B-9000 Ghent, Belgium. Electronic mail may be sent to jan.dehouwer@rug.ac.be

REFERENCES

Bargh, J. A., Chaiken, S., Govender, R., & Pratto, F. (1992). The generality of the attitude activation effect. *Journal of Personality and Social Psychology, 62,* 893–912.

Bower, G. H. (1991). Mood congruity of social judgements. In J. P. Forgas (Ed.), *Emotion and social judgements* (pp. 31–54). Oxford: Pergamon Press.

Cameron, J. A., Alvarez, J. M., & Bargh, J. A. (2000). *Examining the Validity of Implicit Measures of Prejudice.* Poster presented at the first annual meeting for the Society of Personality and Social Psychology, Nashville, TN.

Chen, M., & Bargh, J. A. (1999). Consequences of automatic evaluation: Immediate behavioral predispositions to approach or avoid the stimulus. *Personality and Social Psychology Bulletin, 25,* 215–224.

Cohen, J. D., Dunbar, K., & McClelland, J. L. (1990). On the control of automatic processes: A parallel distributed processing account of the Stroop effect. *Psychological Review, 97,* 332–361.

Collins, A. M., & Quillian, M. R. (1969). Retrieval time from semantic memory. *Journal of Verbal Learning and Verbal Behavior, 8*, 240–248.

Craft, J. L., & Simon, J. R. (1970). Processing symbolic information from a visual display: Interference from an irrelevant directional cue. *Journal of Experimental Psychology, 83*, 415–420.

Cunningham, W. A., Preacher, K. J., & Banaji, M. R. (2001). Implicit attitude measures: Consistency, stability, and convergent validity. *Psychological Science, 12*, 163–170.

Dasgupta, N., McGhee, D. E., Greenwald, A. G., & Banaji, M. R. (2000). Automatic White preference: Eliminating the familiarity explanation. *Journal of Experimental Social Psychology, 36*, 316–328.

De Houwer, J. (1997). *Automatic affect and cognition.* Unpublished doctoral dissertation, University of Leuven, Belgium.

De Houwer, J. (1998). The semantic Simon effect. *Quarterly Journal of Experimental Psychology, 51A*, 683–688.

De Houwer, J. (2001). A structural and process analysis of the Implicit Association Test. *Journal of Experimental Social Psychology, 37*, 443–451.

De Houwer, J. (2001a). Stimulus-response compatibility effects without dimensional overlap. Manuscript in preparation.

De Houwer, J., Crombez, G., Baeyens, F., & Hermans, D. (2001). On the generality of the affective Simon effect. *Cognition and Emotion, 15*, 189–206.

De Houwer, J., & Eelen, P. (1998). An affective variant of the Simon paradigm. *Cognition and Emotion, 12*, 45–61.

De Houwer, J., & Hermans, D. (1994). Differences in the affective processing of words and pictures. *Cognition and Emotion, 8*, 1–20.

De Houwer, J., Hermans, D., & Eelen, P. (1998). Affective Simon effects using facial expressions as affective stimuli. *Zeitschrift für Experimentelle Psychologie, 45*, 88–98.

De Houwer, J., Hermans, D., Rothermund, K., & Wentura, D. (in press). Affective priming of semantic categorization responses. *Cognition and Emotion.*

Dovidio, J. F., & Fazio, R. H. (1992). New technologies for the direct and indirect assessment of attitudes. In J. Tanur (Ed.), *Questions about questions: Meaning, memory, expression and social interaction in surveys* (pp. 204–237). New York: Sage.

Eriksen, B. A., & Eriksen, C. W. (1974). Effects of noise letters upon the identification of a target letter in a nonsearch task. *Perception and Psychophysics, 16*, 143–147.

Farnham, S. D., Greenwald, A. G., & Banaji, M. R. (1999). Implicit self-esteem. In D. Abrams & M. A. Hogg (Eds.), *Social identity and social cognition* (pp. 230–248). Oxford, UK: Blackwell.

Fazio, R. H. (1986). How do attitudes guide behavior? In R. M. Sorrentino & E. T. Higgins (Eds.), *Handbook of Motivation and Cognition* (Vol. 1, pp. 204–243). New York: Guilford Press.

Fazio, R. H., Jackson, J. R., Dunton, B. C., & Williams, C. J. (1995). Variability in automatic activation as an unobtrusive measure of racial attitudes: A bona fide pipeline? *Journal of Personality and Social Psychology, 69*, 1013–1027.

Fazio, R. H., Sanbonmatsu, D. M., Powell, M. C., & Kardes, F. R. (1986). On the automatic activation of attitudes. *Journal of Personality and Social Psychology, 50*, 229–238.

Fitts, P. M., & Seeger, C. M. (1953). SR compatibility: Spatial characteristics of stimulus and response codes. *Journal of Experimental Psychology, 46*, 199–210.

Glaser, W. R., & Glaser, M. O. (1989). Context effects in Stroop-like word an picture processing. *Journal of Experimental Psychology: General, 118*, 13–42.

Greenwald, A. G., & Banaji, M. R. (1995). Implicit social cognition: Attitudes, self-esteem, and stereotypes. *Psychological Review, 102*, 4–27.

Greenwald, A. G., McGhee, D. E., & Schwartz, J. L. K. (1998). Measuring individual differences in implicit cognition: The Implicit Association Test. *Journal of Personality and Social Psychology, 74*, 1464–1480.

Hermans, D., De Houwer, J., & Eelen, P. (1994). The affective priming effect: Automatic activation of evaluative information in memory. *Cognition and Emotion, 8,* 515–533.

Hommel, B. (1995). Stimulus-response compatibility and the Simon effect: Toward an empirical clarification. *Journal of Experimental Psychology: Human Perception and Performance, 21,* 764–775.

Hommel, B. (1997). Toward an action-concept model of stimulus-response compatibility. In B. Hommel & W. Prinz (Eds.), *Theoretical issues in stimulus-response compatibility* (pp. 281–320). Amsterdam: North-Holland.

Klauer, K. C., & Musch, J. (2001). On the goal-dependence of automatic attitude activation: A model of affective priming by two mechanisms. Manuscript submitted for publication.

Klauer, K. C., Roßnagel, C., & Musch, J. (1997). List-context effects in evaluative priming. *Journal of Experimental Psychology: Learning, Memory, and Cognition, 23,* 246–255.

Kornblum, S., Hasbroucq, T., & Osman, A. (1990). Dimensional overlap: Cognitive basis for stimulus-response compatibility: A model and taxonomy. *Psychological Review, 97,* 253–270.

Kornblum, S., & Lee, J. W. (1995). Stimulus-Response compatibility with relevant and irrelevant stimulus dimensions that do and do not overlap with the response. *Journal of Experimental Psychology: Human Perception and Performance, 21,* 855–875.

Lu, C. H., & Proctor, R. W. (1995). The influence of irrelevant location information on performance: A review of the Simon and spatial Stroop effects. *Psychonomic Bulletin and Review, 2,* 174–207.

MacLeod, C. M. (1991). Half a century of research on the Stroop effect: An integrative review. *Psychological Bulletin, 109,* 163–203.

Mathews, A., & Klug, F. (1992). Emotionality and interference with color-naming in anxiety. *Behaviour Research and Therapy, 31,* 57–62.

Mathews, A., & MacLeod, C. (1985). Selective processing of threat cues in anxiety states. *Behaviour Research and Therapy, 23,* 563–569.

Mogg, K., Mathews, A., & Weinman, J. (1989). Selective processing of threat cues in anxiety states: A replication. *Behaviour Research and Therapy, 27,* 317–323.

Neely, J. H. (1991). Semantic priming effects in visual word recognition: A selective review of current findings and theories. In D. Besner & G. W. Humphreys (Eds.), *Basic processes in reading: Visual word recognition* (pp. 264–336). Hillsdale, NJ: Lawrence Erlbaum Associates.

Nuttin, J. M. (1985). Narcissism beyond Gestalt and awareness: The name letter effect. *European Journal of Social Psychology, 15,* 353–361.

Pratto, F. (1994). Consciousness and automatic evaluation. In P. M. Niedenthal & S. Kitayama (Eds.), *The heart's eye: Emotional influences in perception and attention* (pp. 115–143). San Diego, CA: Academic Press.

Pratto, F., & John, O. P. (1991). Automatic vigilance: The attention grabbing power of negative social information. *Journal of Personality and Social Psychology, 61,* 380–391.

Proctor, R. W., & Lu, K. P. L. (in press). Eliminating, magnifying, and reversing spatial compatibility effects with mixed location-relevant and irrelevant trials. In W. Prinz & B. Hommel (Eds.), *Attention and Performance XIX.*

Rudman, L. A., Greenwald, A. G., Mellott, D. S., Schwartz, J. L. K. (1999). Measuring the automatic components of prejudice: Flexibility and generality of the implicit association test. *Social Cognition, 17,* 437–465.

Simon, J. R. (1990). The effects of an irrelevant directional cue on human information processing. In R. W. Proctor & T. G. Reeve (Eds.), *Stimulus-response compatibility: An integrated perspective* (pp. 31–86). Amsterdam: North-Holland.

Solarz, A. K. (1960). Latency of instrumental responses as a function of compatibility with meaning of eliciting verbal signs. *Journal of Experimental Psychology, 59,* 239–245.

Stroop, J. R. (1935). Studies of interference in serial verbal reactions. *Journal of Experimental Psychology, 18,* 643–662.

Swanson, J. E., Rudman, L. A., & Greenwald, A. G. (2001). Using the Implicit Association Test to investigate attitude-behavior consistency for stigmatized behavior. *Cognition and Emotion, 15,* 207–230.

Wentura, D. (1999). Activation and inhibition of affective information: Evidence for negative priming in the evaluation task. *Cognition and Emotion, 13,* 65–91.

Wentura, D. (2000). Dissociative affective and associative priming effects in the lexical decision task: Responding with "yes" vs. "no" to word targets reveals evaluative judgment tendencies. *Journal of Experimental Psychology: Learning, Memory, and Cognition, 26,* 456–469.

Wentura, D., Rothermund, K., & Bak, P. (2000). Automatic vigilance: The attention-grabbing power of approach- and avoidance-related social information. *Journal of Personality and Social Psychology, 78,* 1024–1037.

Williams, J., Watts, F., MacLeod, C., & Mathews, A. (1996). The emotional Stroop task and psychopathology. *Psychological Bulletin, 120,* 3–24.

Zajonc, R. B. (1980). Feeling and thinking. Preferences need no inferences. *American Psychologist, 35,* 151–175.

Zhang, H., Zhang, J., & Kornblum, S. (1999). A parallel distributed processing model of stimulus-stimulus and stimulus-response compatibility. *Cognitive Psychology, 38,* 386–432.

Zorzi, M., & Umilta, C. (1995). A computational model of the Simon effect. *Psychological Research, 58,* 193–205.

APPENDIX

The taxonomy that I described in this chapter is highly similar to the taxonomy that was proposed by Kornblum (Kornblum et al., 1990; Kornblum & Lee, 1995; Zhang et al., 1999). The main difference between the two taxonomies is that I classify tasks according to the compatibility at the trial level whereas Kornblum classifies tasks according to compatibility at the set level. In all compatibility tasks, there is a set of stimuli that can appear on the various trials and a set of possible responses. Just like one can define the similarity between two individual stimuli, one can also define the similarity between two sets of stimuli. For instance, in a Stroop color-word task, all responses, words, and inkcolors refer to a color. As such, the set of words is similar to the set of responses because all members of the word set and all members of the response set refer to color. There is a similar overlap between the set of inkcolors and the set of words and between the set of inkcolors and the set of responses. Kornblum therefore defines the Stroop task as a task in which there is an overlap (a) between the set of irrelevant stimuli (i.e., the words) and the set of responses (i.e., irrelevant S–R overlap), (b) between the set of relevant stimuli (i.e., the inkcolors) and the set of responses (i.e., relevant S–R overlap), and (c) between the set of irrelevant stimuli and the set of relevant stimuli (i.e., S–S overlap). Assume that one changes the Stroop color-word task in such a way that all words refer to digits rather than to colors (e.g., the words "seven", "two", . . .). In that variant of the task, there would no longer be an overlap between the set of words and the set of inkcolors or responses. Kornblum would define this variant as a task in which there is relevant S–R overlap but not irrelevant S–R overlap or S–S overlap.

There main problem with Kornblum's taxonomy is that it does not take into account extrinsic features of the stimuli and responses. Consider the Eriksen and Eriksen task (Eriksen & Eriksen, 1974). In this task, participants are instructed to give a certain response (e.g., to press a left key) on presentation of certain letters (e.g., the letters F and G) and a different response (e.g., to press a right key) following the presentation of other letters (e.g., the letters R and S). During the testing phase, three letters are presented side by side in the middle of the screen. Participants have to give the response that is associated with the middle letter while ignoring the flanker letters. Nevertheless, responses to the middle letter are slower when it is flanked by letters to which a different response was assigned (e.g., "G R G") than when the same response was assigned to the flanker letters and the middle letter (e.g., "S R S").

Because the all the irrelevant flankers and all the relevant middle letters refer to letters whereas the responses do not refer to letters, Kornblum classifies this task as a task with S–S overlap but without relevant or irrelevant S–R overlap. However, this classification ignores the fact that on some trials, the flankers are extrinsically associated with the correct response (e.g., "G R G") whereas on other trials the flankers and the middle letter are extrinsically associated with a response that differs from the correct response (e.g., "S R S"). Therefore, irrelevant S–R compatibility varies over trials. This crucial fact is overseen because Kornblum only takes into account intrinsic features of the stimuli and response.

One could argue that the taxonomy of Kornblum can be changed in such a way that one can take into account extrinsic features of the stimuli and responses. With regard to the Eriksen and Eriksen task, for instance, one could argue that the set of responses is similar to the set of flankers because the flankers are mapped onto the responses. However, this would undermine the taxonomy of Kornblum. Because all reaction time tasks by definition require that stimuli are mapped onto responses, one would then have to postulate that all reaction time tasks involve relevant S–R overlap. Therefore, it only seems to make sense to classify tasks according to compatibility at the trial level.

Chapter 10

Beyond Verbal Self-Report: Priming Methods in Relationship Research

Rainer Banse
Humboldt-Universität zu Berlin

How do we know in advance that our partner will soothe us when we are sad or that our child will like a birthday present? Sure, we are not always correct, but we do fairly well in predicting the behavior of relationship partners. This capacity is due to a mental representation of personal relationship that has been termed *internal working model* in attachment theory (Bowlby, 1969), or *relational schema* in a more general perspective on relationship representation (Baldwin, 1992). Because relationship research traditionally relies on behavior observation and verbal self-report data, the cognitive representation of relationships has mainly had the status of a postulated background concept and has not been an object of investigation in its own right. This has changed since the 1990s when relationship researchers became increasingly interested in using experimental methods such as affective and semantic priming to study relational schemata. In this chapter I review this work and some of its historical precursors. The aim is to show how priming has been successfully used in relationship research, to discuss the limitations of this approach, and to make some suggestions for future research.

According to Baldwin's (1992) conceptualization of the relational schema this knowledge structure is composed of three distinct parts: relationship-specific representations of the relationship partner, the self, and the interaction between them. Relationship experiences are stored in this knowledge structure not as a record of the historical truth, but as they were seen, interpreted, and memorized by the individual. Based on these stored past experiences the relational schema can be used to simulate interaction sequences in order to predict reactions of the partner. In happy relationships the relational schema provides continuity, security, and trust. Also malfunctioning relationships are reflected in the relational schema. Of course, if the representation of the relationship partner and his or her expected behavior are unrealistic, the relational schema can lead to dysfunctional interactive behavior.

THREE APPROACHES TO STUDY RELATIONAL SCHEMATA

There is a limited number of ways to study the general structure and individual differences in the content of relational schemata. One can observe relationship partners when they interact, one can ask people about their relationships, or one can access the relational schema using experimental methods. All three approaches allow only for indirect inferences about relational schemata, each has specific virtues, problems, and limitations.

Behavior observation has been extensively used to study infant–parent relationships in preverbal infants (Ainsworth, Blehar, Waters, & Wall, 1978) and children up to age 6 (Main & Solomon, 1986). Although this research tradition has resulted in an elaborate theory of mental representation, different types of relational schemata (i.e., working models) were inductively inferred from typical patterns of behavior in mother–child interactions (e.g., of secure, avoidant, and anxious-ambivalent children). However, it seems difficult to use behavior observation alone to empirically test predictions about the structure and content of relational schemata.

The most commonly used method in relationship research is the *explicit* verbal self-report. There is compelling evidence that this approach is an economical, efficient, reliable, and fairly valid way to study relational schemata. However, *explicit* verbal self-reports of relationship quality are often distorted by positive self-presentation, and they are limited to features of relationship quality that can be consciously accessed and verbally reported. These problems can be circumvented using *indirect* verbal self-report measures such as the Adult Attachment Interview (AAI, George, Kaplan, & Main, 1985). In the AAI it is not the content, but rather the relation between content of the interview and formal characteristics, such as incoherence, lack of detail, or inappropriate affect, that are used to infer attachment-specific features of the relational schema. This approach bears many similarities to the diagnosis of the veridicality of eye-witness testimonies used in forensic psychology (e.g., Lamb, Sternberg, & Esplin, 1994; Trankell, 1971). Although based on verbal reports, both approaches are intended to assess mental representations in a way that is robust against voluntary or involuntary distortions of the verbal account. The major disadvantage of the AAI and similar interview techniques is that they are extremely time-consuming.

Finally, the third approach uses experimental methods and response time measures to make inferences about the structure and content of mental representation of relationships. Although the experimental toolbox contains several potentially suitable experimental paradigms such as the Stroop-task (McLeod, 1991), the affective Simon task (De Houwer & Eelen, 1998; De Houwer, Hermans, & Eelen, 1998) or the Implicit Association Test (IAT; Greenwald, McGhee, & Schwartz, 1998; see also De Houwer, chap. , this volume), almost all research reviewed here used various priming paradigms. Priming is a standard method in cognitive psychology and has recently attracted growing interest also in social psychology as an implicit measure of attitudes, stereotypes, and prejudice (e.g., Devine, 1989; for an overview see Brauer, Wasel, & Niedenthal, 2000). More interesting, the first studies using priming of relational schemata date back to the 1960s (Silverman & Silverman, 1964), and built on the "New Look" research tradition of the 1940s rather than the development of priming methods in cognitive psychology (e.g., Meyer & Schvaneveldt, 1971; Neely, 1977).

PRIMING IN RELATIONSHIP RESEARCH

Rationale of the Priming Method

Priming approaches are attractive in the context of relationship research because they may circumvent the two critical problems of verbal report measures, namely their reactivity and limitation to information that can be consciously accessed and verbalized. The term *priming* is used for a broad class of experimental techniques that are used to study the effects of the activation of a specific mental content on subsequent behavior. In general it is assumed that mental representations are organized in some form of associative network. According to such network models, the activation of one node spreads to other nodes as a function of association strength and the distance between nodes. If a node of the network is pre-activated or *primed* by activation spreading from a connected node, it is easier to activate this node subsequently. The facilitation of activating a target concept (or node) can be measured by shortened response latencies or reduced error rates as compared to priming with unrelated concepts or no priming at all. Taking advantage of this basic effect, the priming method uses measures of response facilitation to draw inferences about the content and structure of the associative network.

Priming effects are generally conceived of as reflecting automatic processes (i.e., processes that unfold without requiring awareness), intentionality, or the allocation of attentional resources. Although the behavior that is influenced by the priming can be controlled in principle, priming effects in well-designed experiments are unlikely to be controlled because participants are unaware of the priming or of the relation between the priming and its effects on subsequent behavior (Bargh, 1994).

There are very different methods to activate a specific mental content. These range from procedures that require the active participation of the participant, such as writing down a story (e.g., about rejecting versus supportive friendship experiences, Miller & Noirot, 1999), imagining a supporting versus critical significant other (Baldwin, 1994), or resolving a scrambled sentence task, in which grammatically correct sentences have to be built by choosing four words out of sets of five. If many scrambled sentences contain words relating to the target concept, an unobtrusive priming of this concept can be achieved (Bargh, Chen, & Burrows, 1996; Higgins, Rholes, & Jones, 1977). When using these approaches, care is taken that participants are unaware about the influence of the priming on subsequent behavior by using a cover story that makes it plausible that the priming task and the subsequent task belong to different experiments or are unrelated.

In other approaches, pictures, names or words are presented as primes using a tachistoscope or a computer monitor. The priming procedure can take place before the subsequent task (e.g., Bornstein, Leone, & Galley, 1987), or primes and subsequent task can be presented intermixed (Fazio, Sanbonmatsu, Powell, & Kardes, 1986). To make certain that controlled cognitive processes cannot influence priming effects, targets are presented very shortly after the onset of the prime (e.g., 300 ms), or primes are presented outside of conscious awareness or *subliminally* (*lat.* for "below threshold"). Priming procedures are called subliminal if primes are presented above an objective perception threshold evidenced by an experimental effect of the primes, but below a subjective perception threshold evidenced by ". . . the person's own report of a lack of phenomenal experience of the stimulus" (Bargh, 1992, p. 237), or the incapacity to recognize primes in a direct discrimination task (Cheesman & Merikle, 1986; Greenwald, Draine, & Abrams, 1996; Merikle & Reingold, 1992). More interesting, it has been found often that supraliminal priming produces similar results as subliminal priming. According to Bargh (1994) the crucial point is *not* whether or not participants are aware of primes, but whether they are aware of a possible influence of primes on subsequent behavior. The use of subliminal priming is just an elegant method to eliminate any suspicion that priming effects are influenced by conscious or deliberate cognitive processes.

Three Research Programs

Empirical studies that have used priming methods to investigate the mental representation of relationships can be grouped into three categories. A first line of research has investigated the effects of a subliminal activation of relational schemata on very global outcome measures such as therapy success.

A second line has used the priming method to study the architecture of relational schemata, as well as the connections between relational schemata and other constructs, such as the self-concept, self-esteem, mood, or coping behavior. In a third approach affective priming has been used as a nonreactive, indirect or implicit *measure* of relational schemata (e.g., Banse, 1999; 2001). This approach is conceptually akin to priming methods for assessing implicit attitudes or prejudices (e.g., Dovidio, Kawakami, Johnson, Johnson, & Howard, 1997; Fazio, Jackson, Dunton, & Williams, 1995; Wittenbrink, Judd, & Park, 1997).

SUBLIMINAL PSYCHODYNAMIC ACTIVATION

Somewhat surprisingly, the historically earliest and, up to now, largest research program using subliminal semantic priming in the context of personal relationships is rooted in psychoanalysis and has been conducted in a clinical context. Silverman and Silverman (1964) presented a subliminal psychodynamic activation (SPA) method to experimentally test hypotheses derived from psychoanalytic views of psychopathology. Although this research program has produced an impressive number of studies its impact has been limited. Both relationship researchers and scholars of unconscious cognition have been reluctant to accept the results of this research as empirical facts. This skepticism was probably raised by both ". . . the lack of widespread enthusiasm for the SPA result's proposed psychodynamic interpretation" (Greenwald, 1992, p. 769), and perhaps more important, by the very unusual methodological approach using entire sentences as primes in a subliminal priming procedure. In an informal opinion survey among experts in unconscious cognition (Greenwald, 1992, Appendix B), only a small minority considered the claimed subliminal psychodynamic activation as empirically established.

The evaluation of the empirical status of SPA research could not be more contradictory. Hardaway (1990) presented a meta-analytic review of SPA studies that confirmed a significant SPA effect and concluded somewhat apodictically "Future research designed to replicate basic experimental effects is deemed superfluous" (p. 177), whereas Fudin (1999) raised serious concerns about the internal validity of SPA experiments and underscored ". . . the need to start anew research in this area" (p. 234). So not only the psychoanalytical explanation of subliminal psychodynamic activation, but also the mere existence of the SPA effect have been contested.

According to psychoanalytic theorizing, many adults harbor fantasies to be one or to merge with the comforting, protective, and nurturing "good mother of early childhood" (Silverman & Weinberger, 1985). In a therapeutic setting SPA is claimed to activate such fantasies and to enhance the beneficial effects of the therapy. In typical SPA experiments, the sentence

"Mommy and I are one" is presented repeatedly by a tachistoscope for 4 ms during one or several therapeutic sessions, and a neutral sentence such as "People are walking" is used as a control prime in another session. The priming procedure is double-blind; The experimenter does not know whether the experimental or the control prime is used, and the patient is unable to consciously recognize the prime due to the short exposure time. The priming effects have been assessed using pre–post treatment difference scores in various measures including ratings of psychopathology, well-being, projective tests, smoking abstinence, physiological reactions, or behavior accuracy measures. Most studies have been conducted with participants diagnosed as schizophrenics, other studies included depressive, phobic, or non-clinical samples.

In his meta-analysis Hardaway (1990) reviewed 56 studies containing results of 111 independent samples. Besides the prime sentence "Mommy and I are one" other sentences relating to the mother were used (e.g., "Mommy and I are two", "Mommy feels fine"), and also stimuli that alluded to oneness but did not contain the word *Mommy* (e.g., "my girl and I are one," "Daddy and I are one"). Besides the type of stimuli and the number of priming repetitions, Hardaway coded several potential moderator variables such as sample characteristics, methodological quality, and the laboratory affiliation of the authors.

The effect size of the "Mommy and I are one" primes as compared to control primes was significant and of moderate size ($d = .41$). The effect size for other Mommy stimuli ($d = .14$), and other oneness stimuli ($d = .22$) was still significant but substantially smaller. This result suggests that the "Mommy and I are one" primes activated a specific relational schema and elicited particularly strong effects for primes related to mother *and* oneness. The remaining variance between studies could be attributed to sampling error and the unreliability of measures. No significant influence was found for the researcher's laboratory affiliation or the other potential moderators. Virtually identical results were reported in published and unpublished studies (Weinberger, 1992), and a file-drawer analysis revealed that 2,237 more unpublished studies with zero-effects would be needed to attribute the overall effect to a publication bias for significant results. In another meta-analysis, Bornstein (1990) showed that for patients subliminal priming had significantly larger effects than supraliminal priming, whereas no difference was found for normal controls. Hardaway (1990) stated that experimental effects were also found for normal controls, but unfortunately failed to report the corresponding effect sizes. However, the results of Hardaway's meta-analysis provide evidence that the prime "Mommy and I are one" did positively influence the outcomes of therapeutic and educational interventions, and that the effect sizes of studies were independent of the author's affiliation to Silverman (but see Fudin, 1999).

The most interesting result of the meta-analysis was that the sentence "Mommy and I are one" had more positive effects than primes relating either to Mommy or to oneness. But how is it possible that some extremely brief exposures of a sentence can influence molar constructs such as therapy effects? Weinberger (1992) tried to demystify SPA-results by relating them to accepted phenomena of contemporary mainstream psychology. He proposed that the moderation of therapy effects by subliminal priming may be mediated by a positive mood induction, leading to more flexibility in thinking, better problem solving, and eventually to more positive therapy outcomes (but see Sohlberg, Samuelberg, Sidén, & Thörn, 1998). Weinberger maintains that the genuine psychoanalytic contribution to SPA-effects is the identification of potent stimuli. In fact, whereas one does not need to adhere to psychoanalytic theorizing to accept the word *Mommy* as positive, hardly any other theoretical framework would predict *oneness* to be a potent positive stimulus. This fact may be partly responsible for the vivid scepticism SPA-results have encountered outside the psychoanalytic community.

In this respect a recent study by Glassman and Andersen (1999) is particularly interesting. In this study subliminal multiple word primes were used to activate relational schemata of significant others without referring to psychodynamic assumptions. The primes were short descriptions of significant others (e.g., is usually very insightful, gets depressed sometimes, is very sensitive) that had been generated by the participants at least 1 week before the priming session in an allegedly different experiment. A series of such describing sentences were briefly (71 to 100 ms) presented in parafoveal vision during a mock interactive computer game with a fictitious second person. A subsequent forced choice discrimination task showed that the prime sentences were indeed presented outside of awareness. As in previous research using written person descriptions of significant others (Andersen, Glassman, Chen, & Cole, 1995), participants erroneously assigned attributes of the significant other to a fictitious person who shared some descriptors with the significant other. This was the case although the critical traits were *not* used for priming. This result suggests that the entire significant other schema was activated and then used "to go beyond the information given" about the fictitious interaction partner. Less false positive memory was found in two control groups who were subliminally primed either with descriptions of nonsignificant others, or someone else's significant others. Overall, these results provide strong evidence that schema effects can be attributed to the mental representation of significant others, and not to the self-generation of primes, or specific features of significant-other descriptions.

The results of Glassman and Andersen (1999) have several important implications. First it is noteworthy that the psychoanalytical concept of *transference* can be empirically demonstrated and explained as a "normal" schema effect that can occur with any significant other even if the significant other schema is activated outside of awareness. Second, in two experiments, subliminally presented four-word sentences elicited specific and theoretical meaningful effects. Unlike the "Mommy and I are one" prime in SPA research no controversial theoretical assumptions are required to interpret the observed priming effects. The idiographic prime sentences generated by the participants can be straightforwardly interpreted as a readout of individual relational schemata. However, the basic problem of the complexity of the used primes remains. Is it plausible that subliminally presented sentences can be processed? Greenwald (1992) noted that nothing more complex than "a partial analysis of the meaning of single words" has been empirically established, but that "the task of demonstrating that attentionless unconscious cognition can extract the meaning of a two word sequence poses a theoretically significant challenge (p. 775)".

Unfortunately up to now there is little systematic research taking up Greenwald's "two word-challenge". Draine (1997) and Greenwald and Liu (1985, cf. Greenwald, 1992) found no evidence that subliminal two-word primes had any sentence level priming effects over and beyond the additive effects of individual prime words. However, it may be possible to reconcile the controversy about multiple word primes. I return to this point at the end of this chapter.

EXPLORING THE STRUCTURE AND CONNECTIONS OF RELATIONAL SCHEMATA

Role Schemata, Relational Schemata, and Self-Esteem

A second research program using subliminal priming for studying the structure and connections of relational schemata has mainly been conducted by Mark W. Baldwin and colleagues. These authors have published a series of studies that have explored the effects of chronic individual differences or temporal experimental activation of relational schemata on several cognitive and affective constructs such as the self-concept, self-esteem, anticipated partner reactions, or reported mood and coping behavior during an imagined stressful event.

In an initial study, Baldwin, Carrel, and Lopez (1990) aimed to demonstrate that the cognitive representation of an authority figure can be unobtrusively activated using a subliminal priming procedure, and that the person schema can have a specific effect on the self-concept in an academic context. The experiment began with asking advanced students in psychology to note several research ideas. They then performed a mock reaction time task that consisted in pressing a button as quickly as possible after seeing a light flash before they had to evaluate the quality of one of the previously noted research ideas. The light flash was in fact the picture of the scowling face of a familiar academic authority (Robert Zajonc), the face of a friendly looking postdoctoral fellow, or a blank control slide.

The primes were repeatedly presented for 2 ms and immediately followed by a pattern mask for 10 ms in a fully double blind experimental procedure. The results showed that a subliminal priming with the disapproving face of the academic authority elicited more negative self evaluations than a priming with the friendly face of the research assistant. Although this result confirmed the hypotheses, it did not exclude the possibility that the effect was caused by the facial expressions rather than the social roles of the persons. This point was addressed in a second experiment with catholic female students not familiar with Robert Zajonc. After having read a text describing a sexual dream implying a woman's permissive attitude toward sexuality, the participants were subliminally primed with either the picture of the disapproving Robert Zajonc, a photo of an equally disapproving Pope John Paul II, or a blank control slide. Additionally the participants were asked to describe themselves as "nonpracticing" versus "practicing" Catholics.

As expected, those subliminally primed with the disapproving face of the Pope reported a more negative self concept, and this effect was found only for participants who described themselves as practicing Catholics. The data show that a negative expression *combined* with the status of an authority (academic or religious) was sufficient to lower self-esteem, but not a negative expression alone. In a follow-up study, Baldwin (1994) investigated whether the self-concept lowering effect of common authority figures would generalize to individually chosen significant others. Participants were asked to provide the names of a number of persons including an accepting and a critical significant other that were then used as subliminal primes. After the priming, participants were surprisingly asked to remember and to write down the items presented in a prior incidental learning task, which was much more difficult than expected. Measures of mood, self-esteem, and a self rating on the performance in the memory-task were assessed. The results showed that the self-esteem scores were significantly lower after priming with the individual names of *critical* persons than after priming with the names of *accepting* persons. No effect was found for the self-evaluation of performance or the mood-scales. The latter null-finding made it unlikely that the priming effect of significant other names was mediated by a mood induction, thus suggesting that relational schemata are directly linked to the representation of the self and self-esteem, and not indirectly via affective processes. To investigate whether subliminality was critical for obtaining the observed priming effects, the name of a critical or a supportive significant other was presented supraliminally in a second experiment. Additionally, a self-awareness manipulation was introduced by using a mirror besides the experimental computer that was turned to the participants for half of the sample, and turned away for the other half (Carver & Scheier, 1981), inducing high or low self-awareness, respectively.

Previous research had shown that supraliminal primes have a stronger influence on self-aware participants (Baldwin & Holmes, 1987), and that supraliminal primes yield assimilation effects when presented incidentally, but contrast effects when focused upon (Strack, Schwarz, Bless, Kübler, & Wänke, 1993). In consequence, it was expected that the analysis of self-esteem would show an interaction effect between the factors self-awareness and type of significant other. Only under conditions of high self-awareness should a critical other lower self-esteem. This predicted interaction effect was in fact marginally significant. In the high self-awareness condition (with mirror) self-esteem significantly decreased in the critical other condition, and no significant effect was found for the accepting other condition. In the low self-awareness condition, an opposite trend was found that was presumably due to an overcompensation of the priming effect. In this experiment the manipulation also influenced mood, but a mediation analysis revealed that the effects found for self-esteem remained marginally significant when controlling for mood. The observed cross-over interaction between self-awareness and critical versus supportive relationship underlines the virtue of the subliminal priming technique. Although supraliminal primes may have similar effects as subliminal primes (Bargh, 1994), this is only to be expected if participants are not aware of a possible influence of the prime on subsequent behavior, which is guaranteed if primes are presented outside of awareness.

Navigating in the Social Space: Predicicting Behavior of Relationship Partners

The stored knowledge about the partner, the self, and past interaction patterns between them open a mental theater, in which own actions and partner reactions can be simulated. Attachment theory (Ainsworth et al., 1978; Bartholomew, 1990; Bowlby, 1969; Collins & Read, 1994) provides an elaborated theory of different types of internal "working models" or relational schemata. For example, as compared to secure individuals anxious-ambivalent individuals are characterized by a strong need for closeness and the expectation to be rejected when searching for closeness. This characteristic should be reflected in relational schemata containing corresponding *if–then* contingencies that link own actions to expected partner responses. Baldwin, Fehr, Keedian, Seidel, and Thomson (1993) conducted an elegant study showing that the experimental cognitive approach is in fact a viable method to reveal specific features of relationship representations by using explicit and implicit approaches in parallel.

It was expected that individuals with secure attachment would indicate more optimistic interaction expectations than insecure individuals. Explicit interpersonal expectations in a romantic relationship were measured in three different contexts (trust, dependency, and closeness) using sentences such as "You want to spend more time with your partner . . .". The participants then indicated the frequency of positive (. . . he/she accepts you) and negative outcomes (. . . he/she rejects you).

As expected, anxious-ambivalent individuals reported more negative expectations in the domains of trust and closeness seeking (but not dependency), and avoidant individuals reported more negative expectations in the trust domain. However, these results could be accounted for by individual differences in social desirability or by semantic overlap between reported interpersonal expectations and attachment measures. In a second experiment, these alternative explanations were eliminated by using a lexical decision task to assess interpersonal expectancies. To prime specific interpersonal contexts, sentences were displayed word by word (600 ms each), followed by targets that had to be classified as words or nonwords. As expected, secure individuals responded relatively faster to words denominating positive, and avoidant individuals relatively faster to target words denominating negative partner behavior (the number of anxious-ambivalent participants was not sufficient for analysis). This result is important for attachment theory because it shows that different adult attachment styles are indeed characterized by specific if–then contingencies at the representational level. From a more general perspective it is noteworthy that the priming with the interpersonal contexts facilitated specifically lexical decisions for those target words that represented probable partner behaviors for each attachment style and not just relationship unspecific semantic proximity between primes and targets.

Interpersonal Expectancies and Self-Esteem

Many theories ranging from symbolic interactionism (Cooley, 1902; Mead, 1934) to recent functional accounts of self-esteem (Leary, Tambor, Terdal, & Downs, 1995) have postulated that individual differences in the self-concept and self-esteem reflect the individual's perception of evaluations by significant others. The self is not a homogeneous construct and can be better described as composed of several specific selves (e.g., social, academic, sport, etc.) with corresponding specific self-esteem (Marsh, 1993; Marsh & Yeung, 1998; Pelham & Swann, 1989). In extending the approach described previously, Baldwin and Sinclair (1996) investigated the often postulated relation between interpersonal contingencies and self-esteem in the context of success and failure. Individuals with low self-esteem were expected to have a chronically accessible relational schema in which success is associated with acceptance, and failure with rejection. Individuals with high self-esteem, however, should instead by default expect unconditional acceptance.

In analogy to the study reported previously, Baldwin and Sinclair (1996) postulated that the representation of an individual's own behavior (related to success and failure) should be connected to the representation of responses of the social environment (acceptance vs. rejection) in relational schemata. To prime the first part of these *if–then* contingencies, Baldwin and Sinclair (1996) used words relating to success (e.g., success, win), failure (e.g., lose, incompetent), or control words (begin, estimate). To assess the automatically expected reactions, target words relating to acceptance (e.g., cherished, accepted), rejection (e.g., abandoned, ridiculed), neutral words (e.g., listened, hammer), and nonwords (e.g., lisrened, hammen) were used. A self-esteem measure was obtained and the sample was split at the median in a low and high self-esteem group. As expected, individuals with low-self esteem showed faster responses to rejection targets after failure primes than after success primes.

Because success and failure primes and acceptance and rejection targets are affectively polarized, the results may have been caused by a valence congruency effect (positive primes speed up responses to positive and negative primes to negative targets), making the assumption of a mediating relational schema superfluous. This alternative explanation was excluded in a second experiment by showing that priming effects were specific to interpersonal words and did not occur for other valenced words (e.g., freedom, amuse vs. stealing, decay).

Many developmental theories of self-esteem postulate that self-esteem is shaped by many episodes of acceptance or rejection by significant others contingent on success and failure (e.g., Leary et al., 1995; Rogers, 1959). If this conjecture is true, it should be possible to demonstrate this relation when focusing on a single interaction episode. This hypothesis was tackled in a third experiment. This time Baldwin and Sinclair (1996) did not take an individual difference perspective investigating individuals with high and low trait self-esteem, but manipulated the postulated determinant of self-esteem experimentally. To activate an accepting versus criticizing significant other schema, they asked participants to vividly imagine appropriate significant others. Immediately afterward, participants performed the same lexical decision task as in the second experiment. The results confirmed that the priming effect was again specific to the critical significant other prime and interpersonal target words.

In summary, the study by Baldwin and Sinclair (1996) provides strong evidence for the hypothesis that contingency expectations are part of relational schemata, that an activation of either a specific relational schema or of specific types of interactions can trigger related contingency expectancies, which are in turn related to self-esteem. For the architecture of relational schemata this result suggests that relationship specific if–then contingencies can be generalized and activated in the form of an interaction script with the "generalized significant other."

If–Then Contingencies and Coping Behavior

Although the effects of relational schemata on self-esteem are interesting, one may object that the presumably temporal and subtle changes of self-concept and self-esteem are of academic interest only. The practical relevance of schema activation effects would be much greater if those would directly influence relationship relevant behavior. Pierce and Lydon (1998) have extended the work of Baldwin and colleagues by investigating how priming with elements of relational schemata influences behavior intentions. An unwanted pregnancy situation was chosen as a meaningful stressful situation that could be easily imagined by female students. To prime different interaction expectancies, words indicating either support (e.g., helpful, supportive, caring), rejection (e.g., critical, rejecting, hurtful), or random consonants as control stimuli were presented in alternation with masks similar to Baldwin (1994). Immediately after the priming, participants listened to a scenario describing an unwanted pregnancy, and then answered questions about support seeking and coping strategies they would adopt in this situation.

The significant effects of subliminal priming on reported affect and coping behavior were generally small but in the expected direction. Women primed with negative interaction descriptors reported less positive affect, and marginally less growth-oriented coping than women in the control condition. Women primed with positive interaction descriptors reported more seeking of emotional support, and less self-denigrating coping than women in the control condition. The chosen coping intentions appeared as if the participants would adapt to a social environment showing the primed behavior.

AFFECTIVE PRIMING AS AN IMPLICIT MEASURE OF RELATIONAL SCHEMATA

The research presented previously used priming as a method to explore the internal structural properties of relational schemata, or connections of relational schemata and other constructs. However, besides the empirical demonstration that two mentally represented entities are connected, the priming method can also be used to *measure* specific aspects of relational schemata, thus providing an interesting methodological complement to verbal self-report or behavioral measures commonly used in relationship research. As compared to these methods, the priming approach may be more robust against self-presentation concerns and therefore provide an alternative method to assess strongly socially valued relationship qualities. However, the usefulness of this approach for the analysis of individual differences depends crucially on the psychometric properties of the priming measures. The studies presented in the following used different priming paradigms to investigate whether person-related primes do elicit person-specific priming effects, and whether these effects are sufficiently reliable for the analysis of individual differences.

A very basic aspect of the relational schema is the evaluation of or attitude toward a relationship partner. There is ample evidence that the mere activation of attitude objects or person schemata is sufficient to automatically activate an evaluation that is associated with the object (e.g., Fazio et al., 1986; Fiske, 1981). Under certain circumstances this automatic evaluation can influence subsequent behavior. Affective priming methods take advantage of this effect to measure the automatic evaluation of prime stimuli. Depending on the nature of the subsequent task two affective priming paradigms can be distinguished. In the affective priming paradigm proposed by Murphy and Zajonc (1993) affectively polarized primes (e.g., positive and negative facial expressions) are subliminally presented and immediately followed by affectively neutral target stimuli (Chinese ideographs) that have to be evaluated on a liking scale. Murphy and Zajonc showed that the valence of subliminal primes systematically influenced the subsequent liking rating, positive primes leading to more positive, and negative primes to more negative ratings of the neutral targets.

Banse (1999) adapted this paradigm for measuring the implicit evaluation of relationship partners in a large sample (N = 201). Instead of facial expressions of emotions, the names and affectively neutral faces of good friends or romantic partners were used as critical primes along with the names and faces of the participants and control primes. Deviating from Murphy and Zajonc (1993) who presented the face primes for 4 ms with a tachistoscope, Banse (1999) used PCs to present face and name primes relating to a significant other, the self, and a control for 10.5 ms. Immediately after the primes either a mask or a blank screen followed for 31.5 ms. The visibility of primes was varied using first masked and then unmasked primes. Pretests had shown that unmasked face and name primes relating to self and significant others were relatively easy to recognize. The masked or unmasked primes were then followed by Chinese ideographs that had to be rated on a 6-point liking scale.

To explore the relations between individual differences in affective priming effects and explicit measures of relationship quality, questionnaire measures of relationship satisfaction and adult attachment were obtained. There is an ongoing controversy whether implicit and explicit measures of mental representations should be considered as the same or distinct constructs (e.g., Greenwald & Banaji, 1995; Fazio & Towles-Schwenn, 1999; Wilson, Lindsey, & Schooler, 2000), and in consequence it is not yet clear whether substantial correlations between these measures can be expected. In either case, correlation coefficients can be meaningfully interpreted only if the reliability of both explicit and implicit measures are sufficient. To estimate the retest reliability of the priming procedure, the priming experiment was repeated for a subsample of participants ($N = 66$) 1 to 4 weeks later.

The results showed that masked primes relating to significant others elicited significantly more positive ratings of the Chinese ideographs than primes relating to self, whereas intermediate effects were obtained for control primes. This pattern replicated across relationship types (romantic partners and good friends), and more important, the priming effects were identical for names and faces, thus providing strong evidence that effects were in fact due to an activation of person schemata and not to other features of the primes (e.g., the attractiveness of faces). The unmasked priming block showed a different pattern: For faces, the partner-related primes had much stronger positive effects than self-related primes, for unmasked names no difference was found.

Why was the affective reaction toward the self less positive than toward the partner? It is likely that the implicit partner schema is more positive due to idealization (Murray, Holmes, & Griffin, 1997), and that the self schema contains more negative attributes. The differential priming effect for the self and the other schema was statistically reliable but very small. The priming effect obtained with angry versus happy faces reported by Murphy and Zajonc (1993) was about 20 times stronger. This difference in effect size was most likely due to the much stronger affective difference between angry and happy emotional expression as compared to a significant other and the self.

The results show that the Murphy and Zajonc paradigm can be used to assess partner-specific automatic evaluation at the group level. However, the aim of using the priming effects as a measure of *individual differences* in automatic partner evaluation clearly failed. The retest reliabilities of individual priming indices were marginal at best (ranging from –.06 to .28), and no substantial correlations were found between individual priming measures and explicit measures of relationship quality or adult attachment. The lack of any substantial correlations between individual affective priming effects and explicit measures of relationship quality in Banse (1999) could indicate that this measure is *essentially* uninformative because it reflects only a gross positive–negative distinction, but bears no information about a differentiated evaluation of the relationship partner. Alternatively, the indirect assessment of implicit person evaluation via an evaluation of neutral stimuli could lack sensitivity. As a potentially more sensitive indicator for automatic evaluation, Banse (2001) used an adaptation of the Fazio et al. (1986) affective priming paradigm with an evaluative decision task that had been successfully used as a measure of individual differences in racial prejudice (Fazio et al., 1995).

In this affective priming paradigm participants are briefly presented with affectively polarized prime words (Fazio et al., 1986) or faces of ingroup and outgroup members (Fazio et al., 1995). They then have to decide whether subsequently presented target words have a positive or negative meaning. The response latencies (or error rates) are then used as an indicator of the automatic evaluation of primes. Most studies using this paradigm have found congruency priming effects (i.e., positively evaluated primes facilitate the evaluative decision for positive as compared to negative target words, and negatively evaluated primes for negative as compared to positive target words; for an overview see Klauer & Musch, chap. 2, this volume).

The priming procedure used by Banse (2001) closely paralleled the previous experiment (Banse, 1999) except for three major changes. First, instead of a like–dislike rating task, a good–bad evaluative decision task was used. Participants had to decide whether clearly positive and negative target words had a positive or negative meaning. Second, the name and the face of a disliked person (Saddam Hussein) were added to the three person identities (self, partner, and control) used before. Third, masked and unmasked primes were not blocked but presented intermixed. Some procedural features differed from the standard procedure used by Fazio et al. (1986). A shorter prime exposure time (10.5 ms instead of 200 ms), and prime-target SOA (42 ms instead of 300 ms) was used. As in the previous study, relationship satisfaction and adult attachment self-report measures were obtained to explore the relation between individual differences in priming effects and explicit measures of relationship quality or personality.

The response time difference between negative and positive target word conditions for each prime category was used as priming index. These difference scores were not subtracted from control prime effects because the face control prime (the portrait of an unknown person) was likely to be evaluated more positively than the name control prime (the neutral word *occasion*). Referencing priming effects to the control primes might have been misleading for the analysis of group level treatment effects, as well as for the analysis of individual differences. For example, people reacting more positive to their relationship partner may also tend to react more positively to unknown persons than people with more negative partner schemata.

It was expected that primes relating to significant others (friends or romantic partners) would facilitate the evaluative decision for positive as compared to negative target words, and that primes relating to disliked persons would facilitate the evaluative decision for negative as compared to positive target words. This hypothesis was confirmed for unmasked primes (Fig. 10.1, Panel A). As in the previous study (Banse, 1999), priming effects were very similar for face primes and name primes, providing strong evidence that the effects were caused by the evaluation of person identities and not by other characteristics of the primes such as physical attractiveness of faces. Surprisingly, for masked primes both the liked and the disliked person facilitated the evaluation of positive targets more than self-related and control primes. This unexpected finding was difficult to interpret. Because

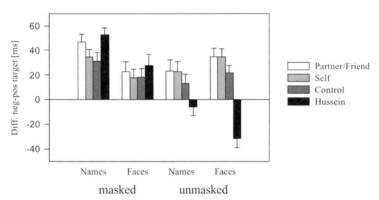

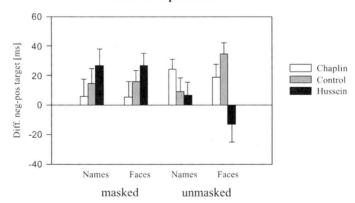

FIG. 10.1. Mean answer latency differences between negative and positive targets as a function of person identity, prime modality, and masking of primes (Banse, 2001; Reprinted by permission of Psychology Press Ltd., Hove, UK).

the positively evaluated significant others were also more familiar than the negatively evaluated Saddam Hussein, prime valence and prime familiarity were confounded.

In a second experiment a liked and a disliked person of roughly comparable familiarity (Charlie Chaplin and Saddam Hussein) were used as primes. The idiographic primes relating to the self and significant others were omitted. With this set of primes a very clear pattern of results emerged (Fig. 10.1, Panel B). Whereas the congruency priming effects of the first experiment could be replicated for unmasked primes, reverse priming effects were found for masked primes. Masked primes relating to the liked person facilitated the evaluation of negative compared to positive targets, and primes relating to the disliked person facilitated the evaluation of positive compared to negative targets. Although such reverse priming effects have been occasionally observed in affective priming studies (see Klauer & Musch, chap. 2, this volume), it is not yet clear why and under which conditions such effects occur (see also the chapters by Glaser, chap. 4, this volume; and Wentura & Rothermund, chap. 3, this volume).

The results show that it is possible to assess the automatic evaluation of persons with the Fazio et al. (1986) affective priming paradigm at the group level. To test the suitability of this approach for the study of individual differences, the reliability of the priming measure and its correlations with questionnaire measures of relationship quality were explored. The consistency coefficients (Cronbach's α) for positive split-half test correlations ranged from .0 to a maximum of .57 in the condition of unmasked priming with the name of the relationship partner. In general, unmasked priming conditions tended to show somewhat higher consistencies than masked priming conditions. Additional analysis with the priming index referenced to control primes yielded similar priming effects, but the internal consistencies were still lower.

Although the consistencies seem to be more substantial than those found in the Murphy and Zajonc paradigm (Banse, 1999), they clearly fall short of the conventionally required standard of .80. In consequence, when the priming indices were simultaneously regressed on the four attachment scales (secure, fearful, preoccupied, and dismissing attachment), few significant regression coefficients were found. Unlike the group level priming effects, regression coefficients were not consistent across name and face primes. Interestingly enough, two out of three significant regression coefficients in Experiment 1 that could be conceptually replicated in Experiment 2 were in fact replicated: Anxious attachment was related to more positive priming effects of the masked face of Hussein (Exp. 1: $b = 46.7$, $p < .01$; Exp. 2: $b = 28.1$, $p < .05$), and dismissing attachment was related to the more positive priming effects of the clearly visible faces of the relationship partner in the first ($b = 28.0$, $p < .05$), and of the clearly visible face of Charlie Chaplin in the second experiment ($b = 29.4$, $p < .01$). As one might expect, significant regression coefficients were generally found for those priming effects with relatively high reliability. It is puzzling, however, that the sign of these regression coefficients was just opposite to expectations. The fact that anxiously attached individuals showed a more positive automatic evaluation of the masked face of Saddam Hussein may be due to the fact that priming effects for masked primes were generally reversed. However, the finding that more dismissive individuals show a more positive automatic evaluation of relationship partners (and Charlie Chaplin) is difficult to reconcile with attachment theory, because according to Bartholomew (1990; Bartholomew & Horowitz, 1991) dismissing attachment is characterized by a relatively *negative* evaluation of the relationship partner.

Although these individual differences results are interesting and certainly merit further investigation, it is obvious that the reliability of the measure of automatic evaluation should be substantially increased. This could be achieved in several ways: First, future studies should limit the number of experimental conditions and maximize the number of trials per condition. Second, in the standard procedure of the evaluative decision task presented here, there is a trade-off between reaction latencies and error frequencies. Greenwald (1995; cf. Musch, 1999) has developed an adaptive "response window technique" that forces participants to react extremely quickly. This approach has been found to concentrate priming effects on error rates, thus providing larger and more robust effects than the standard procedure (e.g., Draine & Greenwald, 1998; Musch, 1999; Otten & Wentura, 1999). Third, experimental standard techniques such as trial order randomization and counterbalancing across subjects are *not* optimal for the analysis of individual differences. In order to maximize the reliability of individual differences all experimental conditions should be kept constant across subjects. One has to chose between optimizing the experimental design for the analysis of treatment effects, or for the analysis of individual differences, both aims are partially incompatible.

An alternative experimental approach for measuring automatic evaluation of relationship partners is the Implicit Association Task (IAT, Greenwald, McGhee, & Schwartz, 1998), which uses a double discrimination task to assess the association between a pair of target concepts and an evaluation dimension or any other attribute dimension (for details see also De Houwer, chap. 9, this volume). It has been shown that IAT measures reach not only psychometrically satisfactory reliability levels (Banse, Seise, & Zerbes, 2001; Cunningham, Preacher, & Banaji, 2001), but also convergent and criterion validity when used as an implicit measure of attitude toward relationship partners (Banse, 2000; Zayas & Shoda, 2001).

PUTTING THE PIECES TOGETHER:
THE ARCHITECTURE OF RELATIONAL SCHEMATA

The empirical studies presented so far have investigated single features of relational schemata, their internal structure, or connections between the relational schema and other constructs. To conclude this chapter I would like to show that many pieces of the presented evidence can be integrated into a coherent picture of the mental representation of relationships schematically illustrated in Fig. 10.2.

As a core concept of the mental representation of relationships we have introduced the relational schema as proposed by Baldwin (1992). The relational schema is composed of the relationship specific representation of the partner (Pa) , the self (S), and the interaction (Int) between the self and the partner. Each of these three elements is in itself conceived of as a

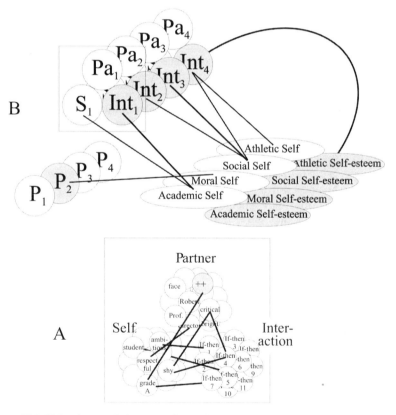

FIG. 10.2.   An associative network containing a relational schema (Panel A), and its interconnections with other relational schemata, person schemata, and the cognitive representation of the self (Panel B).

complex knowledge structure containing declarative knowledge relating to the self and to the partner, as well as procedural knowledge or if-then contingencies in the interaction part (Fig. 10.2, Panel A).

We have seen that the representation of significant others (e.g., romantic partners and friends) and known persons who are not relationship partners (e.g., Saddam Hussein or Charlie Chaplin) contain an evaluative component (++) that can be automatically activated on the mere presentation of the name or the face of this person (Banse, 1999, 2001). In Fig. 10.2, person schemata (P) and the person part of relational schemata (Pa) are conceptualized as basically similar knowledge structures. However, the results of Glassman and Andersen (1999) suggest substantial differences in the internal organization of person versus partner schemata. A priming with the self-generated descriptions of significant others caused transference, whereas primes relating to nonsignificant others did not. This result indicates better accessibility and/or higher interconnectedness of stored person information within relational schemata as compared to mental representations of nonsignificant others (see also Andersen, Glassman, & Gold, 1998).

Due to their asymmetric nature, the cognitive representation of some role relationships have an intermediate status between relational schemata and the representation of unacquainted persons. The representation of distant authorities (e.g., the Pope) may lack the interaction part of a relational schema but nevertheless be connected to the representation of the self. As nicely shown by Baldwin et al. (1990), even a subliminal exposure to a critical moral or academic authority may suffice to temporarily lower self esteem, provided that the moral or academic context is made salient. Panel B in Fig. 10.2 depicts some of the connections between different relational schema, other person schemata, and the self. The different types of relationships are illustrated by the link between a person schema (P_2) symbolizing the Pope and the moral self, and a link between the first relational schema (symbolizing an academic authority) and the academic self/self-esteem. Although the results of Baldwin et al. (1990) did not conclusively show that relational schema were differentially related to those aspects of the self that are directly pertinent for the relationship, other studies have shown that domain-specific selves and self-esteem can be empirically distinguished (e.g., Marsh, 1993; Marsh & Yeung, 1998). It seems therefore reasonable to assume that these different aspects of the self and of self-esteem are more or less related to different significant others. The relational schema of an academic supervisor should be more closely related to the academic self than the schema of the pope, even for practicing Catholics.

There is substantial evidence supporting the representation of interaction as part of specific relational schemata. Baldwin and Sinclair (1996, Exp. 3) demonstrated that if–then contingencies or interpersonal expectancies are relationship-specific. After priming with an evaluative person, a contingency between success and acceptance as well as between failure and rejection became apparent in a lexical decision task. When primed with an unconditionally accepting significant other, no contingency was found.

Baldwin and Sinclair (1996, Exp. 1) have also demonstrated that the representation of if–then contingencies are meaningfully related to individual differences in self-esteem. Only individuals with low self-esteem showed a contingency between success and failure and acceptance and reaction. If–then contingency representations were not only demonstrated for specific relationships but also at a more abstract level. Baldwin et al. (1993) showed that individual differences of secure versus avoidant attachment were meaningfully related to the expectation of positive versus negative partner behavior. Pierce and Lydon (1998) showed that subliminal priming with words describing supportive versus rejecting interaction was related to different intended coping strategies and anticipated affect in a stressful situation. These results strongly suggest an activation of the interaction part of relational schemata *across relationships*, and a connection with *general* self esteem. The organization of such generalized features are illustrated in Fig. 10.2 by the two gray shaded connected rows of interaction units and specific self-esteem units. This simultaneous representation of specific relationships and the "generalized other" is conceptually akin to a hierarchical models of internal working models in attachment theory (e.g., Collins & Read, 1994).

Up to now there seems to be little empirical support for the third postulated element of relational schemata (i.e. a set of different relationship specific representations of the self). It is theoretically plausible that the self-representation of individuals may differ between relationships. For example, a female executive may represent herself as dominant, assertive, and competitive in a close work-relationship, and as nondominant, insecure, and caring in a romantic relationship. However, due to the highly idiosyncratic nature of intra-individual differences of self representations an experimental demonstration using the priming method remains a challenge for future research.

Limitations of the Associative Network Approach

Most of the empirical findings presented previously can be translated into simple structural features of an associative network representation as shown in Fig. 10.2. However, some of the presented results seem to require a more complex model. For example, the results of SPA research as summarized by Hardaway (1990) suggest that the relational schema representing the mother relationship may have a privileged status. SPA researchers presume that the power of the "Mother and I are one" prime lies in the unconscious motive to merge with "the good mother of early childhood" (Silverman &

Weinberger, 1985), and that the specific priming effects of this schema on therapy success and other global outcome measures is mediated by positive mood (Weinberger, 1992). Moreover, these priming effects seem to be stronger under subliminal than under supraliminal priming conditions (Bornstein, 1990). Although it may be possible to handle such conditional activation effects as well as general effects of mood and motivation in an associative network model, alternative approaches such as connectionist or parallel distributed processing models could prove to be more adequate (see for example Smith, 1996).

APPARENT INCONSISTENCIES, LIMITATIONS, AND DIRECTIONS FOR FUTURE RESEARCH

Multiple Word Primes

Scholars of unconscious cognition (e.g., Draine, 1997; Greenwald, 1992) have raised serious doubts that the multiple word primes used in SPA research (e.g., "Mommy and I are one") have any effects at sentence level that go beyond the additive effects of individual words. Draine (1997) noted that the existence of sentence level effects has in fact never been explicitly tested in SPA research. He concludes from his own research that it is very improbable that sentence level information can be processed outside of awareness. However, perhaps these apparently contradictive positions can be reconciled. First, neither SPA results nor the multiple word priming effects reported by Glassman and Andersen (1999) provide unambiguous evidence that primes have been processed at sentence level, the effects may in fact be due to single word effects. The "Mommy and I are one" prime may be more effective than primes of the type "Daddy and I are one" because of stronger effects of the word *Mommy* as compared to *Daddy*; and primes related to oneness (e.g., "My Girl and I are one"; "Father and I are one)" may have substantial but weaker effects due to the prime words referring to other relationship partners, and not to oneness. Also the finding that the prime sentence "Mommy and I are one" was found to be more effective than "Mommy is gone" (Weinberger, 1992) can be explained in terms of single word effects. For example, the word *gone* may reduce the priming effect of *Mommy* relative to the word primes *I, Are,* and *One*). Draine (1997) has found additive single word effects with affectively polarized words for both supraliminal and subliminal priming procedures. As long as multiple word primes are able to activate relational schemata, the implications of SPA results and those of Glassman and Andersen (1999) for relationship research would remain the same even if the effects were eventually found to be due to single word effects.

Second, it is important to note that almost all studies reporting subliminal priming effects of relational schemata (Baldwin, 1994; Baldwin et al., 1990, 1993; Baldwin & Sinclair, 1996; Glassman & Andersen, 1999; Hardaway, 1990; Pierce & Lydon, 1998) differed from the standard priming method as used in unconscious cognition research (e.g., Draine, 1997). In the research tradition of the latter, subliminal priming effects are typically assessed immediately after *each single* trial, and primes with opposite effects are presented intermixed. The typical priming approach in relationship research, however, uses a repeated presentation of *a single* prime, or a set of *functionally equivalent* primes, ranging from several presentations to very massive repetitions of up to 300 (Baldwin, 1994) before assessing priming effects. In other words, whereas primes in relationship research tend to be *consistent* with respect to the activated mental content, the default procedure in experimental cognitive and social psychology uses *inconsistent* sets of stimuli including primes and targets. It may be that the repetition of subliminal primes is critical to process even multiword strings in a piecemeal fashion, either at sentence or at single word level. Moreover, there is evidence that priming effects increase as a function of the frequency of consistent subliminal primes (Bargh & Pietromonaco, 1982; Devine, 1989). In other words, priming effects seem to accumulate across trials. The procedural difference between consistent and inconsistent priming may explain the apparent contradiction between subliminal priming effects in relationship research, which often last up to several minutes, and the very fast decay of subliminal priming effects in experimental psychology, which seem hardly ever to survive 1000 ms. In the light of the evidence presented here it seems promising to consider the effects of prime consistency and prime repetition in future attempts to tackle Greenwald's (1992) still fascinating "two-word-challenge".

Limitations of the Priming Approach

The studies presented here provide convincing evidence that the priming method is a valid approach for the investigation of the mental representation of relationships. However, like any other method in psychology, the priming approach has problems and limitations. A general problem concerns the notoriously weak effect sizes. In many of the studies presented here, expected effects were only marginally significant, or significant effects were not found for all conditions or for all dependent variables for which effects were expected. This may indicate that experiments often operate at the minimal level of required statistical power.

Unlike verbal self-report measures, priming effects seem to be quite robust against voluntary distortions caused, for example, by positive self-presentation. Subliminal priming procedures exclude that results are influenced by voluntary behavior, but also supraliminal priming yields valid and generally similar results if participants are unaware of the relation between the priming and the subsequent assessment of priming effects. If this relation becomes obvious (e.g., Banse, 1999; Baldwin, 1994; Bornstein, 1990) a dissociation between subliminal and supraliminal priming may result. There is also evidence that supraliminal and subliminal priming may lead to different priming effects even if the supraliminal method is considered to preclude any deliberate voluntarily control about the dependent measure (Banse, 2001). In consequence, the internal validity of priming measures should not be taken for granted. Especially in subliminal priming, effects may depend on nonobvious boundary conditions. Even subtle and apparently peripheral procedural modifications may have dramatic effects. Moreover, prime stimuli may not activate the intended mental content but instead other mental structures thus leading to unpredicted or even opposite priming effects (see Fiedler, chap. 5, this volume). For these reasons it is advisable to use strong research designs to establish the internal validity of priming effects by demonstrating the specificity of effects, their internal replication, or convergence with other measures.

Suggestions for Future Research

As pointed out earlier, there are two main reasons to use priming methods in relationship research. One is to avoid that the assessment of relational schemata is distorted by self-presentation concerns. Some of the studies presented before took advantage of the low controllability of priming effects to exclude alternative explanations of results obtained using explicit verbal self-report measures. A second potential advantage of priming methods consists in their potential capacity to assess aspects of mental representation that are *not* consciously accessible. Here still lies a major challenge for the "relational cognition" approach. In a first step it seems necessary to develop implicit measures that are sufficiently reliable for assessing relational schemata at the individual level. It remains to be seen whether such measures will be based on improved priming paradigms (e.g., Draine & Greenwald, 1998), other approaches such as the Implicit Association Test (Greenwald, McGhee, & Schwartz, 1998), or entirely new techniques.

Although proponents of the subliminal psychodynamic activation paradigm claim that their experimental results are due to an activation of unconscious content, to my knowledge it has not yet been conclusively demonstrated that priming or other response time based measures are able to assess unconscious contents of relational schemata. A first obstacle in this endeavor is to define an empirical criterion that allows to distinguish between truly unconscious content and content that is consciously accessible but not reported. Here attachment theory could offer a pragmatic test: An implicit measure could be considered to tap unconscious aspects of a relational schema if it were able to identify individuals classified as insecure in the Adult Attachment Interview or analogue indirect interview techniques, but as secure in explicit self-report measures. Obviously such an implicit measure would be extremely interesting for relationship research because it would provide a second avenue to investigate empirically the discrepancies between conscious and unconscious mental representations of relationships.

ACKNOWLEDGMENTS

I thank Jack Glaser, Mark W. Baldwin, Jochen Musch, Jens Asendorpf, Iain Glen, Bertram Gawronski, Hartmut Leuthold, and Christine Rebetez Banse for their critical comments on drafts of this chapter.

REFERENCES

Ainsworth, M. D. S., Blehar, M. C., Waters, E., & Wall, S. (1978). *Patterns of attachment.* Hillsdale, NJ: Lawrence Erlbaum Associates.

Andersen, S. M., Glassman, N. S., Chen, S., & Cole, S. W. (1995). Transference in social perception: The role of chronic accessibility in significant-other representations. *Journal of Personality and Social Psychology, 69,* 41–57.

Andersen, S. M., Glassman, N. S., & Gold, D. A., (1998). Mental representations of the self, significant others, and nonsignificant others: Structure and processing of private and public aspects. *Journal of Personality and Social Psychology, 75,* 845–861.

Baldwin, M. W. (1992). Relational schemas and the processing of social information. *Psychological Bulletin, 112,* 461–484.

Baldwin, M. W. (1994). Primed relationship schemas as a source of self-evaluative reactions. *Journal of Social and Clinical Psychology, 13,* 380–403.

Baldwin, M. W., Carrel, S. E., & Lopez, D. F. (1990). Priming relationship schemas: My advisor and the pope are watching me from the back of my mind. *Journal of Experimental Social Psychology, 26,* 435–454.

Baldwin, M. W., Fehr, B., Keedian, E., Seidel, M., & Thomson, D. W. (1993). An exploration of the relational schema underlying attachment styles: self-report and lexical decision approaches. *Personality and Social Psychology Bulletin, 19,* 746–754.

Baldwin, M. W., & Holmes, J. G. (1987). Salient private audiences and awareness of the self. *Journal of Personality and Social Psychology, 53,* 1087–1098.

Baldwin, M. W., & Sinclair, L. (1996). Self esteem and "If–Then" contingencies of interpersonal acceptance. *Journal of Personality and Social Psychology, 71,* 1130–1141.

Banse, R. (1999). Automatic evaluation of self and significant others: Affective priming in close relationships. *Journal of Social and Personal Relationships, 16,* 803–821.

Banse, R. (2000). *Implicit attitudes towards romantic partners and ex-partners: A test of the reliability and validity of the IAT.* Unpublished manuscript, Humboldt Universität zu Berlin.

Banse, (2001). Affective priming with liked and disliked persons: Prime visibility determines congruency and incongruency effects. *Cognition and Emotion, 15,* 501–520.

Banse, R., Seise, J., & Zerbes, N. (2001). Implicit and explicit attitudes towards homosexuality: Reliability, validity, and controllability of the IAT. *Zeitschrift für Experimentelle Psychologie, 48*, 145–160.

Bargh, J. A. (1992). Does subliminality matter to social psychology? Awareness of the stimulus versus awareness of its influences. In R. F. Bornstein & T. S. Pittman (Eds.), *Perception without awareness: Cognitive, clinical, and social perspectives* (pp. 236–255). New York: Guilford Press.

Bargh, J. A. (1994). The four horseman of automaticity: Awareness, intention, efficiency, and control in social cognition. In R. S. Wyer & T. K. Srull (Eds.), *Handbook of Social Cognition* (2nd ed.; Vol. 1, pp. 1–40). Hillsdale, NJ: Lawrence Erlbaum Associates.

Bargh, J. A., Chen, M., & Burrows, L. (1996). Automaticity of social behavior: Direct effects of trait construct and stereotype activation. *Journal of Personality and Social Psychology, 71*, 230–244.

Bargh, J. A., & Pietromonaco, P. (1982). Automatic information processing and social perception: The influence of trait information presented outside of conscious awareness on impression formation. *Journal of Personality and Social Psychology, 22*, 293–311.

Bartholomew, K. (1990). Avoidance of intimacy: An attachment perspective. *Journal of Social and Personal Relationships, 7*, 147–178.

Bartholomew, K., & Horowitz, L. M. (1991). Attachment styles among young adults: A test of a four-category model. *Journal of Personality and Social Psychology, 61*, 226–244.

Bornstein, R. F. (1990). Critical importance of stimulus unawareness for the production of subliminal psychodynamic activation effects: A meta-analytic review. *Journal of Clinical Psychology, 46*, 201–210.

Bornstein, R. F., Leone, D. R., & Galley, D. J. (1987). The generalizability of subliminal mere exposure effects: Influence of stimuli perceived without awareness on social behavior. *Journal of Personality and Social Psychology, 53*, 1070–1079.

Bowlby, J. (1969). *Attachment and loss: Vol. 1. Attachment*. New York: Basic Books.

Brauer, M., Wasel, W., & Niedenthal, P. (2000). Implicit and explicit components of prejudice. *Review of General Psychology, 4*, 79–101.

Carver, C. S., & Scheier, M. F. (1981). *Attention and self-regulation: A control-theory approach to human behavior*. New York: Springer.

Cheesman, J., & Merikle, P. M. (1986). Distinguishing conscious from unconscious perceptual processes. *Canadian Journal of Psychology, 40*, 343–367.

Collins, N. L., & Read, S. J. (1994). Cognitive representations of attachment: the structure and function of working models. In K. Bartholomew & B. D. Pearlman (Eds.), *Advances in Personal Relationships* (Vol. 5, pp. 53–90). London, UK: Jessica Kingsley.

Cooley, C. H. (1902). *Human nature and the social order*. New York: Schocken.

Cunningham, W. A., Preacher, K. J., & Banaji, M. R. (2001). Implicit attitude measures: Consistency, stability, and convergent validity. *Psychological Science, 12*, 163–170.

Devine, P. (1989). Stereotypes and prejudice: Their automatic and controlled components. *Journal of Personality and Social Psychology, 56*, 5–18.

De Houwer, J., & Eelen, P. (1998). An affective variant of the Simon paradigm. *Cognition and Emotion, 12*, 45–61.

De Houwer, J., Hermans, D., & Eelen, P. (1998). Affective Simon effects using facial expressions as affective stimuli. *Zeitschrift für Experimentelle Psychologie, 45*, 88–98.

Dovidio, J. F., Kawakami, K., Johnson, C., Johnson, B., & Howard, A. (1997). On the nature of prejudice: Automatic and controlled processes. *Journal of Experimental Social Psychology, 33*, 510–540.

Draine, S. C. (1997). *Analytic Limitations of Unconscious Language Processing*. Doctoral Dissertation, University of Washington.

Draine, S. C., & Greenwald, A. G. (1998). Replicable unconscious semantic priming. *Journal of Experimental Psychology: General, 127*, 286–303.

Fazio, R. H., Jackson, J. R., Dunton, B. C., & Williams, C. J. (1995). Variability in automatic activation as an unobtrusive measure of racial attitudes: A bona fide pipeline? *Journal of Personality and Social Psychology, 69*, 1013–1027.

Fazio, R. H., Sanbonmatsu, D. M., Powell, M. C., & Kardes, F. R. (1986). On the automatic activation of attitudes. *Journal of Personality and Social Psychology, 50*, 229–238.

Fazio, R. H., & Towles-Schwenn, T. (1999). The MODE model of attitude-behavior processes. In S. Chaiken & Y. Trope (Eds.), *Dual process theories in social psychology* (pp. 97–116). New York: Guilford Press.

Fiske, S. T. (1981). Schema-triggered affect: Applications to social perception. In M. S. Clark & S. T. Fiske (Eds.), *Affect and cognition. The seventeenth annual Carnegie symposium on cognition* (pp. 55–78). Hillsdale, NJ: Lawrence Erlbaum Associates.

Fudin, R. (1999). Subliminal psychodynamic activation: Methodological problems and questions in Silverman's experiments. *Perceptual and Motor Skills, 89*, 235–244.

George, C., Kaplan, N., & Main, M. (1985). *The adult attachment interview*. Unpublished manuscript, University f California, Berkeley.

Glassman, N. S. & Andersen, S. M. (1999). Activating transference without consciousness: Using significant other representations to go beyond what is subliminally given. *Journal of Personality and Social Psychology, 77*, 1146–1162.

Greenwald, A. G. (1992). New look 3: Unconscious cognition reclaimed. *American Psychologist, 47*, 766–779.

Greenwald, A. G. (1995). *Informal report of a "response window" procedure to produce large supraliminal and subliminal semantic priming effects*. Unpublished manuscript, University of Seattle.

Greenwald, A. G., & Banaji, M. R. (1995). Implicit social cognition: Attitudes, self-esteem, and stereotypes. *Psychological Review, 102*, 4–27.

Greenwald, A. G., Draine, S. C., & Abrams, R. L. (1996). Three cognitive markers of unconscious semantic activation. *Science, 273*, 1699–1702.

Greenwald, A. G., McGhee, D. E. & Schwartz, J. L. K. (1998). Measuring individual differences in implicit cognition: The Implicit Association Test. *Journal of Personality and Social Psychology, 74*, 1464–1480.

Greenwald, A. G., & Liu, T. J. (1985, November). *Limited unconscious processing of meaning*. Paper presented at the meeting of the Psyconomic Society, Boston.

Hardaway, R. A. (1990). Subliminally activated symbiotic fantasies: Facts and artifacts. *Psychological Bulletin, 107*, 177–195.

Higgins, E. T., Rholes, W. S., & Jones, C. R. (1977). Category accessibility and impression formation. *Journal of Experimental Social Psychology, 13*, 35–47.

Lamb, M. E., Sternberg, K. J., & Esplin, P. W. (1994). Factors influencing the reliability and validity of statements made by young victims of sexual maltreatment. *Journal of Applied Developmental Psychology, 15*, 255–280.

Leary, M. R., Tambor, E. S., Terdal, S. K., & Downs, D. L. (1995). Self-esteem as an interpersonal monitor: The sociometer hypothesis. *Journal of Personality and Social Psychology, 68*, 518–530.

Main, M., & Solomon, J. (1986). Discovery of an insecure disorganized/disoriented attachment pattern: Procedures, findings, and implications for classification of behavior. In T. B. Brazelton & M. Yogman (Eds.), *Affective development in infancy* (pp. 95–124). Norrwood, NJ: Ablex.

Marsh, H. W. (1993). relations between global and specific domains of self: The importance of individual importance, certainty, and ideals. *Journal of Personality and Social Psychology, 65*, 975–992.

Marsh, H. W., & Yeung, A. S. (1998). Top-down, bottom-up, and horizontal models: The direction of causality in multidimensional, hierarchical self concepts models. *Journal of Personality and Social Psychology, 75*, 509–527.

McLeod, C. M. (1991). Half a century of research on the Stroop-effect: An integrative review. *Psychological Bulletin, 109,* 163–203.

Mead, G. H. (1934). *Mind, self, and society.* Chicago: University of Chicago Press.

Meyer, D. E., & Schvaneveldt, R. W. (1971). Facilitation in recognizing pairs of words: Evidence of a dependence between retrieval operations. *Journal of Experimental Psychology, 90,* 227–234.

Merikle, P. M., & Reingold, E. M. (1992). Measuring unconscious perceptual processes. In R. F. Bornstein & T. S. Pittman (Eds.), *Perception without awareness* (pp. 55–80). New York: Guilford Press.

Miller, J. B., & Noirot, M. (1999). Attachment memories, models, and information processing. *Journal of Social and Personal Relationship, 12,* 147–173.

Murphy, S. T., & Zajonc, R. B. (1993). Affect, cognition, and awareness: Affective priming with optimal and suboptimal stimulus exposures. *Journal of Personality and Social Psychology, 64,* 723–739.

Murray, S. L., Holmes, J. G., & Griffin, D. W. (1997). The self-fulfilling nature of positive illusions in romantic relationships: Love is not blind but prescient. *Journal of Personality and Social Psychology, 71,* 1155–1180.

Musch, J. (1999). *Affektives Priming: Kongruenzeffekte bei der evaluativen Bewertung [Affective priming: Congruence effects in evaluative decisions].* Unpublished doctoral dissertation: University of Bonn.

Neely, J. H. (1977). Semantic priming and retrieval from lexical memory: Roles of inhibitionless spreading activation ad limited-capacity attention. *Journal of Experimental Psychology: General, 106,* 226–254.

Otten, S., & Wentura, D. (1999). About the impact of automaticity in the minimal group paradigm: Evidence from affective priming tasks. *European Journal of Social Psychology, 29,* 1049–1071.

Pelham, B. W., & Swann, W. B., Jr. (1989). From self conceptions to self worth: On the sources and structure of global self esteem. *Journal of Personality and Social Psychology, 57,* 672–680.

Pierce, T., & Lydon, J. (1998). Priming relational schemas: Effects of contextually activated and chronically accessible interpersonal expectations and responses to a stressful event. *Journal of Personality and Social Psychology, 75,* 1441–1448.

Rogers, C. R. (1959). Therapy, personality, and interpersonal relationships. In S. Koch (Ed.), *Psychology: A study of a science* (Vol. 3, pp. 184–256). Toronto: Ontario, Canada: McGraw Hill.

Silverman, L. H., & Silverman, D. K. (1964). A clinical-experimental approach to the study of subliminal stimulation: The effects of a drive-related stimulus upon Rorschach responses. *Journal of Abnormal and Social Psychology, 69,* 158–172.

Silverman, L. H., & Weinberger, J. (1985). Mommy and I Are One: Implications for Psychotherapy. *American Psychologist, 40,* 1296–1308.

Smith, E. R. (1996). What do connectionism and social psychology offer each other? *Journal of Personality and Social Psychology, 70,* 893–912.

Sohlberg, S., Samuelberg, P., Sidén, Y., & Thörn, C. (1998). Caveat medicus—let the subliminal healer beware: Two experiments suggesting conditions when the effects of Silverman's Mommy and I Are One phrase are negative. *Psychoanalytic Psychology, 15,* 93–114.

Strack, F., Schwarz, N., Bless, H., Kübler, A., & Wänke, M. (1993). Awareness of the influence as a determinant of assimiliation versus contrast. *European Journal of Social Psychology, 23,* 53–62.

Trankell, A. (1971). *Der Realitätsgehalt von Zeugenaussagen [The validity of eye-witness testimonies].* Göttingen: Vandenhoeck & Ruprecht.

Weinberger, J. (1992). Validating and demystifying subliminal psychodynamic activation. In R. F. Bornstein & T. S. Pittman (Eds.), *Perception without awareness: Cognitive, clinical, and social perspectives* (pp. 170–188). New York: Guilford Press.

Wilson, T., Lindsey, S., & Schooler, T. Y. (2000). A model of dual attitudes. *Psychological Review, 107,* 101–126.

Wittenbrink, B., Judd, C. M., & Park, B. (1997). Evidence for racial prejudice at the implicit level and its relationship with questionnaire measures. *Journal of Personality and Social Psychology, 72,* 262–274.

Zayas, V., & Shoda, Y. (2001). *Automatic evaluative reactions toward mother and romantic partner: Testing attachment theory's predictions.* Paper submitted for publication.

IV: The Role of Evaluation in Mood, Emotion, and Behavior

Putting Process Into Personality, Appraisal, and Emotion: Evaluative Processing as a Missing Link

Michael D. Robinson
North Dakota State University

Patrick T. Vargas
Emily G. Crawford
University of Illinois

INTRODUCTION

People differ in how they process affective information, but such differences are not necessarily captured by personality traits. Nevertheless, such differences (e.g., speed to recognize rewards or threats) have the potential to influence emotional behavior and experience. For these reasons, it is important to supplement personality self-report with evaluative processing paradigms in order to develop a more complete understanding of how and why people differ in their emotional reactions. In the present chapter, we will set an agenda for future evaluative processing research, one in which individual differences play a central role. We will argue that it may be mistaken to assume that self-reported traits (e.g., extraversion, neuroticism) will necessarily covary with evaluative processing tendencies. Despite these often meager relationships between traits and processing tendencies, both may predict emotional states and, equally important, may do so interactively. If this is the case, the emotional consequences of a given trait, as well as the emotional consequences of a given processing style, are not invariant, but depend on each other. A focus on individual differences in evaluative processing is likely to lead to a more differentiated understanding of both traits and processing tendencies on the one hand and appraisal and emotional states on the other. The present chapter discusses such issues and presents relevant findings from a number of recent studies.

Traits and Processes

Consider the following hypothetical experiment. Professor E assumes that extraverts tend to be happier in part because they automatically and habitually attend to rewarding information in the environment. She obtains self-reports of extraversion (e.g., "I am the life of the party") and also constructs an emotional Stroop task with positive (e.g., "love"), negative (e.g., "criticism"), and neutral (e.g., "sound") words (see Williams, Mathews, & MacLeod, 1996, for a review of the emotional Stoop task). Attention to reward is operationalized as the difference between color-naming latencies to rewarding words versus neutral words.

Let us consider the different possible outcomes of Professor E's experiment. A first possibility is that extraverts are slower to name the color of rewarding words (indicating attention to word meaning) relative to introverts. This is a happy state of affairs for Professor E, who writes up the results announcing the .30 correlation. What have we learned as a result of this experiment? We have learned that extraverts do have a tendency to automatically attend to rewarding information. However, recall that Professor E proposed a mediational hypothesis, as depicted in the top panel of Fig. 11.1. That is, extraverts experience more positive affect in life in part *because* they automatically attend to rewards.

Even after obtaining a .30 correlation, a number of issues remain. Most obvious perhaps is that a .30 correlation means that only 9% of the variance is shared. This would seem to imply that extraversion and attention to reward are largely orthogonal constructs. Even more critical, Professor E has not provided support for the mediation hypothesis. The mediation hypothesis requires that: (1) extraversion correlates with attention to reward (established); (2) extraversion correlates with positive affect (not established, but likely); (3) attention to reward correlates with positive affect (not established); and (4) attention to reward still predicts positive affect with extraversion simultaneously controlled (not established).

In other words, without a measure of the person's emotional experiences, preferably in daily life, we cannot test Professor E's mediation hypothesis. Note that we are also placing additional requirements on the attention to reward measure. If such a measure indeed has affective consequences, one might expect it to predict positive mood states in daily life. Again, measurement of a third variable—mood states—is required to demonstrate the affective consequences of attention to reward. A simple correlation with extraversion does not demonstrate these affective consequences.

Let us suppose, instead, that Professor E obtains no correlation between extraversion and attention to reward. Such a null findings is, in fact, typical of the personality/processing literature (Rusting, 1998). Does this mean that extraversion doesn't measure attention to reward? Provided that we have a psychometrically useful processing measure (i.e., a measure of how a person processes emotional information), we think the answer is yes. Traits and affective processes do not necessarily correlate, precisely because they tap different constructs. Does this mean that attention to reward is irrelevant to positive affect? Such a conclusion is warranted only if we obtain a measure of positive affect. In our experience, processing measures often do predict emotional experience even when they do not correlate with self-reported traits. This possibility is diagrammed in the middle panel of Fig. 11.1.

The middle panel of Fig. 11.1 depicts what we think to be an exciting possibility. Evaluative processing measures, broadly defined, may yield a new understanding of individual differences in emotional experience. Furthermore, because processing measures can be understood as mechanisms, whereas traits cannot, we have learned something about the causes of posi-

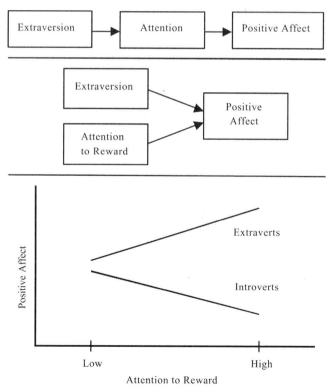

FIG. 11.1. Extraversion, Attention to Reward, and Positive Affect: Mediation (top), Independent Effects (middle), or Moderation (bottom).

tive affect. Specifically, attention to rewarding information is a proximate cause of positive affect. Among other implications, if we can train individuals to focus on rewards within the environment, we might expect them to experience a greater degree of subjective well-being.

Let us finally entertain a third pattern of findings, one that we have seen many times in our own work. Professor E finds no correlation between extraversion and attention to reward. However, perhaps because she read this chapter, Professor E obtains measures of daily positive affect. In predicting positive affect, she enters extraversion, attention to reward, and their interaction. The result is a main effect for extraversion (extraverts experience more positive affect), no main effect for attention to reward, but a significant interaction between the two measures. Specifically, attention to reward appears to have *opposite* implications for those low versus high in extraversion. The happiest person is an extravert who is high in attention to reward. The unhappiest person is an introvert who is high in attention to reward. This pattern of hypothetical findings is depicted in the bottom panel of Fig. 11.1.

The pattern of findings depicted in the bottom panel of Fig. 11.1 is interesting for several reasons. The measure of attention to reward splits both extraverts and introverts into two types. There are extraverts who automatically attend to rewards (happy) and those who do not (less happy). There are introverts who automatically attend to rewards (not happy) and those who do not (more happy). Thus, the effects of extraversion on happiness are not invariant, but depend on attentional style. The effects of attentional style, likewise, cannot be viewed as a main effect, but must be viewed as a moderator of extraversion. If we view extraversion as measuring a person's capacity to obtain rewards (Winter, John, Stewart, Klohnen, & Duncan, 1998), we may assert that extraverts who attend to rewards are like kids in the candy store: They notice good things and possess the skills to obtain them. The introvert, by contrast, generally does not possess the capacity or skills to obtain rewards (Winter et al., 1998). We may assert that introverts who attend to rewards are like kids locked out of the candy store: They notice good things, but are acutely aware of not being able to obtain them. Thus, the consequences of reward sensitivity are opposite for introverts and extraverts.

Our discussion of Professor E's experiment is meant to illustrate the value of treating evaluative processing as an independent variable. The typical personality/processing study precludes this possibility because only measures of traits and processing tendencies are obtained. More to the point, without a measure of emotional experience, an investigation can provide no proof for the critical assumptions that individual differences in processing: (1) produce individual differences in emotional states; and (2) are responsible for (i.e., mediate) trait differences in emotional states. As suggested previously, we believe that traits and processing tendencies are largely orthogonal constructs, rendering the mediation hypothesis (traits to processing tendencies to states) not only unproven, but *untenable.*

Our discussion, in addition to suggesting limitations to the standard personality/processing framework, points to an exciting new direction in personality research. Specifically, by measuring processing tendencies and emotional experience, we can begin to forge links between these constructs. For example, we can show that a tendency to automatically attend to threatening information is a cause of anxiety in daily life (MacLeod, 1999). From this perspective, how a person processes emotional information is a personality variable, regardless of whether such processes correlate with emotional traits or not.

To summarize, we propose the following main points:

1. Emotional traits (e.g., extraversion, neuroticism) are largely independent of processing tendencies (e.g., individual differences in attention to reward).

2. Processing tendencies (e.g., individual differences in attention to reward) can have hedonic consequences (e.g., relate to individual differences in positive affect) regardless of whether they correlate with emotional traits or not.

3. Trait/state relations are unlikely to be mediated by processing tendencies, oftentimes because traits and processing tendencies don't correlate in the first place. However, traits and processing may interact in determining emotional experience.

Overview of Chapter

In the first major section that follows we review previous research on traits and processing tendencies. A major aim of this review will be to establish that it is reasonable to view traits and processing tendencies as largely independent constructs. Second, we turn to a consideration of why this should be so. In brief, we propose that people have introspective insight into certain regularities in feeling and behavior, but that they do not, in principle, know how they process evaluative information. Third, we turn to evidence from our lab that demonstrates the value of a process-oriented approach to personality. The pattern of findings will suggest that, although traits and processing tendencies are independent, they do interact with each other in predicting emotional experience. For this reason, a complete understanding of personality requires our knowledge of *both* a person's traits and their processing tendencies. Fourth, and finally, we summarize the main points of the chapter and present recommendations for future research.

THE INDEPENDENCE OF TRAITS AND PROCESSES: PRIOR RESEARCH

Emotional Traits and Evaluative Processing

Of the "Big 5" personality traits, extraversion and neuroticism have the most consistent relations with mood states (Watson, 2000). The higher a person's level of extraversion, the more he or she tends to experience positive affect. The higher a person's level of neuroticism, the more he or she tends to experience negative affect. Although European personality psychologists have been keenly interested in why such relations exist (Eysenck & Eysenck, 1985; Gray, 1991), extant theories, which are largely neurological, have received only mixed support at best (Gale & Edwards, 1986; Matthews & Gilliland, 1999; Stelmack, 1990). American personality psychologists, by contrast, have traditionally been more concerned with psychometric and taxonomic considerations (Digman, 1990). As a result, we know surprisingly little about *why* emotional traits and states tend to be linked (Pervin, 1999; Revelle, 1995). In this regard, consider a quote from Ozer and Reise (1994): "Modern personality research is predominantly trait-oriented. In the absence of theory, measured traits are static variables, good for describing what someone is like . . . but poor at providing a rich and deep understanding of personality processes and dynamics" (p. 367).

Evaluative processing, broadly construed, may provide mechanisms linking traits to states. For example, extraverts may experience more positive affect because they are more likely to attend to, identify, or categorize rewarding stimuli. Similarly, neurotics may experience more negative affect because they are more likely to attend to, identify, or categorize punishing stimuli (Rusting & Larsen, 1998). Other possibilities are also evident. Neurotics may be impaired at discriminating threats from nonthreats, resulting in the unfortunate consequence that even neutral events are regarded as threatening (Clark & Watson, 1999). Extraverts may have a difficult time discriminating neutral events from rewarding ones, resulting in the fortunate consequence that even neutral events are regarded as rewarding (Pavot, Diener, & Fujita, 1990).

What do we know about traits and evaluative processing? In this connection, we consider two recent literature reviews, one by Matthews and Gilliland (1999) and one by Rusting (1998). Matthews and Gilliland reviewed a variety of studies aimed at providing support for the neurocognitive theories of Eysenck (Eysenck & Eysenck, 1985) and Gray (1987). Of particular importance in the present context, Gray (1987) linked the trait of extraversion to the Behavioral Approach System (BAS), a neurocognitive system that is sensitive to signals of reward and influences the probability of approach behavior. By contrast, Gray linked the trait of neuroticism to the Behavioral Inhibition System (BIS), a neurocognitive system that is sensitive to punishment and influences the probability of behavioral inhibition. Furthermore, Gray (1987) proposed two mediation models consistent with the top panel of Fig. 11.1. Specifically, extraverts may experience more positive affect because of their higher BAS activity. Similarly, neurotics may experience more negative affect because of their higher BIS activity.[1]

Gray's (1987) theory has clear implications for evaluative processing. Extraverts should be more sensitive to potential rewards, whereas neurotics should be more sensitive to potential punishments (Zelenski & Larsen, 1999). These predictions have been tested using central (e.g., evoked potentials) and peripheral (e.g., electrodermal activity) measures of physiology, as well as behavioral measures designed to reveal differences in attention, learning, and memory. Some particular studies have supported Gray's theory, but usually only if certain post hoc assumptions are made (e.g., Derryberry & Reed, 1994). Encouraging findings have proven difficult to replicate (e.g., Bartussek, Becker, Diedrich, Naumann, & Maier, 1996). Finally, a good deal of the evidence is either disappointingly complicated or contrary to Gray's theory (Matthews & Gilliland, 1999). On the basis of such evidence, Matthews and Gilliland suggested that we should consider abandoning the neurocognitive approach to personality advocated by Gray. In summary, they state: "It remains to be seen whether either theory (Eysenck's or Gray's) provides a comprehensive explanation for the correlates of traits" (p. 620).

In a second review of the relations between traits and processing tendencies, Rusting (1998) contrasted three models linking traits and mood states to evaluative processing. Relevant dependent measures included emotional Stroop performance (attention), lexical decisions for positive and negative words (identification), and the valence of recalled words in incidental encoding tasks (retrieval). She concluded that there was little evidence for the idea that traits, or mood states, are always associated with certain evaluative processing tendencies. In her words: "This literature has yielded mixed findings across perception, attention, interpretation/judgment, recall and recognition, and autobiographical memory. Although many studies do ob-

---

[1]We simplified Gray's theory for present purposes. In actuality, Gray (1987) linked BAS to impulsivity, a trait that is similar to, but slightly different than, extraversion. He also linked BIS to anxiety, a trait that is similar to, but slightly different than, neuroticism. A problem with Gray's personality traits is that there are no personality scales that are sufficiently validated as measures BIS and BAS function (Matthews & Gilliland, 1999). Because impulsivity and extraversion on the one hand and anxiety and neuroticism on the other are closely aligned, various authors have proposed that standard extraversion scales measure BAS activity, whereas standard neuroticism scales measure BIS activity (Matthews & Gilliland, 1999; Rusting & Larsen, 1997; Watson, 2000). Psychometric considerations appear to support this move (Zelenski & Larsen, 1999).

tain evidence for mood-congruency and trait-congruency, some studies have found mood-incongruency effects, and others have found no effects of mood or personality at all" (p. 189).

In summary, both reviews (Matthews & Gilliland, 1999; Rusting, 1998) suggest that it may be difficult, if not impossible, to link emotional traits to *consistent* styles of evaluative processing. What is particularly problematic in this regard is that situational variables (e.g., task difficulty—Matthews & Gilliland, 1999; mood states—Rusting, 1998) often modify, eliminate, or reverse straightforward trait/processing relations. As we shall see next, similar difficulties arise in the literature on mood disorders (anxiety and depression) and evaluative processing.

Mood Disorders and Evaluative Processing

Since the mid 1980s, clinical psychologists have made large strides in understanding the processing tendencies that are sometimes associated with anxiety and depression (Mathews & MacLeod, 1994). Anxiety-related disorders are often associated with a tendency to automatically attend to threatening information. This link has been established using the emotional Stroop task (Williams et al., 1996), the dot probe task of attention (Mogg & Bradley, 1998), and the dichotic listening task (Mathews & MacLeod, 1986). Mood disorders, on the other hand, are often associated with a tendency to automatically associate the self with negative information. This link has been established using a modified Stroop task (Segal, Gemar, Truchon, Guirguis, & Horowitz, 1995), self-referent encoding and retrieval tasks (Bargh & Tota, 1988; Watkins, Mathews, Williamson, & Fuller, 1992), and autobiographical memory tasks (Kuyken & Brewin, 1995; Williams & Dritschel, 1988).

Such links, however, are not invariantly obtained. Whether normal or abnormal emotional traits have been the focus of investigation, processing tendencies often interact with situational factors (Bradley, Mogg, Galbraith, & Parrett, 1993; Gotlib & Cane, 1987; Mathews & Sebastian, 1993; Richards, French, Johnson, Naparstek, & Williams, 1992; Rusting, 1998; Segal & Ingram, 1994). Under some circumstances, stressors seem to enhance trait-related differences in processing (Gotlib & Cane, 1987; Segal & Ingram, 1994). However, under other circumstances, stressors seem to minimize trait-related differences (Mathews & Sebastian, 1993). Thus, the impact of state factors on trait-related differences in processing is far from clear at this point (Mogg & Bradley, 1998; Williams, Watts, MacLeod, & Mathews, 1997). At the very least, these findings suggest that stable markers of psychopathic processing are difficult to find.

On the basis of results suggesting that processing biases in depression are far more state-dependent than generally assumed, Segal and Ingram

(1994) suggested that processing biases represent markers rather than causes of depressed affect. Similarly, Mogg and Bradley (1998) suggested that anxiety-related processing biases may perpetuate anxious symptoms when present, but probably do not produce such anxious symptoms in the first place. From our perspective, such proposals are largely a function of existing methodologies, which have tended to look for associations between traits and processing tendencies rather than for associations between processing tendencies and state affect (see also MacLeod, 1993, 1999). As we demonstrate later in the chapter, processing tendencies do not have to be correlated with traits in order to predict important emotional outcomes.

Conclusions

In both the personality and the psychopathology literatures, investigators have typically operated under the assumption that evaluative processing tendencies should correlate with emotional traits. Trait/processing correlations, however, are sufficiently inconsistent from study to study that one might propose that traits and processing tendencies measure distinct aspects of personality. In the next part of this chapter, we develop theoretical arguments in support of this possibility.

THE INDEPENDENCE OF TRAITS AND PROCESSES: THEORETICAL CONSIDERATIONS

In the previous sections, we reviewed evidence for the frequent independence of traits and processing tendencies. For example, extraversion typically does not correlate with attention to reward in the emotional Stroop task. This is despite the fact that both of these measures (extraversion and attention to reward) are designed to capture individual differences in reward sensitivity. In the following sections, we consider why such outcomes should be expected rather than viewed as surprising or disappointing.

More specifically, we advance a three-part argument for independence. First, we suggest that people make trait ratings by retrieving semantic, rather than episodic, self-knowledge. Semantic self-knowledge is abstract and general and does not capture how a person appraises specific events. Second, we suggest that processing measures are designed to capture the latter aspects of personality, what we call the *episodic* self. And third, we suggest that these two aspects of personality—episodic and semantic—are fundamentally dissociated. This is for the simple reason that people cannot introspect on their mental processes. Given these arguments, we would not expect traits to be related to processing tendencies. Instead, the two capture distinct aspects of personality.

The Abstract Nature of Trait Knowledge

In accounting for the independence of traits and processing tendencies, it is useful to examine how trait self-reports are made. A key question is whether people retrieve episodic or semantic self-knowledge in making generalizations about themselves (Robinson & Clore, 2001). Episodic self-knowledge is particular to a given time and place. For example, in answering an extraversion item, I might remember my choice to skip a party last Friday night. Semantic self-knowledge is not particular to any given time and place, but rather consists of certain generalizations or beliefs that I have formed about myself. For example, I may have formed the belief that I prefer small, intimate gatherings to large, wild parties. It is important to note that this generalized belief does not reference any particular Friday night, nor Friday nights in general, and might reasonably be expected to characterize my future preferences as well as my past preferences. That is, this generalized belief is abstract and decontextual in nature.

How are trait self-reports made? The available evidence suggests that they are made by retrieving semantic, rather than episodic, self-knowledge. Two sources of evidence are particularly relevant. First, amnesiacs, who exhibit marked deficiencies in recalling past behavior, can nevertheless describe themselves with relative ease (Cermak & O'Connor, 1983; Stuss & Benson, 1984; Tulving, Schacter, McLachlan, & Moscovitch, 1988). Furthermore, their trait judgments are reliable and valid despite their inability to recall a single relevant behavior from the past (Klein, Loftus, & Kihlstrom, 1996; Tulving, 1993). A second source of evidence comes from reaction time studies with normal individuals (Klein & Loftus, 1993; Klein, Loftus, & Sherman, 1993; Klein, Loftus, Trafton, & Fuhrman, 1992; Schell, Klein, & Babey, 1996). Klein and colleagues have repeatedly found that recalling a life event (e.g., my choice to skip a party) does not facilitate my ability to make a relevant trait judgment (e.g., my level of extraversion). Furthermore, making a trait judgment (e.g., my level of extraversion) does not facilitate my ability to recall a relevant life event (e.g., my choice to skip a party).

Two key points follow from this research. First, episodic and semantic self-knowledge are fundamentally dissociated in memory (Robinson & Clore, 2001). That is, retrieving one source of information does not activate the other source. And second, trait self-reports are made by retrieving semantic, rather than episodic, self-knowledge. A person can make trait judgments only because they have formed certain beliefs about themselves, not because they can remember their behavior on particular occasions. Thus, trait reports tap generalizations about the self, but do not tap how a person experiences any particular event.

The independence of episodic and semantic self-knowledge allows us to understand why trait self-reports often diverge from daily experiences. On trait scales, for example, neurotics often report more negative affect (Feldman Barrett, 1997) and somatic distress (Larsen, 1992) than is evident in their daily reports. In a related vein, women report more intense emotions than men on trait scales, but not following daily interactions (Feldman Barrett, Robin, Pietromonaco, & Eyssell, 1998). In the realm of coping styles, people report trait coping strategies that bear little relation to their actual coping attempts in daily life (Schwartz, Neale, Marco, Shiffman, & Stone, 1999). Finally, people consult inaccurate self-theories when reporting on the causes of their mood states (Wilson & Stone, 1985) and problematic behaviors (Shiffman, 2000). Trait self-reports, then, can be systematically biased with respect to daily experiences because they are based on beliefs about the self rather than concrete daily experiences (Robinson & Clore, 2001).

We suggest that a key reason for the independence of traits and processing tendencies is that they tap fundamentally different aspects of the self. Whereas trait self-reports tap semantic self-knowledge, processing measures tap the episodic self, the self that appraises specific events. We expand on this argument in the next section.

Processing Tendencies and the Episodic Self

Self-report is the predominant method for measuring the traits of the individual. There are consequences to this method that have only begun to receive systematic investigation (Robinson & Clore, 2001). In this regard, consider the proposal of William James (1890) that there are at least two, nonoverlapping aspects of personality. There is the "me", which is the self that can be observed and characterized. Self-reported traits arguably capture this aspect of personality. In addition, however, the self also consists of an "I" that processes events. In principle, the "I" cannot be directly observed, but rather consists of the processes, mechanisms, and unconscious inferences that characterize the individual.

One cannot study the "I" by asking people to characterize themselves. Rather, the "I" can only be studied by observing how a person construes particular events. It is here where processing measures of personality become relevant. They are designed to reveal how people process concrete events. For example, emotional Stroop and dot probe measures assess the sources of information that capture attention (Mogg & Bradley, 1998); evaluative priming measures assess the degree to which people automatically categorize evaluative information (Bargh, 1997); and evaluative categorization measures assess the degree to which people are efficient in evaluating valenced material (Fazio & Powell, 1997). All of these measures, as well as others, are essentially concerned with how individuals attribute meaning to particular events.

Individual difference measures based on reaction times are relatively new. For example, the implicit association test, a measure of the degree to which two categories are associated in memory (see De Houwer, chap. 9, this volume), was first introduced in 1998 by Greenwald, McGhee, and Schwartz. Because such measures are new, we are only beginning to understand the unique aspects of personality that can be studied using such techniques. However, there is an older body of work on *implicit motivation* that is relevant to the present discussion. In the Thematic Apperception Test (TAT), individuals are asked to tell stories about ambiguous pictures. By analyzing the content and structure of such stories, the investigator hopes to gain insight into the habitual themes and categories that a person uses to encode (ambiguous) events. Thus, TAT measures of motivation are similar to reaction time measures in the sense that they are designed to capture individual differences in how people attribute meaning to particular events.

Consistent with a major theme of this chapter, McClelland and colleagues have repeated found that self-reported and TAT measures of motivation are independent (see McClelland, Koestner, & Weinberger, 1989, for a review). For example, self-reports of achievement motivation (e.g., "I strongly value achievement") are uncorrelated with the use of achievement themes in understanding ambiguous pictures (McClelland et al., 1989; Spangler, 1992). Consistent with another major theme of the chapter, however, both types of motivation measures are useful in predicting a person's behavior (Bornstein, 1999; McClelland et al., 1989; Spangler, 1992). Thus, self-reported and TAT measures of motivation offer unique views of the self (McAdams, Hoffman, Mansfield, & Day, 1996; Woike, Gershkovich, Piorkowski, & Polo, 1999).

In summary, we suggest that trait self-report measures are valid, but that they capture only one major aspect of personality. Because they require conscious access to semantic self-knowledge, they are limited in what they can reveal about how a person processes particular events. To study how a person processes events, we need to turn to process-based measures of personality. Simply put, people do not have conscious access to how they process information, a point that should become especially clear in the next section.

The Unconscious Nature of Cognitive Processes

Near the turn of the century, psychologists believed that they could observe their own cognitive processes (e.g., Wundt, 1888). This *introspective* methodology involved carefully monitoring the mind as events were apprehended, classified, and evaluated. Psychologists hoped to document the micromomentary transformations that characterize cognitive processing much as present cognitive psychology does. Despite this common interest, there are key methodological differences between turn-of-the-century and modern cognitive psychology. Whereas introspectionists offered self-report accounts of mental operations, modern cognitive psychology rejects these in favor of reaction time and brain imaging techniques (Posner & Raichle, 1997). Why? Simply put, introspective accounts of cognitive processes proved to be extremely unreliable in that they could not be replicated from one lab to another (Boring, 1953).

The failures of the introspective method were so spectacular, in fact, that commentators concluded that mental events could not be studied scientifically (e.g., Watson, 1914, 1924). Such conclusions were persuasive, leading experimental psychologists to abandon the study of covert mental events in favor of studying overt behaviors. Overt behaviors could be measured objectively and did not require a person's subjective analysis. Relatedly, although cognitive psychology eventually made a comeback, it did so by adhering to key tenants of the behaviorist approach. Rather than studying mental events through the use of introspective methods, modern cognitive psychologists instead infer mental events from publicly observable (and hence verifiable) behaviors (MacLeod, 1993). For example, a reaction time is a behavioral record, not a subjective report.

Thus, cognitive psychology became a science precisely because it turned to behavioral records, rather than subjective reports, in making inferences about cognitive processes (MacLeod, 1993). It is now an established axiom that people do not know how they process information. For example, I don't know *how* I read; I only know that I can.

The same principles apply to individual differences in evaluative processing, the key topic of this chapter. If we want to understand individual differences in *how* people process events, we have to use behavioral paradigms (e.g., based on RT) to do so. Although we might expect people to have some insight into regularities in their behavior and experiences, we should not expect people to have insight into how they attribute meaning to emotional events. Such mental events are simply not observable. Such points were forcefully stated in a review by MacLeod (1993, pp. 189–190):

> Asking an individual whether he or she can introspectively detect any attentional bias towards threatening stimuli might at best generate data of indeterminate validity. However, asking such an individual to report whether this attentional effect might reflect a biased allocation of priorities to the integrative processing of threatening representations rather than, say, a tendency to selectively process such representations elaboratively, or may perhaps be due to the automatic spread of activation through a semantic memory network, could generate only ridicule!

Conclusions

Trait self-knowledge is abstract, semantic information about the self. Such knowledge is fundamentally limited in what it can reveal about emotional cognition. People simply do not have conscious access to the processes that give rise to their emotional states (e.g., Lazarus, 1995). If we want to understand how individuals process emotional events, we have to use process-based paradigms to do so.

We see fundamental limitations to the standard approach to personality and processing. We should not expect traits to correlate with processing tendencies. If processing tendencies are meaningful, however, they should predict emotional outcomes. As we show in the next major portion of the chapter, they do. The results illustrate the benefits of a process-based understanding of personality and emotion.

PERSONALITY AS CATEGORIZATION

Theoretical Background and Overview of Studies

Following Kelly's (1963) lead, we may assert that a person's personality is reflected in the categories habitually used to interpret events. For example, one person might tend to classify events as threatening or not, whereas another person might tend to classify events according to whether they are positive or not. How do we measure the habitual use of certain categories? A possible operationalization is suggested by Bruner (1957), who stated that category accessibility is marked by the speed or ease with which a person can place an exemplar in a relevant category. For example, the word *knife* can either be categorized as a utensil or as a potential threat. For one person (e.g., a cook), the utensil category may be chronically accessible; this person should be quick to categorize *knife* as a utensil. For another person (e.g., a victim of repeated abuse), the threat category may be chronically accessible; this person should be quick to categorize *knife* as a threatening weapon.

Based on the work of Kelly (1963) and Bruner (1957), then, we should be able to determine a person's habitual categories by asking them, as quickly as possible, to categorize words according to experimenter-provided categories. In a certain block, for example, they could be asked to determine whether words represent substantial threats or not. An individual who is well-practiced at making the given distinction should be fast; by contrast, an individual who is not well-practiced at making the distinction should be slow. Thus, we can operationalize category accessibility in terms of individual differences in categorization speed.[2]

---

[2]We believe that categorization speed measures a person's habitual, or accessible, categories (e.g., see Fazio & Powell, 1997). On this basis, we would conclude that, if a person were slow on a given categorization task (e.g., threat vs. not), he or she is not well-practiced at making this distinction. In our experience, this interpretation of categorization speed is generally

In the following sections, we demonstrate that such categorization tendencies have hedonic consequences. We start with the observation that traits and categorization tendencies were uncorrelated in all of our data sets. Thus, consistent with a major theme of this chapter, traits and processing tendencies capture distinct aspects of personality. By measuring state, in addition to trait, emotionality, however, we show that categorization tendencies allow us to predict individual differences in emotional experience. Thus, categorization tendencies capture meaningful aspects of personality that traits do not. We illustrate the benefits of a process-based approach to personality by reporting two sets of findings from our lab.

In one set of findings, we target the appraisal tendencies that are sometimes ascribed to neuroticism and extraversion. Because neurotics may be "threat" experts, we asked participants to quickly categorize words as threatening (e.g., *knife*) or not (e.g., *mildew*). Because extraverts may be "reward" experts, we asked participants to quickly categorize words as neutral (e.g., *coffee*) or positive (e.g., *candy*). We then examined the joint influence of neuroticism and threat speed on the one hand, and extraversion and neutral/positive speed on the other, on emotional experience. In both sets of analyses, we observed an interaction between the relevant trait and the relevant processing measure. To foreshadow these results, we find that trait main effects (e.g., for neuroticism) are reduced among participants who are fast at making trait-relevant distinctions (e.g., not threat vs. threat). It appears that fast participants respond similarly to events, regardless of their trait predispositions. We term this effect the *episodic construal* hypothesis.

Because traits and processing tendencies measure distinct aspects of personality, it is quite possible for one to possess processing tendencies that are incongruent with one's traits. In a second set of findings, we show that this degree of congruence or incongruence has hedonic consequences. Specifically, we show that "implicit self-esteem", as measured by a version of the implicit association test, has opposite effects among those low versus high in trait self-esteem. Consistent with a *personality congruence* hypothesis, individuals experience more positive, and less negative, emotional states if they are matched on trait and implicit self-esteem (i.e., high in both or low in both). Mismatched individuals, by contrast, appear to suffer. We then replicate this *personality congruence* effect with the trait of femininity in combina-

---

supported by error rates. Although error rates are quite low on the tasks, people who tend to be faster also tend to make fewer errors. Thus, there is no speed–accuracy tradeoff in relation to these measures. However, given the preliminary nature of our results, other interpretations of categorization speed should not be ruled out. For example, fast responders may be engaging in more shallow, less elaborative processing, perhaps as a way of defending against threatening information. Although error rates would seem to argue against this interpretation of categorization speed, it is nevertheless worth keeping this interpretation in mind, especially with regard to future research.

tion with a categorization task designed to assess feminine expertise. The findings suggest that there are both conscious (i.e., traits) and unconscious (i.e., processing tendencies) aspects of identity and that the two aspects jointly determine emotional well-being.

Methodological Details

Participants in the following studies were college undergraduates. The procedures for each study were generally as follows. At time 1, participants were asked to perform the categorization tasks and complete trait self-reports (independent variables). Because there is some evidence that filling out a trait scale can influence processing tendencies (e.g., Bargh, 1992), we always assess categorization tendencies before obtaining trait self-reports. At time 2, we measured a person's emotional states, either in daily life or in the lab (dependent variables). Times 1 and 2 were typically separated by several weeks. This insures that: (1) participants do not connect the two sessions in any specific way; and (2) the processing measures have to be relatively stable to predict emotional states.

The trait scales were standard ones. The processing measures are described in more detail later. However, one general point is worth emphasizing here. When using categorization speed as an independent measure (see also Fazio & Powell, 1997), it is important to control for "baseline" speed in responding. Certain people might be fast because their motivation to do well is higher; some are more fluent with the language and so on. To remove such erroneous sources of influence, we have used a neutral categorization task—typically not animal versus animal—and regressed out the influence of baseline speed when computing scores of interest (Fazio, 1990). For example, a person would get a negative score if he or she was faster on a threat block than would be predicted on the basis of his or her neutral block performance; a positive score would indicate the opposite.

Study 1: Neuroticism and Speed in Distinguishing Threats from Non-Threats. Neurotics tend to worry about the occurrence of negative events. They also experience more distress-related emotions. We might therefore predict that neurotics would be fast in distinguishing threats from non-threats due to their habitual orientation to life. Alternatively, we might expect them to be slower on the task precisely because they tend to approach all events as somewhat threatening (Clark & Watson, 1999). However, based on the idea that trait self-reports and categorization tendencies are distinct constructs, we expected no correlation. As expected, we did not find a significant correlation between neuroticism and threat speed.

What are the consequences of neuroticism and threat speed? To examine this question, participants were asked to fill out daily reports of distress for 14 days. Of particular interest is how much "fear" and "tension" the participant experiences in daily life. In our test of personality effects, we centered the variables, computed an interaction term, and entered both main effects and the interaction term as simultaneous predictors of the particular emotion in question (see Aiken & West, 1991). In both cases, we found a significant main effect for neuroticism, no significant main effect for threat speed, but a significant interaction between the two predictors. Figure 11.2 displays these results.

As Fig. 11.2 shows, neuroticism plays a relatively small role in feelings of distress among individuals who are fast to distinguish threats from nonthreats. By contrast, neuroticism has a pronounced effect on fear and ten-

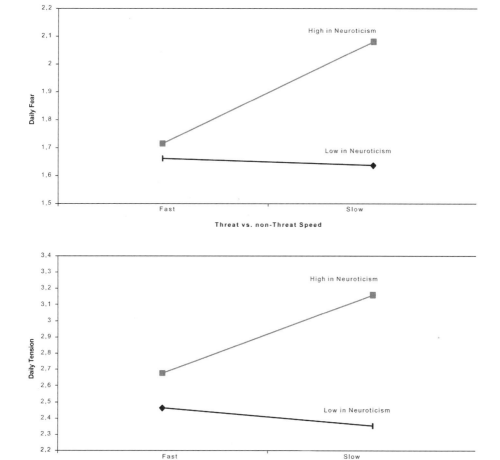

FIG. 11.2. Neuroticism, Threat/Non-Threat Speed, and Daily Experiences of Fear and Tension.

sion if the individual is also slow to make the distinction. This view of the results is consistent with the following interpretation. Let us assume that threat speed measures a person's ability to accurately assess the threat value of new events. If so, we might assume that fast individuals would respond to each new event with reference to that event's threat value. If the event is non-threatening, the person would experience little fear. If the event is threatening, by contrast, the person would experience a good deal of fear.

By contrast, participants slow to make the distinction seem to be assimilating the events of daily life to their affective dispositions. For the slow stable individual, events would, as a default, be viewed as non-threatening. For the slow neurotic individual, events would, as a default, be viewed as threatening. In other words, not possessing the ability to quickly determine the threat value of new events, slow participants may be instead projecting their trait affect onto new events. We thus have the intriguing idea that affective traits are likely to produce trait-consistent experiences only among individuals who are inefficient in making trait-relevant distinctions.

Stated another way, those who are fast at distinguishing threats from non-threats appear to be episodic construers, determining threat on the basis of events rather than dispositions. On the other hand, those who are slow at making this distinction appear to be semantic construers, determining threat on the basis of their trait dispositions rather than particular events. Together, we term this effect the *episodic construal* hypothesis.

Clearly, future work will be necessary to verify this pattern of results. However, it is encouraging that a similar pattern of findings emerges when we examine the joint influence of extraversion and speed in distinguishing positive from neutral words.

Study 2: Extraversion and Speed in Distinguishing Positive From Neutral Words.   Extraverts tend to anticipate the possibility of positive events. They also experience more positive affect. We might therefore predict that extraverts would be fast to distinguish neutral and positive events, precisely because they are positive event experts. On the other hand, one might predict that extraverts would be slower at the task, precisely because they tend to view even neutral events as positive in valence. However, we expected no correlation between extraversion and speed on the task; we have never found such a correlation in our data.

What are the consequences of extraversion and neutral/positive speed? To assess this, we asked participants to report on (1) positive affect within a laboratory setting, (2) their levels of depression during the previous week; and (3) their levels of happiness in momentary daily experience (see Stone, Shiffman, & DeVries, 1999, for an overview of momentary experience sampling). With reference to each of these sources of data, we centered the two predictors, computed an interaction term, and entered these terms into a regression equation predicting each dependent measure separately. As Fig. 11.3 shows, parallel interactions emerged in each regression.

Among people fast to distinguish neutral and positive events, extraversion appears not to matter. Among people slow to make the distinction, extraversion matters to a much greater extent. We may explain these results by offering the following specific interpretation. Much of life falls somewhere between neutral and positive. Mundane daily events are interspersed with minor "uplifts" such as conversations with friends, minor achievements, dates, and so on. If one makes a distinction between neutral and positive events, the person is likely to alternate between neutral and positive states, in essence responding to the events at hand, some of which are neutral and some of which are positive.

Among those slow to distinguish neutral and positive events, by contrast, we might expect dispositional affect to matter to a greater extent, precisely because the neutral versus positive distinction is not habitually made. For the extravert, this would mean that neutral events would be viewed as positive, resulting in more positive affect. For the introvert, by contrast, this would mean that positive events would be viewed as neutral, resulting in less positive affect. The results of Fig. 11.3 are entirely consistent with this interpretation. As such, they provide further support for the idea that affective dispositions matter most among individuals who are inefficient at making trait-relevant distinctions.

Discussion of Studies 1 and 2. We began this research by assuming that affective categorization tendencies would be associated with main effects on emotional experience. For example, it seems reasonable to propose that distressed individuals would either be fast or slow to distinguish threatening versus non-threatening events. If speed on the task measures the "accessibility" of threat-related cognitions, we would expect fast individuals to experience more stress and fear (Higgins, 1996; Mathews & MacLeod, 1994). If speed on the task measures an action-oriented, rather than a state-oriented, approach to stress, we might expect exactly the opposite findings (Kuhl & Koch, 1984).

In each case, however, categorization performance interacted with established emotional traits. For example, neurotic individuals fast to distinguish threats from non-threats experienced less fear and tension in daily life; an opposite, although less pronounced, tendency was found among stable individuals who were fast to make this distinction. Such results suggest at least three conclusions. First, consistent with a main theme of this chapter, we should not expect personality traits to reveal the affective processing tendencies of the individual. As our results demonstrate, however, this does not mean that affective processing has no consequences for emotional experience. One needs to measure emotional experience to establish this conclusion.

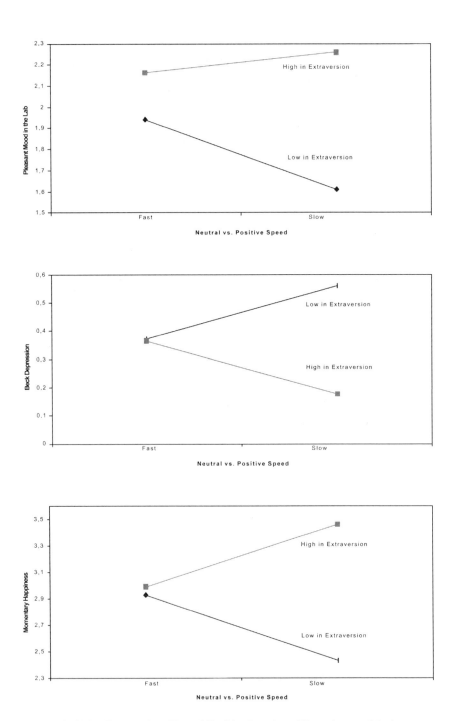

FIG. 11.3. Extraversion, Neutral/Positive Speed, and Experiences of Positive Affect and Depression.

Second, the meaning of an emotional processing measure may be different depending on affective traits. This is an important qualification to the straightforward idea that a given style of emotional processing would be invariantly associated with a given type of affect. For example, it is widely assumed that "attention to threat" tendencies predispose individuals to anxiety and distress (Mogg & Bradley, 1998) and initial results are promising in this regard (MacLeod, 1999). However, we should not preclude the possibility that attention to threat could be potentially beneficial to certain individuals. It is functional, at least in terms of personal safety, to attend to threats within the environment (Mogg & Bradley, 1998; Robinson, 1998). The present results suggest that the greatest anxiety might be experienced by someone who worries about, but cannot efficiently identify, substantial threats (Barlow, 1991; Clark & Watson, 1999).

Third, the meaning of a given personality trait may not be invariant, but may depend on the person's affective processing tendencies. Indeed, in the present results, one saw striking support for the idea that affective traits matter most among individuals who are inefficient at making trait-relevant distinctions. Such results suggest a "fill in" function for dispositional affect especially in the absence of discriminating episodic construal. This view of trait affect is compatible with research showing that affective expectations matter most when the contingencies of reward and punishment are not known (Alloy & Tabachnik, 1984; Chan & Lovibond, 1996).

A related, but distinct, suggestion is that there are at least two forms of trait anxiety or neuroticism (Barlow, 1991; Heller & Nitschke, 1998; Robinson, Robertson, & Syty, 2001; Westen, 1998). Concretely, the present results show that neurotics fast to distinguish threats from non-threats reported less fear and tension in daily life. These individuals are likely to experience transient moments of fear when concrete threats do exist, but may experience relatively little fear at other times. The slow neurotic, by contrast, may experience more chronic anxiety precisely because of the tendency to regard all events as potential threats. By this account, emotional processing measures are key to distinguishing these two forms of neuroticism.

Study 3: Trait and Implicit Self-Esteem. Whereas Studies 1 and 2 were concerned with the *episodic construal* hypothesis, Studies 3 and 4 are concerned with the *personality congruence* hypothesis. Generally, and in agreement with psychodynamic conceptions of the self (Westen, 1998), we assume that there are both conscious (i.e., traits) and unconscious (i.e., processing tendencies) aspects of personality. Furthermore, these aspects of identity can either be congruent with each other or incongruent. Finally, we hypothesize that incongruence is a source of anxiety and distress. We first tested this hypothesis in the context of self-esteem.

Trait self-esteem is characterized by the endorsement of a positive self-view. Implicit (or process-based) self-esteem, by contrast, is thought to measure a person's automatic tendency to associate the self with positive information. Greenwald et al.'s (1998) implicit association test has recently been adapted to the study the latter construct. Participants are asked to classify words as pleasant (e.g., sunshine) or unpleasant (e.g., vomit) and, during the same block, are asked to classify other words as "me" words (e.g., me) or "not me" words (e.g., they). Implicit self-esteem is operationalized as the difference in block speed when "me" and pleasant words are categorized with the same finger versus opposite fingers. To the extent that representations of the self and positive information are compatible, one should be faster when the same finger is used for both types of items (see De Houwer, chap. , this volume).

It is generally assumed that implicit self-esteem should operate as a main effect in predicting esteem-related outcomes (e.g., Bosson, Swann, & Pennebaker, 2000). By contrast, we are predicting an interaction between trait and implicit self-esteem. Among participants high in trait self-esteem, implicit self-esteem should separate those who are "truly" high in esteem versus those who are not. Such a proposal, although somewhat novel, is not controversial. Among participants low in trait self-esteem, we predicted the counterintuitive finding that low, rather than high, implicit self-esteem would be associated with greater well-being. According to the congruence hypothesis, this would be because a mismatch between trait and implicit levels of identity creates tension and confusion on the part of the individual. The *personality congruence* hypothesis stands in contrast to a "main effect" interpretation of implicit self-esteem.

In assessing the *personality congruence* hypothesis, we measured trait and implicit self-esteem in one session. Then, at time 2, we collected reports of various measures of happiness. The results were markedly in support of the congruence hypothesis. In Fig. 11.4, we show two confirmations of the hypothesis. The predicted interaction was obtained on a laboratory measure of happiness. It was also obtained in an experience sampling study in which participants reported on momentary feelings of pleasant affect.

As predicted, implicit self-esteem had opposite effects for those low versus high in trait self-esteem. Among participants high in trait self-esteem, greater implicit self-esteem was associated with more pleasant affect. However, among participants low in trait self-esteem, just the opposite pattern obtained. Specifically, participants low in trait self-esteem experienced greater pleasant affect if they were low, rather than high, in implicit self-esteem. Obviously, such results suggest that implicit self-esteem does not measure the same tendency among all participants. Instead, consistent with an emerging theme in this chapter, the impact of implicit self-esteem on

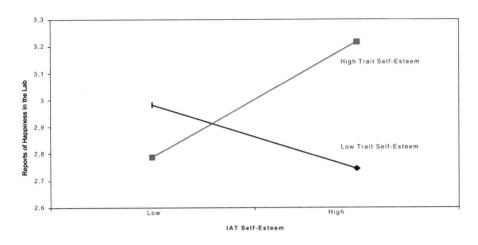

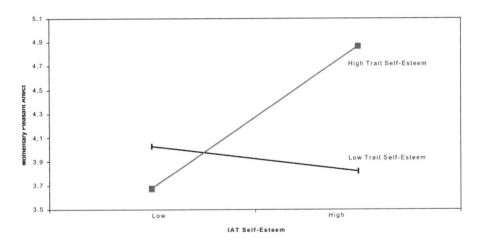

FIG. 11.4.   Trait and Implicit Self-Esteem Interact in Predicting Positive Affect.

positive affect depended on participant's level of trait self-esteem. The results, in summary, provide positive support for the congruence hypothesis.

Study 4: Trait and Implicit Femininity.   To provide further support for the
congruence hypothesis, we assessed the hypothesis with reference to trait
and implicit femininity. Trait femininity was assessed by a short form of the
Bem femininity scale (Bem, 1974). Implicit femininity was assessed by a categorization task. Specifically, we asked participants to quickly determine
whether words represented feminine (e.g., caring) or masculine (e.g., inde-

pendent) attributes. Because we were specifically interested in femininity, we computed a latency score for feminine words only. We then controlled for speed on a compatible baseline task (Fazio, 1990).

Trait and implicit femininity were assessed at time 1. We used these scores to predict experiences of pleasant and unpleasant affect in momentary daily experiences. Participants were asked to carry a Palm Pilot computer for 1 week and report on their momentary affective states when prompted by the computer. They received five prompts per day, determined at random times. Thus, through the use of experience-sampling procedures, we get a representative view of the person's daily affective experiences (Stone et al., 1999). We predicted that trait and implicit femininity would interact in predicting momentary affect. As Fig. 11.5 shows, the results were in accord with predictions.

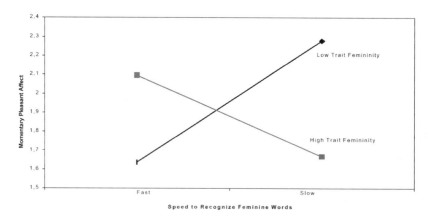

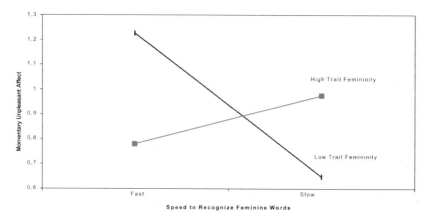

FIG. 11.5. Trait and Implicit Femininity Interact in Predicting Momentary Experiences of Pleasant and Unpleasant Affect.

As predicted, participants low in trait femininity experienced more positive affect and less negative affect if they were slow to recognize feminine words in the categorization task. By contrast, participants high in trait femininity experienced more positive affect and less negative affect if they were fast to recognize feminine words in the categorization task. Clearly, these results offer positive support for the *personality congruence* hypothesis.

Discussion of Studies 3 and 4. Throughout this chapter, we have argued that trait and process-based components of personality are fundamentally distinct constructs. In terms of identity, this raises the distinct probability that some individuals will view themselves in a manner that is congruent with their processing tendencies, whereas others will not. Such matches or mismatches appear to have profound consequences for emotional well-being. When traits and processing tendencies match, the world may seem subjectively more predictable and friendly to one's identity concerns. When they mismatch, by contrast, one may find oneself pursuing outcomes that are inconsistent with important aspects of the self-concept.

On the basis of these ideas, we offered a *personality congruence* hypothesis. Results involving both self-esteem and femininity offer support for the hypothesis. In the former regard, it was notable that some individuals low in trait self-esteem appeared to be happier than some individuals high in trait self-esteem. Specifically, participants low in both types of self-esteem tended to be happier than participants high in trait self-esteem, but low in implicit self-esteem. Such results offer striking evidence for the hedonic importance of process-based aspects of personality.

CONCLUSIONS

In this chapter, we have proposed that individual differences should play a central role in future research on evaluative processing. Such an approach can allow us to demonstrate the affective consequences of certain processing tendencies. Such an approach can also allow us to test mediation and moderation models of personality/emotion relations. Finally, in this chapter, we have presented evidence that traits and processing tendencies interact in determining emotional experience. Such results imply that traits on the one hand and processing tendencies on the other do not have invariant effects on emotional experience, but instead jointly determine emotional outcomes.

The ideas that we have advanced in this chapter are not easy to pursue. However, the benefits of such an approach are extensive. To illustrate both the benefits and costs of our proposal, we revisit several key research areas that our proposal addresses.

Traits and Processing Tendencies

We hope that other investigators are coming to recognize the limits of standard approaches to personality. A trait in itself does not provide a mechanism for linking persons to outcomes (Cervone & Shoda, 1999; Revelle, 1995). Perhaps recognizing this limitation to traits, an emerging number of studies have sought to link traits to processing mechanisms that might mediate trait/state relations (e.g., Rusting & Larsen, 1998). However, these studies have typically found rather meager relationships, suggesting that traits and emotional mechanisms are largely independent constructs.

Let us consider some of the obstacles to establishing a mechanistic approach to trait/state relations. Typically, investigations have sought to link traits to emotional processing tendencies, presumably under the assumption that trait effects on state affect are mediated by emotional processing tendencies. However, such research, even when it has found significant trait/processing correlations, is very far from establishing the crucial mediation hypothesis. Most important, mediation requires the measurement of the dependent measure of ultimate interest, namely people's affective experiences in daily lives. Let us assume some generous correlations between traits and processing tendencies (.3) on the one hand and processing tendencies and emotional experience (.3) on the other. Assuming a complete mediation hypothesis, we would predict a $.3 \times .3 = .09$ correlation between emotional traits and emotional states. Typically, trait/state correlations are considerably higher than this (Watson, 2000), suggesting that no substantial mediator has been measured to date.

Once we assume that traits and processing tendencies are separable constructs, we free ourselves from some restrictive assumptions (Greenwald & Banaji, 1995). We can now entertain the possibility that we can gain insight into the emotional life of the individual by knowing how he or she processes evaluative information. This approach, in turn, suggests some new directions for evaluative processing research.

Evaluative Processing (Considered Broadly)

A broad perspective on evaluative processing entails two important, although difficult, methodological requirements. One, the standard evaluative processing paradigm (see Klauer & Musch, chap. , this volume)—namely, prime-target pairs that match or mismatch in valence—has uncertain relevance to emotional experience. For the most part, we have not shown that such an automatic tendency to evaluate short SOA (i.e., prime-target onset lag) primes has important emotional consequences. By measuring "outcome" variables such as emotional experience in daily life, we can show that the automaticity of evaluation indeed has hedonic consequences (e.g., see Fazio & Powell, 1997).

We note that the typical evaluative processing paradigms may be ideally designed for revealing people's automatic tendency to evaluate, but may be less ideally designed for revealing important individual differences (Fazio, 2001). At the very least, the addition of neutral primes and targets could allow one to separate reactions to positive events versus negative events, a critical distinction in personality and mood research (Watson, 2000). More important, it is reasonable to assume that we gain distinct views of the individual by employing priming, attention, accessibility, identification, and categorization paradigms. Furthermore, many of these paradigms can be crossed with the task at hand (e.g., lexical decision vs. pronunciation), manner of presentation (e.g., subliminal vs. supraliminal), and the content of stimuli (e.g., reward- vs. punishment-related). Thus, we have a dizzying array of views on the individual. We should not limit ourselves to any one paradigm or content area in studying evaluative processing.

By treating evaluative processing as an independent measure, we also face new issues centered around reliability and validity. It is crucial to obtain test–retest data so that we can learn which aspects of emotional processing are relatively stable and which aspects are not. Only stable processing tendencies should be regarded as individual differences. In terms of validity, the consequences of evaluative processing are largely unknown. It is not easy to obtain evidence for convergent and discriminant validity when it is not exactly clear what is being measured (Bosson et al., 2000). Indeed, we know very little about the convergent validity of even well-established processing measures like those centered around attention to threat. In this connection, do attention to threat scores based on the Stroop task, the dot probe task, and the dichotic listening task correlate positively? Only if this were the case would we feel comfortable labeling their common component *attention to threat.*

In terms of predictive validity, we have argued for a third variable approach. This requires measuring emotional behavior and/or experience in the laboratory as well as in daily life. The collection of such data obviously makes the study more difficult to complete. However, one needs to collect such data for the purposes of predictive validity. Given the early state of this area of research, we hope investigators keep an open mind in such studies. Although one may enter a study looking for main effects of processing performance, one may leave the study with interactions. As we showed previously, such interactions can be of interest in their own right.

An analogy to the TAT literature would seem to be useful here. It is always easier to collect self-report measures of a given personality construct. Partly because people give consistent responses when they know what is being measured (Knowles & Byers, 1996), and partly because people do have accurate self-knowledge (Fuhrman & Funder, 1995), reliability for trait scales tends to be high. Such trait scales also possess immediate face validity. McClelland and colleagues (McClelland et al., 1989), however, pursued the hypothesis that motivation has important implicit components that are not captured by trait scales. Over the years, their TAT measures of implicit motivation have been strongly critiqued, both on reliability and validity grounds. Such critiques led to refinements of scoring procedures as well as careful and insightful "third variable" studies. As a result, we now know a great deal about the separable consequences of trait and implicit motivation (Bornstein, 1999; McClelland et al., 1989; Spangler, 1992). We hope similar success stories befall measures of evaluative processing tendencies.

Individual Differences in Evaluative Processing

Despite repeated claims that emotional appraisal is an unconscious process, existing research has relied too heavily on self-reports of appraisal, often in response to hypothetical or recalled emotions rather than emotions experienced within the moment (Lazarus, 1995; Parkinson, 1997; Robinson, 1998). It is also the case that individual differences in appraisal have been largely neglected (Lazarus, 1995; van Reekum & Scherer, 1997). Fortunately, the situation is changing, as illustrated by the present volume. Increasingly, we want to know how people evaluate and interpret events within their environment, a goal that requires us to develop nonself-report measures of emotional cognition. As a result, we are increasingly able to peer into the "black box" of emotional cognition. We suggest that a broad perspective on emotional cognition, one that embraces individual differences, is likely to be especially generative in the future.

REFERENCES

Aiken, L. S., & West, S. G. (1991). *Multiple regression: Testing and interpreting interactions.* Newbury Park, CA: Sage.

Alloy, L. B., & Tabachnik, N. (1984). Assessment of covariation by humans and animals: The joint influence of prior expectations and current situational information. *Psychological Review, 91,* 112–149.

Bargh, J. A. (1992). The ecology of automaticity: Toward establishing the conditions needed to produce automatic processing effects. *American Journal of Psychology, 105,* 181–199.

Bargh, J. A. (1997). The automaticity of everyday life. In R. S. Wyer (Ed.), *Advances in social cognition* (Vol. 10, pp. 1–61). Mahwah, NJ: Lawrence Erlbaum Associates.

Bargh, J. A., & Tota, M. E. (1988). Context-dependent automatic processing in depression: Accessibility of negative constructs with regard to self and others. *Journal of Personality and Social Psychology, 54,* 925–939.

Barlow, D. H. (1991). Disorders of emotion. *Psychological Inquiry, 2,* 58–71.

Bartussek, D., Becker, G., Diedrich, O., Naumann, E., & Maier, S. (1996). Extraversion, neuroticism and event-related potentials in response to emotional stimuli. *Personality and Individual Differences, 20*, 301–312.

Bem, S. L. (1974). The measurement of psychological androgyny. *Journal of Consulting and Clinical Psychology, 42*, 155–162.

Boring, E. G. (1953). A history of introspection. *Psychological Bulletin, 50*, 169–189.

Bornstein, R. F. (1999). Criterion validity of objective and projective dependency tests: A meta-analytic assessment of behavioral prediction. *Psychological Assessment, 11*, 48–57.

Bosson, J. K., Swann, W. B., & Pennebaker, J. W. (2000). Stalking the perfect measure of implicit self-esteem: The blind men and the elephant revisited? *Journal of Personality and Social Psychology, 79*, 631–643.

Bradley, B., Mogg, K., Galbraith, M., & Parrett, A. (1993). Negative recall bias and neuroticism: State vs. trait effects. *Behaviour Research and Therapy, 31*, 125–127.

Bruner, J. S. (1957). On perceptual readiness. *Psychological Review, 64*, 123–152.

Cermak, L. S., & O'Connor, M. (1983). The anterograde and retrograde retrieval ability of a patient with amnesia due to encephalitis. *Neuropsychologia, 21*, 213–234.

Cervone, D., & Shoda, Y. (1999). *The coherence of personality.* New York: Guilford Press.

Chan, C. K. Y., & Lovibond, P. F. (1996). Expectancy bias in trait anxiety. *Journal of Abnormal Psychology, 105*, 637–647.

Clark, L. A., & Watson, D. (1999). Temperament: A new paradigm for trait psychology. In L. A. Pervin & O. P. John (Eds.), *Handbook of personality: Theory and research* (2nd ed., pp. 399–423). New York: Guilford Press.

Derryberry, D., & Reed, M. A. (1994). Temperament and attention: Orienting toward and away from positive and negative signals. *Journal of Personality and Social Psychology, 66*, 1128–1139.

Digman, J. M. (1990). Personality structure: The emergence of the five-factor model. *Annual Review of Psychology, 41*, 417–440.

Eysenck, H. J., & Eysenck, M. W. (1985). *Personality and individual differences: A natural science approach.* New York: Plenum.

Fazio, R. H. (1990). A practical guide to the use of response latency in social psychological research. In C. Hendrick & M. S. Clark (Eds.), *Review of personality and social psychology* (Vol. 11, pp. 74–97). Newbury Park, CA: Sage.

Fazio, R. H. (2001). On the automatic activation of associated evaluations: An overview. *Cognition and Emotion, 15*, 114–141.

Fazio, R. H., & Powell, M. C. (1997). On the value of knowing one's likes and dislikes: Attitude accessibility, stress, and health in college. *Psychological Science, 8*, 430–436.

Feldman Barrett, L. (1997). The relationships among momentary emotion experience, personality descriptions, and retrospective ratings of emotion. *Personality and Social Psychology Bulletin, 23*, 1100–1110.

Feldman Barrett, L., Robin, L., Pietromonaco, P. R., & Eyssell, K. M. (1998). Are women the "more emotional" sex?: Evidence from emotional experiences in social context. *Cognition and Emotion, 12*, 555–578.

Fuhrman, R. W., & Funder, D. C. (1995). Convergence between self and peer in the response-time processing of trait-relevant information. *Journal of Personality and Social Psychology, 69*, 961–974.

Gale, A., & Edwards, J. A. (1986). Individual differences. In M. G. H. Coles, E. Donchin, & S. W. Porges (Eds.), *Psychophysiology: Systems, processes, and applications* (pp. 431–507). New York: Guilford Press.

Gotlib, I. H., & Cane, D. B. (1987). Construct accessibility and clinical depression: A longitudinal investigation. *Journal of Abnormal Psychology, 96*, 199–204.

Gray, J. A. (1987). *The psychology of fear and stress* (2nd ed.). Cambridge, UK: Cambridge University Press.

Gray, J. A. (1991). Neural systems, emotion, and personality. In J. Madden IV (Ed.), *Neurobiology of learning, emotion, and affect* (pp. 273–306). New York: Raven Press.

Greenwald, A. G., & Banaji, M. R. (1995). Implicit social cognition: Attitudes, self-esteem, and stereotypes. *Psychological Review, 102*, 4–27.

Greenwald, A. G., McGhee, D. E., & Schwartz, J. L. (1998). Measuring individual differences in implicit cognition: The implicit association task. *Journal of Personality and Social Psychology, 74*, 1464–1480.

Heller, W., & Nitschke, J. B. (1998). The puzzle of regional brain activity in depression and anxiety: The importance of subtypes and comorbidity. *Cognition and Emotion, 12*, 421–447.

Higgins, E. T. (1996). Knowledge activation: Accessibility, applicability, and salience. In E. T. Higgins & A. W. Kruglanski (Eds.), *Social psychology: Handbook of basic principles* (pp. 133–168). New York: Guilford Press.

James, W. (1890). *Principles of psychology.* New York: Holt.

Kelly, G. A. (1963). *A theory of personality: The psychology of personal constructs.* New York: Norton & Company.

Klein, S. B., & Loftus, J. (1993). Behavioral experience and trait judgments about the self. *Personality and Social Psychology Bulletin, 19*, 740–745.

Klein, S. B., Loftus, J., & Kihlstrom, J. F. (1996). Self-knowledge of an amnesic patient: Toward a neuropsychology of personality and social psychology. *Journal of Experimental Psychology: General, 125*, 250–260.

Klein, S. B., Loftus, J., & Sherman, J. W. (1993). The role of summary and specific behavioral memories in trait judgments about the self. *Personality and Social Psychology Bulletin, 19*, 305–311.

Klein, S. B., Loftus, J., Trafton, R. G., & Fuhrman, R. W. (1992). The use of exemplars and abstractions in trait judgments: A model of trait knowledge about the self and others. *Journal of Personality and Social Psychology, 63*, 739–753.

Knowles, E. S., & Byers, B. (1996). Reliability shifts in measurement reactivity: Driven by content engagement or self-engagement? *Journal of Personality and Social Psychology, 70*, 1080–1090.

Kuhl, J., & Koch, B. (1984). Motivational determinants of motor performance: The hidden second task. *Psychological Research, 46*, 143–153.

Kuyken, W., & Brewin, C. R. (1995). Autobiographical memory functioning in depression and reports of early abuse. *Journal of Abnormal Psychology, 104*, 585–591.

Larsen, R. J. (1992). Neuroticism and selective encoding and recall of symptoms: Evidence from a combined concurrent-retrospective study. *Journal of Personality and Social Psychology, 62*, 480–488.

Lazarus, R. S. (1995). Vexing research problems inherent in cognitive-mediational theories of emotion—and some solutions. *Psychological Inquiry, 6*, 183–196.

MacLeod, C. (1993). Cognition in clinical psychology: Measures, methods or models? *Behaviour Change, 10*, 169–195.

MacLeod, C. (1999). Anxiety and anxiety disorders. In T. Dalgleish & M. J. Power (Eds.), *Handbook of cognition and emotion* (pp. 447–477). Chichester, England: John Wiley & Sons.

Mathews, A., & MacLeod, C. (1986). Discrimination of threat cues without awareness in anxiety states. *Journal of Abnormal Psychology, 95*, 131–138.

Mathews, A., & MacLeod, C. (1994). Cognitive approaches to emotion and emotional disorders. *Annual Review of Psychology, 45*, 25–50.

Mathews, A. M., & Sebastian, S. (1993). Suppression of emotional Stroop effects by fear arousal. *Cognition and Emotion, 7*, 517–530.

Matthews, G., & Gilliland, K. (1999). The personality theories of H. J. Eysenck and J. A. Gray: A comparative review. *Personality and Individual Differences, 26*, 583–626.

McAdams, D. P., Hoffman, B. J., Mansfield, E. D., & Day, R. (1996). Themes of agency and communion in significant autobiographical scenes. *Journal of Personality, 64*, 339–377.

McClelland, D. C., Koestner, R., & Weinberger, J. (1989). How do self-attributed and implicit motives differ? *Psychological Review, 96*, 690–702.

Mogg, K., & Bradley, B. P. (1998). A cognitive-motivational analysis of anxiety. *Behaviour Research and Therapy, 36*, 809–848.

Ozer, D. J., & Reise, S. P. (1994). Personality assessment. *Annual Review of Psychology, 45*, 357–388.

Parkinson, B. (1997). Untangling the appraisal-emotion connection. *Personality and Social Psychology Review, 1*, 62–79.

Pavot, W., Diener, E., & Fujita, F. (1990). Extraversion and happiness. *Personality and Individual Differences, 11*, 1299–1306.

Pervin, L. A. (1999). Epilogue: Constancy and change in personality theory and research. In L. A. Pervin & O. P. John (Eds.), *Handbook of personality: Theory and research* (2nd ed., pp. 689–704). New York: Guilford Press.

Posner, M. I., & Raichle, M. E. (1997). *Images of mind.* New York: Scientific American Library.

Revelle, W. (1995). Personality processes. *Annual Review of Psychology, 46*, 295–328.

Richards, A., French, C. C., Johnson, W., Naparstek, J., & Williams, J. (1992). Effects of mood manipulation and anxiety on performance of an emotional Stroop task. *British Journal of Psychology, 83*, 479–491.

Robinson, M. D. (1998). Running from William James' bear: A review of preattentive mechanisms and their contributions to emotional experience. *Cognition and Emotion, 12*, 667–696.

Robinson, M. D., & Clore, G. L. (in press). Belief and feeling: Evidence for an accessibility model of emotional self-report. *Psychological Bulletin.*

Robinson, M. D., Robertson, D. A., & Syty, N. A. (2001). *Personality as belief: Evidence for situation-contingent activation.* Unpublished manuscript, North Dakota State University.

Rusting, C. L. (1998). Personality, mood, and cognitive processing of emotional information: Three conceptual frameworks. *Psychological Bulletin, 124*, 165–196.

Rusting, C. L., & Larsen, R. J. (1997). Extraversion, neuroticism and susceptibility to positive and negative affect: A test of two theoretical models. *Personality and Individual Differences, 22*, 607–612.

Rusting, C. L., & Larsen, R. J. (1998). Personality and cognitive processing of affective information. *Personality and Social Psychology Bulletin, 24*, 200–213.

Schell, T. L., Klein, S. B., & Babey, S. H. (1996). Testing a hierarchical model of self-knowledge. *Psychological Science, 7*, 170–173.

Schwartz, J. E., Neale, J., Marco, C., Shiffman, S. S., & Stone, A. A. (1999). Does trait coping exist?: A momentary assessment approach to the evaluation of traits. *Journal of Personality and Social Psychology, 77*, 360–369.

Segal, Z. V., Gemar, M., Truchon, C., Guirguis, M., & Horowitz, L. M. (1995). A priming methodology for studying self-representation in major depressive disorder. *Journal of Abnormal Psychology, 104*, 205–213.

Segal, Z. V., & Ingram, R. E. (1994). Mood priming and construct activation in tests of cognitive vulnerability to unipolar depression. *Clinical Psychology Review, 14*, 663–695.

Shiffman, S. (2000). Real-time self-report of momentary states in the natural environment: Computerized ecological momentary assessment. In A. Stone, J. S. Turkkan, C. A. Bachrach, J. B. Jobe, H. S. Kurtzman, & V. S. Cain (Eds.), *The science of self-report: Implications for research and practice* (pp. 277–296). Mahwah, NJ: Lawrence Erlbaum Associates.

Spangler, W. D. (1992). Validity of questionnaire and TAT measures of need for achievement: Two meta-analyses. *Psychological Bulletin, 112*, 140–154.

Stelmack, R. M. (1990). The biological basis of extraversion: Psychophysiological evidence. *Journal of Personality, 58*, 293–311.

Stone, A. A., Shiffman, S. S., & DeVries, M. W. (1999). Ecological momentary assessment. In D. Kahneman, E. Diener, & N. Schwarz (Eds.), *Well-being: The foundation of hedonic psychology* (pp. 26–39). New York: Russell Sage Foundation.

Stuss, D. T., & Benson, D. F. (1984). Neuropsychological studies of the frontal lobes. *Psychological Bulletin, 95*, 3–28.

Tulving, E. (1993). Self-knowledge of an amnesic is represented abstractly. In T. K. Srull & R. S. Wyer (Eds.), *Advances in social cognition* (Vol. 5, pp. 147–156). Hillsdale, NJ: Lawrence Erlbaum Associates.

Tulving, E., Schacter, D. L., McLachlan, D. R., & Moscovitch, M. (1988). Priming of semantic autobiographical memories: A case study of retrograde amnesia. *Brain and Cognition, 8*, 3–20.

van Reekum, C. M., & Scherer, K. R. (1997). Levels of processing in emotion-antecedent appraisal. In G. Matthews (Ed.), *Cognitive science perspectives on personality and emotion* (pp. 259–300). New York: Elsevier.

Watkins, P., Mathews, A. M., Williamson, D. A., & Fuller, R. (1992). Mood congruent memory in depression: Emotional priming or elaboration? *Journal of Abnormal Psychology, 101*, 581–586.

Watson, D. (2000). *Mood and temperament.* New York: Guilford Press.

Watson, J. B. (1914). *Behavior: An introduction in comparative psychology.* New York: Holt, Rinehart, & Winston.

Watson, J. B. (1924). *Behaviorism.* Chicago, IL: University of Chicago Press.

Westen, D. (1998). The scientific legacy of Sigmund Freud: Toward a psychodynamically informed psychological science. *Psychological Bulletin, 124*, 333–371.

Williams, J. M. G., & Dritschel, B. H. (1988). Emotional disturbance and the specificity of autobiographical memory. *Cognition and Emotion, 2*, 221–234.

Williams, J. M. G., Mathews, A., & MacLeod, C. (1996). The emotional Stroop task and psychopathology. *Psychological Bulletin, 120*, 3–24.

Williams, J. M. G., Watts, F. N., MacLeod, C., & Mathews, A. (1997). *Cognitive psychology and the emotional disorders* (2nd ed.). Chichester, England: Wiley & Sons.

Wilson, T. D., & Stone, J. I. (1985). More on telling more than we can know. In P. Shaver (Ed.), *Review of personality and social psychology* (Vol. 6, pp. 167–183). Beverly Hills, CA: Sage.

Winter, D. G., John, O. P., Stewart, A. J., Klohnen, E. C., & Duncan, L. E. (1998). Traits and motives: Toward an integration of two traditions in personality research. *Psychological Review, 105*, 230–250.

Woike, B., Gershkovich, I., Piorkowski, R., & Polo, M. (1999). The role of motives in the content and structure of autobiographical memory. *Journal of Personality and Social Psychology, 76*, 600–612.

Wundt, W. (1888). Selbstbeobachtung und innere wahrnehmung. *Philosphische Studien, 4*, 292–309.

Zelenski, J. M., & Larsen, R. J. (1999). Susceptibility to affect: A comparison of three personality taxonomies. *Journal of Personality, 67*, 761–791.

Chapter 12

What Is Primed by Emotion Concepts and Emotion Words?*

Paula M. Niedenthal
CNRS and the University of Clermont-Ferrand, France

Anette Rohmann
University of Münster, Germany

Nathalie Dalle
University of Clermont-Ferrand, France

When we use emotional language and when we read emotion words, when we invoke emotion concepts and when we recount emotional stories, what happens to our emotional states? Just what is the relation between the processing of emotion concepts and emotion words, and other emotion processes such as feelings? This question has implications for the modeling of the representation and processing of emotion. It also has implications for how we interpret a number of different findings in the affect-cognition and attitudes literature that purport to show effects—automatic and controlled—of emotion, affect, and attitude on subsequent information processing and subsequent affective experience.

In order to answer these questions, first, a theory of the function of language and comprehension generally, and also of emotional language specifically, is required. Just why have we developed the capacity to talk about emotions given that we have so many other channels through which emotions can be expressed and communicated (e.g., emotional prosody, facial expression, posture, and the signs of vascular events such as blushing)? One

Preparation of this chapter was supported by a Programme Cognitique-2000 grant from the Minister of Research and Technology, France. The authors thank Markus Brauer, Jerry Clore, and Piotr Winkielman for helpful comments on a previous version of the chapter. Correspondence may be addressed to Paula M. Niedenthal, LAPSCO/ UFR Psychologie, Université Blaise Pascal, 34, avenue Carnot, 63037 Clermont-Ferrand Cedex, France. E-mail: niedenthal@srvpsy.univ-bpclermont.fr.

possibility is that language about emotion developed as yet another chan-nel by which a faithful representation of an internal state can be communi-cated. If language is a veridical readout of ongoing emotional states, this implies one representational model, and certain relations between emo-tional feelings and emotional language. If language serves another func-tion, for example, to channel or otherwise control emotion, or if it serves several of these functions, then this implies a more complex relationship between the representations of emotional feelings and emotional language and concepts. Second, one must have a theory of concepts that maps onto the adopted theory of language. How are emotions and emotion concepts represented and what do these representations contain? How are different representations of emotions activated? And what are the consequences of the activation of a concept?

With these two theoretical positions—a theory of language and a theory of concepts—initially clarified, one can then proceed to propose and test models of the different representations of emotion and the ways in which they interact. In this chapter we present ideas that encourage a good look at the processing of emotional states, emotion concepts, and emotional and affective words. After discussing theoretical accounts of language and con-cepts, as applied to emotion, we consider the role of emotion and affect in certain conceptual tasks. We then report experimental evidence from our laboratory that suggests that the experience of emotional feelings and the activation of emotion concepts and words do not have the same conse-quences for subsequent information processing. The implications of this work for understanding emotion representation is then discussed.

WHAT GOOD IS EMOTIONAL LANGUAGE?

Why do we have words for our emotions at all? Although there is debate over the meaning of facial expressions of emotion (Ekman, 1994; Fridlund, 1990, 1991; Izard, 1994, Russell, 1994), it is the case that facial expressions seen in context communicate an enormous amount of information about the subjective experience of the expresser (Carroll & Russell, 1996; Fer-nandez-Dols & Carroll, 1997; Wallbott, 1988). It has also been demon-strated that tone of voice, or emotional prosody, determines the nature and impact of a vocal communication, sometimes more than the content of the utterance itself (Argyle, 1975). And other nonverbal cues such as posture may be equally informative (e.g., Weisfeld & Beresford, 1982). Given the existence of these channels of expression, what is the function of emotional words and emotional language? Is there a unique function?

It can certainly not be denied that emotion words provide a readout of emotional state, and thus overlap in their function with that of other channels of emotional communication. The emotion lexicon does a good job of representing emotional life and of faithfully preserving something about the affective experiences to which it refers. This is why emotion psychologists study the emotion lexicon in the first place (e.g., Fehr & Russell, 1984; Ortony & Clore, 1989; Shaver, Schwartz, Kirson, & O'Connor, 1987). It appears to ground psychological experience, and to correspond to individual differences in emotional experience in ways that make sense (Feldman, 1995a, 1995b; Feldman Barrett & Russell, 1998). So, one nonunique function of emotional language is to faithfully preserve something about the nature of the experiences that they denote and support communication about those experiences.

But Semin (2000), considering the purpose of language in general, argued that language is a more complex social tool that is used to transform reality and manipulate the environment. Indeed, it is a device that evolved in order to enhance social coordination (Corballis, 1998; Tomasello, Kruger, & Ratner, 1993). In employing a particular content and a particular structure of language, individuals are able to create a social context and understanding, and thereby meet and convince others to meet their current goals and needs (see also Barsalou, in press, for a related argument).

This analysis extends to understanding the functions of emotional language. Emotional language is also about social coordination, and the creation of a temporary and a permanent social structure designed to meet ones present goals. Consistent with this idea, Semin and colleagues (Semin, Görts, Naddram, & Semin-Goossens, 2002) recently demonstrated that the use of emotional language varies with culture, such that cultural requirements for self-realization and independence, versus for enhancing relationships and interrelatedness, significantly influence its use. For example, in one study Semin and colleagues (Semin et al., 2002, Experiment 1) found that individuals from a collectivist culture tended to use verbs of state (e.g., to love, to hate) that imply both an object and a subject, and therefore, relationships with others. In contrast, individuals from individualistic cultures, more often used nouns and adjectives (e.g., I am ashamed, I am happy), which implicate the self, and which do not make direct reference to an object of the emotion. These findings suggest that different cultures use emotional language to serve the aim of fulfilling cultural imperatives and maintaining the societal structure.

Thus, it appears that emotions are represented and expressed by use of emotion words and language, not only in order to communicate that a particular state is being experienced, but also as a way to (re)create a context in which the state can be regulated. In the discussion of an emotional situation, emotional language can locate the cause of the agent, the likelihood of action, and, perhaps most important, behavioral requirements on the part of the listener (Frijda, 1987; Gehm & Scherer, 1988; Scherer, 1988;

Smith & Ellsworth, 1987). Therefore, the way in which one talks about emotion, and even the specific emotion word one chooses to utter, has a number of psychological consequences.

Consequences for the individual who translates the situation into emotional language were demonstrated by Mendolia and Kleck (1993), who showed that what a person talks about when describing an emotional event has an impact on his subsequent emotional reaction to the same event at a later point in time. In their study (Mendolia & Kleck, 1993, Experiment 2) participants were exposed to a stress-inducing film and then asked to talk either about fact-relevant issues of the film or about their emotions. Two days later they watched the film again and their emotions were assessed in several ways. The number of times participants thought about the stimulus was also measured. Participants who talked about their emotional reactions and reported that mental images of the film disrupted their thoughts between the two sessions were less autonomically aroused while watching the film a second time 2 days later. Furthermore, they reported more positive affect when confronted with and when talking about the film a second time. Participants who talked about the factual sequence of events in the film, and who did not experience repetitive thoughts about the episode in between the two sessions, were more autonomically aroused when they viewed the stimulus 2 days later. This suggests that the translation of an emotional event into emotional language regulates future emotional responding (for similar findings, see Johnson & Leventhal, 1974 and Leventhal, Brown, Shacham, & Engquist, 1979).

Halberstadt and Niedenthal (2001) demonstrated another influence of emotional language in the emotional experience of an individual. In three experiments, the researchers tested the hypothesis that the application of a specific emotion label or category in the perceptual encoding of an ambiguous emotional expression influences the way in which the expression is represented in perceptual memory. In one experiment, for example, participants viewed faces expressing a blend of happiness and anger. Some participants then created stories (either aloud or in their heads) to explain why the target person was expressing one of the two emotions, according to a label provided by the experimenter (i.e., either happiness or anger). Other participants merely looked at the faces. Later, all participants attempted to identify the initially seen facial expressions in computer movies in which the faces changed continuously from anger to happiness (or the reverse). Just one of the frames in the movies showed the facial expressions initially seen by the participants. Facial expressions conceptualized in terms of anger were remembered as displaying more anger than the same facial expressions conceptualized in terms of happiness, regardless of whether the explanations were told aloud or imagined. A second experiment extended this finding to anger–sad expressions, an emotion blend more commonly encountered in real life. Furthermore, a similar, but reduced bias was observed in participants who received biasing emotion labels (e.g., "this person is angry") but who did not have to explain the emotion.

An implication of Halberstadt and Niedenthal's research for considering the relationships between emotion and language is that the emotional language used to encode an event can determine its emotional meaning, and even perceptual memory of the event. This can in turn justify measures that are taken to cope with the emotional event. For example, suppose that an individual tells a friend that a person with whom an angry interaction just took placed "looked so enraged I thought he was about to hit me." First, the perceiver's memory of the facial expression should converge on the perceptual implication of this categorization, as suggested by the results of Halberstadt and Niedenthal (2001) just described. Furthermore, a number of responses from the listener (e.g., "if he had hit you, I would have called the police") and from the perceiver him or herself, would now be justified. The process of labeling and thus categorizing an event, even a perceptually ambiguous event, can determine the social reality, to the point of creating new perceptual evidence in its favor. What these kinds of results and other like them suggest is that the relationship between emotional experience and emotional language is not a simple one. Words can transform emotions and interpersonal interaction about them, and quite probably, emotional words evolved just for that purpose. The multifunction, multi-influence character of emotional language requires a powerful approach to the representation of emotion and emotion concepts, one that can handle the complexity of the relations between emotion and language. It is to this problem that we turn next.

EMOTION CONCEPTS AS PERCEPTUAL SIMULATORS

The present analysis of emotion words and language is not unmanageable if wedded with a sufficiently powerful theory of concepts. Barsalou (1999a, 1999b) has presented a perceptual symbols approach to representing concepts that we believe is particularly useful for modeling emotion concepts (Niedenthal, Ric, & Krauth-Gruber, 2002). The approach departs in two important senses from most recent models of concept representation. First, most extant models assume amodal concept representation. That is, they make the assumption that there is no particular relation between the sensory experience (visual, haptic, olfactory, and so on) with an instance of a concept, and the information actually stored in long-term memory. Furthermore, in such models, representation is arbitrary. That is, there is no particular reason that one representational code might be favored over another. Due to the amodal, arbitrary nature of representation in such models, similarity between the symbols bears no relation to the similarity between perceptual states. As an example, in an amodal model a concept might be represented by a series of Xs and Os (e.g., Medin & Schaffer, 1978). Similarity between concepts is then represented by an overlap in the pattern, but this pattern bears no relationship to the perceptual or conceptual similarity between the actual concepts. Thus, an arbitrary code might reflect the fact that fruits and pastries are similar because they both taste sweet, but nothing about the representation preserves anything analogical about sweetness.

In contrast, in Barsalou's (1999a) approach, subsets of perceptual states, perceptual symbols, are assumed to ground concepts and to be combined to support higher cognitive functions such as inference and judgment. The symbols have the same structure as perceptual states (they are *modal*) and their structure is informative about what they denote; similarity between them corresponds to similarity between perceptual states (they are *analogical*). Concepts are thus not simply mental receptacles for incoming information, or lists and bins for the performance of conceptual tasks, but they are essentially perceptual simulators; they support the mental replaying of the perceptual features of the concept. Not all perceptual aspects of a concept will be simulated at any given time, however. This is determined by the focus of selective attention (Barsalou, 1999a).

Evidence for the viability of this approach to concepts has been obtained in experiments using *property verification* tasks (Solomon & Barsalou, 2000), in which participants indicate whether a member of a category possesses a given characteristic. Additional evidence comes from experiments involving *property generation* tasks (Wu & Barsalou, 2000), in which participants freely produce characteristics of typical members of categories. Two indicators seem to support the conclusion that individuals perceptually simulate concepts. One of these indicators is *perceptual effort*. When generating properties of a concept, for instance, the modal approach uniquely predicts that easily observable properties are more likely to be mentioned because they are more likely to be part of an image. Hidden, or occluded, properties are less likely to be produced because they are not likely to be part of the image. The other indicator is *instructional equivalence*. In a test of instructional equivalence, some experimental participants are directed to create a perceptual image of the concept. Other participants are given no instructions at all. If the behavior of the two groups of participants is similar (and different from other controls), this suggests that participants in both groups perceptually simulate the concept. Results of a number of studies provide evidence of both perceptual effort and instructional equivalence (e.g., Barsalou, Solomon, & Wu, 1999).

All of this does not mean that amodal systems of concepts, such as feature lists, schemas, and semantic networks, have no place in cognitive processing, indeed they may. In all likelihood the tendency to rely on perceptual symbols versus amodal representations depends on the conceptual task at hand (Solomon & Barsalou, 2000). For some simple tasks in which meaning is not necessary for task performance, processing may be based on something like amodal representations. But even in more complex conceptual tasks, modal representations are used, or simulated, to different degrees. For the present analysis we rely on the following principles in understanding emotion concepts: (1) perceptually grounded concepts are simulated to different extents in the performance of different conceptual tasks, (2) the aspects of the tasks that influence extent of simulation are exposure (or time), motivation, and instruction (see below), (3) the extent to which a concept is simulated determines the involvement of perceptual properties contained in the resulting output. Thus, concepts can be processed superficially, such that many perceptual aspects of the concepts are not simulated or re-experienced, and concepts can also be simulated in such a way so as to implicate much of its deep structure.

This approach is useful for conceptualizing emotion concepts (Niedenthal et al., 2002). Because perception can be introspective, a modal account supports understanding of the representation of both the internal (e.g., feelings) and external (e.g., eliciting events) aspects of emotions. In addition, the approach allows one to imagine the use of emotion words without making recourse to the deeper perceptual properties of the concept, and in turn to imagine the simulation of many features of an emotion concept, which might in the extreme evoke the represented emotional state.

This view is consistent with models of emotion processing that conceptualize emotion as represented on different levels, such as the motor, schematic, and conceptual levels proposed by Leventhal and Scherer (1987; see Buck, 1985, and Niedenthal, Setterlund, & Jones, 1994 for similar approaches). It is also consistent with Lang's (1979, 1984) bio-informational network theory. In Lang's approach a semantic network for an emotion is seen as organizing prototypical information for that emotion. The informational units (or "nodes") are of three kinds: (1) stimulus units, (2) response units, and (3) meaning units. The stimulus units contain information about the kinds of external stimuli and contexts that could evoke that emotion (emotion antecedents). Thus the prototype network for fear reactions may contain "snakes" as a fear stimulus. Response units contain information on how one reacts to a particular emotion-inducing stimulus. The responses include verbal utterances and behavioral routines, as well as physiological responses. In the case of a fear response to a snake, the response units might contain visceral reactions such as increased heart rate, and the urge to flee. The meaning units are used to interpret the information from the activated stimulus and response nodes. For example, a snake phobic might interpret the meaning of a stuffed, mounted snake in a museum differently from viewing someone walking down the street with a live python wrapped around their neck. Also, the stuffed snake will be responded to differently if the snake phobic already feels somewhat aroused compared to when feeling calm. When a sufficient number of informational units are activated, the emotion program is processed, and an emotion is experienced. The emotion itself in this model is conceived of as a consequence of the activation of a sufficient number of units of information.

As with other associative network accounts of emotion, Lang's approach does not specify exactly how internal and external perceptual information is represented in the network. Barsalou's approach adds this important dimension and perhaps constitutes a more parsimonious way to model certain phenomena (Niedenthal et al., 2002). Furthermore, it allows emotion concepts to be directly compared and contrasted to other artifactual and natural concepts.

WHAT DETERMINES THE EXTENT OF PERCEPTUAL SIMULATION OF AN EMOTION CONCEPT?

The extent of perceptual simulation of an emotion concept, or possibly any other concept, is likely determined by the degree of exposure to the concept (or time to simulate it), motivation, and task requirements. Extent of exposure is merely the repetition or duration of exposure to information relevant to a particular concept, or time allowed for its processing. Thus, for example, if one is exposed to an emotion word, or a cue to an emotion concept, once, for a very brief time (such as a subliminal exposure to a single word), then very little perceptual simulation of the concept should occur. This is not because simulation can not occur unconsciously, in theory it can (Barsalou, 1999a). It is merely that the use of the word, and perhaps the concept, is very short lived and does not require that many aspects of the perceptual grounding of the concept be accessed. In contrast, if one is exposed repeatedly to subliminal emotion words, all closely related to the same emotion, then the concept will be more often unconsciously simulated and more of the perceptual properties of the concepts might be accessed (Bargh & Chartrand, 1999).

Perhaps more interesting is the motivation to simulate a concept. It is conceivable that one might want to use emotional language and concepts with no intention to produce the perceptual grounding of the concept in experience. As an example, imagine an encounter with a person who has recently learned the English language. Some of the first emotion terms that are learned are the basic emotion terms such as happiness and sadness. So, suppose further that the person has already learned the meaning of these terms. If he or she now asks me to explain the meaning of the English word *grief,* I can rely on a simple, perhaps even amodal, representation of emotion, and say "grief is like sadness, only stronger and sometimes longer-lasting." This may be all that it takes to understand the meaning of *grief* if one knows the meaning of *sadness.* On the other hand, if the person has not yet learned the word for sadness, my motivation to reexperience and generate a reexperience of the perceptual properties of this concept might be enhanced. Now I might evoke for both of us a condition under which grief is felt (such as the death of a loved one), and I might encourage the listener to simulate the concept by reference to this, or several related situations. In such a case, both of us may actually relive a type of grief, and by this process the listener has learned a new label for a known emotion experience. Motivation to perceptually simulate a concept might also be influenced by the degree to which the concept is related to the self. That is, the notion of "my experiences of grief" might be more likely to be simulated, and the perceptual properties of grief might thus be more likely to be replayed and reexperienced, than the notion of "ones experience of grief."

Finally, the type of conceptual task to be performed will influence the extent to which the simulation of a concept occurs. This is illustrated by an example presented in Solomon and Barsalou (2000). The authors described a property verification task used by Kossyln (1976, 1980). As mentioned previously, the task involves the determination of whether a feature is true of a target category. Details of the Kosslyn experiments are unnecessary for making the point, which is that in the property verification task the nature of the "false" trials can determine the way in which the information on the "true" trials is processed. If on all "false" trials the presented features have nothing whatsoever to do with the target category (e.g., is "feathers" a property of "hammer"?) this influences how much processing is required to determine the truth value of "true" trials. Specifically, any time a mere association is detected between the feature and the target category, a positive response will necessarily be correct. Thus the task can be performed with almost no processing of the target concepts at all and no evidence of perceptual simulation will be observed. However, if false properties are also associated with the target category (e.g., is "litter" a property of "cat"?), then the concept must be processed more deeply in order to make a correct response on "true" trials (Solomon & Barsalou, 2000). If mere association is used, then when the question "is 'litter' a property of 'cat'?" is posed, an incorrect "true" response will be generated. If the detection of association allows individuals to correctly perform a property verification task, then in the task so constructed, perceptual simulation will not be necessary. If however, simpler processing is not sufficient, then perceptual simulation will be necessary for correct performance. Thus, clearly, task requirements can determine what kind of representation is accessed (e.g., amodal versus modal) and also the degree to which a modal representation is actually simulated.

The foregoing analysis, relying as it does on a modeal approach to concepts, was recently used to propose a way to conceptualize the occurrence (and nonoccurrence) of emotion congruence effects in impression formation and judgment (Niedenthal et al., 2002). According to Niedenthal and colleagues, the induction of an emotion activates or brings to mind the relevant emotion concept, which involves the simulation of aspects of this particular emotional experience. The simulation of a happy concept by an individual in a happy state, for instance, might implicate the simulation of a happy face, a friendly social interaction, or a state felt during a recent vacation. Whether selective attention is focused on perceptual aspects of faces, aspects of social interaction, or those of asking favors will depend on the demands of whatever information processing task is required next. So, if we ask happy participants in a laboratory experiment to make judgments about pictures of couples (e.g., Forgas, 1993), they will focus attention on aspects of the emotion concept that is associated with romantic relationships in order to generate their inferences.

The detection of *emotion congruence* is then determined by the extent to which the target of judgment must be simulated in order to produce the inference. Extensive simulation will bring more perceptual aspects into the simulation and thereby produce greater, or more easily detectable, emotion congruence. Less simulation will yield a response with fewer perceptual aspects of the concept. Thus, if an individual has to make judgments about a series of romantic couples, and he has seen many such couples before (because they are statistically frequent), very little simulation will be required. Few perceptual aspects of the activated emotion concept will be focused on, and consequently the judgments will contain little evidence of the emotional aspects of the concept (Forgas, 1993; 1995; Forgas & Moylan, 1991). If, however, judgments must be made about couples about which very little is known (because they are statistically infrequent, such as interracial couples) more simulation will occur and more perceptual aspects of the activated emotion concept will be generated. Consequently the influence of the emotion concept on the judgment will be greater. Emotion congruence will thus not be observed when judgments are based on superficial simulation of a concept, but emotion congruence will be more likely seen in judgments based on deeper simulation of a concept (Niedenthal et al., 2002).

The fact that extent of exposure, motivation, and conceptual task requirements can yield different degrees of perceptual simulation of concepts has important consequences for the interpretation of a number of studies that purport to, in one way or another, involve affect or emotion. In the next section we consider several conceptual tasks the performance of which is at least sometimes assumed to engage affective processes. Specifically, we consider the emotional consequences of (1) sentence unscrambling tasks, and (2) automatic affective priming. Following that, we report some recent research from our laboratory that tests effects of the activation of different emotion representations (i.e., the priming of emotion concepts vs. emotion states) in subsequent information processing.

THE SENTENCE UNSCRAMBLING TASK

Sentence unscrambling is a task that has been used to prime concepts, usually social or trait categories, which are of interest to the researcher. Such tasks have been successfully used to activate concepts such as kindness and hostility (Srull & Wyer, 1979), gender stereotypes (Banaji, Hardin, & Rothman, 1993), and stereotypes of the elderly (Bargh, Chen, & Burrows, 1996; Stapel, Koomen, & Van der Plight, 1996). In the task, individuals are presented with a series of words listed in random order. They then construct grammatically correct sentences or phrases out of a subset of the words. Critical sentences form statements that are associated with the concept to be primed. What would happen if the words and sentences referred to emotional states and "core" emotion themes? Would such a task activate emotion concepts such that very little or no perceptual simulation was performed? Or would such a treatment yield essentially the reliving of an emotional state?

The conceptual basis of emotion has been studied by researchers interested in the cognitive structure of emotions (Oatley & Johnson-Laird, 1987; Ortony, Clore & Collins, 1988), the appraisal dimensions of emotions (e.g., Roseman, Antoniou, & Jose, 1996; Scherer, 1999; Smith, Haynes, Lazarus, & Pope, 1993), the prototypicality of emotions (e.g., Russell, 1980; Shaver et al. 1987), and the antecedents of, experience of, and coping strategies for emotion (e.g., Scherer, Wallbott, & Summerfield, 1986; Mesquita & Frijda, 1992). Based on this literature, we recently constructed a sentence unscrambling task with the aim of activating emotion concepts (Innes-Ker & Niedenthal, in press). Four-word sentences were constructed that described the situations, behaviors, reactions, and appraisals associated with happiness and sadness. A fifth word was added to each sentence to create groups of five scrambled words. The fifth word always had the same emotional connotation as the sentence itself. That is, if a four-word sentence described a happy situation, the fifth word was also associated with happiness. Thirty such sentences were created for each emotion. Examples appear in Table 12.1. Fifteen sentences with neutral content were added to each set to obscure the interest in emotion, resulting in 45 sentence in each set. A set of 45 sentences with neutral content was created for the control condition. The words for each sentence and the fifth filler word were presented in scrambled order in the actual task.

TABLE 12.1
Example Sentences (Already Unscrambled) That
Were Used in the Sentence Unscrambling Task

Happy sentences	
Sentences	Filler word
The guests felt satisfied	ease
The audience was ecstatic	interest
A nice summer evening	smile
The crowd cheered loudly	harmony
A long pleasure cruise	insight
She shouted with exuberance	kind
Sad sentences	
Sentences	Filler word
The man felt lonely	affliction
The child looked dejected	slump
He sunk into melancholy	fate
She had strong regrets	sigh
The man was despondent	blight
Her distress was visible	refuse

We predicted that performance of this conceptual task would *not* encourage individuals to perceptually simulate emotion concepts such that their own emotional state would be detectably influenced. Our prediction was based on the requirements of the task, as well as participant motivation. First, the task requires that an individual put together a coherent sentence, and superficial conceptual processing can be engaged in when the goal is to form a sentence. Second, the subjects and objects of the sentences were completely hypothetical. The self of the participants was not involved at all (as, for instance, in the Velton mood induction procedure; see later discussion). That is, individuals formed sentences such as "She shouted with exuberance," and not "I shouted with exuberance," a sentence that, it might be predicted, would and could be simulated extensively.

A pilot study was then conducted to investigate the effects of the sentence unscrambling task on emotional state (Innes-Ker & Niedenthal, in press). In particular, approximately 25 individuals each unscrambled the happy, sad, or neutral sentences. They all then completed a scale designed to measure their emotional state. There was no effect of unscrambling sentences about happiness or sadness on emotional state. And this finding was replicated in many subsequent studies, using different sentences and different numbers of sentences. Thus, apparently participants could construct sentences that represented the core theme of a particular emotion concept without simulating the concept sufficiently to relive the emotional experience, at least as measured on a self-report inventory of felt emotional state.

But the objection could of course be made that no representation of emotion of any type was activated by the task. A second pilot study was therefore conducted to examine the influences of the task on lexical processing. In this study, participants unscrambled one set of emotion sentences (happy, sad, or neutral). Afterward they performed a lexical decision task, which contained words related to happiness, sadness, and neutral ideas. Results indicated that participants who had unscrambled happy sentences made lexical decisions about happy words faster than participants in the other conditions. Those who had unscrambled sad sentences made lexical decisions about sad words faster than participants in the other conditions.

The Innes-Ker and Niedenthal findings regarding the sentence unscrambling task are consistent with other recent findings. For example, participants in a study by Bargh, Chaiken, Raymond, and Hymes (1996) were instructed to unscramble sentences that contained words associated with the stereotype of the elderly, such as *lonely*, *dependent*, and *helpless*, or sentences containing neutral words. They were then ostensibly dismissed from the experiment, but were surreptitiously timed as they walked down the hall to the elevator to leave the building. Those who had unscrambled sentences with words evocative of the elderly stereotype walked more slowly than control participants presumably because activation of the stereotype of the elderly was accompanied by the activation of associated behavioral scripts (e.g., retarded motor movements). In Barsalou's account, the stereotype of the elderly was simulated such that behavioral/motoric aspects of the stereotype were subsequently generated.

However, many of the words associated with the stereotype possess a sad connotation. Thus, perhaps it was the simulation of emotion concepts and not the stereotype of the elderly that caused the slower walking. That is, simulation of the concept *sad* could also cause slow walking, because sadness is associated with retarded motor movement. Just which concepts were the participants simulating? Bargh and colleagues conducted a follow-up study in which they exposed new participants to the sentence-unscrambling task and then measured their mood states. Exposure to the sentences did not induce a sad mood. Thus, the sentence unscrambling task used by Bargh and colleagues, like that used in the Innes-Ker and Niedenthal work, also did not appear to constitute a task in which emotion concepts are perceptually simulated, despite the conscious processing of emotionally charged words.

Now, compare the findings just described to those of Stapel and Koomen (2000, Study 2b) who employed a sentence-unscrambling task that included sentences taken from the Velton (1968) mood induction procedure. These sentences, such as "My life is wonderful" and "Everybody understands me" specifically involve the self. Furthermore, the instructions to the participants directed them to try to generate the emotion suggested by the sentences. It would seem that the combined involvement of the self and the instructions constitutes a situation in which perceptual simulation should occur. For example, an individual might imagine how and why his life was wonderful, or aspects of the very people who are understanding, and also the feelings associated with these images. Indeed, participants who took part in the Stapel and Koomen study did report feeling the emotional states described by the words and concepts used in this sentence unscrambling task.

In summary, results of recent studies using sentence unscrambling tasks suggest that motivation and task requirements can cause the emotion concepts involved to be extensively simulated, with all the experiential consequences of those simulations. However, in addition, the concepts can be used without extensive simulation, and in this case, reliving of the affective experience may not detectably occur.

THE EVALUATIVE PRIMING TASKS

Fazio and colleagues (Fazio, Sanbonmatsu, Powell, & Kardes, 1986) originally demonstrated that the presentation of a word that denotes an object toward which an individual holds an accessible attitude can facilitate the processing of a subsequent word that carries the same affective/attitudinal value. The task that Fazio and colleagues used was one in which participants were aware of the initial priming word, committed it to memory, and then made an evaluative judgment (positive, negative) about the target word. In follow-up research, different aspects of the task and the stimuli were varied (e.g., Bargh, Chaiken, Raymond, & Hymes, 1996; Hermans, De Houwer, & Eelen, 1996; Klauer, Rossnagel, & Musch, 1997; Wentura, 1999). It appears now that evaluative priming is an automatic effect, produced by strong and by weak evaluative primes, observed in a variety of tasks, including those in which the target is not explicitly evaluated (e.g., the word naming task), with a variety of stimuli serving as primes and targets. More recently, the results of extensive research cast doubt on the possibility that an affective prime of the same valence as a target actually facilitates responding in the naming task (Klauer & Musch, in press), however. Thus, the effect may not be observable in all tasks that are held to measure the automatic influences of prior information on the processing of subsequent information. And this has implications for the viability of one of the preferred mechanistic accounts of the effect, specifically the spreading activation account (Fazio, 2001; see also Klauer & Musch, chap. , Wentura, & Rothermund, and Ferguson, chap. , & Bargh, chap. , this volume).

Where is the place of affect in the evaluative priming effect? Is automatic evaluation due to affective responses that are automatically evoked by exposure to stimuli toward which strong and weak attitudes are held? Or is the evaluative response or organizing principle purely cognitive in nature. Clore and colleagues (2001) think that it is not necessary to assume that affect is involved at all. They note, as we mentioned previously, that the effect has been observed for subliminally presented stimuli with very weak evaluations that would not, in any event, induce affect when processed consciously. Clore and colleagues also argued that because in similar tasks the priming of gender expectations by male and female names has also been observed, it is not necessary to think of the evaluative priming effect as being due to affect.

We agree with Clore et al. (2001) and would broaden their arguments by appealing to the perceptual symbols account of concepts. Consistent with our prior reasoning about sentence unscrambling tasks, it might be most accurate to say that affective responses sometimes accompany, but probably do not account for the range of evaluative priming effects observed at this point. The determinants of the involvement of any affective process at all probably include the nature of the task required, the kinds of stimuli involved, and several other task parameters that can influence the extent of simulation of the concepts labeled by the primes and the targets used as experimental stimuli.

With regard to the demands of the conceptual task, a basic distinction can be drawn between the requirement of an evaluative versus nonevaluative judgment of the target stimuli. Recall that in the original research, Fazio and colleagues (1986) instructed participants to make a positive/negative categorization of the target words. Extensive research by Cacioppo and his colleagues (e.g., Cacioppo, Crites, Berntson, & Coles, 1993; Cacioppo, Crites, Gardner, & Berntson, 1994) has demonstrated that measures of the late positive potentials (LPPs) of the event-related brain potential show important differences between evaluative and nonevaluative categorizations. Specifically, LPPs measured during evaluative categorizations are relatively larger over the right hemisphere suggesting greater involvement in that region during evaluative than nonevaluative categorizations (Crites & Cacioppo, 1996). Given that neural units in the right hemisphere are active in affective perception and judgment (Tucker & Frederickson, 1989), such a result implicates a greater role of affect in evaluative than in nonevaluative judgment processes. In Barsalou's account this suggests that different perceptual features of concepts are attended to during evaluative judgments and that these are sufficient to reinstantiate part of the affective experience. There is no necessity to simulate affective aspects of objects when nonevaluative categorizations or judgments are made. Therefore the reexperience of the affective feature of a concept does not necessarily occur if the concept is processed in this way. When it is argued that the evaluative priming effect does not require the intention to evaluate (e.g.,

Bargh, Chaiken, Govender, & Pratto, 1992; Hermans, De Houwer, & Eelen, 1994), this suggests to us that the processing involved in the performance of tasks used to make this claim (e.g., the naming task, the lexical decision task) are not fundamentally affective in nature.

In this chapter we are focusing on the affect-eliciting power of words and the concepts to which they refer. However, in recent evaluative priming studies, researchers have used other types of stimuli either as primes, targets, or both. Such stimuli vary quite dramatically in their signal value for emotions and in their likelihood of motivating conceptual simulation. Pictures (e.g., Hermans et al., 1994) and odors (Hermans, Baeyens, & Eelen, 1998) may be more likely to produce emotional responses as they are processed quite differently from affective words (De Houwer & Hermans, 1994). As Hermans and colleagues note in their chapter (chap. , this volume), the processing of words can occur without any involvement of evaluative information (we would add, in certain tasks). In contrast, pictures have more direct access to evaluative information (e.g., Spruyt, Hermans, De Houwer, & Eelen, 2001). Thus, when pictures are processed it is perhaps more likely that affective responses are activated.

Of course, even the nature of the word stimuli, when used in evaluative priming research, has varied in terms of the accessibility of the associated attitudes (e.g., Bargh et al., 1992, 1996; Fazio, 1993). It would seem that it is easier and more likely to stimulate aspects of words associated with easily accessible attitudes. Furthermore, the higher accessibility may be correlated with the representation of more perceptual grounding of the concept in the first place, and a greater likelihood of reproducing affective features of the concept.

Finally, other task factors may influence whether affect is experienced in the context of evaluative priming tasks. Notably, in much initial evaluative priming research, the same primes and targets were seen repeatedly throughout the task (Bargh et al., 1996; Fazio et al., 1986). Meanwhile, in other research the primes and targets were seen only once (e.g., Klauer & Musch, in press). If an individual is repeatedly exposed to the same words, the possibility that the perceptual grounding of the labeled concept is simulated sufficiently to provoke the experiential aspects of the concept is enhanced. Such simulation may also be enhanced when the priming stimuli are presented at supraliminal levels rather than subliminal levels.

One possible conclusion to be drawn from the present analysis is that the more evaluative priming is shown to be independent of the nature of the task requirements, stimuli, and other procedural factors, the more likely that the effect is not caused by the production of an automatic affective response. Evaluative priming might be a basic cognitive priming phenomenon, one in which the organizational structure (based on good–bad assessments) bears some similarities and some differences to associative priming. Another possibility is to suggest that the entire literature on evaluative priming be organized according to the present predictions regarding the conditions under which affect is most likely to be elicited. It might then be easier to determine whether, in fact, strong evaluative priming is only observed when the conditions are right for the reexperience of affect associated with the experimental stimuli. Finally, one could draw the conclusion that, in the end, too many phenomena are currently included under the rubric of "evaluative priming," a conclusion that is related to Fiedler's analysis (Fiedler, chap. , this volume). It may be that "affective" priming and other sorts of priming have all been thrown into the same pile. It is the separation of some of these types of priming to which we turn next.

EMOTION–COGNITION INTERACTIONS

There is now a substantial literature that reports a number of emotion–cognition interactions (e.g., Eich, Kihlstrom, Bower, Forgas, & Niedenthal, 2000; Fiedler & Forgas, 1988; Niedenthal & Kitayama, 1994). In addition to the effects discussed earlier, emotions influence the content of judgment and impression formation (e.g., Forgas & Moylan, 1987; Hirt, Levine, McDonald, & Melton, 1997; Isen, Shalker, Clark, & Karp, 1978; Laird, Wagener, Halal, & Szegda, 1982; Martin, Abend, Sedikides, & Green, 1997; Schwarz & Clore, 1983). Emotions have also been associated with different strategies for information processing (e.g., Bless, Schwartz, & Kemmelmeier, 1996; Bodenhausen, Kramer, & Suesser, 1994; Bodenhausen, Sheppard, & Kramer, 1994; Fiedler, 2000; Mackie & Worth, 1991; Petty, Gleicher, & Baker, 1991; Schwarz & Bless, 1991). And they influence the organization of semantic material in memory (Isen, 1987; Niedenthal, Halberstadt, & Innes-Ker, 1999; Niedenthal & Setterlund, 1994).

But a reasonable and repeated criticism of such work is that emotional states and feelings are not implicated in the effects at all. Maybe, rather, semantic emotion concepts—the amodal representations of emotions—activated directly by the induction procedure itself, or self-activated by the experimental participant, underlie the effects (Clore et al., 2001; Wyer & Carlston, 1979). If this is true, then affect-cognition researchers should be much more modest about the implications of their findings.

Emotion-Congruent Judgment. For example, Forgas and colleagues (Forgas & Bower, 1987; Forgas, Bower, & Krantz, 1984) have observed emotion-congruent impression formation. Other research has shown that people interpret neutral facial expressions in emotion-congruent ways (Isen et

al., 1978; Niedenthal, Halberstadt, Margolin, & Innes-Ker, 2000; Schiffenbauer, 1974). Emotion network models of emotion processing (e.g., Bower,
1981), predict emotion congruent social judgment due to the activation of
units representing emotional states in memory that have been activated by
the corresponding emotional state (Niedenthal & Showers, 1991). But suppose that laboratory manipulations of emotion prime amodal representations of emotional knowledge, or concepts that are not accompanied by
much of the affective grounding. Perhaps then, the findings of "emotion"
congruence are all due to such concept activation, and no emotional state
is required for their observation.

Emotional Response Categorization.   The same interpretation could be applied to research purporting to find support for Niedenthal, Halberstadt,
and Innes-Ker's (1999; also Niedenthal & Halberstadt, 1995, 2000a, 2000b)
theory of emotional response categorization. Those researchers argued
that emotional states serve to ground categories such that objects and
events in the world that have elicited the same specific emotion are
grouped together and treated as "the same sort of thing" (Bruner, Goodnow, & Austin, 1956). The theory is comprised of three claims. The first of
these is that a set of specific emotions provides the structure for emotional
response categorization. That is, people treat as equivalent those things
that have elicited specific feelings of anger, sadness, happiness, fear, and so
forth. The second claim is that the subjective experience of one of the specific emotions causes a reorganization of the conceptual space into emotional response categories. The final claim is that such a conceptual (re)or-
ganization is due to selective attention to the emotional responses
associated with already-represented concepts, and the emotional response
to perceived objects and events.

To evaluate the reorganization of conceptual relations during states of
emotion, Niedenthal et al. (1999) conducted experiments in which experimental participants were presented with target concepts (X) and judged
which of two comparison concepts, A or B, the target was most similar to.
Critical triads were constructed such that A shared an emotional relation to
X (e.g., both were associated with happiness). In contrast, B shared a distant, nonemotional, taxonomic, or associative relation to X. Findings revealed that, compared to individuals who were in a relatively neutral emotional state, individuals in emotional states of happiness, sadness, and fear
were systematically more likely to group together X with A. Thus, for example, individuals in happy and sad emotion conditions were more likely to
group the target concept *kiss* with the comparison concept *fortune* than with
the comparison concept *handshake*. They were also more likely to group *am-
bulance* with the concept *poverty* rather than *wheelbarrow*, and to group together *vulture* with *insanity* rather than *parakeet*.

Research by Halberstadt and Niedenthal (1997) supports the claim that the preferential categorization of stimuli in terms of emotional response during emotional states is due to selective attention to emotional response equivalence. In three studies, participants in whom happiness, sadness or neutral emotion had been experimentally induced were presented with all possible pairs of a set of female and male faces expressing happiness and sadness, and rated the similarity of each pair. Multidimensional scaling analyses revealed that the primary dimensions of similarity were *expressed emotion* and *gender of face*. However, participants in the two emotion conditions weighted emotional expression (both the expression of happiness and that of sadness) more heavily in their similarity judgments than did participants in the control condition. In contrast, the latter participants tended to weight gender of face in their judgments more than those in the emotion conditions.

Emotion congruence and emotional response categorization are two effects that have been assumed to be due to the effects of emotion on the activation of information in memory and on the allocation of selective attention, respectively. But to date no research has tested the actual role of emotion in these effects. Recently Innes-Ker and Niedenthal (in press) attempted to do just that.

Experimental Tests of Effects of Emotions versus Emotion Concepts. Specifically, two large-scale experiments were conducted to examine the influences of emotional states and the priming of emotion concepts in social judgment and in emotional response categorization (Innes-Ker & Niedenthal, 2001; Experiments 1 and 2). The question in each of the two major experiments was whether the activation of semantic emotion knowledge about happiness and sadness has the same effects on cognitive processes, as do induced states of happiness and sadness.

In the first experiment (N = 196), participants either unscrambled sentences related to happiness, sadness, or neutral ideas, as described previously, or were exposed to films that induced happiness, sadness, or a neutral state. They then read a story about the day in the life of a woman called M that could be understood as comprised of rather happy or rather sad events. Later participants rated their impressions of the feelings and experiences of the hypothetical character, and other elements and outcomes represented in the story. Although the manipulation of emotional state strongly influenced participants' impressions of the emotions experienced by the hypothetical character, and the emotional nature of the described events, the priming of emotion concepts did not at all (see Table 12.2).

Thus, it appears that when emotion concepts are accessed, but no particular affective experience is relived, subsequent effects on cognitive processing are not ones that would be called emotion congruent; in Forgas' (2000) terms, no affect infusion occurs.

TABLE 12.2
Average Ratings of Nine Items That Assessed the Happiness,
Contentment, and Pleasantness of All Elements in the Story
of M. Ratings Were Made on –2 to 2 Scales.
From Innes-Ker and Niedenthal (2001).

	Emotion Condition		
	Happy	Control	Sad
Format			
Emotion Induction	.889	.734	.496
Sentence Unscrambling	.599	.588	.752

In the second experiment, participants (N = 195) again either unscrambled happy, sad, or neutral sentences or watched films designed to induce emotional states. Afterward, they performed the triad task describe previously, and used in Niedenthal et al. (1999). Table 12.3 presents examples of happy and sad triads. The results, which are illustrated in Fig. 12.1, were consistent with the findings of the impression formation experiment. Specifically, individuals who were in induced emotional states showed effects of these states in their performance on the triad task. As in the Niedenthal et al. (1999) studies, happy and sad condition participants more often thought that the emotionally related concept was more similar to the target concept than did neutral condition participants. On the other hand, participants in the three sentence-unscrambling conditions (happy, sad, neutral), all performed the triad task in the same way. No effect of sentence unscrambling was observed.

Thus, in two large-scale studies in which the effects of feeling states versus the activation of emotion knowledge were compared, previously observed effects of emotion (emotion congruence judgment and emotional response categorization) were observed for emotional state conditions but not for concept activation conditions. This clarifies the mechanisms under-

TABLE 12.3
Example Triads Presented in the Order {X: A, B} Where X
Is the Target Concept, A Is the Emotion Alternative, and B
Is the Taxonomic Alternative. From Niedenthal et al. (1999).

Triad Type	Examples
Happy triads	joke: sunbeam, speech
	puppy: parade, beetle
	waterski: celebration, elevator
Sad triads	cancer: divorce, pulse
	ambulance: poverty, wheel barrow
	bankruptcy: tomb, teller

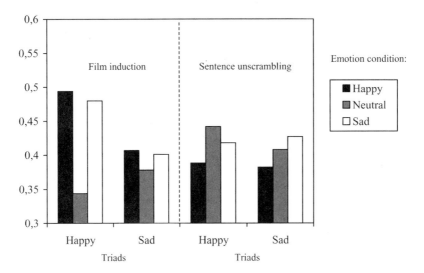

FIG. 12.1. Percentage of emotion concepts selected as most similar to the target concept, for happy and sad triads, and by individuals in happy, sad, and neutral emotional states.

lying some affect-cognition interactions. It seems that affect infusion in general requires that the perceptual aspects of an emotion are experienced, not merely the semantic aspects. This could be due to an emotion caused by external signal stimuli, or an emotion caused by sufficient simulation of a stored emotion concept. For instance, emotional states and effects of emotion on subsequent cognition processes have been observed when participants are asked to recall emotional autobiographical memories (e.g., Bodenhausen, Kramer, & Suesser, 1994; Strack, Schwarz, & Gschneidinger, 1985). The rehearsal of emotional autobiographical memories should, in the present approach, produce an emotion, or parts of an emotional state.

CONCLUSION

Recently many different tasks have been used to explore effects involving words and concepts that are affectively charged, with the aim of better understanding certain cognitive processes, such as attitude activation, evaluation, and mood. Our point in this chapter is that a powerful theory of conceptual representation and processing is required in order to study the conditions under which the treatment of emotional words and concepts will result in the reexperience of some affect.

We endorsed Barsalou's recent perceptual symbols approach to modeling concept representation, and his simulation view of conceptual processing

(Barsalou, 1999a, 1999b, in press). The value of the approach is that it is well adapted to studying emotion and emotion concepts because it makes explicit the role of perceptual representation, including that based in introspection, in the grounding of concepts. Thus, unlike some models of concepts, the approach can handle the representation of simple concrete concepts, as well as much more abstract concepts, such as emotion concepts. In addition, rather than positing many different types of emotion representation, the approach implies that the extent of perceptual simulation of a concept is an important determining factor of the influence of that concept on subsequent processing and behavior. Thus, the approach is parsimonious.

We suggested that many affect-cognition interactions and many accounts of affective processing can be understood in terms of the degree of simulation involved in using a concept. More extensive simulation, or even greater simulation competence (Barsalou, 1999a), will yield, as result, access to more and deeper perceptual features of a concept. Tasks that require extensive simulation of emotion concepts, due to protracted exposure, heightened motivation to imagine the concept, or the complexity of conceptual processing necessary for their performance may even result in the reexperience of an emotional state. More superficial treatment may not. Thus, the use of emotional words, language, and concepts may indeed be very flexible and susceptible to adaptation to the individuals current goals in ways that are at the same time more sophisticated and more basic than previously thought.

REFERENCES

Argyle, M. (1975). *Bodily Communication.* London: Methuen.

Banaji, M. R., Hardin, C., & Rothman, A. J. (1993). Implicit stereotyping in person judgement. *Journal of Personality and Social Psychology, 65,* 272–281.

Bargh, J. A., Chaiken, S., Govender, R., & Pratto, F. (1992). The generality of the attitude activation effect. *Journal of Personality and Social Psychology, 62,* 893–912.

Bargh, J. A., Chaiken, S., Raymond, P. R., & Hymes, C. (1996). The automatic evaluation effect: Unconditioned automatic attitude activation with a pronunciation task. *Journal of Experimental Social Psychology, 32,* 104–128.

Bargh, J. A., & Chartrand, T. L. (1999). The unbearable automaticity of being. *American Psychologist, 54,* 462–479.

Bargh, J. A., Chen, M., & Burrows, L. (1996). Automaticity of social behavior: Direct effects of trait construct and stereotype activation on action. *Journal of Personality and Social Psychology, 71,* 230–244.

Barsalou, L. W. (1999a). Perceptual symbol systems. *Behavioral and Brain Sciences, 22,* 577–609.

Barsalou, L. W. (1999b). Language comprehension: Archival memory or preparation for situated action? *Discourse Processes, 28,* 61–80.

Barsalou, L. W. (in press). Being there conceptually: Simulating categories in preparation for situated action. In N. L. Stein, P. J. Bauer, & M. Rabinowitz (Eds.), *Representation, memory, and development: Essays in honor of Jean Mandler.* Mahwah, NJ: Lawrence Erlbaum Associates.

Barsalou, L. W., Solomon, K. O., & Wu, L. L. (1999). Perceptual simulation in conceptual tasks. In M. K. Hiraga, C. Sinha, & S. Wilcox (Eds.), *Cultural, typological, and psychological perspectives in cognitive linguistics: The proceedings of the 4th conference of the International Cognitive Linguistics Association* (Vol. 3, pp. 209–228). Amsterdam: John Benjamins.

Bless, H., Schwartz, N., & Kemmelmeier, M. (1996). Mood and stereotyping: Affective states and the use of general knowledge structures. In W. Stroebe & M. Hewstone (Eds.), *European review of social psychology* (Vol. 7, pp. 63–93). Chichester, England: Wiley.

Bodenhausen, G. V., Kramer, G. P., & Suesser, K. (1994). Happiness and stereotypic thinking in social judgement. *Journal of Personality and Social Psychology, 66*, 621–632.

Bodenhausen, G. V., Sheppard, L. A., & Kramer, G. P. (1994). Negative affect and social judgement: The differential impact of anger and sadness. *European Journal of Social Psychology, 24*, 45–62.

Bower, G. H. (1981). Mood and memory. *American Psychologist, 36*, 129–148.

Bruner, J. S., Goodnow, J. J., & Austin, G. A. (1956). *A study of thinking.* New York: Wiley.

Buck, R. (1985). Prime theory: An integrated view of motivation and emotion. *Psychological Review, 92*, 389–413.

Cacioppo, J. T., Crites, S. L., Berntson, G. G., & Coles, M. G. H. (1993). If attitudes affect how stimuli are processed, should they not affective the event-related potential? *Psychological Science, 4*, 108–112.

Cacioppo, J. T., Crites, S. L., Gardner, W. L., & Berntson, G. G. (1994). Bio-electrical echoes from evaluative categorizations: A late potential brain potential that varies as a function of negativity and extremity. *Journal of Personality and Social Psychology, 67*, 115–125.

Carroll, J. M., & Russell, J. A. (1996). Do facial expressions signal specific emotions? Judging emotion from the face in context. *Journal of Personality and Social Psychology, 70*, 205–218.

Clore, G. L., Wyer, R. S., Dienes, B., Gasper, K., Gohm, C., & Isbell, L. (2001). Affective feelings as feedback: Some cognitive consequences. In L. L. Martin & G. L. Clore (Eds.), *Mood and social cognition: Contrasting theories.* Mahwah, NJ: Lawrence Erlbaum Associates.

Corballis, M. C. (1998). Evolution of the human mind. In M. Sabourin, M. Robert, & F. Craik (Eds.), *Advances in psychological science, Vol. 2: Biological and cognitive aspects* (pp. 31–62). Hove, England UK: Psychology Press.

Crites, S. L., & Cacioppo, J. T. (1996). Electrocortical differentiation of evaluative and nonevaluative categorizations. *Psychological Science, 7*, 318–321.

De Houwer, J., & Hermans, D. (1994). Differences in the affective processing of words and pictures. *Cognition and Emotion, 8*, 1–20.

Eich, E., Kihlstrom, J. F., Bower, G. H., Forgas, J. P., Niedenthal, P. M. (2000). *Cognition and Emotion.* New York: Oxford University Press.

Ekman, P. (1994). Strong evidence for universals in facial expression: A reply to Russell's mistaken critique. *Psychological Bulletin, 115*, 268–287.

Fazio, R. H. (1993). Variability in the likelihood of automatic attitude activation: Data reanalysis and commentary on Bargh, Chaiken, Govender, and Pratto (1992). *Journal of Personality and Social Psychology, 64*, 753–765.

Fazio, R. H. (2001). On the automatic activation of associated evaluations: An overview. *Cognition and Emotion, 15*, 115–141.

Fazio, R. H., Sanbonmatsu, D. M., Powell, M. C., & Kardes, F. R. (1986). On the automatic activation of attitudes. *Journal of Personality and Social Psychology, 50*, 229–238.

Fehr, B., & Russell, J. A. (1984). The concept of emotion viewed from a prototype perspective. *Journal of Experimental Psychology, General, 113*, 464–486.

Feldman, L. A. (1995a). Variations in the circumplex structure of emotion. *Personality and Social Psychology Bulletin, 21*, 806–817.

Feldman, L. A. (1995b). Valence focus and arousal focus: Individual differences in the structure of affective experience. *Journal of Personality and Social Psychology, 69*, 153–166.

Feldman Barrett, L., & Russell, J. A., (1998). Independence and bipolarity in the structure of affect. *Journal of Personality and Social Psychology, 74,* 967–984.

Fernandez-Dols, J. M., & Carroll, J. M. (1997). Context and Meaning. In J. A. Russell & J. M. Fernandez-Dols (Eds.), *The Psychology of Facial Expression.* Cambridge, UK: Cambridge University Press.

Fiedler, K. (2000). Toward an integrative account of affecta and cognition phenomena using the BIAS computer algorithm. In J. P. Forgas (Ed.), *Feeling and thinking. The role of affect in social cognition* (pp. 223–252). Cambridge, UK: Cambridge University Press.

Fiedler, K., & Forgas, J. (1988). *Affect, Cognition and Social Behavior.* Toronto, Canada: Hogrefe.

Forgas, J. P. (1993). On making sense of odd couples: Mood effects on the perception of mismatched relationships. *Personality and Social Psychology Bulletin, 19,* 59–70.

Forgas, J. P. (1995). Strange couples: Mood effects on judgements and memory about prototypical and atypical relationships. *Personality and Social Psychology Bulletin, 21,* 747–765.

Forgas, J. P. (2000). *Feeling and thinking: The role of affect in social cognition.* Cambridge, UK: Cambridge University Press.

Forgas, J. P., & Bower, G. H. (1987) Mood effects on person-perception judgements. *Journal of Personality and Social Psychology, 53,* 53–60.

Forgas, J. P., Bower, G. H., & Krantz, S. E. (1984). The influence of mood on perceptions of social interactions. *Journal of Experimental Social Psychology, 20,* 497–513.

Forgas, J. P., & Moylan, S. (1987). After the movies: Transient mood on social judgements. *Personality and Social Psychology Bulletin, 13,* 467–477.

Forgas, J. P., & Moylan, S. J. (1991) Affective influences on stereotype judgements. *Cognition and Emotion, 5,* 379–397.

Fridlund A. J. (1990). The behavioral ecology and sociality of human faces. *Personality and Social Psychology Review, 2,* 90–122.

Fridlund, A. J. (1991). Evolution and facial action in reflex, social motive, and paralanguage. *Biological Psychology, 32,* 1–96.

Frijda, N. H. (1987). Emotion, cognitive structure, and action tendency. *Cognition and Emotion, 1,* 115–143.

Gehm, T., & Scherer, K. R. (1988). Factors determining the dimensions of subjective emotional space. In K. R. Scherer (Ed.), *Facets of emotion: Recent research* (pp. 99–114). Hillsdale, NJ: Lawrence Erlbaum Associates.

Halberstadt, J. B., & Niedenthal, P. M. (1997). Emotional state and the use of stimulus dimensions in judgement. *Journal of Personality and Social Psychology, 72,* 1017–1033.

Halberstadt, J. B., & Niedenthal, P. M. (2001). Effects of emotion concepts on perceptual memory for emotional expressions. *Journal of Personality and Social Psychology, 81,* 587–598.

Hermans, D., Baeyens, F., & Eelen, P. (1998). Odors as affective processing context for word evaluation: A case of cross-modal affective priming. *Cognition and Emotion, 12,* 601–613.

Hermans, D., De Houwer, J., Eelen, P. (1994). The affective priming effect: Automatic activation of evaluative information in memory. *Cognition and Emotion, 8,* 515–533.

Hermans, D., De Houwer, J., & Eelen, P. (1996). Evaluative decision latencies mediated by induced affective states. *Behaviour Research and Therapy, 34,* 483–488.

Hirt, E. R., Levine, G. M., McDonald, H. E., & Melton, R. J. (1997). The role of mood in quantitative and qualitative aspects of performance: Single or multiple mechanisms? *Journal of Experimental Social Psychology, 33,* 602–629.

Innes-Ker, Å. H., & Niedenthal, P. M. (in press). Emotion concepts and emotional states in social judgment and categorization. *Journal of Personality and Social Psychology.*

Isen, A. M. (1987). Positive affect, cognitive processes, and social behavior. In L. Berkowitz (Ed.), *Advances in Experimental Social Psychology, Vol. 20* (pp. 203–253). New York: Academic Press.

Isen, A. M., Shalker, T. E., Clark, M., & Karp, L. (1978) Affect, accessibility of material in memory and behavior: A cognitive loop? *Journal of Personality and Social Psychology, 36,* 1–12.

Izard, C. E. (1994). Innate and universal facial expressions: Evidence from developmental and cross-cultural research. *Psychological Bulletin, 115*, 288–299.

Johnson, J. E., & Leventhal, H. (1974). Effects of accurate expectations and behavioral instructions on reactions during a noxious medical examination. *Journal of Personality and Social Psychology, 29*, 710–718.

Klauer, K. C., & Musch, J. (in press). Does sunshine prime loyal? Affective priming in the naming task. *Quarterly Journal of Experimental Psychology, 54A*, 727–751.

Klauer, K. C., Rossnagel, C., & Musch, J. (1997). List-context effects in evaluative priming. *Journal of Experimental Psychology: Learning, Memory, and Cognition, 23*, 246–255.

Kosslyn, S. M. (1976). Can imagery be distinguished from other forms of conceptual representation? Evidence from studies of information retrieval times. *Memory & Cognition, 4*, 291–297.

Kosslyn, S. M. (1980). *Image and Mind.* Cambridge, MA: Harvard University Press.

Laird, L. D., Wagener, J. J., Halal, M., & Szegda, M. (1982). Remembering what you feel: Effects of emotion on memory. *Journal of Personality and Social Psychology, 42*, 646–657.

Lang, P. J. (1979). A bio-informational theory of emotional imagery. *Psychophysiology, 16*, 495–512.

Lang, P. J. (1984). Cognition in emotion: Concept and action. In C. Izard, J. Kagan, & R. B. Zajonc (Eds.), *Emotions, cognition, and behavior.* New York: Cambridge University Press.

Leventhal, H., Brown, P., Shacham, S., & Engquist, G. (1979). Effects of preparatory information about sensations, threat of pain, and attention on cold pressor distress. *Journal of Personality and Social Psychology, 37*, 688–714.

Leventhal, H., & Scherer, K. (1987). The relationship of emotion to cognition: A functional approach to a semantic controversy. *Cognition and Emotion, 1*, 3–28.

Mackie, D. M., & Worth, L. T. (1991). Feeling good, but not thinking straight: The impact of positive mood on persuasion. In J. P. Forgas (Ed.), *Emotion and Social Judgement* (pp. 201–219). Oxford, UK: Pergamon Press.

Martin, L. L., Abend, T., Sedikides, C., & Green, J. D. (1997). How would I feel if . . . ? Mood as input to a role fulfillment evaluation process. *Journal of Personality and Social Psychology, 73*, 242–253.

Medin, D. D., & Schaffer, M. (1978). A context theory of classification learning. *Psychological Review, 85*, 207–238.

Mendolia, M., & Kleck, R. E. (1993). Effects of talking about a stressful event on arousal: Does what we talk about make a difference? *Journal of Personality and Social Psychology, 64*, 283–292.

Mesquita, B., & Frijda, N. H. (1992). Cultural variations in emotions: A review. *Psychological Bulletin, 112*, 179–204.

Niedenthal, P. M., & Halberstadt, J. B. (1995). The acquisition and structure of emotional response categories. In D. L. Medin (Ed.), *The psychology of learning and motivation, Vol. 33* (pp. 23–64). New York: Academic Press.

Niedenthal, P. M., & Halberstadt, J. B. (2000a). Grounding categories in emotional response. In J. Forgas (Ed.), *Feeling and thinking: The role of affect in social cognition.* Cambridge, UK: Cambridge University Press.

Niedenthal, P. M., & Halberstadt, J. B. (2000b). Emotional response as conceptual coherence. In E. Eich, J. F. Kihlstrom, G. H. Bower, J. P. Forgas, P. M. Niedenthal, *Cognition/emotion interactions.* New York: Oxford University Press.

Niedenthal, P. M., Halberstadt, J. B., & Innes-Ker, Å. H. (1999). Emotional response categorization. *Psychological Review, 106*, 337–361.

Niedenthal, P. M., Halberstadt, J. B., Margolin, J., & Innes-Ker, Å. H. (2000). Emotional State and the Detection of Change in Facial Expression of Emotion. *European Journal of Social Psychology, 30*, 211–222.

Niedenthal, P. M., & Kitayama, S. (1994). *The heart's eye: Emotional influences in perception and attention.* San Diego, CA: Academic Press.

Niedenthal, P. M., Ric, F., & Krauth-Gruber, S. (2002). Explaining emotion congruence (and its absence) in terms of perceptual simulation. *Psychological Inquiry, 13,* 80–83.

Niedenthal, P. M., & Setterlund, M. B. (1994). Emotion congruence in perception. *Personality and Social Psychology Bulletin, 20,* 401–410.

Niedenthal, P. M., Setterlund, M. B., & Jones, D. E. (1994). Emotional organization of perceptual memory. In P. M. Niedenthal & S. Kitayama (Eds.), *The heart's eye: Emotional influences in perception and attention* (pp. 87–113). San Diego, CA: Academic Press.

Niedenthal, P. M., & Showers, C. (1991) The perception and processing of the affective information and its influences on social judgement. In J. P. Forgas (Ed.), *Emotion and Social Judgements* (pp. 125–143). Oxford: Pergamon Press, Inc.

Oatley, K., & Johnson-Laird, P. N. (1987). Towards a cognitive theory of emotions. *Cognition and Emotion, 1,* 29–50.

Ortony, A., & Clore, G. L. (1989). Emotions, moods, and conscious awareness: Comment on Johnson-Laird and Oatley's "The language of emotions: An analysis of a semantic field." *Cognition and Emotion, 3,* 125–169.

Ortony, A., Clore, G. L., & Collins, A. (1988). *The Cognitive Structure of Emotions.* New York: Cambridge University Press.

Petty, R. E., Gleicher, F., & Baker, S. M. (1991). Multiple roles for affect in persuasion. In J. P. Forgas (Ed.), *Emotion and social judgement* (pp. 181–200). Oxford, UK: Pergamon Press.

Roseman, I. J., Antoniou, A. A., & Jose, P. E. (1996). Appraisal determinants of emotions: Constructing a more accurate and comprehensive theory. *Cognition and Emotion, 10,* 241–277.

Russell, J. A. (1980). A circumplex model of affect. *Journal of Personality and Social Psychology, 39,* 1161–1178.

Russell, J. A. (1994). Is there universal recognition of emotion from facial expression? A review of the cross-cultural studies. *Psychological Bulletin, 115,* 102–141.

Scherer, K. R. (1988). *Facets of Emotion. Recent Research.* Hillsdale, NJ: Lawrence Erlbaum Associates.

Scherer, K. R. (1999). Appraisal theory. In T. Dalgleish and M. Power (Eds.), *Handbook of cognition and emotion.* New York: John Wiley & Sons.

Scherer, K. R., Wallbott, H. G., & Summerfield, A. B. (1986). *Experiencing emotion.* Cambridge, UK: Cambridge University Press.

Schiffenbauer, A. (1974). Effect of observer's emotional state on judgements of the emotional state of others. *Journal of Personality and Social Psychology, 30,* 31–35.

Schwarz, N., & Bless, H. (1991). Happy and mindless, but sad and smart? The impact of affective states on analytic reasoning. In J. Forgas (Ed.), *Emotion and social judgement* (pp. 55–71). Oxford, UK: Pergamon Press.

Schwarz, N., & Clore, G. L. (1983). Mood, misattribution, and judgements of well-being: Informative and directive functions of affective states. *Journal of Personality and Social Psychology, 45,* 513–523.

Semin, G. R. (2000). Communication: Language as an implementational device for cognition. *European Journal of Social Psychology, 30,* 595–612.

Semin, G. R., Görts, C. A., Nandram, S., & Semin-Goossens, A. (2002). Cultural perspectives on the linguistic representation of emotion and emotion events. *Cognition and Emotion, 16,* 11–28.

Shaver, P., Schwartz., J., Kirson, D., & O'Connor, G. (1987). Emotion knowledge: Further exploration of a prototype approach. *Journal of Personality and Social Psychology, 52,* 1061–1086.

Smith, C. A., & Ellsworth, P. C. (1987). Patterns of appraisal and emotion related to taking an exam. *Journal of Personality and Social Psychology, 52,* 475–488.

Smith, C. A., Haynes, K. N., Lazarus, R. S., & Pope, L. K. (1993). In search of the "hot" cognitions: Attributions, appraisals, and their relation to emotion. *Journal of Personality and Social Psychology, 65,* 916–929.

Solomon, K. O., & Barsalou, L. W. (2000). Grounding concepts in perceptual simulation: II. Evidence from property verification. *Under revision.*

Spruyt, A., Hermans, D., De Houwer, J., & Eelen, P. (2001). Explaining the affective priming effect: Affective priming in a picture naming task. Manuscript submitted for publication.

Srull, T. K., & Wyer, R. S. (1979). The role of category accessibility in the interpretation of information about persons: Some determinants and implications. *Journal of Personality and Social Psychology, 37,* 1660–1672.

Stapel, D. A., & Koomen, W. (2000). How far do we go beyond the information given? The impact of knowledge activation on interpretation and inference. *Journal of Personality and Social Psychology, 78,* 19–37.

Stapel, D. A., Koomen, W., & Van der Plight, J. (1996). The referents of trait inferences: The impact of trait concepts versus actor-trait links on subsequent judgements. *Journal of Personality and Social Psychology, 70,* 437–450.

Strack, F., Schwarz, N., & Gschneidinger, E. (1985). Happiness and reminiscing: The role of time perspective, affect, and mode of thinking. *Journal of Personality and Social Psychology, 49,* 1460–1469.

Tomasello, M., Kruger, A., & Ratner, H. (1993). Cultural learning. *Behavioral and Brain Sciences, 16,* 495–552.

Velton, E. (1968). A laboratory task for induction of mood states. *Behavioral Research and Therapy, 6,* 473–482.

Wallbott, H. G. (1988). In and out of context—Influences of facial expression and context information on emotion attributions. *British Journal of Social Psychology, 27,* 357–369.

Wentura, D. (1999). Activation and inhibition of affective information: Evidence for negative priming in the evaluation task. *Cognition and Emotion, 13,* 65–91.

Weisfeld, G. E., & Beresford, J. M. (1982). Erectness of posture as an indicator of dominance or success in humans. *Motivation and Emotion, 6,* 113–131.

Wu, L. L., & Barsalou, L. W. (2000). Grounding concepts in perceptual simulation: Evidence from property generation. *Under revision.*

Wyer, R. S., & Carltson, D. E. (1979). *Social cognition, inference, and attribution.* Hillsdale, NJ: Lawrence Erlbaum Associates.

Chapter 13

The Parallel Worlds of Affective Concepts and Feelings*

Gerald L. Clore
University of Virginia

Stanley Colcombe
University of Illinois at Urbana-Champaign

In conversation, what is left unsaid is sometimes more powerful than what is said, because the hearer must supply the meaning. When the hearer does so, the message can be especially compelling. We suggest that this process is evident in certain instances of unconscious affective priming. Specifically, when the source of an activated affective meaning is not apparent, it may be experienced as having an internal source. This, we argue, gives unconscious affective primes their interesting and powerful effects. In the current chapter, we summarize some of our own recent work in this area and suggest some principles for understanding the work of others. In general, we take a skeptical view of some of the claims that have been made about suboptimal priming. Rather than displaying hidden emotional processes (e.g., Bargh, 1997; Murphy & Zajonc, 1993), we assume that subliminal stimulation involves quite ordinary cognitive processes (Clore & Ketelaar, 1997). This is not to say that unconscious priming has ordinary effects. But the intriguing effects that it does produce, we suggest, may be understood by thinking of the process as the activation of semantic meaning without episodic constraints,[1] a message without a messenger, one might say.

We are concerned in this chapter with affective feelings and affective concepts, and with their parallel effects on judgment and processing. Moods are affective states that are temporally extended and that have no salient object or focus. As a result, their possible meanings are relatively un-

---

* Support is acknowledged from NSF Grant SBR 96-01298 and NIMH Grant MH50074.
[1]This conception arose initially in conversation with Leonard Martin in the Spring of 1984.

constrained. We propose that the information from induced mood and from primed concepts can have similarly broad influences, because both are unconstrained by salient knowledge about their sources.

Emotions are also affective states, but, in contrast to moods, they do have salient objects. This feature makes them powerful in ways that moods are not. The experience of emotion provides insistent information that some specific object is good or bad in some specific way. The experience is located in the body, but its meaning is situated in the world. As a result, emotions can both motivate and direct problem-focused coping. In contrast, the diffuse feelings that characterize moods have no clear anchor either in the body or in the world. Thus, emotions can be powerful because they have focus, whereas moods lack both urgency and focus. But this affective myopia makes them powerful in a different way. Moods can have broad and general effects precisely because they lack such constraints (e.g., Schwarz & Clore, 1983). Experiences of good and bad moods convey information that something (possibly everything) relevant to oneself is good or bad in unspecified ways. A decade or two of research on mood by social and cognitive psychologists shows that the unconstrained nature of the information involved allows mood to play a role in judgment and decision-making, as well as in cognitive processing more generally (see Clore, Schwarz, & Conway, 1994, for a review).

This chapter is not primarily about mood and emotion, but about the mood-like effects that sometimes occur when evaluative concepts are unconsciously primed. We propose that moods and primed evaluative concepts have parallel effects, because affective feelings and affective meaning obey the same rules (Clore, Gasper, & Garvin, 2001). Our basic argument rests on two hypotheses, the first of which is: *Like affective feelings of mood, unconsciously primed affective meaning can have broad influence, because the value conveyed about potential objects is generally unconstrained by awareness of its source.* This hypothesis concerns the observation that both mood-based feelings and subtly primed concepts can have general effects on evaluative judgments. In addition to explaining the generality of their effects, we also need to explain their compellingness. Hence, the second hypothesis is that: *The information from affective mood and the information from affective priming share important phenomenological qualities that make them both especially compelling.* We suggest that the feelings and thoughts are persuasive, because in the absence of a salient, external source, they are experienced as internally generated.

EXPLANATIONS OF PARALLELISM

The phenomenon of interest concerns the parallelism in the results of mood studies and priming studies. Possible explanations for the parallelism are (1) that both are really examples of conceptual priming, (2) that both are really examples of induced feeling, or (3) that both are caused by a third factor shared by affective concepts and affective feelings. The most common approach has been the first of these, explaining the effects of mood on judgment in terms of cognitive priming (Bower, Montiero, & Gilligan, 1978; Forgas & Bower, 1988; Isen, Shalker, Clark, & Karp, 1978). The priming hypothesis holds that mood selectively activates mood-congruent material in memory, which in turn leads to mood-congruent judgments. In contrast, the second approach posits the reverse causal flow, suggesting that subliminal priming works by inducing affect (e.g., Bargh, 1997; Winkielman, Zajonc, & Schwarz, 1997). That approach holds that subliminal exposure to affective concepts allows the affective part (assumed to be fast), but not the cognitive part (assumed to be slow) to be processed. Thus, instead of assuming that induced feelings prime affective concepts, this approach assumes that primed affective concepts induce feelings (or some unconscious version of affect). In contrast to either of these, we propose the third possibility, which assumes that induced mood and subliminal affective priming have comparable effects because they are alternative forms of the same information, namely, they are alternative representations of value (see Table 13.1). According to this view, the influence of the induced feelings and primed concepts flows from the fact that both are unconstrained in their source and hence in their applicability. We turn to this issue next.

CONSTRAINTS AND AFFECT APPLICABILITY

Our proposal is that affective feelings and evaluative concepts are both ways of representing goodness and badness. Positive feelings serve as experiential information that something about the object of one's attention is good

TABLE 13.1
Comparison of Explanations for Mood
and Priming Effects on Judgment

Phenomenon	Alternative Theories	Explanation
Unconscious affective priming influences evaluative judgment	Zajonc-Bargh-Winkielman	Affective concepts elicit (unconscious) affect
	Affect-as-Information	Affective concepts convey evaluative information
Mood Induction influences evaluative judgment	Bower-Forgas-Isen	Moods activate affective concepts in declarative memory
	Affect-as-Information	Affective feelings convey evaluative information

in some way. Similarly, positive concepts that come to mind may serve as conceptual information that something is good. Induced mood and subliminal affective priming both convey information about value, and neither typically has an object. We argue that the critical element in both mood studies and unconscious priming studies is this lack of constraint, which allows wide latitude in the situated meaning of affective feelings and affective thoughts. For example, when diverse primes are used in either unconscious or subtle priming studies, evaluative meaning may be the only thing they have in common, so that positivity and negativity become primed with no well-defined source. Being unconstrained as to its source, such primed evaluative meaning may be experienced as a reaction to whatever is currently in focus. Similarly, and for the same reason, the feelings of mood may also be experienced as a reaction to whatever is in mind at the time (Clore, Gasper & Garrin, 2001a).

A consequence of this lack of constraint is that, depending on one's focus, one may experience affective feelings and thoughts as information about one's current situation, about one's general knowledge, or about one's initial responses on a task, or, if engaged in routine self-monitoring, as information about oneself. Thus, positive mood or activated positive concepts, for example, may be experienced as evidence of the benignness of the situation (Schwarz & Clore, 1996), of the applicability of one's general knowledge (Bless, Clore, Golisano, Rabel, & Schwarz, 1996), of the correctness of one's expectations and initial responses (Clore, Wyer, Dienes, Gasper, Gohm, & Isbell, 2001; Wyer, Clore, & Isbell, 1999), or perhaps of one's general self-confidence or well-being.

In line with these considerations, various forms of experiential and conceptual information can be differentiated in terms of the presence and absence of constraints or limits on the range of possible objects. Table 13.2 depicts four affective conditions that differ with respect to whether they have a salient object and whether they refer only to the present.

This table indicates that *emotions* and *attitudes* differ from *moods* and *affective temperament* in part because the former confer value on specific objects, whereas the latter leave the object of value unspecified. Looking at the table the other way, *emotions* and *moods* both differ from *attitudes* and *affective*

TABLE 13.2
Object Specificity and Temporal Duration as Constraints
on the Meaning of Experiential Information

Sources of Felt Affective Information		
	Current	*Chronic*
Salient Object	Emotions	Attitudes
No Salient Object	Moods	Temperament

TABLE 13.3
Object Specificity and Temporal Duration as Constraints on the
Meaning of Information From Activated Affective Concepts

	Sources of Conceptual Affective Information	
	Current	Chronic
Salient Object	Perceptions	Beliefs
No Salient Object	Primes	Traits

temperament in that the value conferred by the former is constrained to be about something in the present (i.e., they are states), whereas the object of value for attitudes and temperaments need not be in the present (i.e., they are dispositions).

The logic about the constraints on the meaning of affective feelings also applies to affective concepts. An analogous table spells out the implications for ideas rather than feelings. According to Table 13.3, the affective concepts involved in everyday affective *thoughts* and *beliefs* have objects; that is, they are generally about something. In contrast, subtly *primed affective concepts* and those chronically activated in *affective traits* do not have salient objects. As a result, the possible application of their affective meaning is relatively unconstrained. Looking at the table the other way, *thoughts* and *primes* may be immediate and fleeting, whereas *affective beliefs* and *traits* endure and may or may not be activated in a given moment. As a result, the evaluative meanings rooted in affective beliefs and traits are not as temporally constrained as those rooted in perception.

We believe that the parallelism of the conditions that differentiate among forms of felt affect and forms of conceptualized affect helps explain the parallelism in the dynamics of induced feelings and primed concepts. Thus, Tables 13.2 and 13.3 represent a proposal in which the principles of the affect-as-information approach (Clore, et al., 2001) can accommodate affective concepts as well as affective feelings. In both cases, the information conveyed by affective concepts and feelings depends on attributions about their sources.[2]

The tables suggest that we have different labels for feelings and accessible concepts depending on whether they are current or chronic and whether they are experienced as being about a particular object or not. Thus, primed elements of meaning should obey the same principles as mood-based affect. This proposal has been formalized (Clore et al., 2001) as the Episodic Con-

---

[2]Appealing to causal attributions does not implicate active, explicit cognitive operations. Attributions are often implicit, existing simply as an implication of whatever world knowledge a situation elicits or whatever perceptual grouping arises on the basis of proximity in time and space, as outlined by gestalt psychologists (e.g., Heider, 1958).

straint Principle, which says that, *Primed concepts and affective feelings have similar effects when the obscurity of their sources leaves their potential meanings similarly unconstrained.* Several recent studies test whether these principles (from an informational analysis of mood) also provide an informational analysis of subliminal priming. These are described in the final sections.

We have focused in this discussion largely on one kind of constraint, namely, whether or not affective feelings and concepts have objects. This focus is appropriate because it is one of the primary ways in which feelings of mood and the subliminal priming of meaning are similar. But before proceeding, let us note that we assume that the distinctiveness of particular emotional feelings reflects the unique meaning of the situations in which such emotions arise, and this distinctiveness is also an important constraint on their indiscriminant applicability. In a similar way, the evaluative meaning of affective concepts is also constrained in its influence on other evaluations, not only by whether or not it is cognitively bound to a particular object, but also by its descriptive meaning. Thus, the word *intelligent* describes a particular kind of goodness, and *kind* describes another. Saying that someone is intelligent carries little or no implication about their kindness. We return to this point later, but first we turn to the second characteristic that induced moods and primed thoughts have in common, namely, that they are credible because they are experienced as one's own.

SPONTANEITY AND CONVINCINGNESS

William James (1890), referring to his own depression, commented on the "appalling convincingness of feelings." We suggest that the information from feelings is convincing because it is experienced as arising spontaneously from within. We know from research on persuasion (Petty & Cacioppo, 1986), that source credibility is an important factor in persuasiveness, and we presumably find ourselves to be particularly credible sources. More specifically, we find our automatic, unbidden reactions to be convincing. This is true both interpersonally and intrapersonally. We find compliments from others more credible when they appear spontaneous than when they seem dictated by other considerations. According to attribution theory (e.g., Jones & Nisbett, 1971), we usually see our own behavior as due to situational factors. However, for subliminally primed ideas and thoughts, there is usually no support in awareness for making a situational attribution, although a situational attribution would be appropriate. As in the case of feelings, the apparent spontaneity and internal origin of subliminally primed ideas should make them compelling.

A dramatic illustration of the credibility of spontaneous inner experience comes from disorders such as the Capgrass syndrome in which individuals become convinced that everyone close to them, including spouses, friends, and family are imposters (Feinberg, 2001). As a result of stroke damage, visual recognition of others can remain intact, although the connections that allow one to experience affective reactions to them do not. To cope with the distressing experience of recognition without affection, otherwise sensible individuals find themselves entertaining bizarre hypotheses that their loved ones have become occupied by extraterrestrials or are clones of themselves. The extreme attempts of sufferers to make sense of their feelings suggest that our spontaneous inner experience is the one source of information we rarely question.

We are arguing that the information from induced mood and the information from primed ideas are similarly believable when they are experienced as spontaneous and hence as one's own. Of course, in the case of unconscious priming, this proposition requires elaboration. Is a phenomenological explanation applicable to unconscious stimuli? We believe that it is, because although the unconscious primes are not experienced, the meaning they activate is experienced as an attribute of the next thing to occupy attention. We argue that when feelings and activated meanings are cognitively unconstrained, they may be experienced as attributes of whatever is in mind at the time. We turn to this issue next.

Affect-as-Information About Objects

Our perceptual system is dedicated to modeling the world of objects around us. By and large, people do not dwell on sensations by themselves. They serve as a means of knowing about other things, rather than as ends in themselves. In a similar manner, affective feelings and meanings provide information about the objects of one's attention, functioning more like adjectives than like nouns. They represent the goodness or badness of things. They are experienced as the goodness or badness of objects, including, of course, of aspects of ourselves and our responses when these are in focus.

We are arguing that in the canonical situation, affective information is experienced as being about some object. In addition, we are suggesting that the object about which affect provides information depends on what is salient at the time. Indeed, emotions would be even more problematic than they are if the information they provided was about something other than our current cognitive content.

Higgins (1996, p. 161) makes a similar point about the informativeness of thoughts that come to mind: "People naturally assume, for example, that a category comes to mind in the presence of a stimulus because the stimulus is a member of the category. This is a reasonable and adaptive assumption. Indeed, a loss of this assumption would create an existential crisis."

Affective Montage

A useful metaphor for thinking about how we form a single reality from individual experiences is that of montage in film-making. The montage effect occurs when two images following one another closely in time are grouped together in experience. It is this kind of effect, along with other visual illusions, that fascinated the Gestalt psychologists of the 19th century. They observed that we automatically perceive things as grouped together when they occupy our minds simultaneously as a result of being associated in time and space. In early silent films, this montage effect became an indispensable tool for story telling. They discovered that images of a menacing figure followed by images of a heroine shrinking in fear tended to be experienced as a single event. Indeed, the tendency is so pronounced, that when such a connection was not desired, film-makers had to insert a brief delay from one scene to the next to disrupt the effect. Presumably our ability to find coherence in the flow of sounds in speech or in music involves a similar principle.

In subliminal priming too, affective meanings tend to become attached to whatever else is in mind at the time. The meaning that is primed is unconstrained because the brief exposure times used in priming along with backward masking procedures tend to interfere with the transfer of the experience to memory. As a result of this interference, neither the stimulus nor the exposure event can be explicitly recalled (Bornstein, 1992). Some decoding often does take place, however, so that if the stimulus is similar to something that has stored meaning, that stored information may be activated. The information most likely to be activated is a gross categorization of the stimulus as good or bad, a process that Bargh (1997) has dubbed the *automatic evaluation effect.*

Bargh's terminology implies that one is actively engaged in some kind of bottom-up evaluation process. However, most of what we encounter already has evaluative meaning, so that the *automatic evaluation effect* usually involves reading off evaluative meaning that is already inherent in the meaning of the stimulus. It is not clear, therefore, to what extent there is another active unconscious evaluation process. Moreover, it is not clear whether the effect of such procedures is to cause activation to spread to evaluatively similar stimuli in memory (Greenwald, Draine, & Abrams, 1996), to prepare one to make evaluatively similar responses (Klinger, Burton, & Pitts, 2000), or simply to cause one to make response errors (Franks, Roskos-Ewoldsen, Bilbrey, & Roskos-Ewoldsen, 1999). In this regard, Fiedler (chap. , this volume) points out that priming accounts have generally focused only on category activation, and that they need also to consider the explicit or implicit instructions about what to do with primed material. Under different conditions, the same prime may result in either assimilation or contrast. The correct interpretation presumably depends on the procedure used. In our discussion, we assume that repeated suboptimal presentation of positive or negative stimuli activates evaluative meaning. Being objectless, it may become attached to whatever comes to mind next. When a novel or neutral stimulus is presented next (e.g., Murphy & Zajonc, 1993), the primed evaluation may adhere to it, so that it is rated more positively or negatively than it otherwise would have been.

Summary

In this section, we have argued that: (1) Affective feelings of mood and unconsciously primed affective meanings can both have broad influence because their true sources are not salient; (2) the apparent spontaneity of the feelings of mood and of primed meaning makes the information they convey especially convincing; (3) because evaluative reactions are ordinarily about something, the information from induced feelings and primed concepts are readily attached to whatever is in mind at the time. These common properties should allow mood and subliminally primed concepts to produce parallel effects, the topic to which we turn next. We discuss first explanations for the effects of mood on judgment and then review issues about priming and judgment.

PARALLELISM IN STUDIES OF JUDGMENT

Mood and Judgment

One of the most reliable effects of mood is the tendency for people to make mood-congruent evaluative judgments. Investigators often use films or music to induce mood so that individuals experience positive or negative feelings that are independent of whatever cognitive content is also active at the time (e.g., Gouaux, 1971). There are two primary explanations for the resulting mood-congruent judgments, one that proposes that feelings of mood are used directly as information in judgment, and one that assumes that the role of mood is indirect. In the latter view, mood primes cognitive content, which in turn is the basis of judgments.

Affect-as-Information.   The affect-as-information approach (Clore, 1992; Clore et al., 2001a, 2001b; Schwarz & Clore, 1983, 1988, 1996) assumes that for many evaluative judgments, the process is one in which feelings are used directly as answers to the implicit question, "How do I feel about that?" Tests of this view often vary the attributions that participants make for their feelings (e.g., Keltner, Locke, & Audrain, 1993). The point of such experiments is to show that mood effects depend on the apparent information conveyed in feelings about people's reactions to objects of judgment. When, at the moment of judgment, the feelings are experienced as due to something else, then mood effects on judgment tend to disappear.

Critiques. Because of its emphasis on the role of attributions and on the manipulation of attributions in experiments, the affect-as-information position is sometimes misunderstood to imply that in everyday life, the objects of one's feelings are arbitrary, and hence show great plasticity. On the contrary, we assume that emotional reactions are usually firmly wedded to the objects to which they are responses and are therefore quite resistant to misattribution and change (e.g., Gasper & Clore, 1998). Mood is a useful tool for examining the role of attribution in affective judgments, because the feelings of mood (as opposed to those of emotions) are not already dedicated to specific objects.

The position is also sometimes misunderstood to imply that mood effects should occur only under conditions in which inquisitive participants would be unable to deduce the true cause of their feelings. The critical variable, however, is not whether the true cause would be obvious to an analytic participant or an uninvolved observer, but whether the individuals actually involved focus on the feelings and their causes at the right moment. In most such experiments, induced moods are sufficiently mild and participants are sufficiently preoccupied that feelings become objects of focus only when evaluative judgments are called for.

It may also be important to clarify what is implied in an informational analysis of affective influence. Because almost anything might be classified as information, does the assertion that affect serves as information say anything? Does it rule out anything? These are fair questions for any scientific claim. One claim of the affect-as-information approach is simply that judgments and decisions are often based directly on feelings, which we view as embodied information. An alternative hypothesis is that judgments are not based on how one feels, but on what one knows about the object of judgment. In that view, the role of affect is to make affect-congruent beliefs more accessible in memory. In the first view, affective feeling is the embodied information on which judgments are made, and in the second, affect activates in memory the information on which judgments are made. The claim, then, is not that judgments are based on information, which would be empty, but rather that affect can itself be that information.

Affect-as-Prime. An alternative account of mood effects on judgment (e.g., Bower et al., 1978; Forgas & Bower, 1988; Isen et al., 1978), focuses on the hypothesis that mood influences judgment indirectly by priming mood-congruent concepts and beliefs in memory. It assumes that judgments are made on a biased sample of information from memory, which is automatically activated by mood.

Traditional judgment and decision theory has also assumed that judgments are based on stored beliefs about objects of judgment (e.g., Anderson, 1971; Fishbein & Ajzen, 1975). Social-cognitive accounts too assume that judgments reflect the accessibility of particular concepts (e.g., Higgins, Rholes, & Jones, 1977). Thus, when psychologists turned their attention to mood, it was natural to assume that mood effects also were reflections of the accessibility in memory of mood-congruent concepts and beliefs (Bower, 1981; Isen, 1984).

Critiques. The priming view has the advantage of incorporating mood within general cognitive theory (Bower, 1981). Also, it has stimulated a great deal of research. Some evidence, however, seems to conflict with a memory-based approach. For example, little or no relationship is generally found between memory and judgment, leading to the inference that many judgments may not be based on memory (Wyer & Srull, 1989). Also, if mood effects are due to priming, then mood effects (like priming effects) should occur only at encoding (Srull & Wyer, 1979), but mood effects have been shown to occur when mood is introduced at the judgment stage (Clore & Wilkin, 1985; Fiedler & Stroehm, 1986). In addition, if mood congruent effects occur through selective retrieval from memory, they should be found only when both mood-congruent and mood-incongruent material exist in memory, so that one or the other can be selectively activated (Bower, 1981; Isen et al., 1978). However, some research (Schwarz, Robbins, & Clore, 1985) shows that mood effects may be just as large for affectively homogeneous stimuli as for mixed stimuli, suggesting that a biased selection of material from memory may not be the mediator of mood effects. In addition, a wealth of evidence has emerged from other sources suggesting that affective and "visceral" factors are used directly in judgment (e.g., Clore et al., 1994; Loewenstein, 1996).

More generally, the basic premise of priming accounts (that affective feelings automatically prime material from declarative memory) is not as well-documented as generally assumed. A review of the evidence (Wyer et al., 1999) shows that studies have often inadvertently confounded primed mood-congruent concepts with induced feelings of mood. Studies that have disentangled feelings from concepts (e.g., Parrott & Sabini, 1990) find that the effects on memory are carried by the concepts and not by the feelings. Thus, although mood-congruent content may play a role as one attempts to understand one's feelings about an object of judgment, such activation of mood-congruent cognitive material is elaborative rather than automatic. For these reasons, we are not inclined to view primed concepts as the primary explanation for the effects of mood on judgment (but see Forgas, 2001, for a clear statement of an alternate view).

It should be noted that Forgas's (2001) current framework includes both affect-as-information and priming explanations in one framework. The affect infusion model classifies mood effects as either "heuristic" or "substantive," and identifies affect-as-information as relevant to heuristic effects, and mood-congruent priming as relevant to substantive processing. Forgas (2001) reported evidence against a heuristic, interpretation by showing that mood effects are more likely to occur when judgments take longer to make. This evidence is inconsistent with the use of mood as a short-cut or heuristic. However, it also seems inconsistent with the hypothesis that affect influences judgment through automatic priming, because that process should be very rapid. Presumably, the time-consuming part of the mood-based judgments could reflect either the time to formulate thoughts about one's feelings for use as retrieval cues, or the time to integrate embodied and conceptual affective information into one judgment. More important, as Wyer et al. (1999) indicate, affect-as-information processes are not restricted to heuristic processing. Rather, how we feel about something is often the information of choice in judgments. Thus, affect-as-information processes need to be included as substantive processes of judgment.

In this section, we have indicated that there is ample data to show that mood influences evaluative judgments. In addition, we have digressed to compare two of the explanations for such effects. In the next section, we change the topic from mood influences on judgment to affective priming influences on judgment. Specifically, we examine how priming effects that parallel those of mood emerge when suboptimal affective priming activates information about value that is similarly unconstrained in its object, but which is conceptual rather than embodied.

Priming and Judgment

Within social psychology, priming paradigms have been the methodological mainstay of social cognition for more than 20 years (e.g., Higgins et al., 1977; Higgins, 1996). The underlying idea is that that concepts vary in their cognitive accessibility, and that such variations in accessibility explain many social judgment phenomena (Wyer & Srull, 1989). In their original study, Higgins et al. (1977) asked participants to engage in a color-naming task in which they were exposed to several evaluative terms that served as primes. Afterward, they read an ambiguous passage about a person named Donald, and were asked to give their impression. The passage allowed them to see Donald either positively or negatively. The results showed that as long as the primes were the same words as those used to rate the character, they influenced the ratings. However, no evaluative priming occurred for traits unless they shared descriptive meaning. Thus, there was evidence for descriptive priming, but not for evaluative priming. That is, the applicability of primed evaluative meanings was limited by the salience of the primed descriptive meaning, suggesting that evaluative priming might not occur when respondents have some awareness of the priming stimuli.

Storbeck and Robinson (2001) have shown that when descriptive priming and affective priming are assessed independently, descriptive priming takes precedence over affective priming. In four experiments, they showed that descriptive priming trumps evaluative priming in lexical decision tasks and object identification tasks regardless of whether the stimuli are words or pictures.

Other research is generally consistent with these findings (see Wyer & Srull, 1989 for a review). There are many demonstrations of descriptive priming in which, for example, exposure to synonyms of a term such as *hostile* on one task elevates ratings of that same attribute (hostility) in subsequent judgments. However, such studies do not show general evaluative priming, because they do not find evidence of similarly negative ratings on other trait dimensions. Of course, if the other trait ratings were collected after having rated someone as *hostile*, then the ratings on hostility might serve as a basis for other negative ratings. However, it is important to distinguish real affective priming (e.g., the increased accessibility of the concept *hostile* after earlier use of other terms with hostile meaning) from mere evaluative inference (inferring other negative traits from one's perception of the person as hostile).

By contrast, using non-optimal priming, Krosnick, Betz, Jussim, and Lynn (1992) did show that exposure to evaluative primes resulted in prime-congruent evaluations of liking for a person appearing in a subsequent neutral photograph. The primes were emotional pictures, and they were presented subliminally. The results suggest that true evaluative priming might occur provided that primes are presented subliminally, because participants would remain unaware of the descriptive content that would otherwise constrain the evaluative priming.

In general, we assume that processing a word used as a prime activates all of its various elements of meaning, its semantic associates, and so on. This also apparently happens during ordinary reading. Such diffuse activation does not cause confusion in reading, because previously encountered words place constraints on which of the possible meanings and nuances emerge. Thus constrained, only the contextually relevant aspects of meaning emerge into consciousness. But in unconscious priming (suboptimal exposure) procedures, the meaning that emerges from an exposed word is presumably less finely tuned by context.

With optimal (conscious) exposure times, the descriptive meaning of the primes often dominates the evaluative aspects, resulting in descriptive, but not evaluative priming. However, if the priming terms were evaluatively more extreme, so that descriptive meanings were not dominant, then general evaluative priming might be more likely. Evidence consistent with that possibility has been reported by Stapel and Koomen (2000), who found that when evaluatively more extreme stimuli are used as primes, the evaluative as well as descriptive implications of the concepts are activated. Extreme primes (*malevolent, warm,* etc.) increased the accessibility of the general evaluative concepts of *good* and *bad* that they exemplified. Once activated, these concepts stimulated participants to interpret the target's behavior along specific trait dimensions in a manner that was evaluatively consistent with them.

It should be noted that Bargh (1997) proposed that extremity of evaluation is not a factor in affective priming. He argued that the same effects occur with mild or extreme evaluative primes. Indeed, he argued for a separate, precognitive stage in which people categorize stimuli into simple good or bad categories. However, the data reviewed by Klauer and Musch (chap. XX, this volume) show that investigators differ with respect to whether they do or do not find effects for evaluative extremity.

Additional questions have arisen concerning whether affective priming occurs on nonevaluative tasks (Fazio, 2001). Bargh, Chaiken, Raymond, and Hymes (1996) reported evaluative congruence effects on latencies for pronouncing target words after exposure to evaluatively similar and dissimilar priming words. However, some others have been unable to find such effects (e.g., Klauer, 1998) or have found the reverse (e.g., Glaser & Banaji, 1999). More important, as investigators have begun to examine affective priming using different tasks, it has become apparent that priming paradigms are not about stimulus meaning alone. Wentura and Rothermund (chap. 3, this volume) suggest that the affect system is concerned with stimulus meaning, not in the abstract, but in the service of behavior. As a result, measures of affective priming are necessarily also measures of the relevance of stimuli to possible responses. Indeed, Wentura (2000) found that he could produce reversals in affective congruence or incongruence in a lexical decision task simply by reversing the response required to indicate whether a word or nonword had been seen. Thus, although we are focusing on the constraints on affective meaning that are provided by the stimulus context, there appear to be a corresponding set of constraints coming from the response end. Nevertheless, the focus in this chapter is restricted to a discussion of stimulus constraints on evaluative meaning.

For our purposes, a study by Winkielman et al. (1997) is especially informative. Participants rated how much they liked particular Chinese ideographs after brief, masked exposures to photographs of smiling or frowning faces. The positive and negative affective meaning conveyed in the expressions was found to influence liking and disliking of the Chinese ideographs that appeared immediately afterward. In such procedures, participants are generally unaware of having seen the priming stimuli. Participants may show above-chance accuracy in recognizing whether they had seen smiling or frowning faces, but they cannot reliably identify specific faces. In other words, the evaluative, but not the descriptive, meaning gets through. Under the right circumstances, then, we expect that the evaluative rather than the descriptive aspects of the primes will govern priming, a finding that would parallel the results found for mood. Thus, when evaluative meaning is a dominant feature, we expect general evaluative priming (e.g., in experiments using explicit primes that are extreme in evaluative meaning Stapel and Koomen [2000] or with subliminal evaluative primes where only the evaluative meaning is retained.).

We also hypothesize that the similarities between the results for mood and for evaluative priming are due to the affective information conveyed in affective feelings and thoughts. A test of that hypothesis is whether or not changes in attributions for the occurrence of the feelings and thoughts result in corresponding changes in evaluative ratings, findings to which we turn next.

Attributions and Judgment

We know from extensive research that mood effects can be expected only when the true cause of the mood-based feelings is not salient to participants as they form their judgments. When an extraneous source of the feelings of mood is made salient, mood effects often disappear or even reverse (e.g., Schwarz & Clore, 1983). The same pattern is evident in studies of explicit priming. Martin (1986) studied the effects of priming concepts blatantly rather than subtly, and found contrast effects. After blatant priming with positive concepts, people made negative ratings, and after blatant priming with negative concepts, they made positive ratings. A similar observation was made by Lombardi, Higgins, and Bargh (1987), who divided participants according to whether or not they remembered the priming event. They found priming effects among those who did not recall the primes, and they found contrast effects among those who did recall them.

The critical factor, however, is not actually awareness, but whether participants make correct attributions at the time of judgment. For example, Martin, Seta, and Crelia (1990) used a blatant priming procedure that made the true cause of the concept accessibility obvious. That procedure tended to produce contrast effects, but when the investigators introduced a cognitive load so that participants were kept mentally busy during judgment, they were prevented from making the correct attribution. As a result, priming effects were still obtained. These studies suggest that successful priming requires that participants do not attend to possible constraints on the applicability of the primed concept. This occurs in instances of suboptimal or unconscious priming, because the constraints are unavailable, and it may occur in blatant priming if attention is occupied by a secondary task.

Attribution and Subliminal Priming

Murphy and Zajonc (1993) observed that subjects evaluated unknown Chinese ideographs more positively when they were preceded by the subliminal presentation of smiling rather than frowning faces. Consistent with an affect-as-information approach, our interpretation is that participants misattributed whatever affective meaning was activated by the subliminal faces to the ideographs, because their subliminal presentation made a correct attribution unlikely. Said another way, the primed affective meaning attached itself to the experience of the ideographs, because participants could not remember the brief exposure to smiling or scowling faces, which was its true source. Consistent with this explanation, the effect was obtained only when the faces were presented suboptimally, and not when they were presented optimally. Apparently, optimal exposure allowed subjects to identify the actual source of their reactions, rendering them nondiagnostic for evaluating the ideographs.

These results appear consistent with a feelings-as-information account, but as a test, Winkielman et al. (1997) conducted an extended replication of the study with an explicit attribution manipulation. They found that the observed effect remained unchanged. Specifically, they either informed subjects that a smiling (or frowning) face would precede each ideograph (Experiment 1), or they exposed subjects to music, which they said would elicit positive or negative feelings (Experiment 2). Neither misattribution manipulation resulted in augmentation or discounting effects. However, it turns out that subjects did not report having any subjective experience of affect in the experiment. Such faces, although they may convey affective meaning when presented suboptimally, do not necessarily elicit affective feelings.

Because subjects did not report being in a mood or having affective feelings in these studies, it is not surprising that opportunities to misattribute their feelings to an irrelevant source did not eliminate the effect. In addition, the failure to find attribution effects aimed at feelings when there were no feelings suggests that the usual attribution effects in studies of mood do not represent demand artifacts.

Winkielman et al. (1997) interpreted their data as evidence for the role of "unconscious affect" and implied that the active ingredient in mood and judgment studies too might be unconscious affective forces that operate outside of awareness, rather than the information from feelings, as hypothesized in the affect-as-information approach. We are inclined to think, however, that the Winkielman et al. study, as well as many other intriguing and important studies in the Zajonc tradition, may be studies of semantic priming so that they are not uniquely relevant to emotion. Indeed, evidence from Greenwald et al. (1996), shows that the same effects can be obtained with nonaffective stimuli, including priming a readiness to respond to gender by subliminal exposure to male and female names. We view unconscious priming as a fascinating phenomenon with some especially interesting properties, but perhaps not as a royal road to understanding affect.

A premise of this chapter is that the way in which primed affective concepts influence judgment is not that different from the way feelings of mood do so. However, since the feelings of mood are available to consciousness, one may become aware of them independently of an object. But one becomes aware of primed meaning only when it emerges as an attribute of whatever comes to consciousness next. As shown by Murphy and Zajonc (1993), when the words or faces used to prime affective meaning are made conscious, then attributional processes operate exactly as they do with the feelings of mood, eliminating or reversing affective priming.

Summary. Thus far, we have discussed the parallel effects of mood and affective priming on judgment. We have suggested that mood effects may not be primarily due to the mediation of primed, mood-congruent concepts as proposed by Bower (1981), Isen (1984), or Forgas (2001). We have suggested that the reverse hypothesis, that affective priming induces affective feelings (or some unconscious counterpart), may also not be the pivotal process. It seems unlikely that merely being exposed to evaluative words creates emotional moods. Indeed, if it did, reading a dictionary might be a much more exciting experience than it is. In this regard, the chapter by Niedenthal, Rohmann, and Dalle (chap. 12, this volume) gives a plausible account of the conditions that may be required for isolated words and other stimuli to elicit affect. We propose that an important feature of both moods and unconscious affective primes is that they convey information about value. More important, these representations of value are also unconstrained in their applicability. As a result, the principles that we have found to govern mood effects should also govern affective priming.

APPLYING INFORMATIONAL PRINCIPLES TO PRIMING

We have recently formalized several principles to account for phenomena in the mood and cognition literature (Clore et al., 2001a, 2001b). For example, the *Experience Principle* and the *Information Principle* propose that emotional feelings convey embodied information about one's unconscious appraisals. In addition, the *Attribution Principle* proposes that when the true source of affective cues is not salient, the affect may be misattributed to other cognitively accessible objects. Because they are about mood, these principles tend to be framed in terms of the experience of affect, but they can be extended to apply to primed affective meaning. We argue that, like the evaluative information from induced feelings, the evaluative information from primed affective meanings can be comingled with descriptive information during one's experience of an object. One might reasonably object to this equation on the grounds that unconsciously primed affective meaning cannot be experienced by itself in the same way as affective feelings of mood can be, and hence that primed meaning is not available to be attributed in the same way? We think that it is not a problem, because mood also influences judgment only when one attends to one's feelings in conjunction with the object of judgment. When the feelings of mood are experienced separately as moods, the effects on judgment tend to disappear (e.g., Schwarz & Clore, 1983). In this regard, priming effects are fully parallel. They occur only when primed affective meaning emerges in one's experience as a reaction to the object of judgment. Both mood and primed meaning therefore obey the same attribution principle. Drawing attention to mood and its induction tends to eliminate or reverse its influence on judgment, and altering the priming procedure so that participants are aware of the link between primed concepts and the priming manipulation also tends to eliminate or reverse their influence.

Another key principle is the *Immediacy Principle*, which says that *Affective feelings tend to be experienced as reactions to current mental content* (Clore et al., 2001a, 2001b). We live in a stream of affective and other sensory feedback, each of which conveys potentially important information. For example, feeling sick to one's stomach might be appropriately attributed to whatever one happened to have eaten 2 hours earlier. Similarly, feeling the symptoms of influenza might be appropriately attributed to whatever ill person one happened to be with 2 weeks ago. But when one feels an emotion such as fear or anger, it is invariably about whatever happens to be in mind at that moment. The presumed purpose of such affective cues is to indicate the significance of the stimuli to which one is attending. However, when the affective cues come from mood, or when they are triggered by background ideation of which one is only dimly aware, the proper object of attribution is open. Under those conditions, as we have seen, affective cues may influence judgments of liking, provided that one is focusing on an object with a goal of evaluating it. But what happens when one's focus is not on an object to be evaluated, but on a task to be performed or a problem to be solved? Changing one's focus from judgment stimuli to problem-solving responses leads to very different effects, as summarized in the *Processing Principle* to which we turn next.

Mood and Processing

When one is focused on performance, rather than on judgment, the same affective feelings may be experienced as information about the performance task. As a result, one's processing strategy becomes "tuned" to the processing requirements of the situation (Schwarz & Clore, 1996). Such tuning may occur when positive or negative affective cues are experienced as positive or negative feedback about one's expectations and inclinations about the task (Clore et al., 2001b). In general, information processing tasks require both drawing on one's existing knowledge and using new information from the environment. For example, as the eyes of readers skim along a page, what they already know must be interwoven with new information. They must assimilate new information to existing expectations, but also accommodate existing beliefs to new data (Fielder & Bless, 2000). We assume that in any given moment the weighting given to each is guided by one's subjective experience of the task. For example, the breezy experience of reading something one finds easy to understand privileges the knowledge one is bringing to the task, whereas an effortful experience of reading something one finds challenging inhibits reliance on expectations so that one's agenda shifts to picking up new information. If subjective experiences of ease and difficulty do influence shifts in processing strategy, then positive and negative feelings of mood may have similar effects. According to the Processing Principle (Clore et al., 2001b; Wyer et al., 1999), when one is task-focused with a performance goal, affective feelings may be experienced as feedback about performance or about the value of accessible information.

Isbell (e.g., Isbell, 1999; Isbell, Clore, & Wyer, 2000) has conducted research designed to test this hypothesis. She examined the hypothesis in the context of an experiment on the extent to which people relied on stereotypes or on new behavioral evidence. To induce moods, she asked participants to recall and describe in detail a happy or sad event in their recent past. Then they read a story about a day in the life of a woman described either as an introverted librarian or as an extraverted sales person. This initial information was intended to activate stereotypic beliefs about persons in such roles. However, the story actually contained an equal number of introverted and extraverted actions by the woman.

Participants indicated their impression of the woman by rating her on various extraverted or introverted characteristics. The results showed that individuals made to feel happy focused on their stereotyped beliefs about librarians and salespersons, whereas individuals made to feel sad focused more on the specific actions of the woman as described in the story (Fig. 13.1).

Moreover, as a further test of the affect-as-information interpretation of the results, Isbell conducted a follow-up study in which she made salient to participants the true cause of their affective feelings. Consistent with an attribution approach, mood no longer showed the same effects. In fact they were now reversed, suggesting that whether greater weight is placed on stereotype-based expectations or on actual behaviors depends on whether par-

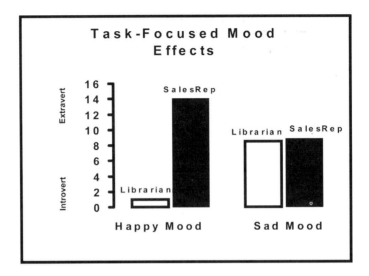

FIG. 13.1.   Happy mood leads to reliance on stereotyped expectations; sad
mood leads to reliance on behaviors (Isbell, 1999).

ticipants experience the affect as feedback about their beliefs or as coming
from extraneous sources.

In the section on judgment, we alluded to the fact that induced positive
or negative feelings and suboptimally primed positive or negative concepts
can both produce positive or negative judgments. We also pointed out that
drawing respondents' attention to the true cause of their thoughts or feelings could eliminate both of these effects. Such attributional results show
that affective influences on judgment require affective feelings or thoughts
to be attributed to (experienced as reactions to) the object of judgment.
They are consistent with the hypothesis that the active agent in both cases is
the information conveyed by the affective thoughts and feelings, because
changing the information value changes the effects. However, with the exception of the study we describe next, no one has previously shown parallel
effects for affective priming on processing.

Unconscious Priming and Processing

The experiments by Isbell (Isbell, 1999; Isbell et al., 2000) showed mood effects on stereotyping. Our interpretation is that these effects occur because
participants who are task-focused experience the cues from their mood as
feedback about the value of their accessible beliefs (see Clore et al., 2001a,
2001b). Such mood and stereotyping effects have also been shown by
Bodenhausen, Sheppard, and Kramer, 1994. Related results have also been

obtained for expectations based on scripts for behavior in common situations, such as the essential restaurant script (Bless, Clore, Golisano, Rabe, & Schwarz, 1996).

To assess whether unconscious affective primes might produce similar effects in the absence of changes in mood, Colcombe, Isbell, and Clore (2001) employed the same basic design as that used by Isbell (which was described previously), except that an unconscious priming paradigm was used instead of a mood induction paradigm.

For the priming task, four slight variations on a schematic smiley face (☺) and four variations on a schematic frowny face (☹) were constructed. These were shown foveally as part of a task requiring participants to specify which of two colors (red or blue) was most numerous in an array of circles on each of 32 trials. To start each trial, a white fixation dot appeared at the center of the computer screen. After a delay of 100–160 msecs., a schematic face appeared centered on the computer screen The face stimulus remained on the screen for 32 msecs., followed by a random pixilated black and white pattern that served as the backward mask. Then, participants were presented with an array of 7 circles, each of which was colored either red or blue. Participants then hit one of two keys on a computer keyboard to indicate whether the most numerous color was red or blue. The same procedure was used in two separate studies. The first was designed to assess the effect of priming on mood. Immediately after the color-naming task in which the priming occurred, participants rated their moods. Scales included happy, sad, good mood, bad mood, relaxed, and tense, each rated on 11-point scales. In addition, participants rated how they felt "overall" on a –5 to +5 scale anchored at one end by a frowny face and at the other by a smiley face. Although there was some tendency for exposure to smiley faces to report higher mood afterward, the differences were not significant. Thus, we conclude from this experiment that this affective priming procedure does not induce mood.

The second experiment employed the same priming methodology, but immediately after the color naming (priming) task, participants read the story previously used in the studies by Isbell (Isbell, 1999; Isbell et al., 2000). The story was about a day in the life of a woman named Carol, who was described either as an introverted librarian or as an extraverted sales person. The narrative included mention of an equal number of extraverted and introverted (prescaled) behaviors as well as a number of neutral behaviors. After a brief filler task, participants were asked to rate Carol on the same dimensions relating to introversion–extraversion as in the mood studies by Isbell. It was predicted that despite the fact that unconscious priming with the smiley and frowny faces did not affect mood, the unconstrained affective meaning of the primes would produce effects similar to those found for mood.

The results concerned ratings on scales relevant to introversion and extraversion. The predicted interaction was obtained between the valence of the unconsciously exposed faces and the expectations set up by the initial description of Carol as an introverted librarian or an extraverted sales person (see Fig. 13.2). As in the case of positive mood, subliminal exposure to smiley faces appeared to confer positive value on the expectations and inclinations of respondents. Similarly, as in the case of sad mood, subliminal exposure to frowny faces inhibited reliance on stereotyped expectations and resulted in ratings that were based on the individual behaviors mentioned in the story, behaviors that were equally often introverted and extraverted.

The results of the unconscious priming study show that the parallelism seen in the effects of mood and unconscious priming on judgment are also evident in their effects on processing. What accounts for this parallelism? Earlier we suggested that the parallelism in the judgment data might still be explained by assuming that mood effects are mediated by priming (as proposed by Bower et al., 1978; Forgas, 2001; and Isen et al., 1978). The same ambiguity does not apply to the parallel influences found for mood and priming on processing styles. It is not clear how priming explanations can account for the processing effects of mood. The only directly relevant means by which priming might mediate mood effects on processing is the suggestion that, "Affectively primed thoughts and associations may take up scarce attentional and memory resources" (Forgas, 2001, p. 122). This attentional capacity explanation has been offered for the processing conse-

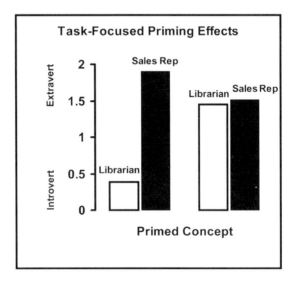

FIG. 13.2.   Suboptimally presented images of smiley faces lead to reliance on stereotyped expectations, and frowny faces lead to reliance on behaviors (Colcombe, Isbell, & Clore, 2001).

quences of negative mood (Ellis & Ashbrook, 1988) as well as of positive mood (Isen, 1984; Mackie & Worth, 1989). However, the adequacy of this approach is undermined by studies that rule out capacity explanations but still find the same mood effects on processing (Bless et al., 1996).

It is less easy to rule out the reverse explanation, that unconscious priming effects are mediated by mood. Unconscious priming effects on both judgment (Winkielman et al., 1997) and processing (Colcombe, Isbell, & Clore, 2001) have been reported without corresponding variations in mood. Some studies of unconscious affective priming have reported effects on mood, but it is quite possible that priming positive affective meaning would lead to affirmative answers to such questions regardless of whether mood had actually been induced. Also, of course, if positive affective priming led to better task performance, the performance might induce positive mood. However, in that case, mood would simply be co-active rather than causal with respect to strategy or performance changes.

One way to show that positive and negative information value (rather than mood) is the important variable, is to show that processing effects can be produced with other affective cues that do not involve mood. An example is research showing that slight muscular effort with approach versus avoidance meaning (arm flexion vs. extension) can influence processing in the same way as positive and negative mood, but without being mediated by mood (Friedman & Forster, 2000). Another example is the effect of posed facial expressions relevant to happiness and anger on judgments of jokes without mood changes (Strack, Martin, & Stepper, 1988). In addition, similar mood-like processing effects have been shown in persuasion situations simply by having materials printed on red versus blue paper (Soldat & Sinclair, 2001). These tasks appear to involve affectively relevant information, but not necessarily felt affect. In this regard, Martin, Ward, Achee, and Wyer (1993) suggest that positive and negative affective cues may influence processing by serving as answers to implicit questions about processing, such as, "Have I done enough?" It seems likely that any number of positive and negative thoughts, feelings, or other affective cues might serve as affirmative or negative answers to such processing questions.

Summary. In an earlier section we showed that mood induction and suboptimal affective priming have parallel effects on evaluative judgments, and we showed that both are subject to the same attributional effects. In the succeeding section, we showed that induced moods and suboptimal affective priming also have parallel effects on strategic information processing. In the final section, we present further evidence of parallelism by testing whether the Immediacy Principle (from the affect-as-information account of mood effects) is applicable to the suboptimal priming situation. The research examines further whether the influence of primed affective information depends on its apparent information value. Specifically, it tests the hypothesis that varying focus of attention during priming governs whether priming affects evaluative judgment or strategic processing. We expected that such processes would be equally applicable to mood and suboptimal priming because the applicability and meaning of both are similarly unconstrained.

Varying the Object of Primed Information

As a final examination of the informational view of mood and priming effects, we conducted two experiments to test the Immediacy Principle (Clore et al., 2001a, 2001b) in a priming paradigm. According to the Immediacy Principle, affective feelings tend to be experienced as reactions to current mental content. Numerous experiments show that affective influences are mediated by implicit attributions about the source and hence the meaning of the affect. Attributions to objects give feelings their specific information value because such attributions constrain the evaluative message of feelings to be about something in particular. In experiments from the affect-as-information perspective, we intentionally arrange for the misattribution of feelings in order to examine the effects of variations in their information value. Emotional feelings are not easily misattributed in real life, because they are often closely tied to the objects that elicited them. Similarly, affective conceptual meaning is usually linked to particular descriptive content. However, the repeated suboptimal exposure of affective stimuli varying in descriptive content does appear to prime evaluative meaning by itself. Under such conditions, we predict that its impact should depend on the context provided by the attentional focus of the individual at the time.

The first experiment in this series (Colcombe & Clore, 2001) was a conceptual replication and extension of the Colcombe, Isbell, & Clore priming study described previously. In this experiment, we exposed participants suboptimally to primes that were synonyms of the word *happy* (happy, glad, smiley, joyful, gleeful, elated, merry) or of the word *sad* (sad, down, depressed, gloomy, glum, mope, dismal). These were presented in a parafoveal priming paradigm as part of a visual search task similar to those used elsewhere (e.g., Bargh & Pietromonaco, 1982; Devine, 1989). However, this experiment was conducted in a group setting in a large classroom.

Stimuli were projected on a screen approximately 15×10 feet in size. Participants were run in-groups of 17 to 25 and recorded their own responses with pencil and paper. Respondents were asked to look at a fixation dot that abruptly appeared in the middle of the screen, and to identify the color of an ellipse appearing at approximately 6–8 degrees of visual angle from the fixation dot in one of the four quadrants of the screen 200 milliseconds later. The ellipse remained on the screen for 1.5 seconds and there was a 1.5 second intertrial interval. There were 48 trials. Again, the nominal task of the subject was simply to record the color of the disk as quickly and accurately as possible. However, on two thirds of the trials, 125 milliseconds before the colored disk appeared, one of the happy or sad priming words appeared. These brief, masked presentations of positive or negative affective words should have activated positive and negative semantic meaning. Participants then read a story about a character named Paul, who relates events from his childhood to a psychotherapist. The story was adapted from one used by Bower, Gilligan, and Montiero (1981). The memories were equally divided into happy (e.g., getting his first bicycle) and sad memories (e.g., his grandmother dying). To vary participants' expectations or accessible ideas about Paul, the materials that they read included notes from Paul's previous counselor. The notes indicated, among other things, that the counselor considered Paul to be basically a happy person or basically a sad person.

We expected that during the color-naming task, participants' attention would be focused on their own responses. Hence, any activated evaluative meaning should be experienced as task fluency (or disfluency), or as a belief that they were doing satisfactorily (or not). We assumed that positive performance feedback would lead participants to follow their current expectations and inclinations, and that negative feedback would inhibit reliance on such expectations in favor of attending to new information from the environment. If so, then we should expect task-focused participants with positive primes to rely more on their expectations (that Paul was a happy or a sad person).

The results can be seen in Fig. 13.3, which depicts a significant interaction between the expectation and the prime variables. As predicted, variation in whether participants expected the character to be happy or sad influenced judgments after positive primes, but not after negative primes. The results suggest that when task-focused, individuals use primed affective information as feedback about the value of their expectations, happy concepts leading them to rely on their expectations and sad concepts leading them to ignore their expectations and rely on their memory for specific events.

The results of this experiment show again that priming affective concepts unconsciously can influence processing styles in the same way as inducing affective feelings can. Moreover, they show that the effects are robust. They replicate the effects of affective priming on processing found by Colcombe, Isbell, and Clore (2001), but using a different story and different rating scales. In addition, the experiment was conducted in groups as opposed to individually. But the main function of this experiment was to serve as a comparison for a second experiment using the same judgments and the same story, but varying the attentional focus of participants.

The second experiment used the same materials, but it was conducted at individual computers, and the primes were presented as the story appeared

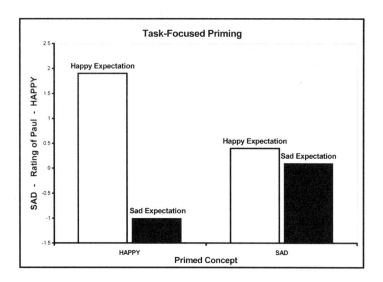

FIG. 13.3. When task-focused, suboptimally presented words denoting happiness or sadness produce the same effects as mood on processing, but without changes in mood.

on the computer screens. Presenting the primes during the story ensured that participants' attention during priming would be on Paul, the central character, rather than on themselves and their task performance. Participants pressed the space bar to progress through the story, which appeared one line at a time. Just before each line appeared, a synonym of the words *happy* or *sad* appeared in the same spatial location as Paul's name (or a personal pronoun that referred to him) was about to appear. The words were presented for 50 milliseconds, then masked with Paul's name or a pronoun referring to him. As before, an expectation was first established by having them read a note from his prior counselor indicating his opinion that Paul was basically either a happy person or a sad person.

By using Paul's name as the mask for the unconscious primes, we expected that the primed evaluative information would become attached to Paul as an object. If so, priming should influence judgment rather than processing styles, as in the previous experiment. That is, rather than governing whether or not respondents rely on expectations (a prime by expectation interaction), we expected the primes in this procedure to influence impressions of Paul directly (a prime main effect).

The results can be seen in Fig. 13.4, which shows the obtained main effect for the valence of the primes. As expected, the interaction with expectation seen in the previous experiment (when participants focused on their color-naming performance) did not occur. Instead, the change in the focus of the respondents also changed the situated meaning of the primed con-

Person-Focused Priming

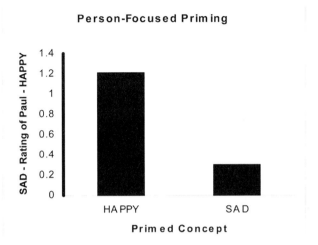

FIG. 13.4.   When person-focused, suboptimally presented words denoting happiness or sadness produce judgment effects comparable to those found for mood, but without changes in mood.

cepts. By shifting their primary point of focus, we were able to shift the primed meaning from being information about the value of respondents' expectations about the character to being an attribute of the character himself. As a result, the same priming stimuli that had produced processing effects in the first experiment, now produced judgment effects. Because priming did not influence respondents' self-reports of mood, the effects do not appear to be due to mood, but to the information conveyed by primed affective meaning. The results indicate that the Immediacy Principle is as applicable to unconsciously primed concepts as it is to affective feelings from induced moods.

The results validate the hypothesis that affect-as-information principles (e.g., Bless, 2001; Clore et al., 2001a; Martin, 2001, Schwarz, 2001; Wyer et al., 1999) also apply to affective thoughts. Affect concerns value, and affective feelings and affective concepts are simply two ways of representing value. When affective feelings arise from moods and affective concepts are primed outside of awareness, the objects of value are unconstrained and unspecified until they are experienced in conjunction with an object. The process is rather like that described in Shakespeare's *Midsummer Night's Dream.* Much of the play hinges on a love potion, which, when applied to the eyes of a sleeping person, makes them fall in love with whomever their eyes fall on as the person awakes. In a similar way, the primed positive meanings and induced positive feelings in our experiments conferred positive value on whatever happened to occupy the attention of participants at the time. The same thing happened for both unconscious primes (Fig. 2) and induced moods (Fig. 1) and in both judgment (Fig. 4) and processing (Fig. 3) situations. The surprising extent of this parallelism leads us to conclude that the observed effects are due neither to feelings nor to primes as such, but to the affective information they convey when experienced as attributes of whatever objects are currently in mind.

CONSTRAINTS ON MEANING

We have proposed that when evaluative information is activated without a focus on its form, object, or source, it becomes a loose cannon, likely to have an impact on any object it bumps into. We have focused on the idea that affective feelings from mood and affective concepts from priming can have similarly broad effects, because their meaning is similarly unconstrained. This idea, that meaning is constrained by the cognitive and perceptual context in which it is activated, is a thoroughly general one, as discussed further in this chapter.

Freud also believed that the vicissitudes of affect are dependent on their mental context. In Freud's (1915) early theory, conscious thought required both a qualitative idea and quantitative energy. Repression was a form of thought control achieved by cutting off affective energy from an idea. Once the repressed affect lost its object, however, it was free to become attached (or attributed) to other substitute ideas. The affect could then emerge into consciousness as part of a new idea. Affect that failed to find a substitute object might leak into consciousness as objectless anxiety, or it might take a bodily part as an object and create hysterical symptoms. Alternatively, affect might find expression in artistic creativity by attaching itself to objects symbolically related to repressed urges.

Of course, some objects are more problematic than others. The talking therapy was intended to help patients reconnect their misattributed affect to its original source. The goal was to restrict runaway affect to a single specific meaning, a meaning usually found by exploring the patient's past. What was important, of course, was not that the therapist made the correct attribution, but that the patient did. Freud concluded that it was not sufficient to take short-cuts, as he attempted to do in the early use of hypnosis. To really change the information value of affective reactions required a time-consuming process of re-plumbing the whole network of supporting connections so that appropriate constraints on the flow of affective significance could be instituted. Our point in taking this brief detour into Freud is to show some precedence for our concern with the importance of the episodic constraints on the semantic meaning of affect. A secondary point is to note the similarity between the affect-as-information approach and Freud's approach in the importance given to attributions in establishing informational value. He explained illness in terms of misattributions and saw psychotherapy as a process of reestablishing correct attributions to constrain the flow of affective meaning.

In a larger context, any form of communication, whether through direct conversation or indirect priming, involves both activating some aspect of meaning and inhibiting its application. The process of reading, for example, provides a useful model. Apparently all of the meanings of all of the words encountered on a page get activated while reading. It is then up to the context provided by neighboring words and sentences to constrain the activated meaning, so that only the most contextually appropriate reading wins out. In some forms of text, such as instructions for assembling toys or furniture, the goal is to be as specific as possible. Instructions should avoid any ambiguity so that one can execute actions in the correct order, using the correct parts. In contrast, poetry and metaphor may require retaining some ambiguity. For example, the analogy "love is like a rose" is poetically satisfying because it is sufficiently concrete to evoke specific images, but sufficiently multifaceted to leave unspecified the specific ways in which love and roses might be alike. An analogy that constrained the similarity further should be rated less profound and satisfying (e.g., "love is like a rose, because both are beautiful"). Presumably, poems must be sufficiently concrete to evoke strong feelings and images, but sufficiently spare to allow the particulars to echo into the general. Is these ways, poetry, and other art forms, involve the management of subjective experience to create meaning that is only partially constrained.

This tension between generality and constraint in establishing the information value of affect has been a central theme in attribution theory. Most relevant is the literature on attributions for success and failure and their role in depression (Abramson, Metalsky, & Alloy, 1989) and optimism (Seligman, 1990). Attribution theorists agree that the meaning that one finds in the affective experience of failure creates problems when it is attributed to causes that are internal to the individual, general in nature, and uncontrollable. But if attributions for failure constrain the information to be about specific, controllable responses, rather than general, uncontrollable abilities, failure can even be energizing and motivating (Dweck & Leggett, 1988).

A related theme can be found in various Eastern religions. A Buddhist approach to coping with pain is to focus directly on the source of the pain. Rather than trying to avoid the pain by diverting one's attention, distress is more effectively diminished by attending directly to the pain. If its meaning is left unconstrained, the negative affect from the pain may generate greater distress. By focusing directly on the site of the pain, the negative affective reaction is experienced as being about the injury and nothing more. Taking the same logic even further, trying to experience the constituent sensations involved in the pain, rather than the pain as a whole, may further localize and constrain the experience and its meaning and significance.

A similar argument can be given for the beneficial effects of social interaction and psychotherapy for individuals suffering trauma, loss, or shame. Attempts to suppress unpleasant memories and concerns are often unsuccessful (Wegner, 1989) and when practiced over long periods can lead to psychological dysfunction. But focusing directly on the distressing events in spoken or written communications can have dramatic benefits (Pennebaker, 1990). The benefit presumably occurs when one's communication about the distressing event becomes specific. As it becomes situated in time and place through communication, its affective meaning becomes more appropriately constrained. Such localization may have no effect on the problem itself, of course, but it may circumscribe the otherwise widening circle of affective meaning, constraining it to be about its true source and therefore not about other things.

Finally, although cognitively constraining negative affect by focusing on the particular has important psychological consequences, the yoga teachings in Hindu culture advise seeking to transcend the particular. A spiritual goal is be able to divorce oneself from the world, believing that caring about particulars is an impediment to caring about essences. In meditation, one might focus on a leaf, a pool of rainwater, or some other physical object, but the goal is to transcend those physical constraints to experience the unfettered oneness of beauty and truth. Writers in that tradition speak of detaching themselves from the particular, from sense impressions and from the content of one's thoughts and feelings. They seek to let go of perceptions of the outer world and let timeless truth expand within (Anantananda, 1996).

Speaking from outside that tradition, psychologists might also imagine that just as a focus on particulars can be useful for coping with negative affect, such a focus might not be useful in positive states. Wilson and Kraft (1993) have shown, for example, that feelings of love for one's mate are diminished by listing the particular reasons for loving, presumably because love requires a sense of innumerable and yet-to-be-experienced ways in which the relationship and the partner are good. An embodied experience of positive affect can be experienced as love, loyalty, or trust only if the experience remains partially unexplained, so that it serves as evidence of a well-spring of good within the other, the full implications of which are yet to be experienced.

CONCLUSIONS

Induced moods and unconscious affective primes have parallel effects on judgment and processing. Rather than explaining mood effects on the basis of implicit priming or explaining priming effects on the basis of mood, we offer an affect-as-information account for both. Both affective feelings and affective concepts convey information about goodness and badness. However, because the sources of moods and primed concepts are generally unclear or inaccessible, the situated meaning of the evaluative information they carry is unconstrained. As a result, it may be experienced as information about whatever is in mind at the time. In conscious priming paradigms, the constraints provided by the descriptive meanings of the primes prevent general evaluative priming from occurring. But studies suggest that evaluative priming may occur either when exposure to the prime is unconscious or when the dominant meaning of the stimulus is evaluative. Evidence that the critical factor is the evaluative information conveyed in moods and primes comes from studies showing that their effects occur only when people are unable to attend to the true sources of the evaluative information.

In this chapter, we extend these observations by adding new parallels in the domain of affective processing to the known parallels in the domain of affective judgment. We used stereotyping as the target phenomenon and showed that affective primes can have the same effects on styles of information processing as induced moods, but without the mediation of mood. A final experiment shows that the factor determining whether unconscious primes produce evaluative judgment effects or strategic processing effects is the participants' focus at the time of priming. That focus, in turn, governs the object about which primed affective meaning is experienced as informative.

REFERENCES

Abramson, L. Y., Metalsky, G. I., & Alloy, L. B. (1989). Hopelessness depression: A theory-based subtype of depression. *Psychological Review, 96,* 358–372.

Anantananda, S. (1996). *What's on my mind? Becoming inspired with new perception.* South Fallsburg, NY: Syda Foundation.

Anderson, N. H. (1971). Integration theory and attitude change. *Psychological Review, 78,* 171–206.

Bargh, J. A. (1997). The automaticity of everyday life. In R. S. Wyer (Ed.), *Advances in social cognition* (Vol. 10, pp. 1–61). Mahwah, NJ: Lawrence Erlbaum Associates.

Bargh, J. A., Chaiken, S., Raymond, P., & Hymes, C. (1996). The automatic evaluation effect: Unconscious automatic attitude activation with a pronounciation task. *Journal of Experimental Social Psychology, 32,* 104–128.

Bargh, J. A., & Pietromonaco, P. (1982). Automatic information processing and social perception: The influence of trait information presented outside of conscious awareness on impression formation. *Journal of Personality and Social Psychology, 43,* 437–449.

Bless, H. (2001). Mood and the use of general knowledge structures. In L. L. Martin & G. L. Clore (Eds.). *Theories of mood and cognition: A user's handbook* (pp. 9–26). Mahwah, NJ: Lawrence Erlbaum Associates.

Bless, H., Clore, G. L., Golisano, V., Rabel, C., & Schwarz, N. (1996). Mood and the use of scripts: Do happy moods really make people mindless?. *Journal of Personality and Social Psychology, 71,* 665–678.

Bodenhausen, G., Sheppard, L. A., & Kramer, G. P. (1994). Negative affect and social judgment: The differential impact of anger and sadness. *European Journal of Social Psychology, 24,* 45–62.

Bornstein, R. F. (1992). Inhibitory effects of awareness on affective responding: Implications for the affect-cognition relationship. In M. Clark (Ed.), *Emotion: Review of personality and social psychology, 13.* Newbury Park, CA: Sage.

Bower, G. H. (1981). Mood and memory. *American Psychologist, 36,* 129–148.

Bower, G. H., Gilligan, S. G., & Monteiro, K. P. (1981). Selectivity of learning caused by affective states. *Journal of Experimental Psychology: General, 110,* 451–473.

Bower, G. H., Monteiro, K. P., & Gilligan, S. G. (1978). *Emotional mood as a context of learning and recall. Journal of Verbal Learning and Verbal Behavior, 17,* 573–585.

Clore, G. L. (1992). Cognitive phenomenology: Feelings and the construction of judgment. In L. L. Martin & A. Tesser (Eds.), *The construction of social judgments* (pp. 133–163). Hillsdale, NJ: Lawrence Erlbaum Associates.

Clore, G. L., Gasper, K., & Garvin, E. (2001). Affect as information. In J. P. Forgas (Ed.), *Handbook of Affect and Social Cognition* (pp. 121–144). Mahwah, NJ: Lawrence Erlbaum Associates.

Clore, G. L., & Ketelaar, T. (1997). Minding our emotions: On the role of automatic, unconscious affect. In R. S. Wyer (Ed.), *Advances in social cognition* (Vol. 10, pp. 105–120). Mahwah, NJ: Lawrence Erlbaum Associates.

Clore, G. L., Schwarz, N., & Conway, M. (1994). The affective causes and consequences of social information processing. In Wyer & T. K. Srull (Eds.), *Handbook of social cognition, 2nd ed.* (Vol. 1, pp. 323–417). Hillsdale, NJ: Lawrence Erlbaum Associates.

Clore, G. L., & Wilkin, N. (1985, May). *Does emotional bias occur during encoding or judgment?* Midwestern Psychological Association, Chicago.

Clore, G. L., Wyer R. S., Dienes, B., Gasper, K., Gohm, C., & Isbell, L. (2001b). Affective Feelings as Feedback: Some Cognitive Consequences. In L. L. Martin & G. L. Clore (Eds.), *Theories of mood and cognition: A user's handbook* (pp. 27–62). Mahwah, NJ: Lawrence Erlbaum Associates.

Colcombe, S., & Clore, G. L. (2001). *The role of context in suboptimal affective priming.* Unpublished manuscript. University of Illinois.

Colcombe, S., Isbell, L., & Clore, G. L. (2001). *The effects of suboptimal exposure to smiles and frowns on information processing.* Unpublished manuscript. University of Illinois at Urbana-Champaign.

Devine, P. G. (1989). Stereotype and prejudice: Their automatic and controlled components. *Journal of Personality and Social Psychology, 56,* 5–18.

Dweck, C., & Leggett, E. (1988). A social cognitive approach to motivation and personality. *Psychological Review, 66,* 183–201.

Ellis, H. C., & Ashbrook, P. W. (1988). Resource allocation model of the effects of depressed mood states on memory. In K. Fiedler & J. Forgas (Eds.), *Affect, cognition, and social behavior* (pp. 25–43). Toronto, CA: C. J. Hogrefe.

Fazio, R. H. (2001) On the automatic activation of associated evaluations: An Overview. *Cognition and Emotion, 15,* 115–142.

Fiedler, K., & Bless, H. (2000). The formation of beliefs at the interface of affective and cognitive processes. In N. H. Frijda, A. S. R. Manstead, & S. Bem (Eds.), *Emotions and beliefs: How feelings influence thoughts* (pp. 144–170). Paris, France: Cambridge University Press.

Fiedler, K., & Stroehm, W. (1986). What kind of mood influences what kind of memory: The role of arousal and information structure. *Memory & Cognition, 14,* 181–188.

Feinberg, T. E. (2001). *Altered egos: How the brain creates the self.* Oxford, UK: Oxford University Press.

Fishbein, M., & Ajzen, I. (1975). *Belief, attitude, intention and behavior.* Reading, MA: Addison-Wesley.

Forgas, J. P. (2001). Feeling and Doing: Affective influences on interpersonal behavior. *Psychological Inquiry, xx, xxx–xxx*.

Forgas, J. P., & Bower, G. H. (1988). Affect in social and personal judgments. In K. Fiedler & J. Forgas (Eds.), *Affect, cognition, and social behavior* (pp. 183–207). Toronto, CA: Hogrefe International.

Franks, J. F., Roskos-Ewoldsen, R., Bilbrey, C. W., & Roskos-Ewoldsen, B. (1999). *Attitude priming: Spreading activation or response competition.* Unpublished manuscript. Vanderbilt University.

Freud, S. (1915). Instincts and their vicissitudes. *Collected papers* (pp. 60–83). New York: Basic Books.

Friedman, R. S., & Forster, J. (2000). The effects of approach and avoidance motor actions on the elements of creative insight. *Journal of Personality and Social Psychology, 79,* 477–492.

Gasper, K., & Clore, G. L. (1998). The persistent use of negative affect by anxious individuals to estimate risk. *Journal of Personality and Social Psychology, 74,* 1350–1363.

Glaser, J., & Banaji, M. R. (1999). When fair is foul and foul is fair: Reverse priming in automatic evaluation. *Journal of Personality and Social Psychology, 77,* 669–687.

Gouaux, C. (1971). Induced affective states and interpersonal attraction. *Journal of Personality and Social Psychology, 20,* 37–43

Greenwald, A. G., Draine, S. C., & Abrams, R. L. (1996). Three cognitive markers of unconscious semantic activation. *Science, 273,* 1699–1702.

Heider, F. (1958) *The psychology of interpersonal relations.* New York: Wiley.

Higgins, E. T., Rholes, W. S., & Jones, C. R. (1977). Category accessibility and impression formation. *Journal of Experimental Social Psychology, 13,* 141–154.

Higgins, E. T. (1996). Knowledge activation: Accessibility, applicability, and salience. In E. T. Higgins & A. Kruglanski (Eds.), *Social Psychology: A handbook of basic principles* (pp. 133–168). New York: Guilford

Isbell, L. M. (1999). *Beyond heuristic information processing: Systematic processing in happy and sad moods.* Doctoral dissertation, University of Illinois at Urbana-Champaign.

Isbell, L. M., Clore, G. L., & Wyer, R. S. (2000). *Mood and stereotyping.* Unpublished manuscript, University of Illinois at Urbana-Champaign.

Isen, A. M. (1984). Toward understanding the role of affect in cognition. In R. S. Wyer & T. K. Srull (Eds.), *Handbook of social cognition* (Vol. 3, pp. 179–236). Hillsdale, NJ: Lawrence Erlbaum Associates.

Isen, A. M., Shalker, T. E., Clark, M. S., & Karp, L. (1978). Affect, accessibility of material in memory and behavior: A cognitive loop? *Journal of Personality and Social Psychology, 36,* 1–12.

James, W. (1890). *Principles of psychology.* New York: Henry Holt.

Jones, E. E., & Nisbett, R. E. (1971). *The actor and the observer: Divergent perceptions of the causes of behavior.* Morristown, NJ: General Learning Press.

Klauer, K. C. (1998). Affective priming. *European Journal of Social Psychology, 8,* 63–107.

Keltner, D., Lock, K. D., & Audrain, P. C. (1993). The influence of attributions on the relevance of negative feelings to satisfaction. *Personality and Social Psychology Bulletin, 19,* 21–30.

Klinger, M. R., Burton, P. C., & Pitts, G. S. (2000). Mechanisms of unconscious priming: I. Response competition, not spreading activation. *Journal of Experimental Psychology: Learning, Memory, & Cognition, 26,* 441–455.

Krosnick, J. A., Betz, A. L., Jussim, L. J., & Lynn, A. R. (1992). Subliminal conditioning of attitudes. *Personality and Social Psychology Bulletin, 18,* 152–162.

Lombardi, W. J., Higgins, E. T., & Bargh, J. A. (1987). The role of consciousness in priming effects on categorization: Assimilation versus contrast as a function of awareness of the priming task. *Personality and Social Psychology Bulletin, 13,* 411–429.

Loewenstein, G. (1996). Out of control: Visceral influences on behavior. *Organizational Behavior and Human Decision Processes, 65,* 272–292.

Mackie, D. M., & Worth, L. T. (1989). Cognitive deficits and the mediation of positive affect in persuasion. *Journal of Personality and Social Psychology, 57,* 27–40.

Martin, L. L. (1986). Set/reset: Use and disuse of concepts in impression formation. *Journal of Personality and Social Psychology, 51,* 493–504.

Martin, L. L. (2001). Mood as input: A configural view of mood effects. In L. L. Martin & G. L. Clore (Eds.), *Theories of mood and cognition: A user's handbook* (pp. 135–158). Mahwah, NJ: Lawrence Erlbaum Associates.

Martin, L. L., Seta, J. J., & Crelia, R. A. (1990). Assimilation and contrast as a function of people's willingness and ability to expend effort in forming an impression. *Journal of Personality and Social Psychology, 59,* 27–37.

Martin, L. L., Ward, D. W., Achee, J. W., & Wyer, R. S. (1993). Mood as input: People have to interpret the motivational implications of their moods. *Journal of Personality and Social Psychology, 64,* 317–326.

Murphy, S., & Zajonc, R. B. (1993). Affect, cognition, and awareness: Affective priming with optimal and suboptimal stimulus exposures. *Journal of Personality and Social Psychology, 64,* 723–739.

Parrott, G., & Sabini, J. (1990). Mood and memory under natural conditions: Evidence for mood and incongruent recall. *Journal of Personality and Social Psychology, 59,* 321–336.

Pennebaker, J. W. (1990). *Opening up: The healing power of confiding in others.* New York: William Morrow.

Petty, R. E., & Cacioppo, J. T. (1986). *Communication and persuasion: Central and peripheral routes to attitude change.* New York: Springer-Verlag.

Schwarz, N. (2001). Feels as information: Implications for affective influences on information processing. In L. L. Martin & G. L. Clore (Eds.), *Theories of mood and cognition: A user's handbook* (pp. 159–176). Mahwah, NJ: Lawrence Erlbaum Associates.

Schwarz, N., & Clore, G. L. (1983). Mood, misattribution, and judgments of well-being: Informative and directive functions of affective states. *Journal of Personality and Social Psychology, 45,* 513–523.

Schwarz, N., & Clore, G. L. (1988). How do I feel about it? Informative functions of affective states. In K. Fiedler & J. Forgas (Eds.), *Affect, cognition, and social behavior* (pp. 44–62). Toronto, CA: Hofgrefe International.

Schwarz, N., & Clore, G. L. (1996). Feelings and phenomenal experiences. In E. T. Higgins & A. Kruglanski (Eds.), *Social Psychology: A handbook of basic principles.* New York: Guilford.

Schwarz, N., Robbins, M., & Clore, G. L. (1985, May). Explaining the effects of mood on social judgment. Midwestern Psychological Association, Chicago.

Seligman, M. E. P. (1990). *Learned Optimism.* New York: Pocket Books.

Soldat, A. S., & Sinclair, R. C. (2001). *Colors, smiles, frowns: External affective cues can directly affect responses to persuasive communications in a mood-like manner without affecting mood.* Unpublished manuscript. University of Alberta.

Srull, T. K., & Wyer, R. S., Jr. (1979). The role of category accessibility in the interpretation of information about persons: Some determinants and implications. *Journal of Personality and Social Psychology, 37,* 1660–1672.

Stapel, D. A., & Koomen, W. (2000). How far do we go beyond the information given? The impact of knowledge activation on interpretation and inference. *Journal of Personality and Social Psychology, 78,* 19–37.

Storbeck, J. L., & Robinson, M. D. (2001). *When preferences need inferences: A direct comparison of the automaticity of cognitive versus affective priming.* Unpublished manuscript. University of Virginia.

Strack, F., Martin, L. L., & Stepper, S. (1988). Inhibiting and facilitating conditions of the human smile: A nonobtrusive test of the facial feedback hypothesi. *Journal of Personality and Social Psychology, 54,* 768–777.

Wegner, D. M. (1989). *White bears and other unwanted thoughts: Suppression, obsession, and the psychology of mental control.* New York: Penguin Books.

Wentura, D. (2000). Dissociative affective and associative priming effects in the lexical decision task: Responding with "yes" vs. "no" to word targets reveal evaluative judgment tendencies. *Journal of Experimental Psychology: Learning, Memory, and Cognition, 26,* 456–469.

Wilson, T. D., & Kraft, D. (1993). Why do I love thee? Effects of repeated introspections on attitudes toward the relationship. *Personality and Social Psychology Bulletin, 19,* 409–418.

Winkielman, P., Zajonc, R. B., & Schwarz, N. (1997). Subliminal affective priming resists attributional interventions. *Cognition and Emotion, 11,* 433–465.

Wyer, R. S., Clore, & G. L., & Isbell, L. (1999). Affect and information processing. In M. Zanna (Ed.), *Advances in Experimental Social Psychology.* New York: Academic Press.

Wyer, R. S., & Srull, T. K. (1989). *Memory and cognition in its social context.* Hillsdale, NJ: Lawrence Erlbaum Associates.

Chapter 14

Motor Compatibility: The Bidirectional Link Between Behavior and Evaluation

Roland Neumann
Jens Förster
Fritz Strack*
University of Würzburg

EVALUATIVE PROCESSES AND BEHAVIOR

Evaluation is a pervasive phenomenon in everyday life and it is difficult to imagine objects that are not evaluated. In fact, it appears that evaluation represents the most important aspect of the information enclosed in language (Osgood, Suci, & Tannenbaum, 1957). Zajonc (1980) has speculated that even in life the most important decisions in life hinge on evaluative processes. The pervasiveness of evaluative processes is further illustrated by the fact that they contribute to both emotions and attitudes (Eagly & Chaiken, 1998; Lazarus, 1991; Ortony, Clore, & Collins, 1988). Emotions are assumed to emerge from appraisal processes, which represent a sequence of stimulus evaluation checks that deal with the interaction of evaluative and descriptive processes (Scherer, 1988). Attitudes can be conceived of as a link between evaluation and an attitude object in memory (Fazio, 1989). Both attitudes and emotions can be activated automatically on the perception of relevant cues in the environment. This might be due to the fact that the evaluative processes underlying emotions and attitudes are, at least in part, elicited automatically.

*This research was supported by Grant DFG Ne 721/1-1 from the German Science Foundation. We thank Roland Deutsch, Jack Glaser, Michael Häfner, Beate Seibt, and Piotr Winkielman who gave valuable suggestions.

Consistent with this assumption, a vast amount of research has documented that the evaluative meaning of objects in our environment is automatically extracted (for an overview see Bargh, 1997). Thus, the affective meaning of pictures (Fazio, Jackson, Dunton, & Williams, 1995; Giner-Sorolla, Garcia, & Bargh, 1999; Krosnick, Betz, Jussim, & Lynn, 1992; Niedenthal, 1990; Murphy & Zajonc, 1993), odors (Hermans, DeHouwer, & Eelen, 1998), or words (Bargh, Litt, Pratto, & Spielman, 1989; Fazio, Sonabatsu, Powell, & Kardes, 1986; Greenwald, Klinger, & Liu, 1989; Klauer, Roßnagel, & Musch, 1997) can influence subsequent responses and judgments. This automatic extraction of affect, however, differs in several aspects from semantic processing (Bargh, 1997; Klauer, 1998; Wentura, 1999). For example, Bargh, Litt, Pratto, and Spielman (1989) have demonstrated that individuals had access to the valence of subliminally presented words although they were unable to specify their meaning. It would therefore seem that the valence of information is extracted prior to its semantic content (Murphy & Zajonc, 1993). Moreover, a central characteristic in spreading-activation models of semantic memory is that activation spreads to adjacent rather than to remote concepts in the associative network. However, semantic association does not play a role in affective priming studies, because, for example, all positive primes influence subsequent targets independent of whether they are semantically related or not. In short, there are important differences between semantic and evaluative processing, which suggest that they possess different functions in the processing of information. But why is this the case?

One answer is that the automatic evaluation of objects in our environment serves adaptive purposes in that they provide the fast responses to the current challenges. Our natural three-dimensional environment provides us with hospitable as well as hostile stimuli. A basic requirement for avoiding the effects of harmful objects and using the benefits of hospitable objects is the ability to initiate appropriate behavior quickly and without much cognitive effort. According to evolutionary approaches (Buck, 1980; Buss & Schmidt, 1993; Ekman, 1975; Izard, 1977; Plutchik, 1980; Tesser, 1993), the main function of attitudes and emotions is to prepare individuals to act in accordance with the requirements of a given situation. Plutchik (1980), for example, postulated that fear prepares the individual for flight responses, whereas anger leads to tendencies to act aggressively. In addition to these more general action tendencies, Darwin (1872/1965) observed that several emotions can be characterized by a specific emotional expression. For example, happy people raise the corners of their mouth (contract their zygomaticus muscle) and angry people furrow their brow (contract their corrugator muscle). Darwin (1872/1965) was convinced that emotional expressions and action tendencies both represent innate response patterns that are activated by evaluative processes.

Notably, according to Darwin (1872/1965), these response patterns are not exclusively determined by evaluative processes. Individuals are capable of controlling their expressive behavior to a considerable degree. Contemporary research has shown that emotional expressions are shaped by evaluative processes, communicational attempts, and display rules that reflect voluntary attempts to control one's behavior (Ekman & Friesen, 1975; Hess, Banse, & Kappas, 1995). Still, the question of whether expressive behavior is actually related to emotions is under debate (Buck, Jeffrey, Losow, Mark, Murphy, & Constanzo, 1993; Fridlund, 1994). For example, Fridlund (1994) has fundamental doubts that emotional expressions are due to emotions and underlying evaluative processes. He defends the position that emotional expressions are exclusively communicational attempts that possess a function for social interaction, but are not expressions of underlying emotions.

Yet, the correspondence between attitudes, emotions, and behavior might be much closer than it appears in light of these arguments. From the perspective of dual-process models in social cognition (Chaiken & Trope, 1999) it is not uncommon that behavior is determined by a mixture of automatic and controlled processes. Derived from dual processing models, we propose that overt behavior such as facial expressions hinge on an automatic affective component and a controlled component that includes intentional aspects of self-control. In this chapter we propose that the relationship between evaluative process and behavior might be much closer at a representational level than it seems at the level of overt behavior. We therefore adopt a level of analysis that is entirely mental in assuming that automatic affective processes are directly related to the representation of compatible adaptive behavior.

Most critical is therefore the use of measures that taps processes that are unavailable to introspection so that the controlled components of behavior are eliminated. Given the possibility that attitudes and emotions automatically elicit compatible action tendencies or expressions, methods that are not based on introspective reports might be better suited for revealing this relationship.

Except for controllability, however, the correspondence between attitude, emotion, and behavior might be lower than evolutionary approaches have claimed, because widely different behavioral patterns can be associated with the same emotion. To meet this problem, Lang et al. (1990) proposed that the basic processes underlying both attitudes and emotions are closely related to broader behavioral orientations such as approach and avoidance behavior. Lewin (1935/1967) suggested as much and argued that

> . . . one might distinguish two large groups of valences according to the sort of initial behavior they elicit: the positive valences (+), those effecting approach; and the negative (–), or those producing withdrawal or retreat. The

actions in the direction of the valence may have the form of uncontrolled im-
pulsive behavior or of directed voluntary activity; they may be "appropriate"
or "inappropriate." (Lewin, 1935/1967, p. 81)

Accordingly, it is not the specific behavior that is related to evaluative
processes but rather broad classes of behavioral orientations. More important, we assume that the relationship between evaluative processes and behavioral orientations of approach and avoidance orientations is realized at
the mental level. Notably, this level of analysis allows for the possibility that
evaluative processes can activate the representation of approach or avoidance behavior without any peripheral activity in the muscles. Because attempts to control one's behavior should not matter at this level of analysis,
it might therefore be possible to clarify whether evaluative processes are directly linked to behavioral orientations (Darwin, 1872/1965).

TWO INDEPENDENT MOTIVATIONAL ORIENTATIONS

So how can we conceive of a relationship between evaluative processes and
behavioral orientations at a mental level? It is perhaps one of the most basic
assumption in psychology that people are motivated to approach pleasure
and avoid pain in order to meet the requirement of survival (Bargh, 1997;
Cacioppo, Gardner, & Berntson, 1997; Davidson, Ekman, Saron, Senulis, &
Friesen, 1990; Gray, 1990; Lang, Bradley, & Cuthbert, 1990; Miller, 1959).
Therefore, our starting point is that the relationship between evaluative
processes and behavioral orientations is realized within two motivational
orientations: the approach and the avoidance orientation. These two motivational orientations, because they are involved in the processing of affect
and the generation of appropriate behavior, occupy a central function in
the regulation of a person's needs. We assume that the processing of
affectively positive concepts immediately triggers the approach orientation
and thereby facilitates all kinds of approach behaviors. Conversely, the
processing of affectively negative concepts activates the avoidance orientation and thereby facilitates all kinds of avoidance behaviors. Moreover, the
two behavioral orientations are not only a consequence, but also a cause of
evaluative processes. This reversed causal relationship was first proposed by
Charles Darwin (1872/1965), who assumed that expressive behavior, in addition to its adaptive function (for example, opening the eyes in surprise
improves the reception of information), regulates the intensity of one's
current feeling. In line with this assumption, we suggest that a *bidirectional*
causal relationship exists between evaluative processes and approach–
avoidance behavior such that evaluative processes might not only facilitate

compatible behavior. Conversely, behavior might also facilitate compatible evaluative processes.

In what follows, we summarize evidence for the bidirectional relationship between evaluative processes and behavioral orientation on the approach–avoidance dimension. More specifically, we first provide some evidence that evaluative processes exert an immediate impact on approach–avoidance tendencies. Next, we focus on the influence of approach–avoidance behavior on evaluative processes and summarize evidence that this reverse causal relationship also exists. Finally, we discuss the implications of the bidirectional relationship between evaluative processes and behavior.

THE INFLUENCE OF EVALUATIVE PROCESSES ON APPROACH OR AVOIDANCE RESPONSES

As a part of the physiological efferent system, reflexes represent automatic behavioral responses that indicate the current prevailing motivational orientation (Lang et al., 1990). Thus, defensive reflexes such as the blink reflex can be thought of as the most primitive form of avoidance behavior. The assumption that the blink reflex should be facilitated when a person is processing negative as compared to neutral information was tested in a series of studies by Lang et al. (1990). In these studies the startle reflex was repeatedly elicited by a flash of light or an acoustic signal while subjects were processing affective information. The authors observed higher activity over the orbicularis oris muscle (which wrinkles the skin around the eye) as an index of the blink reflex if unpleasant rather than neutral information is processed. These findings can be taken as a first piece of evidence that avoidance responses are facilitated while a person is processing negative information. In support of our framework, these results suggest that avoidance behavior is closely linked to the processing of negative information.

But is there any evidence that positive evaluation is linked to approach behavior? Support for this thesis comes from a study by Solarz (1960), in which participants were required to push cards with words that were mounted on a movable stage either toward themselves or away from themselves. In this study, participants were faster at moving words forward (approach) when the words were positive rather than negative; when the task was to push the words away (avoidance), they responded faster to negative than to positive words.

Similar findings were obtained in a recent study by Chen and Bargh (1999), in which participants had to evaluate words on a computer screen as "good" or "bad" by either pushing or pulling a lever. Consistent with Solarz's findings (1960), participants were faster at evaluating positive words when pulling the lever toward themselves but were faster at evaluating negative words when pushing the lever away.

In a further study, Chen and Bargh (1999) demonstrated that such effects do not depend on the conscious evaluation of the presented words. Even if the word evaluation task was replaced by the task of eliminating any stimulus as soon as it appeared on the screen by either pushing or pulling a lever, the same pattern of results was observed. These findings support the assumption that evaluative processes immediately produce compatible behavioral responses without any conscious mediation. Taken together, the correspondence between evaluation and approach–avoidance tendencies is much closer if this behavior is accessed at a level of automatic processes.

However, approach and avoidance behavior as instantiated in these experiments is afflicted with the problem of the reference point of body movements. That is, as Chen and Bargh (1999) coincide "a reframing of the instructions could well have produced the opposite relationship between attitude and behavior as long as laws within the psychological situation remain intact" (p. 222). Thus, one can for example define body movements in relation to an external object, so that body movements away from the own body can be regarded as approach toward the object and body movements toward the own body as avoidance of the object.

Therefore, we sought for behavioral responses that reflect more unambiguously the approach–avoidance dimension likewise for both attitudes and emotions. Facial expressions meet this criterion for both emotions and attitudes in that they reflect approach or avoidance orientations more unambiguously than movements of the arm. It does not depend on the point of reference that a smile reflects an approach and a frown an avoidance orientation. Hence, to use facial expressions allows to test whether the processing of evaluative information activates one of the two motivational orientations and thereby facilitates the execution of compatible facial action.

Thus, to find out whether the processing of positive information activates the approach orientation and thereby facilitates smiling whereas the processing of negative information activates the avoidance orientation and thereby facilitates frowning, Neumann and Hess (2000) recently conducted a series of experiments in which the latency to contract either the zygomaticus (which is involved in smiling) or the corrugator muscle (which is involved in frowning) was assessed by employing an EMG procedure. In the first study, participants had to categorize as fast as possible whether a word on the computer screen was either positive or negative. However, instead of pressing a key they learned to respond to the words by contracting their zygomaticus muscle or their corrugator muscle. For each participant the EMG activity of both muscles was therefore assessed in a relaxed and in a contracted state. The computer recorded the amount of time that elapsed between the presentation of a word and 70% of the EMG activity over the contracted muscle.

In support of our assumption that the processing of affective information triggers one of the two motivational orientations and thereby facilitate the referring facial expression, we found that participants responded faster to positive than to negative words if they had to contract their zygomaticus muscle. The response to negative words was faster than to positive words if the corrugator muscle was contracted (see Fig. 14.1). This supports the assumption that the processing of positive information activates the approach orientation and thereby facilitates smiling, whereas the processing of negative information activates the avoidance orientation and thereby facilitates frowning.

One might object, however, that emotions and the referring emotional expressions arise from specific combinations of evaluative and descriptive processes (e.g., Ortony et al., 1988). Therefore, it may seem reasonable to assume that emotional expressions are not facilitated by unspecific evaluative information but by emotion-specific knowledge. Although relevant research remains to be done, we think this is unlikely because the words employed in our studies did not possess a direct semantic relation to a single emotion such as sadness, anger, disgust or anxiety but to a more unspecific valence.

But how is it then conceivable that evaluative processes along the good-bad or pleasant-unpleasant dimension give rise to a variety of qualitatively different emotions such as sadness, anger, disgust, or anxiety? Much in line with the assumptions of other emotion researchers (Scherer, 1988; Weiner,

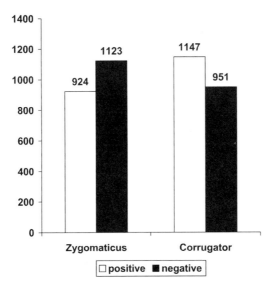

FIG. 14.1.   The influence of the valence of the words on the response latency of facial muscle contractions.

1986), we suggest that the specificity of full blown emotions unfolds temporally after the basic evaluative processes. Thus, consciously experienced feelings can be conceived of as a relatively late outcome (Berridge & Winkielman, in press; LeDoux, 1998) of a process that integrates evaluative and descriptive information. Accordingly, although descriptive features are extracted temporarily after evaluative features as was described previously, descriptive features are necessary to specify the emerging feeling (Neumann, 2000) and to select a concrete and appropriate instantiation of approach or avoidance behavior. From this point of view, an early negative evaluation can result in anxiety and thereby elicit overt avoidance behavior or can alternatively result in anger and elicit overt approach behavior. Thus, in the case of anger semantic information for instance about the violation of norms or the blocking of goals is able to switch the behavioral orientation that was activated by the early negative evaluation.[1] Thus, both evaluative and semantic processes serves adaptive functions, however, the former precedes the later and determines the general behavioral orientation whereas the later selects the more context specific strategy.

That emotions get increasingly differentiated across time is also reflected in facial action. Research in subthreshold activation of specific facial muscle regions revealed that at weak levels of emotional intensity and at early stages of processing facial efference varies only as a function of emotional valence (Cacioppo, Petty, & Marshall-Goodell, 1984). Thus, consistent with the so-called motor recruitment hypotheses (Tassinary & Cacioppo, 1992) contractions of the zygomaticus and the corrugator muscle precede the emotion specific differentiation of the facial muscle. These assumptions are further supported by the finding that the same two facial expressions are closely associated with two different neural structures that are assumed to be involved in the generation of approach and avoidance behavior (Davidson, Ekman, Saron, Senulis, & Friesen, 1990).

Although our findings provide evidence that the two motivational orientations were activated whenever participants had the task of evaluating affective words, it is not clear whether they would be activated automatically in the absence of an evaluative task. Therefore, we conducted a second experiment in which participants were instructed to respond as fast as possible with either the corrugator muscle or the zygomaticus muscle whenever they saw something on the computer screen. Consistent with Study 1, participants responded faster to positive than to negative words if they had to contract the zygomaticus muscle. And they responded faster to negative

---

[1]Notably, not every form of anger is associated with unequivocal approach behavior (Davidson, Ekman, Saron, Senulis, & Friesen, 1990) and it might be interesting whether such forms of anger involves conflicts between early elicited avoidance and later activated approach tendencies.

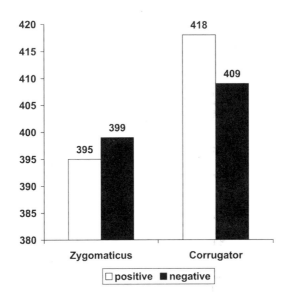

FIG. 14.2.   The influence of the valence of the words on the response latency of facial muscle contractions.

than to positive words if asked to contract the corrugator muscle (see Fig. 14.2).

In summary, these findings support our assumption that evaluative processes automatically trigger compatible expressions and behavioral tendencies. Moreover, the summarized studies corroborate the suggestion that two separate motivational orientations are involved in the processing of affective information and the selection of compatible behavioral response. This early selection process is evident in the facilitation of behavioral responses to compatible affective stimuli.

THE INFLUENCE OF APPROACH OR AVOIDANCE
RESPONSES ON EVALUATIVE PROCESSES

Darwin (1872/1965) thought that behavior might not only be a consequence, but also a cause of evaluative processes. As outlined earlier, he assumed that the intensity of emotions was a function of the interaction of evaluative processes *and* emotional expressions. An even more extreme position was advocated by William James (1890), who proposed that emotional expressions and action tendencies trigger emotions in the absence of evaluative processes. Both approaches are corroborated by a considerable amount of contemporary research using varying sorts of facial, postural, and vocal expressions (for a review see Adelman & Zajonc, 1989). James' assumption that emotional expression can initiate emotions is supported by a study conducted by Duncan and Laird (1980). In this study, participants study put on smiles, frowns, and neutral faces and had to indicate their elation and surgency afterward. The authors observed that participants in the smiling condition were more elated than those in the neutral condition, while the frowning condition lead to more anger than the neutral condition. In a similar vein, Zajonc, Murphy, and Inglehart (1989) required participants to pronounce or listen to various phonems. Some of the phonems either facilitate smiling (pronouncing the vowel "e") or inhibit smiling (pronouncing the German vowel "ü"). In support of James' assumption, participants preferred those phomens that facilitated smiling.[2]

On the other hand, there are several studies supporting Darwins' view that emotional expressions moderate the evaluative processes underlying emotions. In one such study, Strack, Martin, and Stepper (1988) manipulated the contraction of the zygomaticus muscle while subjects rated cartoons on their funniness. For this purpose, participants had to hold a pen in their mouth in a way that either facilitated or inhibited smiling. More specifically, one group held the pen between their teeth (which facilitates smiling), while the other group held it between their lips (which inhibits smiling). Although participants did not recognize the meaning of their facial expression, they judged cartoons to be funnier when smiling was facilitated than when smiling was inhibited. Thus, the intensity of the emotional experience was influenced by both the cartoon and the facial expression.

Such interactive effect have been documented not only for facial expressions. In a postural feedback study, Stepper and Strack (1993) induced either an upright or a slumped body position. In addition, participants received either moderate or above-average feedback about their achievement in an intelligence test. As expected, participants who received their above-average feedback in an upright rather than in a slumped position experienced more pride. Most interesting, however, the manipulation of the posture had no effect on those who received average feedback about their achievement. In order to feel proud it is therefore not sufficient to adopt an

---

[2]As we have pointed out elsewhere (Neumann & Strack, 2000b) dissenting views exist on how these expressions influence emotional responses. Duncan and Laird (1980) have advocated the view that a self-perception process mediates the impact of expressions on subjective experience. According to this position, individuals have to infer their subjective experience from their expression when internal cues are weak. One important precondition for such inferences to occur is that people be aware of the meaning of their facial expression. This approach, however, is not easily reconciled with findings demonstrating that similar effects are obtained in the absence of the recognition that an emotional expression was activated. Zajonc et al. (1989) proposed a physiological explanation for facial feedback effects. This explanation, however, is quite specific to facial expressions but can hardly account for effects of the body posture or arm position later reported in this chapter.

upright posture. Rather, it is necessary that individuals attribute a positive outcome to their own efforts (Weiner, 1986).

These studies, however, do not allow us to decide whether or not evaluative processes mediate the influence of expressions on emotions. In line with Darwin's proposals, we suggested that a bidirectional link exists among evaluative and behavioral processes. Is there in fact any support for the idea that approach–avoidance responses directly influence evaluative processes? Support for such a direct impact comes from a series of studies conducted by Cacioppo, Priester, and Berntson (1993). The researchers observed that neutral Chinese ideographs presented during arm flexion were subsequently evaluated more favorably than ideographs presented during arm extension. They assumed that arm flexion is usually more closely coupled temporally with the consumption of desired goods, and thus argued that movements toward the body such as arm flexion can be interpreted as approach behavior, whereas movement of the hand away from the body can be interpreted as avoidance behavior. In summary, these studies corroborate the assumption that evaluative processes are directly influenced by activated approach–avoidance responses, and that it is therefore likely that facial and postural feedback effect on emotions are also mediated by evaluations.

In the studies conducted by Cacioppo et al. (1993) participants are assumed to have no attitude toward Chinese ideographs because they were most likely seeing most of them for the first time. However, what happens if the same body posture is induced in participants while they are forming an impression of physically attractive and unattractive persons? We have postulated that the processing of positive information is facilitated when the approach orientation is activated. Given that this facilitation effect results in an accumulation of more positive information about the person, she/he should be evaluated more positively. Consistent with this assumption, Förster (1998) demonstrated that participants flexing their arm evaluated only attractive persons depicted on photos more positively. Notably, and inconsistent with Cacioppo et al. (1993), these findings were obtained for online judgments as well as for memory based judgments. These findings therefore point to the importance of compatibility between evaluation and behavior such that compatible combinations are facilitated.

As was pointed out previously, many different forms of nonverbal interactive behavior can be regarded as a form of approach or avoidance behavior. For example, shaking the head horizontally or vertically may be seen as a different manifestation of this general tendency because such movements are habitually performed in Western cultures when people accept or refuse a proposition. That such movements of the head might be capable of activating evaluative processes was suggested by a study that examined the effect of nodding and shaking of the head on the effect of persuasive messages (Wells & Petty, 1980). This study revealed that nodding while listening to persuasive messages led to more positive attitudes toward the content of the message than shaking the head.

In a similar vein, Förster and Strack (1996) found that participants who nodded while encoding positive and negative words were more likely to show enhanced recognition of positive words. In contrast, participants who shook their head while encoding were better at recognizing negative words. Most important, a signal-detection analysis revealed that this effect was due to the discrimination of whether a word was presented in the learning list, but not to a response bias. Therefore, it is likely that these head movements have their impact at the encoding stage rather than the retrieval stage.

To further scrutinize whether such effects actually operate at the encoding stage, we conducted an experiment in which participants were required to either flex or extend their arm as in the Cacioppo et al. (1993) studies (Neumann & Strack, 2000a). While performing this task, participants had to judge as fast as possible whether the meaning of a series of words presented on the computer screen was pleasant or unpleasant. We reasoned that contractions of the flexor might be able to activate the approach orientation and thereby facilitate the categorization of positive words, whereas the tensor muscle might trigger the avoidance orientation and thereby facilitate the categorization of negative words. In line with these expectations we found that positive words were categorized faster than negative words when participants flexed the arm, while negative words were categorized faster than positive words when participants extended the arm (Neumann & Strack, 2000a). We concluded that approach and avoidance movements activate the compatible motivational orientation and thereby facilitate the categorization task.

Nevertheless, one might still doubt that head movements or arm contractions can be conceived of as approach or avoidance behavior that activate one of the two motivational orientations. To validate that the approach and the avoidance orientation are actually activated by these behaviors, we tried to activate them by visual cues that also signal approach or avoidance. We assumed that approach and avoidance can be conceived of as movement that regulates the distance toward important objects, and that afferent feedback and visual information might be an equivalent in this respect. Therefore, we conducted a second study in which participants were again required to judge as fast as possible whether the meaning of a series of words presented on the computer screen was pleasant or unpleasant. To test our thesis that visual cues of approach or avoidance would produce the same congruency effect as in the prior study, we replaced the task of flexing or extending the arm by a visual illusion that made participants believe they were moving either toward or away from the computer screen. Keeping the size of the words constant, this was achieved through a background of concentric circles that were either increasing or decreasing. In the condition where participants had the impression that they were moving toward the computer screen, participants were faster at categorizing positive words, the oppositive was the case in the condition where participants had the sense that they were moving away from the screen (Neumann & Strack, 2000a).

These findings suggest that the two motivational orientations can be activated by different forms of input related to approach or avoidance. Cues about approach or avoidance exert an impact on the processing of affective information whether mediated by proprioceptive or by exteroceptive feedback.

We have argued that the facilitation of evaluative processing occurs immediately on the activation of the referring motivational orientation by relevant feedback. However, the findings reported so far allow for the alternative interpretation that the influence of the feedback on processing depends to the evaluation task. That is, participants were required to categorized the words as positive or negative and it is therefore conceivable that the influence depends on an evaluative mindset or the goal to evaluate the stimuli. To find out whether the influence of feedback on evaluative processes is goal dependent, we conducted a third study that replaced the evaluative task by a lexical decision task and included a set of evaluatively neutral words.[3] In this study we replicated the pattern of the previous two studies in that participants were faster at responding to positive words while seemingly moving toward the computer screen; the opposite was the case when they appeared to be moving away from the screen (Neumann & Strack, 2000a). Therefore, it seems warranted to assume that the facilitation of evaluative processing occurs immediately on the activation of the referring motivational orientation by relevant feedback.

In summary, these findings support our assumption that perceived movement along the approach–avoidance dimension directly triggers compatible evaluative processes. From this point of view, it seems more likely that facial and postural feedback effects are also mediated by evaluative processes, as Darwin (1872/1965) suggested. From the perspective of the position (James, 1890) that only specific emotional expressions can influence their referring specific emotion it is hard to imagine how unspecific movements of the head or arm can exert an influence on different emotional experiences. However, given that (a) such movements directly influence evaluative processes, and (b) evaluative processes play a central role in the elicitation of emotions (Lazarus, 1991), such unspecific arm movements should also exert an influence on emotional experience.

To test the assumption that arm movements influence the intensity of experienced emotions, we conducted two experiments in which emotions were elicited while participants had to either flex or extend their arm (Seibt

---

[3]Evaluatively neutral words were employed together with positive words, negative words and nonwords.

& Neumann, 2000). Because we found that arm flexion activates the approach orientation and arm extension activates the avoidance orientation (Neumann & Strack, 2000a), we predicted in the first experiment that processes underlying the elicitation of happiness should be influenced by contraction of the forearm. More specifically, we expected that the contraction of the flexor muscle would increase the amusement elicited by a cartoon, whereas the contraction of the tensor muscle would decrease the amusement. Consistent with these expectations, we found that participants who contracted their tensor muscle felt less amused by a cartoon than those who hold their forearm relaxed (see Fig. 14.3).

Moreover, those who contracted their flexor muscle felt more amused by the cartoon than those in the control condition. These findings can be taken as a first piece of evidence that movements of the arm on the approach–avoidance dimension are able to influence the intensity of experienced emotions.

However, this influence on the experienced intensity of a positive emotion cannot be regarded as compelling evidence that two separate motivational orientations mediate the obtained effects, because it is still conceivable that negative emotions might also be intensified by contractions of the flexor muscle. Thus, to find out whether the contraction of the tensor muscle is able to intensify feelings of anxiety, we conducted a second study in which we tried to induce social anxiety by telling participants that they had to speak in front of an audience. While waiting for their speech, half of the participants contracted the flexor muscle of their forearm while the other

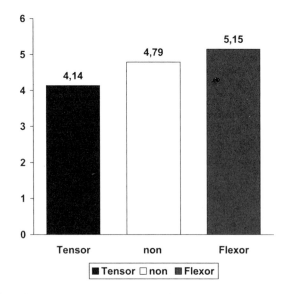

FIG. 14.3.   Reported amusement as a function of somatic activation.

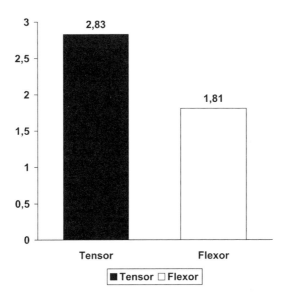

FIG. 14.4.   Reported anxiety as a function of somatic activation.

half was required to contract the tensor muscle. Again we found a compatibility effect (see Fig. 14.4) in that those contracting their tensor muscle indicated that they were more anxious than those contracting their flexor muscle (Seibt & Neumann, 2000).

In summary, these experiments show that the activation of various forms of behavior along the approach–avoidance dimension may exert an immediate impact on evaluative processes. The rule we identified is that approach behavior facilitated the processing of positive information and avoidance behavior facilitated the processing of negative information. These findings corroborate the assumption that the activation of approach or avoidance responses triggers two separate motivational orientations that facilitate compatible evaluative processes.

THE BIDIRECTIONAL LINK BETWEEN BEHAVIOR AND EVALUATION

Derived from dual processing models in social cognition (Chaiken & Trope, 1999) we proposed that overt behavior along the approach avoidance dimension hinge on two stages of processing: an automatic affective component and a controlled component that includes intentional aspects of self-control. We suggest that affective processes immediately trigger the representation of approach–avoidance behavior. Whether the activated representations result in of overt behavior depends on effortful voluntary attempts. The research reported in this chapter was concerned with the automatic affective component in that implicit measure employed allows to study the relationship of affect and behavior at the representational level.

Drawing on Darwin (1872/1965), we proposed that evaluative processes underlying attitudes and emotions are directly connected to the representation of approach–avoidance responses through a bidirectional link. Therefore, we suggested that evaluative processes facilitate congruent approach or avoidance behavior. In addition, activated approach or avoidance responses might also facilitate compatible evaluative processes. We assumed that the feedback mechanism between positive evaluations and approach behavior constitutes the approach orientation, and that the feedback loop between negative evaluations and avoidance behavior forms the avoidance orientation.

Consistent with these proposals, we reported evidence that evaluative processes exert an immediate impact on approach or avoidance responses. Moreover, a considerable amount of research has documented that approach or avoidance responses exert a direct impact on evaluative processes. These findings corroborate the thesis of a bidirectional relationship between evaluative processes and approach–avoidance responses.

In the case of expressive behavior, it seems reasonable to assume that the link between evaluative processes and action tendencies is hardwired. However, it is implausible that gestures such as nodding and shaking of the head are hardwired with evaluative processes because there are cultural differences in this behavior (Förster & Strack, 1996). Rather, it is likely that the frequency of the contingency of behavior and affective consequences determines the associative strength of the link. Bidirectional relationships should result whenever there is an isomorphic (one-to-one) contingency between behavior and evaluation, so that whenever one part of the link is present, the other is also.

From that point of view, it is conceivable that all kinds of behavioral responses are linked to evaluative processes, and that, in principle, it should be possible to establish the opposite relationship, namely that approach behavior is shown to negative stimuli and avoidance behavior to positive stimuli. However, we expect that it is more effortful to change hardwired evaluation–behavior links than acquired links.

We suggest that the bidirectional relationships within the two separate orientations possess the function of reaching a stable motivational state given either an evaluative or a behavioral input. For adaptive reasons it might be important to amplify each input into the two motivational orientations in order to prevent ambiguities. Moreover, as was pointed out previously, the mechanisms operating within these orientations differs in important points from what we know about associative memory. We suggested that these differences in the mechanisms have evolved in order to increase the fitness to the requirements of the environment. In summary, the assumption that two separate motivational orientations moderate the relationship between evaluation and approach or avoidance responses provides a coherent explanation for the various relationships between attitudes, emotions, and behavioral responses.

Which alternative explanations can account for the examined link between evaluative processes and approach or avoidance responses? It is still conceivable that one single mechanism generates the two opposite behavioral orientations. Such an objection, however, has to deal with the overwhelming evidence that positive and negative evaluations are not just different ends on a bipolar dimension but are often unrelated (Cacioppo et al., 1997) and that psychophysiological research usually finds evidence for different neural substrates that generate approach and avoidance orientations respectively (Davidson et al., 1990; Lang et al., 1990). Moreover, we think that such a single mechanism cannot be reconciled easily with the finding that behavioral responses exert an influence on evaluative processes. What processes mediate such an influence of opposite behavioral orientations and what is the mechanism that selects the evaluative process that is facilitated? One possibility is to reframe part of the research reported in terms of *response competition tasks,* in which two different responses can be provided to one of two different stimuli. For example, Klinger, Burton, and Pitts (2000) recently suggested a response competition view for affective priming effects. According to this view, unconsciously perceived words automatically activate response tendencies that facilitate or interfere with target responding. Is it therefore conceivable that it is not the mediation by motivational orientations that provides an explanation for the reported findings, but the competition of two incompatible motor responses that differ in the amount of accumulated evidence?

We think that response competition mechanism do not provide a sufficient explanation because the studies of Chen and Bargh (1999, Experiment 2) and Neumann and Hess (2000, Experiment 2) clearly can not be regarded as response competition tasks. Participants in both studies were required to perform just one single response to both positive and negative affective words. Because similar patterns of results were obtained with and without response competition tasks in these experiments, it is unlikely that response competition mechanisms are sufficient to explain these effects. Furthermore, the behavioral responses in the research reported in this chapter represent different forms of approach or avoidance behavior and are therefore much more specific than in typical response competition tasks. In summary, it is difficult to explain our findings with a single mechanism because it is unclear in such a model how an evaluative process is transformed into a behavioral orientation and how a behavioral orientation is transformed into an evaluative process.

The research summarized in this chapter was exclusively concerned with the automatic interplay between evaluative processes and behavioral responses. As was pointed out in the introduction, we do not deny that behavior is also determined by conscious processes. Even spontaneous behavioral responses such as facial expressions can be voluntarily controlled to a considerable degree.

Nevertheless, we wanted to stress the point that the representation of behavior can be automatically activated on the processing of affective information independent of whether the decisive behavior is actually executed or not. In applying dual processing models to the relationship of evaluative processes and behavioral responses we find evidence that the selection of an appropriate response (controlled process) temporally follows rather than precedes the activation of this response (automatic process).

Thus, not every motor behavior that is activated at the representational level is actually selected and executed afterward. Instead, individuals can control their behavior and display an emotional expression that is incompatible with their current emotion. In this case the behavioral response elicited automatically by evaluative processes might be opposite to the direction that is actually executed. However, as was demonstrated in Förster and Strack (1996), it would require more capacity to execute an action that is incompatible with the affective cues in the environment. In a similar vein, attempts to suppress one's emotional expression while experiencing a negative emotion impairs memory for emotional events (Richards & Gross, 2000).

The bidirectional relationship between evaluation and behavior might provide a clue for understanding the synchronization between the evaluative and the behavioral components of both attitudes and emotions. Thus, the bidirectional relationship enables recursive processes between evaluation and behavior, allowing them to be activated in close temporal proximity, and providing for the rapid exchange of activation through this loop. These processes of synchronization might help to find a stable state, which is probably important for adaptive reasons.

Accordingly, the two motivational orientations described in this chapter are shaped by the requirement of survival and the exigencies of the human environment (Glenberg, 1997). The delineated approach not only provides an integrative framework for the regulation of highly adaptive behavior, but also offers an explanation of self-regulative processes such as facial and postural feedback effects.

REFERENCES

Adelmann, P. K., & Zajonc, R. B. (1989). Facial efference and the experience of emotion. *Annual Review of Psychology, 40*, 249–280.

Bargh, J. A. (1997). The automaticity of everyday life. In R. S. Wyer (Ed.), *Advances in Social Cognition, 10* (pp. 1–62). NJ: Lawrence Erlbaum Associates.

Bargh, J. A., Litt, J., Pratto, F., & Spielman, L. A. (1989). On the preconscious evaluation of social stimuli. In A. F. Bennett & K. M. McConkey (Eds.), *Cognition in individual and social contexts.* Amsterdam, Netherlands: Elsevier/North-Holland.

Berrigde K. C., & Winkielman, P. (in press). What is an unconscious emotion? *Cognition and Emotion.*

Buck, R. (1980). Nonverbal behavior and the theory of emotion: The facial feedback hypothesis. *Journal of Personality and Social Psychology, 38,* 811–824.

Buck, R., Losow, J. I., Murphy, M. M., & Constanzo, P. (1993). Social Facilation and Inhibition of Emotional Expression and Communication. *Journal of Personality and Social Psychology, 63,* 962–968.

Buss, D. M., & Schmitt, D. P. (1993). Sexual Strategies Theory: An evolutionary perspective on human mating. *Psychological Review, 100,* 204–232.

Cacioppo, J. T., Gardner, W. L., & Berntson, G. G. (1997). Beyond bipolar conceptualizations and measures: The case of attitudes and evaluative space. *Personality and Social Psychology Review, 1,* 3–25.

Cacioppo, J. T., Petty, R. E., Marshall-Goodell, B. (1984). Electromygraphic specificity during simple physical and attitudinal tasks: Location and topographical features of integrated EMG responses. *Biological Psychology, 19,* 1–37.

Cacioppo, J. T., Priester, J. R., & Berntson, G. G. (1993). Rudimentary determinants of attitudes. Arm flexion and extension have differential effects on attitudes. *Journal of Personality and Social Psychology, 65,* 5–17.

Chaiken, S., & Trope, Y. (1999). *Dual-process theories in social psychology.* New York: Guilford Press.

Chen, M., & Bargh, J. A. (1999). Consequences of automatic evaluation: Immediate behavioral predispositions to approach or avoid the stimulus. *Personality and Social Psychology Bulletin, 25,* 215–224.

Darwin, C. (1872). *The expression of emotion in man and animals.* New York: Philosophical Library.

Davidson, R. J., Ekman, P., Saron, C. D., Senulis, J. A., & Friesen, W. V. (1990). Approach-Withdrawal and Cerebral Asymmetry: Emotional Expression and Brain Physiology. *Journal of Personality and Social Psychology, 58,* 330–341.

Duncan, J., & Laird, J. D. (1980). Positive and reversed placebo effects as a function of differences in cues used in self-perception. *Journal of Personality and Social Psychology, 39,* 1024–1036.

Eagly, A. H., & Chaiken, S. (1998). Attitude structure and function. In D. T. Gilbert & S. T. Fiske (Eds.), *The handbook of social psychology* (Vol. 1, 4th ed., pp. 269–322). Boston: Mcgraw-Hill.

Ekman, P. (1975). *Unmasking the face.* Englewood Cliffs: Prentice-Hall.

Fazio, R. H. (1989). On the power and functionality of attitudes: The role of attitude accessibility. In A. R. Pratkanis, S. J. Breckler, & A. G. Greenwald (Eds.), *Attitude structure and function* (pp. 153–179). Hillsdale: Lawrence Erlbaum Associates.

Fazio, R. H., Jackson, J. R., Dunton, B. C., & Williams, C. J. (1995). Variability in automatic activation as an unobtrusive measure of racial attitudes: A bona fide pipeline? *Journal of Personality and Social Psychology, 69,* 1013–1027.

Fazio, R. H., Sanbonmatsu, B. M., Powell, M. C., & Kardes, F. R. (1986). On the automatic activation of attitudes. *Journal of Personality and Social Psychology, 50,* 229–238.

Förster, J. (1998). Der Einfluß motorischer Perzeptionen auf Sympathie-Urteile attraktiver und unattraktiver Portraits [The influence of motor perception on likeability judgments of attractive and inactractive portraits]. *Zeitschrift für Experimentelle Psychologie, 45,* 167–182.

Förster, J., & Strack, F. (1997). Motor actions in retrieval of valenced information: A motor congruence effect. *Perceptual and Motor Skills, 85,* 1419–1427.

Fridlund, A. J. (1994). *Human facial expression: An evolutionary view.* San Diego: Academic Press.

Giner-Sorolla, R., Garcia, M. T., & Bargh, J. A. (1999). The automatic evaluation of pictures. *Social Cognition, 17,* 76–96.

Glenberg, A. (1997). What memory is for. *Behavioral and Brain Sciences, 20,* 1–55.

Gray, J. A. (1990). *Psychobiological aspects of relationships between emotion and cognition.* Hillsdale: Lawrence Erlbaum Associates.

Greenwald, A., Klinger, M. R., & Liu, T. J. (1989). Unconscious processing of dichoptically masked words. *Memory and Cognition, 17,* 35–47.

Hermans, D., Baeyens, F., & Eelen, P. (1998). Odours as affective processing context for word evaluation: A case of cross-modal affective priming. *Cognition and Emotion, 12,* 601–613.

Hermans, D., De Houwer, J., & Eelen, P. (1994). The affective priming effect: Automatic activation of evaluative information in memory. *Cognition and Emotion, 8,* 515–533.

Hess, U., Banse, R., & Kappas, A. (1995). The intensity of facial expression is determined by underlying affective state and social situation. *Journal of Personality and Social Psychology, 69*(2), 280–288.

Izard, C. (1977). *Human emotions.* New York: Plenum Press.

James, W. (1890). *The principles of psychology.* New York: Holt.

Klauer, K. C. (1998). Affective Priming. In W. Stroebe & M. Hewstone (Eds.), *European Review of Social Psychology* (pp. 67–103). New York: Wiley.

Klauer, K. C., Roßnagel, C., & Musch, J. (1997). List-context effects in evaluative priming. *Journal of Experimental Psychology: Learning, Memory, and Cognition, 23,* 246–255.

Klinger, M. R., Burton, P. C., & Pitts, G. S. (2000). Mechanisms of unconscious priming: Response competition, not spreading activation. *Journal of Experimental Psychology: Learning, Memory, and Cognition, 26,* 441–455.

Lang, P. J., Bradley, M. M., & Cuthbert, B. N. (1990). Emotion, attention, and the startle reflex. *Psychological Review, 97,* 377–395.

Lazarus, R. S. (1991). Progress on a cognitive-motivational-relational theory of emotion. *American Psychologist, 46*(8), 819–834.

LeDoux, J. (1998). Fear and the brain: Where have we been, and where are we going? *Biological Psychiatry, 44,* 1229–1238.

Lewin, K. (1935). *A dynamic theory of personality: Selected papers of Kurt Lewin.* New York: McGraw-Hill.

Miller, N. E. (1959). Liberalization of basic S-R concepts: Extensions to conflict behavior, motivation and social learning. In S. Koch (Eds.), *Psychology: A study of science, Study 1* (pp. 198–292). New York: McGraw Hill.

Murphy, S. T., & Zajonc, R. B. (1993). Affect, cognition, and awareness: Priming with optimal and suboptimal stimulus exposures. *Journal of Personality and Social Psychology, 64,* 723–739.

Neumann, R. (2000). The Causal Influences of Attributions on Emotions: A Procedural Priming Approach. *Psychological Science, 11,* 179–182.

Neumann, R., & Hess, M. (2000). *The latency of facial contractions as an index of affective information processing.* Unpublished Manuscript. Universität Würzburg.

Neumann, R., & Strack, F. (2000a). Approach and avoidance: The influence of proprioceptive and exteroceptive cues on affective processing. *Journal of Personality and Social Psychology, 79,* 39–48.

Neumann, R., & Strack, F. (2000b). Experiential and non-experiential routes of motor influences on affect and evaluation. In H. Bless & J. P. Forgas (Eds.), *The message within: Subjective experiences and social cognition* (pp. 52–68). Philadelphia: Psychology Press.

Niedenthal, P. M. (1990). Implicit perception of affective information. *Journal of Experimental Social Psychology, 26,* 505–527.

Ortony, A., Clore, G. L., & Collins, A. (1988). *The Cognitive Structure of Emotions.* Cambridge, UK: Cambridge University Press.

Osgood, C. E., Suci, G. J., & Tannenbaum, P. H. (1957). *The measurement of meaning.* Urbana: University of Illinois Press.

Plutchik, R. (1980). *Emotions: A psychoevolutionary synthesis.* New York: Harper & Row.

Richards, J. M., & Gross, J. J. (2000). Emotion regulation and memory: The cognitive costs of keeping one's cool. *Journal of Personality and Social Psychology, 79,* 410–424.

Scherer, K. R. (1988). *Facets of emotion: Recent research.* Hillsdale, Lawrence Erlbaum Associates.

Seibt, B., & Neumann, R. (2000). *The influence of unspecific body postures on emotions.* Unpublished Manuscript. Universität Würzburg.

Solarz, A. K. (1960). Latency of instrumental responses as a function of compatibility with the meaning of eliciting verbal signs. *Journal of Experimental Psychology, 59,* 239–245.

Stepper, S., & Strack, F. (1993). Proprioceptive determinants of emotional and nonemotional feelings. *Journal of Personality and Social Psychology, 64,* 211–220.

Strack, F., Martin, L. L., & Stepper, S. (1988). Inhibiting and facilitating conditions of human smile: A nonobtrusive test of the facial feedback hypothesis. *Journal of Personality and Social Psychology, 54,* 768–777.

Tassinary, L. G., & Cacioppo, J. T. (1992). Unobservable facial actions and emotions. *Psychological Science, 3,* 28–33.

Tesser, A. (1993). The importance of heritability in psychological research: The case of attitudes. *Psychological Review, 100,* 129–142.

Weiner, B. (1986). *An attribution theory of motivation and emotion,* New York: Springer.

Wells, G. L., & Petty, R. E. (1980). The effects of overt head movements on persuasion: Compatibility and incompatibility of responses. *Basic and Applied Social Psychology, 1,* 219–230.

Wentua, D. (1999). Activation and inhibition of affective information: Evidence for negative priming in the evaluative task. *Cognition and Emotion, 13,* 65–91.

Zajonc, R. B. (1980). Feeling and thinking: Preferences need no inferences. *American Psychologist, 35,* 151–175.

Zajonc, R. B., Murphy, S. T., & Inglehart, M. (1989). Feelings and facial efference: Implications of a vascular theory of emotion. *Psychological Review, 96,* 395–416.

Author Index

H

N

Nakamura, Y., 142, 153, *167*, 199, 200, 201, 202, 210, *214*

Nandram, S., 309, *332*

Naparstek, J., 282, *305*

Naumann, E., 281, *303*

Naumann, U., 127, 128, *135*

Neale, J., 285, *305*

Neely, J. H., 20, 21, 22, 23, 25, *35*, 52, 53, 54, 66, *84*, 88, 92, *107*, 170, 171, 175, *187*, 223, *242, 247, 273*

Neill, W. T., 64, *84*

Nelson, T. O., 193, *214*

Neuberg, S. L., 114, *136*

Neumann, O., 27, *35*, 51, *84*

Neumann, R., 376, 380, 382, 383, 384, 385, 387, *390, 391*

Newman, L. S., 96, *107*

Nickel, S., 110, 127, 129, *135*

Niedenthal, P. M., 247, *271*, 310, 311, 313, 314, 316, 317, 318, 323, *330, 332*, 372, *390*

Nisbett, R. E., 25, *35, 367*

Nitzchke, J. B., 295, *304*

Noirot, M., 248, *273*

Norman, K. A., 195, 196, 209, *214*

Nowak, A., 195, 196, 197, 209, *214, 216*

Nuttin, J. M., 235, *242*

O

Oatley, K., 317, *332*

O'Connor, M., 284, *303*, 309, 317, *332*

Oden, G. C., 55, *84*

Öhman, A., 139, 141, 145, *167*

Olson, J. M., 181, *187*

Olson, M. A., 157, 162, *167*

O'Reilly, R. C., 122, *136*, 195, 196, 209, *214*

Ortony, A., 190, *214*, 309, 317, *332*, 371, 377, *390*

Osgood, C. E., 371, *390*

Osman, A., 221, *242*, 243

Ostrin, R. K., 147, *167*

Otten, S., 8, *35*, 73, 75, *84*, 141, *167*, 263, *273*

Ozer, D. J., 280, *305*

P

Palmer, S. E., 196, *214*

Park, B., 114, *137*, 169, 170, 171, *188, 249, 274*

Parkinson, B., 302, *305*

Parott, G., 368

Parrett, A., 282, *303*

Pavelchak, M. A., 140, 147, *165*, 169, 170, 175, 179, 181, 185, *186*

Pavot, W., 280, *305*

Peeters, G., 57, 75, *84*

Pelham, B. W., 255, *273*

Pendry, L. F., 7, *36*

Pennebaker, J. W., 296, *303*, 364, *368*

Pervin, L. A., 280, *305*

Petty, R. E., 11, *34*, 202, *212*, 323, *368*, 378, 381, *389, 391*

Petzold, P., 132, *136*

Phaf, R. H., 196, *214*

Pichler, A., 71, *82*

Pierce, T., 257, 266, 268, *273*

Pietromonaco, P., 268, *271*, 358, *365*

Pietromonaco, P. R., 285, *303*

Piorkowski, R., 286, *306*

Pitts, G. S., 10, 18, 19, 22, 30, *35*, 47, 173, *187, 367*, 387, *390*

Plutchik, R., 372, *391*

Poldrack, R. A., 194, 206, *214*

Polo, M., 286, *306*

Pope, L. K., 317, *332*

Popper, K., 109, *136*

Posner, M. I., 88, *107*, 175, *187*, 193, 196, *213, 214*, 287, *305*

Postmes, T., 115, 123, *135*

Powell, M. C., 8, 9, 10, 16, 22, 31, *33*, 40, 52, 53, *82*, 87, 88, 90, 98, 102, 103, 104, *106*, 139, 140, 148, 149, 152, 154, *165*, 169, 171, 175, *186*, 220, 225, 226, *241*, 248, 258, 260, 262, *272*, 285, 288, 290, 301, *303*, 320, 321, 322, 372, *389*

Pratto, F., 9, 11, *32*, 38, 52, 53, 55, 56, *81*, 85, 87, 89, 90, 102, 103, 104, *106, 107*, 151, 152, *163, 167*, 169, 170, 171, 175, 176, 179, 182, *185*, 219, 220, 227, *240, 242*, 322, 372, *389*

Preacher, K. J., 238, *241*, 263, *271*

Priester, J. R., 381, 382, *389*

Presser, S., 181, *187*

Proctor, R. W., 224, 226, *242*

Subject Index